55

8712

7518

8267

Kristin Pochman
2.9 Offenhaven East
372-6293

Children
and Their
World

Children and Their World

Strategies for Teaching Social Studies

Second Edition

David A. Welton
Texas Tech University

John T. Mallan
Syracuse University

Houghton Mifflin Company   Boston
Dallas   Geneva, Illinois   Hopewell, New Jersey   Palo Alto   London

B. Othanel Smith, Advisory Editor

Printed in the U.S.A.

Library of Congress Catalog Card Number: 79-7429

ISBN: 0-395-30769-4

To ...
David Jr., Stephen, Christopher,
Lynda and Shawn ♡

... as they encounter their world.

Contents

**PART 2
Instructional
Management**

Preface

It was on a fine September morning several hundreds of students ago that we sat in an empty classroom nervously awaiting the arrival of our first class. That long-awaited day had finally arrived! Little did we think then that some twenty years later we would be writing the second edition of a social studies methods text. Yet during those intervening years we've learned a lot (or at least we'd like to think so), no small portion of which came from our former students—elementary pupils, in-service teachers, and prospective teachers alike.

During our first year of teaching, we learned that being called upon to teach something has a profound way of revealing what one doesn't know but must quickly learn, just to stay ahead of the students. We also learned another humbling fact; namely, that just because we happened to be teaching something didn't necessarily mean that our students were eager to learn it. They could ignore us just as easily as we had ignored some of our teachers. But then we also learned of those countless "little things" that make teaching so satisfying—that glow students radiate when they *finally* understand something, like the look of pleasure when, at Christmastime, you are presented with yet another brightly wrapped package that will complete your year's supply of after-shave lotion or cologne.

As we were preparing the original manuscript for this book, we found—as one often finds in teaching—that we had to be selective. Indeed, if we hadn't practiced "selective neglect," this book would be the size of an unabridged dictionary—and that was unacceptable. Some of the easiest decisions as to what we would neglect involved material that was readily available elsewhere. Because instructions for making an overhead projector transparency are readily available elsewhere, for example, you will not find information of that nature in this book. With the easy decisions out of the way, the task of deciding what to emphasize grew considerably more complex. Inasmuch as this book—or any book for that matter—is based on a set of assumptions and positions, we think that you should know of these in advance, since they will undoubtedly influence the way you approach the text.

About This Book

We have written this book out of the conviction that social studies can be approached as something students do and use, not simply as something they are expected to know. In no way are we suggesting that social studies content is unimportant; on the contrary, we think it's more important than ever.

With the continued expansion of the so-called knowledge explosion, we have become increasingly aware of the need for an approach to social studies in which the legitimate "know about" dimensions are balanced with an emphasis on developing the skills children can use to deal with any kind of information, knowledge, or experience they may encounter. Helping prospective teachers develop and manage such an approach is one of the major purposes of this book.

This book is also premised on the notion that learning is an active—as opposed to a passive—process. That's hardly an earthshaking idea, and to pursue it further is to risk beating a dead horse. Yet for such an obvious premise, it's amazing how often it is violated. As you continue on in this book, you'll find that our approach to it and to social studies is geared to involvement—of students, of teachers, and of you, the reader.

Provoking involvement through a book format poses some challenges not typically encountered in classroom settings; that is, we are denied perhaps the most critical element in maintaining involvement—direct feedback from you. If your students experience difficulty, for example, you can stop and go back until you're satisfied that it's safe to go on. However, since we are denied the luxury of direct feedback here (although obviously you have the option of rereading a section before going on), we have done several things that we hope will promote your involvement with this book.

For one thing, we've decided to say "we think" instead of "it is thought that," for such a change is overdue in textbook writing. In addition, at the beginning of each chapter we've included a brief outline of the key ideas and key questions that we plan to consider. If you are one of those people who likes to know what's coming, you should find these tools to be of value.

Another thing that makes this book different from others in the field is the inclusion of exemplary student activities. All of them have been used successfully with students (naturally, we've omitted those that didn't work out quite as well as we had expected). More importantly, and although you may wish to use the activities as we have presented them, they also serve as *models* —as exemplary lesson formats that can be adapted and modified to other topics and other content or subject areas.

After 12 to 14 years of watching social studies teachers in action, we also have assumed that—for better or worse—you could, if need be (and without any formal teacher training), stand before a class and "tell 'em what they need to know." That thought may raise the hackles of a lot of teacher educators, but nonetheless it was a fairly common practice not too long ago. Now, however, in view of the really superb teacher's guides that accompany most textbook series, almost everyone who can read directions could probably teach a conventional social studies program. They might even do a fairly decent job of it. Of course, upon encountering one of the new concept-based social studies programs, they might face some problems. But even if they didn't understand why some third graders study the Eskimo, the Spanish monarchy, and the Mayflower Compact almost simultaneously they could, by following the teacher's guide, probably muddle through.

We have assumed that most readers of this book want to go beyond "muddling," beyond a conventional "follow-the-recipe" approach to social studies.

In fact, our expectation is that your intent is to create a vigorous, interesting, integrated, and challenging social studies program. That assumption may not be entirely valid, we know, but this book has been written in the hope that it is.

Theory? Because *theory,* its role, and the way it functions are considered "delicate" topics by many prospective teachers, we feel that our position in this area needs to be especially clear at the outset. The contention that methods texts are "too theoretical," and that what teachers need is not more theory but just some "good, practical ideas," has an element of validity to it. The underlying assumption, however, appears to be that everyone, perhaps intuitively, knows how to teach and that there's just not that much to it. Any agreement or dispute with this assumption is based on an implicit definition of what it means "to teach," but to make that definition explicit in the absence of feedback from you would not be especially productive at this point. What we think "to teach" means should become apparent from the kinds of approaches and activities we recommend throughout this book.

Consider, for a moment, the following situation: *You have been assigned to teach a series of inductive lessons on economics to a first-grade class.* What might seem to be an outlandish assignment may take on a different meaning when you learn that this is precisely what's required by one of the newer social studies textbook series.

But why economics?

And why inductive lessons?

If you know next to nothing about economics, you obviously have a problem—regardless of whatever teaching strategy you're expected to employ. On the other hand, if you are fortunate enough to be a whiz at economics, at least half the problem is resolved. But you may still have the problem of developing a teaching strategy.

At the risk of burdening you with what may seem a truism, it is apparent that content and method go hand in hand. They are perhaps the most vital components of teaching. Which is more important—content or method? Neither! It's not an either-or issue; both are critical.

Almost all of us have had occasion to witness truly brilliant scholars who, when standing before a class of students, turned out to be among the poorest teachers on record. Yet most of us have also had teachers, brilliant or not, who have stimulated our interest and generated greater productivity and more real learning than any of us might have thought possible. The key here is not only content, not only method, but a third, less obvious component— the ability to relate content and teaching method and then *apply* them in the classroom. The key is *application.* In a sense, content, method, and application form the triumvirate of teaching; each is necessary but not sufficient in and of itself.

The problem here is that it's you, not us, who has to do the applying. If you have no classroom responsibilities at the moment—and we suspect that many readers don't—we recognize that the absence of a situation that demands that you begin applying what you know clearly affects the way you will approach this book. Indeed, some readers will probably succumb to the tendency to take the easy way out, to treat content and method as separate entities. For them, the end result could well be the addition of two more discrete sets of information—sometimes on a level equivalent to the name of the Lone Ranger's horse—to their storehouse of apparently useless data that is filed away or forgotten for lack of an opportunity to apply the data somewhere.

Because we view teaching as an applied skill, you will find us making every effort to relate subject-matter content with teaching methods, and teaching theory with actual practice. We may not always be entirely successful, but our focus is on the synthesis of content and methods as they are demonstrated in practice.

We have also assumed that there is not one, single, "right, true, and always effective" way to teach social studies. We know that each of you brings to teaching a different style, different needs, and different expectations, all of which will influence the way you teach in your own classroom. We also know that whatever teaching strategy you ultimately feel comfortable with is, in the final analysis, a personal decision. Our reason for mentioning this is twofold. First is the notion of *choice* that is implicit in selecting a teaching strategy. We hope that the teaching strategies you employ are chosen from a repertoire of different ways to teach and, accordingly, that you are not limited to just one approach. Secondly, we forewarn you that although we will present a range of possible teaching strategies, we also advocate the use of some methods and approaches over others, and will spare no effort to convince you of their appropriateness. Finally, we suggest that you reread portions of this book sometime during your first year of teaching. Although this suggestion may seem presumptuous now, we suspect that your perspective will have changed and that what once seemed irrelevant could suddenly take on new meaning.

How This Book Is Organized

This edition is organized into two major sections. Part I is intended to help establish a framework—a way of looking at social studies as a subject area—as well as to identify some of the tasks involved in teaching it. Part II, the longer section, approaches social studies from a nuts-and-bolts, management-oriented perspective. Exemplary student activities and exemplary teaching materials have been integrated throughout both sections of the book.

Readers who are familiar with the first edition of this book will notice several significant changes in this volume. First, the simplified design and format of this edition is intended to eliminate the problems with continuity that occasionally arose with the first edition. Second, a major organizational change was accomplished by moving the treatment of instructional planning (Chapter Three) to a much earlier and more prominent location, so that it corresponds more closely to the sequence in which many methods courses are taught. Third, and although appearances might suggest otherwise, this edition is considerably shorter than the first.

New to this edition are treatments of sex-role stereotyping, oral history, global/international education, consumer education, law-related education, and career education. Also new to this edition are expanded and updated treatments of multicultural/multiethnic education, individualized instruction, values education, map and globe skills, the diagnosis of reading-related problems, and evaluation.

Acknowledgments   In preparing this manuscript, we became keenly aware of our indebtedness to many people. As is probably true for many authors, we sometimes found ourselves wondering whether an idea we were dealing with was really ours or one we had adopted from a source long since forgotten. Although we have documented our sources, we accept full responsibility for this manuscript. In addition, we acknowledge the debt of gratitude we owe to the students, teachers, and colleagues who have influenced and inspired us in countless ways.

We gratefully acknowledge the contributions and suggestions provided by Elmer Williams, University of Georgia; Lowell Horton, Northern Illinois University; and Vivian Dutton, University of Arizona, as they reviewed portions of the manuscript.

We owe a special acknowledgment to our families, and especially to our wives, Kathleen Welton and Diane Mallan, who know only too well the trials and joys associated with producing a manuscript such as this, and with whom we intend to become reacquainted.

David A. Welton
John T. Mallan

Children
and Their
World

Prologue

Remember when you

... couldn't understand why Australia was a continent but Greenland wasn't?

... thought Paris, Boston, and Chicago were states?

... "had" current events every Friday?

... constructed an Eskimo igloo from sugar cubes?

... memorized the state capitals, the Preamble to the Constitution, the Gettysburg Address, or the presidents of the United States, in order?

... were taught that "mail carriers deliver the mail," when you already knew it?

... made a chart of the explorers, where they went, when they went, and who they went for?

... couldn't remember the capital of Afghanistan or Ethiopia's major export?

... laboriously recopied from at least two encyclopedias your report on mythology, "the South," or Andrew Jackson?

Introduction: Reflecting on What's Ahead

A lot of things are done in the name of teaching social studies, some of which you may remember fondly and others that you've long since forgotten. Quite frankly, some of what you once learned might not have been taught at all, were it not for the "Joan of Arc" syndrome. This syndrome is a fairly common occurrence in schools generally and in social studies particularly, and is illustrated in the following conversation. Note that it really doesn't make much difference who is talking here; it could be two teachers, a parent and a teacher, or even two students. The only essential qualification is that at least one of them has spent some time studying the topic under consideration.

Joan of Arc syndrome

"I hear that they're taking Joan of Arc [or any other topic] out of the social studies curriculum. Kids won't be studying about her in school any more."
"What are they doing that for?"
"I guess it's because they can't figure out why they should keep her in."
"Why they should keep her in? Isn't it obvious? I learned about Joan of Arc—you did too—and I think that every American should learn about

her. I mean, well . . . look at what it's done for us! Look at where *we* are today! Success depends on learning the kinds of things that *everyone* should know, including Joan of Arc."

"So you're saying that because we learned it, students today should learn it too."

"Exactly! I learned it, they should learn it too!"

Why then would you typically find sixth graders studying various nations around the world? The answer, in part, lies in the "Joan of Arc" syndrome; it's what sixth graders have traditionally studied in social studies for almost as long as there has been something called "social studies" (or "sixth grade"). At the turn of the century, of course, many students left school at the end of Grade 6 or shortly thereafter. Therefore, it was essential to "cover the earth" prior to the end of sixth grade lest students end their public schooling with significant gaps in their knowledge of world geography. For most students today, of course, sixth grade is the midpoint, not the end of their school careers. Yet what continues to be taught as social studies is often little more than an updated version of what sixth graders studied in earlier eras.

There's some "Joan of Arc" in each of us, we suspect, which is reflected in a certain unwillingness to examine rationally some of the things we do. It's often more comfortable to continue doing what we've always done because—well because that's the way we've always done it. Occasionally we make adjustments, to be sure. What were once taught as facts, for example, may now be presented as the myths they really are. Columbus's "discovery" of America and George Washington's involvement with that infamous cherry tree are probably two of the best examples of this.

Facts and myths

We are not suggesting here that everything about the past is outdated, inaccurate, or old-fashioned, nor are we suggesting that everything in our educational heritage is "good, sacred, and beyond question" the sort of thing that should be included in a contemporary educational experience. But then we don't think that every new idea that comes along is necessarily good and worthwhile either. Rather, our purpose is to indicate that the "Joan of Arc" syndrome often operates as an interfering mechanism which tends to keep us from critically examining what we do and what we have done in the name of teaching social studies.

A concern for balance

Unfortunately, "looking critically" at our own experiences and at social studies teaching in particular, is sometimes interpreted to mean "finding fault with" in a negative, degrading kind of way. We'll take occasional potshots at some of the things that have been done; in fact, we've taken a couple already. However, our intent is to be critical in the spirit of critical thinking —that is, to examine what teachers and students do from a balanced and reasoned approach to teaching social studies.

Consider, for example, the igloo-building activity that we "remembered" at the opening of this chapter. On the surface it might seem to be an eminently reasonable social studies activity. Although we've already cued you to the fact that we think otherwise, permit us to examine it in a broader context. And, for a moment, put yourself in the place of a teacher whose program calls for the study of the Eskimos.

Building model igloos from sugar cubes (which are the color and texture of snow without painting) lacks most of the physical danger that could be associated with an activity like harpoon building, for example, particularly if your students are inclined toward overly enthusiastic role playing. Igloo building is not without its problems, however. First, you'll need to decide if every student must build an igloo, including those students who detest model building. This is a management-type problem to be sure, but as a teacher you would need to determine in advance whether students will be free to do whatever they want to do, or whether they must select among other activities that you make available.

Once these decisions have been made and the igloo building gets under way, you're apt to encounter "the glue problem." Unless you've built something out of sugar cubes lately, it will probably take some experimenting to find a glue that works satisfactorily. Using plastic model cement, for example, almost guarantees disaster. Elmer's-type glues will work if used in moderation *and* if your students have the patience needed to hold the sugar cubes in place until the glue has set. (Note that having easily frustrated children hold sugar cubes for 10–15 minutes or so until the glue sets does *not* "teach" patience.) Instead of Elmer's, try a fast-setting household cement—the faster setting, the better.

Getting rectangular sugar cubes to slope inward to form the igloo's roof can also present a problem. This can be solved in a couple of ways: students could cut pieces of styrofoam to an igloo shape, and then glue the sugar cubes to it, or they could simply draw lines on the styrofoam to indicate blocks of snow, eliminating the sugar entirely. Either way, the models will resemble igloos even though they lack a hollow interior and even though no self-respecting Eskimo would probably approve of them. To produce a more realistic finished product, it's necessary to cut off one edge of each sugar cube so that it leans inward properly. Cutting sugar cubes without crumbling them can be accomplished with saw-toothed steak knives, but in view of all the cutting that must be done, the activity could well prove to be as dangerous as harpoon building, perhaps more so.

If it isn't apparent already, notice that seemingly trivial problems like those we've mentioned can become as time-consuming as problems of major consequence. In any event, once your students' igloos have begun to take shape, someone is sure to discover that real igloos are not built from blocks of snow stacked like bricks, as shown in Figure A, which is the way most students build them. Rather, real igloos are constructed in a continuous upward spiral, as is illustrated in Figure B. And so, what began as an apparently simple activity has probably become a classic example of Murphy's Law—"Anything that can go wrong will, usually at the worst possible time."

Some teachers justify model-building activities, such as the igloo-building activity we've described here, by indicating that in doing them their students will learn about life in whatever area they are studying (in this case, life in the Arctic). Actually, whether students learn anything about life in the Arctic—about what it's like to find shelter in a land of scarce resources—by building model igloos is debatable at best. In fact, unless students research the igloo-building process *prior* to starting construction, what they actually

Prologue 1

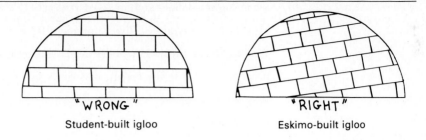

"WRONG"

Student-built igloo

"RIGHT"

Eskimo-built igloo

learn from the activity may have little or nothing to do with its stated purpose. Rather, as in this case, the activity may simply become a lesson in construction, in how to cut and glue sugar cubes.

Despite the problems we've noted, you might decide to continue the activity anyway. It's the kind of thing that's difficult to stop in midstream. And, should your class study the Far East, you might have your students sit on the floor as they eat an "Oriental meal" complete with chopsticks, even though the connection between that experience and your students' "broader understanding" of Oriental cultures is also doubtful. We're not trying to take the "fun" activities out of social studies, but we are suggesting that unless those activities are part of a well-integrated, well-thought-through program of study, they can easily lead to what James Banks (1976) has called "the chitlin's and tepee approach" to multiethnic education. No matter how appealing they may seem, activities such as an occasional ethnic meal, a day set aside to honor a certain cultural or ethnic group, or even some model-building activities can have the unintended effect of teaching inaccurate information and negative stereotypes. Eskimos today, for example, no longer live in igloos, just as Plains Indians no longer live in tepees. Thus, teachers who have their students build igloos or tepees need to make certain their students clearly understand that they are re-creating a historical event. If they don't, the potential for teaching misinformation looms large.

The underlying issue here concerns putting social studies activities into a perspective that balances the unique and picturesque—Eskimos and igloos, Native Americans and tepees—with the world as it really is. The basic question deals with identifying ways in which you, as a teacher, can plan, select, and develop activities that become a meaningful part of a child's social studies experience. That, in part, is what this book is about.

Earlier we suggested that some of what you learned in the name of social studies might better have been left out or forgotten. The other side of that coin deals with what might be included in a social studies program but usually isn't. At times there may be things that bother students—questions they think are important but that are typically not part of a school's program. Their questions may be similar to the ones listed below:

Is it O.K. to lie sometimes? When?

How do other people feel about me? Can I be sure?

"The chitlin's and tepee approach"

The questions students ask

Why do I need to know the century in which Julius Caesar was killed, by whom he was killed, and for what reason?

Must I like everybody? What happens if I don't?

Why do stores always have sales after Christmas but not before?

If cooperation is so important, why don't you get graded on it in school?

Why are most of the "good" movies rated "PG"?

Is anyone really free?

Why can't everyone have all the money they need?

Underlying each of these questions is a legitimate human and social concern. Many of the questions relate to the kinds of things that students think about and, in some cases, even worry about. A more fundamental issue, however, is whether or not such concerns should have a place in a social studies program—or a school's program. Some folks argue that schools have no business dealing with questions and concerns such as these, and that to do so is an invasion of the rights and responsibilities of the home. We disagree. We're not suggesting that such concerns should become the sole basis for social studies programs—far from it—but that they can play legitimate roles.

Whether children's concerns should or should not play a significant role in social studies programs leads to an even more basic question: what *is* social studies anyway? Is it simply another name for history and geography? Identifying what social studies is and what it can be is a major thrust of this book. This question is something we deal with directly in Chapter One and implicitly throughout the balance of the book. An equally important concern relates to how one goes about teaching social studies. As we deal with these questions—what social studies is and how one teaches it—our intent is to provide the background, the skills, and the experiences that will enable you to plan and teach a dynamic social studies program.

Social Studies As A School Subject

In this section we examine how social studies fits in with other subjects taught in elementary and middle schools. To do this, we've organized this section around three key questions: (1) How does social studies compare with other subjects? (2) How do students feel about it as a subject? and (3) Why do students seem to feel as they do?

Social Studies and "The Basics"

In some ways, American public education can be likened to a grandfather clock with its pendulum swinging in one direction and then reversing its course. Various educational movements have tended to reflect a "pendulum effect." During the 1920s and early 1930s, for example, the progressive education movement was in full swing. Although progressive education took many different forms, some of which were far from what its supporters ever dreamed of, the essential idea underlying progressive education was to move

Stricter discipline encouraged by "back to the basics" would reduce opportunities for informality in the classroom.

away from a lockstep, "stand-beside-your-desk-when-you-recite" approach to teaching and to move toward a style of teaching that was more responsive to students' interests and needs. As is often true of movements of this sort, some educators went to extremes. Instead of a prescribed curriculum, for example, schooling sometimes became a case of "what would you like to learn about today, kids?" If students weren't interested in learning math, they didn't learn math; it was almost that simple. But as is also true of movements of this sort, most schools never went to such extremes; for them it was business as usual. Nevertheless, during the late 1930s and throughout the 1940s there was a distinct movement away from "progressive education," a reverse swing not unlike the "back to the basics" emphasis that prevails in many areas of the country today.

"Back to the basics"

The current "back to the basics" movement is ill-defined. There isn't a single group or spokesperson we could point to as being totally representative of it. But then, it isn't totally clear what we are moving back *from*. As an expression, *back to the basics* implies that American schools have somehow moved away from an emphasis on teaching basic skills. However, many educators argue that teachers have never stopped emphasizing "the basics" to begin with, and thus there's nothing to move back from. Despite these claims, an even larger body of Americans seems to believe that schools should exhibit most (but not necessarily all) of the following characteristics: (1) an emphasis on the "three Rs"; (2) strict discipline; (3) promotion from one grade level to the next based on demonstrated achievement (no social promotion); (4) teaching techniques that include drill, recitation, homework, and frequent testing; (5) elimination of "frills" (e.g., basket weaving, igloo

Prologue Table 1
Curriculum Materials
Used by 65 Fifth
Graders, by Subject
Matter, Percentage
of Use, and
Percentage of Time

Subject Matter	Number of Times Used	Percentage of Use*	Percentage of Time*
Language–Literature	365	40	39
Aesthetics–Recreation (includes music, recess and physical education)	152	17	17
Social Studies (includes history, geography, social-behavioral science, philosophy, religion, values, and psychology)	143	16	16
Mathematics	135	15	17
Science (includes biological and physical science/technology)	93	10	11
Not Classified	16	2	
Total	904	100	100

*Rounded

Source: O. L. Davis, Jack R. Frymier, and David Clinefelter. "Curriculum Materials Used by Eleven-Year-Old Pupils: An Analysis Using the Annehurst Curriculum Classification System." Paper delivered at the American Educational Research Association Annual Meeting, April 6, 1977.

building, etc.), which corresponds with greater emphasis on the three Rs; and (6) an emphasis on patriotism and other traditional American values (Brodinsky, 1977, pp. 522–23).

Because it's difficult to get an accurate breakdown on the time allotted to teaching the various subject areas, it's not entirely clear how elementary social studies has been affected by "the basics" movement. It appears, however, that a greater emphasis on the three Rs has been gained at the expense of two subjects: social studies and science (c.f., Shaver, Davis, and Helburn, 1979; Welton, 1978; Gross, 1977).

Time devoted to social studies

Some investigators (c.f., Gross, 1977, p. 198) have indicated that social studies is sometimes taught for only one hour per week (and sometimes less). This doesn't compare very favorably with reading and language-related instruction, which often takes in excess of two hours per day. However, in a study that investigated how children actually spend their time in school, the picture doesn't look quite as bleak. In that study (Davis, Frymier, and Clinefelter, 1977), the researchers "shadowed" 65 eleven-year-old students from schools in six states over a three-week period. Each time a child used any kind of instructional material the observers noted this on a special form. Table P.1 illustrates what these researchers found in terms of how often students used curriculum materials associated with the different subject areas and in terms of the percentage of time spent working with those materials.

This study confirms the strong emphasis placed on teaching language-related subjects. Interestingly enough, it also indicates that mathematics and social studies receive somewhat similar emphasis. Note, however, that the fact that this study involved fifth graders is more important than it might seem, because at *lower* grade levels more time is apt to be devoted to

*"What's to worry about? They'll teach sex like they do
the rest of the subjects and the kids will lose interest."*

*The relationship
between time
and grade level*

instruction in reading, the language arts, and math. Since the length of the school day hasn't changed recently, that extra time appears to have been gained at the expense of social studies. Richard Gross (1977, p. 198), for example, cited surveys from two states indicating that 70 percent or more of the teachers in Grades K–4 did little or nothing with social studies. Although it is possible to teach reading and other language-related skills using social studies materials—which we illustrate in Chapter Eight—many teachers have apparently not chosen to do so.

In summary, the amount of time devoted to teaching social studies in elementary schools seems to partially depend on the grade level; the higher the grade level, the more attention social studies is likely to receive. At the middle school level, the picture is more clear-cut; the tendency is to require one period (approximately 40 minutes) of social studies each day.

Students' Attitudes Toward Social Studies

How do students feel about the different subjects they study, especially social studies? Many investigators (c.f., Jersild and Tasch, 1949; Rice, 1963; Harris, 1969; McTeer, Blanton, and Lee, 1975) have attempted to answer that question, and with few exceptions they have found that social studies is the subject students like least. In most instances, these researchers and others (c.f., Herman, 1963) also found a sex-related difference: as a rule, girls tended to like social studies even less than boys. Incidentally, in many of those studies the most popular subject was spelling.

There are exceptions to almost every rule, and such is the case here. For example, when John Calvert (1970) asked fourth graders to rank the subjects they studied from most-liked to least-liked, social studies once again occupied its usual position at the bottom of the heap. But when Calvert asked fifth graders to do the same thing, social studies was ranked as the subject they liked best. Why such a drastic change from one year to the next? In this instance, the fifth graders had been using a social studies program entitled "Man: A Course of Study" (MACOS), which apparently was much more to their liking. The irony here is that even though MACOS has proven popular with many students (and teachers), it has also proven to be so controversial that in some communities it has either been modified substantially or dropped entirely, a situation we examine in detail in Chapters Four and Five.

From least-liked to most-liked

Although students' responses to MACOS are clearly an exception to the general rule, they also illustrate that social studies doesn't have to be dull. Not reflected in most of the other studies either, we suspect, are teachers who make social studies interesting for their students. It may take some effort on a teacher's part, but we think that a subject that deals with people and places around the globe should be at least as interesting and useful as a subject like spelling.

Why Students Feel As They Do.   Reflect for a moment on your own experience with social studies. Restrict yourself to your elementary school experience if you can (if you remember it), and try to identify several reasons that might explain why children tend to rank social studies among their least-liked subjects. Use the space below if you wish.

_____

_____

Perhaps children feel as they do because when they study arithmetic or spelling their answers are either right or wrong, while in social studies they are never quite sure. Or perhaps it's because in science they deal with butterflies and bugs—real, living things—not with places far removed and people long since dead. Or maybe it's because in reading and language arts they deal with interesting stories—stories with plots—while in social studies their books resemble miniature encyclopedias. The list could go on and on.

Some of the problems you noted above may relate to the content, to what is taught as social studies. For example, it's the rare American child who hasn't watched with fascination as a fire engine raced down the street, lights ablaze and siren screaming. It's also the rare child who cannot readily explain what fire fighters do: "They put out fires, of course." Nevertheless, some primary-level social studies programs include a lengthy unit on community helpers that deals in part with fire fighters, often in a way that adds little, if anything, to what students already know. In other words, some social studies programs focus on teaching children that milk trucks carry milk, when they are already well aware of what milk trucks carry. On the other hand, when social studies programs deal with content that is new to children, they sometimes go to the opposite extreme. Identifying the five provinces of Australia, for example, is apt to pose a problem for most adults, to say nothing of children. Thus, children (and many adults) are unlikely to care much about learning such information, even though it would be "new" to them. Even if students don't ask "What do we gotta learn this stuff for?" it's

Irrelevant content?

a safe bet they are thinking such thoughts. The tendency of some social studies programs to deal with content (information) that children don't care about, is, we think, one of the main reasons why they give them such low ratings.

Telling children that they should care about the information presented in a social studies program isn't a very persuasive motivator, at least not for very long. The fact of the matter is that children very often don't care, and this, you'll find, is one of the problems we address throughout this book. It's not essential that children come away liking social studies, although we'd be extremely pleased if they did, but rather that they care about it and see it as worthwhile.

Liking and caring

It's important in this context to distinguish between *liking* a subject and *caring* about it. Some of us don't like arithmetic, for example, yet despite our dislike, we care about it. Arithmetic has utility; it's something one does or must do from time to time, and this alone may be sufficient to make us care about it. By contrast, social studies tends to be something one *knows* but seldom does. If we are never expected to "do" social studies, it becomes all too easy to shrug our shoulders and say, "who cares." To avoid this kind of situation, social studies must be seen as something useful, as something we use or "do" every day.

Skill subjects

Subjects that we use or "do," like arithmetic, can be described as *skills* (or skill subjects). Such subjects have a knowledge base, as does virtually everything taught in schools, but they go a step further; skill subjects require that you apply what you know in problem-solving situations. It's in the applying —in the application—that the actual skill enters the picture. Thus, the ultimate test of your arithmetic ability lies not in your knowledge of the number system or of the additive principle (to cite two of arithmetic's knowledge elements). Rather, the real test comes when you must apply your knowledge in a problem-solving situation. The fact that some of us occasionally bounce checks at the bank isn't necessarily an indication of our lack of arithmetic knowledge (although it can be); it's more likely to be an indication of our inability (or unwillingness) to apply what we know. Indeed, most of us know our arithmetic facts ($2 + 2 = 4$, etc.); it's just that some of us don't "do" them very well!

Social studies as something you *do?* Is it possible to teach social studies in many of the same ways that arithmetic is taught, that is, as something children know *and* do?

"Doing" social studies

We don't advocate throwing out the traditional "knowing about" elements of social studies—including the five provinces of Australia or the capital of Afghanistan—for to do so is tantamount to throwing the baby out with the bath. Rather, we believe that the social sciences offer a wealth of information about the human experience that children can use to interpret the world in which all of us live. Our aim is to strike a balance between the factual knowledge traditionally associated with social studies and opportunities for students to apply that information, that is, to create situations in which students can actually *do* social studies. Of course, such an approach may differ somewhat from the way most of us learned social studies, and to think that we might actually have an opportunity to apply some of the history and geography we have supposedly learned can be a bit mind-boggling. Nevertheless, our intent throughout the balance of this book is to show you how you can teach the *use* of social studies.

Suggested Activities

1 "Well I taught it, they just didn't learn it" is a remark heard in teachers' lounges across the country. Try wrestling with the question of whether teaching can take place in the absence of learning.

2 Classifying all subjects taught in elementary schools according to the criteria of "to do" and "to know," as discussed in the Prologue, should enable you to generate an interesting perspective on the curriculum as a whole. For example, was handwriting (penmanship) something you were expected to know? Or was it something you were expected to do? Classify the subjects listed below into one of the two categories. (Note that we've separated language arts, science, and social studies into some of their major components, e.g., grammar, spelling, history, chemistry. We realize that few elementary schools have a separate course entitled "Chemistry"; nevertheless, elements of chemistry are taught under the more general label of "science.")

Subjects

Anthropology	Geography	Physics
Arithmetic	Geology	Poetry
Art (drawing)	Grammar	Political science
Astronomy	History	Reading
Biology	International relations	Social psychology
Botany	Literature	Sociology
Chemistry	Music (vocal/instrumental)	Spelling
Economics	Penmanship	Zoology
	Physical education	

Subjects one "Does"

_____
_____
_____
_____
_____
_____
_____
_____
_____
_____

Subjects one "Knows"

_____
_____
_____
_____
_____
_____
_____
_____
_____
_____

3   Although the "Joan of Arc" syndrome may well be responsible for the inclusion of some things in the social studies curriculum that might not be necessary, the reverse is probably just as true; some of the things presently taught as social studies should continue to be taught as such. Identify and place in rank order at least five major ideas or topics that you feel should continue to be taught in social studies programs. In a small group, use your rankings as a basis for developing a single list that incorporates all suggestions.

References

Banks, James A. "Multiethnic Education: Practices and Promises." Paper delivered at the Annual Meeting of the National Council for the Social Studies, Washington, D.C., November, 1976.

Brodinsky, Ben. "Back to the Basics: The Movement and Its Meaning." *Phi Delta Kappan* 58 (March 1977): 522–26.

Calvert, John. *Change in Student Perceptions of the "Social Studies."* Syracuse, NY: Eastern Regional Institute for Education, 1970.

Davis, O. L., Jr.; Frymier, Jack R.; and Clinefelter, David. "Curriculum Materials Used by Eleven-Year-Old Pupils: An Analysis Using the Annehurst Curriculum Classification System." Paper delivered at the American Educational Research Association Annual Meeting, April 6, 1977.

Gross, Richard E. "The Status of the Social Studies in the Public Schools of the United States: Facts and Impressions of a National Survey." *Social Education* 41 (March 1977): 194–200.

Harris, Louis. "What People Think About Their High Schools." *Life* 66 (May 16, 1969): 23–33.

Herman, Wayne L., Jr. "How Intermediate Children Rank the Subjects." *Journal of Educational Research* 56 (April 1963): 435–36.

Jersild, Arthur, and Tasch, Ruth. *Children's Interests and What They Suggest for Education.* New York: Bureau of Publications, Teachers College, Columbia University, 1949.

McTeer, J. Hugh; Blanton, F. Lamar; and Lee, H. Wayne. "The Relationship of Selected Variables to Student Interest in Social Studies in Comparison with Other Academic Areas." *Journal of Educational Research* 68 (February 1975): 238–40.

Rice, Joseph P., Jr. "A Comparative Study of Academic Interest Patterns Among Selected Groups of Exceptional and Normal Intermediate Children." *California Journal of Educational Research* 14 (May 1963): 131–37.

Shaver, James P.; Davis, O. L., Jr.; and Helburn, Suzanne W. "The Status of Social Studies Education: Impressions from Three NSF Studies." *Social Education* 43 (February 1979): 150–53.

Silberman, Charles E. *Crisis in the Classroom.* New York: Random House, 1970.

Welton, David A. "A Brief Pause for Station Identification." *The Social Studies* LXIX (January/February 1978): 12–13.

Social Studies:
A Teaching
Framework

Part 1

1 The Dynamics of Social Studies

Key Questions

What is social studies?

What is "citizenship education"?

What can someone who "knows" social studies be expected to do?

Key Ideas

Social studies is an area characterized by conflicting and, at times, contradictory aims and purposes.

Social studies is generally thought to have three basic purposes: (*a*) the preparation of future citizens, (*b*) teaching children to think, and (*c*) teaching our cultural heritage.

Contemporary social studies programs tend to place less emphasis on memorized information and more emphasis on individual involvement, decision making, and skills acquisition.

Social studies goals are often so broadly stated that they may offer little guidance to prospective teachers.

Introduction: Searching for Definition

What is social studies and why is it taught? These are the major questions this chapter deals with. The reason we have included the term *dynamics* in the title of this chapter is to suggest the movement or action that has taken place in social studies over the years. Social studies has changed from what it once was, and it is changing still. Since it was introduced over sixty years ago, social studies has evolved to the point that there are currently several different views regarding what it is and why it's taught.

Differing views

That different conceptions of social studies have emerged is neither unusual nor unexpected. In fact, a somewhat similar situation exists to varying degrees in the fields of mathematics, science, and some of the other subject areas. Sir Julian Huxley, for example, once described the field of psychology as "a confused assemblage of warring heresies" (1967, p. 32). Although "warring" is too strong a word to describe the situation in social studies, the fact that there are differing conceptions of social studies effectively prevents us from identifying one of them as *the* prevailing point of view.

This situation may help to explain why, in your twelve or so years of experience with social studies as a student, you probably found teachers who approached it in different ways. Some of them may have emphasized the need to learn names, dates, and places, while others more or less ignored such things and tried to focus on main ideas, basic concepts, self-awareness, and so forth. Still other teachers probably fell somewhere between these extremes. Our point here is to suggest that, despite your experiences with social studies as a student, you probably were not privy to the instructional decisions that were made about it—about what social studies is and how it would be approached. Possibly you weren't aware that such decisions even existed, yet the social studies you studied clearly resulted from them. Our intent is to clarify some of the options and alternatives that may (or should) have been considered by your teachers and that, ultimately, will have a bearing on the kind of social studies program you provide for your students.

Who Is Qualified for the Presidency?

Model student activity

Overview This activity, which is adapted from Marsha Hobin (1974), asks you (or better yet, a group) to select from eight candidates whom you feel is best qualified to be president of the United States. In this and many other social studies lessons, the sequence of activities is important. Although there is nothing to stop you from altering the suggested sequence—in fact doing so could enhance the activity's effectiveness—on your first encounter we suggest that you follow the recommended sequence.

On the cards that follow are some basic biographical data about people who have been or are still active in American life. For this activity, their names and sex have been omitted. All of them, however, have met the three constitutional requirements for the presidency; they are all natural-born citizens, at least thirty-five years old, and have resided in the United States for at least fourteen years.

[Note: The candidates' age and career data were determined by selecting a significant point in the individual's career and then using that date as the basis for subsequent calculations. For candidates who were elected to the presidency, for example, the date used for determining their age and career data was just prior to their election to that office. Hence, the expression "Age as of this date" refers to the candidate's age at a particular point in historical time, not today. To reveal more information than this—such as the actual date—would heighten the guessing-game effect and limit the effectiveness of this activity.]

Procedure: phase one

Introduction Before considering the candidates, you should identify any additional qualifications (beyond those established in the Constitution) you think a president of the United States should possess. For example, should presidents have college degrees? Or prior political experience?

List additional qualifications here:

_____   _____

_____   _____

Phase two

Selection Which of these eight *individuals* do you think would be *best* qualified to serve as president of the United States? Which individual do you feel would be *least* qualified? (The candidates' identities appear in Appendix A.)

CARD 1

College Attended: Harvard University, Columbia University
Religion: Protestant
Career (Major Occupations): Farmer, Lawyer, State Senator, Assistant Secretary of Navy, Governor, Vice-Presidential candidate
Married: 27 years   **Children:** 6
Age as of this date: 50

CARD 2

College Attended: None
Religion: Protestant
Career (Major Occupations): Investor, Druggist, Bookseller, Brigadier General in U.S. Army
Married: 1st spouse: 5 years until spouse's death
          2nd spouse: 1 year
Children: 3 by first marriage
Age as of this date: 38

Source: *Dictionary of American Biography*, Charles Scribner's Sons, 1928, pp. 362–67.

CARD 3

Colleges Attended: Morehouse College, A.B. and L.H.D., Crozer Theological Seminary, B.D., University of Pennsylvania, Boston University, Ph.D., D.D., Harvard University, L.L.D., Central State College, Morgan State College
Religion: Protestant
Career (Major Occupations): Protestant minister, Teacher of Philosophy at Harvard, President of a civil rights organization, 1 of 10 outstanding men for the year according to *Time* magazine, Nobel Prize winner, Noted public speaker
Married: 15 years   **Children:** 4
Age as of this date: 37

CARD 4

College Attended: None
Religion: No specific denomination
Career (Major Occupations): Land speculator and farmer, Lawyer, Member of U.S. House of Representatives, U.S. Senator, U.S. Judge, Commander of U.S. Armed Forces
Married: 38 years   **Children:** none
Age as of this date: 62

Source: *Dictionary of American Biography,* IX, Charles Scribner's Sons, 1932, pp. 526–31.

CARD 5

College Attended: Columbia University
Religion: No specific denomination
Career (Major Occupations): Writer, Served as Lieutenant Colonel in Army, Lawyer, Member of a congress. Member of a constitutional convention, Secretary of the Treasury
Married: 24 years   **Children:** 8
Age as of this date: 47

Source: *Dictionary of American Biography,* VIII, Charles Scribner's Sons, 1932, pp. 171–79.

CARD 6

College Attended: None (Private secondary school in England)
Religion: Protestant
Career (Major Occupations): Teacher, Journalist, Member of a labor union (trade union league), United States delegate to the United Nations, Chairman of the United Nations Commission on Human Rights, Endorsed by a President for the Nobel Peace Prize, Noted public speaker
Married: 27 years   **Children:** 6
Age as of this date: 65

Source: *Current Biography: Who's News and Why, 1949,* The H. W. Wilson Co., 1950, pp. 528–32.

CARD 7

College Attended: University of Alabama

Religion: Protestant

Career (Major Occupations): Lawyer, State Assistant Attorney General, State legislator, U.S. Judge, State Governor, Party Candidate for Presidency, Served in U.S. Air Force, Noted public speaker

Married: 1st spouse: 26 years until spouse's death
2nd spouse: 3 years

Children: 4 by first marriage

Age as of this date: 55

Sources: *Who's Who in America*, II, Marquis Who's Who, Inc., 1972, p. 3300; *Current Biography, Yearbook 1963*, H. W. Wilson Co., 1964, pp. 454–56.

CARD 8

College Attended: None

Religion: No specific denomination

Career (Major Occupations): Postmaster, Lawyer, U.S. Representative, Store owner, State congressman, Served as Captain in U.S. Army, Noted public speaker

Married: 19 years   **Children:** 4

Age as of this date: 51

Source: *Dictionary of American Biography*, XI, Charles Scribner's Sons, 1933, pp. 242–49.

Phase three

Summarizing questions

1 To what extent did your choices reflect the qualifications you listed in Phase One?

2 Would you modify your original list in any way?

3 Should any of the following factors be considered in selecting a presidential candidate?

3.1 Age

3.2 Religion

3.3 Sex

3.4 Educational background

3.5 Number of children

3.6 Previous occupations

3.7 Personal appearance

3.8 Personality

3.9 Ethnic background

3.10 Marital status

4 Should other factors be considered, e.g., mental health? a police record?

5 What qualifications do you think are *most* important?

6 Which are *least* important?

Optional questions and extending activities

1 Is your list of qualifications representative of the beliefs of most individuals in your community? In your class? How would you find out?

2 Could you develop a similar lesson for another political office (or for someone applying for an elementary social studies position)?

Nature of activity   Decision making/values clarification.

Suggested format   Small groups (5–7) to consider presidential qualifications and the data cards. Discussion questions can be considered in small groups and then summarized in a teacher-led, large-group activity.

Objectives

1 Given the constitutional qualifications for president, the individual will:
1.1 identify any additional qualifications he feels to be appropriate, and
1.2 determine if these are acceptable to a group of his peers.

2 Given biographical data for eight individuals, all of whom meet the constitutional qualifications for president, students will select the one person they feel to be best qualified and the person they feel to be least qualified for that office. They must then defend and/or modify their selection to reach group consensus.

3 Upon completion of this activity, each individual will list at least seven factors (in addition to those in the Constitution) that might influence voters in determining which candidates are best qualified to be president of the United States.

Descriptors

Two interest-arousing techniques

In addition to raising some fundamental issues about the presidency and the person who might fill that office, the previous activity also illustrates two techniques that can help to enhance student interest and involvement. Briefly, those techniques are: (1) *creating mystery-type situations,* which, in this instance, is achieved by limiting information at the outset (intentionally omitting the candidates' name and sex), and (2) *providing choices (alternatives) for students to select among.* Separately, creating puzzle- or mystery-type situations and/or providing opportunities for realistic decision making are powerful interest-arousing devices. When combined, as they are in this activity, success is almost guaranteed. We'll provide additional examples of how you might adapt and apply these devices to other student activities throughout the balance of the book.

"Who is Qualified for the Presidency" also illustrates some of the basic issues that will be raised in this chapter. The fact that we included it here, for example, is probably a sufficient basis to presume that it has something to do with social studies. But, *what makes it a social studies activity?* Is it because the presidency (and politics) usually falls within the realm of political science? (Yes.) And is it because political science is one of the social sciences, which makes it a part of social studies too? (Yes, again.)

The presidency activity has no previously established "right" answers. You had to determine the best and least qualified candidate according to the criteria that you—not someone else—established. *Is it still social studies now?* (Certainly! Helping students identify the criteria on which to base rational decisions is considered a prime goal of social studies.)

The presidency activity didn't require that you memorize any facts, although you probably remember some nevertheless. Nor did it require that you research anything. Between the data it provided and the experiences you brought to the activity, virtually everything you needed was there. But *is it still social studies?* (Sure, social studies is no more likely to require that students memorize information or do research than English, science, or any other subject taught in elementary schools. In fact, rather than ignore students' previous experiences, why not actively draw upon them?)

The social science disciplines

At the heart of social studies lie the social science disciplines—history, geography, economics, political science, sociology, anthropology, and social psychology. (Note that not everyone agrees that history should be included as one of the social sciences, despite the prominent role it plays in most social studies programs.) We've already suggested that some aspects of political science appear in the presidency activity, but it doesn't stop there. Of the following, which are present in either a major or minor role?

Yes   No

____ ____ The use of historical data (history).

____ ____ A concern for the interaction of people and their physical environment (geography).

____ ____ A concern for systems of trading and distributing resources (economics).

____ ____ A concern for various aspects of government and political behavior (political science).

____ ____ A concern for individual and group values and group behavior (sociology).

____ ____ A concern for the study of cultures and cultural change (anthropology).

____ ____ A concern for human relationships and interpersonal affairs (social psychology).

Multi-disciplinary approach

To one degree or another, at least five social science disciplines can play a role in this activity. Each provides a slightly different perspective from which to examine the human experience. Even though determining where one discipline ends and another begins is sometimes a problem for specialists in the field, those fuzzy boundaries are seldom a concern to most teachers. In fact, unless they must teach courses in single social science disciplines (e.g., "pure" economics), which rarely happens, elementary teachers are more likely to be concerned with providing an integrated, *multidisciplinary* approach to studying the human (social) experience. At the same time, the possible involvement of one or more of the social science disciplines, as illustrated by the presidency activity, is a distinguishing characteristic of most social studies activities, and of social studies itself.

In dealing with elementary and middle school social studies, the problem is not one of determining where the boundaries separating each of the social science disciplines lie. Rather, as John Dewey noted in 1936 (p. 367), "in the proper emphasis upon social studies, the primary problem . . . is to determine the scope and range of the subject matter designated 'social.' "

Social Studies: The Study of Things Social

What is social studies? The amount of time that's been devoted to answering this question is almost incalculable. Just when a group seems to be reaching agreement, someone is apt to say, "but we haven't taken such-and-such into consideration," and the struggle for an acceptable definition is likely to begin anew. We do not detail most of those battles here since they are well documented elsewhere (see the Suggested Readings at the end of this chapter for some excellent accounts). Instead, we highlight only those aspects of the efforts to define social studies that have clear implications for what you might do in your classroom.

Edgar Wesley produced one of the most widely quoted (and shortest!) answers to the question "what is social studies?" when he said, "The social studies are the social sciences simplified for pedagogical purposes" (Wesley and Wronski, 1958, p. 3). Note that you could substitute "teaching" for "pedagogical" without affecting the meaning unduly. Wesley's definition was aimed primarily at the high school level where it is most applicable. In most secondary schools, social studies is typically made up of separate courses in subjects such as history, government, economics, social psychology, sociology, and so forth. Each course tends to be a somewhat simplified version of a similar social science course taught at the college level, although just how much watering-down there may be varies considerably—sometimes it's very little.

Simplified social science

Prior to about 1920 and in selected instances since that time (see box, pages 33–35), Wesley's "simplified social sciences" definition would have applied to elementary social studies too. At that time, what we now call "social studies" usually referred to two subjects, history and geography, both of which were typically taught as separate courses. Figure 1.1 illustrates a page from an elementary geography text that was published in 1896. Note that each "fact" is stated so definitely that its accuracy isn't likely to be questioned, and that each sentence is numbered separately to facilitate recitation.

Mental discipline

The study of history and geography was thought to provide a form of religious and moral training, inspire patriotism, and afford training for citizenship. Some of these reasons are still cited today, but at that time another important reason was cited for teaching those subjects; namely, for the

Figure 1.1   Page from an 1896 Geography Textbook

AFRICA.

Ruins at Karnak, Egypt.

DESCRIPTION.

Map Questions on Page 75.

1. **Africa** is the south-western grand-division of the Eastern continent. It is three times as large as Europe.

2. This grand-division is a **vast table-land,** with narrow low plains along the coasts. The principal mountain ranges are on the margin of the table-land, which is higher in the southern and eastern than in the northern and western parts.

3. The principal **rivers** are the Niger, the Nile, the Kongo, and the Zambezi. The principal lakes are Victoria, Tanganyika, Nyassa, and Tchad.

4. Africa is situated chiefly in the torrid zone, and has a hotter **climate** than any other grand-division. A moist region lies on both sides of the equator. This is covered with prairies or dense tropical forests. North and south of this belt, the climate is hot and dry.

5. The principal wild **animals** are the elephant, the giraffe, the hippopotamus, the rhinoceros, the lion, the leopard, the hyena, the zebra, the crocodile, the gorilla, and the ostrich.

In the southern part of Africa, ostriches are raised upon "ostrich farms" for their feathers.

6. Most of the **inhabitants** of Africa belong to the Ethiopian, or black, race. The Caucasian race inhabits the countries bordering on the Mediterranean and Red seas.

QUESTIONS.—1. In what part of the Eastern continent is Africa? What is said of its size? Bound it.—2. Describe the surface.—3. Describe the Niger River. The Nile. The Kongo. The Zambezi. The Orange. Where is Lake Albert? Victoria? Tanganyika? Nyassa? Tchad?—4. Describe the climate of Africa. Where is the moist region?—5. Name some of the principal wild animals.—6. To what race do most of the inhabitants belong? What countries do the whites inhabit?

(73)

"mind training," or mental discipline, they offered. According to mental-discipline theory, the mind is like a muscle that must be trained or disciplined. Oftimes that "training" consisted of long—sometimes deliberately prolonged—and distasteful lessons which, when completed, would produce students who were somehow better off as a result of their experience. Indeed, for some teachers of that era, the epitome of mental discipline might be demonstrated when students were able to recite, verbatim, complete pages from the geography book illustrated in Figure 1.1.

Transfer

Mental discipline's demise as a learning theory was speeded when psychologists discovered that mind training in one subject area didn't necessarily transfer to other subject areas, that memorizing Latin, for example, did not influence a student's performance in history, or vice versa. Mental-discipline approaches did not disappear overnight, however. In fact, some teachers today still require their students to memorize the Preamble to the Constitution, the Gettysburg Address, or the presidents of the United States, in order, all in the name of patriotism and mind training. Note, however, that when children are given the opportunity to memorize something, be it the Gettysburg Address, "By the shores of Gitche Gumee," or whatever, *some* of them love it. They seem to enjoy the challenge that memorizing poses. Other children, however, despise such activities with equal passion.

Memorization = understanding?

Another fallacy of the mental-discipline approach was its tendency to equate memorization with understanding. The error in equating the two is well illustrated by children who can recite the Pledge of Allegiance flawlessly, yet who haven't the faintest idea of what "one nation, indivisible" means.

Even though mental discipline declined during the early decades of this century, history and geography continued to play a major role in most schools. The reasons for teaching them, however, tended to become more utilitarian. It was argued, for example, that studying history would produce individuals who were more socially intelligent and historically-minded (Wehlage and Anderson, 1972, p. 3). This shift, slight as it was, was further aided during the 1920s, '30s, and '40s by an increased emphasis on education for "life adjustment." Instead of teaching subjects for their intrinsic value, teachers were called on to provide schooling that addressed the practical problems individuals would face in an increasingly technological society.

Intrinsic or practical value?

The emphasis on life adjustment influenced social studies teaching to the extent that it was no longer assumed that there were bodies of knowledge from the disciplines—history as history, etc.—that had to be taught for their own sake. Agreement on this point was not universal, however; it still isn't. But generally, as Wehlage and Anderson (1972) noted, the emphasis shifted toward helping students learn such personal and social skills as "being good family members, making wise vocational choices, and managing money intelligently." Today, some forty to fifty years later, "making wise vocational choices" and "managing one's money intelligently" are major goals of *career education* and *consumer education* programs respectively.

The emphasis on helping students cope with problems they might encounter in the real world was accompanied by a corresponding deemphasis on teaching the social science disciplines separately. Instead of teaching geography as a separate subject, for example, elements from geography, history, political science, or any of the other social science disciplines would be drawn upon as needed and merged into something that became known as "social studies." With such merging, Wesley's "social sciences simplified" definition no longer accurately described the nature of elementary social studies.

Merging

With few exceptions, elementary social studies today reflects a *unified-studies,* or integrated, approach. Typically it consists of a little economics, a little anthropology and archaeology, some history and political science, and, at times, quite a lot of geography. And although everything contained in most social studies programs is drawn from the parent social science disciplines, it isn't always clear what criteria were used to do the "drawing." As a result, Keller (1961, p. 60) described social studies as a "federation of subjects often merged in inexact and confusing ways." Or as Milton Ploghoft (1965) put it, social studies became curriculum's "foggy bottom."

Unified studies

Shirley Engle (1965, p. 1) described the situation this way:

> There is confusion, if not open disagreement, about the nature and hence the purpose of the social studies. On the one hand are those, principally academicians, who see the term social studies as no more than a general name of a collection of separate but somewhat related disciplines—history, sociology, economics, political science, etc. To many at this extreme, the very name social studies is anathema because it does not refer to a particular subject. At the other extreme are those who see social studies as a discipline in its own right, intermingling knowledge from all of the social science disciplines and dealing directly with social ideas and problems as these occur to the average citizen.

There are still plenty of people—not all of them academicians—who feel that as a subject "social studies" is for the birds. Generally, these individuals yearn for a return to the days when history was taught as history, economics as economics, and so on. Max Rafferty (1973, p. 22) once described such individuals as those who ". . . see these ancient and highly differentiated disciplines being hanged, drawn, quartered, and mixed up all together in a steaming witches' brew labeled 'social studies,' which offers the children dubious gobbets of undigested and variegated information designed to confuse them completely about virtually everything."

"Social hash"?

In the fifty-or-so year interval since the life-adjustment emphasis first emerged, it appears that the educational pendulum (which we referred to earlier) has swung a couple of times. In the early 1950s, for example, Arthur Bestor (1953) was describing the schools as "Educational Wastelands." Instead of dealing with immediate problems such as "managing one's money," Bestor and others of similar persuasion argued that the schools should focus on basic intellectual development. In other words, the critics of that era argued that a well-established foundation in "the basics" would enable students to deal with whatever kinds of immediate problems they might encounter. We're not trying to suggest that history necessarily repeats itself, but the argument that schools should focus on skills, not frills, is essentially similar to the argument put forth by "back-to-the-basics" supporters today.

After the Russians launched their satellite in 1957, thereby beating the United States in the space race, national attention turned to the so-called "crisis in our schools." America's solution was a massive, federally funded, curriculum development effort throughout the 1960s and early 1970s, a movement that began in mathematics and the "hard" sciences—physics, chemistry, etc.—and was later extended to the humanities and social

"Project Social Studies"

sciences. The funds to pay for the development of new social studies teaching materials were funneled through the U. S. Office of Education (U.S.O.E.) and the National Science Foundation (N.S.F.) in what became known as "Project Social Studies."

The boxed material on pages 29–31, entitled "What Causes Unfriendliness," illustrates sample student material from one of the elementary curriculum-development projects funded under Project Social Studies. These materials, which are part of the *Social Science Laboratory* series, were produced by the Michigan Social Science Curriculum Project (1969). Like instructional materials developed by some of the other curriculum projects, they reflect an attempt to introduce a relatively new discipline into the social studies curriculum. In this instance, that discipline was social psychology. Note that although some of the teaching materials developed during the 1960s have become somewhat dated, many of the approaches and techniques have since been revised and incorporated into the text materials currently available from commercial publishers.

The disciplines change, too

The increased emphasis on teaching the social science disciplines that emerged in the 1960s by no means reflected a return to the kind of social studies taught at the turn of the century. For one thing, the social science disciplines themselves had changed. One of the best illustrations of this is found in political science. It's oversimplified but essentially correct to say that for many years political science was dominated by an emphasis on "structure." This means that most political scientists focused their attention on how political institutions were (and are) organized. And, as "structuralists," their interest was expressed in questions such as "How many members are in the United States Senate?" and "How are those seats allocated?" More recently, many political scientists have shifted their concern toward *political socialization,* the way in which we develop our political beliefs and attitudes. (This shift in focus is readily apparent in some of the newer teaching materials produced by the High School Political Science Curriculum Project at Indiana University, such as *Comparing Political Experiences.*) Instead of focusing on questions of structure, a political socializationist would be likely to ask: "When (and how) does a person become a Republican, a Democrat, or an independent?" This doesn't mean that socializationists totally ignore questions of structure or vice versa; it's a case of changing emphases, not exclusion.

The changing nature of social studies (the "dynamic" we referred to earlier) is reflected in part by changing emphases in the social science disciplines, such as the one we illustrated above, and by changing conceptions as to why social studies should be taught—which is the topic we'll get into momentarily. That dynamic is also illustrated by a recent change in what some consider to be the "official" definition of social studies. Prior to 1978, the National Council for the Social Studies, the preeminent organization of social studies educators, defined social studies as including "history, economics, sociology, civics, geography, and all modifications or combinations of subjects whose content as well as aim is predominantly social." This was subsequently changed to: "the social science disciplines and those areas of inquiry which relate to the role of the individual in a democratic society designed to protect his and her integrity and dignity and which are concerned with the understanding and solution of problems dealing with social issues and human relationships" (*Social Studies Professional*, 1979).

Social studies defined

Why don't the people in social studies education produce a definition that is short and sweet? We can't say for certain, of course, but we suspect that it has to do with that dynamic we've been talking about here. Personally, we feel that scholars in each of the social science disciplines have identified findings and procedures that can help elementary and middle school students deal with their world. The effort in elementary and middle school social studies, we feel, should be directed toward "orchestrating the social sciences," to borrow a phrase from Lawrence Senesh (1971). The teacher, like a conductor, must bring in the strings (history), the brass (geography), the reeds (political science), or the percussion (economics) as they are needed. Together they make music.

We also feel that the way one goes about studying social phenomena is just as important as what is being studied. We think traditional social studies has tended to be extremely product-oriented, almost overly concerned with "the facts." In many instances, students can engage in some of the processes and procedures that social scientists use to produce their findings, and thus gain insight to how "the facts" were produced. At the same time, however, we don't believe it appropriate to attempt to train elementary children to become miniature historians, miniature political scientists, or the like. For one thing, the kids are almost sure to resist. John Fiorino (1970, p. 17) noted that "history and the social sciences are producers of knowledge while social studies is largely a consumer." We contend that providing students with experience and an awareness of how knowledge is produced, no matter how limited such experience is, will contribute to making them more intelligent consumers in the marketplace of ideas.

Adding a process emphasis

Why do we advocate such an approach? We think it parallels the kinds of questions elementary students tend to ask and the way that they learn. When students inquire, "Is it O.K. to lie sometimes?" you can bet that they're not especially interested in whether their question is economic, political, historical, or geographic. They want an answer—or a way to get at an answer—regardless of the disciplinary label we attach to the question. *How* you answer their question may be as important as what you say, just as how you go about teaching social studies may be as important as what you choose to teach.

Social Psychology in Elementary Schools

For years, efforts to teach interpersonal relations in elementary schools were piecemeal affairs, typically consisting of discussions on "Why we should cooperate," or "Why we shouldn't fight on the playground." Then in the mid-1960s, the Michigan Social Science Curriculum Project, directed by Ronald Lippitt and the late Robert Fox, developed curricular materials designed to help fourth, fifth, or sixth-grade children use the research strategies of social psychology. In part, their intent was to bring the processes of social science into elementary classrooms. The original question motivating the development of this program was, "What can be done with the child who has trouble in the classroom because he does not relate well with other pupils and/or the teacher?" Underlying that, of course, was a concern for what the social and behavioral sciences had to offer, but this wasn't necessarily treated in traditional classrooms.

Sample instructional materials

Their materials, the *Social Science Laboratory Units* (Lippitt, Fox, & Schaible, 1969), are geared toward making the classroom a living laboratory where children systematically gather, organize, and interpret information on their own behavior as well as the behavior of others. The seven lab units are designed to use immediate events in the child's life— the "here and now"—as their basic substantive content.

Everything begins with a unit entitled "Learning to Use Social Science," in which students examine data-gathering processes— interviewing, sampling, etc. They then move into one of the human-relations units, some of which are entitled: "Discovering Differences," "Friendly and Unfriendly Behavior," "Being and Becoming," "Individuals and Groups," "Deciding and Doing," and "Influencing Each Other."

The following is a sample student activity from the unit "Friendly and Unfriendly Behavior" (pp. 1–2).

"What Causes Unfriendliness?"

Julia Julia was tired of standing in line. Why doesn't the teacher open the door and let us in? she wondered. The bell rang a long time ago, and besides, it's cold outside.

Julia looked at Wendy, who was standing ahead of her in line. She was talking to Dick. Why doesn't she turn around and talk to me? Julia thought.

Model student activity

Dick and Wendy started to laugh. Julia became angry. I bet they're laughing at me, she told herself. They were probably talking about me. I'll get even with them!

Finally the teacher opened the door and the line started to move. Julia gave Wendy a hard push. Wendy fell against Dick and almost knocked him down.

Dick glared at Wendy. "What's the matter with you!" he exclaimed.

"Julia pushed me," said Wendy.

"I did not," Julia said. "Caroline pushed me and I couldn't help hitting you."

Figure 1.2 Circular Process—Julia

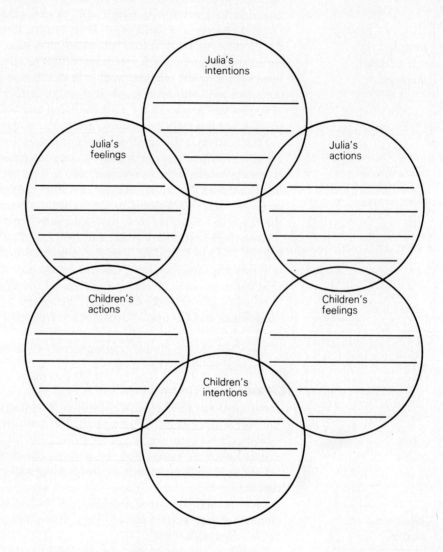

Source: Lippitt et al., Social Science Laboratory Units, *Project Book 3. Chicago: Science Research Associates, Inc., 1969, p. 2. © 1969, Science Research Associates, Inc. Reproduced by permission of the publisher.*

"I did not," Caroline protested. Several children had seen what happened. "Liar! Liar!" they cried, "Julia is a liar!"

The teacher came to see what was the matter. "What's going on here?" she said.

Caroline's best friend, Martha, spoke up. "Julia pushed Wendy. I saw her do it, and now she's trying to blame it on Caroline."

Julia began to cry. Nobody likes me, she thought. I don't know why, but nobody likes me.

Directions   As you read the story about Julia, you probably noticed that Julia's *feelings, intentions,* and *actions* formed a circular process as she interacted with the other children. Fill in tne *feelings, intentions,* and *actions* of Julia and the other children in the appropriate circles in Figure 1.2.

Social Studies: The Quest for Purpose

In the post-Sputnik frenzy of the 1960s, the teaching of mathematics was in a turmoil of sorts. Math specialists were arguing that children's knowledge of mathematics should extend beyond rote learning, beyond $2 + 2 = 4$ or $9 \times 9 = 81$. It was argued that the ability to manipulate numbers accurately was insufficient; rather, students must better understand the nature of mathematics. One of the things that differentiated the so-called "new math" from traditional math was its additional emphasis on "understanding."

Computation vs. understanding

To support this change in emphasis, a host of "new math" instructional materials were developed. Many of these materials introduced topics, such as set theory and number bases, that had rarely been studied in elementary schools before. In some cases, the topics were as new to teachers as they were to students. The implicit, and sometimes explicit, message of the "new math" was something akin to "Don't worry about computational skills—they'll take care of themselves once children understand the nature of mathematics." With the fortunate perspective that hindsight offers, it now appears that "the message" of the new math, though sometimes stated as a fact, was actually a theory—and that usually *wasn't* stated. As teachers shifted their focus toward understanding the nature of math, many children's computational skills suffered, often declining drastically. True, many children could now cite the additive principle, for example, but they couldn't multiply 9×7, with either accuracy or speed. The result? By the 1970s, many schools had begun backing away from the almost exclusive emphasis on "understanding" in order to bring students' computational skills into a better balance. In oversimplified form, the "new" new math of the 1970s and '80s now reflects a dual focus, the computational-skills thrust of traditional arithmetic and an emphasis on "understanding" that is a legacy of the "new math" of the 1960s.

Multiple purposes

Our foray through the realms of mathematics is intended to illustrate a phenomenon also found in social studies; namely, the need to strike a balance between multiple purposes. The overarching concern of social studies is perhaps best described by the term *citizenship education.* Citizenship education, however, suffers from the vagueness inherent in certain broadly stated educational goals. When you try to be more specific, as in trying to identify what schools and teachers should teach to produce the knowledge and behavior good citizens should exhibit, you are almost certain to encounter a situation similar to the "computation-understanding" phenomenon that math education has faced.

Three approaches

Within the overarching framework of citizenship education, there are three generally recognized approaches to social studies. They are: (1) teaching our cultural heritage; (2) teaching the social science disciplines; and (3) teaching children how to think, how to engage in reflective inquiry. These approaches are obviously related. American history, for example, is both a social science discipline and a repository of information about our cultural heritage. Thus, by teaching history one could theoretically kill two birds with one stone. In other instances, however, the interrelationships are less obvious or don't exist at all. In the following sections we examine the nature of citizenship education and the various approaches to it.

Technician Teaching

Over the years we've met our share of teachers who have little or no idea of the different conceptions of social studies. As a general rule, their approach consists of opening the teacher's guide (which accompanies the textbook) and doing what it says. If the guide says to talk about a certain picture in the text, they "talk" about the picture. Since anyone with a high school diploma and the ability to read the teacher's guide could do what they do, we call these individuals "technician-teachers."

When students ask "What do we gotta learn this stuff for?" as you can be certain they will, the technician-teacher's response is often "Because it's in the book." Because they haven't thought about why they are teaching something, and because they haven't decided why their students must learn it, technician-teachers often lack an adequate answer. "Because it's in the book" isn't a very effective student motivator, in social studies or in anything else. (This is a factor that probably helps account for social studies' low ratings.) And because technician-teachers may not understand *why* they're doing whatever it is they are trying to do, we suspect that they have more than their fair share of discipline problems too.

More to learn?

It's also been our experience that when prospective teachers explore some of the different approaches to teaching social studies, they sometimes approach the task as if it were merely more stuff to learn. Considering the "computation vs. understanding" situation in math education, we suggest that you consider a slightly different approach. Realistically, just as some math teachers put most of their emphasis on teaching computation skills, others tend to lean more heavily toward helping children understand the nature of mathematics. Whichever approach they take probably depends a lot on where they have the most competence and feel most comfortable. When we, as authors, are asked to teach children (not college students)—which we are regularly—you can be sure that we seldom venture into areas or approaches we don't believe in or with which we don't feel comfortable. If we did venture into such areas, our lack of commitment and the phoniness that accompanies it would be too readily visible. We've got better things to do than spend our time "faking it," and we suspect that you do too. Consider approaching the different conceptions of social studies as options, as alternatives that you can emphasize in relation to your competence and where you feel most comfortable.

For better or for worse, remember that elementary social studies is eclectic; it can be put together in a lot of different ways. In the long run we think that it will be to your advantage to regard this as an asset, not a liability. Indeed, doing so will, we think, be more effective than trying to teach something you neither understand nor believe in.

Social Studies as Citizenship Education

Social studies and citizenship education have gone hand in hand ever since the term *social studies* was introduced in 1916. The purpose of social studies, like the purpose of schools themselves, has been to educate children and youth in the attributes of good citizenship. However, until the attributes of good citizenship—what responsible citizens should know and be able to do —are identified, we lack the concrete guidelines necessary to determine what should be taught in the schools.

What are the components of responsible citizenship? Over the years various groups have sought to identify these characteristics, and often their results have been quite similar. The products of two such efforts, one by Edwin Carr and Edgar Wesley (1950, p. 1219), and another by Daniel Roselle (1966) who was reporting the efforts of the Civic Education Project, are shown below. Note that we have reordered the original lists somewhat in order to present essentially similar characteristics as matched pairs.

Good Citizenship

The Attributes of Citizenship
A responsible citizen is one who:

(Carr and Wesley)	(Roselle)
Respects the rights and opinions of others.	Believes in BOTH liberty of the individual and equality of rights for all.
Is skillful in securing, sifting, evaluating, organizing, and presenting information.	
Assumes social and civic responsibility.	Accepts the responsibility to participate in decision making by informing representatives, experts, and specialists of his [or her] reactions to alternative public policies.

Acts in accord with democratic principles and values.

Develops a set of principles consistent with his [or her] democratic heritage, and applies them conscientiously in . . . daily life.

Becomes a judicious consumer.

Understands principal economic, social, and political problems.

Develops skills and acquires knowledge to assist in the solution of political, economic, social and cultural problems . . .

Learns about vocational activities and opportunities.

Understands the interdependence of peoples and groups.

Understands that the continuation of human existence depends upon the reduction of national rivalries, and works for international cooperation and order.

Becomes a happy member of a home.

Makes intelligent adjustments to change.

Recognizes that we live in an "open-end" world, and is receptive to new facts, new ideas, and new processes of living.

Makes value judgments that enable him to function constructively in a changing world.

Gets along with individuals and groups.

Has compassion for other human beings, and is sensitive to their needs, feelings, and aspirations.

Uses basic social studies skills.

Exercises critical judgment.

Understands and promotes social progress.

Remains constantly aware of the tremendous effects of scientific discoveries on American and world civilizations, and works for use in the quest of improved living for all mankind.

Takes pride in the achievements of the United States, and at the same time appreciates the contributions to civilization of other people.

Realizes the importance of economic security and economic opportunity in the lives of every human being and registers concern himself [or herself] with strengthening both.

Uses the creative arts to sensitize himself [or herself] to human experience and to develop the uniqueness of his [or her] personality.

Sources: Edwin R. Carr and Edgar B. Wesley, "Social Studies," In Walter S. Monroe (ed.), Encyclopedia of Educational Research *(Rev. ed.) New York: Macmillan, 1950; and Daniel Roselle, "Citizenship Goals for a New Age,"* Social Education, *Vol. 30 (October 1966): 415–20.*

School-wide purposes

Make no mistake about it: These attributes extend far beyond the scope of social studies alone. *They reflect the purposes for which we have schools.* Less than half of the attributes seem to be clearly within the province of social studies, and even then social studies does not have the sole responsibility for treating most of these. The problem becomes one of identifying the elements that social studies can contribute to the training of responsible citizens. This is where the different conceptions of social studies—teaching the cultural heritage, teaching the social science disciplines, and teaching children to think—enter the picture. We examine each of these in the next sections.

Social Studies as Teaching the Cultural Heritage

In nations where governments have been thrown from power, one of the first things the new governments do is order that the schools' history books be rewritten. It's important that the nation's future citizens get the "correct" view of their nation's history. It doesn't take much imagination to determine which government is depicted in the most favorable light.

Schools everywhere are concerned with producing "good citizens," however that expression may be defined. One of the few things common to schools around the globe is the expectation that they teach about how their respective societies came into being. Many things may be a part of that story, including the nation's literary heritage and its scientific and technological development, but the most formal treatment usually occurs as a course or courses in the nation's social, economic, and political history. Thus, the Russians study Russian history, the British study British history, Americans study American history, and so forth around the globe.

In the United States, students often study American history at least three times: first at Grade 5, then at about Grade 8, and then again at Grade 11 or 12. All fifty states have laws of one sort or another that require the study of American history and government during the student's school career (High, 1962, p. 209). Some states go even further by requiring the study of American or state history before students leave elementary school. Legislation of this type seems to be motivated at least in part by political considerations, not solely by the educational merit of certain topics. This phenomenon is further illustrated by some state laws requiring that the study of democracy must precede the study of communism, socialism, or other governmental forms. We aren't aware of any teachers who have been prosecuted for violating such laws, probably because the laws are difficult to enforce and because most of their impact is on the overall organization of the curriculum. Nevertheless, legal requirements such as these, which are sometimes referred to as "Spirit of '76" laws, suggest that when it comes to dealing with our cultural heritage, there are certain topics that governments and, presumably, the people they represent want taught in the schools.

"Spirit of '76" legislation

Except for the "democracy-before-communism" type of legislation, there is an interesting quirk in some of these "Spirit of '76" laws; although they may call for the study of American history, for example, they don't always specify the topics to be taught. State departments of education sometimes produce more specific guidelines, but teachers don't always have to follow these either. So in many instances, teachers have considerably more flexibility than it might seem.

What, then, should every citizen know about our cultural heritage? For example, should every citizen know about Christopher Columbus, the Declaration of Independence, the Constitution, and the Civil War? This may not seem too difficult, so we'll assume you agree.

If you do, you're trapped! Now you face the prospect of identifying *what*, specifically, we should know about these topics. What, for example, should every citizen know about Columbus? That he "discovered" America? That he was born in Venice of questionable parentage? That he sailed in 1492? That he thought he was in the Indies? That his three ships were the *Nina*, the *Pinta*, and the *Santa Maria*? That he was reputed to have had a "thing" going with Queen Isabella? Any of the above? Or all of them? (Note: there's an intentional error in the data above. Did you find it?)

Deciding what to teach

The question of what to teach about Christopher Columbus is difficult to deal with, and to say that children should learn what's most important doesn't help much either. What's more important or less important? When we, as authors, ask ourselves why we know this information, we are equally hard put to come up with a satisfactory response. We know it, apparently because somebody in our past decided that it was important to know.

By the examples used thus far we may have implied that studying our cultural heritage is limited to American history. It isn't, of course, since our heritage extends to the very origins of *Homo sapiens.* When "our cultural heritage" is broadly defined, as it usually is, it encompasses virtually *all* knowledge that is a part of the human experience. *Selecting* which knowledge shall be taught is not a minor problem, as well you might imagine.

Social studies as teaching the cultural heritage is based on two related but essentially untested assumptions. They are: (1) that knowledge is good because it leads to understanding and wisdom; and (2) that studying the past produces responsible and patriotic citizens. It's impossible to prove the cause-effect relationships inherent in these assumptions, since schools have always dealt with our cultural heritage in one form or another. To expect that the schools will stop teaching history, for example, so as to test these assumptions seems to border on the absurd. As a consequence, we will probably continue to accept them as valid in the forseeable future.

Involvement can enhance students' interest in concrete information.

The Image-of-Greatness Approach

A popular approach to teaching our cultural heritage, in the primary grades especially, involves an in-depth study of prominent Americans from our near and distant past. George Washington, Thomas Jefferson, Ben Franklin, and Abraham Lincoln, for example, receive extensive treatment in many social studies programs. More recently, individuals such as Crispus Attucks, George Washington Carver, Susan B. Anthony, and John Glenn have been added to the list.

To explain why these individuals play such a prominent role in social studies, Donald Oliver (1960) identified what he called the "image-of-greatness" approach. Oliver stated that "the central objective of the great image approach is to provide young people with inspiring symbols which dramatically present basic human problems and the particular cultural solutions of our society." By using narrative history, the hope is that children will be projected into situations where they will develop a sense of historical reality that binds them to their compatriots of the past.

Expecting children to mimic American heroes probably isn't very realistic, especially since the society in which most of those individuals achieved prominence is not the society in which we live today. Nevertheless, the fact that American heroes were real people, and the fact that narrative history tends to focus on concrete events—as opposed to analytic history's tendency to focus on broader, more abstract trends and issues—helps make the image-of-greatness approach something that children can relate to. Incidentally, certain aspects of history, such as George Washington's dental problems, have probably received more attention and prominence through this approach that they otherwise would have.

"I pledge allegiance to the flag. . . ."

Most Americans are familiar with the events leading up to the signing of the Constitution and the Declaration of Independence, since they are common topics in American history and because we are reminded of them every Fourth of July. While most Americans can recite the Pledge of Allegiance, how many of us know of its origins? Apparently this aspect of history has not yet been judged of sufficient importance to be included in most history books. However, we'll fill you in if you're interested.

Compared with the Magna Carta or the Declaration of Independence, the Pledge of Allegiance is of recent origin. It was written by James B. Upham, head of the promotion department of *Youth's Companion Magazine,* to help support that magazine's campaign "to place a flag over every American school." The Pledge was first used when some twelve million school children recited it simultaneously, reading from *Companion* leaflets, upon the opening of the Columbian Exposition in 1892.

What was the Columbian Exposition? Perhaps the need to explain that, which is another story entirely, also explains why the history of the Pledge is not yet in many American history books.

Emphasis on Multicultural Education

For many years, our collective view of ourselves was reflected in the "melting pot" notion. The basic thrust of that view was that the cultures brought to this country by immigrants were somehow merged and melded together, in a big pot so to speak. The school did much of that cultural melding since it was the institution that dealt with immigrants on a regular basis. What came out of the school was an individual who supposedly reflected *the* American culture and value system.

Social studies textbooks have long been one of the major vehicles for projecting what it means to be an American. Fitzgerald (1979, p. 43) indicates that prior to the mid-1960s our nation was populated by two kinds of people according to the textbooks: "we Americans," and "the immigrants." Turning immigrants into "Americans" was typically presented as "a problem." Black Americans were seldom mentioned in social studies texts prior to the mid-1960s, and when they were, it was often as "the slaves"—as individuals who had somehow magically appeared in this country. Few women, other than Jane Addams and Dolley Madison, were presented, while the Spanish colonizers of Mexico and the Southwest were typically cast as gold-hungry villains. In short, the American history presented in social studies textbooks was largely an Anglo-Saxon, male-dominated enterprise.

"Us" and "them"

"Discoveries" of the 1960s

With the coming of the civil rights movement of the 1960s, most textbooks stopped distinguishing between "we Americans" and "the immigrants" and began reflecting a different point of view; namely, that we are a nation of immigrants. As Fitzgerald (1979, p. 49) stated, "The textbooks made many discoveries about Americans during the nineteen sixties. The country they had conceived as male and Anglo-Saxon turned out to be filled with blacks, 'ethnics,' Indians, Asians, and women. . . . The country also turned out to be filled with Spanish-speaking people who had come from Mexico, Puerto Rico, and other countries of the Caribbean basin. This last of their discoveries was—at least, to judge from the space they gave it—the most important one next to the discovery of blacks."

The multicultural-education emphasis in social studies is intended to reflect the fact that we are, as a nation, a multicultural, multiethnic society. Even though it might seem to be a play on words, the multicultural-education emphasis shifts the overall approach slightly, from teaching our cultural heritage to the more accurate, "teaching our *multicultural* heritage."

Multicultural/ multiethnic education

For most purposes, *multicultural education* and *multiethnic education* are virtually synonymous. As such they share a common goal of sensitizing students to the cultures, contributions, and heritages of blacks, Hispanic people, and other minorities. One technique for reaching that goal, particularly at the high school level, is through *ethnic studies;* that is, courses in black history, Spanish-speaking cultures, and the like. At the elementary level, where separate courses are less common, the study of various ethnic groups is likely to be conducted in an integrated fashion. In fact, if multicultural-multiethnic education is not integrated into a broader program of studies, we run the risk of teaching inaccurate stereotypes through what James Banks (1976) called the "chitlin's and tepee" approach we referred to earlier.

Coping with the Knowledge Explosion

One of the most perplexing problems teachers face in teaching our cultural heritage is that of "coverage," of getting everything in. This problem is perhaps best illustrated in American history courses where, faced with an almost encyclopedic textbook, many teachers are seldom able to get beyond World War II. It's the rare history course that deals with the Korean conflict, the Eisenhower years, Vietnam, or the civil rights movement of the 1960s in something other than a hurried, once-over fashion. Because there's not time to cover everything, something must be left out. Often it's recent history that is omitted. The problem, of course, is created by the fact that the school year has remained an almost-constant 180 days while history just keeps on rolling along. Thus, a teacher in the mid-1930s had some fifty fewer years of history to deal with, and the events that affect us today were somewhere in the distant future.

Selective neglect

One solution to the problem created by the cumulative nature of history is what we call "selective neglect." Since total coverage is virtually impossible, you select the topics you *don't* plan to deal with—those you intend to neglect. This then enables you to devote more time and attention to the areas you do cover. Even if you use this strategy, however, you are apt to feel constant pressure to move on. Another option you could employ takes "selective neglect" one step further and is called *postholing.* Here, you identify one or more topics that you and your students will engage in an intensive, long-term (in-depth) study of—you really "dig into" a topic. One example of such a postholing technique is found in the "Man: A Course of Study" (MACOS) program in which students spend roughly an entire semester studying the Netselik Eskimos. In this case, however, and although survey courses can be criticized for lacking depth, spending a semester st udying Eskimos is, for some students at least, a case of going overboard in the other direction.

Prospective teachers sometimes resist the notion that they have a role in selecting what they teach, be it in social studies, reading, math, or what have you. The common assumption seems to be that all of the selecting has been done beforehand, either by principals, curriculum committees, or authors of the textbooks being used. It's true that *some* selecting will have been done, as reflected by the textbook and perhaps by state or local curriculum guides. Still, many of these materials will present more content than you could reasonably expect to cover in a school year, and thus it is likely that you need to select even further.

During your first year of teaching, you may find yourself following the text and the teacher's guide fairly closely, learning the material with your students as other teachers have done in the past. Then, as you feel more comfortable, you may begin to branch out a bit, adding some things and deleting others. It's when teachers reach this second phase that they sometimes begin looking in earnest for criteria that will help them select what to teach.

Ever-expanding body of knowledge

Despite changing views of what is or isn't important, the cumulative nature of history is further affected by the widely-heralded knowledge explosion. You've undoubtedly heard that the amount of information available to us is multiplying at an increasing rate. Biologist Bentley Glass (1962, p. 6) has estimated that by the year 2000 biological knowledge will be one hundred times greater than it was in the early 1900s. And that's just in biology. Add to that the knowledge generated in other disciplines and you have a tremendously expanded "reservoir of knowledge" to deal with. We have illustrated this situation in pictorial form in Figure 1.3.

Were we to "pump" all of this information into children, even in small doses, they'd likely drown. There's just too much of it. Thus, the need to *select* the information to be taught becomes apparent once again.

If we could deal only with the smaller reservoir of knowledge, selecting what to teach might be less of a problem. The information in the smaller reservoir is "older" and, by some accounts, less likely to change. We don't buy the "old knowledge is good knowledge" argument in its entirety, however, primarily because information in the new reservoir—new knowledge —has changed that in the old. For a firsthand example of this phenomenon, look back at that 1896 geography text (Figure 1.1) and determine how many of the "facts" have been changed by new information. Not everything has changed, of course, but enough has that it seems essential that we select to teach the information and skills that will help a child survive in today's society and tomorrow's world.

Social Studies as Teaching the Social Sciences

A persistent criticism of traditional social studies programs is that they tend to emphasize isolated bits and pieces of information without providing a framework (or structure) that enables students to organize all of that information into some kind of meaningful whole. It's almost a case of being unable

Figure 1.3 The Knowledge Explosion

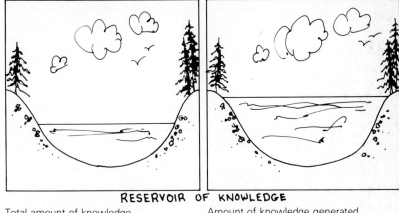

RESERVOIR OF KNOWLEDGE

Total amount of knowledge prior to 1925

Amount of knowledge generated during last fifty years

to see the forest for the trees. The structures, or frameworks, that could help students "put it all together" already exist, it is held, in the form of the social science disciplines. Barr, Barth, and Shermis (1977) captured the essence of this approach by stating that, "The various social science disciplines . . . offer not only the most reliable, responsible, and precise way of knowing the world, they also guarantee that the knowledge that students learn will not be obsolete in a few years. That is, as students learn the process by which social scientists function, they will be gifted with a *way of knowing* that will endure. They will understand the world in the deepest meaning of the term *understand;* and they will, thereby, become better citizens, capable of making decisions about problems around them."

A way of knowing

The two essential components of the social science disciplines approach are: (1) findings from the social sciences—the facts, the concepts, and the generalizations that social scientists have produced in their quest for knowledge; and (2) the processes and techniques that social scientists employ to produce and validate their findings. It is the inclusion of this second component, the processes of the social sciences, that distinguishes this from other approaches to citizenship education.

Findings and processes

As we noted earlier, the disciplines approach to social studies drew considerable interest during the 1960s. The emphasis on (1) "process," and (2) student-centered teaching techniques were major components of the so-called "new" social studies. Its ultimate goal, citizenship education, was (and is) shared with the other approaches to social studies. It differs from other approaches through its emphasis on helping students look at the world through the eyes of social scientists.

Criticism

The disciplinary approach to social studies has been criticized on several grounds, among the most prominent of which is the claim that schools are not in the business of producing miniature historians, sociologists, and so forth. Related criticism involves the contention that most of us deal with events holistically; that is, we deal with human encounters in their totality.

As Brubaker, Simon, and Williams (1977, p. 204) noted, "Citizens in the world do not divide their decision-making into various disciplines." When confronted with decisions, we don't tend to say "I must look at this as a historian would, or a sociologist would, etc." Rather, we tend to react immediately, based upon what our senses and experiences tell us is most appropriate.

Too narrow?

A related criticism of the disciplinary approach is based on the contention that, by emphasizing a narrow view of the *science* aspects of social studies, the tendency is to deemphasize or even exclude more impressionistic (nondisciplined) ways of knowing (Newmann, 1970, p. 119). Even Nobel prize-winning scientists, it is claimed, employ non-logical, nondisciplined ways of knowing—things like intuition, emotion, and even fantasy (Rothenberg, 1979)—and to ignore these methods, either intentionally or unintentionally, is to exclude some of the tools people use most often. In fairness, however, we have been unable to find an advocate of the disciplinary approach who also advocates the exclusion of intuition, emotion, or other nondisciplined ways of knowing. Note also that emphasizing the processes of science does *not* automatically exclude someone's "bright idea."

A practical problem related to the disciplinary conception of social studies involves teachers who, because of their previous experience with traditional, knowledge-oriented social studies programs as students, might understandably lack the skills needed to teach a process-oriented program. If you've never participated in taking a survey, for example, you might be hesitant to conduct one with your students. Like igloo building, survey taking can become more complicated than you might expect. Note, however, that this isn't a criticism of the disciplinary approach, but rather a problem one encounters when using it.

Process: an added dimension

Back-to-the-basics supporters may object to the "newfangled processes" that are part of the social-science-disciplines approach and argue that we should go back to teaching the Constitution, the Civil War, etc. They either ignore or are unaware of the fact that study of the Constitution, the Civil War, or anything else is not excluded in the disciplinary approach. By no means does the disciplinary approach ignore the "basics;" rather it is a matter of adding a dimension that hasn't been systematically presented previously.

Aspects of the social science disciplines typically appear in social studies textbooks under "An Investigation" or some similar heading. First-grade students, for example, might be asked to gather data on their physical characteristics—height, weight, hair color, etc.—and then present that information in simple chart or graph form. Another common technique is a straightforward presentation of information about what social scientists do, in sections with titles such as "What do archaeologists do?" Where it's appropriate, both techniques may be combined. Methods of observing and recording tend to be emphasized, as illustrated by the student materials "What Causes Unfriendliness?" (pages 29–31). The overall intent is to bring the processes and findings of the social science disciplines into the elementary classroom. We'll take a more detailed look at the nature of those processes and findings in the next chapter.

Social Studies as Teaching Children How to Think

Facts change. They go out of date. Skills don't! So to provide children with effective tools that they can use for the rest of their lives, teach them the skills that go into effective decision making. That is a basic premise for using social studies to teach children how to think.

Teaching children to think effectively is a total-school responsibility, not the province of social studies alone, by any means. Thus the appropriate question is: What is it that social studies can contribute to teaching children to think effectively?

One of the most influential advocates of using social studies as a means for teaching thinking skills was the late Hilda Taba. Her study of how children think will probably stand as one of the landmarks of educational research (Taba, Levine, and Elzey, 1964).

Role of background information

Taba (1967, p. 27) expressed her position this way: "One of the most widely accepted (and highly questionable) assumptions is that thinking cannot take place until a sufficient body of factual information has been accumulated to 'think with' later." This is the "lack of background" idea that some teachers complain about. You've undoubtedly met teachers who got so caught up in presenting "a little background information" that there was never time left to *do* anything with the information. In this context, Taba goes on to say that "Teaching that follows this assumption stresses coverage of factual knowledge, thus burdening the student's memory with an unorganized, perishable, and obsolescent assemblage of facts."

Information processing

Taba is not alone as an advocate of teaching effective thinking. A host of others support the idea. Often, however, they emphasize different aspects of thinking, and as a consequence adopt different terminology to reflect those emphases. Hence, you will find some authorities using the terms *inquiry* or *reflective inquiry*, others advocating *decision making*, some supporting *reflective thinking*, and still others using *critical thinking* and/or *problem solving*. For us to explain the differences among these, some of which hinge on subtle nuances and emphases, would probably require a book as long as this one. We will point out some of the differences where appropriate in later chapters, but for the moment suffice it to say that some form of information processing is common to them all.

If you set out to teach children to think effectively, what, specifically, would you teach? Various groups can offer some help in this respect through their attempts to identify the component skills of thinking. The list below, for instance, is abridged from one developed by a committee of the National Council for the Social Studies (1962, pp. 318–27). It identifies some of the basic information-processing skills that you might teach students.

I. Skills centering on *ways and means of handling social studies materials*

    A. Skills of locating and gathering information from a variety of sources, such as using books and libraries effectively, taking notes, using the mechanics of footnoting and compiling bibliographies

    B. Skills of interpreting graphic materials, such as using and interpreting maps, globes, atlases; using and interpreting charts, graphs, cartoons, numerical data, and converting "raw data" into these graphic forms

C. Skills needed to develop a sense of time and chronology, such as developing a time vocabulary and understanding time systems; perceiving time relationships between periods or eras and between contemporaneous developments in various countries or parts of the world

D. Skills of presenting social studies materials, such as writing a defensible paper and presenting an effective speech; participating in a discussion involving social problems

II. Skills of *reflective thinking as applied to social studies problems*

A. Skills of comprehension, such as identifying the central issues in a problem or argument; arriving at warranted conclusions and drawing valid inferences

B. Skills of analysis and evaluation of social studies materials, such as recognizing underlying and unstated assumptions or premises, attitudes, outlooks, motives, points of view, or bias; distinguishing facts from hypotheses, judgments, or opinions, and checking the consistency of hypotheses with given information and assumptions; distinguishing a conclusion from the evidence which supports it; separating relevant from irrelevant, essential from incidental information used to form a conclusion, judgment, or thesis; assessing the adequacy of data used to support a given conclusion

C. Skills of synthesis and application of social studies materials, such as formulating valid hypotheses and generalizations, and marshaling main points, arguments, central issues; comparing and contrasting points of view, theories, generalizations, and facts; distinguishing cause-and-effect relationships from other types of relationships, such as means and ends; combining elements, drawing inferences and conclusions, and comparing with previous conclusions and inferences

III. Skills of *effective group participation*

A. Assuming different roles in the group, such as gadfly or summarizer, as these roles are needed for the group to progress

B. Using parliamentary procedures effectively

C. Helping resolve differences within the group

D. Suggesting and using means of evaluating group progress

Criticism

There isn't much criticism directed toward using social studies as a vehicle to teach thinking skills; it's the kind of thing that few would oppose. If there's any controversy at all, it involves the question of which thinking skills should get the most emphasis. The absence of apparent controversy and criticism does *not* mean that thinking skills get a lot of attention, however. In other words, despite considerable lip service as to how important thinking skills are, we suspect that there are some important, though usually unstated, reasons for the neglect or incidental treatment these skills receive. Some of these are suggested below.

1   *Thinking skills are not really valued (despite what people may say to the contrary).* Imagine yourself in the following situation: You have been accused of a crime and have been offered two methods of trial. One is by a jury of your peers; the other is by a computer, that is, a computer that is accurately programmed to analyze all of the available information and to render a verdict wholly consistent with the data.

Which option would you choose—the jury of your peers or the computer? Would it make a difference if you were guilty? Or innocent?

2   *Thinking skills are difficult; they are too much work, and besides, the kids can't do them.* If students could apply thinking skills prior to instruction, there would be little need to teach them. But the fact that children may have difficulty recognizing an underlying assumption or distinguishing between a fact and an opinion, for example, is not a sufficient basis for avoiding such skills. Applying thinking skills is sometimes difficult; it can be "hard work." It's a curious kind of logic, however, that uses this phenomenon as a basis for not teaching such skills.

The situation is further complicated by a comment which you've undoubtedly heard from time to time: "Don't bother me with all of *that,* just tell me the answer." Our concern for getting answers—the quicker the better—and our corresponding lack of concern for the processes used to produce those answers, may help to explain why thinking skills don't get more attention than they do.

3   *Thinking skills are cold, abstract, and impersonal.* Thinking is one of the few quiet activities (sleeping is another one) children engage in. You can't necessarily tell when it is taking place. Indeed, thinking can be a highly personal kind of thing. It's doubtful, however, that thinking skills are any more abstract than, say, the skills involved in long division. They may be more difficult at times, but not inherently "colder" or lacking in emotion. Were some people more intimate with thinking skills, perhaps they would become more personal and less "distant."

[handwritten margin note: England = Americans speak before they think.]

Zig-Zag Thinking

We suspect that those of us who consider ourselves to be logical thinkers typically start at one point and then move, step by step, toward an end point. Edward de Bono (1970) has suggested that logical thinking, the kind most of us use, is actually a form of "vertical thinking." de Bono doesn't dispute the value of vertical thinking but indicates that it isn't the only effective way to think. His alternative? Lateral (sideways) thinking!

Sideways thinking?

de Bono uses a hole-digging analogy to illustrate the difference between vertical and lateral thinking. In vertical (logical) thinking, one begins with a hole in a given spot and proceeds to dig it deeper and deeper. In sideways (lateral) thinking, one doesn't dig the same hole deeper but looks instead for different places to dig.

de Bono supports his case with several anecdotes, one of which involves an office building that was built with too few elevators. Because of long waits for an elevator at the beginning and end of the day, some employees became disgusted and quit. Several solutions to the problem were considered, such as staggering working hours, adjusting the elevators so they stopped only at certain floors, and even adding additional elevators.

The final solution consisted of installing large mirrors in the elevator waiting areas. The result, according to de Bono, was that the employees became "so preoccupied with looking at themselves (or surreptitiously at others) that no one noticed the long wait for elevators anymore."

Whether de Bono is actually dealing with two totally different kinds of thinking is debatable. In the skyscraper case, the real problem was in dealing with the effect—the impatience of employees—created by the shortage of elevators, not simply with the elevator shortage itself. The implication is that we be especially careful to identify problems in their totality.

Thinking and Social Action

The interesting thing about thinking as an objective for teaching social studies is that it is not an end in itself. To have a child say, for example, "O.K., I've thought about it"—period—should leave you dangling as it does us. The question is, "O.K., now that you've thought about it, what's going to happen?" In other words, what will be the visible result—the product—of that invisible process called "thinking" that (supposedly) went on inside a child's head? Unless thinking results in some kind of action, in the child's doing something visible, the effort may be regarded as a kind of academic exercise.

What children do with the results of their thinking has two situational dimensions. The first occurs in the classroom where they must somehow demonstrate that they have thought, that they can, for example, distinguish between a fact and an opinion or identify the central issue in a problem or argument. The second dimension occurs in a broader societal context where students, because they have been trained to think effectively, can be expected to engage in some type of social action. As a committee for the National Council for the Social Studies (1962, p. 318) put it, "... the purpose of teaching skills in social studies is to enable the individual to gain knowledge concerning his [or her] society, to think reflectively about problems and issues, and *to apply this thinking in constructive action*" (italics ours).

Action

Student councils are sometimes cited as appropriate avenues of constructive action for elementary students. And as a form of action, student councils are generally controversy-free. The antinuclear protests of the late 1970s can also be viewed as civic or social actions, but they are certainly far from controversy-free. One of the dangers in any civic or social action, in schools or beyond, occurs when individuals move into action without analyzing the alternatives open to them. In other words, constructive action should be the result of thought—of intelligent, reflective thinking. If it isn't, we invite a form of chaos.

**Values
Education**

What things are most important to you? What kinds of things do you prize, cherish, and value? When faced with choosing among alternatives—things like selecting a college, a wardrobe, or even a mate—what kinds of things do you consider in making your decision? Helping students to answer questions like these is a major thrust of values education.

We've included values education as an emphasis within the "teaching-children-to-think" approach to social studies because answering the kinds of questions posed above cannot be done without a certain amount of thinking. But because we devote an entire chapter to values education, we deal only briefly with it here.

On the surface, values education would seem to be another way of saying "teaching values." For some, that is exactly what it means. Countless individuals believe that one of the most important components of social studies involves teaching children to believe in the core values of a democratic society. Some of those core values are the belief in the dignity and equality of the individual, the belief in the value of hard work (sometimes referred to as the Protestant ethic), and allegiance to democratic principles.

Teaching children what they should value and believe in can be a touchy issue, particularly because the school is only one of several institutions (including the home and church) associated with teaching values. In addition, it's one thing to teach that democracy is one of several governmental forms, for example, but quite another to teach that democracy is the *superior* form. The latter reflects a value judgment which, when presented uncritically and as if everyone everywhere believes it to be true, represents a form of *indoctrination*.

Indoctrination?

Actually, it's impossible for teachers not to teach values. Everytime teachers decide to teach something they are in effect saying "This is important and worth knowing." From the students' point of view, if something were not important and worth knowing, teachers wouldn't spend time teaching it, would they? In addition, every action teachers take, every behavior they model, serves as an implicit indicator of ways in which students should conduct themselves. In other words, teaching values is an inescapable fact of life.

When you or other teachers consciously, explicitly, and uncritically set out to teach certain values, e.g., "democracy is the superior form of government," you enter the arena of indoctrination. As Barr, Barth, and Shermis (1977, p. 16) noted, "By far the most important issue in social studies has been the question of indoctrination. No other single issue has so dominated discussions and debates in their field." In the event that it isn't clear from what we've said already, teaching values is on one hand an unavoidable aspect of teaching, and on the other hand an area of some considerable risk.

*Values
clarification*

Instead of trying to teach values as such, another approach to values education focuses on *values clarification*. Stated as simply as possible, the goal of values clarification is twofold: (1) helping students to clarify (become aware of) the values they hold, and (2) teaching them a process for doing that (clarifying what they think is important). The key to values clarification lies not in teaching students what *others* value, but rather in helping students identify what they themselves think is important.

Figure 1.4   The Organization of Elementary Social Studies

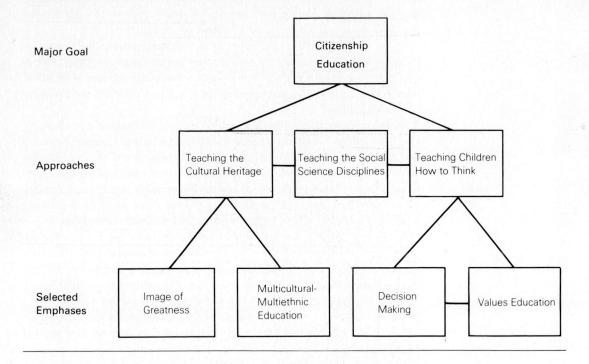

Opportunities for reflecting either of these approaches to values education are present in the "Who is Qualified for the Presidency" activity presented at the beginning of this chapter. For example, if a teacher were to say something such as "Candidate Four is obviously the best choice because . . ." that teacher would be reflecting an indoctrination approach to values education. On the other hand, if a teacher were to say something like, "Let's look at how we weighed the candidates' characteristics"—where the emphasis is clearly on the decision-making process—that teacher would more nearly reflect a values-clarification approach to values education. The distinction is subtle but important. We'll say more about values education and the role it plays in social studies teaching in Chapter Five.

Summary

If it wasn't clear when we started, it's probably very clear now that describing the nature of social studies can be a complex and sometimes confusing proposition. On the assumption that further clarification will be helpful, we have summarized the basic elements of social studies in graphic form in Figure 1.4.

We indicated earlier that social studies is dynamic. It has changed, in both form and substance, in the past and it is changing still. Amidst these changes at least one thing has remained constant: the goal of producing effective citizens. As Figure 1.4 illustrates, that goal has come through unscathed.

Figure 1.4 also illustrates the major approaches to social studies—teaching the cultural heritage, teaching the social science disciplines, and teaching children how to think. It is important to note that all of these approaches are reflected in why we have schools and, thus, may involve every subject taught in schools, not just social studies.

Several emphases that fall within the major approaches to social studies are also indicated in Figure 1.4. One aspect of teaching our cultural heritage may involve the study of prominent Americans and reflect what Donald Oliver called "the image of greatness approach." Another aspect of studying our heritage reflects the view that our society is a composite of cultures. Although we may be "one nation, under God," we are a multiethnic society, a phenomenon that is reflected in the multicultural, multiethnic-education emphasis of social studies. Two additional emphases of social studies that involve teaching children to think (and which are also illustrated in Figure 1.4) reflect a concern for helping children to make decisions (decision making) as well as for helping them to determine what's important (values education).

There are probably as many different social studies programs as there are teachers in this country. As a result, some of the dynamics we have referred to in this chapter may appear in some areas but not in others. Some of the changes in social studies can be summarized as follows:

Trends

from programs based primarily on history and geography, to *programs involving more of the social science disciplines;*

from programs based mainly on transmitting knowledge from the social science disciplines to *programs involving the information-handling processes of the social science disciplines;*

from a concern for "knowing" to *a concern for finding out;*

from programs that present a narrow approach to American culture to *programs that reflect a multicultural emphasis;* and

from programs that try to teach the reservoir of knowledge to *programs that select from the reservoir of findings from the social and behavioral sciences.*

In the next chapter we examine the social science disciplines, the kinds of human endeavor they study, and, perhaps most importantly, how the disciplines *go about* studying the human experience.

Suggested Activities

1   Stuart Chase has said that "formal history, with its Caesars and Napoleons, tends to be a record of the abnormal, the geniuses, sports, freaks, and misfits; the glandular cases of mankind." (*The Proper Study of Mankind,* p. 65.) How would you react to Chase's contention in light of your own experience?

2   American schools have traditionally taught that "saving for a rainy day" is a good and desirable practice. Some schools even invite local banks in for "banking day" in support of that practice. At the present time, however, inflation is eroding the value of the dollar to the point that it may not be worth what it was when it was placed in a bank; instead it may be more valuable if spent when earned. Would you openly support "bank day," remain neutral, or what?

References

Banks, James A. *Teaching Strategies for Ethnic Studies* (2nd ed.). Boston: Allyn & Bacon, 1979. See also, "Multiethnic Education Across Cultures." *Social Education* 42 (March 1978):177–87.

Barr, Robert D., Barth, James L., and Shermis, S. Samuel. *Defining the Social Studies.* Bulletin 51. Washington, D.C.: National Council for the Social Studies, 1977.

Bestor, Arthur. *Educational Wastelands.* Urbana: University of Illinois Press, 1953.

Brubaker, Dale L., Simon, Lawrence H., and Williams, Jo Watts. "A Conceptual Framework for Social Studies Curriculum and Instruction." *Social Education* 41 (November–December, 1977):201–05.

Carr, Edwin R. and Wesley, Edgar B. "Social Studies." In Walter S. Monroe (ed.) *Encyclopedia of Educational Research.* Rev. ed. New York: Macmillan, 1950. Also reported in Gross, Richard B., and Badgen, W. V. "Social Studies." In Charles W. Harris (ed.) *Encyclopedia of Educational Research.* 3rd ed. New York: Macmillan, 1960.

de Bono, Edward. *Lateral Thinking: Creativity Step by Step.* New York: Harper & Row, 1970.

Dewey, John, "What is Social Study?" *Progressive Education* 15 (May 1938):367–69.

Engle, Shirley H. "Objectives of the Social Studies." In Massialas, Byron G., and Smith, Frederick R. (eds.) *New Challenges in the Social Studies: Implications for Research for Teaching.* Belmont, CA: Wadsworth, 1965.

Fiorino, John A. "Why Social Studies?" In McLendon, Jonathon C., Joyce, William W., and Lee, John R. (eds.) *Readings in Elementary Social Studies: Emerging Changes* (2nd ed.). Boston: Allyn & Bacon, 1970.

Fitzgerald, Frances. "Onward and Upward with the Arts; Rewriting American History —II." *The New Yorker* (March 5, 1979):40–92.

Glass, Bentley. "Information Crisis in Biology." *Bulletin of the Atomic Scientist* 18 (October 1962):6–12.

High, James. *Teaching Secondary School Social Studies.* New York: John Wiley and Sons, 1962.

Hobin, Marsha. "Clarifying What is Important." In Kownslar, Allan O. (ed.) *Teaching American History: The Quest for Relevancy.* Washington, D.C.: National Council for the Social Studies Yearbook 44 (1974):169–88.

Huxley, Julian. "The Scientific Synthesis." In *Science and Synthesis.* New York: Springer–Verlag, 1967,

Jarolimek, John (ed.). "The Status of Social Studies Education: Six Case Studies." *Social Education* 41 (November–December, 1977):574–601.

Keller, Charles R. "Needed: Revolution in the Social Studies." *Saturday Review* 44 (September 16, 1961):60–62.

Lippitt, Ronald, Fox, Robert, and Schaible, Lucille. *Social Science Laboratory Units: Project Book Three.* Chicago: Science Research Associates, 1969.

Metcalf, Lawrence E. "Some Guidelines for Changing Social Education." *Social Education* 27 (April 1963):197–201.

Metcalf, Lawrence E. "Research in Teaching Social Studies." In Gage, N. L. (ed.) *Handbook of Research on Teaching.* Chicago: Rand McNally & Co. (1963):929–65.

National Council for the Social Studies. "The Role of the Social Studies." *Social Education* 26 (October 1962):315–18, 327.

Newmann, Fred M. "Questioning the Place of Social Science Disciplines in Education." In Gardner, W. E. and Johnson, F. A. (eds.) *Social Studies in Secondary Schools.* Boston: Allyn & Bacon, 1970.

Oliver, Donald W. "Categories of Social Science Instruction." *High School Journal* 43, (April 1960):387–97.

Ploghoft, Milton E. "Social Studies: Curriculum's Foggy Bottom." *Social Education* 29 (December 1965):540–44.

Roselle, Daniel. "Citizenship Goals for a New Age." *Social Education* 30 (October 1966):415–20.

Rothenberg, Albert. "Creative Contradictions." *Psychology Today* 13 (June 1979): 54–62.

Senesh, Lawrence. "Orchestration of Social Science in the Curriculum." In Morrisset, Irving, and Stevens, W. William, Jr. (eds.) *Social Science in the Schools: A Search for Rationale.* New York: Holt, Rinehart and Winston, 1971.

Social Studies Professional, A Newsletter of the National Council for the Social Studies 52 (September 1979).

Taba, Hilda. "Implementing Thinking As An Objective in Social Studies." In Fair, Jean, and Shaftels, Fannie R. (eds.) *Effective Thinking in the Social Studies.* Washington, D.C.: National Council for the Social Studies Yearbook 37 (1967):25–49.

Taba, Hilda, Levine, Samuel, and Elezy, Freeman F. *Thinking in Elementary School Children.* U. S. Office of Education Cooperative Research Project No. 1574. San Francisco: San Francisco State College, 1964.

Taylor, Bob L. "Is Citizenship Education Obsolete? A Commentary." *Educational Leadership* 31 (February 1974):466–69.

Wehlage, Gary, and Anderson, Eugene M. *Social Studies Curriculum in Perspective: A Conceptual Analysis.* Englewood Cliffs, N.J.: Prentice–Hall, 1972.

Wesley, Edgar B., and Wronski, Stanley P. *Teaching Social Studies in High Schools.* Boston: D. C. Heath, 1958.

Suggested Readings

Robert D. Barr, James L. Barth, and S. Samuel Shermis. *Defining the Social Studies.* Bulletin 51. Washington, D.C.: National Council for the Social Studies, 1977. As Shirley Engle noted, this book has managed "to clarify the lines of battle between the competing philosophies of the social studies and to point up the irreconcilable nature of the issues that separate them" (p. 103). For a more concise treatment, see James L. Barth, and Samuel Shermis. "Defining the Social Studies: An Exploration of Three Traditions." *Social Education* 34 (November 1970):743–51.

Jerome Bruner. *The Process of Education.* New York: Vintage College Books, 1960. A short, eminently readable book that helped to make "process" the focus of the post-Sputnik curriculum reforms.

Edwin Fenton. *The New Social Studies.* New York: Holt, Rinehart and Winston, 1967. This is a concise summary of the "new" social studies and what it's all about.

Frances Fitzgerald. "Onward and Upward With the Arts: Rewriting American History" Parts I, II, and III. *The New Yorker* (February 27, March 5, and March 12, 1979). This three-part series is a fascinating, detailed account of how social studies textbooks treat various topics.

John D. Hass. *The Era of the New Social Studies.* Boulder, CO: ERIC Clearinghouse for Social Studies/Social Science/ and the Social Science Education Consortium, Inc., 1977. This superb, thoroughly documented and detailed account traces the rise and fall of the so-called "new" social studies.

Maurice P. Hunt, and Lawrence Metcalf. *Teaching High School Social Studies.* (2nd ed.) New York: Harper & Row, 1968. Despite the fact that its title indicates its orientation, this book's treatment of reflective thinking, "closed areas," and the techniques of value analysis are excellent.

Mark M. Krug. *History and the Social Sciences.* Waltham. MA: Blaisdell Publishing Company, 1967. Professor Krug has some serious doubts about the merits of the "new" social studies, doubts which he clearly exposes in this book.

2 Social Studies and the Human Experience: The Disciplinary Foundations

Key Questions

What have we learned from the human experience, and what implications does this have for social studies education?

How do the social sciences differ from the humanities?

How does an *analytic* discipline, such as mathematics, differ from *synthetic* disciplines, such as social studies, and what does this mean for anyone who will teach them?

What are alternative ways one might approach social studies content?

Key Ideas

Humans have the potential to learn from experience—individual and collective.

The human experience is the source of content for social studies programs.

Different ways of examining the human experience have emerged over time, ways which collectively constitute the social science disciplines.

The nature of social studies differs considerably from an analytic discipline, such as mathematics. To approach them as similar is to misunderstand their nature.

Findings (concepts and generalizations) drawn from the social science disciplines are the primary basis for social studies content.

Introduction: On Studying Ourselves

We humans are really a remarkable species; we devote lifetimes to collecting things. Some of us, like pack rats, gather artifacts from the past, artifacts which, once they have aged properly, we call "antiques." This permits us to sell them for three times what we paid for them or, in some cases, three times what they're worth.

Others of us literally risk our lives collecting information about ourselves and our habitats. In fact, some of us question the sanity of those individuals who risk life and limb to be the first to stand on an invisible spot called the South Pole. Likely to garner the same response are those who traverse steaming jungles in search of "lost bands" of people. Yet others regard such actions as "brave," "courageous," and "dedicated to the cause of science."

Lifelong quests

Some of us, though, neither collect antiques nor feel sufficiently curious to want to seek out new, and in some cases original knowledge. Still we are, from birth onward, collectors, repositories, and processors of information about our individual and collective selves. True, we may not have the training of professional anthropologists or sociologists, but all of us nevertheless engage in a lifelong study of human behavior and the human experience.

Our purpose in this chapter is to examine the human experience, to consider how we have devised increasingly specialized ways for looking at it, and to see what has been found as a result of that examination. Finally, we look at what all of this means in terms of those portions of the human experience we select to pass on to the young—what we call social studies.

The Scope of the Human Experience

To say that you as a prospective teacher have been charged with the responsibility for interpreting and transmitting the human experience to the young of our culture has a grandiose and almost pompous ring to it. But once you get beyond the mechanics—the "how to do it"—of schooling, that's the name of the game. Admittedly, schools share some responsibility with other institutions in our culture—the family, the government, etc.—but a significant role in the transmission and interpretation of the human experience has been relegated to the schools, and to you as a prospective teacher in those schools.

Actually our efforts to pass on our cultural legacy have been indelibly inscribed in the annals of history. First through word of mouth and then through written history, we have transmitted portions of our collective social and cultural heritage to the young. But cast against the backdrop of historical time, our efforts to systematically examine the human experience are comparatively recent. In other words, we managed to govern ourselves well before there was something called political science, and we functioned in groups well before there was something called sociology. Indeed, it is only relatively lately that we have been afforded the luxury and security of devising ever more specialized ways for studying ourselves.

The recent past

It can be helpful to look at our experience through the metaphor of a clock. (This material is adapted from Postman and Weingartner [1969].) So imagine, if you will, the face of a clock on which every minute represents fifty years, substantially the best part of an individual's lifetime. On such a scale, the printing press would have been invented about nine minutes ago (Figure 2.1). And in medicine, it would have been only about three minutes ago that doctors began to be able to cure people of a variety of illnesses. In fact, in

Figure 2.1 The
Sequence of
Inventions

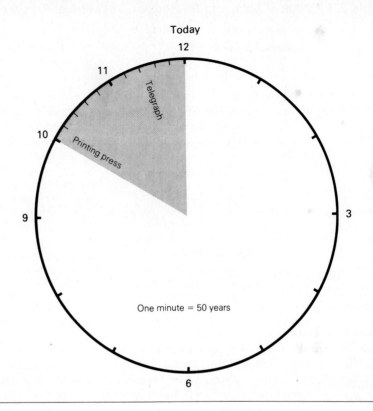

One minute = 50 years

the sweep of medical history, it has been only seconds since medicine achieved some of its most significant developments—organ transplants, laser beam surgery, and some of the other things we take for granted today.

The same scenario can be replayed for other areas. In the field of communications, for example, imagine what life would be like if we didn't have television. Not only would we be denied almost instantaneous access to events in the world (and beyond) but, with the television set gone, many of us would find ourselves rearranging the living room furniture so as not to be facing a blank spot on the wall (or, more importantly, attending to nourishing primary relationships).

Despite our penchant for the past, we are suggesting that many of those things that afford us our current lifestyle are of comparatively recent origin. Similarly, much of what we know about ourselves is also of comparatively recent origin. It is only recently that we have had a sufficient grasp of our experience to recognize that our view of what it means to be human has changed over time. The information in Table 2.1 is oversimplified to some extent, but it reveals some of those changes.

Table 2.1 What It Means to Be Human: A Historical Perspective

When	Conceptual Framework	Implications
Ancient	Without necessarily making any reference to the real world about them, human beings were believed to be able to use their "unique" mind to reason about their condition.	The world was what human beings said it was. Humans were unique and set apart from the rest of the world. The concept of science at this time was the application of reason to morality and virtue.
Early Christian Era	Religious frameworks found men and women to be part of a larger scheme and to serve purposes for existence that transcended their earthly experience. The application of the human mind and reasoning ability found rational reasons for following reasoned authority and authorities.	Mind was pure and good and physical needs and desires were viewed as evil. Humans were seen as having two dimensions—the soul and the body. Men and women were born in sin and human effort was directed toward redemption and the "other" world.
Renaissance	The political framework found men and women recognizing social realities found in existing social conditions. Power, control, leadership, and forms of social organization were based on political realities. Machiavelli's precepts emerge. Note: some argue that Machiavelli was the first political *scientist*—a scientist because he built his framework by observing and generalizing from the real world.	Beginning of the nation state and nourishment of loyalty to earthly concerns now ran parallel to religious ideals. Beginning to use observed and observable information upon which to build ideas, people started to become increasingly aware of the complexity of their world. This movement modified their "way of knowing."
18th & 19th Centuries	The economic framework emerged. The human condition began to focus on industrializing, on ideological justifications for property and the accumulation/distribution of wealth. The industrial revolution was under way. Adam Smith, Karl Marx, and others observed and interpreted the human experience as basically economic. Economic activity was part of the "natural" world. Human behavior was subject to "laws" just as the natural world was.	There was a definite relationship between people's "daily bread" and their larger conceptual frameworks of politics and religion. Class distinctions emerged, and economic mobility was related to social mobility. The organization and rules for economic activity fed nation-state rivalry, the need for justifying imperialism, and the need for explaining differing economic "levels." Natural laws pertaining to government, economics, and social class emerged as "right" when viewed as a larger, observed pattern of human experience. This led to a view of natural progress that human beings couldn't control.

When	Conceptual Framework	Implications
Early 20th Century	The psychoanalytic conceptual framework found men and women at the mercy of their subconscious and deterministically influenced by experiences. The framework reintroduced the individual and raised concern with ego, superego, and id. Each individual was a product of his or her environment—especially the early environment that acted in screening subsequent experiences. Freud's interpretation helped sharpen this framework.	The primary focus appeared to be on the individual and this seemed compatible with political and economic world views that seemed to carry weight. Emphasis was *not* on the individual deliberately interacting with experience but on the impact of early experiences that "conditioned" the psychological sets an individual carried through life—stress was on the inner person and the psychological impact one's life history carried.
Middle 20th Century	The physical sciences had struggled into maturity. The social sciences commenced to scientifically (empirically) study human behavior. Instead of emerging with set and unchanging "laws" of human behavior, the social sciences, through systematic research, came up with findings stated in "if . . . then . . . " terms—findings stated in probability rather than certainty. Aspects of human behavior became the provinces of specific disciplines, as potential sources for understanding and explaining the human condition. The proper study of man was man. Previous conceptual frameworks that focused on absolution external to human beings became challenged through the application of a maturing science to the area of human behavior.	The social science concept of man freed people from any sort of absolute determinism. It portrayed human beings as organisms interacting with man-made and natural environments. Rational applications of social science findings again brought focus to Homo sapiens as a learning/ teaching and valuing species. Social concern moved from "other worldliness" to the human condition on this planet. Ways of "knowing" shifted from logic and reason to observable human phenomenon. With a continuing struggle, men and women assumed responsibility for their life chances. As John Dewey maintained, the purpose of life is life. Social science provided different information with which to help adapt and control. The choices, difficult as they are, are ours to make.

Jacob Bronowski, in *The Ascent of Man,* has indicated that the human experience has provided us with some basic lessons, the most fundamental of which he called the "principle of tolerance." Bronowski (1973, p. 20) states that:

> There is no absolute knowledge. And those who claim it, whether they are scientists or dogmatists, open the door to tragedy. All information is imperfect. We have to treat it with humility. That is the human condition.

Imperfect information can be disconcerting for those of us who favor certainty and absolutes, a situation that becomes more awesome should we violate the human experience by teaching lessons of false certainty to the young. Indeed we could be courting tragedy by failing to heed the principle of tolerance. In summary form, the lessons learned from the human experience may seem obvious; but from a longer-range view, they can have a profound effect on what we do in schools. What is it we've learned about the human experience? The following seem most apparent:

Lessons from the human experience

1. Human nature is culturally defined.

2. Humans demonstrate a variety of adaptive behaviors.

3. Our view of what it means to be human has changed over time.

4. We are concerned not only with survival but also with the quality of life.

5. We have developed different ways of knowing, and conceptual tools with which to process information and experience.

6. We can learn from our experience; we have the ability to change.

Social Science as a Way of Studying Human Experience

During our undergraduate days, we took an introductory psychology course in which the professor spent three lectures defending psychology's qualifications as a science. At the time, it seemed odd to us that someone would devote so much effort to defending a field of study when most of us (as students) approached psychology as another body of information to learn, another course to pass. Most students in that class, we suspect, were not aware of who could be attacking psychology in a way that justified such a vigorous defense. It certainly wasn't the students.

Hindsight has enabled us to put that teacher's behavior into perspective; that is, apparently her concern was with the academic respectability that a particular way of examining the human experience gains when it matures to the point that it is regarded as valid. We discovered that, at one time, psychologists were frowned upon, regarded as upstarts who really had nothing to contribute to the fund of human knowledge. Today, however, we doubt that anyone would take three class periods to defend psychology's qualifications as a legitimate body of knowledge. In fact, we suspect that today you will find the even more specialized areas of psychology—such as

Coming of age

psycholinguistics, the study of language as a reflection of one's attitudes and motivations—vying for increased recognition as legitimate ways for studying the human experience.

We are suggesting two things: first, that various ways of looking at ourselves tend to gain respectability over time and, second, that we have evolved ever more specialized ways of doing so. This has, we feel, resulted in a situation where it becomes difficult to determine what is or is not social studies. There was a time, for example, when social studies (and social science) was made up of history, geography, political science, and perhaps philosophy. Then along came some of the "newer" social sciences—anthropology, sociology, etc. Today, in addition to psycholinguistics, we have law, psychiatry, consumer education, citizenship education, and a host of others. As a result, it's difficult to know where to draw a boundary around the social sciences, if indeed it can (or should) be drawn.

At another time, we could conveniently separate the social from the natural sciences. But today, with our capability for managing "genetic surgery," for example, the distinction is less clear. "Genetic surgery" certainly has social consequences, and thus what might seem to be a biological question at the outset finds itself squarely in the social domain.

The social implications of science

Is something such as "population education" (see, e.g., Massialas, 1972; Viederman, 1972) a science question with social implications or a social question with technological and scientific implications? It depends on how you want to look at it. It depends, also, on the way in which you view science itself. One view, based on the 1930 edition of the *Encyclopaedia of the Social Sciences*, is depicted in Figure 2.2. Although this view of science is over fifty years old, the intervening years have offered little reason to question it. And, presented in the form illustrated in Figure 2.2, several ideas are suggested:

The nature of science

All science is an offspring of philosophy. At the time of the Greeks, science was equated with moral philosophy.

Natural and social science, although perceived as two distinct and separate categories, are (in theory and in fact) functionally related. That is, findings in the natural sciences influence social science methodologies and findings, while findings from the social sciences influence the methodologies and findings of the natural sciences. Thus, academic disciplines are reciprocal.

The basic tools of science are applicable in both natural and social science.

The extent to which a particular discipline uses the tools of science and is committed to the systematic use of observation and measurement influences whether or not it is classified as a social science.

A social studies curriculum could include, if one accepts the categories and classification system of the *Encyclopaedia of the Social Sciences,* elements of the methods and findings of any or all of the disciplines and areas presented in Figure 2.2.

The scope of the social sciences depends upon whose list you happen to be using; authorities don't agree. For our purposes, we have selected the listing presented in the *International Encyclopedia of the Social Sciences* (Sills, 1968, p. xxii). It identified the following disciplines:

*The social
sciences*

Anthropology—including cultural, economic, physical, political, social, and applied anthropology as well as archaeology, ethnography, ethnology, and linguistics.

Economics—including econometrics, economic history, the history of economic thought, economic development, agricultural economics, industrial economics, international economics, labor economics, money and banking, public finance, and certain aspects of business management.

Geography—including cultural, economic, political, and social geography (but not physical geography).

History—including the traditional subject matter fields of history and the scope and methods of historiography.

Law—including jurisprudence, the major legal systems, legal theory, and the relation of law to the other social sciences.

Political Science—including public administration, public law, international relations, comparative politics, political theory, and the study of policy making and political behavior.

Psychiatry—including theories and descriptions of the principal mental disorders and methods of diagnosis and treatment.

Psychology—including clinical, counseling, educational, experimental, physiological, social, and applied psychology.

Sociology—including economic, organizational, political, rural, and urban sociology; the sociologies of knowledge, law, religion, and medicine; human ecology; the history of social thought; sociometry and other small-group research; survey research; and such special fields as criminology and demography.

Statistics—including theoretical statistics, the design of experiments, nonsampling errors, sample surveys, governmental statistics, and the use of statistical methods in social science research.

The Behavioral Sciences

Some scholars suggest that several of the disciplines listed under the social sciences should be clustered under the label "behavioral sciences," a phrase that gained popularity when the Ford Foundation subsidized a Behavioral Science Program in the 1950s. Bernard Berelson (1963, p. 4), for example, distinguishes between the social and behavioral sciences as follows:

> The behavioral sciences are typically more devoted to the collection of original data reflecting the direct behavior of individuals or small groups as against the more aggregative, indirect, and documentary practices of economists, political scientists, and historians.

Figure 2.2 The Fields of Science

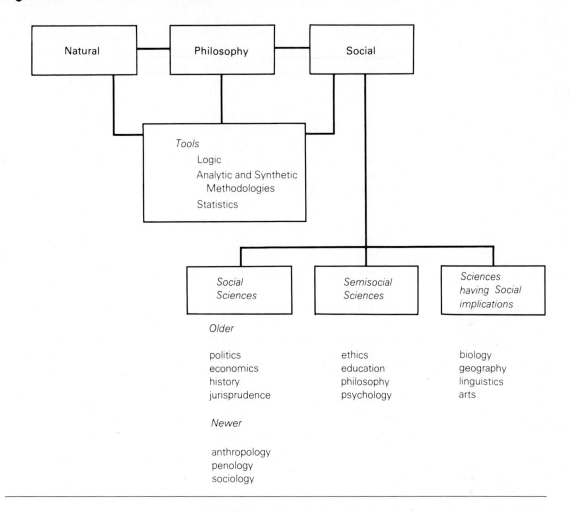

Within Berelson's scheme, it would seem that sociology, anthropology, psychology, and some of the other disciplines would be subsumed under a behavioral science category.

The expression *behavioral sciences* is used more frequently than it was ten to fifteen years ago, and we suspect it would gain even wider usage and acceptance were it not for its manipulative connotations—"I don't want any behavioral scientists studying me. What d'ya think I am, crazy or something?" To some it smacks of a subversive plot. Indeed it may be some time before the legitimacy of the behavioral sciences extends very far beyond the academic community.

Social Studies, Social Science, or Both: A Question of Emphasis

Although the problem of defining the scope of the social sciences still exists, social scientists are continually adding to the fund of knowledge we call the human experience. While individual efforts may be systematic and well organized, we have no systematic way of managing the information that social scientists are producing. Thus we find the results of their efforts scattered throughout hundreds of journals and magazines. Some of these findings eventually appear in textbooks.

The nature of information about the human experience can take many forms. In some cases it consists of *factual data*—pure, uninterpreted, documentary information. You could, for example, determine how many acres of American farmland were harvested in 1957, assuming you have a need for such information. In other cases, information takes the form of reinterpretations of existing information—a new look at the role slavery played as a cause of the Civil War, or a new explanation for why Indians might further complicate their food problem if they were allowed to eat their sacred cows.

Generalized findings

Still other data are combined in the form of generalizable statements (generalizations) that are applicable to all of us at all times and in all places; for example, all cultures develop a means of social control, ways in which the conduct of their members is governed, etc. Still other data about the human experience exist in the form of probability statements, descriptions of the ways in which we *tend* to behave. We know, for example, that the members of a group will *tend* to perceive the group's opinion as being closer to their own than it actually is (Berelson and Steiner, 1964, p. 336), just as we know that when two cultures come into contact, a certain amount of change and diffusion will take place. We also know that things learned early in life will *tend* to change less readily than those things learned later in life (Berelson and Steiner, 1964, p. 653). By knowing these things, we have a basis for anticipating and interpreting human behavior.

We deal with the different forms of knowledge from the social and behavioral sciences in considerably greater detail in Chapter Seven. Here, our intent is to suggest that social science findings come in such a variety of forms. This has implications for you as a prospective social studies teacher. In the next section we go one step further and suggest that approaching social studies as you might approach a subject such as mathematics is to misunderstand the nature of the beast.

Analytic Disciplines

For our purposes, permit us to suggest mathematics as an illustration of a school subject that reflects a relatively "closed" system. In other words, math's principles, its rules, and its axioms are givens: $1 + 1$ will always equal 2. We suggest further that mathematics is also a "language," a means by which we can express logically consistent relationships. And to carry this out even further, you will find that the algorithms of arithmetic ($1 + 1 = 2$, or $3 \times 3 = 9$) can be construed as the "grammar" of mathematics. They reflect the way in which mathematics "fits" together to the extent that $2 + 2 = 5$ is as wrong as saying "We *is* here" or "He *are* there."

Mathematics also exemplifies a discipline that has an identifiable hierarchy, as can be illustrated by those knowledges prerequisite to doing long division. In other words, the nature of mathematics is such that you can analyze and identify what a child must know in order to enter the system and thereby communicate (and compute) in mathematical terms. Somewhat the same situation also exists in music; if you don't understand the concept of "staff," you can anticipate problems.

We refer to subjects like mathematics as *analytic* disciplines: bodies of knowledge that exhibit the following characteristics:

Characteristics of analytic disciplines

1   The entire scheme of the discipline rests upon abstract constructs and rules. A student is not required to observe and check similarities and differences among real-world objects to find that there are agreed-upon rules—for example, that all circles, by definition, have 360 degrees, and that a degree is 1/360 of a circle. In like manner, one never sees a degree but rather has a mental picture of what a degree is. One can "do" mathematics without ever referring to a real-world object or relationship (and even though children sometimes persist in counting on their fingers).

2   The principles, rules, or axioms are given, and are logically related. These logically consistent rules govern the products and processes in an analytic discipline.

3   Once students learn (and follow) the logical rules of an analytic system, they are able to manipulate abstractions to arrive at "set" answers—answers that are correct and right because they are based on the total system.

Teaching implications

4   The implications for teaching and learning in analytic disciplines include:

4.1   The presence of correct answers that can be verified as such

4.2   The existence of correct procedures that can be evaluated as such

4.3   A situation where each aspect of a procedure is dependent upon a preceding aspect, which necessitates teaching (and learning) the content in sequence; in a real sense, an analytic system is the basis of a taxonomy.

4.4   If there are "set" rules and "set" procedures and correct responses, and if there is a logical sequence to what must be learned, then teaching tasks and student assessment are dependent, to some degree, on the "order" imposed by the content.

Some of us function well in analytic systems, while others of us have considerable difficulty manipulating abstractions. In fact some of us, apparently because of our experience with analytic subjects such as mathematics, attempt to force other subject areas into an analytic mold. Sometimes the "fit" leaves a lot to be desired.

With one major exception, social studies generally does not "fit" the characteristics of an analytic discipline. This does not mean that the skill of analysis is alien to social studies—far from it. What it does mean is that the *basis* for saying one knows something is different in most social studies. The major exception to this is the area of map and globe skills. Longitude and latitude, for example, fit the characteristics of an analytic system. It is relatively "closed," and either you understand it or you don't.

Synthetic Disciplines

Each of us, in our own way, adds something to the human experience. And each of us will tend to look at the human experience a little differently. Our perceptual "blinders" will permit us to see some elements while ignoring others. In other words, each of us builds—synthesizes, if you will—a personal view of the world in which we live. And although each of us perceives the world differently, it becomes difficult to say that a particular view is "wrong": different, yes, but not necessarily wrong.

To the extent that social studies involves elements of the human experience, and to the extent that it is nearly impossible to point to a student and say, "She knows social studies," with the same security as one could say, "She knows arithmetic," we consider social studies as falling into the category of a *synthetic* discipline. Again, we are referring here to the source and the referents used in an academic study. Synthetic disciplines can be characterized as follows:

Characteristics

1 The basis of the discipline rests upon observed, real-world phenomena; mental constructs or generalizations are developed to bring order to what has been observed. Thus a student is *not* confined to working with abstract mental constructs that have no necessary basis in real-world or observable phenomena.

2 The concepts, generalizations, and findings of a synthetic discipline are not given (in the philosophical sense) *prior* to observation. The processes of a study are controlled by logic, but there is no necessary logical relationship among findings. However, the more generalizable the finding, the more *probable* it is that the finding is an explanation of the phenomenon.

3 Students using a synthetic discipline learn the tools (including logic and analysis) for systematically conducting inquiry. Through the manipulation of skills, the results or "products" of the inquiry emerge. However, the results are not considered "correct" (as would be the case in an analytic discipline) but rather are judged in terms of the procedures used in the study.

Teaching implications

4 The implications for teaching and learning include:

4.1 A more limited idea of what constitutes a "correct" answer: a finding from the social sciences is different than a principle in mathematics—the latter being a logical mental construct while the former is based on ideas rising from observing the world around us.

4.2 There are valid procedures to follow and these can be evaluated as such.

4.3 The generalizations and findings in a synthetic discipline are generally *not* dependent upon a highly structured network of preceding generalizations that must be mastered before moving on. Consequently, content need not be learned in a set sequence, nor does the discipline readily lend itself to task analysis.

4.4 The ordering of observed phenomena is created rather than imposed. The order itself can be modified and changed.

We referred to analytic disciplines as "closed" systems; that is, built upon given mental constructs. Synthetic disciplines are more "open" systems; that is, they deal with human experience in terms of tendencies (probabilities) rather than static givens. A problem with this kind of differentiation emerges by virtue of the fact that an analytic system such as mathematics also has a history—its process of change. In addition, some social science disciplines (economics, for example), tend to be more analytic than some of the other disciplines. Thus differences in the "openness" and "closedness" of the disciplines are a matter of degree more than kind.

Searching for the Structure of the Disciplines

During the 1960s we witnessed considerable interest among social scientists in the structure of their respective disciplines. At least a part of their interest can be attributed to a statement made by Jerome Bruner in his landmark book, *The Process of Education* (1960, p. 31): ". . . the curriculum of a subject should be determined by the most fundamental understanding that can be achieved of the underlying principles that give structure to that subject."

Considerable controversy has surrounded the search for structure, and to a certain extent it continues still. Some scholars are unwilling to accept the notion that the disciplines have structures, while among those who do, there is little agreement as to what those structures are. Still others argue that teaching the structure of a discipline is not what social studies is all about, and that the intent of social studies is not to produce miniature historians, economists, political scientists, and so forth, but should be directed toward teaching children how to use findings from the various social science disciplines.

Why do we bother differentiating between analytic and synthetic disciplines? First, because school programs seem to be organized as if all subject areas were analytic, as if the organizational structure for a math program, for example, would be equally appropriate for social studies, literature, and science (natural or physical science, that is). Second, we differentiate because one begins with a different set of assumptions when teaching synthetic (as opposed to analytic) disciplines; and third, because we think you should be aware of one of the differences between social studies and subjects such as math—a difference you may have been aware of intuitively but were probably unable to explain in more specific terms.

Actually, the fact that social studies is a synthetic discipline offers a number of alternative approaches to social studies content; it affords us a number of different entry points to the human experience. Some of these are identified in Table 2.2.

Starting with a listing from any column as an entry point, over three thousand alternative configurations are possible, each reflecting a different orientation and a different blending of content and instructional purposes. Our list is not exhaustive; for instance, just by listing the major components of each discipline (social psychology, etc.) we could double the number of possible configurations. Six thousand? With so many possibilities (some more preferable than others) it's little wonder that some individuals go to the other extreme and define social studies simplistically—as just history and geography. Yet to do so is to deny the nature of the human experience.

Table 2.2 Alternative Ways of Looking at Social Studies

Objects of Study	Disciplines	Major Findings and Ways of Knowing	Instructional Purposes
the community	anthropology	value statements	miniature scholars
native Americans	economics	descriptions	cognitive skill development
area studies	geography	nonempirical-based feelings	accumulation of knowledge
the United States	history	principles (analytic or empirical)	concept development and testing
non-western civilization	philosophy	generalizations based on observations and probability	creative use of indvidual and collective experience
the environment	political science		indoctrination
change processes	psychology		social control
minorities	sociology		
local, state, and national government			
citizenship			
consumer economics			

The Program-Content Game
(This activity can be done alone or in a small group.)

Directions At random, select one item from each column in Table 2.2 (four elements in all). Choose one of these, at random, as your primary instructional focus. Then plan a social studies lesson using just these elements.

If done in groups, share your lessons with one another and, as a group, identify the "lesson" implicit in the game.

The X Y Z of Social Studies Content

Considering all the social science disciplines, the possible topics for study, and the other alternative ways of approaching social studies content, it becomes apparent that we need something that can help pull all of these together. In other words, we need some common element that can help bridge content, methods, and goals. We, like others before us, suggest that the major findings from the social science disciplines can serve as this common element.

Major Findings from the Social Sciences

The following are some major findings which we have stated in nonacademic terminology. We have selected some of the most general findings, those that seem to hold for most human beings and human activities regardless of unique social situations, cultural backgrounds, or geographic locations. Ultimately these findings serve as the foundation (or part of it) for virtually every social studies program.

A People all over the world are the same in some ways and different in other ways. People respond to the same problems. The ways people respond may differ.

B Human beings *learn* to behave the way they do. The ways human beings think and act depend more on their experiences than on being born with differences.

C Most human beings learn social habits. Some of these habits are performed automatically and without thought. When people behave in habitual ways, there are patterns to their behavior; these patterns help others to predict how people will behave.

D Most people think that their own way of doing things and their own ways of thinking are "natural" and right.

E Every habit, pattern of behavior, and idea people have makes "sense" to them and to their living situation. The habits, behaviors, and ideas of other people not in the same life situation may *not* make the same sense.

F All people have the ability to learn from past experience; people can accept or change their ways of living.

G When a change takes place in one part of a person's life, it is likely to make changes in other parts of his or her life. Some intended changes bring about unintended changes.

H People usually respond to what they *think* things are and not to what things really are.

I Most people live in group settings. A person may live in a number of different group settings at the same time. This may cause conflict for a person, especially if different groups expect opposite kinds of behavior.

J Most people carry a "map" of their social worlds in their mind. This helps make social living different from just being in the physical presence of others.

K Most groups in which people live are dependent upon other groups (in which they don't live). This can lead to cooperation or conflict.

L People learn to play certain roles. Other people expect the roles to be played in certain ways. The roles a person plays (and the rewards and punishments that go with the roles) may change over time and with new situations.

M A person seldom behaves in a certain manner for only one reason. Why individuals behave as they do usually involves a number of factors. Behavior is not a simple thing to understand.

N Most human behavior is done to satisfy some purpose. Humans behave in order to achieve goals.

O All human beings are born with the same physical needs. Ways of satisfying these needs differ from one person to another, from one group to another.

P   A person's personality is usually made up of physical traits, life experiences, and the physical setting in which the person lives.

Q   Individual human beings differ from each other in what they value and in how they behave. People living in the same group have a tendency to share values and behaviors that are quite similar.

R   The groups in which people live have definite ways to teach group members what to think and how to behave. Most people both influence others and are influenced by others.

S   Every human group has some way of handling how people work, how resources are used and distributed, and how the group's "wealth" is to be managed. All this is related to what the group values.

T   In most groups, individual group members depend upon one another for satisfying needs and wants.

U   How people use their physical environment depends upon what is available, what is wanted, and how the group manages itself. How people use their physical and social environments depends upon their value system.

V   How people think and behave depends, in part, on past experience. People can use past experience a number of ways: (1) to learn how and when to change, (2) to find reasons for continuing certain things, (3) to provide answers to problems, (4) to make people feel unique and part of a common, shared past.

W   All people live under some form of control. There are basic rules of behavior and basic ways of enforcing the rules. In all groups of people there are rules for individual behavior and rules for conducting group behavior. How rules are made and enforced often depends upon what people value.

X   In all human groups there are ways of handling disagreements.

Y   In order for human beings to live with one another, there is need for a common language that allows peoples to share ideas in ways that allow understanding.

Z   Most people and groups of people believe in myths and legends that help them interpret the world and that help them make sense of their own world.

Content

These findings could become the content around which instruction is geared. Notice, however, that as we have used the term *content* in this chapter it has referred to two different but mutually supporting ideas: (1) the information and ideas contained in a particular subject area, such as social studies, and (2) the subjects or topics that matter in a specific field of study. If you think about the two different meanings, a rather crucial aspect of social studies teaching begins to emerge (if, that is, you are not already aware of it): being a teacher is different from being a scholar. Teachers must identify and use specific information and ideas to ensure that *others* learn to identify and use information and ideas, whereas scholars usually identify information and ideas to be used in developing more content and more effective modes of inquiry.

An Eskimo classroom. What do you notice?

We are not suggesting that scholars can't teach, nor are we suggesting that teachers cannot also be scholars. Our point is that while teachers have some dependency upon the scholars' work, teachers and scholars may view content from different perspectives.

Teaching and scholarship

To a large extent, the social (and behavioral) sciences are constructs developed to aid in the scholarly pursuit of knowledge. Yet in a very basic sense, the information and findings from the academic disciplines become the raw materials upon which social studies programs are built. How one chooses to select, organize, and use this raw material will determine the nature of that program.

Social Studies Education and Social Science Education

It can be argued that social studies education is an applied version of social and behavioral science—that the results of systematic study of the human experience become the content of the social studies and that the disciplined ways of studying human behavior become skills to be developed. Yet some authorities will suggest that what we have just described is not social *studies* education but rather social *science* education. Although this might seem to be another case of academic hairsplitting, distinguishing between the two will make a difference in the kind of program you teach.

In distinguishing between social studies and social science, it's important to recognize that *science* has at least two meanings. The first and most obvious describes certain courses—biology, chemistry, and the like—that all

Kristin Poolman
203 Offenhauer
East
372-6298

of us have taken at one time or another. But *science* is also defined as a set of procedures or processes for dealing with data. It's this second element, the systematic procedures for securing and processing information, that social scientists and natural and physical scientists have in common. A chemist and an economist, for example, may both test certain theories, the chemist using test tubes and the economist using statistical graphs and tables. It's not the hardware—the test tubes, the tables, or the other paraphernalia—that makes someone a scientist; rather it's the rigorous way in which the individual secures and processes information.

Science: courses and processes

The kind of social studies programs that many of us experienced probably did not focus on the procedures used in investigating human phenomena, nor are they likely to have focused on identifying conditional (probable) explanations for human behavior. Rather, the focus tended to be on categorical "laws" and past achievements. In other words, most traditional social studies programs seem geared to what can be called a humanities approach. We have always had some difficulty pinpointing just what "the humanities" are, since they have tended to become a curricular catchall in much the same way social studies has. For our purposes, however, we have accepted the definition of the humanities provided in the handbook of *Standard Terminology for Curriculum and Instruction in Local and State School Systems,* which states, "The study of a group of related subjects such as literature, art, music, religion, history, philosophy, and classical and modern languages . . ." (Putnam and Chrismore, 1970).

The humanities approach

The primary concern of the humanities seems to be with peoples' individual cultural achievements and values as distinguished from their social institutions. The humanities would seem to offer a repository for our collective cultural experience. The key difference between the humanities and the sciences rests, we think, with the latter's concern for processes of investigation and the former's concern with the products of previous investigations. Note that our distinction here is descriptive, *not* judgmental.

From our perspective then, *social studies education* can be defined as the transmission of the human experience from a humanities perspective, with the knowledge and appreciation of our social, political, cultural, and technological achievements as its primary goal. *Social science education,* on the other hand, can be regarded as more inclusive since it incorporates the application of science as a way of studying social phenomena and the human experience.

Definitions

To distinguish between social studies and social science does not imply the existence of mutually exclusive, hostile camps. Our intent is to describe an orientation, an emphasis that the program you teach can reflect.

The way in which you ultimately teach the human experience will depend on a lot of factors, obviously. The resources you have available, the community's expectations, your own background in the social sciences, and whatever curriculum guide your school uses can all play a part in that decision. And, if most of your course work and experience is in the humanities, you may be more comfortable with that approach to social studies. Yet one of the most crucial factors in that decision will rest upon what your values tell you is important and worthwhile for kids to know.

Summary

What do we known about ourselves? How can and should we go about selecting and teaching what we know about ourselves? Our intent in this chapter has been to blend these two questions in an examination of the human experience, that colossus from which all social studies stem.

We looked first at some of the ways in which we examine the human experience; namely, the social science disciplines. We focused particularly on the ways in which information gleaned from the social science disciplines differs from other disciplines, such as mathematics. We suggested, also, that while differentiating between analytic and synthetic disciplines could very well be meaningless for students, it has some important ramifications for those of us faced with teaching those disciplines. Finally, we differentiated between social studies education and social science education, and suggested that traditional social studies instruction has reflected a humanities approach, one that does not give primary emphasis to the processes of science. We also suggested that the way most teachers approach social studies reflects, to one degree or another, a blending of social studies and social science.

References

Berelson, Bernard (ed.). *The Behavioral Sciences Today.* New York: Basic Books, 1963.

Berelson, Bernard, and Steiner, Gary A. *Human Behavior: An Inventory of Scientific Findings.* New York: Harcourt, Brace and World, 1964.

Bronowski, Jacob *The Ascent of Man.* Boston: Little, Brown, 1973.

Bruner, Jerome. *The Process of Education.* Cambridge, MA.: Harvard University Press, 1960.

Massialas, Byron. "Population Education as Exploration of Alternatives." *Social Education* 26 (April, 1972):347–56.

Postman, Neil, and Weingartner, Charles. *Teaching As A Subversive Activity.* New York: Dell Publishing, 1969.

Putnam, John F., and Chismore, W. Dale (eds.) *Standard Terminology for Curriculum and Instruction in Local and State School Systems, Handbook 6.* Washington, D.C.: U.S. Government Printing Office, 1970.

Seligman, Edwin R. A. "What Are the Social Sciences?" In E. R. A. Seligman (ed.), *Encyclopaedia of the Social Sciences.* Vol. 1. New York: Macmillan, 1930: pp. 3–7.

Sills, D. E. Introduction. In D. E. Sills (ed.), *International Encyclopedia of the Social Sciences.* Vol. 1. New York: Macmillan, 1968.

Viederman, Stephen. "Population Education in the United States." *Social Education* 36(April, 1972):337–46.

Suggested Reading

Stuart Chase, *The Proper Study of Mankind: An Inquiry into the Science of Human Relations.* (rev. ed.) New York: Harper & Row, 1967. Long one of our favorites—we have difficulty keeping a copy around. An excellent introduction to how the social sciences look at experience.

3

Planning: Organizing a Teaching Framework

Key Questions

How does one plan social studies lessons and units?

How do teachers deal systematically with the complex aspects of planning?

Where do teachers get their objectives?

How do teachers *use* content?

In planning, where do teachers begin?

Key Ideas

Instructional planning is a systematic process in which each aspect of planning interacts with every other aspect.

Planning is a complex process mainly because of the number of elements that one must deal with. Complex, yes. Complicated? No.

The key to successful planning lies in clearly specifying one's intent.

Goals and objectives reflect different levels of specificity in stating instructional outcomes; goals are general, objectives are more explicit.

Planning begins with the identification of what students will be able to do *after* instruction.

Social studies content is something that teachers *use*, and not merely something that students are expected to know.

Introduction: Beginning at the End

The natural place to start something—whether it's teaching, this chapter, or anything else—is at the beginning. Such an obvious statement hardly demands elaboration, but when it comes to instructional planning, things are not quite as obvious as they might seem. When teachers plan for instruction they do *not* begin by deciding what they'll have their students do on the first, the second, and then the third day of class. Sooner or later, those decisions must be made, of course, but in planning, most teachers begin at the "end," with the identification of what students should know, feel, and be able to do *after* instruction. The first phase of planning begins at the "ends," at the destinations that teachers want their students to reach. Once those "ends" are determined, the balance of a teacher's planning can work backward from those points. When teachers actually teach, the pattern may be reversed. Through instruction, teachers attempt to reach the destinations—the goals and objectives—they have identified through the planning process.

Teaching and writing actually share some of the same characteristics. For instance, when we started to write this chapter, we did not begin with the words you have just read. In fact, before we could even think of starting this chapter we had to know what it would say and where it would lead. Only then could we determine what should go into the introduction you're reading now. In addition to a detailed outline, a list of key ideas, and a pile of notes, we have already written a rough draft of the summary for this chapter. Thus, we've actually started this chapter at the end, by writing the summary first. We've also learned that as we write the balance of the chapter things will sometimes change a bit. Occasionally we deviate from our plan (our outline) and end up giving more or less emphasis to some topics than we had originally planned. The same kind of thing often occurs in teaching. In any event, we don't write the final draft of the summary until after we've written the rest of the chapter.

Planning: key questions

Whether you are planning to teach social studies or anything else, the planning process involves three basic elements. Simply stated, they are: (1) identifying *where* you (and your students) are going; (2) identifying *how* you (and your students) will get there; and (3) identifying *how well* you got to wherever you were going. All three components are essential, but the key to the entire process is Element One—determining where you are going. Unless you are able to identify clear goals and objectives, you could very well end up somewhere else. Like Robert Mager's fabled sea horse, you need to know where you are going before you begin.

Fable of the sea horse

Once upon a time a Sea Horse gathered up his seven pieces of eight and cantered out to find his fortune. Before he had traveled very far he met an Eel, who said,

"Psst. Hey, bud. Where 'ya going?"

"I'm going out to find my fortune," replied the Sea Horse proudly.

"You're in luck," said the Eel. "For four pieces of eight you can have this speedy flipper, and then you'll be able to get there a lot faster."

"Gee, that's swell," said the Sea Horse, and paid the money and put on the flipper, and slithered off at twice the speed. Soon he came upon a Sponge, who said,

"Psst. Hey bud. Where 'ya goin'?"

"I'm going out to find my fortune," replied the Sea Horse.

"You're in luck," said the Sponge. "For a small fee I will let you have this jet-propelled scooter so that you will be able to travel a lot faster."

So the Sea Horse bought the scooter with his remaining money and went zooming through the sea five times as fast. Soon he came upon a Shark, who said,

"Psst. Hey, bud. Where 'ya going?"

"I'm going out to find my fortune," replied the Sea Horse.

"You're in luck. If you'll take this short cut," said the Shark, pointing to his open mouth, "you'll save yourself a lot of time."

"Gee, thanks," said the Sea Horse, and zoomed off into the interior of the Shark, there to be devoured.

The moral of this fable is: if you're not sure where you're going, you're liable to end up someplace else—and not even know it (Mager, 1975, preface).

Overview

In this chapter we will examine the elements of planning for instruction, paying particular attention to the process of identifying goals and objectives. We will also examine the different types of products that result from the planning process, particularly unit plans and daily lesson plans. We deal only briefly with Elements Two and Three of the planning process outlined above. Element Two, figuring out how to reach your goals and objectives, is actually another way of saying "selecting and developing instructional activities," which is something we deal with throughout the balance of the book. Likewise, we don't deal extensively with evaluation—with figuring out *how well* you and your students reached your goals and objectives—since that aspect of planning is the focus of Chapter Fifteen.

Managing Multiple Goals and Objectives

Typically, three expectations are held for children who have studied social studies (or anything else): they will be expected to *know* something about the facts, concepts, and generalizations of social studies; they will be expected to apply *skills* that enable them to use the knowledge they have acquired; and they will be expected to acquire certain *attitudes* or beliefs that will guide them in the future. Children will, for example, be expected to know something about history, geography, and human behavior, just as they will be expected to be able to use a map or to differentiate between facts and opinions. And, typically, they will be expected to be effective, responsible citizens. The problem teachers face is that it is virtually impossible to deal with each of these expectations separately; they must be dealt with simultaneously. It's not an insurmountable problem, of course, but does take a bit of getting used to.

The three major categories of expectations (knowledge, skills, and attitudes) all reflect purposes for which instruction is undertaken. But as will soon become evident, there are purposes and then there are purposes. "To produce effective citizens" and "To name forty-five of the fifty state capitals" are both purposes, for example, but the former is considerably different from the latter. The first is a general aim or goal, while the other is a much more specific statement of purpose. Both have a role in teaching social studies, but they serve quite different functions.

The function of goals

The purpose of broad statements such as those relating to "effective citizenship" or "understanding American history" is to identify goals or aims. Goals establish a general purpose, a general direction toward which teaching should be aimed. Unfortunately, goals are usually so generally stated that it's difficult to tell when they have been reached. Though we might want to say, for example, that by virtue of their social studies experience children will "understand American history," we are also confronted with the specter of historians for whom "understanding American history" is a lifelong quest.

At the opposite end of the spectrum are much more specific statements such as "From memory, the child will name forty-five of the fifty state capitals." It differs from the broadly stated goal in that it is measurable and precisely specifies the behavior the child is expected to exhibit. Such statements are referred to as *objectives,* and because they usually describe how the child is expected to perform or behave, they may also be referred to as *performance objectives* or *behavioral objectives.*

Objectives

The distinction between goals and objectives is illustrated in the following conversation which we have titled, "I Want to Be the Best Archer in the World."

Robin: Some day I'm going to be the best archer in the world.
Mr. Hood: That's a great goal, son, but how will you know when you reach it?
Robin (scratching his head): What do you mean, Dad? By practicin', I guess.
Mr. Hood: O.K. But how will you know when you have become the world's best archer?
Robin: C'mon Dad. Even Coach says I'm good.
Mr. Hood: I mean *specifically.* Don't give me this judgment stuff. Give me something that I can see, something so that I'll know when you've reached your goal.
Robin: Ya' mean like hitting the target most of the time?
Mr. Hood: Don't give me any of this "most of the time" business. How many times do you need to hit it?
Robin: Say, like 99 times out of 100 tries?
Mr. Hood: Now that's more like it. That's your objective!
Robin: But some people can hit the target 100 times in 100 tries.
Mr. Hood: In that case, maybe you'd better change your objective to, say, 999 times out of 1000. Maybe that's closer to your goal.
Robin: Or maybe I could win an Olympic gold medal.
Mr. Hood: That sounds good to me, son. Your objectives are measurable and you'll know when you've reached them. But can you do it? Are they reasonable?
Robin: Hmmmm.

Objectives such as "From memory, the child will name forty-five of the fifty state capitals," identify a *condition* (from memory), a *standard* (forty-five of the fifty state capitals), and an identifiable *task* (to name) for which it is possible to say either yes or no—the child either did or did not complete the task successfully. Any one or all three of the elements could be changed, which might result in an objective such as "Using a map (condition), the child will list (a task) the names of all fifty state capitals (the standard) of the United States."

If two or more people might disagree as to whether or not a student "appreciates" or "really understands" something, you are in all likelihood dealing with a goal, not an objective. To *really* understand something obviously implies a greater depth of comprehension than "understanding," but then the most immediate problem lies in providing specific indicators for "understanding." What it all boils down to is the specificity of the verb that is used in stating the goal or objective.

Below we have provided two lists of verbs. In one of them, the terms are more precise and therefore more closely associated with objectives. In the other, the verbs are more global, more open to differing interpretations. Which list would you associate with goals? With objectives?

*Identifying
behavior
precisely*

List 1 goals

to grasp the significance of
to really understand
to recognize
to appreciate or to enjoy
to believe or to have faith in
to comprehend or to understand
to know (or to know thoroughly)
to be aware of
to esteem or to take satisfaction in

List. 2 objectives

to write or list
to illustrate
to define
to predict or to suggest
to name or identify
to locate or to rate
to restate or to tell why
to distinguish or to discuss
to differentiate or to ask

The verbs in List 2 reflect the kind of precision you could associate with objectives, while List 1 reflects less specific terms that would be associated with aims or goals. In reality, as Sawin (1969, p. 59) has suggested, teachers usually find themselves dealing with expectations that range from the very explicit (objectives) to the very general (goals). These levels are identified below.

*Levels of goals
and objectives*

objectives- very explicit

Goals- very general

> Level 1: *Very Explicit.* Example: given a number of factual statements and a list of generalizations (only some of which are supported by the factual statements), the student is able to identify which generalizations are supported by the facts, and able to tell why this is so. (Specific Unit or Lesson Objective)
> Level II: *Specific.* Example: the student is able to judge the extent to which certain generalizations about social phenomena are warranted. (Course Objective)
> Level III: *General.* Example: the student is able to communicate effectively with others. (School Objective)
> Level IV: *Very General.* Example: the student is able to cope with the problems of life. (Lifelong Objective)

*Judging
appropriateness*

It is overly simplistic to suggest that goals are goals and objectives are objectives, because to do so ignores the relationship between the two. More specifically, even though our exemplary objective, "Naming forty-five of the fifty state capitals from memory" illustrates the characteristics of a properly stated objective, this does *not* necessarily mean that it is a "good" and acceptable objective. Every objective must be judged in terms of the goals to which it relates. One needs to decide, for example, whether memorizing the state capitals will necessarily contribute to one's understanding of United States geography. If it will, it is probably an appropriate objective. If it will not, it's probably inappropriate and should be dropped accordingly, behaviorally-stated or otherwise. Because goals are stated in such general terms, teachers usually find it necessary to judge how a particular objective relates to their instructional goals; the nature of that relationship determines whether the objective is worthy of being studied.

<u>Stating objectives in behavioral terms lends precision to instruction.</u> Occasionally, less precise objectives may be acceptable; probably the most frequent instances of this will occur in relation to creative, open-ended activities, activities where there isn't a single "right answer." Writing behavioral objectives for creative-writing assignments, for example, is difficult, to say the least; you may very well find yourself in the position of trying to cast the dimensions of creativity in behavioral terms. Indeed, to indicate that "The student will write a four-paragraph story using correct grammar, punctuation, and spelling, and having an identifiable theme, plot, and climax, on a specified topic," might be enough to stifle anyone's creativity. The conditions expressed in such objectives tend to focus on *form,* not content, and correct form, at least as it is reflected in "correct" grammar, is anything but open-ended. In light of this, and despite the desirability of precisely stated objectives, there will be times when stating your expectations in behavioral form isn't worth the time and effort it takes. It's clearly a trade-off. Determining when such a trade-off is called for is largely a matter of your own good judgment.

Trading off

Can You Tell a Goal from an Objective?

Self-test

Some of the following statements and tasks are goals, and some are objectives. Place a *G* in the space provided for those that are goal-related, and an *O* for those that are objectives.

  O   1. The student will list, in chronological order, the full names of the four U.S. presidents whose last names begin with the letter J.

  G   2. The student will really understand "critical thinking."

  O   3. Given the following concept statements, the student will circle each statement that is testable in the form presented.

    3.1 Capital punishment deters homicide.

    3.2 Individuals who oppose nuclear energy are unpatriotic.

    3.3 Most societies have a code that determines acceptable and unacceptable behavior.

  O   4. The student will identify one assumption in each of the following statements:

    4.1. People without children should not pay school taxes.

    4.2 One person's opinion is as good as another's.

    4.3. Teachers should not be permitted to strike.

  O   5. The student will form a hypothesis using the following information:

    5.1 Boston is located on the Charles River.

    5.2 Moscow is located on the Volga River.

    5.3 London is located on the Thames River.

    5.4 Cincinnati is located on the Ohio River.

    5.5 Paris is located on the Seine River.

    Hypothesis: _____

  O   6. Using the hypothesis developed in Task 5, the student will identify one exception to that hypothesis.

_G_ 7. The student will demonstrate proper respect for the rights and opinions of others.

_G_ 8. The student will grasp the significance of any three of the following holidays:
8.1 Thanksgiving
8.2 Christmas
8.3 George Washington's Birthday
8.4 Memorial Day
8.5 The Fourth of July

Cognitive and affective domains

Of the three expectations generally associated with social studies, the first two—the development of knowledge and skills—involve remembering or thinking. Activities that involve the knowing dimension are said to fall within the _cognitive_ domain. Attitudes and values, on the other hand, involve one's feelings and emotions (as opposed to thinking or knowing as such). Thus, attitudes and values are considered to fall within the _affective_ domain.

For analytical and planning purposes, one can deal with the cognitive (knowing) and affective (feeling) domains separately. In practice, however, the domains tend to merge together. This often becomes evident in instances where a teacher's attitudes and feelings about certain subject matter, either positive or negative, come across as strongly as the subject matter itself.

Taxonomy: an organizational scheme

To better enable teachers to describe and deal with the different kinds of behavior they expect of their students, Benjamin Bloom and his associates developed a system of organizing and classifying educational objectives. Their work is entitled _Taxonomy of Educational Objectives: The Classification of Educational Goals,_ and is divided into the two parts dealt with here: _Handbook I: Cognitive Domain_ (1956) and _Handbook II: Affective Domain_ (1964). Although the term _taxonomy_ may sound imposing, it refers to a classification scheme, of which the phyla in biology is one example. The biological phyla reflect a system for categorizing and classifying living creatures—for distinguishing the lowest, one-celled bacteria from higher forms. In the same way, the _Taxonomy_ offers a hierarchical scheme for classifying educational goals and objectives; a taxonomical scheme is hierarchical because each level builds upon and is more complex than the previous level.

The major categories in the Cognitive Domain of the _Taxonomy of Educational Objectives_ (Bloom, 1956), as well as illustrative general objectives and illustrative behavioral terms for stating specific learning outcomes, are shown in Table 3.1 (Gronlund, 1970). Similar elements for the Affective Domain (Krathwohl, 1964) are shown in Table 3.2 (Gronlund, 1970).

Knowledge objectives

Knowledge-level objectives are relatively easy to formulate. One must identify whatever information the students will be expected to know, and then state the conditions under which they will be expected to know it, stating, for example, "The child will, from memory, identify two ways in which housing in a desert area is similar to and different from housing in a mountainous region." Similarly, skill objectives can usually be formulated

Table 3.1 The Cognitive Domain of *Knowing and thinking* the *Taxonomy of Educational Objectives* (Bloom, 1956)

Descriptions of the Major Categories in the Cognitive Domain	Illustrative General Instructional Objectives	Illustrative Behavioral Terms for Stating Specific Learning Outcomes
1 *Knowledge.* Knowledge is defined as the remembering of previously learned material. This may involve the recall of a wide range of material, from specific facts to complete theories, but all that is required is the bringing to mind of the appropriate information. Knowledge represents the lowest level of learning outcomes in the cognitive domain.	Knows common terms Knows specific facts Knows methods and procedures Knows basic concepts Knows principles	Defines, describes, identifies, labels, lists, matches, names, outlines, reproduces, selects, states
2 *Comprehension.* Comprehension is defined as the ability to grasp the meaning of material. This may be shown by translating material from one form to another (words to numbers), by interpreting material (explaining or summarizing), and by estimating future trends (predicting consequences or effects). These learning outcomes go one step beyond the simple remembering of material, and represent the lowest level of understanding.	Understands facts and principles Interprets verbal material Interprets charts and graphs Translates verbal material to mathematical formulas Estimates future consequences implied in data Justifies methods and procedures	Converts, defends, distinguishes, estimates, explains, extends, generalizes, gives examples, infers, paraphrases, predicts, rewrites, summarizes
3 *Application.* Application refers to the ability to use learned material in new and concrete situations. This may include the application of such things as rules, methods, concepts, principles, laws, and theories. Learning outcomes in this area requires a higher level of understanding than those under comprehension.	Applies concepts and principles to new situations Applies laws and theories to practical situations Solves mathematical problems Constructs charts and graphs Demonstrates correct usage of a method or procedure	Changes, computes, demonstrates, discovers, manipulates, modifies, operates, predicts, prepares, produces, relates, shows, solves, uses
4 *Analysis.* Analysis refers to the ability to break down material into its component parts so that its organizational structure may be understood. This may include the identification of the parts, analysis of the relationships between parts, and recognition of the organizational principles involved. Learning outcomes here represent a higher intellectual level than comprehension and application because they require an understanding of both the content and the structural form of the material.	Recognizes unstated assumptions Recognizes logical fallacies in reasoning Distinguishes between facts and inferences Evaluates the relevancy of data Analyzes the organizational structure of a work (art, music, writing)	Breaks down, diagrams, differentiates, discriminates, distinguishes, identifies, illustrates, infers, outlines, points out, relates, selects, separates, subdivides.

Descriptions of the Major Categories in the Cognitive Domain	Illustrative General Instructional Objectives	Illustrative Behavioral Terms for Stating Specific Learning Outcomes
5 *Synthesis.* Synthesis refers to the ability to put parts together to form a new whole. This may involve the production of a unique communication (theme or speech), a plan of operations (research proposal), or a set of abstract relations (scheme for classifying information). Learning outcomes in this area stress creative behaviors, with major emphasis on the formulation of *new* patterns or structures.	Writes a well organized theme Gives a well organized speech Writes a creative short story (or poem, or music) Proposes a plan for an experiment Integrates learning from different areas into a plan for solving a problem Formulates a new scheme for classifying objects (or events, or ideas)	Categorizes, combines, compiles, composes, creates, divises, designs, explains, generates, modifies, organizes, plans, rearranges, reconstructs, relates, reorganizes, revises, rewrites, summarizes, tells, writes
6 *Evaluation.* Evaluation is concerned with the ability to judge the value of material (statement, novel, poem, research report) for a given purpose. The judgments are to be based on definite criteria. These may be internal criteria (organization) or external criteria (relevance to the purpose) and the student may determine the criteria or be given them. Learning outcomes in this area are highest in the cognitive hierarchy because they contain elements of all of the other categories, plus conscious value judgments based on clearly defined criteria.	Judges the logical consistency of written material Judges the adequacy with which conclusions are supported by data Judges the value of a work (art, music, writing) by use of internal criteria Judges the value of a work (art, music, writing) by use of external standards of excellence	Appraises, compares, concludes, contrasts, criticizes, describes, discriminates, explains, justifies, interprets, relates, summarizes, supports

Source: Reprinted with permission of The Macmillan Company from Stating Behavioral Objectives for Classroom Instruction *by Norman E. Gronlund. Copyright © 1970 by Norman E. Gronlund.*

with relative ease, especially if you use the descriptors supplied in Table 3.1. Developing attitudinal objectives, however, usually presents a more perplexing problem. When teachers attempt to influence a child's attitude, they are consciously attempting to alter the child's state of being—a situation fraught with moral overtones. And although it's one thing to state a desired attitude or behavior—"being a good classroom citizen," for example—it is quite another to identify appropriate ways in which children can demonstrate such attitudes.

Attitudinal objectives: a problem

Students who talk continually, who interrupt whenever the spirit moves them, or who run in the halls or fight on the playground are exhibiting characteristics that deviate from the generalized notion of "responsible school citizens." From a planning perspective, the problem becomes one of translating generalized notions such as "responsible school citizens" into specific behavioral statements. It's true that we could indicate, for example, that a "good school citizen" is one who pays attention, turns work in on time,

Table 3.2 The **Affective** Domain of *attitudes + values* the *Taxonomy of Educational Objectives* (Krathwohl, 1964)

Descriptions of the Major Categories in the Affective Domain	Illustrative General Instructional Objectives	Illustrative Behavioral Terms for Stating Specific Learning Outcomes
1 *Receiving.* Receiving refers to the student's willingness to attend to particular phenomena or stimuli (classroom activities, textbook, music, etc.). From a teaching standpoint, it is concerned with getting, holding, and directing the student's attention. Learning outcomes in this area range from the simple awareness that a thing exists to selective attention on the part of the learner. Receiving represents the lowest level of learning outcomes in the affective domain.	Listens attentively Shows awareness of the importance of learning Shows sensitivity to human needs and social problems Accepts differences of race and culture Attends closely to the classroom activities	Asks, chooses, describes, follows, gives, holds, identifies, locates, names, points to, selects, sits erect, replies, uses
2 *Responding.* Responding refers to active participation on the part of the student. At this level he not only attends to a particular phenomenon but also reacts to it in some way. Learning outcomes in this area may emphasize acquiescence in responding (reads assigned material), willingness to respond (voluntarily reads beyond assignment), or satisfaction in responding (reads for pleasure or enjoyment). The higher levels of this category include those instructional objectives that are commonly classified under "interests"; that is, those that stress the seeking out and enjoyment of particular activities.	Completes assigned homework Obeys school rules Participates in class discussion Completes laboratory work Volunteers for special tasks Shows interest in subject Enjoys helping others	Answers, assists, complies, conforms, discusses, greets, helps, labels, performs, practices, presents, reads, recites, reports, selects, tells, writes
3 *Valuing.* Valuing is concerned with the worth or value a student attaches to a particular object, phenomenon, or behavior. This ranges in degree from the more simple acceptance of a value (desires to improve group skills) to the more complex level of commitment (assumes responsibility for the effective functioning of the group). Valuing is based on the internalization of a set of specified values, but clues to these values are expressed in the student's overt behavior. Learning outcomes in this area are concerned with behavior that is consistent and stable enough to make the value clearly identifiable. Instructional objectives that are commonly classified under "attitudes" and "appreciation" would fall into this category.	Demonstrates belief in the democratic process Appreciates good literature (art or music) Appreciates the role of science (or other subjects) in everyday life Shows concern for the welfare of others Demonstrates problem-solving attitude Demonstrates commitment to social improvement	Completes, describes, differentiates, explains, follows, forms, initiates, invites, joins, justifies, proposes, reads, reports, selects, shares, studies, works

Descriptions of the Major Categories in the Affective Domain	Illustrative General Instructional Objectives	Illustrative Behavioral Terms for Stating Specific Learning Outcomes
4 *Organization.* Organization is concerned with bringing together different values, resolving conflicts between them, and beginning the building of an internally consistent value system. Thus the emphasis is on comparing, relating, and synthesizing values. Learning outcomes may be concerned with the conceptualization of a value (recognizes the responsibility of each individual for improving human relations) or with the organization of a value system (develops a vocational plan that satisfies his need for both economic security and social service). Instructional objectives relating to the development of a philosophy of life would fall into this category.	Recognizes the need for balance between freedom and responsibility in a democracy Recognizes the role of systematic planning in solving problems Accepts responsibility for his own behavior Understands and accepts his own strengths and limitations Formulates a life plan in harmony with his abilities, interests, and beliefs	Adheres, alters, arranges, combines, compares, completes, defends, explains, generalizes, identifies, integrates, modifies, orders, organizes, prepares, relates, synthesizes
5 *Characterization by a Value or Value Complex.* At this level of the affective domain, the individual has a value system that has controlled his behavior for a sufficiently long time for him to have developed a characteristic "life style." Thus the behavior is pervasive, consistent, and predictable. Learning outcomes at this level cover a broad range of activities, but the major emphasis is on the fact that the behavior is typical or characteristic of the student. Instructional objectives that are concerned with the student's general patterns of adjustment (personal, social, emotional) would be appropriate here.	Displays safety consciousness Demonstrates self-reliance in working independently Practices cooperation in group activities Uses objective approach in problem solving Demonstrates industry, punctuality and self-discipline Maintains good health habits	Acts, discriminates, displays, influences, listens, modifies, performs, practices, proposes, qualifies, questions, revises, serves, solves, uses, verifies

Source: Reprinted with permission of The Macmillan Company from Stating Behavioral Objectives for Classroom Instruction *by Norman E. Gronlund. Copyright © 1970 by Norman E. Gronlund.*

etc., but it usually isn't long before we reach the point of stating behaviors that a student should *not* exhibit—does not interrupt, etc. When things reach that point, we may find ourselves in the position of doing nothing for students who *don't* misbehave; who do not do what the deviators from a notion of responsible class citizen do. If this is confusing, it's probably because the number of negatives in the previous statement reflects the problem of stating affective objectives in terms of behaviors students will *not* exhibit. Yet, if you try to phrase potential objectives as positive statements, such as "The student will stop interrupting the teacher whenever the teacher is talking," they often take on a "have you stopped browbeating your spouse yet?" flavor.

Affective goals

Our point here is that most affective goals serve a valid and valuable function when stated as goals. Further, we are suggesting that most attitudinal changes occur over time, not after just one or two twenty-minute activities. In other words, children's attitudes usually reflect behavior patterns that have been developed over time and that are, in many instances, resistant to rapid change.

Modeling

How, then, do teachers deal with affective goals and objectives? We suspect that for the most part they *model* the desired behaviors. Consistency between what teachers say and what they do is the key here. For example, a teacher who mouths the need to respect rights and opinions of others but who also, perhaps unintentionally, "puts Sarah down" every time Sarah says something, can hardly be said to exhibit behavior that is consistent with the stated goal. The need for consistency and the recognition that actions do indeed speak louder than words is particularly crucial in the area of planning for affective goals and objectives.

Sources of Goals and Objectives

Many prospective teachers think that most of the instructional goals and objectives they might need have already been developed and are written down somewhere. The problem, as they see it, lies in finding that source. Most teachers soon discover that there are several sources of previously identified goals and objectives. They include: state and local curriculum guides; prepackaged teaching units, some of which are available commercially; teacher's editions of social studies textbooks; the school system itself; and the social science disciplines. Materials from any of these potential sources can provide a point of departure for your planning needs, but they may present certain limitations too.

State and local guides - good source of pre-planned goals and objectives

State and local curriculum guides provide a good source of preplanned goals, objectives, and potential learning activities. Just how helpful these can be will probably depend on their level of specificity, which can vary considerably. An exemplary segment of a local curriculum guide, in this case one that was developed cooperatively by teachers from several school systems, appears in Appendix B. We placed it in the appendix to preserve the format, which is one that many teachers seem to prefer. In addition to the format, note that the unit segment is so specific that it includes almost everything a teacher might need. Other state and locally developed curriculum guides may be considerably less specific, however. Some of them present only a list of desirable goals, a brief outline of recommended content, and several suggested learning activities. Before they can be used for day-to-day teaching purposes, a good deal of additional teacher planning may be required.

Some teachers prefer step-by-step, recipe-type curriculum guides while others like the briefer outline-type guides they can adapt to fit the needs of their classes. In either instance, and particularly among materials designed for wide circulation (such as over an entire state), you may find that the suggested teaching activities are inappropriate for your class. When that happens, and when it becomes necessary to adapt teaching materials for your students, you'll probably find yourself writing your own instructional goals and objectives.

The teacher's editions of *some* social studies textbooks, like *some* curriculum guides, contain excellent instructional objectives. Don't be too surprised, however, if you happen across some that say, "Help the child understand the geography of the United States," or "Help the student appreciate the contributions of Athenian democracy." Although these can be acceptable as goals, they leave much to be desired in terms of helping you plan tomorrow's lesson.

The school as a source of goals and objectives presents an equally mixed picture. Virtually every school system in the country has stated goals, as well they should, but often these are of the long-range type, such as "Develop each student to the fullest extent of his or her capability." Some schools, of course, go much further and support the development of detailed curriculum guides, such as the one illustrated in Appendix B. In other instances, the social studies curriculum guide—if indeed there is one—may so closely duplicate the teacher's edition of the textbook series that it is virtually useless. Such guides usually end up gathering dust on a shelf somewhere. The point here is that while some school systems go to great lengths to help teachers identify appropriate goals and objectives for social studies instruction, such efforts are by no means universal.

The social science disciplines as a source of goals and objectives also present a mixed picture. Insofar as goals are concerned, the basic approaches to social studies—teaching children to think, teaching the cultural heritage, etc.—often parallel the kinds of educational goals that schools establish. From time to time, various social studies groups have attempted to make those broadly stated goals more specific, but their efforts have typically stopped just short of the precise objectives you could readily adopt for day-to-day instruction. To indicate that students should be able to distinguish between facts and opinions, for example, does *not* specify what materials they should use to do this. Will they use a videotaped TV commercial? A political campaign speech? Or what? Since teachers could use many different types of materials to help their students distinguish between facts and opinions, it becomes necessary to include the materials or content dimension in order to create instructional objectives that have a satisfactory degree of precision.

In planning for instruction, especially in formulating instructional objectives, it is important to recognize the dual role social studies content can play. On one hand, social studies content may reflect what children can be expected to know, such as the composition and operation of the electoral college. On the other hand, content is also something that teachers *use,* that they teach with. When teachers use a campaign speech to help children distinguish between facts and opinions, as in our example above, the speech itself is merely a vehicle. The emphasis is *not* on having students learn the speech itself; it's something they *use.* The teacher selected it as a basis for determining which statements represent facts and which represent the candidate's opinions.

From our perspective, a basic ingredient in the know-how of teaching lies in knowing how to use social studies content in different ways and for differ-

The disciplines

Dual role for content

ent purposes. Further, when children "know" social studies, their "knowing" should enable them to go beyond simply regurgitating factual information. Kids, too, can use content to serve different functions: to defend a position, to identify assumptions, facts, or opinions, to test hypotheses, etc. Indeed, when children learn to use social studies content in such ways, they are in fact using social studies.

Content Utilization

Mike Mulligan and His Steam Shovel (Virginia Burton, 1939) is a delightful children's book in which Mike's steam shovel, Mary Anne, is nearly sent to steam shovel heaven because the new, engine-powered shovels are getting most of the jobs. In the story, Mike and Mary Anne agree to dig the cellar of the new Popperville town hall. They also agree to finish the job in just one day, or else they won't get paid. By digging furiously, they manage to complete the job within a day, except for one thing. In their haste, Mike forgets to leave a way to get Mary Anne out of the cellar. So there she sits, quietly belching smoke, at the bottom of the hole they dug.

An argument between Mike and Henry B. Swap, a member of the town council, quickly follows. Swap claims that since Mary Anne is still in the cellar, the job isn't finished and Mike shouldn't get paid. The day is saved, however, when a little boy suggests that they build the new town hall around Mary Anne and make her its new furnace. And Mike? He could become the new janitor.

The idea of using a former steam shovel as a furnace illustrates a concept found in some of the newer social studies programs. That concept—structure and function—reflects the fact that a particular structure, such as a steam shovel, could be used to serve a number of different purposes or functions (such as a hole digger, a *very* slow form of transportation, or even a furnace).

Children at the earliest primary levels can readily handle the idea of

Structure and function

structure and function. For example, when we asked a group of first graders to indicate the different functions a twelve-inch ruler could serve, here's what they suggested:

1   to measure
2   to make straight lines
3   to spank someone
4   to stir something
5   to mark your place when reading
6   as wood to build something, like a birdhouse
7   to dig holes with
8   to prop up something (like a window)
9   to use when hanging things like mobiles when you can't reach
10 to use as a weapon
11 as a stake in a garden
12 you could carve it and make things
13 as a perch in a birdcage
14 as a pointer when talking at the board
15 as a number line for doing math
16 as a pattern for making a ruler of your own
17 as a turner when cooking
18 as a paint stirrer
19 tie a cloth around it and use as a shoeshiner
20 use it to jam something closed (like a door)
21 put under the corner of a table to stop it from wiggling
22 cut in two lengthwise and use the parts to make a kite
23 as drumsticks

You could undoubtedly add several more functions to the students' list. The problem for most of us, however, is that our culture and our previous experiences tend to limit the way we view certain structures. For example, in our culture dogs are used as pets, not as sources of food. Likewise, horses, which could readily serve as sources of protein, are typically used for work or pleasure when alive, and for dog food when dead. Moving to an educational context, we find that content—subject matter—is usually viewed as having a single function, as something that "teachers teach and kids are expected to know."

Our point in this section, which is particularly important to planning, is to show how the concept of structure and function also applies to content. Social studies content need not be viewed only as something that teachers teach and that students are expected to know, but can, like steam shovels and rulers, be used to serve a number of different functions.

The dual usage of content, which we call *content utilization*, is reflected in the fact that both a noun form and a verb form of the phrase can apply. As a noun, content utilization refers to the *idea* that social studies content can be used in different ways. In verb form, it refers to the *process* of selecting and using subject matter for one or more possible purposes.

Content utilization has three key elements:

Perceptual blinders

limits how we
view certain
structures

dual use of content —
content utilization

Three components

1 *selection* of the content to use with your students
2 *use* of the content (that is, how you plan to go about dealing with it)
3 *purposes* for which you intend to use the content

All of these elements are interrelated. Thus, how you use a particular content selection will depend on your purpose, just as the materials that you have available will largely determine which ones you use with students. If your only resource is a textbook, you obviously don't have much to select from, a situation that probably explains why teachers often become collectors on a grand scale. Pictures, catalogs, magazines—in fact almost anything—can furnish potential content for use with your classes.

Content Utilization and Planning

One of the best ways to understand the nature of content utilization and its relationship to instructional planning is to actually do some. Together we will plan a segment of a skills-oriented unit of study. To do this, we have selected a vehicle that isn't commonly associated with social studies teaching: two cans of Green Giant Niblets corn (see Figure 3.1).

Why corn? Why not a more common topic such as community helpers? Our reasons are twofold: first, we can avoid that "it's something that every child should know" syndrome that so often influences what's taught as social studies; and, secondly, we can illustrate that it is quite possible to teach legitimate skills by using neutral—or even mundane—content. Recognize that in this instance, canned corn serves as a vehicle, nothing more.

Our immediate task is to *use* the two cans of corn as a basis for questions which, as students try to answer them, can serve as a basis for teaching a variety of different skills. Instead of posing possible questions, you could identify potential activities, like "Design a new label" or "Try to determine a more appealing color scheme for the existing label." Or you could do both.

Potential questions or activities

We usually begin with key questions because they give a clear focus for lessons or activities. Posing a question such as "How many words can be made from the word *niblets*?" clearly implies an activity that students could do. In actually presenting the activity to students, however, it isn't essential that the question be asked. Rather, the teacher could say something such as, "Let's see how many words we can make from the letters in *niblets.*" Since teachers tend to bombard students with questions throughout any given day, we think it's sometimes preferable to present an instructional activity as a task and not as a question. Our point is to indicate that key questions underlie most instructional activities, regardless of the subject area.

For the purposes of this activity, try your hand at identifying "key" questions or potential student activities *in each of the major subject areas taught in elementary schools:* language arts (including reading), mathematics, science, and social studies.

We have suggested some sample questions and potential activities that could be based on them below. Note that as you identify key questions, it is *not* essential that you be able to answer them in advance. In fact, some of your best questions may be those you can't answer. Questions like "Why

Figure 3.1 The Basis for the Corn Curriculum

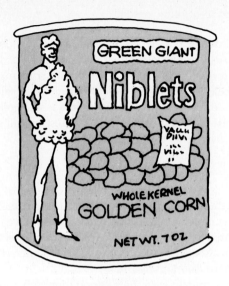

NET WT. 7 OZ. 200 GRAMS HEAT & SERVE
Ingredients:
Golden Whole Kernel Corn, Water, Sugar, Salt.
NUTRITION INFORMATION
Serving Size . . . 1 cup (6 oz.)
Servings per Container . . 1¹/₁₆ (or 2 3½ oz. Servings)
Per One-Cup Serving:
Calories 150   Carbohydrate . . . . 35 grams
Protein . . . . . 3 grams   Fat . . . . 2 grams
PERCENTAGE OF U.S. RECOMMENDED DAILY ALLOWANCE (U.S. RDA)
Protein 4   Vitamin C . . 20   Riboflavin . . 6   Calcium . *
Vitamin A . . 4   Thiamine . . . 2   Niacin 6   Iron 4
*Contains less than 2 percent of the U.S. RDA of this
nutrient.
DISTRIBUTED BY **GREEN GIANT COMPANY** LE SUEUR, MINN. 56058
Packed in U.S.A.   Printed in U.S.A.

NET WT. 12 OZ. 340 GRAMS HEAT & SERVE
Ingredients:
Golden Whole Kernel Corn, Water, Sugar, Salt.
NUTRITION INFORMATION
Serving Size . . . 1 cup
Servings per Container . . . . . . 2 (or 4 3-oz. Servings)
Per One-Cup Serving:
Calories 150   Carbohydrate . . . . 30 grams
Protein . . . . . 4 grams   Fat . . . . 1 gram
PERCENTAGE OF U.S. RECOMMENDED DAILY ALLOWANCE (U.S. RDA)
Protein 6   Vitamin C . . 25   Riboflavin . . 6   Calcium . . 0
Vitamin A . . 4   Thiamine . . . 2   Niacin 6   Iron 4
DISTRIBUTED BY **GREEN GIANT COMPANY** LE SUEUR, MINN. 56058
Packed in U.S.A.   Printed in U.S.A.

do most cans have ridges (or rings)?" can serve as unknowns, as things to inquire about. Concern for "the answers" can come later, after your students (or you) have inquired.

Language Arts

How many different words could you make from the letters in *niblets*?

Write a story entitled "The Day the Green Giant Turned Blue" (creative writing).

Create a new advertising jingle for Green Giant products.

Classify the words on the label beginning with *G* as nouns, verbs, or adjectives. Star those that fit into more than one category.

Other language arts questions/activities

_____

_____

_____

Mathematics

Identify three different ways to determine the number of kernels in the large can. Then determine which way is the most accurate.

How could you measure the length of the label without taking it off the can?

When would purchasing the large can be a bad buy?

How much corn would a person have to eat to get their recommended daily allowance of iron?

Other math questions/activities

Cost per ounce of each can?

_____

_____

Science

What else is in these cans besides corn? How could you find out? Why would this be important to know?

Does "net weight" include the liquid the corn is packed in? How could you find out?

Are tin cans really made from tin? How could you find out?

What is vacuum packing? What other products are vacuum-packed? Why?

Other science questions/activities

_____

_____

_____

Social Studies

Do most of the people in this class prefer canned corn or frozen corn? How could we find out?

What information on the label is there by law? When did labeling laws come into effect? Why?

When were safe canning processes developed? How did they change our way of life?

What role does corn play in our diet? How could we find out?

How many different occupations are involved in getting corn from the Giant's valley to us?

Questions like "How could you find out?" and "How do you know?" serve to effectively shift the focus of these activities from a concern for "the answer" to a concern for finding the answers. In other words, the answers to many of these questions, such as "What else is in these cans besides corn?" (water, salt, etc.), probably have less utility and transfer value than the processes students engage in to arrive at their answers. Indeed, how *do* you know what is in these cans besides corn? How could you find out?

In their present form, the questions and/or potential tasks we've just developed are really nothing more than an amorphous collection. There is no sequence to most of them, so it isn't essential for students to have completed one activity before moving on to another. Recognizing that content can be used for a remarkable variety of purposes, the planning problem we now face lies in organizing all of these elements in a way that makes sense, both to us as teachers and for students.

Ensuring a process emphasis

Answers have less utility than process.

Linear vs. Systematic Planning

A particularly troublesome idea for prospective teachers is the mistaken notion that the planning process follows the same sequence in which the products of planning—written lesson plans and units—are presented. A preplanned unit, for example, is usually presented in the following order: first there is apt to be a list of broad goals followed closely by a list of concepts or generalizations. These are typically followed by a list of behavioral objectives that may or may not be keyed to a series of suggested student activities. The last element usually includes sample test items or other kinds of suggested evaluation activities. The step-by-step format of written unit plans is convenient and logical, but prospective teachers are sometimes led to believe that the planning process also follows the same linear, step-like sequence. It can, but it doesn't have to. In fact, trying to plan your own units in the same sequence in which written units are presented is apt to give you more headaches than you might imagine and make the task more complicated than it already is.

Instead of approaching instructional planning as a series of discrete steps, which is the way some texts tend to present it, we suggest that you consider approaching planning as an interactive *system,* as a process where each dimension of planning interacts with every other dimension. Furthermore, where you enter the system is not all that important; what is most important is that everything "hangs together" when you are done. To illustrate our point here, think back to those times just before the first test in some of the classes you've taken. Didn't you sometimes find yourself wondering what questions the instructor would ask? However, based on your experience with that first test, you probably approached the second test with a much clearer sense of what would be expected of you. Perhaps the reason "test anxiety" is such a common phenomenon lies in some teachers' unwillingness (or perhaps their

Planning as a system

inability) to specify their expectations precisely. From a planning perspective, however, *every test question reflects an instructional objective*—it indicates what the teacher expects the student to know or be able to do. So by analyzing a teacher's test questions, you can readily identify at least some of that teacher's instructional objectives. Despite the fact that tests usually mark the end of something—a unit, a course, or even a semester—the relationship between objectives and test items is such that some teachers actually begin their planning by devising a preliminary test. This procedure then allows them to determine how clearly they have identified their objectives.

At times in your own planning, you may be able to identify and design a great student activity based on a goal or objective you have in mind. At other times you may put most of your initial emphasis on identifying possible learning activities, and *then* develop objectives and evaluation strategies to fit them. Once you are satisfied that you've dealt with your overall goals, you can evaluate your plan in terms of its consistency. Your concern here will rest with whether you have planned so that everything "hangs together" and does what you started out to do.

Organizing for Instruction

Organizing something for instructional purposes, whether it's questions you plan to ask, possible student activities, or whatever, is the essence of planning. Throughout the entire process, the focus is on students. Sometimes they are participants in the planning process—in fact, we recommend that you involve students whenever and to whatever extent you can. Whichever planning process you follow, your students will be the ultimate benefactors.

The intent of all planning is to identify what students will do (or be doing), and then to identify courses of action that will permit them to do it. The end result of a teacher's planning—their unit or lesson—typically consists of a series of goal-related learning experiences that have a common theme or focus. Sometimes that theme is phrased as a question, such as "How do people manipulate the behavior of others?" More typically, the activities and experiences deal with selected aspects of a topic: "transportation," "community helpers," "life in Colonial America," etc. (We'll take a detailed look at the topics typically taught in elementary social studies programs in Chapter Four.)

Unit teaching, which is the practice of organizing instruction around selected themes, questions, or topics, is such a well-entrenched practice that the terminology should be familiar. The units you experienced as students were, as the term implies, a series of learning activities and experiences that were related to a common focus. As students, though, you were on the receiving end of a *teaching unit*, that is, what you experienced were the activities and materials your teachers used with your class. In all likelihood, your teachers selected those activities and materials from larger, more encompassing resource units. A *resource unit* is a planning aid that teachers usually develop for themselves and that includes possible learning activities,

Types of units

materials to support those activities (lists of films, filmstrips, and other teaching aids and resources), as well as references or background material.

If a teacher wanted to develop a teaching unit on canned corn, he might very well create a file that would ultimately become the basis for his resource unit. Every time that teacher happened upon an article about corn, canning, or anything related to the topic, he might clip it and add it to the resource file. If that article were usable by children or could be rewritten for them, it might one day be incorporated into the teaching unit. Until then it would remain a part of that teacher's resource unit.

Unit: long-range plan

Unit planning is a way of ensuring that a teacher's day-to-day activities will come together to form a meaningful experience for students. As such, the unit serves to provide an overall organizer for the individual lesson plans from which it is built. In fact, the overall organization that a detailed unit plan provides usually eliminates the what-am-I-going-to-do-tomorrow dilemma teachers might otherwise face. Teachers must, of course, plan on a day-to-day basis, making adjustments in tomorrow's lesson based on what happened today. But with a unit to provide a long-range plan, those daily adjustments will be minor, especially as compared to what is involved in planning from scratch. In the absence of long-range plans, one continually faces the question of what to do tomorrow.

Unit Planning

Our purpose in this section is to work through some of the various phases of the unit planning process. For the purposes of this illustration we have chosen to follow up on our previous example that dealt with canned corn. Note again that although a unit on corn isn't something you would normally find in most elementary schools, by using it as our vehicle we are able to illustrate aspects of the planning process (particularly the principles of content utilization) with greater clarity than would be true using a more traditional topic. Unfortunately, developing a unit in the absence of a specified group of children lends an air of artificiality to this activity that doesn't exist in real life. A unit developed for a class of poor readers, for example, might be considerably different from one developed for a class of students reading at or above grade level. For the purpose of this activity, we have assumed that we are teaching at the primary grades and that our students are poor-to-average readers. This assumption doesn't change the way we would plan, but it does mean we can't use activities that depend heavily on reading.

Identifying a Focus.   One of the most important decisions in unit planning concerns which way we should go with our topic or vehicle—in this case, corn. Should we focus on the governmental regulation of food products (labeling laws, etc.), the development of food processing (canning, freezing, etc.) and its influence on our way of life, or should we examine the relationship between transportation and trade (the various aspects of shipping and selling corn)? Of the many possible ways to go, two factors will influence our decision: (1) what students already know about these topics and (2) the skills that may be required to complete potential learning activities. In the case of governmental regulation of the food industry we can be fairly certain that we are dealing with something unknown to most primary-age students. If we

Which way to go?

Team planning: six heads may be better than one!

are uncertain about that, a pretest should remove any doubt. Then, too, government regulations may be something students don't care about. If that's a problem, which it could very well be, we'll need to pay particular attention to developing activities that whet their appetites—which is often easier said than done.

Studying how the government regulates the food industry could be a way of helping students broaden their awareness of government itself. However, if this is one of our ultimate goals, there is probably a better vehicle than canned corn to help teach it. Besides, potential learning activities relating to governmental functioning and food regulation would likely involve considerable reading. For these reasons, we can discard the government-regulation focus and turn to something somewhat less sophisticated.

Alternative focuses

The different modes of transportation involved in producing canned corn might be an appealing focus, especially since we could probably devise some non-reading (pictorial) activities dealing with trucks, trains, ships, and other forms of transport. On the other hand, most primary-level students are quite aware of trucks, trains, ships, etc., and unless we are careful, we might find ourselves boring students with discussions about how milk trucks carry milk.

Primary-level students are probably not aware of how heavily any kind of trade depends upon transportation. Should we decide to pursue this focus, we would need to do the same type of *task analysis* as for government regulation of the food industry. We need to determine what children must understand before they can deal with the role of transportation in any kind of trade. An obvious prerequisite here is the need to understand the notion of trade as the exchange of goods and services. Then students must understand the notion of transportation, not solely in terms of trucks and trains, but also in terms of its function—the movement of goods and people. And if students are to understand why things are transported, they must also understand why goods are traded. These understandings get us into the concepts of self-sufficiency and interdependence. If everyone were self-sufficient, for example, there would be little need for either trade or transportation.

We may also want children to understand the role of the transporter in trade: that is, the conditions under which truckers, railroads, airlines, or shipping companies offer their service—transportation—in exchange for something, usually money. This could also get us into the notion that transportation companies don't own the goods they transport; rather, they are selling a service.

If all of this seems to have gotten very complex, you're right. Our task analysis reveals that we've opened Pandora's box! In terms of possible topics and concepts to be dealt with, we have identified the following: trade, transportation, self-sufficiency, interdependence, goods and services, exchange, and communication. Separately, none of these concepts is beyond the grasp of primary children; in fact, primary-level teaching materials already exist for most of them. But when it comes to helping children understand how these ideas are interrelated, it appears that we've tackled something much more complex than we bargained for, something that is unnecessarily complex for exemplary purposes. In other words, although we could develop a teaching unit along the lines we've suggested, it's not the kind of thing most prospective teachers tackle for their first planning effort.

By examining the key questions/activities we posed earlier (pp. 88–89), it appears that one of them involving the type of corn that most people might buy (canned or frozen) can serve as the keystone for a unit that follows a more manageable tack. Implicit in that question is the concept of *choice:* the fact that people satisfy their wants and needs in different ways. By expanding that idea to a context that goes beyond a consumer's decision as to which kind of corn to buy, it becomes apparent that many choices (decisions) were made in the production of the canned corn. These extend to a farmer's decision to grow corn instead of something else, or to the fact that the wood from which the paper label was made could have been used for something else (or not used at all). The resources that went into making the metal can could also have been used differently.

From a specific instance, the choice of what kind of corn to buy, we have actually worked backward to a general principle: decisions are involved in the allocation of human and natural resources. In other words, the two cans of corn can serve as visible indicators of resources that were allocated and used in particular ways. And by considering products other than corn, we should be able to develop a teaching unit that illustrates how people make a variety of decisions in using resources to satisfy their needs.

Analyzing what is involved

What backround do children need first? Pretest Possibility.

Too complex

A new focus: using resources

Notice that in addition to identifying a unit focus, resource utilization, we have also begun to identify some cognitive goals for our unit. These include (to cite just two of them), the desire to have students understand that human and natural resources are allocated, and that the way in which resources are used involves a variety of decisions.

Before primary-age children could even begin to comprehend some of the goals stated above, a lot of terminology would need to be clarified. This would include "resources," "natural resources," "needs," "allocation," and the like. By making a list of these terms as we go, we can use that list as we review the learning activities we've developed to see that we have made adequate provisions for addressing terminology. Then, too, we could deemphasize vocabulary by using expressions such as "divide up" in place of "allocate."

There are several different routes we could pursue in developing our unit from this point, such as identifying instructional objectives more precisely, or developing possible learning activities. We prefer to identify additional guiding (key) questions, simply because they tend to lend direction and specificity to our unit at this stage in its development. Some of those key questions are:

Key questions

1   What resources were used to produce the two cans of corn?
2   What resources are used to produce other common products?
3   What other things could be produced from those same resources?
4   What are resources, and where do they come from?
5   How are resources used differently?

These questions are not necessarily in the order we may finally put them in, nor is it entirely essential that we deal with all of them.

In the course of this unit, the children may come to appreciate the fact that, although humans may have an almost unlimited supply of needs and desires to be satisfied, we do not have an unlimited supply of resources. The scarcity of resources, especially as it is reflected in the current energy crunch, is something that students should both understand and appreciate. Note that if we choose to we could get into the different types of energy required to produce those two cans of corn, thereby integrating current events into our unit. Whether we deal with the energy crisis or not, we have nevertheless implicitly identified at least two affective (attitudinal) goals for our fledgling unit: an appreciation of the scarcity of resources and of the need to allocate them wisely.

Review

Progress Report: Unit Development
After a couple of false starts, we've finally laid the foundation for our unit. It's far from complete, but thus far we have identified:
   Unit title: (Undecided)
   Grade level: Primary (2nd)
   Unit focus: Using resources (resource utilization)
   Major vehicle: Canned corn
   Secondary vehicle: Other products (yet to be decided) commonly
found around the home and school

Unit Goals: Cognitive: Knowing or Thinking

1   The child will understand the nature of resources.
2   The child will understand that the use of resources always involves choices and decisions.

Unit Goals: Affective: Attitudes or Values.

3   The child will appreciate the scarcity of resources, our widespread dependence on them, and the need to use resources wisely.

Instructional Objectives and Learning Activities: (yet to be decided)

Formulating Objectives and Activities   With a broad framework for the unit established, the planning problem now becomes one of filling in the gaps. Recognize that there isn't necessarily any one *best* way to proceed from this point. Some teachers may prefer to specify objectives with greater clarity, some may wish to identify potential student activities, and others may wish to identify possible resources and teaching materials. Instead of working with just one element of the plan, some experienced teachers shift back and forth, working on the various components simultaneously.

Alternate paths

Our preference is to identify a way to initiate the unit, a way that not only grabs the students' attention but also helps establish a direction for the activities that follow. It has been our experience with both unit planning and daily lesson plans that if we can get an activity or lesson off to a good start, and if we know what that activity or lesson should lead to, then the middle will almost sustain itself.

Initiating the unit

Of the several possible ways to initiate this unit, our first decision is *not* to begin with the usual defining of terms. We'll need to deal with definitions eventually, of course, but beginning with them is about as dull a way of starting a unit that we can think of. Our inclination is instead to begin the unit by identifying the resources that went into producing the cans of corn. (Note that we're using adult language here, not necessarily what we'd use with students.) Presenting a list of "things" (resources) that went into producing the canned corn is one alternative, or we could develop a kind of "family tree" for canned corn as is illustrated in Figure 3.2.

Choosing between starting with a list, the family tree, or something else is just one of the countless decisions that planning requires. In this instance, we would use the family tree activity because it illustrates both the resources used in producing canned corn and their sequence of use. Also, in our judgment, it's a more appealing format for presenting data. Finally, developing a family tree for canned corn in a whole-class setting could serve as a model for follow-up activities in which small groups of students could create similar charts for other familiar products—furniture, clothing, agricultural products, or almost anything else. Note that our reason for going into such detail here is to indicate some of the factors we considered in arriving at our decision. Of course, if the notion of a family tree is totally foreign to our students, a preliminary activity in which students learn to create their own family trees may be advisable. This decision would hinge on our awareness of our students' previous experiences (with family trees), which is something

What if we're wrong?

Figure 3.2 A
Family Tree for a
Can of Corn

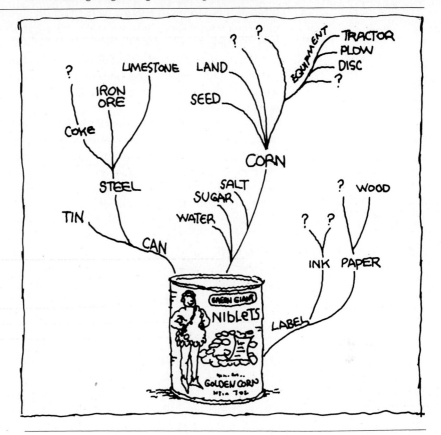

teachers gain simply by working with their classes. Since the students' experiences are unknown to us here, we are forced to make assumptions. If we assume incorrectly or don't make provisions (emergency plans?) for instances where we have assumed improperly, we may find ourselves up that proverbial creek. Enough said about the critically important role that students' past experiences play in instructional planning.

Once students have identified some of the natural resources used in the production of various products, they could then compare their charts to determine what resources are common among the products. They could then produce pictorial charts (pictures cut from magazines, perhaps) or murals showing the different products produced from a particular resource and that have titles such as "Things Made from Wood." Lest the children tire from all of this chart making, we would intersperse some of the numerous films and filmstrips that deal with how we use natural resources. A particularly good film, for example, is *The New House: Where It Comes From* (Coronet Films). Other films and filmstrips, some with generic titles such as *The Story of . . . (Bread, Wood, Steel,* etc.) might also be suitable.

What we have done, thus far, is begin to identify a rough sequence of potential student learning experiences. Upon reexamining our key "corn" questions (pp. 88–89), you will find some ideas that we have not yet woven

*Possible
activities*

into our unit. For example, we have not dealt specifically with people (services) as a resource, nor have we said anything about money as a mechanism for allocating resources. Trying to deal with money at this point in our unit's development could create another planning nightmare, so we will hold it in abeyance until our unit takes better form. Then, we will include it if we can work it in. If we can't, money as a medium of exchange can become the focus of another unit.

Thus far, we've hinted at several teaching activities, but for the most part our planning has been in fairly general terms. Our intent has been to build a foundation, a basis for day-to-day teaching activities. We have also tried to illustrate that the progression of unit planning moves from the "whole," the unit, to the "parts," or specific teaching activities—not the other way around.

A special note about the role of *daily* lesson plans in unit planning is in order here. You will notice below that we have presented our teaching episodes on an activity basis, not on a lesson plan basis. The reason for this is that each activity is intended to reflect a meaningful learning episode. However, we cannot determine ahead of time how long each activity will actually take. Some may take a day, some two days, and some considerably longer. Because of this, and because the unit plan provides the overall organizational framework, the teacher's daily lesson plans will merely indicate where the class is in relation to the overall unit plan. The teacher's daily lesson plans might read, for example, "Continue Activity Two." Teachers who do *not* use unit planning are necessarily forced to follow a much more elaborate daily lesson-planning procedure (see p. 106).

Developing and sequencing learning activities is neither more nor less important than any other aspect of planning. Unfortunately, we know of no formula or procedure to help you do it. In most instances, it seems to be a matter of what makes the most sense to an individual (teacher). Below we have indicated the sequence of activities *we* would use, but this isn't the only way such a unit could be organized or taught. In fact, if things don't go the way we've planned, we'll undoubtedly face some hasty reorganizing.

Sample Unit Plan: "Using Resources"

Note: The following activities are described in adult terms, not necessarily as we would present them to children. In developing your own units, you may wish to include key questions in the language you would use with students. We have included some key student questions as examples. We have also included some exemplary behavioral objectives where appropriate. What we have not done, however, is identify activities on a day-to-day basis. The reason for this, as we noted earlier, is because the activities flow together. Just how much time you devote to an activity will depend on a lot of things, including your students' interest and the time you have available. It is one of those things you may need to play by ear.

Initiating activity   *Identifying the components of canned corn*
Divide the class into small groups and (if possible) provide each with an identical can of corn. Ask each group to identify as many "things" as possible that went into making the corn. (If a group member can list the

group's ideas, great; if not, it's not essential.) Gauge the length of time spent on this activity by your students' interest: five minutes or less may be sufficient, depending on the group.

Then, have the various groups identify what they have found (list the components on the chalkboard as each group reports). Probe, cajole, and stimulate as necessary. After the groups have gone as far as they seem able, ask if any of the items seem to go together. For classes that have worked in small groups, this portion of the activity could be done on that basis. Otherwise, doing it as a large group may be your alternative. (Note: Some items may go into more than one category.)

The intent of this activity is to have the children identify components, and only secondarily have them classify and label groups of those components.

Behavioral objective: Not applicable. This is a group activity, not one focusing on the skill levels of individual students. Note: we do not mean to imply that behavioral objectives are wholly foreign to group activities.

Special note

They are not. Unless you plan to assess the performance of individual students, however, it doesn't seem reasonable to state the objectives in those terms. In instances where some of your students evidence skill deficiencies in areas related to the activity, you might very well want to cast behavioral objectives for them. In other words, you could indicate that "After the group activity in which the possible components of canned corn are enumerated, the student will identify two (three or more) components with similar characteristics ('things that seem to go together')." Note also that when you evaluate group activities, as you should, the results may suggest specific behavioral objectives for some of your students who don't fare too well.

Skill areas:
observation
analyzing
inferring
(classifying—identifying patterns)

Activity 2   A "family tree" for canned corn

Working with the "things" previously identified, the teacher and students will locate components on a "family tree" chart similar to the one illustrated in Figure 3.2. As a group, students will identify all of the "things" (not yet defined as resources) they can think of that were involved in producing the two cans of corn (displayed). Have a good reader read the label. Items the students identify should be listed on the board, and may include such things as *farmer, metal, paper, ink,* etc. Don't push too far here. For example, accept *paper* without going into paper's components (wood, etc.) unless the children insist on it. This will be picked up again in Activity 3.

Behavioral objective: Not applicable. Again, this is a group activity intended to establish a "model" for later individual activities.

Optional initiating activity: If students are unfamiliar with a "family tree" flow chart, the unit could be begun by having each student make family tree charts of their own, using either snapshots, if available, or names of relatives. This activity, however, is usually more appropriate in the context of the study of families, and can be built upon if done at an earlier time or at an earlier grade level.

Note: The next three activities are extensions of Activity 2, and will depend upon how far back the children went with the canned corn's components. Were they, for example, satisfied with paper (for the label) as a component? If so, the basic question in the following activities is, "Have we really identified everything that went into the cans of corn?" For paper, for example, the question is, "Is paper made from anything?"

Activities 3, 4, and 5 each follow a similar format. The children should tentatively identify the resources and processes that go into producing the various components of the cans of corn—paper, metal, etc. These group hypotheses should be recorded for later reference. The exact nature of subsequent activities will depend on the materials and resources available, but the most important will relate to the production of:

1 paper
2 metal (tin cans)
3 corn

This is where a data bank may prove especially helpful.

In these activities, the students' hypotheses are tested against data (on paper making, etc.) provided through films, filmstrips, or other media.

Activity 3   *Paper*
The intent of this activity is to test the children's ideas about the resources used in making paper.
Key question: What do you think paper is made from?
List components the students identify. Use any of the following materials (as available).
Possible materials:
Film: *Paper and Pulp Making* (Coronet)
8mm. film loop: *Products from Trees* (Doubleday)
encyclopedia article
Add the resources to the master "family tree" chart.
Behavioral objective: Another group activity!
Skill areas: Comparing and contrasting their speculations (hypotheses) with the data presented.
Optional extending activity: Making paper
Follow instructions for making paper in *Teaching Social Studies in the Elementary School* by R. C. Preston and W. Herman (1974, pp. 568–70).

Activity 4   *Tin cans*
Follows the same format as Activity 3.
Possible materials:
Films: *Tin from the Malayan Jungle* (International Film Bureau); *Steel & America* (Disney Productions)
Filmstrip: *Rocks, Minerals & Mining* (Encyclopaedia Britannica Films)
other: Selections from Ema Green, *Let's Go To a Steel Mill.* New York: Putnam, 1961.

Behavioral objective: Same as for Activity 3.
Skill areas: Same as for Activity 3.

Activity 5   *Corn*
Follows the same format as Activities 3 and 4.
Possible materials
Films: *Farmer* (Encyclopaedia Britannica Films); *Farmer Don and the City* (Film Associates)
Filmstrips: *Farming in Indiana* (Jam Handy); *Where Food Comes From* (Encyclopaedia Britannica Films); *The Corn Belt* (Society for Visual Education)
Behavioral objective: Same as for Activities 3 and 4.
Skill areas: Same as for Activities 3 and 4.
Optional extending activities: Consider the nature of salt, ink, or any other component in the production of canned corn as interest warrants. Follow same format as Activities 3 through 5.

Behavioral objective for activities 3, 4, and 5 (taken as a group): At the conclusion of these activities, the child will name at least five resources used in the production of the canned corn (knowledge level).

Activity 6   *Where do things come from?*
Each child (or small group) will select a common object or article and make a "family tree" chart for it similar to the one done for corn. Note that for some things, such as articles of clothing, this activity may involve identifying the steps in its production.
   Children should explain and display their charts.
Behavioral objective: Given a common object or article of their choice, the student will identify either: (1) the components that were used to produce it, or (2) the steps involved in its production.
Skill Areas:
observing different objects
analyzing
inferring

Activity 7   *Mini-synthesis*
Using the corn charts and those the children constructed for Activity 6, develop a discussion-oriented activity that will help the children to recognize that: (1) the "things" (materials) that went into making the canned corn all ultimately originated in the land, (2) all goods ultimately have their origin in the land, and (3) people were involved at every step along the way. If the occasion has not arisen previously, the term *resources* can be identified as a label for "things," and the term *goods* associated with objects or products produced from natural resources.
Key questions:
1. Do you notice anything about those "things" our cans of corn were made from?
2. Can you think of anything that does not come from the land?
Behavioral objective: At the conclusion of this activity, the student will list at least five resources originating in the land.

Skill areas:
classifying and labeling
analyzing
inferring (dependency on the land)
Optional extending activities:
1. Show the film: *Man's Basic Need: Natural Resources* (Encyclopaedia Britannica Films)
2. Show the film loop: *Our Productive Resources* (Doubleday)

Activity 8   *What would happen if?*
The intent of this activity is to have children speculate on how things would be different if we didn't have certain things, especially certain natural resources.
Key question: What would happen if we didn't have any wood? electricity? water? bicycles? corn? iron?
Behavioral objective: Not applicable—a group activity.
Skill areas:
analyzing
inferring

Activity 9   *What we do with what we've got*
The intent of this activity is to extend the notion that goods and basic resources are used in different ways. For example, a tree, while reflecting the use of the land in a particular way, can itself be used in a number of different ways.
Description: Provide individual students or groups with labeled pictures (cut from magazines, etc.) of various resources—land, a tree, steel (which really isn't a resource per se), water, etc. The students are then asked to make a collage of pictures illustrating different ways in which the product or resource can be used. The teacher should also make a chart showing land being used in different ways—for a playground, for growing crops, for housing, for parking lots, etc. (Note: Instruct students *not* to include their original picture in their collage until after the class has had an opportunity to identify what resource each collage deals with. This may take several days.)
Behavioral objective: Given a picture of one product or basic natural resource, the student will identify at least seven other pictures of that resource being used in different ways.
Skill areas:
observing
interpreting

Activity 10   *What could we do with the playground?*
The intent of this discussion format activity is to illustrate that people have decided to use a particular piece of land, the school playground, in a certain way. In other words, if oil were discovered beneath the school playground, the land might be used for other than playground purposes —in this case, to hold an oil well. The way in which the playground might be used is subject to several limitations, not the least of which in

our oil well example is the presence of oil. Certain value issues also enter the picture. For example, if gold or oil were discovered on the school playground, it *could* be turned into a gold mine or an oil field; but *should* it? The physical determiners—climate, etc.—should be dealt with first through questions such as "Could our playground be used as an orange grove (or a corn field)?" Such questions will vary according to climatic regions.

Value considerations can be introduced through role playing. For example, the following situation could be presented to students.

Gold Discovered on School Playground
"Gold has been discovered on the _____ School playground. The Acme Mining Company wants to buy the playground and build a gold mine there. They are willing to pay a lot of money for the property. Your group must decide if the playground should be sold."
Behavioral objective: At the conclusion of this activity, the student will identify three factors which might influence the ways in which resources are used.
Skill areas:
analyzing
inferring

Culminating activities   Returning to the master "family tree" chart (for the cans of corn), the children should:
1 Identify the primary decision-makers involved in the production of the canned corn; e.g., the farmer, the lumberman, the food processor.
2 Identify alternative decisions these individuals might have made in terms of the way they used the resources available to them.

Then, given a series of pictures of people in different occupations—a machinist, a dairy farmer, a baker, etc.—the students will identify the resources each is using.

Transition to next unit

Culminating activities provide students with opportunities to apply and extend some of the ideas previously dealt with in different contexts. In this unit, we began with canned corn as the primary vehicle, and then returned to it in the culminating activity. It wasn't essential to do that, but it seemed to round things out rather nicely. It is helpful, but not essential, if the culminating activities can provide a "bridge" to the next unit, which might focus on conservation (the use and abuse of resources), the role of tools in using resources to produce goods and services, or perhaps the role of money as a medium for allocating resources. Once again, the way in which students respond to portions of the unit we have just planned could well be a cue to the way we should go in the next one.

Unit Planning Checklist

Once teachers have decided how they will culminate their unit, a vital phase of planning still remains. Having dealt with the various parts of their unit, it now becomes important to examine the whole, to go back over what they've developed to see that it does what they hope it will do. To facilitate

this preliminary review, we have developed the following unit-plan checklist. We suggest that you use it to evaluate the unit we've just developed. If
you can't answer "yes" to every criterion, we apparently have left some
planning undone.

*Does it all fit
together?*

General

Yes No   *Goals*

___ ___   Have we identified in general terms what students should know
at the end of this unit?

___ ___   Have we identified in general terms what skills students should
be able to demonstrate at the end of this unit?

___ ___   Have we identified affective goals for this unit?

___ ___   Have we identified what should be done for students who cannot demonstrate what is indicated above?

Unit Objectives

___ ___   Have we identified cognitive and affective objectives for this
unit?

Specific

Yes No

___ ___   1 Have we identified a vehicle or focus for the unit?

___ ___   2 Have we identified a main idea or generalization for the
unit?

___ ___   3 Have we task-analyzed the elements of this unit in terms of
prerequisite understandings?

___ ___   4 Have we stated instructional objectives in performance
terms?

___ ___   5 Have we identified and sequenced learning activities?

___ ___   6 Have we identified guiding (key) questions
6.1 for planning purposes?
6.2 for instructional use with students?

___ ___   7 Have we identified teaching materials and resources?

___ ___   8 Have we identified a way to initiate the unit?

___ ___   9 Have we identified the means for student evaluation?

___ ___   10 Have we devised a means for evaluating the unit for internal
and external consistency (such as this checklist)?

___ ___   10.1 Do the various sections of the unit "fit together"; e.g.,
no "hidden" objectives (internal consistency)?

___ ___   10.2 Is the unit, as a whole, justifiable? Can it be defended
as worthy of being studied (external consistency)?

On Winging It

We would be remiss if we didn't indicate that some teachers don't
bother with (or don't know how to do) unit planning. Instead, they read
the chapter in the text, list a few so-called "discussion questions," order a
film or filmstrip just to break up the monotony, and then may find
themselves making out a test the night before it is to be given. Without a
textbook that does most of the organizing for them, they'd be lost.

At one time or another most teachers find themselves in a predicament when what they've planned doesn't seem appropriate or when, for one reason or another, they haven't planned at all. What you do then is "wing" it.

Quite frankly, we have "winged" a few lessons in our time, some that went spectacularly well and others that "bombed" so badly that we wanted to crawl under the desk. Indeed, few things are worse than the feeling you get when something is going poorly but you have nothing prepared that might rescue you (and your class) from almost certain disaster. One of the ironies of teaching is that after teachers have spent untold hours planning, things don't always go as planned. Students may go off on a tangent, a film won't arrive on time, or any one of a thousand other things may go amiss. None of these makes planning any less valuable, but it does reemphasize the need for flexibility and making adjustments as you go.

For days when things don't go as planned, we suggest that you keep a couple of all-purpose, "emergency activities" in your file. By and large they will almost certainly be better than that widely used alternative, "OK, kids, open your books to page so-and-so, and we'll start reading."

Beware of Murphy's Law

Lesson Planning

With unit plans to provide the overall organization, lesson planning is seldom a tedious task. Without a unit plan, however, lesson planning requires that you duplicate much of what you might otherwise have done in preparing a teaching unit.

In developing daily lesson plans, we suggest that you *not* succumb to the practice of listing every question you might ask of students in the sequence in which you plan to ask them. No matter how logical it might seem, when teachers do this, their questions—not the students' responses—tend to become the focal point of the lesson. When this happens the possibility of building on a student's previous response is often lost. Thus, listing your questions in the sequence in which you plan to ask them could very well limit your ability to respond to changes in direction suggested by the students' responses. Our experience indicates that if you know where a lesson should go and what it's leading to, then only four or five key questions should be sufficient.

Caution!

For prospective teachers, it's important to recognize that lesson plans are not for your use alone. Often, those plans must communicate what you intend to do to your cooperating teacher, a college supervisor, and some-times even the principal (some of whom collect daily or weekly lesson plans from all of their teachers). This sometimes results in lesson plans that are, in our judgment at least, more detailed than they would otherwise need to be for effective teaching. Quality teaching demands quality planning. Recognize, though, that the length and scope of your lesson plans may be a function of the dual purpose they serve: (1) as a plan for the students you teach and (2) to communicate your intent to those who observe you.

Not for you alone

The following is a sample daily lesson plan in a format that should enable you to deal effectively with students *and* communicate your intent to those who evaluate your planning. In this instance, our example comes from Activity 9, "What we do with what we've got," from our unit plan.

Exemplary Daily Lesson Plan

Sample

Unit generalization: Resource utilization results from choices among alternatives, choices made by human beings. (It is not essential that the unit generalization be repeated on each lesson plan, just helpful.)

Lesson focus: Alternative utilization of resources and goods.

Objective: To extend the notion that basic resources and goods are used in different ways.

Performance objective: Given a picture of one product or basic natural resource, the student will identify at least seven pictures of the product or resource being used in different ways.

Advance preparation:

1 Locate pictures of products or basic resources—farmland, a tree, water, an ingot of iron, etc. Label these appropriately.
2 Gather needed materials: magazines (you'll need a variety, and lots of them); tagboard, large newsprint, or colored paper (on which to mount the collage); scissors (if the kids don't have their own); rubber cement (for mounting pictures without wrinkling).

Procedure: Distribute pictures and then identify the students' task: "Make a collage showing different ways in which the product or resource shown on your picture is used." (If students have not made collages previously, you may need to show them a sample—such as the one you are making for land usage.)
(Reminder: Be sure to tell students not to mount their original pictures on their collage. They should keep them "hidden.")

Follow-up: Have children share their collage with the rest of the class. When the product or resource has been identified, add the original picture to the collection.

Evaluation: As per performance objective.

Summary

Instructional planning is something that isn't complete until teachers see what they have planned come to fruition. Most of a teacher's planning takes place prior to instruction, but a substantial amount also takes place during instruction, usually in the form of day-to-day adjustments. Some planning may even take place after instruction, when you decide what should be changed when the unit is taught again. In this chapter, we have identified the various components of planning and indicated how those components fit together. We also illustrated formats in which the products of one's planning —teaching units and daily lesson plans—can be organized and presented.

The instructional-planning process begins at the "end," with the identification of what students should be able to do after instruction. These "ends," which reflect the purposes for undertaking instruction, are usually expressed in two forms—as instructional goals and as instructional objectives. Goals were identified as generalized and ofttimes unmeasurable statements that indicate a general direction teaching should take. Examples of goals include having students "Appreciate the contributions of American patriots," or "Understand the impact that technology has had on the American way of life." Instructional objectives, on the other hand, describe specific behaviors students will demonstrate as they move toward a certain goal. Statements such as "The student will, from memory, identify three factors that led to the Civil War," or "Given a list of statements, the student will identify those that are facts and those that reflect opinions," are examples of instructional (behaviorally-stated) objectives. The fact that objectives are phrased in behavioral terms, however, does *not* necessarily mean that they are good and worthy of instruction. Rather, teachers must evaluate potential objectives, no matter how they are stated, in terms of the goals to which they relate.

The way that teachers approach and use social studies content plays an important role in the planning process. *Content utilization,* which refers to the fact that teachers and students can *use* content in a variety of different ways and for many different purposes, is what we are referring to here. We are not suggesting that you should develop a unit on canned corn, as we did in this chapter, although you might wish to if it were appropriate. Rather, our intent was to illustrate how corn could serve as one of several possible *vehicles* that would permit us to reach our goals. Using content as a vehicle is an important facet of contemporary social studies programs, and is something we examine in the next chapter.

Suggested Activities

1 Most colleges of education maintain collections of social studies curriculum guides and textbook series. If not, the local school system might loan you copies. Where possible, get two different curriculum guides or texts (preferably teacher's editions) *for the same grade level.* Compare and contrast them in terms of the following:
a. the nature and clarity of their goals and objectives
b. the relationship of suggested student activities to the stated goals and objectives
c. the similarities and differences in format, suggested topics, and suggested teaching approaches.

2 Occasionally schools in some parts of the country periodically suspend their regular curriculum for a day. In place of it teachers develop variations on the "can of corn" curriculum we dealt with in this chapter. On those days, the entire curriculum is developed around a single vehicle, such as apples, pumpkins, breakfast cereals, sports, or almost anything you could imagine (including corn). You may never be called upon to teach "apple math" or "soccer social studies," but the prospect can be intriguing.

Using the procedures we suggested earlier (pp. 87–91), try your hand at identifying possible questions and student activities for each subject in the curriculum for the topic/vehicle of your choice.

References

Bloom, Benjamin S. (ed.) *Taxonomy of Educational Objectives: The Classification of Educational Goals: Handbook I: Cognitive Domain.* New York: Longmans, 1956.

Burton, Virginia Lee. *Mike Mulligan and His Steam Shovel.* Boston: Houghton Mifflin, 1939.

Fraenkel, Jack R. *Helping Students Think and Value: Strategies for Teaching the Social Studies.* Englewood Cliffs, NJ: Prentice-Hall, 1973.

Gronlund, Norman. *Stating Behavioral Objectives for Classroom Instruction.* New York: Macmillan, 1970.

Mager, Robert F. *Preparing Instructional Objectives* (2nd ed.) Palo Alto, CA: Fearon, 1975.

Krathwohl, David R. (ed.) *Taxonomy of Educational Objectives: The Classification of Educational Goals: Handbook II: The Affective Domain.* New York: Longmans, 1964.

Preston, R. C., and Herman, W. *Teaching Social Studies in the Elementary School.* (4th ed.) New York: Holt, Rinehart and Winston, 1974.

Sawin, Enoch I. *Evaluation and the Work of the Teacher.* Belmont, CA: Wadsworth, 1969.

Suggested Readings

James E. Davis, and Frances Haley. (eds.) *Planning A Social Studies Program: Activities, Guidelines, and Resources.* Boulder, CO: ERIC Clearinghouse for Social Studies/Social Science Education/Social Science Education Consortium, Inc., 1977. This is an eminently practical guide to developing or modifying a social studies program. It's probably the finest publication of its type that we've seen.

Every social studies methods text deals with planning in one fashion or another. Some that complement your text in this area are listed below:

William Joyce, and Janet Alleman-Brooks. *Teaching Social Studies in the Elementary and Middle Schools.* New York: Holt, Rinehart and Winston, 1979.

Peter Martorella. *Elementary Social Studies As A Learning System.* New York: Harper & Row, 1976.

Lavonne A. Hanna, Gladys L. Potter, and Robert W. Reynolds. *Dynamic Elementary Social Studies: Unit Teaching.* (3rd ed.) New York: Holt, Rinehart and Winston, 1973.

4 Social Studies Programs: Who Teaches What, When?

Key Questions

What is taught when in social studies?

How important is *sequence* to a social studies program?

Key Ideas

For years, the dominant pattern among elementary social studies programs has been the "expanding environments" approach.

In general, we are too close to ourselves to study ourselves effectively.

New social studies programs, at least those that vary from the expanding environments approach, exhibit some of the following characteristics:

1 They use content as a vehicle and as a means to contrast new events and information with a child's previous experience.

2 They may follow a concept-based approach that uses some form of spiral curriculum development.

Introduction

The time and place: 3:30 on a mid-September afternoon in an elementary school somewhere in the Midwest. *The scene:* After a long day, John Clark, a new sixth-grade teacher, hails his principal, Mr. Warren Immel, who is passing by in the hall.

John: Hey, Mr. Immel. Got a minute?
Warren: Sure. What's up?
John: We've got to do something about this social studies program.
Warren: I know! Those books are really getting beat up. I guess it's time we budgeted some money for social studies.
John: Yes ... but it's more than just some new books. I think we'd better look at the entire program.
Warren: What do you mean?
John: Well, it finally dawned on me what I'm supposed to teach this year. I've already begun with a unit on early man, and then I'm supposed to move to Egypt, Greece and Rome—the cradles of civilization—and then to units on religions, the Middle Ages, forms of government, the early history of our country, and a unit on technology— major inventions like the printing press, the spinning jenny, and that sort of thing. And *then,* I have to teach a huge unit on world history since about 1900.

Warren: I know—and you have to get through all that before February because then you move to the geography of the Eastern Hemisphere.

John: Right! The *entire* Eastern Hemisphere. Do you know how many nations there are? That's a lot of stuff to cover in a year, much less a single semester.

Warren: Yes, it is, but on the other hand we have a fairly conventional social studies program. It's not much different from what's taught in most elementary schools I know of.

John: Maybe we should be unconventional.

Warren: Well . . . but there are some other things to consider. In the primary grades, for example, some kids can't read a social studies text; they need a program based on experience.

John: Some of my kids can't read their books either.

Warren: True, but that's another problem. You see, our social studies program is based on what's called the "expanding environments" approach. It starts in the primary grades with experiences and activities that are based on the children's experiences, and then moves toward increasingly more abstract and distant areas in the upper grades. We sort of begin with what's closest to the child—the concrete—and move to the abstract. (Turning toward the chalkboard) it looks something like this. (See Figure 4.1.)

John: O.K. I see the point. But how were you able to do that so easily—without looking it up or something?

Warren: It's easy if you remember the organizing principle. You begin in first grade with the community closest to the children—family—and then work upward and outward from there.

John: O.K. So one last question. If my students finish the world this year, what's left? This pattern seems to end with Grade 6. What do they do next year? Start all over?

Warren: In this district, seventh graders study state history, and eighth graders study American history.

John (Interrupting.) But they studied state history in fourth grade, and U.S. history in Grade 5!

Warren: Well, maybe it doesn't fit the pattern. But as far as we're concerned, we have a logical program we've followed for years. Even if you have to skim over some things at times, at least we've exposed children to the world—even if they don't understand everything completely. Now . . . about those new books . . .

Exploring ever-expanding environments

Note: This episode is based on a real incident. The principal, despite the fact that we disagree with some of his views, has earned our respect and admiration.

The social studies program outlined in Figure 4.1 has been *and continues to be* the dominant elementary social studies program in this country today. Occasionally you may find variations, to be sure (some of which we'll examine later in this chapter) but for the most part, the *expanding environments* approach to elementary social studies is so common that it is tantamount to a national curriculum (see Superka, Hawke, and Morrisett, 1980). This means that if you know what grade level you plan to teach, Figure 4.1 can provide a general indication of what will be expected of you. If you don't know what

A national curriculum

Figure 4.1
Expanding-Environments Approach to Social Studies (K-6), plus Grades 7 and 8

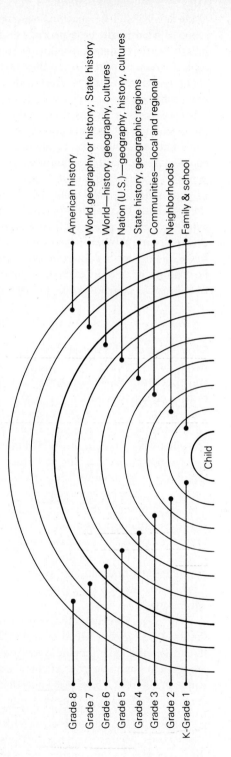

grade level you'll be teaching—as most prospective teachers don't—the scope of what might be expected of you broadens considerably. If you fall into this latter category, take heart. As we illustrate later in this chapter, the topical sequence of the expanding environments approach to social studies is *not* as important as it is often made out to be, which means that you may have considerably more latitude than you might otherwise suspect.

Curriculum or program?

Social studies programs, the way they are organized, and other factors that influence them are our major concern in this chapter. As we examine them, you'll notice that we tend to use the terms *program* and *curriculum* interchangeably. Authorities sometimes distinguish between the two, *curriculum* being the broader framework within which teachers develop their own programs. Among public school personnel, however, you often hear expressions such as "Our math program," "Our social studies program," or "Our career education program." In many instances, they are referring to an existing curriculum that has been adapted by the teachers in a school or school district for their particular purposes. Inasmuch as *program* seems to be edging out the more formal *curriculum* in common usage, we have opted to follow that convention in the balance of this chapter.

Organizing Social Studies Programs

Developing a social studies curriculum is much like unit planning but on a *much* larger scale. Many of the same activities, such as determining goals and specifying objectives, apply. However, instead of deciding on the sequence of activities within a unit, the concern in program planning shifts to the sequence of units to be taught in a given year. Of equal concern is how what is taught during one year relates to what was taught the previous year and what will be taught the following year. Just as the parts of unit planning —goals, objectives, learning activities, etc.—must fit together into a meaningful whole, so too must the parts of curriculum planning—units from the current year, the previous year, and the following year—fit together to form a meaningful social studies experience.

The essential aspects of any curriculum or program are captured in four little words: *what, why, when,* and *how.* You could actually add a fifth word, *where,* which has generally been assumed to be "in school." Teaching is not something that can take place only in classrooms, but with few exceptions, we really haven't witnessed a stampede to take advantage of the alternatives.

What should be taught? *Why* should something be taught (and, why should *it* be taught instead of *something else*)? *When* (in what sequence) should something be taught? And, *how* should something be taught? These are the four basic questions of curriculum planning. In slightly altered form and with different labels, these questions are basic to analyzing social studies curriculum offerings. In this case they become:

Scope

1 How much of the universe of social studies knowledge will be taught? In other words, what is the *scope* of the subject matter? On a practical level, the question is one of whether, for example, a unit on "the farm" or "desert communities" will or will not be included in a social studies program. To

answer questions related to scope, one needs to have already addressed the question of *why* (or why not).

2   Why is something to be included in or excluded from a social studies program? Is it because the topic reflects information that happens to be available, because it is something that has always been taught in schools (Joan of Arc), or is there some other reason children should study it?

Rationale

The question *why* functions as a request for a *rationale*, or statement of justification. When students ask "What do we have to study this stuff for?" they are asking for a reasoned (and convincing) statement as to why something is worth being studied. Responding adequately isn't always easy, as we noted earlier.

3   When (at what grade level) will something be taught? This is the *sequence* question which, in terms of curriculum, is one of the thorniest to deal with. Sequence, the order in which topics or units will be dealt with, has two dimensions: within-grade levels and between-grade levels. Having decided to teach a unit on "the farm," for example, the between-grade-level question asks at which grade level it should (and will) be taught. Placing topics (or units) at a particular grade level can be influenced by many factors, which we will examine shortly.

Two dimensions of sequencing

The within-grade-level sequence dimension is concerned with the year's sequence of activities. Having decided that Greece, Rome, and ancient Egypt should be taught at a certain grade level, for instance, the within-grade-level sequencing then involves determining the *order* in which they should be taught. Whenever history is involved, as in this example, the sequence is typically based on chronology. On that basis, ancient Egypt occurred first, and would thus be taught first. But which came next—Greece or Rome?

4   How will everything be pulled together into a meaningful whole? This is the basic organizational question of curriculum and teaching. To illustrate how important this dimension can be, consider a social studies program that asks you to teach the following sequence of topics to a third grade class:
a) a unit on explorers
b) a unit on the history and geography of Japan
c) a unit on community helpers
d) a unit on transportation
e) a unit on the Civil War

Consistency

If there's something—a theme, a vehicle, an approach, anything—that can pull these topics together so that they make sense, it certainly isn't obvious. What we seem to have is a disjointed collection of discrete topics. And, were students to complete such a program, they too would likely have in their possession a disjointed collection of discrete pieces of information. In this case, whoever determined the scope of the program may have had some good reasons, but they also seem to have some odd ideas about how and why those topics should be sequenced.

There probably isn't any one best basis for organizing social studies programs. But at least one thing should be apparent from this example—social studies programs must be organized around something.

During the early decades of the 20th century, the prevailing practice was to determine what content was to be taught—ancient, colonial, medieval, modern, or world history, for example—and then divide that content into a logical sequence that would fit the time available. If one could reasonably expect to have a child in school for six years (which was fairly common at the time) that six-year period became the time available. Whatever the schools wished to teach had to be squeezed into that six-year period.

When attending junior high and high schools became more common, the time available increased considerably. For some students, it doubled—from six years to twelve. With few exceptions, however, drastic changes in the elementary social studies curriculum did *not* occur. In fact, remnants of the 19th-century pattern of curriculum organization can still be found in many schools today. What did change, however, was the purpose. Instead of preparing students to function in the outside world at the end of Grade 6, many schools shifted (perhaps unwittingly) to a "getting 'em ready for" stance. The purpose of elementary schools became "getting students ready for" the next level of schooling, be it middle school, junior high, or high school. This stance still permeates much of what goes on in schools today, so that one of the real purposes of kindergarten, for example, is to prepare students for first grade. It's a phenomenon repeated over and over again as students move up the educational ladder. There are legitimate elements to "getting 'em ready for," to be sure, but as schools have become increasingly bureaucratic in their organization, it becomes all too easy to slip into the frame of mind where the main purpose of school is to prepare students for more schooling, and where anything else they get in that process almost becomes secondary.

Legitimate elements of "getting 'em ready for" are evident in topics traditionally treated in the expanding environments approach (or *expanding horizons, expanding communities of man*—all refer to essentially similar programs) to social studies (see Figure 4.1, p. 111). In logical progression, each community (or environment) appears to be built upon the previously studied community. Through an adult's eyes, then, understanding the concept of *state* at Grade 4 should enable children to better understand the concept of *nation* when they meet it in Grade 5. The logic is apparently faultless. A problem arises, however, from the fact that most children do *not* view their world through an adult's eyes. What might seem logical to an adult can be totally lost to children for whom tomorrow is the immediate future and next week is "way off" in the distant future. Whether students *should* be concerned with what they will study in the future is not the issue here; their immediate concern is with the present—with the here and now —and not with something they may need "next year." From a child's perspective, next year can be so far in the future that it is virtually meaningless. Thus, how children develop a sense of time—including their perception of the present, the future, and the past—should play an important role in organizing a social studies program.

Similarly, the way in which children develop their conception of space— their perception of how they fit into their environment—should have a bearing on the organization of social studies programs, especially on the sequence of the environments they study. For many children, distance is measured by the number of *fars* they attach to *away;* as any child will tell

Time available

The "getting 'em ready for" syndrome

Children's perceptions

you, "far, far away" is much farther than plain old "far away." When both time and space are involved, the situation can become yet even more complicated. In the next section we examine some of the developmental considerations that influence—or should influence—the organization of social studies programs.

Developmental Considerations

Have you noticed that your birthdays seem to come around much faster than they did when you were younger? And do you remember when you measured your age in half-years—when being seven and a half was a whole lot older than being seven? Or, remember the day of Halloween or Christmas Eve, when it seemed as if it would never get dark? Time just seemed to creep along. In the intervening years, time hasn't sped up, of course, but what has changed is the way in which we perceive time.

A world of opposites

Developing Concepts of Time and Space   It isn't entirely clear how children develop a sense of time. Apparently, the ability to deal with time, especially historical time, develops so gradually that children are quite unaware of what is taking place. The evidence suggests that very young children begin to preceive their world in terms of polar opposites such as "hot–cold," "now–then," "good–bad," etc. (Levi-Strauss, 1966, and Egan, 1979.) At first, things are either "hot" or "cold." Then, as children gain experience, it appears that they gradually differentiate and refine the opposites so as to form a continuum. They learn that "warm" lies somewhere between "hot" and "cold," while "*very* hot" and "*very* cold" become new ways for expressing the extremes of temperature.

Conceptions of time apparently develop from an initial "now–then" orientation to the world. "Now" is the easiest for children to deal with, for it refers to the present moment. "Then" usually refers to anything not happening "now," and thus includes both past and future. (If lumping the past and the future together seems illogical to us as adults, it also serves to illustrate that logic, itself, is a learned behavior.) This is further illustrated by the fact that most children have no problem shifting from the real world to a storybook world filled with witches, dragons, and animals that talk, feel, and express many of the same emotions they do. As Egan (1979, p. 131) notes:

> The world is not perceived as an impersonal, objective entity. Such a conception is the achievement of a mature rationality, and depends on the secure development of what have been called concepts of 'otherness'—historical time, geographical place, causality, logical relationships, etc. The child's world is full of entities charged with, and given meaning by, those things the child knows best: love, hate, joy, fear, good, bad. Things are often perceived as feelings, willing, and thinking like the child.

The past

In the child's world of the "here and now"—a world in which time just creeps along—it seems to take considerable experience for the child to differentiate between "then–future" and "then–past." Logic suggests that conceptions of "the past" should be easier for children to deal with, since their past is made up of events that have already happened, events the child

© 1956, United Feature Syndicate

has actually experienced. "The future," on the other hand, is further removed from reality—it hasn't happened yet—and hence is more abstract. Logical or not, it appears that both concepts are equally difficult for children to comprehend.

Our observations indicate that when most children enter elementary school they have a fairly secure conception of "yesterday." Something that happened to them two weeks ago, however, took place "a long time ago," somewhere in a distant, undifferentiated past. Something that occurred two months or two years previous *also* took place "a long time ago." Although children's conception of the past may be likened to a big blur, this does not necessarily mean they have forgotten what happened to them. Children can often describe events—vacations, experiences, etc.—in amazing detail. They can tell you *what* happened, but typically cannot provide an accurate time frame for *when* the events took place. Until children develop the necessary time frame, which appears to be at around age 10 or 11, trying to teach something that happened two centuries ago is apt to be as frustrating as teaching the concept of "snow" to someone from Jamaica. Don't assume that history must be ignored, however. Young children can often relate to the events and individuals of history, particularly if the emphasis is on events and individuals, and if they are presented in story form. But trying to emphasize how long ago those events took place may go right over their heads.

In many respects, the way in which children develop a conception of the future is similar to how they develop notions of the past. Just as events that took place two weeks or two months ago may be regarded as "a long time ago," young children often view events that will take place two weeks or two

What, but not when

The future

months hence as being somewhere in the distant future. Because of this, primary teachers often learn *not* to respond to a child's request for help with "I'll be there in just a minute." From a perspective in which time creeps, a minute is an eternity. Approximately ten seconds later the student is likely to be back asking, "Will you help me now?" From the student's perspective, the minute has passed. Unless the teacher is aware of what's going on, her reply is apt to be an exasperated "I told you I'd be with you in a minute." The entire situation can be avoided (though nothing is guaranteed) if you refrain from using time referents that could be confusing. Instead of "I'll be with you in a minute," a statement such as "I'll be with you as soon as I can" may do much to avoid problems of this kind.

How long is a minute?

How children develop a conception of the past is important inasmuch as historical time is a component of most elementary social studies programs. The future, however, normally isn't a subject as such, although you sometimes find "future studies" taught in high schools and colleges. How children perceive the future can play a role if we expect them to comprehend how a topic they are currently studying fits into a broader picture. Given the way children perceive their world, however, telling a second grader that this year's study of neighborhoods will be important to next year's study of communities, is probably wasted effort.

Piaget's Stages of Intellectual Development   How children develop conceptions of time and space appears to be closely related to their overall intellectual development. Some of the most substantive research on the development of children's thinking was done by the Swiss psychologist, Jean Piaget. Piaget's early interest was in zoology, particularly snails, clams, and other mollusks, but he shifted to children after he began working with Alfred Binet, the developer of the first intelligence tests. Binet wanted to determine how children of various ages responded to the questions on his test, and he hired Piaget to do the research.

After working with several hundred children, Piaget observed that children at certain age levels would consistently use quite different reasons to justify their answers. Four-year-olds would respond quite differently from eight-year-olds, whose answers would be different still from responses provided by teenagers. When children between the ages of two and seven were provided with three objects of different shapes labeled "A," "B," and "C," those children could almost always point out which object was the tallest. But when confronted with a hypothetical proposition such as "If A is bigger than B but smaller than C," for example, those children could almost never tell which item was the largest. In fact, Piaget found that children could not deal with such a problem until about age eleven. Actually, their responses were so consistent that Piaget was able to predict how children of certain ages would respond to specific questions. From these observations, Piaget developed his basic theory of how children's thinking develops.

Cognitive development

Piaget identified four developmental stages that all children progress through as they mature. These stages are illustrated in Table 4.1. Piaget also determined that all children pass through each of the four stages in order—from sensorimotor to preoperational, to concrete operations, to for-

Table 4.1 Stages of Cognitive Development as Described by Piaget

Stage and Age Range	Description
Sensorimotor (Birth to 2 years)	Children learn what things are like through their senses, through what they touch, feel, taste, smell, and manipulate. If they can't see, feel, or touch an object, they believe it doesn't exist.
Preoperational (2–7 years)	Children in this stage gradually acquire the ability to think of more than one thing at a time (decenter). They also begin to master symbols which permit mental manipulation. However, reasoning is still dominated by perception. For example, children in this stage will maintain that a tall, thin tumbler holds more liquid than a short, fat glass even if shown that they hold the same amount. Language is egocentric; words have unique meanings, which limit children's ability to consider others' points of view.
Concrete Operations (7–11 years)	Children are able to decenter, conserve (understand that two differently shaped objects may have the same volume), and reverse (understand that a ball of clay that's been rolled into a long snake, for example, can be reformed into the original ball). Such thinking is limited to concrete objects, however, with little or no ability to generalize beyond them.
Formal Operations (11 years and older)	Children are able to consider the hypothetical, things that don't exist except as mental abstractions. They also become increasingly capable of dealing with propositional thinking and of developing hypotheses.

mal operations—with each stage serving as a basis for the next. There is nothing hard and fast about the age range for a particular stage; children tend to move from stage to stage in a gradual progression. They never skip a stage, however.

To the extent that space (geographical place) and historical time involve the ability to deal with abstractions, Piaget's research indicates that most children would be better able to comprehend them at about fifth or sixth grade—age ten or eleven. Other social studies research tends to confirm Piaget's findings, though perhaps not intentionally.

Time zones

In one study, Davis (1963) sought to teach several classes of fourth, fifth, and sixth graders about geographic time zones. Davis found that all groups benefited from the instruction, though the sixth graders did retain more than the fifth, and the fifth graders more than the fourth. As a result, Davis noted that children may be able to profit from instruction about time zones earlier than was previously thought. Several other studies involving time and spatial concepts have made similar recommendations (Arnsdorf, 1961; Rushdoony, 1963). Other authorities, however, argue that time and space concepts are too difficult to be taught to children prior to the intermediate grades, and that instruction should be delayed, preferably, until the junior high school level (see e.g., Wesley and Adams, 1952).

Figure 4.2 "Ideal" Emphasis for Space and Time, by Grade Level

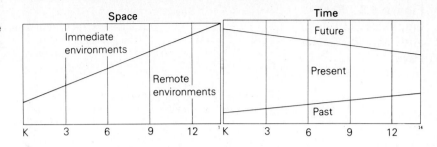

Source: Adapted from Estvan, 1968.

For the majority of their years in elementary school, children are functioning at the concrete-operational level. For primary children, especially six-year-olds, the majority may be functioning at the preoperational level. In light of this, we need to be especially cautious that we do not provide a social studies program which, though it makes sense to us as adults, makes intellectual demands of children that go beyond their abilities. Sooner or later, of course, children must gain experience in looking at the world from an adult perspective. But by forcing this perspective too soon, we risk winning the battle and losing the war—and producing children who hate social studies in the process.

Other Curricular Implications   The two graphs in Figure 4.2 (Estvan, 1968) illustrate what could be called an "ideal" progression with which two of the major elements of social studies—space and time—could be organized. Unfortunately, what may look so "neat and clean" in theory doesn't always work out that way in practice. In an expanding-environment approach, for example, an interesting thing takes place between Grades 3 and 4. In third grade, when children study their community, they are learning about something fairly concrete, something most children have experienced simply by having lived in a community. By looking out the classroom window, they can see at least a part of the reality they are studying. Upon moving to "the state" in fourth grade, however, they move to something that often isn't part of their view of the world. Despite the fact that states have physical dimensions —boundaries, a capitol, etc.—the state is actually a phenomenon of political organization. It is lines on a map, lines you can't see anywhere except on a map. And so, even though the state is a smaller, closer environment than the nation (which the children will study in fifth grade), and while children may indeed live in "the state," these factors do not make it any less an abstraction.

Space and time —ideal and real

Neither can the fifth-grade child "see" the United States, except by looking at a map that is itself an abstracted representation of our country. Nor can we expect that world history and the geography of the Eastern Hemisphere will be any closer to a sixth-grade child's view of reality. Add to this a historical time dimension—studying the European origins of American exploration (1400–1600 A.D.) in fifth grade and ancient Egypt in sixth grade, which is almost as far back in recorded history as it is possible to go—and the apparently systematic progression of time seems spurious at best. Thus,

Dealing with abstractions

Figure 4.3 Real Emphasis for Space and Time, by Grade Level

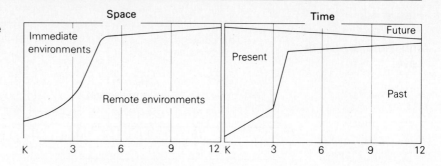

Source: Adapted from Estvan, 1968.

what would seem to be an "ideal progression" in theory (Figure 4.2) becomes a journey of steep inclines and sharp curves in actual practice (see Figure 4.3).

Supporters of the traditional expanding-environments approach to social studies sometimes argue that the sequence in which children study the various environments is important. We fail to see why it is necessary for primary-level children to study their families (or *the* family) before studying the (their) neighborhood. Rather, we think that if families are the focus of study an excellent way to approach them is by examining various families in the neighborhood. Ask yourself also what an intermediate-level child must know about United States history or geography prior to studying ancient Greece or the Middle Ages. The fact that we are unable to identify any essential prerequisites leads us to suggest that a rigid sequence separating the various environments actually increases the chance that children will *not* see the interrelationships that exist between and among families, neighborhoods, communities, states, and nations. As we noted in Chapter Two, social studies is a synthetic discipline. It lacks the preestablished structure found in subjects such as mathematics, and as a consequence can be organized and sequenced in many different ways.

Role of sequence

We are not the first to challenge the expanding-environments approach to social studies (see Smith and Cardinell, 1964). Despite the problems we have identified here, it is still the dominant approach to social studies and will probably continue to be for the forseeable future. There are occasional bright spots on the horizon, programs that use different organizational bases, which we will examine in the next section. But because the expanding-environments approach is so dominant, most of the balance of this book is geared to it. Our continuing emphasis will be on developing concrete learning experiences for children, experiences that can help move social studies out of the realm of the abstract.

Guidelines for Social Studies Programs

If an ideal social studies program actually existed, what would it look like? What characteristics would it exhibit? In 1971 and then again in

1979, the National Council for the Social Studies (NCSS) addressed these questions by developing a set of standards for social studies programs. Highlights from the guidelines are reproduced below.

1   The social studies program should be directly related to the age, maturity, and concerns of students.
2   The social studies program should deal with the real social world.
3   The social studies program should draw from currently valid knowledge representative of human experience, culture, and beliefs.
4   Objectives should be thoughtfully selected and clearly stated in such form as to furnish direction to the program.
5   Learning activities should engage the student directly and actively in the learning process.
6   Strategies of instruction and learning activities should rely on a broad range of learning resources.
7   The social studies program must facilitate the organization of experience.
8   Evaluation should be useful, systematic, comprehensive, and valid for the objectives of the programs.
9   Social studies education should receive vigorous support as a vital and responsible part of the school program (NCSS, 1979, 261–73).

Variations on a Theme

There are countless variations in social studies programs. The most common pattern, which we will illustrate momentarily, reflects a kind of "curricular tinkering." Using the traditional expanding-environments approach as an overall organizer, teachers, school systems, or whoever is responsible for curriculum decision making, begin making minor adjustments so that the program better fits their needs. These adjustments, not incidentally, are often the result of teachers' complaints that their students don't understand what they are supposed to be learning.

Replacement

The least radical source of variation stems from the minor surgery performed by curriculum developers in which units that don't go well are removed and replaced by units the developers hope will go better. In some instances, the replacement units bear little resemblance to what was taught previously. Thus you might find a unit on taiga communities (communities in the northern forestland) replaced by a unit on career education or one of the other curricular thrusts dealt with later in this chapter. Ofttimes, however, the problem that needs attention lies not with the individual *units* taught at a particular grade level but rather with the overall *topic* or *theme* that is supposed to be taught that year. This situation may lead to a more radical, but not uncommon, source of variation: changing the topic or theme for a particular grade level. This type of variation can be found in the New York State social studies program which is currently being revised, where the traditional fourth-grade topic, state history and geography, was replaced by a year-long study of American people and leaders. (See Table 4.2.) Note also that while New York's fifth-grade program called for the traditional

Table 4.2 Flow Chart of the New York State Social Studies Program (Abridged)

Kindergarten   *Local Environment Studies*

Major Topics: The family and school (social and/or economic organization); rules and laws (political organization); the globe and cardinal directions (geography).

Patriotism: The Pledge of Allegiance; celebrating holidays and festivals.

Grade 1   *Local Environment Studies*

Major topics: Farming, past and present (social and/or economic organization); rules, laws, and the idea of democracy (political organization); geographic features of neighborhoods.

Patriotism: The Pledge, National Anthem, and the flag; celebrating holidays and festivals.

Grade 2   *Community Studies*

Major topics: The nature of communities; social, ethnic, and religious groups; local industries (social and political organization); local government and community services (political organization); local maps, road maps, latitude and longitude (geography).

Patriotism: The Pledge, National Anthem, flag symbolism; celebrating holidays and festivals.

Grade 3   *Community Studies*

Major topics: The equator, latitude and longitude, climate; studies of the location, climate, economic and social organization of desert, northern forest (taiga), tropical rainforest, mountain, and prairie farming communities.

Patriotism: The Pledge, National Anthem, and the flag (history and symbolism); responsibilities of citizenship; celebrating holidays and festivals.

Grade 4   *American People and Leaders*

Major topics: Multicultural origins; discoverers and explorers, colonial leaders, leaders in the fight for human rights, in science, industry, and the arts (Columbus, Ben Franklin, Thomas Jefferson, Martin Luther King, Jacob Riis, Thomas Edison, Stephen Foster, etc.).

Patriotism: Focus of the year's total program; celebrate usual holidays and festivals.

Grade 5   *Major Cultural Regions: Western Hemisphere*

Major topics: Climate and topographical features, special purpose maps (geography); The United States—geography, and social, economic, and political organization (population patterns, resources, federal government, etc.); patriotic citizenship—the Bill of Rights, civil rights and responsibilities—celebrate the usual holidays and festivals; Canada and Latin America—geography, history, and social, economic, and political organization.

Grade 6   *Major Cultural Regions: Middle East and Europe*

Major topics: Geographic introduction; The Middle East—geographic overview, historical summary, social, economic, and political organization; Western Europe and Eastern Europe—interdisciplinary studies organized under same headings as above.

Source: Bureau of Elementary Curriculum Development (1966).

study of American geography (history and government), the scope of the sixth-grade program was reduced from the entire Eastern Hemisphere to a more manageable study of Europe and the Middle East.

Seldom will you find the most radical variation of all, which is throwing out the traditional program and replacing it with a totally new curriculum. No matter how persuasive the arguments for change might be, there are some powerful forces that tend to maintain the status quo. It is appropriate, we think, to pause briefly to examine the factors that limit curricular change.

Forces That Inhibit Innovation

The desire to make minor variations in a social studies program can sometimes lead to major problems. When, for example, New York State was contemplating shifting its fourth-grade program from state history to the American people and leaders it faced a major problem: *the availability of instructional materials.* By far, the overwhelming majority of social studies instructional materials (textbooks, etc.) available from commercial sources are (and were) geared to the traditional expanding-environments approach. There was plenty of material available on "the state," but almost nothing on American leaders—almost nothing suitable for use with fourth graders, that is.

Faced with a lack of materials, the New York State Department of Education could have exercised an obvious option, that of writing and producing its own instructional materials. Many school systems have exercised this option in the past, particularly when the changes they were dealing with were relatively small. However, for many school systems caught up in the current budget crunch this is no longer a viable option. Developing curricular materials can be an expensive proposition; *cost* has increasingly become an inhibiting factor. New York State was not forced to write its own instructional materials because, in view of the sizable market it represented, several educational publishers hurriedly produced materials that would meet the anticipated demand. However, had such a program change been proposed by the Muleshoe Local School District—with its population of 64 fourth graders—it's doubtful that the commercial publishers would have been quite so eager.

Tradition can also play a role in inhibiting curriculum change. Just as parents sometimes expect certain things to be taught at certain grade levels, teachers also develop an affinity for certain topics or units. If teachers enjoy teaching something, and if they do an effective job, should they be urged to change?

College entrance requirements are sometimes mentioned as a factor inhibiting curriculum change. Where elementary students are concerned, we think this is one of the biggest smoke screens going. Colleges so rarely examine elementary school grades that to even suggest that a college admissions officer would examine the content of a second-grade social studies program doesn't border on the absurd, it is absurd!

One of the least obvious factors inhibiting curriculum changes are *standardized achievement tests.* These examinations, which students take at

Cost

Tradition

Entrance requirements

Table 4.3
Elementary Social
Studies Curriculum
—Eugene, Oregon

Grade	Questions Posed	Concepts	Skills	Content
1	*The individual within the group*			
	Who am I?	self, individual	observe, identify	select groups
	What is a group?	groups	communicate, share,	family
	What is my role within the group?	interaction	interact	school
		interdependence	gather information	social
	What relationships exist—between the individuals, between the groups?		compare and contrast generalize	culture
2	*Man in his society*			
	What is my relationship to the larger society?	multiple causation	identify multiple causes	models of causation
		environment		models for knowing
	What is the nature of the larger society?	social self	relate past to present	culture studies
		rules-laws	form and apply rules	law; role of
		needs-wants	identify behaviors	individual
			identify symbols	environment
			critical thinking	needs and wants
3	*The community structure*			
	What is the relationship between the individual and the community?	community	identify likenesses and differences	communities
		environment		Eugene-Lane
		interdependence	critical thinking	selected com-
		structure	map skills	munities from
	What is the nature of the community?		conceptualize community	other parts of the world
	How did it come to be a community?		recognize environ-mental influences	
	How does it differ from other communities?			
4	*Man in a world perspective*			
	What is culture?	beliefs	critical thinking	case studies of various
	How is culture iden-tified?	behaviors	identify customs	cultures
		values	recognize and identify	case studies of cultural
	How does man use the land?	environment	behavior patterns	relationships,
		culture		interdependence,
	How do we examine behavior?			diffusion

Grade	Questions Posed	Concepts	Skills	Content

5	*America, a land of peoples*
	How is a culture made?
	How does a culture change with time and location?
		culture-subculture
		  cultural diffusion
		frontier
		cultural growth
		conflict within a
		  culture
		democracy
			critical thinking
			conceptualize meaning
			  of growth, challenge,
			  conflict, resolution
			  within a developing
			  culture
				case studies:
				  American colonies
				  United States

6	*People and problems of the western hemisphere*
	What is a stereotype?
	  A cultural stereotype?
	How are differences reconciled between diverse cultural groups living in reasonably close proximity?
		stereotypes
		conflict, cooperation
		interdependence
		cultural change
			critical thinking
			analyze and identify
			  resulting conditions
			  of diverse cultures
				contrasting cultures
				within a hemisphere:
				  Latin America and
				  Canada

Source: Eugene Public Schools, Eugene, Oregon.

specified intervals, typically use traditional expanding environments programs as the basis against which academic progress is measured.

Significant deviations from the traditional social studies program *could* be reflected by lower student scores on standardized achievement tests. Supposedly, achievement tests measure students' performance *after* something has been studied, but they can also help determine what students at certain grade levels are expected to know. Combine this with the fact that students' performance on achievement tests can be used as a measure of teaching quality—which is theoretically inappropriate but not all that uncommon—and those standardized tests constitute a potent inhibiting factor.

Achievement tests

Taken individually, there are options for dealing with each of the factors that inhibit curriculum innovations—the availability of materials, cost, tradition, and standardized achievement tests. When taken collectively, we sometimes wonder how teachers and other curriculum developers have been able to accomplish as much as they have.

Exemplary Social Studies Programs

In this section we have included two sample social studies programs that reflect the kinds of variations you can reasonably expect to find among curricula that use expanding environments as an organizational basis. The first of these is the elementary social studies program of the Eugene, Oregon Public Schools (Table 4.3). It was developed by Eugene teachers over a several-year period with assistance from the Cooperative Center for Social Science Education at Ohio University. The second program is the New York State Social Studies Curriculum (see Table 4.2) which we referred to earlier, and that exemplifies a recommended program developed on a statewide basis. Although many school systems in New York have followed the recommended program, individual school districts are permitted to develop alternative programs as they see fit.

As you examine the material in Tables 4.2 and 4.3, recognize that these are curriculum overviews, *not* what teachers are expected to teach with. Both the Eugene Public Schools and the New York State Department of Education have developed social studies curriculum guides for each grade level, which teachers can use on a daily basis.

Trends and variations

By comparing the social studies programs presented in Tables 4.2 and 4.3, it should be noted that some vestiges of the expanding-environments approach are still evident. Nevertheless, these programs also illustrate some of the following trends and variations:

1   *There is a reduction in the scope of what is to be taught, particularly at the intermediate (Grades 4–6) level* In the Eugene program, only Grades 3 and 5 reflect the traditional program. Note that Oregon is one of several states that requires a course in American history in the elementary school. In the New York program, significant deviations and a marked reduction in scope are reflected at Grades 4 and 6.

2   *Greater use of organizing questions* These should be self-evident in the Eugene program. Note especially how the questions for Grade 5 reflect a different approach to what might otherwise be "straight" American history. Similar questions are posed in the New York program.

3   *The identification of key concepts to be stressed during the year's study* These should be evident in both programs.

4   *More attention to the skills and processes children should use* These are stated in the Eugene program, and although not stated in New York's overview, they are contained in the grade-level curriculum guides. Paralleling increased attention to skills is a corresponding decrease in the concern for memorized information. What individual teachers do, however, is anyone's guess.

5   *The continuing presence of the "holiday curriculum"* This element is easy to overlook because it is stated last in New York's program (for Grades K–4) and isn't even listed in Eugene's curriculum. It's a safe bet, however, that teachers in Eugene—like their counterparts in elementary schools across the country—note, observe, and celebrate the holidays and festivals (Halloween, Thanksgiving, Washington's Birthday, etc.) that occur throughout the year.

The "holiday curriculum" is a long-standing practice that has added life and color to elementary classrooms for many years. It's also been the reason for holding countless parties! Unfortunately, instead of making it something that parallels an ongoing social studies program, some teachers, especially at the primary level, make the holiday curriculum their entire program.

Variations on a Different Theme

In the previous section we dealt with social studies programs that were largely variations on the expanding-environments approach. In this section, we examine three elements which, when incorporated into a social studies curriculum, can produce something quite different from the programs dealt with above. Those elements are: (1) the use of content as a vehicle (which we examined earlier in the context of planning) and the use of its associated concept, contrast; (2) the nature of spiral curricula; and (3) concept-based approaches to social studies.

Contrast

Consider the following ideas and then respond as indicated:

Elementary students should:

	Agree	Disagree	Not Sure
complete a thorough study of the American family before studying families in other cultures.	_____	_____	_____
not study other forms of government until they have studied democracy.	_____	_____	_____
"know themselves" before studying about others.	_____	_____	_____

Educational circles are filled with beliefs like those listed above, beliefs which, intuitively at least, may seem to make a lot of sense. After studying the American family, for example, it would seem that a child should have a better basis for studying families in other cultures. What is not so immediately apparent are the problems children encounter in trying to study the American family. Children, and adults for that matter, are so close to the family—so much a part of it—that they often have considerable difficulty studying it.

Studying ourselves by studying others

It is very difficult to study anything that we are extremely close to. This phenomenon holds for our family, our language, ourselves—anything we are very intimate with. One of the major ways we find out about ourselves, is by studying and observing others. We'll elaborate on this in Chapter Five, but illustrate this phenomenon here by two examples.

First, consider the following statement: *The Eskimos have over thirty words for snow.* If you look at it in terms of its face value, this statement could be regarded as another piece of factual trivia. Or you could conclude that snow is very important to Eskimos or they wouldn't bother to be so precise about it. Consider, then, another statement: *The Arabs have over forty words for camel.* More trivia? Perhaps. Apparently camels are to the Arabs as snow is to the Eskimos—important. Our point here relates not to what these statements tell us about the Arabs or the Eskimos, but to what these statements tell us about ourselves and our language. Most of us are so close to our language that we are quite unaware of the fact that we have very few ways to talk about snow or camels. Then again, we may not need to talk about snow or camels any more precisely than we already do. But with this information we have a new awareness of Eskimos, Arabs, and ourselves.

Since we are so close to ourselves and our language, most of us must stop and think a bit to identify what we can describe as precisely as Eskimos can describe the different kinds of snow. To a Peruvian in the remote reaches of the Andes, for example, a car is a car. To Americans, of course, cars can be described with amazing precision—even by use of whole herds of animals (Mustangs, Impalas, Cougars, etc.).

Contrast

We can further illustrate this point by indicating that the Shawnee Indians have a word in their vocabulary, *alak*, that describes the interior of a hole. One word! In English, it takes a phrase to do what the Shawnees can with one word. Again, the point is not to add another word, *alak*, to your vocabulary; what is important is the awareness this information gives us of ourselves and our own language. This is part of the power of *contrast*.

So what bearing does all of this have on social studies programs? It should begin to explain why you may find first graders studying the Japanese family, for example, when ostensibly they are learning about the American family. It is *not* because there are things about Japanese families that every first grader must know, but because of the contrast it provides.

Vehicles

By studying the Japanese family, first graders have a basis for comparing and contrasting it to something they are (or should be) already familiar with —the American family. Confusing as it may seem initially, first graders may actually be studying the American family by using the Japanese family as a *vehicle*. It is not unlike planning a unit on using resources around two cans of corn. The corn wasn't something students were expected to learn about, it was merely a vehicle for teaching about resource utilization. Likewise, when first graders find that Japanese children do not celebrate birthdays every year, they may discover with renewed awareness that we do. In the process of studying others, we are actually learning about ourselves.

An especially effective use of contrast is found in "Man: A Course of Study" (MACOS), the social studies program we mentioned earlier. MACOS has experienced its share of problems: its title is now considered to be sexist, though it wasn't considered so when the program was first developed; it has been the focus of a Congressional investigation; and it has been the source of considerable controversy in many communities where it has been adopted. Yet despite the way this sounds, MACOS is not a bad or faulty program. If anything it ranks among the best social studies programs available today. Because MACOS is a significant *alternative* social studies program, and because it illustrates how contrast can be used with striking effectiveness, the next subsection is devoted to it.

MACOS—Case study

Man: A Course of Study was originally planned as a K–8 social studies program, but after almost 5 million dollars had been spent on its development, the funds were cut off, and MACOS was then reorganized as a one-year course for fifth or sixth graders.

MACOS is organized around three key questions. In slightly adapted form, they are:

What is human about human beings?

How did they get that way?

How can they be made more so?

*Studying
animals to learn
about people*

Based in part on the premise that as humans we are too close to ourselves to study ourselves, MACOS begins its study of human beings by using animals as its vehicle. The intent is to discover what is human about human beings by finding out how we differ from animals; the fact that many children love animal studies only adds to their interest. The first half of MACOS, then, is based on animal studies—the salmon, Herring gulls, and a fascinating unit on baboons—which are intended to help children identify those things that set humans apart from animals. In the second half of MACOS, children further refine what they learned about human beings (by studying animals) in an in-depth, semester-long study of the Netselik Eskimos (see Figure 4.4). Again, the Netselik serve as a vehicle. The intent is not to have children accumulate factual information about the Netselik, although they tend to learn a great deal about the Eskimos anyhow (you can't use something as a vehicle without learning about it too). Rather, the intent is to use the Netselik as a way for finding out more about ourselves.

The initial reaction of parents and others who are used to seeing topics being taught for their face value is to regard MACOS as a science course—studying animals is something one does in science, not social studies. What they don't recognize initially is that the continuing focus is on humans, not animals. Some school systems, however, teach MACOS as a science course or as a combined social studies-science course. It fits well into either category.

*The MACOS
spiral*

Unlike some other social studies programs, once an idea (concept or generalization) is introduced in MACOS, it is built and expanded upon throughout the course. One of the first such ideas is that of "life cycle," the notion that significant events—birth, death, reproduction, etc.—occur in the life of almost every member of a species, human or animal. "Life cycle" is presented first in the introductory lessons, reintroduced and expanded upon as children study the salmon, and then further developed throughout the study of the Herring gulls, the baboons, and eventually the Netselik. In this process children discover that, although individual lifetimes end, life still goes on.

*Learning as an
object of study*

The concept *learning* is studied in a similar manner. It is continually expanded and built upon throughout the course, in a kind of spiral fashion (see Figure 4.5). In their study of the salmon, for example, students find that after the female salmon lays its eggs, which are fertilized by the male, both adult salmon move upstream to die. Of the five to six thousand eggs produced by an adult pair, only two or three baby salmon are likely to survive to maturity. The intent here is not to teach a lot of factual information about fish, even though children often find it fascinating. The purpose of all of this is to get students to ponder the questions "If the adult salmon are dead, how do baby salmon learn?" "Who do they learn from?"

In MACOS, the emphasis is on having students raise their own questions.

Figure 4.4 Time Line for Teaching "Man: A Course of Study"

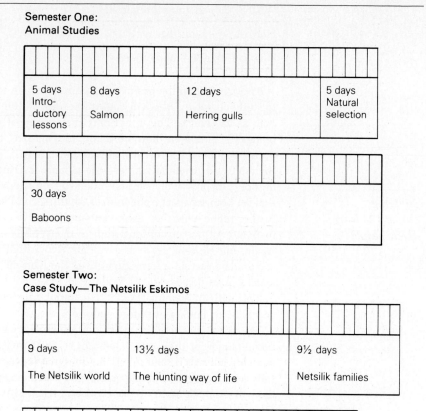

Semester One:
Animal Studies

| 5 days Introductory lessons | 8 days Salmon | 12 days Herring gulls | 5 days Natural selection |

| 30 days Baboons |

Semester Two:
Case Study—The Netsilik Eskimos

| 9 days The Netsilik world | 13½ days The hunting way of life | 9½ days Netsilik families |

| 8 days The dangers of winter | 9 days The hunting way of life in winter | 8 days Winter camp | 3 days The long gaze |

Source: Man: A Course of Study: Guide to the Course *(1968, pp. 2–3).*

Thus, teachers seldom find themselves saying "Boys and girls, today we are going to study learning," because the question "What is learning?" will almost surely have emerged from the students' study of the salmon. Once the "learning" question is raised, students then move to a study of Herring gulls. Why gulls? In one of the films on which MACOS relies heavily, students see the Herring gulls mating (which is a source of no little controversy), laying their eggs, and incubating the eggs until they hatch. Herring gulls are unique in that the adults will not feed their young until the chick pecks at a small red spot on the side of the adult gull's beak. If the chicks don't peck at the red spot, they starve. The obvious question all of this is leading up to is "How do baby Herring gulls learn to peck at that red spot?" The question is guaranteed—even adults who watch the film ask it—and teachers then

Figure 4.5 Development of the Concept *Learning* in Man: A Course of Study

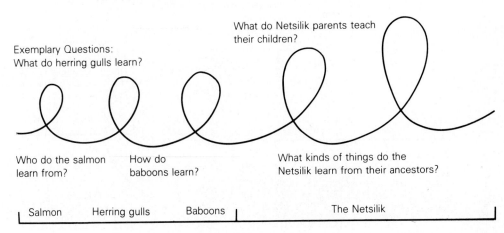

Basic Questions: What is learning?
What is innate and learned behavior?
How do we learn?
Who do we learn from?

What do Netsilik parents teach
their children?

Exemplary Questions:
What do herring gulls learn?

Who do the salmon
learn from?

How do
baboons learn?

What kinds of things do the
Netsilik learn from their ancestors?

| Salmon | Herring gulls | Baboons | The Netsilik |

provide materials relating to the nature of innate and learned behavior. Afterward, the focus temporarily shifts away from learning but returns to it again when students study baboons, and then again as they study the Netselik Eskimos.

Our detailed treatment of MACOS is intended to illustrate two things: (1) how content can serve as a vehicle, which was our original purpose; and (2) the potential for controversy inherent in studying certain aspects of human and animal behavior. The MACOS treatment of the Netselik Eskimos has

Controversy

also come in for its share of criticism. No matter how much emphasis is placed on the Netselik's creative use of scarce resources, or on their ability to survive in one of the harshest environments imaginable, several of the Netselik's practices, such as infanticide, senilicide (leaving the elderly out on the ice to die) or trial marriage, have sometimes been taken out of context and presented as if they were the sole emphasis of the students' study. MACOS does not teach or advocate infanticide, senilicide, etc.; actually, teachers can ignore such topics as they see fit, a fact that often gets lost in the heat of argument. Whether or not elementary children should be exposed to such practices and/or ideas, and whether they should be permitted to deal with questions such as "What makes us human?"—which is really what most of the controversy boils down to—are important issues that we examine in detail in the context of values education (Chapter Five).

*Training
requirements*

Well before the MACOS controversy emerged, its developers were worried that untrained teachers might misuse the materials and direct the course toward purposes other than those for which it was intended. To avoid this, MACOS became one of the first programs to impose a teacher training

Figure 4.6   The Spiral Development of a Generalization

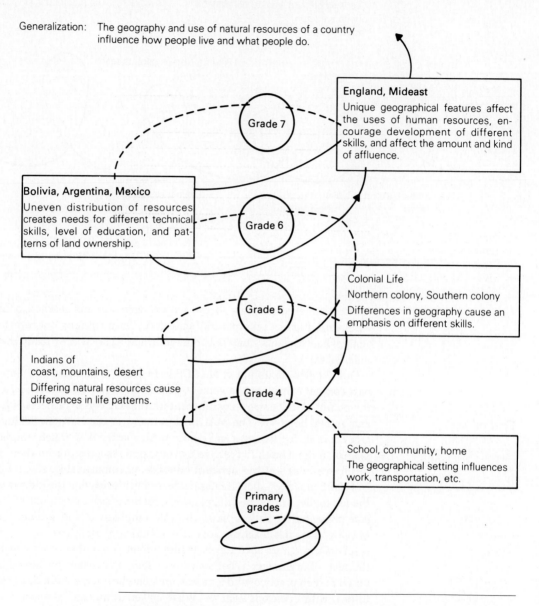

Generalization: The geography and use of natural resources of a country influence how people live and what people do.

Grade 7

England, Mideast
Unique geographical features affect the uses of human resources, encourage development of different skills, and affect the amount and kind of affluence.

Bolivia, Argentina, Mexico
Uneven distribution of resources creates needs for different technical skills, level of education, and patterns of land ownership.

Grade 6

Grade 5

Colonial Life
Northern colony, Southern colony
Differences in geography cause an emphasis on different skills.

Indians of
coast, mountains, desert
Differing natural resources cause differences in life patterns.

Grade 4

School, community, home
The geographical setting influences work, transportation, etc.

Primary grades

Source: Taba (1967, p. 20).

requirement (30 clock hours), which had to be met *before* materials could be purchased. High among the developers' concerns was the fear that untrained teachers would approach the subject matter (animal studies, etc.) as information to be memorized rather than as a vehicle for social study. Uninitiated teachers who required their students to memorize the number of eggs a female salmon lays, for example, would be guilty of perverting the course. In *Man: A Course of Study,* information about animals and the Netselik is not important in and of itself. Rather, it is used as a vehicle to enable children to say something about the nature of human beings.

Spiral Curricula

Earlier we noted that in MACOS, a concept such as learning is introduced and then redeveloped and built upon in new, ever-expanding contexts. The result can be likened to a learning spiral, which we illustrated in Figure 4.5.

Simply stated, the basic idea underlying a spiral curriculum is: "Once students learn something, let's continue to build upon what they already know by introducing new dimensions and by expanding their ideas to new situations." The idea of helping students move from the known to the unknown isn't new, nor is its practice restricted to MACOS. Indeed, the expanding-environments approach to social studies reflects a kind of spiral approach to curriculum. Each community students study is more distant than the previous one and, theoretically, builds upon what was studied the previous year. The problem with the expanding-environments spiral, as we indicated earlier, is that it tends to expand too quickly to communities students are unable to relate to, so that they seldom see any connection between what they are studying this year and what they studied last year.

A building process

Spiral curricula are found in some of the more recent social studies programs, most notably the Taba Social Science Program (Durkin, et. al., 1972), as illustrated in Figure 4.6.

The essential thing to note about the Taba spiral is that generalizations, not communities or environments, are the main focus. For example, the notion that geography and natural resources influence how people live and what they do is first introduced in the primary grades, then expanded upon in different contexts at higher grade levels. Concepts and generalizations are introduced in simple, concrete terms at the primary grades and then continually expanded upon as the children progress from grade to grade.

Concept-Based Social Studies Programs

A significant departure from the topic-to-topic sequence of traditional social studies programs is reflected in the *conceptual* or *concept-based* approach. The nature of a concept-based approach is most apparent if it is contrasted with a traditional topic-to-topic, or expanding-environments approach. The concept-based approach is illustrated in Figure 4.7, and the traditional approach is illustrated in Figure 4.8. For convenience and clarity, we have used the study of nations for our illustration.

What often happens in a topical approach is that once you have studied a nation, region, or what have you, you are usually done with it and seldom return to it again. For instance, you might have studied the geography, history, economy, etc., of the Soviet Union, but once you finished, you probably moved on to another nation and repeated the pattern.

The premise in a concept-based approach is that it is not necessary to study every country in the world, for example, in order to say something about how nations organize their governments, use their resources, or manage their economic systems. Rather, it is possible to establish a pattern among nations by studying only selected nations, not the universe of nations. As Figure 4.7 illustrates, by studying the governments of India and Japan, China and the Soviet Union, or any other combination, it becomes possible to say something about governments in general. In a concept-based approach, then, one of the dimensions that might have been studied in a topic-to-topic approach is selected as the focus of study.

The "parts" vs. the "whole"

In a topic-to-topic approach, students tend to become so concerned with the "parts"—the climate, the government, the customs, etc.—of a particular country that they never see "the whole." In a conceptual approach, the focus shifts to "the whole," and the parts—in this instance, individual nations—become vehicles that enable children to see the whole.

You may recall that earlier we mentioned a widely used third-grade social studies program in which children study the Spanish monarchy, the Mayflower Compact, and the Eskimos simultaneously. If it isn't already apparent, those children were working in a concept-based program. In this instance, the organizing concept is "social control," as illustrated in Figure 4.9. For teachers (or students) who don't understand the basis for conceptual social studies programs, however, trying to understand how Spanish kings, the Mayflower Compact and the Eskimos are related to one another can be a bit bewildering.

The Mayflower Compact, as you recall, was produced by the travelers on the good ship *Mayflower,* who agreed in writing to govern (control) themselves for the common good. The Eskimos, who don't have a written language and couldn't produce a written document even if they wanted to, govern themselves through an elaborate system of myths, beliefs, traditions, and practices handed down from generation to generation. Here we have exemplars of two forms of social control: governance by written mutual agreement and governance by ritual and tradition. The Spanish monarchy serves as an exemplar of absolute control based on the divine right of kings. The fact that these three forms of social control differ so vastly is intended to provide a basis for contrast.

Integrating themes

Among teachers familiar with traditional social studies programs, a concept-based approach sometimes seems a little piecemeal—a little about Eskimos, a little about the Pilgrims, and a little about the kings of Spain—without any integrated or "wholistic" aspects. In addition, the concepts, which are intended to serve as integrators, may be couched in terminology too abstract for children to deal with readily. Thus, in concept-based programs you may also find case studies in which the children conduct an in-depth investigation of a culture, subculture, group or nation. These in-depth investigations provide a single focus for study, rather than the multiple emphases sometimes associated with concept-based approaches.

Figure 4.7 A
Concept-Based
(Selected-
Dimensions)
Approach

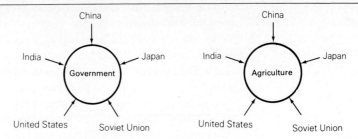

Note: In this approach is it not necessary to study all of the nations listed.

Source: Adapted from Taba (1967, p. 23).

Figure 4.8 A
Traditional,
Topic-to-Topic
Approach

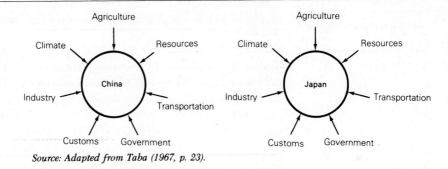

Source: Adapted from Taba (1967, p. 23).

Figure 4.9 An
Approach to the
Concept *Social
Control*

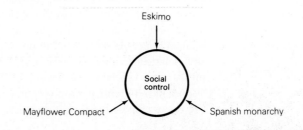

Still More Variations on a Theme Several curriculum-development projects have produced innovative social studies materials for the elementary grades. Some of these are now available from commercial publishers, while others must be obtained from the developers. Your chances of getting free samples are not good, but most developers and publishers have descriptive brochures that convey the essence of these new materials.

A brief description of these materials and a list of possible sources appear at the end of this chapter.

"New" materials

Special Emphases   In addition to the organized social studies programs already examined in this chapter, there are several special emphases that merit attention. These include career education, consumer education, global/international education, and law-related education.

As a general rule, these emphases do not take the form of preexisting programs that teachers simply "plug into" an existing social studies program —otherwise we would have called them "special programs." Rather, they tend to be thrusts, things that teachers emphasize as appropriate, throughout a K–12 program. There are some exceptions, however, and such is the case here. For example, at least four states require that career education be taught in the schools. If you teach in one of those states—Michigan, Iowa, Louisiana, or Kentucky—you may be required to teach a unit, or in some instances an entire course that focuses on career education. Even if you don't teach in those states, you may find yourself integrating career education into your program simply because it is something worth emphasizing.

In this section, we briefly examine the nature of the special emphases noted above. Throughout the balance of the book, we illustrate how these emphases can be integrated into ongoing social studies programs.

Career Education

Among the uninformed, career education is sometimes erroneously assumed to be another way of saying "vocational education." This it is not! Vocational education is a much narrower concept that refers to the practice of providing students with the counseling, skills, and training needed to enter a specific vocation or occupation. Career education, on the other hand, is a much broader concept, one that is sometimes defined so broadly it's difficult to determine precisely what it is (see e.g., Marland, 1971, p. 25).

An expression that often goes hand in hand with career education is "education for the world of work." Here, too, *work* is defined not in terms of one's job or occupation but in a larger societal context. Patrick Good et al. (1977) identify seven characteristics associated with work as it is seen from a career-education perspective. In addition to producing income, these characteristics include: occupying oneself in an interesting way, helping to maintain or increase one's social status, fostering satisfactory social interaction, providing a sense of self-identity, supplying necessary goods and services, and providing opportunities for creative expression and self-fulfillment (Good et al., 1977, p. 136).

Broadly defined

The broad scope reflected in the characteristics associated with *work* is further reflected in the U.S. Office of Education's definition (which some consider as the "official" definition) of career education. It states that career education refers to "the totality of experiences through which one learns about and prepares to engage in work as part of her or his way of living" (Hoyt, 1975, p. 4).

If you consider that schools have long acknowledged a responsibility for helping to prepare students for the world of work, why then should career education receive so much attention today? Several possible explanations have emerged. First, some authorities suggest that schools hadn't done an adequate job in preparing students for the world of work and thus renewed their emphasis on this goal. A second motive becomes apparent in Hoyt's (1977) effort to further clarify career education, when he describes it as "An effort *aimed at refocusing American education* and the actions of the broader community in ways that will help individuals acquire and utilize the

Preparing for the world of work

knowledges, skills, and attitudes necessary for each to make a meaningful and productive and satisfying part of his or her way of life" [emphasis added] (Hoyt, 1977). Using career education as a vehicle to change educational practices was further reflected by Sidney Marland, then U.S. Commissioner of Education, who stated, "If there is a central message in our conception of career education, it is to cry out against this absurd partitioning of the house of education, this separation of subject from subject, of class from class, this false and destructive distinction between the liberal academic tradition on the one hand and the utilitarian-vocational tradition on the other" (Marland, 1973, p. 501). One of the things Marland was referring to, apparently, was the "we teach 'grasslands' in fourth grade" phenomenon often found in the topic-to-topic approach to social studies. A topic like "the grasslands" may be assigned to a grade level, and then once taught there, seldom dealt with again. By defining career education broadly, it can't be dealt with as an isolated topic.

Career education is not a topic, nor is it a course, although it is sometimes approached as such. Neither is career education the sole responsibility of social studies (although it is sometimes approached that way too). It is, as we indicated previously, an emphasis that transcends the entire school program.

How does one approach career education with students who, when asked what they'd like to be when they grow up, respond in terms of locomotive engineers, firefighters, nurses, or pilots? The dominant approach in elementary schools seems to be aimed at developing *career awareness*. There are over twenty thousand different occupations in this country, many of which are beyond the child's scope of experience. At times throughout the year and as appropriate, teachers can draw attention to some of the different occupations (though certainly not to all twenty thousand), thereby building an awareness of the different career choices the children may have open to them. After identifying occupations, teachers can then move on to the skills and/or special training they require. In a unit on transportation, for example, students could investigate the skills required of an intercity truck driver. The teacher could then follow up by inviting a truck driver to talk with the class, preferably a female trucker who, without saying a word about it, can help to destroy the sex-role stereotyping often associated with this particular career. The same holds true for female doctors and male nurses. In our judgment, such approaches can do more to dispel sex-role stereotyping than all the words a teacher might utter. We also hasten to add that integrating career education into an ongoing social studies program is a planned, not an incidental, activity (though don't pass up those spur-of-the-moment opportunities either).

*Career
awareness*

Consumer Education

Compared with career education, consumer education is a considerably narrower, more manageable concept. The goal of consumer education is to provide individuals with knowledge and skills that enable them to understand the nature of the marketplace and to make intelligent decisions in it.

By asking yourself what it takes to be a shrewd buyer, two of the major thrusts of consumer education should become apparent. They are: helping students recognize a rip-off when they see one, and making students aware of what they can do if they feel they've been ripped off. Helping students to become aware of fraudulent or questionable business practices extends the scope of consumer education to include the study of advertising and product packaging techniques, product evaluation (such as that found in *Consumer Reports*), warranties and guarantees, and consumer protection agencies.

*Consumer
decision making*

Consumer education extends beyond recognizing the "traps" that buyers should beware of to include aspects related to intelligent money management, such as budgeting, and aspects related to building an understanding of the consumer's role in the marketplace. For example, helping children understand how consumers' decisions can influence the price of an article or service is an important element of consumer education. Helping children to achieve that understanding, however, also demands an understanding of rudimentary economics on the teacher's part. Unfortunately, economics is not a strength of many elementary teachers; many still regard it as "the dismal science." As a result, we suspect that the economic role consumers play sometimes gets less attention than it merits.

In dealing with topics like misleading advertising or fraudulent business practices, it often takes considerable teacher skill not to project the image that all business people and advertisers are crooks who try to relieve the unwary of their hard-earned money. This is particularly important in teaching primary-level children who tend to think in either-or categories. After examining techniques that advertisers use to manipulate potential buyers, for example, it's all too easy for students to get the impression that consumers are "good" and that all advertising is "bad," as are the businesspeople who advertise their products. Because of this "good guys-bad guys" phenomenon, teachers' statements to the effect that not all advertising is misleading should be accompanied by appropriate examples.

*Children's
perceptions*

The financial aspects of consumer education can also present potential problems, especially for teachers at the primary level again, because of the way in which children perceive money. When asked to choose between a stack of fifteen pennies or a stack of four quarters, primary level children often select the pennies; from their perspective the taller stack is "bigger" and is thus worth more. And when asked to deal with large sums of money, such as $100 (or in some cases, $20) many primary-level children have little comprehension of what that amount will buy. These problems are further complicated by the common misconception that banks "give" people money.

On one hand, children's perceptions and their inexperience and inability to deal with large dollar amounts are consistent with Piaget's findings on cognitive reasoning. On the other hand, correcting misconceptions (about banks, etc.) could very well take place in a consumer-education context. Primary-level children are able to deal with simple comparisons, for example, particularly if the elements being compared are within their realm of experience. More sophisticated analyses, however, may be better left until the intermediate grades or later, when students have achieved a better grasp of the prerequisite understandings.

What is a dollar worth?
What will money buy?
Consumer education begins to address students' questions.

Summary of Consumer Education Goals
1 Develop an understanding of the role consumers play in the economic marketplace.
2 Identify techniques used to influence people, including an analysis of misleading and non-misleading advertising.
3 Identify techniques and processes for evaluating products.
4 Become aware of fraudulent and/or questionable business practices (e.g., bait-and-switch, deceptive packaging).
5 Identify techniques associated with intelligent money management (budgeting, etc.).
6 Identify consumer protection agencies (include their scope and authority).

Global/International Education

The earth is a spaceship; its inhabitants—the people from all nations—face common problems as they journey through the cosmos. Those shared problems, such as pollution, overpopulation, discrimination, the depletion of resources—particularly energy resources—and the denial of human rights, are not American problems alone. They are worldwide problems; to one degree or another they are shared by everyone everywhere. To understand and be able to deal effectively with the complex problems that confront us demands that students develop a global view, one that will permit them to live effectively and creatively in a pluralistic and increasingly interdependent global society (Anderson, 1979, p. 110). This is the goal and the rationale of global/international education.

Building a global perspective

The need for developing a global perspective has become even more apparent with the emergence of two opposing developments in American society. On one hand, the United States has been drawn into an increasingly interdependent stance with other nations. We import more than we export at times, thereby making us more dependent on other nations. Most of the TV sets and cameras and many of the cars purchased in this country, to cite just three examples, are made in Japan. Meanwhile, there is growing concern about foreign investment in the United States. For example, a large proportion of farmland in the American heartland is now owned by foreign corporations and citizens, and many American industries have become subsidiaries of multinational corporations that are based in other countries. The fact that droughts in the Soviet Union (and subsequent purchases of American wheat) have caused the price of a loaf of bread to rise, or that crises in the Middle East have created lines at gasoline pumps, underscores our growing dependence on other nations.

On the other hand, the fact that the United States has been drawn into an increasingly dependent stance, a stance many Americans don't favor, may be partially responsible for the second opposing force noted above; namely, a tendency to turn inward, to become less internationally minded and more provincial in our outlook. There has been a movement toward emphasizing national pluralism, both cultural and ethnic. As a result, for many individuals the very idea that they should identify themselves as Americans *and* as citizens of a global society is repulsive, if not unpatriotic. Global/international education, then, is more likely to be subject to emotionally based attacks than either career or consumer education.

"Spaceship earth"

The spaceship-earth analogy used at the opening of this section has become virtually synonymous with global/international education. The analogy has also become commonplace in global/international instructional materials. As is the case for some of the other special emphases we've dealt with, you sometimes find special units that focus on developing a global perspective (e.g., Senesh, "Spaceship Earth: Our Only Home," 1973; Asimov, "Earth: Our Crowded Spaceship," 1974). But as is true of the other special emphases, global/international education is more than a unit or a course; it's a way of viewing the world.

One of the more difficult problems associated with teaching global interdependence is that of maintaining a balance between what Donald Morris (1974, p. 673) calls the "Doomsday Approach" and oversimplification. By overemphasizing the problems facing the world—energy crises, overpopulation, etc.—students can easily be left with the impression that nothing can be done and that Doomsday is inevitable. At the other extreme is oversimplification. "If only the Arabs would lower their price for oil, there wouldn't be any problem," for example, vastly and inaccurately oversimplifies an exceedingly complex issue. Either extreme can be dangerously misleading, even irresponsible. A balanced, reasoned approach to global/international education is essential.

Law-Related Education

If your experience was anything like ours, you probably sat through your share of boring lessons on such topics as "How a Bill Becomes a Law" or the legal distinction between felonies and misdemeanors. You may also remember when your teachers tried to explain the reasons behind school rules. The fact that lessons may have been boring or that the justifications for school rules sometimes went over the students' heads does not negate our long tradition of teaching about the courts, the legislature, and the legal system. How is law-related (or law-focused) education any different from what schools have been doing all along?

Goals

The current interest in law-focused education is, in part, a reaction against the way in which schools have traditionally approached teaching about the law, which is as a body of theoretical or abstract concepts and processes. Law-related education does not deny the need for students to understand traditional law-related topics such as the structure of our legal system or the lawmaking process, but the goal of law-related education is to move beyond the "parts"—the structural components—to develop an understanding of the basis of law and the vital role it plays in our daily lives.

The ultimate objective of law-focused education is to help students understand that the basis for law rests in morality, and not the other way around. Our laws that punish murderers, for example, are a reflection of the moral principle involving the sacredness of human life. The law itself does not make murder a crime; rather, our sense of morality makes murder a criminal act. Likewise, the "wrongness" of stealing does not grow out of laws that punish those who steal; the "wrongness" of stealing stems from the violation of a moral principle. Since people sometimes violate moral principles, our society has created laws that deal with such violations.

For most elementary children, dealing with abstract concepts such as morality and law, which cannot be seen, touched, tasted or smelled, is difficult if not impossible. No matter how many hours teachers spend telling children about the possibility of hurting someone if they run in the hall, the children usually translate it into terms of what will happen to them if they get caught. The punishment is something they can deal with, something they can feel—painfully at times. On the other hand, the probability that they might hurt someone by running is just that—a probability or possibility that children seem much less able to deal with. Then too, some adult drivers use the same kind of reasoning—they don't exceed the speed limit because they might get caught. The difference between the two (hopefully) is that adults can understand the reasons for speed limits, while to many children "rules are rules."

Summary of Law-Related Education Goals (stated as continuums)

Children move away from:	*Children move toward:*
perceiving law as restrictive, punitive, immutable, and beyond the control and understanding of the people affected	perceiving law as promotive, facilitative, comprehensible, and alterable
perceiving people as powerless before the law and other socio-civic institutions	perceiving people as having potential to control and contribute to the social order
perceiving issues of right and wrong as incomprehensible to ordinary people	perceiving right and wrong as issues all citizens can and should address
perceiving social issues as unproblematic	perceiving the dilemmas inherent in social issues
being impulsive decision-makers and problem solvers who make unreflective commitments	being reflective decision-makers and problem solvers who make grounded commitments
being inarticulate about commitments made or positions taken	being able to give reasoned explanations about commitments made and positions taken
being unable to manage conflict in other than a coercive or destructive manner	being socially responsible conflict managers
being uncritically defiant of authority	being critically responsive to legitimate authority
being illiterate about legal issues and the legal system	being knowledgeable about law, the legal system, and related issues
being egocentric, self-centered, and indifferent to others	being empathetic, socially responsible, and considerate of others
being morally immature in responding to ethical problems	being able to make mature judgments in dealing with ethical and moral problems

Source: Anderson, 1980, p. 384.

The difficulty that elementary children experience in trying to deal with abstract law-related concepts does not imply that law-related education must be delayed until the upper grade levels. On the contrary, there are a host of law-related concepts that elementary children can deal with, if not in their entirety at least in part. Even the youngest elementary students have a concept of fairness, which they will be quick to demonstrate if they feel they're being treated unfairly. In addition to fairness, other law-related concepts that can be built upon include authority, equality, freedom, honesty, participation, property, privacy, responsibility, and tolerance.

Children's literature often provides an excellent vehicle for treating law-related concepts. For instance, you may remember the classic tale, *The Little Red Hen*, in which a hen (one not too little but very red) finds several grains of wheat. Her pleas for assistance in planting and harvesting the wheat and grinding it into flour are ignored, and she is forced to do everything herself. When her loaf of bread finally comes out of the oven, she discovers that lots of volunteers are willing to help her eat it. But since nobody helped her do the work, she decides to eat it herself. And she does!

Using literature as a vehicle

Instead of moralizing about the story, a teacher could work toward building upon the children's concept of fairness by asking, "Was the little red hen fair to the others?" "Was she fair to herself?" Good discussions among primary-level children (to whom such stories are usually told) are difficult to conduct because the children are often more interested in talking than in listening to what others say. So consider using stories like *The Little Red Hen* with older students, even sixth graders. You may be quite surprised at how well they respond.

Interest in law-related education has become so widespread that over 250 local, state, and regional projects have developed instructional materials relating to it. Among your best sources of additional information are: The ERIC Clearinghouse for Social Studies/Social Science Education, 855 Broadway, Boulder, CO, 80302, and *The Directory of Law-related Activities*, 2nd ed., 1974, published by the Special Committee on Youth Citizenship of the American Bar Association, 1155 East 60th St., Chicago, IL, 60637.

Summary

Most elementary social studies programs are based on the expanding-environments (expanding-horizons or expanding-communities-of-man) approach. We indicated that although the traditional program is both logical and sequential from an adult perspective, its logic and sequence may be much less apparent from a child's perspective. We also examined some of the most significant variations found among the new social studies programs, especially those that follow a spiral, or a concept-based approach, and those such as *Man: A Course of Study*, in which the content (subject matter) functions as a vehicle that allows children to contrast new information with something from their own experience.

The notion that information isn't necessarily important in and of itself is often difficult to accept, especially for those who place a premium on information retention. Indeed, the idea that low-level information can be used as a vehicle to get to higher-level, more useful information hasn't been encountered extensively in practice, at least not in our experience. However, we've tried to illustrate some elementary social studies programs that are based on just such an idea.

The research on how children develop concepts of time and space, particularly historical time and geographical space, suggest that they are better able to handle these concepts after they have moved to Piaget's stage of "formal operations," which is somewhere around the age of eleven. How, then, are primary children able to deal with something, such as the Japanese family, that reflects a culture far removed from theirs? First, Japanese families (or families from any other culture) are used for their contrast with American families, and second, the Japanese family is made as concrete and real as possible. Teachers use films, stories, pictures, or anything they can get their hands on to bring the Japanese family within the scope of the child's experience. Third, how far away a Japanese family lives, as well as Japan's location on a map or globe, are secondary if not incidental to the entire study. For primary-level students, the fact that Japanese families live "far, far away" is usually sufficient. The day-to-day activities and the structure of the Japanese family are what's important, especially as they help to clarify the day-to-day activities and structure of American families.

We indicated also that to expect children to "know themselves" before studying others is tantamount to putting the cart before the horse. Those things that we are extremely close to and intimate with, including our families, our language, and ourselves, are very difficult to study objectively or effectively. Therefore, the way to find out about ourselves is by watching and studying others—our friends, our families, and individuals from other cultures. This phenomenon suggests multiple purposes for virtually all social studies content: as information (about families, cultures, communities, history, geography, etc.) that students can be expected to know, and as a means of finding out about ourselves.

Suggested Activities

1   Do you think it makes any difference for children to understand the logic (the "why") of what they are studying? In math? In social studies? In anything?

2   What type of social studies program do you feel is preferable—one based on adult logic, such as expanding environments, one based on the ever-changing interests and abilities of children, or some combination of these?

3   Since most elementary children are in Piaget's concrete-operations stage, what does this suggest about teaching strategies for elementary schools? About social studies in particular?

4   Go to your curriculum library or resource center and get at least three or four texts, each for the same grade level but from different textbook series. Do a content analysis of these, comparing the topics they cover, the approach they take, and the things they do and do not emphasize. If you work in a small group of six or eight members, and each takes a different grade level to study, you will have a composite of the similarities and variations among textbook series, any one of which you might find yourself teaching from.

5   Assume that you are teaching in a school that uses MACOS. A small group of individuals has charged that you are not teaching social studies anymore. They say you are teaching about fish, birds, and monkeys, and, as anyone knows, that's science. How would you respond to them?

6 Review the assumptions upon which the expanding-environments approach to social studies is based—for example, that children should be exposed to the world by Grade 6, etc. Then, in small groups, outline the characteristics of a K–8 social studies program that follows alternative assumptions of your choosing.

Sources of Selected "New" Social Studies Programs

1 "MATCH (Materials and Activities for Teachers and Children) Units." These wonderful, self-contained kits are available for "The City" (K–4), "The Japanese Family" (4–6), "Paddle to the Sea (Indians)" (4–6), "Medieval People" (4–8), "Indians Who Met the Pilgrims," (4–8), and "A House of Ancient Greece," (5–10). The MATCH kits were developed by the Boston Children's Museum and are available from Delta Education, Box M, Nashua, NH 03061.

2 "Concepts and Inquiry." Originally developed as the Greater Cleveland Social Science Program, the materials use a multitext approach that combines basic concepts from all of the social sciences. Grade 2 materials, for example, include "Communities at Home and Abroad" and "American Communities." Available from Allyn and Bacon, Inc., 470 Atlantic Ave., Boston, MA 02210.

3 "Our Working World." These K–6 materials were developed under the leadership of economist Lawrence Senesh, and include, for example, "Families At Work" (Grade 1) and "The American Way of Life" (Grade 5). Economics is the central discipline, especially in the primary grades, but all the social science disciplines are evident. Available from Science Research Associates, 155 N. Wacker Dr., Chicago, IL 60606.

4 "Social Science Laboratory Units." These materials, originally produced as part of the Michigan Elementary Social Science Education Program, were described earlier. Available from Science Research Associates, 155 N. Wacker Dr., Chicago, IL 60606.

5 "Man: A Course of Study." Originally developed by the Education Development Center (E.D.C.), these materials are currently available from Curriculum Development Associates, 1211 Connecticut Ave., N.W., Suite 414, Washington, DC 20036.

6 "People and Technology." This middle-grades (6–9) program uses two in-depth case studies—one of whaling in nineteenth-century Nantucket and the other of the Volta River Dam in the African nation of Ghana—to explore concepts related to technology, tool usage, and acquiring energy. Available from the Education Development Center, 55 Chapel St., Newton, MA 02160.

7 "The Family of Man." This is a K–6 program originally developed by the University of Minnesota Project Social Studies Curriculum Center, directed by Edith West. Materials are available from Selective Educational Equipment, Inc., 3 Bridge St., Newton, MA 02195.

8 "The Georgia Anthropology Curriculum Project." Materials for this project are available from M. J. Rice, 107 Dudley Hall, University of Georgia, Athens, GA 30601.

9 "Taba Program in Social Studies." This interdisciplinary, 1–7 program is keyed to developing children's thinking skills, especially as they involve concept formation, formulating generalizations, and applying principles. Available from Addison-Wesley Publishing Company, 2725 Sand Hill Rd., Menlo Park, CA 94025.

10 "The Elementary School Economics Program." This project has developed materials for Grades 4 and 5. Materials are available from the Allied Education Council, P.O. Box 78, Galien, MI 49113.

References

Anderson, Carrel M. "Will Schools Educate People for Global Understanding and Responsibility?" *Phi Delta Kappan* 61 (October 1979): 110–11.

Anderson, Charlotte C. "Promoting Responsible Citizenship Through Elementary Law-Related Education." *Social Education* 44 (May, 1980): 383–86.

Anderson, Lee F., and Becker, James. "An Examination of the Structure and Objectives of International Education." *Social Education* 33 (November 1968).

Arnsdorf, Val E. "An Investigation of the Teaching of Chronology in the Sixth Grade." *Journal of Experimental Education* 29 (March 1961): 307–13.

Asimov, Isaac. *Earth: Our Crowded Spaceship.* New York: John Day, 1974.

Becker, James, and Mehlinger, Howard (eds.). *International Dimensions in the Social Studies.* Washington, D.C.: National Council for the Social Studies, 38th Yearbook, 1968.

Brolin, Donn E., and D'Alonzo, Bruno J. "Critical Issues in Career Education for Handicapped Students." *Exceptional Children* 45 (January 1979): 246–53.

Bureau of Elementary Curriculum Development. "Tentative Flow Chart of the Social Studies Program." Albany, NY: State Education Department, University of the State of New York, 1966.

Davis, O. L. "Learning About Time Zones in Grades Four, Five, and Six." *Journal of Experimental Education* 31 (Summer, 1963): 407–12.

Durkin, Mary, et al. *Taba Program in Social Science: Concepts, Generalizations, and Skills.* Menlo Park, CA: Addison-Wesley, 1972.

Egan, Kieran. "What Children Know Best." *Social Education* 43 (February, 1979): 130–34.

Estvan, Frank J. *Social Studies in A Changing World.* New York: Harcourt, Brace & World, 1968.

Furth, H. G. *Piaget for Teachers.* Englewood Cliffs, NJ: Prentice-Hall, 1970.

Good, Patrick L.; MacDowell, Michael G.; Senn, Peter R.; and Saper, John C. "Should We Teach About Work in the Social Studies?" *Social Education* 41 (February 1977): 135–37.

Gorman, Richard M. *Discovering Piaget.* Columbus, OH: Charles E. Merrill, 1972.

Hoyt, K. B. *An Introduction to Career Education: A Policy Paper of the U.S. Office of Education.* Washington, D.C.: U.S. Government Printing Office, 1975.

———. *A Primer for Career Education.* Washington, D.C.: U.S. Government Printing Office, 1977.

Lévi-Strauss, Claude. *The Savage Mind.* Chicago: University of Chicago Press, 1966.

Man: A Course of Study: A Guide to the Course. Cambridge, MA: Education Development Center, 1968.

Marland, Sidney P., Jr. "Marland on Career Education: Questions and Answers." *American Education* 7 (November, 1971).

———. "Career Education, Not Job Training." *Social Education* 37 (October, 1973).

Morris, Donald H. "Teaching Global Interdependence in Elementary Social Studies: Old Concept—New Crisis." *Social Education* 38 (November/December, 1974): 672–77.

Piaget, Jean. *The Psychology of Intelligence.* New York: Harcourt, Brace & World, 1950.

Revision of the NCSS Social Studies Curriculum Guidelines. Washington, D.C.: National Council for the Social Studies, 1979.

Rushdoony, Haig A. "Achievement in Map Reading: An Experimental Study." *The Elementary School Journal* 64 (November, 1963): 70–75.

Senesh, Lawrence. *Our Working Worlds; Regions of the World.* Chicago: Science Research Associates, 1973.

Smith, Ronald O., and Cardinell, Charles R. "Challenging the Expanding Environment Theory." *Social Education* 28 (March, 1964): 141–43.

Superka, Douglas P.; Hawke, Sharryl; and Morrissett, Irving. "The Current and Future Status of the Social Studies." *Social Education* 44 (May, 1980): 362–69.

Taba, Hilda. *Teacher's Handbook for Elementary Social Studies.* (Introductory Edition) Menlo Park, CA: Addison-Wesley, 1967.

Taba, Hilda; Levine, Samuel; and Elzey, Freeman F. *Thinking in Elementary School Children.* U.S. Office of Education Cooperative Research Project No. 1574. San Francisco: San Francisco State College, 1964.

Wesley, Edgar B., and Adams, Mary A. *Teaching Social Studies in Elementary Schools.* (rev. ed.) Boston: D. C. Heath, 1952.

Suggested Readings

Two of the best references we know of for examining social studies programs and materials are:

Judith Hedstrom and Frances Haley (eds.). *Social Studies Materials and Resources Data Book.* Boulder, CO: ERIC Clearinghouse for Social Studies/Social Science Education and the Social Science Education Consortium. Annual volumes. Formerly known as the *Social Studies Curriculum Materials Data Book,* this ongoing series of publications offers the most complete set of descriptions and analyses of social studies materials to be found anywhere. A "must" for every curriculum library.

ALERT: A Sourcebook of Elementary Curricula, Programs, and Projects. Pleasantville, NY: Docent Corporation, 1974. Developed by the Far West Laboratory for Educational Research and Development in San Francisco, this guide to elementary programs is one of the finest we've seen.

Dorothy Lungmus, Frances Haley, G. Dale Greenawald, and Jerry Forkner. *Consumer Education Sourcebook*. Boulder, CO: Social Science Education Consortium/ERIC Clearinghouse for Social Studies/Social Science Education, 1980. Like the *Material and Resources Data Book,* this volume provides descriptions, analyses, and sources for consumer education materials.

Turner, Mary Jane. *Law in the Classroom: Activities and Resources*. Boulder, CO: Social Science Education Consortium/ERIC Clearinghouse for Social Studies/Social Science Education, 1979. This is probably the most comprehensive, most easily understood guide to law-related education currently available. Chock-full of exemplary activities and teaching strategies.

5 Values Education and Social Studies

Key Questions

How do we identify the values we hold?

How sensitive must teachers be to parental and community expectations?

How can we teach values systematically, and should we?

Key Ideas

The school's role in teaching values continues to be the source and subject of controversy. Nevertheless, all teachers do teach values, whether implicitly or explicitly.

Community expectations concerning values education are seldom consistent, nor, in most cases, are they known in advance.

The key components of values education are: (1) values themselves, and (2) a process of valuing. General agreement as to the specific nature of these components does not exist.

Four major approaches to values education are: (1) inculcation, (2) values clarification, (3) moral reasoning, and, (4) values analysis.

Whenever teachers select something to teach, they are in effect reflecting a value position, one that their students may be quite unaware of.

Introduction: The MACOS Controversy

On April Fools Day, 1975, newspapers across the country carried James Kilpatrick's syndicated column entitled, "Sex for Fifth-Grade Eskimos." An April Fools joke this was not! Neither was Kilpatrick referring to the precocious behavior of ten-year-old Eskimos. His sensational title notwithstanding, Kilpatrick's topic was the Congressional debate then raging over "Man: A Course of Study" (MACOS).

The Congressional inquiry into MACOS was preceded by local-level controversies in many communities where MACOS had been adopted. At both levels, the controversies focused on two major issues. One of them concerned the federal government's role in developing and disseminating curriculum materials. With financial support from the National Science Foundation (NSF), a federal agency, thousands of teachers had been paid to attend NSF-sponsored training institutes where they learned how to teach courses like MACOS (which had also been developed under grants from the

NSF). Note that MACOS was only one of many federally financed curriculum-development projects undertaken during the 1960s, so it is by no means a unique case. However, it cost approximately $4.5 million to develop MACOS, while another $3.5 million was spent on dissemination activities (teacher training, etc.). The funds for dissemination were usually justified on the grounds that the government's original investment (for development) would have been wasted unless teachers were made aware of and trained to use the new curriculum materials, a justification that has considerable merit. A more basic question, however, dealt with whether the federal government should be in the curriculum development business at all. It was argued, for example, that commercial publishers, the traditional source of teaching materials, couldn't match the government's funding practices and thus were at a decided disadvantage. In an apparent compromise, the federal government has continued to sponsor some curriculum-development projects, although on a *much* more limited scale than in the mid-1960s, and the materials produced are usually published and marketed through commercial publishers.

Who should develop new curriculum?

Man
A
Course
of
Study

The government's role in curriculum development was seldom the major issue in local MACOS controversies. Most of the controversies focused on the content of the course, on what was or was not appropriate subject matter for fifth graders. The main objections were perhaps most succinctly summarized by Congressman John B. Conlan of Arizona, who stated:

Criticism

> The program allots half a year to study the social behavior and mating habits of birds, fish, and baboons, with the implicit view that man not only evolved from lower animals, but also derived his social behavior from them.
>
> Children are then exposed for a full semester to the alien Netselik Eskimo subculture, in which the following practices are rationalized and approvingly examined in free-wheeling classroom discussion: killing the elderly and female infants, wife-swapping and trial marriage; communal living; witchcraft and the occult; cannibalism (1975, p. 388).

In response to these criticisms, Peter Dow, who along with former Harvard psychologist Jerome Bruner had played a significant role in developing MACOS, stated:

Response

> Much has been said ... about the dangers of exposing young children to alleged issues of adultery, bestiality, cannibalism, infanticide, and senilicide in the MACOS materials, but these horrors are in fact the daily fare of our television screen and are shown presumably with no larger purpose than to "entertain" millions of viewers who daily gawk over lurid scenes of man's inhumanity to man without ever being asked to contemplate the relationship between these behaviors and our elusive search for human understanding. In contrast, MACOS may raise troubling questions about the significance of killing, the importance of the partnership between male and female, and the moral dilemmas that all societies

face in caring for the very young and the very old; but these questions are always considered in the context of what they tell us, or fail to tell us, about how humankind can better understand itself and thus improve its plight (1975, p. 80).

Some observers, ourselves included, have suggested that the MACOS controversy would not have been so heated had the course been designed for the senior-high-school level. Indeed, some school systems have adapted MACOS for use at that level, with relatively little controversy. However, any time teachers deal with such topics as sex, religion, or the "isms"—communism, fascism, or in some cases humanism—topics on which people have differing points of view, the potential for controversy always exists. In elementary schools, the situation is further compounded by the "They're not ready for *that* yet" phenomenon. Ask any ten people when they think children should be exposed to sex education, for example, and you'll be apt to get at least eight different answers, probably more. There just isn't consensus on such a potentially controversial topic. So although fifth and sixth graders are often more knowledgeable about sex than many adults suspect, schools usually play it safe by delaying formal instruction in sex education until students are older and, theoretically at least, better able to handle "it."

Differing viewpoints

The question that usually arises with respect to controversial or potentially controversial issues is: "Don't teachers have the right to present the truth to their students?" The answer is a conditional "Yes." Under the principle of *academic freedom,* teachers have the right to present the truth to their students and, more particularly, the truth as they see it. The essential issue of academic freedom, however, concerns the extent to which teachers are entitled to present the truth without being penalized for doing so. In most instances clear and absolute answers don't exist.

Academic freedom

The degree to which your right to teach as you see fit is protected under academic freedom will depend upon the interaction of three factors: (1) the particular subject matter you are dealing with; (2) how you present that subject matter; and (3) prevailing community sentiment. In general, a teacher's treatment of subject matter must be balanced. Teachers cannot use their classrooms as soapboxes for presenting biased treatments that either favor or oppose a particular cause. Determining what constitutes a "biased treatment," however, may depend in part on community sentiment, difficult as that is to determine before the fact. In some communities, for instance, teachers have used MACOS with nary a ripple of interest. But in other communities, just mentioning MACOS has set off a torrent of protest. Thus the "answer" to the degree to which academic freedom guarantees your right to teach as you see fit is "It depends."

Academic freedom is situational

Whatever legal protection that is afforded by academic freedom can be of little consolation if you are looked upon as being morally wrong by segments of the community in which you teach. Being right in the eyes of the law may not put an end to harassing telephone calls at 3:00 A.M., for example. This means that legal rightness must be balanced against the moral outrage that could result from a teacher's insensitivity to community sentiment. The keys to academic freedom are the same keys that operate in every realm of teaching: sensitivity and reasonability. By ignoring either, you could be en route to problems.

By no means are we suggesting that teachers must forego their principles and bow to community sentiment. In fact, various professional organizations have established the means to help teachers who feel that their academic freedom has been violated (the Mary DuShane Legal Defense Fund of the National Council for the Social Studies is one example). Also keep in mind, however, that as someone once said, "When you are up to your waist in alligators, it's difficult to remember that you came to drain the swamp."

What does all of this have to do with values education? Countless surveys have shown that the majority of Americans believe the schools should teach values, or, in some instances, should do a better job of teaching values than they are already doing. There is of course a minority who feel otherwise. For example, Onalee McGraw, the national coordinator for the Coalition of Children and an advocate for parents' rights, has argued that we should "leave the development of the child's social values to the parents, in the home where they belong (Schaar, 1975, p. 1). Note, however, that deciding *not* to include values in the curriculum, even if that were possible, is itself a value position and is thus open to potential controversy. Combine this with the fact that most surveys do not indicate *which* values the schools should teach, only that they should be taught, and the potential for controversy increases even further.

Douglas Superka chose his words carefully when he described values education as "one of the most exciting and explosive new developments in education" (1974, p. 1). As we examine four of the major approaches to values education in the balance of this chapter, we would be remiss if we did not indicate that values teaching is a sensitive area where you would be well advised to proceed carefully. Because values education can be so controversial, we will give equal time to the proponents and critics of the strategies we present.

Whose responsibility is it?

Some say schools, Some say home.

Teaching Values: Moral and Ethical Implications

It is impossible to avoid values and values teaching, even if a teacher would like to. As we noted in Chapter One, everything teachers do and say—what they choose to study and discuss in class, and how they choose to operate their classrooms—implicitly reflect value positions. By their actions and deeds, teachers indicate to children what is important, valuable, and worthwhile, as well as what is not. So for those of us who will intervene in the lives of children, values teaching is an inescapable fact of life.

Before the turn of the century, when a major mission of the schools was to mold recently arrived immigrants into the mainstream of American society, values teaching was usually called *character education*. By modeling desired behaviors, by preaching, and occasionally by mocking children who deviated from what was expected, the intent was to instill in students certain core values such as honesty, truthfulness, obedience to and respect for one's elders, and beliefs in the dignity of the individual and in the value of work. In addition to whatever teachers might say about these values, the hope was that providing an environment (the school) in which these values were reflected would enable the values to be "caught" and thus incorporated into the student's belief (and behavior) structure.

"Caught" or taught?

Whether values are something that should be taught—systematically and intentionally—or left to be "caught," is still an issue today. Some individuals believe, for example, that schools and teachers have an obligation to teach values through any means available. Others believe that the complexity of our society and of the choices citizens must make demands that children be taught a process for analyzing value questions and issues. Still others believe that any attempt to influence what children believe and value smacks of brainwashing or indoctrination, neither of which have any place in schools today.

In light of these different positions, consider what you would do if a child asked the apparently innocent question, "Where did people come from?" (in the historical, not the biological-sexual, sense). Which of the following would you select?

_____ Indicate that the question is something that should be dealt with at home, not in school.

_____ Indicate that the Judeo-Christian (Adam-and-Eve) view is the most widely accepted.

_____ Briefly explain the concept of evolution.

_____ Present both the Judeo-Christian and evolutionary explanations.

_____ Indicate that people answer the question differently, without further elaboration.

_X_ Indicate that people answer the question differently, and then provide examples.

_____ It depends. (Note: This answer is unacceptable unless you are also willing to indicate *what* it depends upon.)

Varied expectations

Note that the Judeo-Christian and evolutionary views of creation are not values; they are types of explanations. Values enter the picture to the extent that some parents value one type of explanation more highly than the other. In fact, some parents prefer that alternative explanations about the origins of the human race be withheld from their children, thereby tacitly and sometimes openly supporting a form of indoctrination. In a parochial school the question is easier to deal with, primarily because parents send their children to parochial schools knowing that a particular point of view will be presented. In public schools, however, parental expectations are typically much more varied.

When students question you about emotion-charged topics like creation, evolution, or abortion, you'll seldom have the luxury of contemplation. In what amounts to a split second, you must respond in a way that both satisfies your student's curiosity and respects reasonable parental expectations. Treading such a fine line is, as well you might suspect, one of the more difficult tasks a teacher faces.

Value issues are so pervasive that they extend to the fundamental goals of the schools. The goal that children should arrive at their own value decisions through rational means, for example, reflects a value position. Why "rational"? Why not something else? Why not let students operate on the basis of faith, hunches, or intuition, as many of us do anyhow? Michael Scriven's eloquent statement is perhaps the best response we've heard. He said:

Why moral reasoning?

> Moral reasoning and the moral behavior it indicates should be taught and taught about, if for no other reason than it is immoral to keep children ignorant of the empirical and logical bases behind the law and institutions which incorporate this country's virtues and permit its vices. But in addition to this intellectual payoff is the practical benefit to a society of possessing members who are skilled in making value judgments. Such a society becomes a moral community offering important benefits to all of its members (Scriven, 1966, p. 2).

There is a lingering doubt among many parents, teachers, school administrators, and even students concerning the school's role in treating values explicitly. So you may find some teachers who approach values education by attempting to instill or inculcate certain values in their students. Instead of attempting to teach values in such a direct manner, other teachers emphasize the process of helping students become aware of the values they already hold; in other words, they emphasize values clarification. Still another group of teachers tends to put the most emphasis on helping children analyze value questions, such as "Is the wartime use of napalm a justifiable means toward peace?" Others put their emphasis on helping children improve the quality of their moral reasoning—or how they justify their actions. Finally, you may find teachers who intermingle these approaches as they see fit.

Multi-dimensional approaches

Values education is the explicit attempt to teach about values and/or valuing. But because teachers may approach values education so differently, values education is a multidimensional movement, not a set program. As such, values education can take many different forms. In general, the goals of values education include helping children (1) to become aware of the values they hold, (2) to identify and analyze the value questions involved in an issue, and (3) to act in accordance with what they know. We examine four of the major approaches to values education in the next section.

Values Education and Controversy

By dealing with educational controversies and values education in the same section, we may have unjustly indicted values education through guilt by association. We should make it clear that although value issues underlie almost every educational controversy, the reverse, that controversy *will* result from treating value issues in your classroom, is not necessarily true. Controversy *can* result to be sure, just as controversy can arise over the way in which you elect to teach something such as reading (for some individuals phonics is the only acceptable way to approach it, for example). But simply because you could become involved in a controversy does not mean that you will. Values education need not be a cause for controversy any more than anything else you teach. But this, like almost anything else, depends largely on how you elect to approach values education.

Approaches to Values Education

No one has ever seen a value. Like concepts and ideas, values exist only in our minds. As Fraenkel (1973, p. 232) has noted, values are standards of conduct, beauty, efficiency, or worth that individuals believe in and try to live up to or maintain. Honesty and truthfulness, for example, are standards that can (but don't always) govern an individual's behavior. Although we can't see the individual's values, we can see the individual's behavior. Thus, when people say that "Honesty is the best policy" and then proceed to lie whenever it is to their advantage to do so, there is an obvious discrepancy between their actions and what they say; their value claims don't "fit" the behavior we can see. The cliché that actions speak louder than words might be trite, but when it comes to values, one's actions are excellent indicators of the standards one tries (or says one tries) to live up to.

In dealing with values, standards for determining beauty are usually treated separately from standards of conduct. What we find beautiful and enjoy, like watching the sun set over the ocean, is said to reflect *aesthetics*. On the other hand, determining whether one's conduct is "right" or "wrong" from a moral standpoint is reflected in the study of *ethics*. Since schools deal with both aesthetics and ethics, distinguishing between the two provides a basis for determining the kind of values a teacher is attempting to influence.

An overview of four major approaches to values education is provided in Table 5.1. We examine each of these approaches in the following sections.

Aesthetics and ethics

[handwritten margin note: Aesthetics — what we find beautiful and enjoy. ethics — determining if one's conduct is "right" or "wrong".]

Inculcation

Throughout human history, inculcation has been a frequently used technique for molding human behavior. It isn't always effective, but then what is? As an approach to values education (or to all human behavior for that matter), *inculcation* refers to the process of making an impression on the mind through frequent repetition or insistent urging. In other words, inculcation is based on the premise that if you tell someone something often enough, sooner or later he or she will believe it (and behave accordingly).

Inculcation is a two-phase process that consists of (1) identifying the desired standard or value, and (2) providing appropriate and consistent reinforcement, either positive or negative. In phase one, an adult might indicate a desired standard such as "Children should respect their elders." In this instance, the standard would probably be expressed verbally, but in other instances, adults could very well establish the expectation through modeling or other nonverbal means.

Reinforcement (phase two) can take a variety of forms—verbal, nonverbal, or physical action. In the case of respecting one's elders, children may learn

Table 5.1
Overview of
Approaches to
Values Education

Approach	Purposes	Possible Methods
Inculcation	To instill or internalize certain values in students; To change the values of students so they more nearly reflect certain desired values.	Modeling; positive and negative reinforcement; mocking; nagging; manipulating alternatives; providing incomplete or biased information; games and simulations; role playing; discovery learning.
Clarification	To help students become aware of and identify their own values and those of others; To help students communicate openly and honestly with others about their values; To help students use both rational thinking and emotional awareness to examine their personal feelings, values, and behavior patterns.	Role-playing games; simulations; contrived or real value-laden situations; in-depth self-analysis exercises; sensitivity activities; out-of-class activities; small group discussion.
Moral Reasoning	To help students develop more complex moral reasoning patterns based on a higher set of values; To urge students to discuss the reasons for their value choices and positions—not merely to share with others, but to foster change in the students' stages of reasoning.	Moral dilemma episodes with relatively structured and argumentative small-group discussion.
Analysis	To help students use logical thinking and scientific investigation in deciding about value issues and questions; To help students use rational, analytical processes in interrelating and conceptualizing their values.	Structured, rational discussions that demand application of reasons as well as evidence; testing principles; analyzing analogous cases; debate; research.

Source: Abridged and adapted from Superka et al. (1976).

what that standard is through negative reinforcement. Adult statements such as "How many times have I told you not to talk back to your elders" (which isn't a question), or "If you sass your father again you'll get a spanking," are examples of negative reinforcers. Observing another child being chastized for being disrespectful of an elder might also serve the same purpose. Adults may supply appropriate nonverbal reinforcers as well—a

Reinforcement

nod, a smile, etc.—but they sometimes neglect to provide positive verbal reinforcers. In other words, adults are often quick to deal with "bad behavior" but may neglect to supply positive verbal reinforcement for desired behavior, such as "You were very respectful of your grandfather." This phenomenon may help to explain why children sometimes look upon desired behaviors as things they should do *because they will be punished if they don't*. Instead of regarding the behavior from a positive frame of reference —such as "respecting one's elders is good"—children sometimes adopt a negative view, as in "If I'm not respectful of my elders I'll be punished."

The nature of teaching puts you in a position to inculcate values, either directly or implicitly. In addition to whatever you say and do as an individual, you are likely to have some help from the teaching materials you use. As Superka (1974, p. 2) notes, "Some form of inculcation is manifested in nearly all curriculum materials. Substantive values such as honesty and respect for

Values in instructional materials

authority are often directly instilled, as are process values such as rationality and intellectual curiosity." Actually, the degree to which teaching materials directly inculcate values such as honesty sometimes becomes a criterion by which they are judged. Be cautious of materials that go overboard in this direction, however, because attempting to emphasize positive virtues—such as honesty—by excluding any mention of dishonesty or cheating, for example, may create a credibility gap that is quite unintended. Even kindergarten children are aware of dishonesty and cheating, though they don't always use these terms, and to pretend that these things don't exist can create a credibility gap, if not in kindergarten then elsewhere in school. No matter how much we might like to see a world based on mutual respect, honesty, and the like, to imply that such a world exists today may paint a picture far different from the world that children know. If such a picture persists, children may reject the school's view in favor of the world they deal with every day; ultimately, they may reject school entirely. So, no matter how desirable it may seem on the surface, trying to inculcate values by presenting a desired but one-sided view of human interaction (the world) may yield results far different from those you might expect.

How "Real" Should Social Studies Be?

Elementary social studies programs have sometimes been criticized for presenting an idealized conception of the world. Sometimes those criticisms appear in unlikely places, as in Robert Goldhammer's supervision text entitled *Clinical Supervision: Special Methods for the Supervision of Teachers,* published by Holt, Rinehart and Winston, Inc., in 1969. Here's what Goldhammer said about social studies:

Imagine a unit of study somewhere in the primary grades, on "The Family ..." How is "family" generally represented in the early grades?

The houses in which families live never, as far as we are told, include toilets. Members of the family never scratch themselves, utter obscenities, cheat on their wives, fix traffic tickets, drink beer, play the horses, falsify their tax returns, strike one another, make love, use deodorants, gossip on the telephone, buy on credit, have ulcers, or manifest a million other signs of life that even the most culturally deprived child knows about in the most intimate detail....

Certainly at their dinner tables, no textbook fathers talk about having out-bargained that New York Jew, about the niggers who are trying to take over the neighborhood, the cops, the Birchers, the hippies, the war, and so on. On the contrary, one may safely expect the textbook family to be disembodied, apolitical, generally without a specific ethnic identity or religious affiliation, free of social prejudice, innocent of grief, economically secure, vocationally stable, antiseptic and law-abiding straight down the middle. It occupies a universe from which disaffection, divorce, cynicism, loneliness, neurosis, bastardy, atheism, tension, self-doubt, wrecked cars, and cockroaches are inevitably absent.

Unless he is downright dull, it is impossible to imagine that at some level of experience the child is not aware of the thundering disparity between the real world and the school's priggish, distorted, emasculated representations of that world. It seems reasonable to suspect that the child's knowledge almost certainly includes the realization that, in plain language, the curriculum is phony, at least in relation to the example we have considered.

What reactions would you anticipate if textbooks actually presented what Goldhammer criticizes them for not presenting? From students? Parents? Teachers?

*Is this
censorship?*

"Textbook" families seem "perfect".

Children aware of difference between this and the "real world"

Values Clarification

Help individuals clarify just what their values are

Most people, we suspect, are so close to themselves that they really don't know themselves—a statement which, though it may seem to contradict itself at first, should take on additional clarity as we go. We contend that you are so close, so intimate with yourself that you are unable to stand back and take a completely objective look at yourself. In fact, we suggest that the major way in which you learn about yourself is by watching others. For example, have you ever found yourself observing someone and then saying to yourself, "Hey, that's me! I do that too," or "I would never want to be like *that*" (and hope you're not trying to convince yourself that you are not like *that* already)?

*Too close to the
forest to see
the trees*

Or consider what often happens when you are asked to describe yourself. Once you get beyond a physical description, which astute observers don't need anyway, and once you get beyond your hobbies, interests, and talents, you will ultimately arrive at your values. And upon being asked what moral characteristics you exhibit, the result is apt to be a watered-down version of the Scout law—trustworthy, loyal, helpful, and obedient (at times). To that, you'll usually encounter the request to "be honest." You may then respond with a statement such as "Well, I'm a little lazy, and I tend to put things off until the last minute."

Thus far, with the exception of your talents, interests, and possibly your hobbies, you've probably described a typical American. What you are not likely to have described are the norms—values, if you will—that are unique to you and set you apart from others. You—and many Americans like you—are so close to yourself that you are probably not aware of what some of your own norms and values actually are—until, that is, you are confronted with situations that force you to use them. Values clarification is an approach to values education that is intended, in part, to do just that—help individuals clarify what their values are in a rational and justifiable way.

Purpose

The values-clarification approach to values education is usually associated with Louis Raths, Merrill Harmin, and Sidney Simon (1966, 1978), coauthors of *Values and Teaching.* The approach is further expanded upon in *Values Clarification: A Handbook of Practical Strategies for Teachers and Students* by Sidney Simon, Leland Howe, and Howard Kirschenbaum (1972), and in other publications.

The values-clarification approach does not try to instill a particular set of values, as is often the case in inculcation, but rather advocates a valuing *process* that incorporates the following seven subprocesses:

Choosing

1 Encourage children to make choices, and to make them *freely.*
2 Help them *discover alternatives* when faced with choices.
3 Help children *weigh* alternatives thoughtfully, reflecting on *the consequences* of each.

Prizing

4 Encourage children to consider what it is that they prize and *cherish.*
5 Give them opportunities to *affirm their choices* to others.

Acting

6 Encourage them to act, *behave,* live *in accordance with their choices.*
7 Help them be aware of repeated behaviors or patterns in their life (Raths, et al. 1978, pp. 28, 38). [Emphasis added.]

Why values clarification?

Why should people be clear about the values they hold? Raths, et al. (1978, p. 10) indicate that "It seems to us that the pace and complexity of modern life has so exacerbated the problem of deciding what is good and what is right and what is desirable that large numbers of children are finding it increasingly bewildering, even overwhelming, to decide what is worth valuing, what is worth their time and energy." Kirschenbaum further elaborated on the major hypothesis of values clarification by stating, "If a person skillfully and consistently uses the 'valuing process' [outlined above], this increases the likelihood that the confusion, conflict, etc. will turn into decisions and living that are both personally satisfying and socially constructive" (Kirschenbaum, 1977, citing Kirschenbaum, Harmin, Howe, and Simon, 1975, p. 398).

The values-clarification approach to values education does not follow a set formula. Rather, it is an *orientation* that teachers adopt, as appropriate, to help students employ the valuing process outlined above. Nor is values clarification something that must be done on a whole-class basis, although teachers can do so if they wish. In many instances, values clarification may be most appropriate when you interact with a single student. In either situation, you may wish to employ the *clarifying response,* as is illustrated in the following exchange:

The clarifying response

Teacher: Bruce, don't you want to go outside and play on the playground?
Student: I dunno. I suppose so.
Teacher: Is there something that you would rather do?
Student: I dunno. Nothing much.
Teacher: You don't seem much to care, Bruce. Is that right?
Student: I suppose so.
Teacher: And mostly anything we do will be all right with you?
Student: I suppose so. Well, not anything, I guess.
Teacher: Well, Bruce, we had better go out to the playground now with the others. You let me know sometime if you think of something you would like to do. (Dialogue adapted from Raths, et al., 1978, p. 55.)

As this exchange illustrates, the intent is not to get the child to adopt the seven-step values-clarifying process in a single 15-second exchange. That's a long-range goal, to be accomplished over a period of time. The intent of the clarifying response is to encourage students to look at their ideas and to think about them without moralizing, criticizing, evaluating, or otherwise suggesting that you, as the teacher, have a "right answer" in mind (Raths, 1978, p. 55). If the whole exchange isn't genuine, it will fall flat on its face.

Productive clarifying responses may include:

Additional clarifying responses

Is this important to you?

Are you happy about that?

Did you think of other (alternative) things you could do?

Would you really do that or are you just talking?

What other possibilities are there?

Would you do the same thing over again?

Is it important enough that you would be willing to share your idea (project, experiences, etc.) with the others? (Raths, et. al., 1978, pp. 59–63.)

Students often find whole-class or small-group values clarification activities to be particularly engaging. The following student activity is adapted from one entitled "The Miracle Workers," which appears in *Values Clarification* (Simon, et al., 1972, pp. 338–42). See if you don't find it enlightening and, in a way, almost a form of self-awareness therapy.

The Miracle Workers

Several world-famous experts have agreed to provide their services to this class. Their skills are so effective that they are considered miracle workers by the people who have used their services. You can be 100 percent sure that they can do what they say they will. However, their services are in such demand that you must choose only those three workers whose gifts you would most like to receive. You should also choose those three workers who are least appealing to you—the ones whose services you don't think you (or other members of the class) will want or need.

After you have chosen on your own, we will do the same thing in small groups. The experts are:

_____ Dr. Face Lift—a famous surgeon who, by using a new painless technique he has invented, can make you look just the way you have always wanted to look. If you want more muscles, he can do that. Or, if you want to be taller, thinner, or to change the color of your eyes, hair, or anything, he will do it for you.

_____ Abby Landers—Her advice will help you be well liked by everyone. Your life will be filled with good friends.

_____ Madame Xavier—You will never have a question about the future and what it holds for you if you select this expert's services. She will return whenever you ask for her, if she is one of your first three choices.

_____ Dr. Gannon Welby—You will never need to worry about sickness or injury if you select this expert. Perfect health will be yours!

_____ Dr. I.Q.—The world-famous thinker will make you brilliant. You might never need to study (or do homework) again.

_____ Mr. Yule Makamint—Wealth—all the money you ever dreamed of—will be yours if you select this expert.

_____ Olive Branch—Peace and harmony will be yours. This expert will stop all fights—on the playground, at home, or anywhere in the world.

_____ Chunky Goodbar—This expert will provide you with a free, lifetime supply of candy, gum, ice cream, and potato chips. He will also make sure you have no cavities on your next ten trips to the dentist.

_____ Ima Starmaker—Did you ever dream of becoming a Joe Namath, a Billy Jean King, or a Jack Nicklaus? Well, you can, and for any sport you choose. Just make Ima Starmaker one of your first three choices.

Procedure:
1. Have the students rank choices individually, then in small groups.
2. Groups should then record choices on chart paper or on the board.
3. Compare groups' choices, both most favorable and least favorable, in terms of similarities and/or unusual choices. Discuss feelings and reactions.

Model student activity

This student activity was adapted from "The Miracle Workers," an activity developed by Mark Phillips, Center for Humanistic Education, University of Massachusetts, and appears in Simon et al. (1972, pp. 338–42).

Being asked to choose among alternatives can indeed bring forth a certain degree of self-awareness. However, an interesting phenomenon emerges if we add another element, such as the following, to the "Miracle Workers" activity.

_____ Dr. Liva Longlife—This expert has the secret of eternal youth and can help you live as long as you wish. His treatment is painless, and some of his previous patients have lived to be over 200 years old.

A new activity

Adding another alternative probably forced you to rearrange your priorities or at least to reexamine them. The addition of Dr. Liva Longlife actually turns the "Miracle Workers" into a new activity; it is not just the original activity with an added alternative. And altering the activity in this way illustrates two aspects of values clarification that have come under criticism: (1) that in the absence of so-called right answers, one value or value system is as good as another; and (2) that each situation determines the merits of a particular value position.

What Critics Say About Values Clarification Values-clarification activities have sometimes generated sufficient enough controversy that their use has been either severely restricted or banned in some school systems. These actions have been largely the result of parental objections, the basis for which should be apparent in the following episode.

"The Cave-In" episode

In a school system in the Southwest, a sixth-grade teacher had decided to use an activity entitled "The Cave-In," which appeared in *Values Clarification* (Simon, et al., 1972). As the instructions for the activity directed, the desks had been moved out of the way and the class was seated on the floor around a single lighted candle. The class was then told that while they were exploring an underground cavern, an earth tremor had caused a cave-in. Only a narrow pathway to the outside world remained, but other rocks loosened by the tremor were expected to fall momentarily. The teacher then informed the class that, in order to escape, they must form a single line. Individuals at the head of the line would be most likely to get out safely, while those at the end of the line faced almost certain death. The students had to decide among themselves which places in the line they should be entitled to. Note that the nature of this assignment places the activity on shaky ground. Those students who agreed to go toward the end of the line were, in effect, agreeing to die.

The instructions for this activity contained a cautionary note to the teacher indicating that this was a powerful activity that should only be used with groups of students who had developed a high mutual-trust level and who were experienced in values-clarification activities. Since the teacher had already used several other values-clarification activities with the class, he apparently thought these criteria were met.

When the activity got underway, several students said "I pass," which was a recognized way for them to indicate that they didn't want to participate in the activity. For a while, nobody said very much, although quite a few glances were exchanged. After several minutes of this, one boy rose and said, "I can't do anything right; I guess I deserve to die," and walked to the end of the line. The class was dumbfounded, as was the teacher, who wisely ended the activity immediately and attempted to counsel the boy individually.

Several parents heard about what had gone on and protested to the teacher, the principal, and the school board. The teacher agreed that things hadn't gone as planned and that he wouldn't use the activity again. However some parents indicated that they didn't want their children placed in such a situation—ever—and to ensure that they were not, the parents requested that such activities be banned from that school system. The school board agreed.

In this case, and in other instances like it, the positive benefits that might result from other, less potent values-clarification techniques have been condemned (and banned) through guilt by association. Nevertheless, two questions must still be asked: (1) to what extent should the positive benefits of values clarification be weighed against the potential of doing psychological harm to a child; and (2) should elementary and middle-school students be confronted with situations where they must participate in making life-and-death decisions?

Privacy Much of the criticism directed against values-clarification activities has focused on the use of techniques that can jeopardize students' rights to privacy, such as requiring students to state their beliefs publicly. If you look at it, it's almost impossible to clarify your values publicly without disclosing personal information about yourself and your relationships with others, including your family. Thus the very nature of values clarification can constitute a threat to the privacy rights of students and their families. This threat may be further compounded by explicit questioning techniques that may ask students to identify such things as who in their family brings them the greatest sadness, or by projective techniques that ask students to complete sentences that begin "If I were a dog . . .," for example.

Students will often voluntarily reveal their innermost fears and secrets to teachers, which then places the teacher in the role of amateur psychologist and counselor. When students do this voluntarily, the role is imposed upon teachers. But many values-clarification activities are specifically designed to elicit students' feelings, beliefs, and fears. Imagine, for example, what you would say to the boy who said that he couldn't do anything right and decided to go to the end of the line in the episode described above. Would you cajole him, reassure him, or what? Notice also that the clarifying responses shown on page 160 are deceptively benign. Those responses and questions are much like the ones trained counselors and psychologists use in group-

Life-or-death decisions?

What role should teachers play?

Having a clear sense of what you want is an element of values education.

therapy sessions. Asking a question like "Is that important to you?" is easy enough, but you may get answers that you're not trained to handle. If that happens, stop everything before you really get in over your head.

Note that with certain exceptions (such as "The Cave-In") student responses to values-clarification activities are often quite positive. Children seem to like the activities and find them involving, and the self-awareness provided can have a therapeutic effect. The questions that remain concern whether or not most teachers have the skills to play the role of therapist, and whether or not the therapist role is a legitimate teacher role.

Moral vs. Nonmoral Issues Values clarification has also been criticized for its failure to distinguish between moral (ethical) and nonmoral (aesthetic) value issues. Some values-clarification activities, for example, ask students to identify their favorite foods, their hobbies, and the like—things that are largely a matter of personal taste. Obviously, there's nothing immoral or unethical about disliking mushrooms. But in activities like the "Cave-In" simulation, moral issues are clearly involved. Helping children decide how they will spend their allowance, and helping them decide which individuals should be permitted to live and which should die, are clearly not issues of equal magnitude. Indeed, unless you are prepared to help students deal with the issues underlying life-or-death decisions, we suggest that you avoid such activities entirely.

Another criticism that has been leveled at the values-clarification approach is that it tends to promote *ethical relativism.* Ethical relativism refers to the belief that individuals' actions are governed by the situations in which they find themselves—by what is practical or expedient, for example—rather than by overarching moral principles, such as the dignity of the individual and the sanctity of human life, that should apply in all situations. This criticism seems to stem from the fact that there is no justification phase in the seven-step valuing process (p. 159). And because students are neither asked nor required to justify or defend their decisions, they could come away with the impression that one person's views are as good as anyone else's, *regardless* of the situation.

It's true that in some values-clarification activities, such as "The Miracle Workers," one person's selection of "experts" isn't necessarily any better or worse than someone else's; the selection can legitimately be a matter of personal taste. However, upon moving to activities where moral questions are involved, as in "The Cave-In" simulation, it seems almost irresponsible to suggest that life-and-death issues should be settled as a matter of personal opinion.

In summary, the major criticisms directed toward the values-clarification approach concern the following:

1. the use of techniques (such as stating beliefs publicly) that could jeopardize the student's right to privacy;
2. the reliance on techniques and methods that sometimes place teachers in the role of a psychological therapist (or psychiatrist);
3. the failure to distinguish moral from nonmoral issues; and
4. the tacit acceptance of all value beliefs as being equally valid (ethical relativism) (Alan Lockwood, 1977, pp. 399–401).

Values-clarification activities can be powerful teaching tools. But, like any tool, they must be used carefully. A chisel in the hands of a sculptor can produce an object of great beauty. In the hands of an amateur, well ... If you have any doubt about your ability to use value-clarification techniques, we recommend that you practice on your peers, not on your students.

Ethical relativism -

> belief that one's actions are govered by the situations in which they find themselves.

Moral Reasoning

> How does an individual's ability to reason morally develop? —Kohlberg.

The *moral-reasoning* approach to values education is closely associated with the work of Lawrence Kohlberg, a Harvard psychologist. Kohlberg and his associates first developed a theory dealing with how children learn to reason morally, and then developed a teaching strategy to help children improve the quality of their moral reasoning. In order to determine what makes one kind of moral reasoning "better" than another it's necessary to understand the theory on which Kohlberg's teaching strategy is based.

Table 5.2   Kohlberg's Stages of Moral Development

Principled Level Concern for fidelity to self-chosen moral principles	**Stage 5**	*Motivator:* Internal commitment to principles of "conscience;" respect for the rights, life, and dignity of all persons. *Awareness:* Particular moral/social rules are social contracts, arrived at through democratic reconciliation of differing viewpoints and open to change. *Assumption:* Moral principles have universal validity; law derives from morality, not vice versa.
Conventional Level Concern for meeting external social expectations	**Stage 4**	*Motivator:* Sense of duty or obligation to live up to socially defined role and maintain existing social order for good of all. *Awareness:* There is a larger social "system" that regulates the behavior of individuals within it. *Assumption:* Authority or the social order is the source of morality.
	Stage 3	*Motivator:* Desire for social approval by living up to good boy/good girl stereotype; meeting expectations of others. *Awareness:* Need to consider intentions and feelings of others; cooperation means ideal reciprocity (golden rule). *Assumption:* Good behavior equals social conformity.
Preconventional Level Concern for external, concrete consequences to self	**Stage 2**	*Motivator:* Self-interest: what's in it for me? *Awareness:* Human relations are governed by concrete reciprocity; let's make a deal; you scratch my back, I'll scratch yours. *Assumption:* Have to look out for self; obligated only to those who help you; each person has own needs and viewpoints.
	Stage 1	*Motivator:* Fear of getting caught; desire to avoid punishment by authority. *Awareness:* There are rules and consequences of breaking them. *Assumption:* Might makes right; what's regarded by those in power is "good;" what's punished is "bad."

Source: Lickona (1977).

*A rational
process*

In many respects, Kohlberg's research is similar to that of Jean Piaget, which we presented in Chapter Four. Piaget was interested in how children learn to think and reason, while Kohlberg narrowed that focus to the question "How does an individual's ability to reason morally (to justify their actions) develop?"

After investigating moral reasoning among individuals of various ages and from various cultures, Kohlberg found sufficient similarities to be able to identify a Piaget-like developmental sequence, which is shown in Table 5.2. Note that at one time there were six stages in Kohlberg's developmental sequence, but these have recently been redefined so that Stage 5 now incorporates what was formerly in Stage 6.

Sooner or later almost everyone reaches Piaget's last developmental stage, formal operations. Kohlberg has found, however, that fewer than twenty-five percent of American adults ever reach Stage 5 (Principled Level); the rest of us consistently operate at lower stages. If you consider that the moral basis of the Bill of Rights reflects Stage 5 reasoning, Kohlberg's findings suggest that we may be living in a society where the majority of citizens neither understand nor appreciate the fundamental moral principles upon which the society was founded. This may also explain why fifth- and eighth-grade teachers often find that teaching a required unit on "the Constitution" is so frustrating; the majority of their students may be operating at Stage 3, the level at which their primary interest is in gaining the social approval of others. In many instances, students are quite unable to deal with the Stage 5 reasoning on which the Constitution is based.

In Kohlberg's scheme, as in Piaget's, each stage serves as a basis for the next. But while Piaget was able to link age and stage and say, for example, that children around the ages of eleven or twelve should be better able to deal with mental abstractions, the age-stage relationship is less evident in moral reasoning. As Lickona has noted, "In general ... Stages 1 and 2 dominate in the primary school years and persist in some individuals long beyond that. Stage 3 gains ground during the upper elementary grades and often remains the major orientation through the end of high school. Stage 4 begins to emerge in adolescence. Only one in four persons moves on in later adolescence or adulthood to Stage 5" (1977, p. 39).

*Developmental
levels*

The situation is further complicated by the fact that although individuals may be *capable* of reasoning at higher levels, they sometimes use lower-level reasoning to justify their actions. Consider, for example, those individuals who feel that the 55 mph speed limit is an unjust law and therefore one they can break as a matter of principle. That's Stage 5 reasoning for the most part. But those same individuals will not exceed the speed limit, even as a matter of principle, unless there's a good chance that they won't get caught. Self-interest, then, appears to be a confounding factor. To the extent that Kohlberg's stages provide rough—and we emphasize *rough*—indicators of the types of moral understanding you can expect from students, the question then becomes one of how you get students to move to higher levels of moral reasoning.

How Do You Justify Your Actions?
The following statements reflect different stages of moral reasoning. Can you identify what the stages are?

Statement	Stage
"I don't oppose busing (for the purpose of integrating the schools) because it's the law."	4
"I never run in the hall because . . .	
I'll be punished if I get caught."	1
someone might get hurt, especially me."	3
it's against the rules."	4
"The only way to make it in a dog-eat-dog world is to cover your flank."	2
"Each of us, as an individual, is entitled to certain rights."	5
"I do what every good teacher should do; I keep my students in line and don't upset the applecart."	3
"I never exceed the speed limit because I might get caught—I even bought a CB radio."	1

Justifying one's beliefs

Using Moral Dilemmas   The intent of this approach to values education is to help students move toward more complex (higher-stage-level) patterns of moral reasoning. Justifying one's value orientation, which was not a critical phase in values clarification, becomes a critical element in moral reasoning. This is because the way in which individuals justify a course of action reflects their stage (or level) of moral development.

Kohlberg's research indicates that students will be stimulated to move to the next stage of moral development upon repeated exposure to higher levels of moral reasoning. Such exposure can be gained by helping students work with moral dilemmas—stories or situations, in which conflicting moral principles are involved—that require students to identify and evaluate alternative courses of action. Note that a dilemma is a situation in which the alternative courses of action are either desirable or undesirable, but not both. When the two elements are mixed, there is no dilemma; the individual merely follows the most desirable course of action.

Moral dilemmas

A simple moral dilemma might involve a seven-year-old girl named Holly who comes upon a small boy whose kitten is stranded in a tree. Tears stream down the boy's cheeks as he pleads with Holly to rescue his kitten. Although Holly is sympathetic, the last time she climbed a tree she fell and sprained her wrist. After that incident Holly promised her father she wouldn't climb any more trees. What should Holly do? (Lickona, 1977, p. 37.)

Holly could do a number of things, including trying to get help from an adult. Or she could break her promise to her father. By exploring such alternatives in group settings, moral dilemmas are intended to provide students with exposure to different (and hopefully higher) stages of moral reasoning. For younger children, the dilemmas should be fairly simple; they should involve relatively few characters and moral principles (obedience to authority vs. helping a friend in need, for instance). Note also that changing just one element in a moral dilemma, such as changing the kitten in a tree to a kitten trapped on a telephone pole, alters the entire situation.

For older students, the moral dilemmas can be much more complex. The example below involves the question of whether a young German girl should hide her Jewish friend from the Nazi Gestapo.

Model student activity

Helga's Dilemma

Helga and Rachel had grown up together. They were best friends despite the fact that Helga's family was Christian and Rachel's was Jewish. For many years, this religious difference didn't seem to matter much in Germany, but after Hitler seized power, the situation changed. Hitler required Jews to wear armbands with the Star of David on them. He began to encourage his followers to destroy the property of Jewish people and to beat them on the street. Finally, he began to arrest Jews and deport them. Rumors went around the city that many Jews were being killed. Hiding Jews for whom the Gestapo (Hitler's secret police) was looking was a serious crime and violated a law of the German government.

One night Helga heard a knock at the door. When she opened it, she found Rachel on the step huddled in a dark coat. Quickly Rachel stepped inside. She had been to a meeting, she said, and when she returned home, she had found Gestapo members all around her house. Her parents and brothers had already been taken away. Knowing her fate if the Gestapo caught her, Rachel ran to her old friend's house.

Now what should Helga do? If she turned Rachel away, the Gestapo would eventually find her. Helga knew that most of the Jews who were sent away had been killed, and she didn't want her best friend to share that fate. But hiding the Jews broke the law. Helga would risk her own security and that of her family if she tried to hide Rachel. But she had a tiny room behind the chimney on the third floor where Rachel might be safe.

Question: *Should Helga hide Rachel?*

Procedure:

1. Ask students to identify what should be done and why. "What should Helga do?"
2. Divide the class into small groups, either in terms of those who support a particular course of action or at random, and then ask them to discuss their reasons and justify the course of action they have chosen. "Why should Helga do what you think she should (do)?"
3. Permit groups to summarize and clarify their positions.
4. Ask additional probing questions. "Is the welfare of one's relatives more important than the welfare of one's friends?"

Students should be encouraged to express reasonable value positions, though it is not necessary that they arrive at consensus.

[This dilemma appears in the audiovisual kit that accompanies the second edition of *The Shaping of Western Society* (Good & Ford, 1970), a course in the Holt Social Studies Curriculum. Each one-semester course in the series contains six moral dilemmas developed at the Social Studies Curriculum Center, Carnegie-Mellon University. "Helga's Dilemma" also appears in Galbraith and Jones (1975, p. 18).]

How students justify what Helga should or should not do will identify their level of moral reasoning, as Galbraith and Jones (1975, p. 20) illustrate in the following:

Levels of moral reasoning

Stage 1: "If Helga lets Rachel in she might also get into trouble with the Gestapo."

Stage 2: "Helga shouldn't let her in because Rachel probably wouldn't let Helga in if she got into trouble with the Gestapo."

Stage 3: "Helga has an obligation to her family. She will really let them down if she gets them in trouble."

Stage 4: "Helga has an obligation to obey the laws of her society."

Stage 5: "Friendship is not the issue. If Helga was really concerned about the problem in her society, she should be helping all the Jews in order to protest the government action. She should not hide Rachel unless she intends to hide other Jews and to make a public protest in opposition to putting Jews in concentration camps."

What the Critics Say About Moral Reasoning Much of the criticism directed toward moral development has questioned either the adequacy of Kohlberg's theory or the validity of claims about what the analysis and discussion of moral dilemmas can or cannot do. Critics have also questioned the contention that higher-stage reasoning is necessarily *better* than lower-stage reasoning (Fraenkel, 1976). With respect to using moral dilemmas, Fraenkel (1976, p. 221) also noted that ". . . we are not even sure that it is the discussion of the [moral] dilemmas themselves which brings about stage movement. It is certainly conceivable that a sensitive concerned teacher, one who continually engages students in conversation and asks them questions, and lets them know by his or her comments and actions that he or she is interested in what they have to say, may be the independent variable in this regard. The discussion of moral dilemmas may be irrelevant. Perhaps the discussion of nonmoral controversial issues would do just as well. At this point, we just don't know."

Is higher also better?

Because most criticism of moral reasoning involves the more theoretical aspects of moral development, we recommend that you examine the publications listed in the "Suggested Readings" section at the end of this chapter.

Values Analysis

"Is it morally right for missionaries to introduce new technology into a primitive culture, when to do so may cause serious disruptions in that culture's way of life?"

This question is an outgrowth of a situation we shall describe in greater detail in Chapter Six, and it also serves as an example of the kind of value issue that can be attacked through values analysis. Recognize, however, that with a couple of minor changes, the question could change to, "Should missionaries introduce new technology into a primitive culture when they know, in advance, that to do so may cause serious disruptions in that culture's way of life?" Voilà! Here's a moral dilemma amenable to the procedures we noted in the previous section.

Emphasis on rational decision making

The fundamental idea of the values-analysis approach is to examine value questions as rationally and unemotionally as possible. The emphasis clearly is on *analysis*—careful, deliberate, discriminating analysis. Whereas the moral-reasoning approach would have students take a position and then justify it, values analysis would have the students refrain from taking a position until after they have analyzed the issues involved.

According to Jerrold Coombs and Milton Meux (1971, p. 29), the following six tasks are essential to the analysis of any value question or issue:

1 Identifying and clarifying the value question
2 Assembling (gathering and organizing) purported facts
3 Assessing the truth of the purported facts
4 Clarifying the relevance of the facts
5 Arriving at a tentative value decision
6 Testing the value principle implied in the decision

There is no "best" way to get students involved in these processes. Any means the teacher can use to get them involved (except browbeating, coercion, etc., of course) is acceptable. Ultimately, the intent is to wean students from the teacher's influence so that they are able to follow the processes on their own.

What the Critics Say about Values Analysis   The critics don't have much to say about values analysis, at least as far as we can determine. However because some elements of this valuing process are similar to those found in values clarification, some of the same cautions may be in order. Whenever teachers ask children questions like "Has something like this ever happened to you?" or "How did you feel about it?" the potential exists of invading the child's privacy or the privacy of the child's family. Young children in particular don't always distinguish between things that should remain private and things that are suitable for public consumption. As a result, even though the child's responses are made honestly and in all innocence, statements such as "Yeah, I feel the same way when my daddy gets drunk and beats up my mommy," could open the way to having that family's affairs become the topic of dinner-table conversation for other students in the class. Upon hearing such statements, the parents may begin wondering what's going on in

Privacy

school, and perhaps more importantly (to them at least), what their child is saying about them.

The potential of having a family's private affairs broadcast around the neighborhood is offset somewhat by the fact that, throughout much of elementary school, students are more interested in talking than they are in listening to what other students say. Though this can be looked upon as a kind of blessing, it also poses some problems of its own. Fraenkel noted these problems (as he was critiquing the moral-reasoning approach) by stating, ". . . discussion does not work very well or for very long with children below the age of 10 or so. You simply can't have much of an intellectual discussion with third or fourth graders" (1976, p. 221). Intellectual or not, notice that the strategies for value identification, dealing with value conflict, and developing empathy are all based on a series of questions. In some instances, it may be necessary for a single student to respond to a sequence of three or four questions (or more, if elaboration or clarification is required). In a class of twenty-seven students, then, a teacher might very well find himself engaged in what amounts to a dialogue with one student. Hopefully, the other twenty-six students will be interested enough to pay attention (without getting into trouble), but the longer the mini-dialogues go on, the more likely young children are to become bored. In light of this, several cautions, which also apply to discussions in general, seem apparent: (1) the teacher will need to be especially sensitive to the interest level of students who are not participating actively; (2) when possible, the techniques should be used in a small-group format; and (3) when student interest begins to sag, the teacher should shift to something else as quickly as possible.

Discussion or dialogue?

Summary

Maxine Dunfee (1978, p. 274) has said, ". . . there is no problem worth studying which does not lend itself admirably to the valuing process." We agree! We hasten to add, however, that there are many different points of view concerning the problems that should or should not be studied in school. These points of view can often conflict and, at times, lead to considerable controversy.

Under the principle of academic freedom, teachers have the right to teach the truth as they know it, even if their views differ from the prevailing community sentiment. Academic freedom does not entitle teachers to knowingly violate state law or to ignore direct orders from principals, superintendents, or other duly constituted authorities, for ignoring such orders could constitute insubordination. Barring these limitations, teachers are generally free to teach as they see fit. However, when what teachers think they should do is at odds with what a community thinks they should do—or with what a small group in the community thinks they should do—the legal protection afforded under academic freedom must be balanced against the emotional trauma that can accompany values-related controversies. It's the kind of problem for which there are no easy solutions.

In this chapter we have tried to do three things: first, to examine the role that values and value conflicts play in the context of teaching; second, to identify four approaches to values education—(1) inculcation, (2) values clarification, (3) moral reasoning, and (4) values analysis; and, third, to identify some criticisms leveled against each of these approaches.

If our treatment of values education has made you a bit cautious about attempting some of the strategies we've described in this chapter, we have succeeded in meeting one of our objectives. Don't misunderstand us; we think values education is important—vitally important. At the same time, it is (1) an area that may require skills that exceed those provided in most teacher training programs, skills similar to those used by trained and licensed psychotherapists, and (2) an area that has the potential to violate the student's right to privacy, no matter how noble our motives. The final chapter on the appropriate role of values education has yet to be written. It's still a matter of concern and, in some cases, controversy. To the extent that moral dilemmas play a significant role in values education, so too is there a dilemma of sorts about values education itself.

Suggested Activities

1   If you are one who likes the challenge of a difficult activity, attempt to identify behavioral objectives for "The Miracle Workers" or for any other activity in Simon, Howe, and Kirschenbaum's *Values Clarification*.

2   Go to your curriculum library or resource center and select an elementary social studies text for the grade level you'd like to teach. For any segment of the book you choose, indicate how you might incorporate values education into your approach to teaching that segment.

References

Conlon, John B. "MACOS: The Push for a Uniform National Curriculum." *Social Education* 39 (October 1975): 386–89.

Coombs, Jerrold R., and Meux, Milton. "Teaching Strategies for Value Analysis." In Metcalf, Lawrence E. (ed.) *Values Education: Rationale Strategies, and Procedures.* National Council for the Social Studies Yearbook 41 (1971): 29–74.

Dow, Peter B. "MACOS: The Study of Human Behavior as One Road to Survival." *Phi Delta Kappan* 57 (October 1975): 80–83.

Dunfee, Maxine. *Social Studies for the Real World.* Columbus, OH: Charles E. Merrill, 1978.

Fraenkel, Jack R. *Helping Students Think and Value: Strategies for Teaching Social Studies* (2nd ed.) Englewood Cliffs, NJ: Prentice-Hall, 1980.

———. "The Kohlberg Bandwagon: Some Reservations." *Social Education* 40 (April 1976): 216–22.

Galbraith, Ronald E., and Jones, Thomas M. "Teaching Strategies for Moral Dilemmas: An Application of Kohlberg's Theory of Moral Development to the Social Studies Classroom." *Social Education* 39 (January 1975): 16–22.

Good, J. M., and Ford B. *Shaping of Western Society,* incl. *Tradition and Change in Four Societies* (2nd ed.) New York: Holt, Rinehart and Winston, 1970.

Kirschenbaum, Howard. "In Support of Values Clarification." *Social Education* 41 (May 1977): 398,401–02.

Kohlberg, Lawrence and Turiel, Elliot. "Moral Development and Moral Education." In Gerald S. Lesser (ed.) *Psychology and Educational Practice.* Glenview, IL: Scott, Foresman, 1970: 410–65.

Lickona, Thomas. "How To Encourage Moral Development." *Learning* 5 (March 1977): 37–43.

Lockwood, Alan L. "What's Wrong With Values Clarification," *Social Education* 41 (May 1977): 399–401.

Raths, Louis E., Harmin, Merrill, and Simon, Sidney B. *Values and Teaching* (2nd ed.) Columbus, OH: Charles Merrill, 1978.

Schaar, Karen. "MACOS: The Controversy Continues." *APA Monitor* 6 (July 1975): 1+.

Scriven, Michael. "Values in the Curriculum." *Social Science Education Consortium Newsletter* 2 (April 1966): 1.

Simon, Sidney, Howe, Leland W., and Kirschenbaum, Howard. *Values Clarification: A Handbook of Practical Strategies for Teacher and Students.* New York: Hart Publishing, 1972.

Superka, Douglas. "Approaches to Values Education." *Social Science Consortium Newsletter* 20 (November 1974): 1–4.

Superka, Douglas P., Ahrens, Christine, Hedstrom, Judith E., with Ford, Luther J., and Johnson, Patricia L. *Values Education Sourcebook.* Boulder, CO: Social Science Education Consortium/ERIC Clearinghouse for Social Studies/Social Science Education, 1976.

Suggested Readings

Diane Divoky. "Affective Education: Are We Going Too Far?" *Learning,* October, 1975, pp. 20–27. A superb article that raises the kinds of questions that need to be asked.

Douglas P. Superka et al. *Values Education Sourcebook: Conceptual Approaches, Materials Analyses, and an Annotated Bibliography.* Boulder, CO: Social Science Education Consortium, 1976. The title says it all—everything you always wanted to know about values education and then some.

Jack R. Fraenkel. *How to Teach About Values.* Englewood Cliffs, NJ: Prentice-Hall, 1977. This volume is an extension of Fraenkel's work with values presented in *Helping Students Think and Value,* Englewood Cliffs, NJ.: Prentice-Hall, 1973. Both of these books are aimed more toward the secondary than the elementary level, but they are helpful nevertheless.

Raymond H. Muessig (ed.). *Controversial Issues in the Social Studies: A Contemporary Perspective.* National Council for the Social Studies Yearbook 45 (1975). This collection of articles deals with strategies and techniques for introducing controversial issues into your classroom. The titles of most articles are presented in question form, as "Should the Study of Death be Necessary Preparation for Living?"

Note: Several journals have devoted an entire issue to the theme of moral education. See one or more of the following: *Phi Delta Kappan* LVI (June, 1975), Kevin Ryan (ed.); *Social Education* 39 (January 1975); "Cognitive-Developmental Approach to Moral Education," Edwin Fenton (ed.), *Social Education* 40 (April 1976).

6 Teaching Strategies: From Exposition to Inquiry

Key Questions:

What teaching strategies work best for which objectives?

What's the difference between teacher-centered and student-centered teaching strategies—in action, that is?

How do teachers decide which questions to ask and when to ask them?

What is inquiry, and how does it differ from discovery learning and problem solving?

Key Ideas:

Teaching techniques—lectures, discussions, etc.—are the stuff from which teaching strategies are built. Teaching strategies reflect overall plans into which the parts (techniques) fit.

Some teaching strategies are more appropriate than others for reaching certain kinds of objectives. (Although there may be many ways to "skin a cat," not all are equally effective.)

The heart of any teaching strategy lies in the questions a teacher asks.

Underlying every question a teacher asks is a purpose for asking it. These purposes may be as varied as the questions.

Teacher-centered strategies tend to be more appropriate for conveying information; student-centered strategies tend to be more appropriate for developing information-processing skills.

Introduction: Symptoms and Ailments

Somewhere in your educational experience, you probably encountered teachers who, even when they resorted to a lung-busting "All right, people! Shut up!" didn't phase kids in the slightest. Substitute teachers are especially prone to such problems, we suspect, because they really don't have much influence in the long-run payoff for students. They may penalize students, to be sure—a list of misdeeds reported back to the regular teacher or even an occasional trip to the principal's office—but these penalties would tend to be short-run, spur-of-the-moment affairs not likely to result in serious consequences like a failing grade, immediate expulsion from school, or, most important of all to kids, being rejected by their peers.

Prospective teachers sometimes experience the haunting fear that they too will suffer the fate so often met by substitute teachers—discipline problems and, more ego-shattering yet, being ignored by students. When student teachers ask, "How can I get children to stop talking?" we suspect that part of their concern is motivated by the substitute-teacher syndrome. It certainly doesn't take a genius to recognize that if you can't get kids to pay attention today, you are probably on the brink of even bigger problems tomorrow. You've had too much experience as a student to believe otherwise.

Identifying the problem

So what do teachers do to get kids to pay attention? A responder to that question really has two options: one, to suggest several attention-getting techniques they might use or, second, to indicate that while getting attention may be *a* problem, it isn't necessarily *the* problem. If the responder chooses the first course of action, the net effect may be similar to using aspirin to treat cancer—the pain (inattention) may go away for a while, but the basic problem will remain. However, if the responder chooses the second course of action, the teacher may feel that his or her immediate problem isn't being dealt with. So, to maintain credibility, the responder should probably take both courses of action, hoping that the teacher will recognize that getting children to pay attention is usually an effect, a symptom of an even more basic problem. It may be a problem, but not necessarily *the* problem.

If inattention is an effect—a symptom—what is *the* problem? It could result from any number of things: the lack of established ground rules in the classroom, or ground rules that are not consistently adhered to (in which case *the* problem is inconsistency), or it could be that the children don't see much point in studying whatever it is they won't pay attention to. Or the cause could be much simpler—a dreary Friday afternoon when the kids are pooped, and even Mickey Mouse couldn't do much to arouse their interest.

Who is at fault?

The connection between some discipline problems and teaching is this: everyone's attention is apt to wander from time to time, but if an entire class is demonstrating an undesirable behavior, don't be too hasty to place all the blame on the students. There are occasional "bad kids," to be sure, but when an entire class is involved, the teacher would be well advised to examine his or her own behavior for possible causes. It could be, for example, that a teacher has just presented four dull lessons in a row, and the students (as you might expect) are not looking forward to a fifth one. (After four dull lessons in a row in some schools, teachers whose *only* problem is with kids not paying attention have been known to offer tributes to their guardian angels.)

We've implied here that discipline problems may sometimes result from the kind of teaching strategy a teacher employs. However, avoiding discipline problems, important as that may be, is actually a secondary focus in this chapter. Our main focus is on teaching strategies, those patterns of daily lesson plans and activities that must somehow fit together into a manageable pattern and that enable teachers (and students) to reach their objectives.

Teaching Strategies

For some people, associating the term *strategy* with teaching has manipulative or even devious overtones. It conjures up images of football coaches devising their "game plan" or of generals developing a plan of battle. Despite these connotations, and although some of the goals we value in education do differ from those of athletics and the military, the planning processes that coaches, generals, and teachers follow are often markedly similar.

In coaching, the ultimate goal is clear-cut—winning the game. To accomplish this, coaches first analyze the strengths and weaknesses of the opposing team (and their own). The information gleaned from this analysis provides the basis for developing an overall strategy. If the opposing team has a weak defensive line and a good pass defense, for example, the coach's game plan (strategy) is apt to be based on keeping the ball on the ground and with relatively little passing. To accomplish this, the coach will probably select several running plays that become the basis of the game plan. If things don't go as planned when the game is actually played, however, the coach will probably make some adjustments or, in some instances, will revise the game plan entirely.

In teaching, the goal is also clear-cut: helping students reach desired goals and objectives. To accomplish this, most teachers follow the planning procedure outlined in Chapter Three. The teacher's unit plan—the overall strategy—is roughly equivalent to a coach's game plan. Once the overall goals are decided, the teacher plans certain lessons (plays) that are intended to lead toward those goals. The individual lessons will undoubtedly reflect a variety of teaching techniques—different day-to-day teaching activities such as role playing, discussions, films, and filmstrips—which, collectively, constitute a teaching strategy. The relationship between teaching techniques and teaching strategies is illustrated in Figure 6.1.

Teachers who have difficulty handling a particular technique, such as role playing, will probably omit it from their overall strategy (just as a football coach whose star quarterback is injured will probably develop a game plan that relies on fewer passing plays). Teachers may also omit a particular teaching technique if they don't understand why it is used, or if they don't understand its potential uses. On the other hand, teachers who base their entire strategy on one technique, such as lecturing—day after day of lecturing—can probably anticipate problems from elementary-age students.

How do you develop a teaching strategy that doesn't overburden a particular technique? The answer to this question is conditioned by a subtle yet crucial aspect of teaching, namely, the tendency to confuse teaching strategies with learning strategies, with what learners do as they try to deal with whatever they are trying to learn. Although there are numerous ways to learn something (memorization, understanding basic concepts, drill, etc.), the way in which you teach something is not necessarily the way in which your students will learn it. The point here is that teachers, who may admittedly learn something while they are trying to teach, are often engaged in different behaviors than their students.

**Figure 6.1
Components of a
Teaching Strategy**

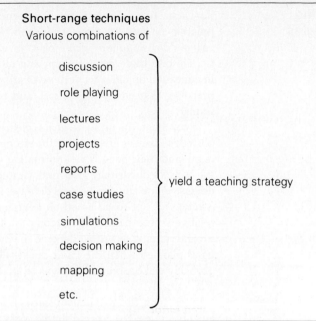

Short-range techniques

Various combinations of

discussion

role playing

lectures

projects

reports

case studies

simulations

decision making

mapping

etc.

} yield a teaching strategy

The distinction between teaching and learning strategies is probably most apparent in the stereotypical college class where the professor's teaching strategy consists of a single technique—lecturing—repeated over and over again. As the professor lectures, students are usually engaged in note taking, and ultimately in memorizing or otherwise comprehending what the professor has said. Thus the students' behavior is likely to differ considerably from the professor's teaching behavior.

There Is Nothing Like a GOOD Lecture

In some educational circles there prevails a notion that lectures are inherently bad and that, should you choose to lecture, you will be committing a grievous sin. (Ironically, it is often in a bad lecture that we are told how bad lecturing is as a teaching strategy.) At the same time, you've undoubtedly witnessed some extremely good lectures in your career as a student—some of which even made eight-o'clock classes worth getting up for. Thus we find ourselves in a situation where on one hand we may be told that lecturing is evil, while on the other hand we have experienced some excellent lectures by superb lecturers. The apparent contradiction seldom goes unnoticed by prospective teachers.

Our experience indicates that the quality of a lecture depends heavily on the ability of the person doing the lecturing. Good lecturers, we've found, must be able to demonstrate most of the following characteristics.

*Qualities of
good lecturers*

1 They must be extremely well versed in their subject. Good lecturers stand at the opposite end of the continuum from students whose reports to the class often reflect the total scope of their knowledge on a topic. Subject-matter expertise is a necessary but not sufficient qualification, however, since

on more than one occasion we have heard subject-matter experts—nationally known specialists in their fields—deliver some absolutely abominable lectures.

② They must have mastered the skills of acting. Good lecturers must be sensitive to timing, pacing, form and style of expression—when to raise their eyebrow or to change their tone of voice. The importance of these elements —the "show-biz" aspects of lecturing—were illustrated in what has been called "The Doctor Fox Effect." To determine if the way a lecture was presented made any difference in how students reacted to it, two researchers hired a Hollywood actor, whom they called Dr. Fox, to present six different types of lecture. The actor first memorized the scripts for three different lectures on the same topic. Each lecture differed in the amount of information it contained; one had very high content, another had some content, while the third contained a lot of verbiage but very little information. The actor then presented each lecture to different groups of students in one of two ways. For one presentation of each type of lecture, Dr. Fox really hammed it up, using gestures, humor, movement, vocal inflection, and considerable enthusiasm. For the second set of lectures, all of the expressive embellishments were omitted and the actor virtually read from the prepared script.

The Doctor Fox effect

What happened? According to Williams and Ware (1977), students who had experienced the highly expressive presentations did significantly better on achievement tests over the material than did students who had experienced the less expressive presentations. In addition, the students almost always rated the expressive presentations as "more effective" than the less-expressive lectures, regardless of the content they contained. The implication, then, is that even if you have little to say on a topic, you should say it with gusto!

Lecturers who have mastered the skills of acting and who have subject-matter expertise are likely to have captured the best of both worlds. Subject-matter expertise is gained through study, while acting skills are developed through practice. For teachers who are not yet accomplished lecturers, pity the poor students who must endure all of that practicing.

Identifying Teaching Strategies

Teaching strategies range from almost complete teacher domination at one extreme to almost complete student involvement at the other. Teachers who approach instruction almost wholly in terms of their own actions—as oriented toward a teaching strategy rather than a learning strategy—will tend to fall toward the left of the continuum shown in Figure 6.2. Here the strategies are characterized by a "telling," or *expository*, orientation. Teachers whose approach to instruction is almost wholly geared toward facilitating the development of their students' skills, and who strive for a high level of student involvement, fall toward the right side of the continuum. Here the strategies are characterized by an *inquiry*, or discovery, orientation. Teach-

Figure 6.2 A
Teaching Continuum

Exposition	Guided Discussion	Inquiry

$\longleftrightarrow$

Teacher-centered	Mixed	Student-centered
(Student passive)		(Teacher facilitated)

Source: Adapted from Fenton (1967, p. 33).

ing strategies that combine elements from both orientations lie somewhere in the middle of the continuum. These "mixed" strategies are difficult to describe precisely but are characterized by the term *guided discussion.*

Exposition In expository (lecture-type) teaching strategies, the primary focus is on the person doing the expositing—the teacher. Hopefully the students are participating mentally and following along with what the teacher is doing, but aside from taking notes, there may be almost no other apparent physical involvement.

Lecture-type strategies

Lecture-type teaching strategies usually follow a Read-Recite-Lecture-Test format. Sometimes the recitation phase is omitted, at the college level especially, and sometimes the teacher will reverse the format and talk about material prior to having the students read it. On other occasions, additional elements may be added—a film, a demonstration, student reports, or current events periods, for example. Such variations notwithstanding, the overall goal of most expository teaching strategies is to present information in an easily understood form.

Expository teaching in its extreme or "purest" form is not often found in elementary schools, probably because the students won't sit still for it, literally or figuratively. Nevertheless, and despite the bad reputation sometimes associated with expository teaching strategies, there are times when lecturing can be extremely useful. Discussions, for example, can become futile exercises in shared ignorance unless students are fully aware of the issues they are dealing with. On other occasions we've seen students flounder hopelessly because their teachers, who favored a discovery approach to teaching, mistakenly thought the students should discover *everything,* including the information necessary to discover whatever they are supposed to discover. In either instance, teachers may avoid such problems by giving short presentations or mini-lectures that bring fresh information to bear on the points in question. We are not suggesting that teachers should provide a daily diet of half-hour speeches—far from it. It's just that in some instances, a mini-lecture could be an appropriate teaching activity.

Mini-lectures

Guided Discussion Guided-discussion teaching strategies reflect a blend of teacher-centered and student-centered teaching techniques. Just how those techniques are "blended" will vary from teacher to teacher, but the following behaviors are characteristic of guided-discussion strategies.

Guided Discussion : (margin note)

Characteristic student behaviors

1 Reading the assignment. (Grades 3 and up.)
2 Asking questions in class about what they don't understand (if they understand it well enough to know what to ask).
3 Listening to the teacher explain, clarify, or add factual details or additional information; recording them if experience shows they will appear on a test.
4 Participating in discussions and/or observing demonstrations.
5 Identifying the essentials (and/or details) of the lesson, memorizing them if necessary.
6 Recalling information from the readings, lectures, and discussions in order to perform satisfactorily on the test.

Characteristic teacher behaviors

1 Organizing topical coverage and assignments so they are manageable for students.
2 Ordering films or other related materials.
3 Determining the objectives toward which the lecture, explanation, discussion, and/or demonstration will be directed.
4 Deciding upon the key questions to get students interested or motivated.
5 Doing some background reading (optional).
6 Delivering lectures, conducting discussions, etc.
7 Preparing, giving, and grading the test (if used).
8 Organizing for the next unit (usually while working on items 1–7 above).

The further a teacher moves away from the more clearly defined roles of expository and guided-discussion strategies, the more difficult it becomes to describe his or her behavior precisely. Shifting the focus to a student-centered teaching strategy necessarily shifts the attention from one individual, the teacher, to the teacher *and* the students. Student-centered (inquiry) strategies are inherently more sensitive to the ways students respond to an activity, and, since it's next to impossible to predict all of the responses students might generate, inquiry-oriented teachers are denied the luxury of being able to predict their students' actions with the same certainty that expository-oriented teachers enjoy.

(margin note) Strategies contrasted

Inquiry Inquiry-oriented teaching strategies focus mainly on developing the students' ability to manipulate and process information from a variety of sources: academic, social, and experiential. An inquiry-oriented teacher is one who gears instructional activities toward maximizing student ability to process information from these sources. Because expository, directed-discussion, and inquiry strategies all are concerned with information processing, it's fair to ask where the difference between them lies. Basically it is in terms of *the kind of processing* students do. In expository classrooms, the processing is generally limited to information storage and retrieval (sometimes described as the ability to regurgitate information on command). Teachers do most of the organizing in an expository classroom, while students are mainly concerned with processing the data for efficient recall.

Guided-discussion strategies are generally aimed at the same processing skills as exposition strategies, namely, information storage and retrieval. The key difference lies in the fact that directed discussion permits students to get clarification on aspects of the information they don't understand.

Inquiry strategies, however, focus on having students organize and process information within a different framework. It is the students who identify problems, generate possible answers, test these answers in the light of available data, and attempt to apply their conclusions to new data, new problems, or new situations. Inquiry strategies focus on *how* students process data instead of on the *products* of someone else's data processing (which is typically the case for expository and guided-discussion strategies).

Exposition and guided discussion are clearly strategies for organizing and presenting information to students. Inquiry is more than that. In an educational context, inquiry is both a noun and a verb—both an act and a *process*. Like discovery, problem solving, and even memorization, inquiry is a learning process, a way in which students and adults can go about solving problems or processing information.

To approach inquiry as a teaching strategy in the same way one might approach exposition—as a teaching strategy from the outset—is to misunderstand the nature of the beast. Inquiry-oriented teachers derive their teaching strategies from the way students engage in inquiry as a learning process. Their strategies grow out of the way students apply inquiry skills. Thus, inquiry is initially a learning process and secondarily a teaching strategy intended to support that process.

The question, then, becomes: *What, specifically, is inquiry?* (And, how does one plan an inquiry strategy?)

What Does an Inquirer Do?   If an inquiry teaching strategy is intended to support a learning process, it's reasonable to ask what someone who uses inquiry does. The scholar in the following example (Olsvanger, 1947) is an inquirer. With nary a word spoken, he identifies the gentleman sitting across from him in a railroad coach. There is no trick in this example, even though it might seem that way at first. As you read it, determine how the scholar figured out who the man sitting across from him was. (Note: To answer "By a process of elimination" or "By deductive reasoning" is to label the process, not describe it. We are asking you to be more specific than that and to *describe* the process the scholar used.)

Focus on process skills

A learner-based strategy

Who is he?

"It Was Obvious"   A Talmudic scholar from Marmaresch was on his way home from a visit to Budapest. Opposite him in the railway carriage sat another Jew, dressed in modern fashion and smoking a cigar. When the conductor came around to collect the tickets the scholar noticed that his neighbor opposite was also on his way to Marmaresch.

This seemed very odd to him.

"Who can it be, and why is he going to Marmaresch?" he wondered.

As it would not be polite to ask outright he tried to figure it out for himself. "Now let me see," he mused. "He is a modern Jew, well dressed, and he smokes a cigar. Whom could a man of this type be visiting in Marmaresch? Possibly he's on his way to our town doctor's wedding. But no, that can't be! That's two weeks off. Certainly this kind of man wouldn't twiddle his thumbs in our town for two weeks!

"Why then is he on his way to Marmaresch? Perhaps he's courting a woman there. But who could it be? Now let me see. Moses Goldman's daughter Esther? Yes definitely, it's she and nobody else . . .! But now that I think of it—that couldn't be! She's too old—he wouldn't have her, under any circumstances! Maybe it's Haikeh Wasservogel? Phooey! She's so ugly! Who then? Could it be Leah, the money-lender's daughter? N—no! What a match for such a nice man! Who then? There aren't any more marriageable girls in Marmaresch. That's settled then, he's not going courting.

"What then brings him?

"Wait, I've got it! It's about Mottell Kohn's bankruptcy case! But what connection can he have with that? Could it be that he is one of his creditors? Hardly! Just look at him sitting there so calmly, reading his newspaper and smiling to himself. Anybody can see nothing worries him! No, he's not a creditor. But I'll bet he has something to do with the bankruptcy! Now what could it be?

"Wait a minute, I think I've got it. Mottell Kohn must have corresponded with a lawyer from Budapest about his bankruptcy. But that swindler Mottell certainly wouldn't confide his business secrets to a stranger! So it stands to reason that the lawyer must be a member of the family.

"Now who could it be? Could it be his sister Shprinzah's son? No, that's impossible. She got married twenty-six years ago—I remember it very well because the wedding took place in the green synagogue. And this man here looks at least thirty-five.

"A funny thing! Who could it be, after all . . .? Wait a minute! It's as clear as day! This is his nephew, his brother Hayyim's son, because Hayyim Kohn got married thirty-seven years and two months ago in the stone synagogue near the market place. Yes, that's who he is!

Aha!

"In a nutshell—he is lawyer Kohn from Budapest. But a lawyer from Budapest surely must have the title 'Doctor'! So, he is Doctor Kohn from Budapest, no? But wait a minute! A lawyer from Budapest who calls himself 'Doctor' won't call himself 'Kohn'! Anybody knows that. It's certain that he has changed his name into Hungarian. Now, what kind of a name could he have made out of Kohn? Kovacs! Yes, that's it—Kovacs! In short, this is Doctor Kovacs from Budapest!"

Eager to start a conversation the scholar turned to his travelling companion and asked, "Doctor Kovacs, do you mind if I open the window?"

"Not at all," answered the other. "But tell me, how do you know that I am Doctor Kovacs?"

"It was obvious," replied the scholar.

How *did* the scholar do it? And is it really all that "obvious"?

Actually, the process the scholar used was very systematic. First he observed the situation—a cigar-smoking, modernly dressed man going to Marmaresch. On the surface there seems nothing unusual about this, but to the scholar, "this seemed very odd." (Could it be that Marmaresch isn't a very swinging place on Saturday night?) We are not told why the scholar found the situation odd, just that it was. *Something* just didn't "fit" and thus became a *discrepant event* which the scholar then tried to explain.

*Cognitive
dissonance*

One's awareness of a discrepant event results from a kind of mental "disturbance" called *cognitive dissonance.* If you've ever heard a clarinet "squeak," you've experienced dissonance; something was out of harmony, musically speaking. A cognitive (or mental) parallel to musical dissonance occurs when you hear a child counting "One, two, three, four, five, seven, eight," for instance. Cognitive dissonance exists when you sense that something is "wrong," or out of harmony with your existing ideas. Upon hearing the child skip the number six, an adult may sense that something is "wrong" (even if the child doesn't) and go back over what was said to determine what the problem was. Note that some people can ignore dissonance, as in the child's counting above, and then there is no discrepant event that needs to be explained. Most of us find dissonance unsettling, however; it so disturbs our equilibrium that we must explain or otherwise resolve the problem. For the Talmudic scholar, explaining the discrepant event became his *problem,* which he then broke down into two more manageable problems: "Who can it be, and why is he going to Marmaresch?"

*Problem
identified!*

Our journey into the nature of cognitive dissonance and discrepant events is intended to emphasize how crucial this phase—awareness of the problem —is to the inquiry process. If the scholar had not sensed a problem there would have been nothing to inquire about, and the story would have ended in the first paragraph. Likewise, if students don't sense that a discrepant event exists, they have nothing to explain. The clear implication is that teachers who wish to use inquiry-oriented teaching strategies may need to structure activities in which they intentionally create cognitive dissonance that provides students with a *motive* for inquiry. Two techniques for creating dissonance (which we noted in Chapter One) are (1) creating mystery-type situations or (2) limiting the information available to students at the outset.

*Reviewing the
data*

Once the problem was identified, our Talmudic scholar reexamined his data—modern dress, cigar-smoking, etc.—and then restated his problem in a way that may be more easily managed: "Whom could a man of this type be visiting in Marmaresch?" Since the scholar has a great deal of information about Marmaresch, he in effect rephrases his question to state, "What's going on in Marmaresch that would bring a man like this to town?"

Hypothesizing

"The town doctor's wedding?" That's a possibility—*a hypothesis,* a tentative answer, an educated guess. But the scholar knows that the wedding is two weeks away, and such an early arrival just doesn't seem very logical. So the scholar rejects Hypothesis 1 and returns to a restatement of his problem, "Why, then, is his fellow passenger on his way to Marmaresch?"

"Courting a woman?" Hypothesis 2. But what woman? Esther Goldman (Hypothesis 2.1)? The scholar's interpretation of Esther's age suggests she would be inappropriate for his railway-carriage companion. Hence, Hypothesis 2.1 is rejected.

But what about Haikeh Wasservogel (Hypothesis 2.2)? Both Haikeh and "Leah, the money-lender's daughter" (Hypothesis 2.3) are rejected. Since there are no more marriageable girls in Marmaresch, Hypothesis 2 is also rejected. The scholar has exhausted the possibilities, at least as he interpreted them. Notice, however, that the scholar's rejection of Haikeh Wasservogel (Hypothesis 2.2) because of her lack of beauty is valid only if his fellow passenger also feels the same way.

After rejecting Hypothesis 2, it's back to the problem once again, "What then brings him?" In a flash of intuition, the scholar decides it has something to do with the bankruptcy case (Hypothesis 3). He tests, rejects, or modifies various subhypotheses until he *concludes,* "In a nutshell—he is Lawyer Kohn from Budapest."

His conclusion, though, is *tentative,* subject to change in light of any additional data. And change it the scholar does. It finally becomes "Doctor Kovacs from Budapest." Now the scholar has an "answer" he can live with. But, is it the right one?

He *tests* his conclusion by asking to open the window. Based on his companion's response, it may be possible to determine if his answer was "right."

But was it?

The Inquiry Process   In the previous episode, the scholar's problem-solving behavior occurred in a number of distinct phases (not steps), all of which reflect the inquiry process. In summary form, they were:

1 Becoming aware of a discrepant event (1.1) which then became a problem to be solved (1.2)
2 Identifying hypotheses (possible explanations or tentative answers)
3 Testing the hypotheses in light of the data
   3.1   If a hypothesis is rejected, the problem may be restated for clarity, and the inquirer goes to Phase 2 again.
   3.2   If the hypothesis is accepted (not rejected), the inquirer proceeds to Phase 4.
4 Modifying the hypothesis, which has become a tentative conclusion, in light of additional data until satisfied that it is a plausible explanation
5 Testing the tentative conclusion (Does it fit? Does it explain the discrepant event?)

For us to suggest that every inquirer follows these procedures in exactly the same sequence would be misleading. People just don't think that way! As Jerome Bruner (1960, p. 63) suggested, "The shrewd guess, the fertile hypothesis, the courageous leap to a tentative conclusion—these are the most valuable coins of the thinker at work." In other words, someone's educated guess—their bright idea—can serve as a legitimate shortcut. Bruner went on to point out, however, that "in most schools, guessing is heavily penalized and is associated somehow with laziness."

There isn't one single "right" way to inquire. Students, like our Talmudic scholar, may shift from trial and error to gradual analysis, and then suddenly be inspired by flashes of insight or intuition. Since none of these methods is necessarily wrong, inquiry teachers don't have a guarantee that every student will approach inquiry-oriented problem solving in the same way.

The Challenge of Inquiry Teaching   Even though students apply informal inquiry skills in their everyday activities, getting them to become aware of problems, to create hypotheses, and to test and modify tentative answers in a more formal way in a classroom is not without some practical problems.

Nonverbal communication enhances the words you utter.

This is especially true for primary-level students who have not yet made the transition to Piaget's stage of formal operations.

Even very young children can become aware of discrepant events, however, particularly if those events do not involve abstract thought. But apparently because there are so many discrepant events in a young child's life—things that are unexplained—children tend to react to them in one of two ways: either they become so interested in something that they insist on sticking with it until it's resolved to their satisfaction, or they dismiss it immediately and for no apparent reason. Unlike many adults, young children do not feel compelled to explain everything and can often live quite happily with things that they don't understand.

Older students, on the other hand, sometimes jump on the first explanation (hypothesis) they create, and cling so tenaciously to it that they ignore other possibilities or data to the contrary. It sometimes becomes a case of "I've already made up my mind, so don't bother me with information!" There's some ego involvement too, we suspect. In a child's world, where things are clearly "right" or "wrong," the very idea of rejecting a tentative

Children's reactions

answer because the data doesn't support it can be construed as being *wrong* (when it is actually *right* to reject it). Even though teachers may say things like "You're not wrong," such statements may not carry much weight if a child is concerned about losing status and prestige for having identified what others regard as an incorrect answer. It takes considerable sophistication to understand why identifying a hypothesis that must be rejected because the data doesn't support it ("He's going to Marmaresch to get married") is a perfectly acceptable, even essential element of inquiry.

Ego involvement

We regard the problems associated with inquiry teaching as a challenge, not as a basis for avoidance. We have suggested, however, that: (1) conducting full-blown inquiry lessons on a whole-class basis may prove difficult, particularly in the primary grades; and (2) helping children develop information-processing skills such as analyzing, inferring, observing, in small segments can equip them to inquire more effectively when they feel the need to do so. Note also that although we've focused on inquiry-oriented strategies here, expository and guided-discussion strategies are not without their challenges too. Good discussions, as opposed to merely sharing personal experiences, for instance, don't just happen; they require considerable skill. And when students are unable to read the major source of informational input, the textbook, any teaching strategy can prove challenging indeed.

Teaching Strategies Revisited   On the surface it might appear that we've outlined three basic teaching strategies and that your task is simply to pick one (or work combinations) and go to it. If only it were that simple! The decision ultimately involves your conception of what it means to teach.

The teacher's role is critical to any teaching strategy, but is especially so in an inquiry-oriented classroom. Skeel and Decaroli (1969, p. 547) captured part of the issue as follows:

*How teachers
view their role*

> Inquiry falters if a teacher views his position as that of a central figure from which knowledge, ideas, value judgments, and conclusions spew forth to be absorbed by young minds. A teacher abdicates this position in an inquiry-centered classroom to accept the less prominent but equally important role of guide.

Carpenter (1967, p. 220) stated much the same position but carried it one step further:

> Thus the inquiry approach views the learner as an active thinker— seeking, probing, processing data from his environment toward a variety of destinations along paths best suited to his own mental characteristics. It rejects passiveness as an ingredient of effective learning and the concept of the mind as a reservoir for the storage of knowledge presented through expository instruction directed toward a predetermined, closed end. The inquiry method seeks to avoid the dangers of rote memorization and verbalization as well as the hazard of fostering dependency in citizens as learners and thinkers.... The measure of ultimate success in education through inquiry lies in the degree to which the teacher becomes unnecessary as a guide.

Inquiry, Discovery, and Problem Solving

When teachers talk about the instructional strategies they use, it's not uncommon to hear some say, "I use a discovery approach," others say, "I use inquiry," and still others say, "I prefer a problem-solving approach." Because universally accepted definitions for inquiry, discovery, and problem solving don't exist, you would need to visit these teachers to find out how they actually teach. You might very well find that, despite the different terminology, the three strategies are more similar than they are different.

The most striking similarity among these approaches is their emphasis on thinking processes and skills. In one form or another, all of them ask students to piece together several items of information in order to identify or discover relationships that may exist among those items.

Discovery

Literally, *discovery* refers to the moment a student perceives a relationship among various data—when the student says, "Aha, I've got it!" The teacher's main role in discovery teaching is creating situations and an environment where students are encouraged to discover and test ideas on their own. If this role sounds like the one we described for inquiry-oriented teachers, it is; a discovery approach is part of a larger process that is similar to the inquiry processes that we outlined earlier.

Problem solving can be confusing because the expression may refer to two somewhat different types of activities. One of these, which is probably the most common, refers to what students do as they answer the problems in a math text. All of us have done this type of relatively short-range problem solving at one time or another. A second type of problem solving involves more complex, longer-range concerns (problems), such as "How could you determine the favorite soft drink in your class?" or "How is a Republican different from a Democrat?"—that

Problem solving

tend to be more closely associated with social studies. Gross and McDonald (1958, p. 262) described this more encompassing approach to problem solving as involving: (1) an awareness of a problem that is personal in character—that is, the problem-solver is disturbed by something (a discrepant event?); (2) a data-gathering phase in which the solver becomes familiar with the task; (3) a hypothesis-formation stage in which the solver formulates solutions; and (4) a hypothesis-testing phase in which possible solutions are tested. The remarkable similarity between this definition and the definition for inquiry (p. 185) should not go unnoticed.

Until the experts straighten out the terminology, suffice it to say that discovery, inquiry, and problem solving all refer to teaching strategies that involve students in the process of search—a search for relationships between and among data.

While expository teaching strategies are most frequently concerned with transmitting large bodies of information to students, those students obviously require skills for dealing with that information. As a result, to say that most expository teachers are concerned only with knowledge transmission is probably inaccurate (although perhaps more likely to be true, we think, than in the case of student-centered strategies).

The changing role of data and skills

Despite the fact that inquiry teaching strategies focus on information-processing skills, such skills cannot be developed in a void; students must have data to work with. In that context, inquiry strategies are vitally concerned with both the kinds of information that kids work with as well as the skills they apply to that information. In moving from expository to inquiry teaching strategies, what changes is not the existence of data, knowledge, or skills, but rather the *role that information and skills play in the teaching strategy.*

Difference Splitting   Rather than associate themselves with either the expository or the inquiry strategy, some teachers hope to select from both inquiry and expository strategies in unique, eclectic ways. However, what might seem to be a safe, middle-of-the road position is not without its hazards. As Rogers (1970, p. 74) stated:

> The notion of inquiry is an intriguing one, and it conjures up images of deeply involved, questioning, bright-eyed children who have finally been rescued from the drudgery of "traditional" classroom teaching. One does not—one cannot—simply insert inquiry lessons, projects or programs into a framework that in its totality is organized to defeat the purposes of the inquiry approach. The situation is analogous, perhaps, to the rejection of a transplanted organ in the human body. The new heart may be perfectly sound, but its new environment is hostile, so it is in fact rejected.

A question of emphasis, not exclusion

Where do you, as a social studies teacher, want to place your emphasis? On knowledge transmission? On the facts kids need to have? An emphasis in which skills may get lost somewhere in the process? Or on the development of information-processing skills? An emphasis that recognizes you will not be able to "cover" all the knowledge in a traditional curriculum? *This decision must be made prior to planning any teaching strategy.*

Dimensions of Expository, Guided-discussion, and Inquiry Strategies

Exposition strategies require that the teacher have:

1 a command of the subject matter
2 the ability to organize subject matter in a way that is understandable when presented to students

Guided-discussion strategies require:

1 a command of the subject matter
2 the ability to organize subject matter in a way that is understandable to students
3 the ability to conduct a discussion

Inquiry strategies require:

1 an understanding of the nature of inquiry
2 a command of the subject matter
3 the ability to relate subject matter to individuals' process-skill levels

"You'll find 'Teaching Methods That Never Fail' under fiction."

Sources

The essential difference among these strategies lies in their source—where they begin. The source of expository teaching strategies lies primarily in *content*—in the subject matter. The source of inquiry strategies, on the other hand, lies in the students' ability to *process* information—to solve problems. Guided-discussion strategies may use either student skills or subject matter as a source; it varies from teacher to teacher. Guided discussion often reflects an effort to increase student involvement and participation, but the strategy itself is usually rooted in subject matter.

Questioning Strategies

As every student knows, questions are a teacher's stock-in-trade. From a student's point of view, teachers always seem to have more questions than they have answers. At the moment, however, our concern is not with answers but rather with the kinds of questions teachers ask, and the relationship between those questions and a teacher's teaching strategy.

The role of questions

The kinds of questions teachers ask are so closely related to their teaching strategy that the two are almost inseparable. Teachers who employ a purely expository strategy are a notable exception, however, because unless they have some type of student recitation, questioning is apt to be almost nonexistent (except on exams). In all other instances, questions and questioning play a key role. A teacher who, for example, continually poses questions like "Who was Henry Hudson, what was the name of his ship, and what river did he sail up?" will have implicitly indicated what he or she thinks is important information for students to know. On the other hand, a teacher who asks the question, "How can we find out who Henry Hudson was and what he did?" has shifted the emphasis considerably. Through the questions they ask, these teachers have indicated two very different purposes.

For Every Question
There Is a Purpose

For every question teachers ask, there is (or at least there should be) an underlying purpose, something the teacher is trying to get at. By analyzing a teacher's questions, we should be able to infer what those purposes are. The reverse is also true: if you know what a teacher's purposes are, you should be able to suggest several questions and/or activities that will enable them to attain them. (If you can't do that right now or if this seems a bit theoretical, take heart—some specific examples are forthcoming.)

Questioning, in the sense of deciding what questions to ask and how to ask them, is at the heart of every student-centered teaching strategy. But before asking a single question, we need something to ask questions about. The following case study, drawn from Stuart Chase's *The Proper Study of Mankind* (1963, pp. 112–13) should serve that purpose. Ultimately, our intent is to illustrate several different ways in which this case study could be used—ways that are reflected in the different kinds of questions we could ask about it. As you read the case study, attempt to identify at least four different kinds of questions (or tasks) you might pose to your students, either before or after they've read it.

Case Study: "Stone Axes"

On the northern coast of Australia lives a tribe of hunters and fishermen called the Yir Yoront. Like most primitive Australians, the tribe enjoyed great stability; they had almost no contact with other cultures. In fact, before the tribe would accept any changes in their beliefs and customs, a myth had to be invented which proved that one's ancestors did things that way, and that the change really wasn't a change at all.

In many ways the tribe was still living in the Stone Age. One of their most important tools was a short-handled stone ax—something they used to build huts, cut firewood, and make other tools for hunting, fishing, and gathering wild honey. The stone heads came from a quarry 400 miles to the south and were obtained from other tribes in an annual fiesta. There, handles were fitted to the axheads and great skill and care. Once finished, the axes were more than just a tool but came to stand for a symbol of being a man; they were something to be treated with great care, handed down from father to son, and almost never loaned to someone else. Not only was the stone ax useful, it became the center of the Yir Yoront belief system.

Just before World War I, missionaries visited the tribe and began distributing steel axes as gifts and rewards. If a man worked very hard he might get an ax, and so might his wife or son. By using the axes as gifts, the missionaries hoped to get the tribe to plant gardens and improve their diets.

New steel axes had an interesting effect on the tribe. Certainly they could cut down trees much faster, but men also lost their importance and dignity. Women and children who had their own axes became independent and disrespectful. The entire tribe was thrown into confusion. The fiesta was no longer held. Crime increased.

Identify four questions and/or tasks you might pose about "Stone Axes":

1 _____

2 _____

3 _____

4 _____

The range of possible questions and tasks certainly isn't endless—after all, it's not a very long case study. Yet there are enough possibilities that we must look at them in terms of categories, not individual questions. As a consequence, you'll have to determine whether or not your questions fit into one or more of our categories, which are based on and identified in terms of the thinking skills students must use to answer them.

Categories of Questions Among the most obvious possible questions are those that follow the form of "What is the name of the tribe living on the northern coast of Australia?" or "How far from the tribe's home was the stone quarry?" The purpose of this type of question is to determine if students can recall factual information. There is little concern with inferring, evaluating, or speculating here; rather, the focus is on the facts and whether or not the students know them. Questions in this category require *memory-recall* skills and are classified accordingly.

Memory-recall

Examples of a second category of possible questions are "Describe (in your own words) what happened to the Yir Yoront when the missionaries began distributing steel axes," or "Explain why you think the missionaries acted as they did." Questions in this category require that students go beyond a literal-level recall of information in order to describe, interpret, or otherwise explain events or actions, and they must do so in their own words. The category is composed of *descriptive-interpretive* questions.

Descriptive-interpretive

A distinguishing feature of "questions" in this category is that the task may not be expressed as a direct question. An alternative format for presenting descriptive-interpretive tasks is as a direct question, like "Can you explain why the missionaries acted as they did?" When posed in this form, the "tasks" must usually be followed by the question, "Why?"

Another category of questions requires that students identify relationships and draw conclusions, bringing in other information as it is appropriate. Examples of questions in this category are: "How would you sum up what happened to the Yir Yoront in general terms (or in as few words as possible?)" or "What general statement could you make about the Yir Yoront's experience?" Because questions of this kind require that students put things together (synthesize) in order to identify relationships or generalizations that go beyond a specific event, the category is labeled *application-synthesis*.

Application-synthesis

In most instances, application-synthesis questions must be preceded by lower-level questions; otherwise they may seem to come from out of the blue. For example, a teacher might state that the introduction of steel axes was a change that affected the Yir Yoront, then ask "What other changes resulted, either directly or indirectly, from the introduction of steel axes?" This question would fall into the descriptive-interpretive category. After students respond, the teacher might summarize by stating, "Introducing the steel axes caused all of these other changes." The teacher could then use an application-synthesis question like "How would you complete a statement that began, 'If one thing changes, then _____ (other changes are likely to occur)." In this example, the teacher is clearly leading students toward making a desired general statement about the nature of change. You might be able to accomplish the same thing with less leading by asking either of the exemplary questions for this category noted above.

Examples of another category of possible questions are: "Were the missionaries right to introduce steel axes into the Yir Yoront way of life?" and "Did the Yir Yoront culture advance after the introduction of the steel-axe technology?" These questions require that students produce an evaluation or render a judgment, and, thus, fall into the *evaluative-judgmental* category. A distinguishing characteristic of evaluative-judgmental questions is that students must identify the criteria they will use in reaching their evaluation. Thus, an evaluative question might be phrased more accurately as follows: "According to what criteria would you decide that the missionaries were either right or wrong?" Even though this might seem to be an unnecessarily long-winded way to pose a question, our intent is to emphasize the need to specify clearly, and in advance, the criteria by which something is being judged. If the evaluative criteria are not explicit, a student's response would be purely personal opinion.

*Evaluative-
judgmental*

A final category of questions asks students to speculate in a hypothetical mode. Examples of questions in this category are: "What might have happened to the Yir Yoront if the missionaries had never come?" or "What if the missionaries had chosen to use beads, mirrors, or objects other than steel axes?" The "what-if" form evident in the examples above is characteristic of questions in this, the *speculative-heuristic* category.

*Speculative-
heuristic*

Speculative-heuristic questions are dillies for generating inquiry, promoting divergent thinking, and getting students to speculate on and analyze alternative courses of action. They also allow students to formulate their own questions, such as "How do missionaries elsewhere get people to change?" or "Where can we find more information on_____?" Once students begin to pose their own questions, you have two options: (1) to attempt to answer them as best as you can—*if* you can; or (2) to guide students in finding answers on their own. The latter option, while preferable in many instances, also requires your judgment as to whether the students' curiosity has been sufficiently aroused to counteract the frustration they may encounter in finding an answer. You'll also need to determine if a student's question is significant enough to warrant a search. For example, a student question such as "What did the steel axes look like?" is a kind of dead-end question. Finding an answer—if that is possible—might lead to satisfaction on the student's part, but very little else.

Caution: speculative-heuristic questions should be used judiciously. Three "what if" questions in a row may be enough to confuse even your most sophisticated students. Instead of speculation, their response may be "Who cares!"

The various categories of questions are illustrated in summary form in Table 6.1.

Table 6.1 Types of Questions by Category and Purpose

Type of Question	Purpose
1 Memory-Recall	To determine if students can recall previously learned information.
2 Descriptive-interpretive	To describe, interpret, and/or explain events or actions in the students' own words, including reasons (nonspeculative) for why individuals acted as they did.
3 Application-synthesis	To identify relationships and to form and draw reasonable conclusions that go beyond the particular action or event.
4 Evaluative-judgmental	To render an evaluation or judgment as to actions or events in light of explicit, previously identified criteria.
5 Speculative-heuristic	To encourage divergent thinking and to speculate on and analyze alternative courses of action.

Other Questions   The categories of questions outlined above were based on the skills required of students in order to answer them. In this section we consider three other categories of questions that are not directly linked to thinking skills but which teachers sometimes employ. Two of these categories, rhetorical and probing questions, are fairly common, while the third, multi-focus questions, is relatively uncommon and should remain so.

Rhetorical questions are actually statements, phrased as if they were questions but for which the teacher really doesn't expect an answer (or for which the teacher supplies the answer). A statement (rhetorical question) such as, "Let's see now, what happened to the Yir Yoront? The missionaries came and . . ." could be used to (1) summarize, (2) refocus, or (3) restructure the lesson in a direction the teacher wishes to pursue.

Probing questions enable the teacher to explore a student's previous responses in greater detail or to bring out elements not previously identified. Examples of probing questions are: "Can you elaborate on that in greater detail?" and "I'm not sure I understand what you just said; can you give an example of what you mean?" Probing questions can also be used to extend discussion or to elicit responses from other students, such as "Does anyone else have anything to add to what Steve just said?"

Multi-focus questions should be avoided whenever possible. The only reason we even mention them is so that you can recognize a multi-focus question when you see (or hear) one. An example of a multi-focus question is: "What differences did you find in the patterns of government and trade in South America and what is similar about these differences?" Formulating the question isn't too difficult, but trying to formulate an answer is something else again; it demands that too many thinking processes be used simultaneously. But that's only one of the things wrong with multi-focus questions. As Taba noted, such a question

> . . . asks the pupil to make several differentiations simultaneously on several levels: (1) differentiation between trade and government; (2) identification of patterns of government for each country; (3) con-

Rhetorical questions

Probing questions

AVOID

trasting trade patterns between three countries, which involves three pairs of contrasts: (4) contrasting governmental patterns in three countries, calling for three pairs of contrasts; (5) isolating the differences in governments from the similarities; and (6) generalizing what is similar about these trade patterns on one hand and governmental patterns on the other (Taba, 1967, pp. 120–21).

After having done all of this—assuming that you understand what must be done *and* can do it—you may be ready to answer the question. The obvious implication is that before asking a question—*any* question—it's essential to consider the skills the students must employ to produce an answer.

Levels of Questions

Can you distinguish between a low-level and a higher-level question? A question like "In what country did the Yir Yoront live?" for example, might be referred to as low-level, while a question like "What do you think happened to the Yir Yoront after the missionaries left?" would be considered higher-level. What makes one question "higher" than another? The basic criterion is complexity—more specifically, the complexity of the cognitive (thinking) skills required to complete the task or answer the question. Thus, higher-level questions require more complex cognitive skills than lower-level questions.

Probably the most common standard for identifying cognitive complexity is the hierarchical ranking of thinking skills provided by *The Taxonomy of Educational Objectives: Cognitive Domain* (Bloom and Krathwohl, 1956), more commonly known as Bloom's Taxonomy. We presented a fairly complete version of the Taxonomy in Chapter Three. A much-shortened version of the Taxonomy is presented here to illustrate how it is possible to identify skills-based questions or tasks that correspond to the various cognitive levels. Once again we have used the content from the Stone Axes case study as the basis for our questions. Note that not all categories of the Taxonomy can (or should) be used with the Stone Axes case study.

1.00 Knowledge
1.10   Knowledge of specifics
    1.11   *Knowledge of terminology*—What terms and symbols will your students need to know?
        Possible question: "What does *technological* mean?"

Knowledge-level questions

    1.12   *Knowledge of specific facts*—What specific facts will your students need to know? (names of the states, chief exports of Brazil, properties of H_2SO_4, etc.)
        Possible question: "In what country did the Yir Yoront live?"
1.20   Knowledge of ways and means of dealing with specifics
    1.21   *Knowledge of conventions*—What sets of rules will your students need to know? (e.g., rules of etiquette, rules of punctuation)
        Possible question: (No previous knowledge of rules or conventions applies.)
    1.22   *Knowledge of trends and sequences*—What awareness of trends and sequences will your students need to have? (e.g., nature of evolution,

changes in attitudes about the role of women in American society)
Possible question: "What has happened in other societies in which technological changes have been introduced?"

1.23 *Knowledge of classifications and categories*—What classification and category schemes will your students need to know? (e.g., types of literature, types of business ownership, types of government)
Possible question: (No previously identified classification or category scheme applies.)

1.24 *Knowledge of criteria*—What sets of criteria will your students need to be able to apply? (e.g., factors to consider in judging the nutritional value of a meal)
Possible question: (No predetermined criteria apply.)

1.25 *Knowledge of methodology*—What sorts of methodology will your students need to master? (ways to solve problems in math, set up an experiment in chemistry, etc.)
Possible task: Identify and formulate a generalizable statement based on the Stone Axes incident.

1.30 Knowledge of the universals and abstractions in a field

1.31 *Knowledge of principles and generalizations*—What general principles will your students need to know? (e.g., laws of heredity, laws of motion)
Possible task: Identify the consequences of technological change.

1.32 *Knowledge of theories and structures*—What general theories will your students need to know? (e.g., nature of free enterprise system, theory of evolution)
Possible question: "What does the situation indicate about the nature of cultural change?"

2.00 Comprehension

2.10 *Translation*—Ability to put a communication into another form. What sorts of translations will your students need to perform? (e.g., state problems in own words, read a musical score, translate words and phrases from a foreign language, interpret a diagram, tell the meaning of a political cartoon)
Possible question: "In your own words, describe what happened to the Yir Yoront."

2.20 *Interpretation*—Ability to reorder ideas, comprehend interrelationships. What sorts of interpretations will your students need to be able to make? (e.g., gather data from a variety of sources and prepare an organized report)
Possible question: "What actually happened to the Yir Yoront?" or "What was the cause of the Yir Yoront predicament?"

2.30 *Extrapolation*—Ability to go beyond given data. What sorts of extrapolations will your students need to make? (e.g., theorize about what might happen if . . ., draw conclusions from given sets of data, predict trends)
Possible question: "What do you think happened to the Yir Yoront after the missionaries left?"

3.00 Application
Ability to apply principles to actual situations. What sorts of applications will your students need to make? (e.g., apply principles of civil liberties to current events)

Higher-level questions

Possible question (assuming a previous study of "change begets change"): "What idea have we studied that explains the Yir Yoront episode?"

4.00 Analysis

Ability to distinguish and comprehend interrelationships, make critical analyses. What kinds of analyses will your students have to make? (e.g., discuss how democracy and communism differ, be able to detect logical fallacies in an argument)

Possible task: Identify at least three "cause-effect" relationships.

5.00 Synthesis

Ability to rearrange component ideas into a new whole. What kinds of syntheses will your students need to make? (plan a program or a panel discussion, write a comprehensive term paper, etc.)

Possible task: Devise a plan that might avoid the "negative" consequences that resulted from the missionaries' actions.

6.00 Evaluation

Ability to make judgments based on internal evidence or external criteria. What sorts of evaluations will your students need to make? (evaluate a work of art, edit a term paper, detect inconsistencies in the speech of a politician or advocate of a given position, etc.)

Possible question: "Were the missionaries right in doing what they did?"

[Source: Adapted from an adaptation/abridgment by Robert Biehler (1974).]

On the Multiple Uses of Social Studies Content

In Chapter Three we illustrated that two cans of corn could be used as the basis for a variety of legitimate instructional activities. In this chapter we have suggested that the Stone Axes case study could also be used in several different ways—ways determined largely by how a teacher might wish to use it, and by the kinds of questions he or she asks about it. In both instances, the principle we are illustrating is that of *content utilization,* the fact that content—in this case, social studies content—can be used in a variety of different ways.

Content utilization revisited

How might you use the Stone Axes case study? Consider the following: (1) as an informal diagnostic reading test (which really isn't social studies); (2) as an ethnographic case study of a primitive tribe; (3) as an example of what may happen when one isolated group comes into contact with another culture, or when a technological innovation is introduced into a culture; (4) as a data base to test previously identified hypotheses (e.g., "Is a change in one thing likely to cause other changes?"); (5) as a vehicle for teaching cognitive skills—hypothesizing, analyzing, inferential thinking, etc.; (6) as a source of speculative-heuristic questions to initiate student inquiry; (7) as a situation or vehicle for asking students to make evaluative judgments (e.g., "Were the missionaries right?"); and (8) as a springboard for further inquiry and research.

When students *use* social studies content, they also learn the content in the process. Students cannot, for example, analyze the Stone Axes case study without learning something about what happened to the Yir

Yoront. In other words, even though we used the case study as a vehicle for illustrating the different levels of questions you could ask, you undoubtedly *learned* something about it as well. Were your students to use the case study as a source for generating hypotheses, for example, they would actually be learning to use social studies content as they go along. Think about it.

For Every Purpose There Is a Question While a purpose underlies every question a teacher asks, the place that teachers begin their planning is not with questions but with their purposes for using content. Once you have a purpose for using content, the questions follow naturally.

To put it algebraically, the issue would be one of:

$$\text{Purpose} + \text{Content} = \text{Questions}$$

Even that is not quite accurate, however, since you may be forced into the situation of determining purposes for using predetermined content such as that found in a social studies textbook. Or, you may have a purpose in mind, such as improving your students' library research skills, but need to identify content on which their research can focus. This will influence the kinds of questions you pose to the students. Thus, the following statement more accurately depicts the situation most teachers face:

$$\text{Purpose} \leftrightarrow \text{Content} = \text{Questions}$$

Question posing acts as a system of relating purposes and content—a key factor in any teaching strategy.

Questioning and Thinking Patterns

The relationship between teachers' questions and children's thinking patterns was the focus of some significant educational research noted earlier, that of the late Hilda Taba and her associates. One of Taba's contributions is the technique of *cognitive mapping,* a way of graphically illustrating the thinking processes that children use in approaching content. For example, when third-grade children were confronted with the heuristic question, "What would happen to the way of life in the desert if sufficient water became available?" the following discussion ensued.

Discussion excerpt

Sequence	Speaker	
(1)	Teacher	Think about the boys and girls of the desert and the big changes that might happen if they had water.
(2)	Gary	Lots of people will start moving there.
(3)		They would have a big city with schools.
(4)		They would have machines and streets and cars.
(5)(6)		They won't need the animals, because the people will go to school and learn how to drive cars.
(7)	Mary	When they have cars and everything they would be more like our country.
(8)		They could learn from the things that we do.

Figure 6.3
Translation of a
Discussion Excerpt
into a Cognitive
Map (Grade 3)

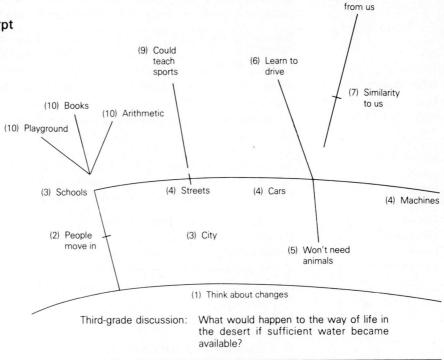

Third-grade discussion: What would happen to the way of life in the desert if sufficient water became available?

Source: Taba (1967, p. 67).

(9)   Alan   If they have streets like we do, we could teach them some of our sports.

(10)   Andria   They could have better schools, bigger playgrounds, and better books to read. They could have a new type of arithmetic (Taba, 1967, p. 67).

This discussion excerpt was then depicted in graphic form (Figure 6.3), with the innermost horizontal representing the most immediate consequences or predictions (e.g., "people will move in") and the most distant horizontal lines reflecting higher levels of cognitive thought, that is, predictions that are several causal leaps beyond the more immediate ones.

In random discussions, where individuals share opinions but the discussion never seems to lead anywhere, a teacher's questions aren't especially important. But in discussions that are intended to help move children from Point A to Point B or Point C, the kinds of questions you ask, as well as the pace or speed at which you ask them, become much more critical. For one thing, there is a tendency for teachers to move to higher levels of questioning once they've received a desired response to a lower-level question. A problem can arise when only one student (the one who answered the lower-level question) is ready to move on to a higher level; the rest of the class may be lost.

Pacing your
questions

As Taba (1967, p. 123) observed, "The decision about how much time to spend on each level—pacing—must take into account the necessity for allowing at least the majority of the class to participate...."

Sequencing Questions The question many prospective teachers ask is "What questions should I ask when?" There are no hard-and-fast answers, but Taba (1967) has suggested a practical, three-question sequence which is applicable to many situations. The questions are: "What?" "Why?" and "What does it mean?"

What? Why? What does it mean?

We have applied this questioning sequence in the example that follows. The purpose of each question is indicated in italics. Notice especially that the questions are *not* asked one after the other, in rapid-fire order, but follow the overall "what-why-what-does-it-mean?" pattern. Note also that we have omitted the student responses for brevity and because our focus is on the functions these questions serve in the lesson.

Sample questioning strategy

T: What happened in *this* incident [the Stone Axe case study]?
(Function: Focusing—What?)
S: Response
T: Did anyone notice anything else?
(Function: Eliciting and extending thought at same level)
S: Response
S: Response
S: Response
T: Is there anything else we've missed?
(Function: Eliciting and extending)
T: OK. But why did this happen?
(Function: Lifting thought to another level—Why?)
S: Response
S: Response
T: You mean you think the missionaries were responsible?
(Function: Clarifying and extending)
S: Response
T: But do you think the missionaries were responsible for increased crime?
(Function: Lifting thought to another level)
S: Response
T: What caused the problems—the steel axes or the missionaries?
(Function: Clarifying and extending)
S: Response
T: Anyone else have a different idea?
(Function: Extending thought at the same level)
S: Response
S: Response
T: OK, but what does all of this mean?
(Function: Lifting thought to another level—What does it mean?)
S: Response
S: Response
S: Response

T: Well, then, are you suggesting that a lot of changes resulted from this one intervention?

(Function: Clarifying and extending)

S: Response

T: If the missionaries were coming anyhow, what might they have used other than steel axes?

(Function: Refocusing)

S: . . . .

The questions you ask will depend on the function you want them to serve; it should be apparent that questions can serve several functions. Those we've used are based primarily on Taba, but we've added some of our own.

Focusing

One of the most important functions questions serve is that of *focusing*. Such questions set the stage for whatever is to follow. The question "What?" serves this function, as well as serving to make certain that students understand the facts of the situation.

The questions "Why?" and "What does it mean?" serve to shift the thinking from one level to another. In the "Stone Axes" example, the question "Why?" lifts the level from the enumeration of facts to a consideration of why the events took place. The *why* question also asks students to analyze the interaction between the events that took place. Finally, the question "What does it mean?" asks students to assess the significance of the incident or events, and may also lead to a generalizable statement such as "A change in one thing may cause lots of other changes."

Wait Time

"Whenever we have a discussion, the same kids participate all of the time and the rest of the class just sits there. Sometimes the students that do talk don't have much to say—it's all very superficial. I don't know. I'm about ready to give up on discussions."

Frustrated teachers have been echoing complaints like this for years. Yet a potential solution to their problem is so simple that it's easily and often overlooked. The solution takes no special skills and has achieved dramatic results where it's been employed. What is it? Doing nothing. Well, almost nothing.

What's the rush?

In some fascinating research conducted several years ago, Mary Budd Rowe (1969, pp. 11–13) examined the relationship between a teacher's wait time and the quality of their classroom discussions. *Wait time* refers to the period of silence between the end of a teacher's question and the teacher's next statement or question. Rowe found that most teachers are apparently unwilling to tolerate silence during a discussion, because their average wait time was only nine-tenths of a second. No wonder students didn't participate! They didn't have time to think before the teacher went on with another comment or question.

After Rowe informed teachers just how short their wait time was, they decided to double it—at least to two seconds. Awkwardly at first, the teachers waited the allotted time. For some of them it seemed like an eternity, but they waited, all two seconds. The results? The number of students participating in class discussions improved dramatically, as did the quality of their contributions. When teachers also lengthened the period of silence between a student's response and the teacher's next comment or question—what Rowe called "Wait Time II"—the results were even more impressive. Even more students responded, including some who almost never participated, while the quality of the discussions improved as well.

The implication is clear: if your discussions don't go well and the same students participate all the time, try lengthening your wait time. If you do that and your discussions still don't go well, you may need to reexamine the kinds of questions you are asking.

Summary

A *teaching strategy* refers to a teacher's overall plan of organization. *Teaching techniques* refer to the day-to-day instructional activities (films, discussions, etc.) teachers use in interacting with students. On any given day, a teacher might use several teaching techniques, such as showing a film, directing a discussion, and presenting a mini-lecture. However, developing a teaching strategy is not simply a matter of mixing together a series of interchangeable teaching techniques. Rather, each of the basic teaching strategies we identified—expository (lecture-type), guided discussion, and inquiry (or discovery)—embodies different assumptions and somewhat different activities on the part of both teachers and students. On a continuum, expository teaching strategies are the most teacher-centered, inquiry-oriented strategies are the most student-centered, and guided discussion falls somewhere between the two extremes.

The more student-centered the strategy a teacher develops is, the more important that teacher's questions become. We identified five categories of questions that teachers might ask, all of which were identified in terms of the skills they require of students in order to answer them. Those categories are: memory-recall, descriptive-interpretive, application-synthesis, evaluative-judgmental, and speculative-heuristic. We also identified two other categories of questions which, although not keyed to thinking skills, a teacher might ask in the course of a lesson. Those categories of questions are: rhetorical and probing. (We actually identified a third type of question—multi-focus —which should be avoided; the questions are too confusing for students to handle.)

In addition to the key role they play in most teaching strategies, the questions teachers pose largely determine the way in which students will use social studies content. If most questions are of the memory-recall type, for example, the teacher's emphasis will be on having children know the content itself, not use it. Higher-level questions—that is, higher in terms of their level on the *Taxonomy of Educational Objectives*—are more likely to demand that your students use content. This doesn't make lower, knowledge-level questions "bad," however. Memory-recall-level (knowledge-level) questions can be used to determine if students have desired information in their possession. The goal, in most instances, however, is to move beyond the knowledge level.

The essence of teaching social studies—or any subject area—is not defined solely in terms of *what* one knows, but also in terms of how one *uses* what one knows. We can't be guaranteed that as students use social studies content in the classroom, they will automatically transfer this use to their outside activities—factors beyond our control will influence that action. However, the hope is that we will have provided students with the skills and training that enable them to make that transfer.

Suggested Activities

1   Select teacher's editions of a first- or second-grade and a fifth- or sixth-grade social studies text. Then, using Bloom's *Taxonomy* as a basis, analyze the recommended questions or tasks for one unit in each book. Determine what proportion of questions/tasks reflects each of the six levels of the *Taxonomy*.

2   Observe a children's television program, such as *Sesame Street, The Electric Company*, etc., and determine what teaching strategies are used most often.

3   Observe a fifteen-minute segment of the television program *Romper Room* (or a video tape of any class in which the teacher interacts with children) and determine what proportion of time is spent on (1) maintaining discipline, (2) direct (teacher-led) instruction, and (3) student interaction.

4   The more student-centered a teacher's strategy, the more important that teacher's questions become. Although their questions are important, inquiry-oriented teachers may actually ask fewer questions in the course of a lesson than teachers who employ other teaching strategies. How would you explain this?

References

Beyer, Barry K. *Inquiry in the Social Studies Classroom.* Columbus, OH: Charles E. Merrill, 1971.

Bloom, Benjamin S., and Krathwohl, David. R. *Taxonomy of Educational Objectives: Classification of Educational Goals: Handbook I: Cognitive Domain.* New York: Longman, 1956.

Bruner, Jerome. *The Process of Education.* Cambridge, MA: Harvard University Press, 1960.

Carpenter, Helen McCracken. "The Role of Skills in Elementary Social Studies." *Social Education* 31 (March 1967): 219–21, 233.

Chase, Stuart. *The Proper Study of Mankind: An Inquiry into the Science of Human Relations.* New York: Harper & Row, 1963.

Fenton, Edwin. *The New Social Studies.* New York: Holt, Rinehart and Winston, 1967.

Gross, Richard E., and McDonald, Frederick J. "Classroom Methods: The Problem-Solving Approach." *Phi Delta Kappan* 34 (March 1958): 259–65.

Olsvanger, Immanuel (Ed.). *Röyte Pomerantsen.* New York: Schocken, 1947. English translation from Nathan Ausbel, *A Treasury of Jewish Folklore.* New York: Crown, 1948.

Rogers, Vincent R. "A Macrocosmic Approach to Inquiry." *Social Education* 34 (January 1970): 74–77.

Rowe, Mary Budd. "Science, Silence, and Sanctions." *Science and Children* 6 (March 1969): 11–13.

Skeel, Dorothy J., and Decaroli, Joseph G. "The Role of the Teacher in an Inquiry Centered Classroom." *Social Education* 33 (May 1969): 547–50.

Taba, Hilda. *Teachers' Handbook for Elementary Social Studies.* (Introductory ed.) Menlo Park, CA: Addison-Wesley, 1967.

Williams, Reed G., and Ware, John E. "An Extended Visit with Dr. Fox: Validity of Student Satisfaction with Instructional Ratings After Repeated Exposures to a Lecturer." *American Educational Research Journal* 41 (Fall 1977): 449–57.

Suggested Readings

Barry K. Beyer. *Inquiry in the Social Studies Classroom.* Columbus, OH: Charles E. Merrill, 1971. This is a well written, step-by-step guide to inquiry teaching. It's aimed more toward secondary school teachers but upper elementary teachers will also find it useful.

Francis P. Hunkins. *Questioning Strategies and Techniques.* Boston: Allyn & Bacon, 1972. If you are interested in exploring further the realms of heuristic questions, cognitive mapping, and how the *Taxonomy* relates to questioning strategies, you will find this slender volume extremely helpful.

Bruce Joyce and Marsha Weil. *Models of Teaching.* Englewood Cliffs, NJ: Prentice-Hall, 1972. This volume will be ranked among the landmark texts in education because it was the first to reduce the mountain of literature dealing with different teaching strategies to manageable terms.

Peter H. Martorella. *Elementary Social Studies As A Learning System.* New York: Harper & Row, 1976. Martorella takes the position that different instructional objectives require different teaching models and strategies, and then demonstrates what he's talking about. Highly recommended.

Frank L. Ryan. *Exemplars for the New Social Studies.* Englewood Cliffs, NJ: Prentice-Hall, 1971. This book is organized around instructional strategies, but its real strength lies in the way it ties these strategies in with lots of practical activities.

Norris Sanders. *Classroom Questions: What Kinds?* New York: Harper & Row, 1966. This was one of the first books to relate classroom tasks and questions to the *Taxonomy of Educational Objectives.* It is still one of the best.

7 Concept-Based Instruction

Key Questions

What are concepts anyhow?

How are facts, concepts, and generalizations related?

What criteria are used in selecting the facts, concepts, and generalizations to be taught?

How do concepts "guide" teachers in instructional management?

What planning procedures are implicit in managing concept-based instruction?

Where do teachers find concepts?

Key Ideas

Concept-based instruction is intended to help students relate factual data in such a way that what they learn is more effectively organized for future use. To the extent that concepts can serve as mental organizers, they become tools for continued learning.

In concept-based instruction, the teacher's role involves the selection of content: data, concepts, and generalizations. The criteria for selection are closely tied to the nature of the social science disciplines.

The nature, kind, and functions of concepts vary according to the different content areas.

Managing concept-based instruction calls for the systematic use of facts, not the dismissal of a factual base for teaching.

Introduction: The Facts of Life, Broadly Speaking

For most children, a *class* is a group of students, a *wing* is something that a bird flies with, and a "dark horse" is just that, a large animal of dark coloration. In social studies, terms such as these have special meanings—meanings that go beyond the concrete representations most children are familiar with. For example, no child (or adult) will ever see a social "class" or a political "wing," since both are abstractions; they are phenomena we can describe in words but for which there are no physical manifestations. And should a child meet a political candidate in person, the explanation as to why that individual is a "dark horse" may involve so many abstractions that the child doesn't understand it either.

With experience, most of us quickly adjust to the fact that many common words and expressions can have multiple meanings. We also become aware that terms such as *capital* or *marginal utility,* can have specialized meanings. Through the medium of language, we are able to describe phenomena that are either real or hypothetical (abstract). Sometimes, we experience a phenomenon, such as a compelling desire for water or other liquids, and then learn of a term to describe that sensation—*thirst.* In other instances, we may become aware of a term, such as *democracy,* first, and then identify the phenomena to which it refers. Yet regardless of how we first learn to connect words with the experiences or things they refer to, most of us continually engage in the process of refining those connections in order to explain ourselves and the things we experience more precisely.

Whether or not we actually think in words is a matter of speculation. Infants who are unable to speak, and yet demonstrate evidence of the ability to think, stand in mute testimony to this question. Nevertheless it is apparent that words, ideas, and clusters of words and ideas play a role in thinking, even if we can't describe that role as precisely as we might like to. Despite this, it's also apparent that all of us organize and process ideas and events, the things we think about and the things that happen to us in the course of our experience. So although we can't see thinking itself, we can see the products of someone's thinking. By analyzing those products—the things that people say and do—it is possible to work backwards and attempt to infer what went on inside someone's brain. As an example of this, reflect on what you do in order to answer the following question: *What day follows the day before yesterday if two days from now will be Sunday?* (Whimbey, 1977). Some individuals break the problem into smaller, more manageable tasks and then deal with each of them separately. Other individuals may try a more wholistic (though random) approach, while still others simply try to guess the correct answer. Of course, those who guess *Thursday* are just as correct as those who work out the answer more systematically.

Many specialists believe that the thinking skills required to answer the problem posed above differ from the sorts of skills required to learn multiple meanings for terms such as *class* or *wing.* These differences form the basis for the *Taxonomy of Educational Objectives: Cognitive Domain* (Bloom, et al., 1956), which we dealt with earlier. In this chapter our focus is on a metaskill, that is, a thinking skill that crosscuts all levels and types of thinking behavior. Our focus is on the different ways in which individuals make sense of and deal with the millions of experiences they have.

Think of what life would be like if we didn't devise systems for organizing and dealing with our experiences. We would have millions of tidbits of information floating randomly around inside our heads; we'd be adrift in a sea of trivia. This doesn't happen, of course, because most of us develop the ability (or metaskill) to cluster related experiences together in some type of personally meaningful way. This process—grouping ideas and experiences in meaningful ways—is called *conceptualizing.* The various clusters (or categories) of ideas or experience are referred to as *concepts.*

The power of language

Conceptualizing –

grouping ideas & experiences in meaningful ways.

In the first part of this chapter, we examine the nature of concepts and conceptualizing and the role they play in teaching social studies. We then examine how concepts are related to facts and generalizations, and look at why some concepts and ideas are considerably easier to teach and learn than others. Finally, we present two examples of how you might organize your teaching around concepts.

The Nature of Concepts

No one has ever seen a concept. But then no one has ever seen an idea either. Both are mental contructs that we presume to exist because we see their effects in what people say and do. In fact, were it not for concepts, we would have nothing with which to organize the vast array of experiences all of us encounter.

The organizing function of concepts can be illustrated through a vastly oversimplified example, one in which the human memory is thought of as a complex conglomeration of mental pigeonholes not unlike a kind of postal sorting system. Each of these mental pigeonholes is labeled with something —usually called a *concept*—that permits us to organize, identify, and cluster the information, experiences, memories, ideas, and whatever else we choose to place in that mental category.

Concept →

Over time, for example, each of us clusters a host of color-related experiences with something called red (or blue, or green). Also included in that cluster is the three-letter word, *red,* which describes and has come to be associated with that color. To eliminate some potential confusion later on, it's important to note that a word is not a concept; it's a symbol that has come to stand for a cluster of ideas and/or experiences, all of which (in this instance) have something about redness associated with them. Our point here is probably best exemplified by the blind, who have heard and learned the word *red* but lack the visual referents and experiences that permit the sighted to build a concept with which red can be associated. As a result, the blind may associate *red, blue, green,* etc., with something called *color* on an abstract level, but it's doubtful that they can go much beyond that.

Concepts as idea clusters

a word is a symbol.

What does all of this have to do with teaching social studies? We'll get to that basic question in a moment, but first we need to develop our redness example a step further.

Early on you attained your concept of red (and we say "your concept" advisedly, since concept formation is a personal thing that takes place inside one's head). That's why no one has ever seen *a* concept, much less your concepts. Anyway, once you thought you understood "redness," you probably tested your discovery by pointing to something, a fire truck perhaps, and saying "red?" The resulting expression of approval confirmed the fact that you had attained the concept, even though you probably didn't think of it in those terms.

Testing concepts

With experience, it usually isn't long before most of us realize that our existing conceptual pigeonholes are inadequate and must be reshuffled or reorganized to accommodate new ideas. After attaining a concept of "redness," for example, it usually isn't too long before one discovers that some things related to *red* just don't fit the existing scheme. An expression such as "seeing red" is only distantly related to color, and referring to a person as "a Red" indicates a great deal that has nothing at all to do with it. This condition, where new information or experience doesn't "fit" our existing conceptual schemes, is an example of the cognitive dissonance discussed in Chapter Six. When individuals say "I don't understand this," they are proba- bly indicating that their existing conceptual structure—their pigeonhole system, if you will—cannot accommodate the new information. In fact, it's doubtful whether children will understand "seeing red" or "redneck" *until* they have expanded their color-related concept while simultaneously rear- ranging, re-cross-referencing, or creating new mental categories to assimi- late these experiences. Once they have done this, we should find (if we could look inside their heads) that, clustered in among the ideas making up their concept cluster "anger," is the expression "to see red." Similarly, their con- cept cluster "Communist" (assuming they have such a concept to begin with) will have grown to incorporate "Red."

Accommodating
new ideas

The process of rearranging our mental pigeonholes to absorb new experi- ences and information (thereby eliminating cognitive dissonance) is what Piaget called *accommodation.* And most of us, like Piaget, would consider it an essential dimension of learning. How does all of this relate to teaching social studies? As John Michaelis (1968, p. 73) put it:

> There is general agreement that fragmented knowledge, isolated facts, and descriptive information should be replaced by a cohesive set of ideas. The learner can use such a set of ideas to organize information, recall facts as needed, and add new concepts as these are discovered.

The relationships among concepts, conceptualizing, and elementary social studies are fundamental to our concern for helping children organize and make manageable what would otherwise be random tidbits of information. Of course, all of us are living proof that humans can conceptualize in the absence of concept-based teaching. But confronted with an ever-expanding body of knowledge about the human experience, we think that teachers have an obligation to organize their teaching in ways that aid the conceptual- ization process.

Facts, Concepts, and Generalizations

At one time, students across America learned that Christopher Columbus (and a bunch of sailors who were with him but whom you've never heard about) discovered America in 1492. Today, a growing body of historical evidence suggests that even though Columbus may have been here in 1492, (and even though we still honor him with a national holiday) he was not the first to discover America. Although many scholars agree that Columbus didn't discover America, they don't agree upon who *did.* Some claim that the Vikings should hold that honor, while others say it belongs to ancestors of the native Americans who migrated here via Alaska.

**"I never quite thought of it that way, son, but yes
. . . you are a bachelor."**

Facts change

What were once taught as facts—as true, reliable, and almost beyond question—are no longer taught as such. But this does not alter the fact that there are still plenty of people who are unwilling to accept the premise that Columbus did *not* discover America in 1492—perhaps because they learned, *as a fact,* that he did.

The Christopher Columbus episode is one of many illustrating that facts can indeed change. It also illustrates the probabilistic nature of almost all the information that social studies teachers deal with. New information is continually changing the way we interpret old information. It's true, of course, that a fact dealing with the length of the Mississippi River, for example, isn't likely to change (although it could), but new information could very well lead historians to reinterpret events that led to the river's discovery. The tentativeness of almost all knowledge—facts or otherwise—is something that every social studies teacher must reckon with.

The *probability* that most facts will accurately reflect whatever they're supposed to is high enough that we need not question it further. However, once you move beyond commonly accepted facts to statements of a more general nature, the probability factor changes. No one can say, for example, that a change in one aspect of life will *always* lead to other changes; a change usually leads to other changes, but not always. That's the nature of generalizations; they are generally true, but not always true. This phenomenon— the probabilistic nature of general statements—may help to explain why social studies is sometimes viewed as a subject area where, once you get beyond the basic facts, there are no "right answers."

Accuracy and reliability

Earlier we suggested that the synthetic nature of social studies is a factor that contributes to the absence of absolute "right" answers. Another facet of that situation should become apparent if you examine some of the different kinds of statements and ideas that social studies deals with, as illustrated below.

Instructions:

1 Complete the following line:

I, _____, was born on _____ _____, _____.
       (name)   (month) (day) (year)

2 Now, compare your statement with the following:

The Declaration of Independence was signed in 1776.

3 What similarities do you notice?

_____

_____

UN: unique and nonrepetitive

Both statements can be considered facts, and both may be equally important, at least to you. But note that both statements also describe unique events, neither of which will ever occur again in exactly the same form. In other words, both are nonrepeatable. Such statements reflect what Mallan and Hersh (1972, pp. 154–156) call UN concepts; they describe an event or experience that is *unique* (U) and *nonrepetitive* (N)—something that happened once and will not happen again.

Elementary social studies books are loaded with UN concept statements, e.g., "The capital of Virginia is Richmond." But they hardly stop there. Included are several other kinds of statements, an assortment of which are shown below. You should be able to spot and identify the UN concept statements with ease, but try your hand at identifying some of the others.

1 The British burned Washington D.C. during the War of 1812.
2 Patriotism.
3 Diminishing marginal utility: as the number of desired articles increases, the less useful or valuable each succeeding one becomes. (In other words, the fifteenth ice-cream cone eaten at a single sitting is likely to add less pleasure and be less desired than the first ice-cream cone.)
4 People should be good neighbors.
5 John F. Kennedy was assassinated in Dallas, Texas.
6 A change in one aspect of life often leads to other changes.
7 A good citizen is one who votes.
8 Community.
9 Community needs are met by groups of people engaged in many related fields (Durkin, et al., 1969).
10 Economics is the study of how resources are allocated.

Facts (UN Concept Statements)

Statements that describe unique events or phenomena which will not occur again are among the easiest to identify. Statements 1 and 5 fall into this category.

A brief note about terminology may be in order here, especially if you find referring to long familiar facts as "UN concept statements" a little troublesome. Our purpose is twofold: (1) to indicate that what people may call *facts* can often include a variety of kinds of statements, and (2) to describe factual statements in terms of their characteristics—as referring to unique (U) and nonrepeatable (N) events or phenomena. As long as you understand those characteristics, it isn't essential that you adopt our terminology.

Cue Concepts

Statements 2 and 8, patriotism and community, may look innocent enough but they are actually among the more difficult to deal with. Traditionally, they would simply be called *concepts,* without any descriptors attached. However, we think that equating a word with a mental construct or category can cause considerable confusion as to the nature of concept-based instruction.

Words such as *community, patriotism,* or *red* serve to *cue* (or point) us to a particular mental idea cluster (assuming, of course, that we've had the necessary prior experience with color or whatever). In other words, a question such as "What is your concept of patriotism (or community)?" actually asks the individual to go into her intellect (pigeonhole system, if you will) to retrieve the ideas, meanings, etc. that are clustered around those terms. We define such terms based on their function; they are concept labels or *cue concepts.*

Once an individual locates the idea cluster she associates with the terms *community* or *patriotism,* which can be done within a fraction of a second, she is usually able to answer the above question with a statement that captures the essential characteristics or qualities of her concept. Ofttimes the verbal rendering of a concept takes the form of a definition, such as those illustrated in Statements 3 and 10. For instance, when asked "What's your concept of community?" an individual might respond, "It's an area where people live." That individual's concept of community may or may not include ideas associated with common interests or work, as in "farming communities," "college communities," or "community of scholars." If not, a teacher could direct instruction toward these ideas, thus adding new and/or related ideas to an individual's existing notion.

Definitions

On one hand, concepts are highly personal; your concepts exist in your intellect and no one else's. On the other hand, one of the purposes of schooling is to depersonalize concepts, that is, to give them something of a standardized meaning. If we didn't standardize concepts to some extent, communication would be, at most, impossible. It would be a world where, as Humpty Dumpty said in *Through the Looking Glass,* everyone would use terms to "mean just what they choose them to mean." The dictionary, of course, reflects a collective attempt to standardize the language. And when you look up a word such as *community,* for which our dictionary lists seven definitions, you may find yourself adding a new idea to your existing idea cluster (concept) while simultaneously participating in standardizing the language, or at least standardizing, to some extent, the way *you* use it.

Standardized meanings

So much of social studies depends on learning the meanings for such cue concepts as economy, capital, and marginal utility (to name just a few) that it has become fairly standard to begin instruction with a definition-learning session. The approach is like that found in many vocabulary lessons: "Here's a new word, and this is what it means." What often happens, however, is that teachers find themselves defining one abstract term with other abstract terms. In fact, it may not be until they get to a practical example, such as the ice-cream cones in our example of diminishing marginal utility (Statement 3) that the children begin to add meaning to the abstractions and, hence, to the definition itself.

The irony here is that the underlying idea of diminishing marginal utility isn't all that difficult to grasp; it's even been successfully taught to first graders in a somewhat modified form. In dealing with definitions, the problem you encounter may stem not from the difficulty of the ideas but from the abstract nature of the terms that describe them.

The first teaching implication here should be fairly obvious: when faced with teaching the definitions for abstract terms, come armed with several practical (concrete) examples that the students will understand. If those examples come from your students' experiences, so much the better. The second implication is probably less obvious and involves the option of *building* definitions as opposed to teaching them by telling. This strategy is illustrated in the following example, drawn from S. I. Hayakawa's *Language in Thought and Action* (1964, p. 64). In this instance, the object in question is a *shrdlu*. Note: The idea here is not to identify a one-word synonym for *shrdlu* but rather to build a more comprehensive definition.

Building a definition

examples!

1   He was exceptionally skillful with a shrdlu.
2   He says he needs a shrdlu to shape the beams.
3   I saw Mr. Jenkins yesterday buying a new handle for his shrdlu.
4   The steel head of Jenkins' shrdlu was badly chipped.
5   Don't bother with a saw or an ax; a shrdlu will do the job faster and better.

Definition: A *shrdlu* _____

_____

By building a definition from examples, you are in effect building a concept—a cluster of related ideas and functions—that can be associated with something, in this case with a *shrdlu*.

Definition learning is clearly an aspect of concept-based instruction, but only one aspect. Just as concepts provide each of us with a way of organizing and making sense out of our experiences, concept-based instruction is a way of organizing teaching so that it focuses on ideas and experiences that are related (or clustered) in some meaningful way. A cue concept, then, can serve as an organizing theme which can help students make sense out of what might otherwise be random tidbits of information. And the purpose of concept-oriented teaching is to provide children with ways in which they can organize the information and experiences they encounter.

Value Concepts

expresses desired or valued behaviors

On the list on page 210, Statements 4 and 7, "People should be good neighbors" and "A good citizen is one who votes," express desired or valued behaviors. In some respects, Statement 7 could be regarded as a definition, but good citizens do more than just vote (or at least we think they should), so it's only a partial definition at best. In fact, the task of providing a complete definition for "good neighbor," "good citizen," or "good anything" involves so many subjective elements that it's nearly impossible to accomplish. Is a "good citizen" one who obeys the law, who protests what he or she feels are unjust laws, or both? Because the criteria for judging "good citizenship" are largely subjective and therefore open to many different interpretations, statements of this type are identified as *value concept statements*.

The difference between value concepts, which are not universally agreed upon, and their more descriptive cousins, UN concepts such as "The Mississippi is the longest river in the United States," lies in the criteria used to assess them. The criteria for determining which ideas or behaviors should be associated with value concepts are largely subjective. The cluster of ideas (concept) that you associate with "good student," for example, may or may not include "getting good grades," "working hard," or "working hard but getting poor grades." Many individuals will offer their opinions on what they think constitutes a "good student," but what *you* think is clearly a matter of your own judgment. The criteria for descriptive concepts tend to be more objective and, hence, considerably more standardized. Although an individual may not be aware of all the attributes of *community,* for example, those characteristics are generally agreed upon and, thus, not likely to generate a heated debate.

Subjective criteria

Distinguishing between descriptive and value concepts has implications for what teachers do in the context of values education. From this perspective, values clarification is a process for identifying and becoming aware of the subjective criteria we associate with value concepts like good citizen, good student, or good neighbor. It also offers students (and others) a perspective from which a teacher's behavior can be observed. When teachers make statements such as, "Good neighbors are people who mow their lawns and keep their yards neat," they may well be treating a value concept (good neighbor) as if it were a descriptive concept. If students come away from a discussion of "good neighbors" thinking of it as a descriptive concept characterized by lawn mowing and keeping one's yard neat, the teacher has probably practiced a subtle form of indoctrination.

Value vs. descriptive concepts

Generalizations (GR Concept Statements)

Statements 6 and 9 on page 210, "A change in one aspect of life often leads to other changes," and "Community needs are met by groups of people engaged in many related fields," are examples of *generalizations.* They are broad, fairly general statements that express very basic relationships among the phenomena of human experience. At times you may see such statements referred to as laws, principles, understandings, or basic findings, but to avoid getting caught up in this morass of terminology, it is helpful to examine generalizations in terms of their characteristics and functions.

"A change in one aspect of life often leads to other changes" (Statement 6) reflects an idea (or concept) that we considered in the Stone Axes case study (p. 191). As we noted there, this statement represents a category of ideas that have broad applicability and reflect things you are likely to find operating in a variety of situations. Statements in this category are also generalized insofar as they describe ways in which humans are likely to behave. A generalization, then, is a statement that describes human behavior that is *likely* to occur in a certain situation.

Functional, "If-then" Concepts   By rearranging its structure slightly, Statement 6 can be cast as an "if-then" statement that posits a functional relationship. In other words, "*If* a change in one aspect of life takes place, *then.* . . ."

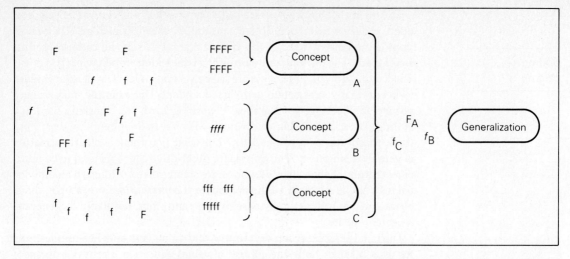

*Tools for
predicting
behavior*

experience

Similarly, the definition portion of diminishing marginal utility is such that it is already in functional form; in this case, as "something" increases, something else is going to decrease. When statements are cast in the functional "if-then" form, they become powerful tools for interpreting, analyzing, and predicting the outcomes of situations and decisions we face every day: "If I spend all of my money on bubble gum, then . . . ," or, "If I change my classroom routine, then I can anticipate . . . ," or, "If I don't study for the test, then. . . ."

Based on your experience, you are in a position to predict what may happen if you don't study for a test, for example. In other words, your experience (as well as everyone else's) can provide the basis for filling in the "then" portion of an "if-then" statement. But your experience may not be the same as everyone else's, and the "thens" are likely to differ somewhat. So it is here that the social sciences, through the systematic study of human behavior and the human enterprise, enter the picture. Based on what the social sciences have identified about human behavior, we are able to predict the "thens" with greater consistency than that provided by individual experience. For example, we are able to say with some assuredness that "If you institute a change in your classroom routine, one of the things that will probably happen is that communication among your students will increase —communication that provides them with mutual emotional support." True, your students might just sit there, apparently doing nothing. But the *probability* is fairly high that they'll talk about the changes among themselves, one way or another; at least that's what the findings from the social and behavioral sciences suggest.

Because "if-then" relationships involve probability to a greater or lesser degree, they can serve as hypotheses to be tested, confirmed, denied, or modified as they apply to specific situations. As such, you may find instances when, for example, one change does *not* lead to other changes. You might also find cases where a child's pleasure isn't satiated until he's eaten at least twenty ice-cream cones. These exceptions don't deny the validity of the general rule; they reflect the variability of the human character.

*GR: generalized
and repetitive*

Statements 6, 9, and the definition for diminishing marginal utility are examples of findings from the social sciences that reflect phenomena that are both *generalized* (G) and *repetitive* (R). As such, they can usually be cast in the form of functional "if-then" statements, even if they don't always appear that way initially. We identify generalizations of this type in terms of their function—as *GR concept statements* (see Mallan and Hersh, 1972, pp. 154–56).

Major Concepts for the Social Studies

In the mid-1960s, the Social Studies Curriculum Center at Syracuse University undertook a project to identify major concepts from the social sciences that appear to be appropriate for elementary and secondary social studies programs. As a result of those efforts, thirty-four concepts were identified within three basic areas: substantive (descriptive) concepts, value concepts, and concepts of method.

Substantive concepts
1 Sovereignty of the nation-state in the community of nations
2 Conflict—its origin, expression, and resolution
3 The industrialization-urbanization syndrome
4 Secularization
5 Compromise and adjustment
6 Comparative advantage
7 Power
8 Morality and choice
9 Scarcity
10 Input and output
11 Saving
12 The modified market economy
13 Habitat and its significance
14 Culture
15 Institution
16 Social control
17 Social change
18 Interaction

Value concepts
1 Dignity of man
2 Empathy
3 Loyalty
4 Government by consent of the governed
5 Freedom and equality

Concepts of method
1 Historical method and point of view
2 The geographical approach
3 Causation
4 Techniques and aspects of method

4.1 Observation, classification, and measurement
4.2 Analysis and synthesis
4.3 Questions and answers
4.4 Objectivity
4.5 Skepticism
4.6 Interpretation
4.7 Evaluation
4.8 Evidence

In identifying these concepts, the Center noted that they are not necessarily the most important concepts, just that they seem especially worthy of further development. To help teachers deal with concepts and concept-based instruction, the Center produced another extremely helpful publication by Verna S. Fancett et al. (1968), entitled, *Social Science Concepts and the Classroom.*

Seeking relationships among data

UN-
unique &
non-repetitive

GR- generalization
concept statement

Creating GR concepts

Teaching Implications   Generalizations are among the most abstract phenomena you will encounter in teaching elementary social studies. Before either you or your students can deal with a generalization such as "Regional specialization encourages interdependent trade relations among nations" (Dempsey, 1972, p. 147), you must bring meaning to at least four cue concepts—*regional specialization, interdependent, trade relations,* and *nations.* Should your students be unable to bring meaning to any one of the cue concepts, the entire statement will be meaningless. What this implies in terms of actual teaching practice is a building process, one in which an ever-increasing body of experience is developed upon which your students can bring meaning to increasingly more general, more sophisticated (and more abstract) concepts. Concepts and generalizations are the result of our ability, as humans, to create abstract relationships among our experiences—the facts of life, if you will—as illustrated below.

On one hand, distinguishing between UN and GR concepts may seem to complicate the never-never land of educational jargon. But the distinction is intended to help simplify a complex situation by operationally defining the different kinds of data that social studies teachers must deal with.

We are of the opinion that once you move beyond the facts—the UN concept statements—most of the information you will be expected to deal with in teaching social studies will be of the GR kind. Some information is just more generalizable and more repetitive than other information, and most generalizations can be stated in a GR form. For example, a generalization like "Regional specialization encourages interdependent trade relations among nations" could be rephrased as "If regional specialization occurs, then interdependent trade relations among nations will be encouraged" and so on. The result is a fundamental and almost universally repetitive (GR) concept statement.

Although we have followed the convention of presenting generalizations as a category separate from concepts, it may not be as separate as we've made it appear. The difference between a GR concept statement and a generalization is more likely to be one of degree, not kind.

Terminology Review

Terms	*Referents*
UN concept statements Also known as facts.	A statement describing unique, nonrepetitive phenomena, e.g., "The first American flag had thirteen white stars"; "Abraham Lincoln was born on February 12, 1809"
Definitions Note: Some definitions (such as the one for diminishing marginal utility) may be expressed as functional, "if-then" statements.	A written or verbal rendering of a concept that expresses its characteristics or attributes, e.g., *bank:* the funds of a gambling establishment; *love:* never having to say you're sorry
Value concept statements Also known as value statements.	A statement expressing a desired behavior, rule of conduct, or judgment, e.g., "A good citizen is one who votes"; "Democrats are better than Republicans"; "Republicans are better than Democrats"
Cue concept Also known as concept, subconcept and, at times, subgeneralization.	A word or phrase that identifies a mental class, a mental construct, or a cluster of related phenomena, e.g., patriotism, interdependence, regional specialization
GR concept statements Also known as principles, laws, functional concepts, theories, "if-then" statements, functional generalizations and, at times, understandings.	A statement expressing, in various degrees of probability, the existence of a generalized and repetitive relationship among phenomena, e.g., "A change in one thing is likely to cause other changes"; "All societies develop a means for governing and judging the conduct of their members"
Generalization Also known as an understanding, basic idea, basic generalization, basic concept, organizing idea, and unifying generalization (especially when used as organizers for a social studies program).	A statement of primary (basic or fundamental) relationships among phenomena, e.g., "Economic behavior depends upon the utilization of resources"; "Change has been a universal condition of human society"

Concepts and Goals

We've shown that the reasons so much primary emphasis is placed on concepts and concept formation are (1) because they are the building blocks from which generalizations are created, and (2) because generalizations such as "Regional specialization encourages interdependent trade relations among nations" will be meaningless unless and until students have had sufficient experience with their component concepts.

Concepts in the primary grades

Students in the primary grades can, for example, begin to bring meaning to *interdependence,* and perhaps to *regional, specialization,* even *regional specialization.* They can also begin to see these phenomena functioning in a number of different settings. The concept of interdependence, for example, certainly isn't restricted to just trade relations among nations or regional specialization. It can also help to identify relationships among the members of a family, the members of a community, and so forth. By beginning with less complex instances, the children can begin to deal with *interdependence* in meaningful ways before they are faced with considering it in relation to the generalization stated above.

The basic issue here is actually a question of where one begins. That is, after identifying a generalization, a teacher could identify the cue concepts that must be understood before the generalization will make any sense. But by beginning instruction in the so-called middle ground, teachers find that most concepts will fit into a *number* of generalizations. Interdependence, to pursue our example still further, can appear in a number of generalized contexts. These can include (but are not restricted to) some of the following generalizations and GR concept statements:

As specialization increases, interdependence also increases.

The members of a family are interdependent.

The members of a community are interdependent.

So one of the goals of social studies instruction is to help children build generalizations that explain the human experience. The route from facts, through concepts, to generalizations is neither straight nor level, however. Indeed, sometimes it's an uphill struggle. The reason social studies programs often spend so much time sightseeing in the concepts neighborhood is because, by nature, a single concept can mark the beginning of progress toward a number of generalizations.

What Makes Something Difficult?

The nature of concepts and concept-based teaching is often a difficult topic to deal with. Because of this we think it is appropriate to examine something that every student alive already knows—that some things are easier to learn than others. The question for us as teachers is *why?* What makes some things easier to learn and other things more difficult?

Teachers can make almost any subject difficult, of course, depending upon what they choose to emphasize. Yet even students whose teachers want them to know the middle names of U.S. presidents may face an easier time of it than students who face the prospect of explaining $e=mc^2$ (Einstein's

The content for generalizations can arise from a variety of media forms; it needn't exist in written words.

general theory of relativity). There is obviously something about $e=mc^2$ that makes it inherently more difficult to deal with than memorizing the fact that the *K* in James K. Polk stands for *Knox,* his mother's maiden name.

To illustrate the various facets of difficulty, we used to ask our classes "What president of the United States wore wooden false teeth?" In unison, the response was "George Washington." We then asked, "What are three major points from Washington's Farewell Address?" The response: silence! We have since learned that Washington's false teeth were constructed of ivory and gold, not wood, so that what we thought was an accurate response to our first question is now inaccurate. Nevertheless, these responses illustrate two factors involved in determining the apparent difficulty of something. First, the fact that Washington wore false teeth is characterized by its ultimate simplicity. It's a straightforward statement, plain and simple. Identifying three points from Washington's Farewell Address, however, is a more complex task that involves a number of related concepts. Not only does the number of elements increase, in this case from one thing (teeth) to three things (major points), but the three points may also involve a host of related subconcepts. When contrasted with false teeth, the notion of sovereignty, for example, is of much broader *scope.* Thus, the scope of concepts is a factor influencing their inherent difficulty: those concepts that are of broader scope are more difficult to manage than those of narrower scope.

Scope of concepts

If placed on a continuum of difficulty, the scope of complexity would look like the figure below.

Scope

Less difficult	More difficult

Narrow scope involving few concepts	Very broad scope involving many concepts

Attempting to make complex concepts or events more manageable by simplifying them or reducing the number of related subconcepts with which students must deal requires a note of caution. Several years ago, we witnessed an attempt to make American history more understandable to a group of so-called slow learners by providing them with simplified outlines of major events. Instead of the simplified "standard" version such groups had received in the past, these students were taught American history in an even more abbreviated form. But to the teachers' surprise, most students experienced even more difficulties working with the outline than they'd had with the more traditional instruction.

Beware of outlines

What had been a well-intended effort to help students actually had the opposite effect. The question, of course, was *why?* Apparently the outline was too simple, too abbreviated. It lacked the factual details that provided a context for putting major events into perspective. Without details with which to build meanings and associations, the kids found themselves confronted with the task of memorizing a list of isolated events. This experience suggests that while an outline can serve as an organizer, it is *not* the thing to be organized. You need to *know* something before its possible to put it in outline form. This may explain why many of us do an outline *after* we've written a paper, not before as we've been taught.

Conceptual distance

The phenomenon of knowing about Washington's false teeth but not knowing the major points of his Farewell Address also illustrates a second facet of conceptual difficulty, namely *conceptual distance.* This refers to the degree to which something is related to the child's experience. On one hand, kids can vicariously relate to and even sympathize with Washington's dental problems (braces wearers know about sore gums). On the other hand, Washington's Farewell Address is unlikely to be part of a child's experience, either directly or vicariously. Our task as teachers is to make it part of their experience. At the outset, however, the Farewell Address is likely to be abstract—unrelated to or at least more distant from children's life experiences—and therefore more difficult for them to deal with.

When conceptual distance is depicted on a difficulty continuum, the result is this:

Distance

Least difficult		Most difficult

Within the child's direct experience	Within the child's vicarious experience	Beyond direct or vicarious experience

Another element contributing to conceptual difficulty is illustrated by the fact that, while every state has a governor, not every city has a mayor. Some cities are run by county executives or by administrators with other titles. It is easier for children to handle concepts in which certain defining attributes are always present, such as governors, than to handle concept statements that deal with probabilities or tendencies.

On a difficulty continuum, the certainty-of-attributes dimension becomes:

Certainty of presence of attributes

Less difficult   More difficult

Attributes always present	Attributes sometimes present

Consistency and certainty also play a role in what can be called the *open-endedness* of concepts. As we noted previously, you will not get much argument about whether or not something is an apple, a table, a car, or a farm. The same is true of the concept "marriage," or at least it used to be. These notions could be considered closed, and therefore less open to misinterpretation. But concepts such as "democratic citizenship" (and "patriotism") are more open, subject to more interpretations, and consequently less reliable for communicating the same thing to different individuals. As a rule, the more open-ended the concept, the more difficult it is for the child to handle.

On our continuum, this dimension becomes:

Open-endedness

Less difficult   More difficult

"Closed," extremely reliable	Open to interpretation, less reliable

These facets of conceptual difficulty suggest that certainty and simplicity contribute to "easiness," while uncertainty and complexity contribute to the "hardness" of something. Although such a statement reeks of common sense, the trap some teachers fall into—unfortunately, we think—lies in their equating easiness with "goodness" and difficulty with "badness." In addition, they sometimes mistakenly assume that children must deal only with reliable, conjunctive, and "closed" concepts *before* they can manage more open-ended, probabilistic, relational concepts. It is really not a case of one or the other, or of one before the other, but rather of meshing both with the child's experience to the degree that it's possible to do so.

Selecting Concepts to Teach

With a universe of teaching possibilities at their disposal, most teachers discover that there just isn't time to teach everything they would like to, want to, or should. As a result, they are forced to make choices, deciding which concepts they are going to teach and which they aren't. In other words, as a teacher you will be forced into the role of selector, whether you want that role or not.

Certainty

Open vs. closed concepts

Any selection process involves identifying the criteria you'll use to do the selecting. Unfortunately, one of the most significant criteria, the *skill levels* of your students, is probably unknown at the moment. As a result, you are forced to defer specific decisions until that vital information becomes known.

Notice, however, that we resisted the temptation to use the expression *ability levels* as a criterion, even though it is sometimes used synonymously with *skills.* We refrained because we know that the problems children often encounter in trying to deal with concept-based instruction don't always depend on their abilities—in the skills sense of the term—as much as they do on their *experiences.* In other words, if you find that your students do not comprehend the concept "dependence," for example, their problem may lie not in their inability to comprehend or associate ideas, but rather in their inexperience with the ideas that, when clustered, reflect the concept. It's all too easy to suggest that by providing your students with experiences—relating to dependence in this case—that your problems will all be solved, but that's the basic idea.

Experience or skill?

Where your students' skills actually come into play—that is, when they influence your decision as to which concepts you are going to deal with—is in selecting the kinds of teaching materials to use with them. It's a situation roughly equivalent to the first time many people encounter a formal legal document. Although what is being described on a deed, for example, may be a piece of property, the terminology and description may be such that many people can't recognize the property even if they are looking at it. In an educational context, the most obvious example of this is a student with a reading skill deficiency. The child's ability to conceptualize *may* be related to his reading difficulty—but don't count on it. It is also possible that the child has difficulty only when building concepts from reading-based materials.

The kinds of experiences your students have had, and the ideas they have derived from those experiences, will play a significant role in determining the concepts they are able to deal with meaningfully. Your students' abilities enter the picture insofar as they provide a basis for determining the kinds of teaching materials to use with them. The situation isn't quite as clear-cut as we may have made it seem here, especially since your students' abilities to handle different kinds of teaching materials may be developed by having them use materials with your guidance; but the basic idea can serve as an operational guideline.

The role of experience

plays role in what concepts they are able to deal with meaningfully.

Other concept (content) selection criteria, some of which are patently obvious, include:

1. *interest*—your's and your students'

2. *values*—what you (and the community in which you teach) think is important

3. the *sophistication* of your students—which is probably related to their experiences

4. the *unifying generalizations*—as found in your curriculum guide

5 the *difficulty* (complexity) of the concepts—as identified in the previous section

6 the degree to which the concepts *reflect the ten guidements of science* (see box below)—to the extent that that is possible

---

Ten Guidements of Science

I   One should not make wild claims about human behavior and about the nature of social environments.

II   One should not pretend to "know" or cheat.

III One should not persuade others at any cost.

IV   Beliefs and knowledge claims should not appeal to prejudice or private authority.

V   One should not "hide" from others that which is not known.

VI   One should establish "truth" with evidence and logic rather than hopes and feelings.

VII One should be willing to communicate not only what one thinks one knows but also the processes and evidence upon which one's knowledge is based.

VIII One should use empirical data as the prime basis for knowing.

IX   One should honor, respect, and welcome others who challenge one's thoughts and thinking with more effective thoughts and thinking.

X   One should live with humility and in an appreciation of tolerance. (Adapted from Bronowski, 1964.)

What do the Ten Guidements have to do with content selection and use? For initial screening, one might decide to use only social studies facts, concepts and generalizations that

1   have an empirical base.

2   do not rely on a proof based on authority and private knowing.

3   do not use emotion-laden words.

4   are amenable to being used as tools in continued studies of human behavior.

5   are amenable to the application of logic in terms of pupils' cognitive development.

6   provide the ingredients for the development of explanatory power among your students.

Using the initial screening guide as a criterion for selecting facts, concepts, and generalizations, determine which, if any, of the following statements meet all six criteria. (Check those you think do, and then discuss your reasons with your colleagues.)

_____   It's raining.

_____   She looks angry.

_____   A stitch in time . . .

_____   As unemployment rises, different types of crime also rise.

_____ Fifty-two percent of eligible voters voted in the last election.

_____ The high rates of interest now being charged are a rip-off.

Exemplars of Concept-Based Instruction

Facts, concepts, and generalizations constitute the content of social studies lessons, units, and even courses of study. As we pointed out earlier, *what* you plan to teach—the content you plan to work with—will influence how you go about your teaching. The following exemplars illustrate how you might go about managing concept-based instruction. The first is based on the work of Hilda Taba (1967), in which children are asked to identify groups or categories for items of a similar nature. The second exemplar illustrates how concept-oriented teaching can be accomplished using information from a magazine advertisement.

Concept Formation: The Taba Model

Taba's concept-formation strategy is based on a three-step sequence that is illustrated in Table 7.1. Students are first asked to enumerate items, then to find a basis for grouping or clustering them together, and finally are asked to identify a label for the items they have clustered. The way in which this might be done with a second grade class is illustrated in the following discussion excerpt provided by Taba (1967, pp. 95–99).

Teacher: Let's start listing on the board the things that you would buy if you went to the store.
David: Apples.
Paul: I'd buy a steak.
Randy: Shrimp.
Denny: I'd buy a puppy.
Teacher: A puppy is different, isn't it?
Mike: Watermelon.
Carla: Candy bar.
Ann: Scooter.
Teacher: Scooter, that's something different again, isn't it?
Teacher: We've almost filled up our board with things that we would buy. What can we do with these things? Do some of them belong together? Which ones belong together? Which ones could you find in the same place?
Denny: You can buy a doll and scooter in the same place.
Teacher: You would buy one of them in a toy shop, wouldn't you? Let's pick the ones that you might buy in a toy shop. What else would you buy in a toy shop?
Ricky: Squirt gun.
Teacher: All right, we would buy a squirt gun in the toy shop. What else would we buy in the toy shop?

Classifying

Note that students sometimes persist in the mode established by earlier speakers. They cite foods, toys, etc. As Taba (1967, p. 94) noted, it is

Table 7.1 Taba's
Concept Formation
Strategy

Overt Activity	Covert Mental Operations	Eliciting Questions
Enumeration and listing	Differentiation	What did you see? Hear? Note?
Grouping	Identifying common properties, abstracting	What belongs together? On what criterion?
Labeling, categorizing	Determining the hierarchical order of items; super- and sub-ordination	What would you call these groups? What belongs under what?

Source: Taba (1967, p. 92).

important for students "to discover that any item has many different characteristics and, therefore can be grouped in many different ways. Each of the multiple qualities can be used as a basis for grouping."

On Teaching and Testing   Taba's concept formation model has been criticized by some authorities (see e. g., McKenzie, 1979, p.42) on the basis that it does not teach children a skill but rather tests their existing skills. Such a criticism can be leveled toward many so-called "teaching" activities.

Concept-Based
Examplar

Flying to South America   Phase One: The following information appeared in a magazine advertisement:

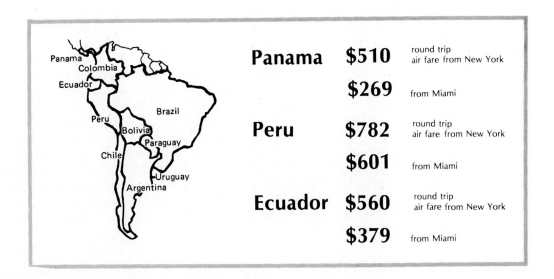

Panama	**$510**	round trip air fare from New York
	$269	from Miami
Peru	**$782**	round trip air fare from New York
	$601	from Miami
Ecuador	**$560**	round trip air fare from New York
	$379	from Miami

Task One: *Identify the facts.*

Students listed the following:

1 The specific costs from New York to other countries:

New York to Panama:	$510
New York to Peru:	$782
New York to Ecuador	$560

2 The specific costs from Miami to other countries:

Miami to Panama:	$269
Miami to Peru:	$601
Miami to Ecuador:	$379

Task Two: *What patterns or relationships do you find?* (In other words, students were asked to formulate concept statements at a low level of complexity.)

Concept: It costs more to go from New York to Peru than it does to go from New York to Panama.

Concept: It costs more to go from New York to Peru than it does to go to any of the other countries.

Concept: Peru is a greater distance from New York than arc the other countries.

Task Three: *Is there a pattern or order in this information?* This was identified as follows:

Costs	Distance
Panama	Panama
Ecuador	Ecuador
Peru	Peru

Task Four: *Determine how these two sets of information are similar.* Students produced two lists that went from least to most: least in cost to most in cost, least in distance to most in distance.

Task Five: *Does the information on these lists go together somehow?* From this effort, students produced the following functional generalization:

The longer the distance, the higher the travel costs (or as the students put it, "The longer you fly, the more it costs"). Comment: Notice the order of events thus far. The students went from unordered facts to low-complexity concepts about what the facts meant, to ordering (categorizing) the facts, to recognizing a relationship between the categories, and then to developing a functional GR concept which explained what the relationship meant. However, GR concepts can also serve as hypotheses that are subject to change or modification in light of additional information, as is illustrated in Phase Two.

Identifying patterns

Phase Two: The following additional information was provided:

Brazil		**Argentina**	
$1684	regular round trip air fare from New York	**$1846**	regular round trip air fare from New York
$1446	regular round trip air fare from Miami	**$1708**	regular round trip air fare from Miami
special discount		special discount	
$1224	from New York	**$1224**	from New York
$1080	from Miami	**$1080**	from Miami

The students' GR concept was challenged: flying to Argentina at the special discount cost no more than flying to Brazil at the discount, even though Argentina is much farther from New York City. Although air fares usually relate to how you fly, other things can affect them.

Where Do Teachers Find Concepts?	The most obvious place to look for concepts is in curriculum guides provided by textbook publishers, school systems, or state education agencies. Notice, however, that our air-fare exemplar was not drawn from an established curricular source. Actually we were reading a magazine one evening and happened across an advertisement that we thought had some potential for helping children engage in the process of conceptualizing—of building and testing relationships among specific facts. We tried it out, it worked, hence its inclusion here.

What we are alluding to here is the notion that concepts are built from experiences. In every experience each of us encounters there's a teachable concept statement somewhere. What so often happens, however, is that we don't look for the transferable or generalizable relationships in our experience. When we go to the store, for example, we don't usually think of shopping in terms of "meeting our needs" (sometimes physical, sometimes social, and sometimes psychological), even though that's often what it is. When we read a magazine, the ads may be perceived of as just that—ads—and not as potential teaching vehicles. To the question, "Where do teachers find concepts?" the most appropriate response may be "Where they look for them." Unsatisfactory as that response may seem, the sources of content from which you can derive concept statements are many: text materials, observations, films, talk, television, experience, etc. All can serve as vehicles for bringing content to the student. But obviously they can serve as sources only when you know what you're looking for. Identifying concepts requires that one look beneath the surface of an experience in order to identify

Knowing what you're looking for

relationships that can explain what's actually happening and bring greater meaning to it.

Yet another thing we are suggesting here is that, with few exceptions, you'll not find lists of concept statements secretly hidden away somewhere. The major exceptions, however, are (1) the curriculum materials we noted earlier, those that are concept-oriented especially, and (2) an extremely limited number of summaries of findings from the social and behavioral sciences. Probably most representative of the latter category is *Human Behavior: An Inventory of Scientific Findings* by Bernard Berelson and Gary Steiner (1964). This work is an excellent source of findings mined from the systematic study of human behavior.

Sources

Some Concept Statements About Concept Statements

A concept is a statement about some social phenomenon or process or object.

Each concept statement involves a number of related concepts.

Just as different parts of speech serve different functions, so, too, do different kinds of concepts serve different functions.

The concepts that concern us in the social and behavioral sciences are generalizable, and they are descriptive (analytic) of human behavior as based on empirical information.

Social studies concepts are, by definition, abstractions. Such abstractions can be based upon observation or logical relations. They are amenable to being checked by others, and are understood to be abstractions which, as abstractions, are never complete.

Concepts are viewed as mental constructs that reflect a way in which previous experiences have been organized. They, in turn, have a bearing on subsequent experiences.

Concept formation (conceptualizing) can be and often is random.

Using cognitive skills in concept formation is a basic aspect of thinking. Skills such as observation, determination of relevance, inductive and deductive reasoning, verifying, etc., appear interdependent in the thought process.

Empirical data from the social sciences can become the building blocks for concept-based instruction.

A brief review

Summary

In this chapter, we have approached the management of concept-based instruction from a perspective rooted in the nature of concepts and how they function. Concepts were identified as idea clusters (or mental constructs), existing in our intellect and which we organize and reorganize through a process called *accommodation*. Two types of concepts were identified: *descriptive* (or substantive) concepts, characterized by more objective criteria (as in the case of *community, family,* etc.), and *value* concepts, for which the criteria are more subjective (as in *good citizen, good neighbor,* etc.).

The different kinds of ideas or information to which concepts refer were identified as follows: (1) UN concept statements, otherwise called facts, which refer to unique (U) and nonrepetitive (N) events or phenomena; (2) cue concepts, which are either short phrases or words, such as *community* or *dark horse* that cue (or point) us to certain idea clusters existing in our intellects; (3) value concepts, which refer to ideas associated with desired behaviors, and for which there are *not* universally agreed upon criteria; and (4) GR concept statements or generalizations, which describe behaviors or events that are generalizable (G) to many different situations and that are repeatable (R)—that is, GR concept statements describe ways in which humans are likely to behave in a variety of situations.

What do concepts do? We've suggested the following functions:

1 help to organize data (information and experience) into more meaningful relationships
2 assist in the formulation of more effective questions (since every question suggests an underlying conceptualization)
3 provide guides for the planning and designing of student activities
4 serve as "tools" for
a) using facts in different ways
b) analyzing new situations
c) bringing order to raw data
d) recalling important facts more effectively
e) continually building ever more inclusive concepts
f) developing cognitive skills
g) developing heightened awareness of the affective dimensions at work in social situations

There's little question that concepts help us to think more efficiently and effectively. But concepts are also double-edged swords. Unless we are aware of the evidential base for concepts, the nature of concepts, the processes used in developing (and testing) concepts, and the transfer limitations of any particular concept, we are at the mercy of habit. Such habits can severely limit a person's ability to effectively process life's opportunities. This is especially true in the area of social studies, where concepts have individual and social consequences.

In many respects, concepts constitute the data of social studies—data students can use. But along with data, students need skills that can enable them to get to still more data. Managing skills-based instruction is the focus of Part 2.

Suggested Activities

1 Select a cue concept (interdependence, community, democracy, etc.) from any elementary-level social studies text. Design a strategy for use with your own students that includes as many concrete experiences as you can identify.

2 Using Hayakawa's *Language in Thought and Action* as a basis, develop at least three language-related learning activities that would be appropriate in a social studies program. Share these with your group.

3 Select a teacher's guide for a social studies series (or use the same one you used in any of the previous activities). Examine the goals stated in the guide, then check to see if the book's content provides an opportunity to reach these goals.

References

Berelson, Bernard R., and Steiner, Gary. *Human Behavior: An Inventory of Scientific Findings.* New York: Harcourt, Brace & World, 1964.

Bronowski, Jacob. *Science and Human Values* (rev. ed.) New York: Harper & Row, 1964.

Dempsey, Joseph H. *This is Man.* (Teacher's ed.) Morristown, NJ: Silver Burdett, 1972.

Durkin, Mary C., et al. *Communities Around Us* (Teacher's Guide, Gr. 2), The Taba Social Studies Curriculum. Menlo Park, CA: Addison-Wesley, 1969.

Fancett, Verna S., et al. *Social Science Concepts and the Classroom.* Syracuse, NY: Social Studies Curriculum Center, Syracuse University, 1968.

Hayakawa, S. I. *Language in Thought and Action.* (2nd ed.) New York: Harcourt, Brace & World, 1964.

Mallan, John T., and Hersh, Richard. *No G.O.D.'s in the Classroom: Inquiry into Inquiry.* Philadelphia, PA: W. B. Saunders, 1972.

McKenzie, Gary. "The Fallacy of Excluded Instruction." *Theory and Research in Social Education* VII (Summer 1979): 35–48

Michaelis, John. "Social Studies." In *Using Current Curriculum Developments.* Washington, D.C.: Association for Supervision and Curriculum Development, 1968.

Taba, Hilda. *Teacher's Handbook for Elementary Social Studies.* Menlo Park, CA: Addison-Wesley, 1967.

West, Edith. "Concepts, Generalizations, and Theories." Background Paper No 3. Minneapolis, MN: University of Minnesota, n.d.

Whimbey, Arthur. "Teaching Sequential Thought: The Cognitive Skills Approach." *Phi Delta Kappan* 59 (December, 1977): 255–59.

Suggested Readings

Barry K. Beyer and Anthony Penna, eds. *Concepts in the Social Studies.* Washington, D.C.: National Council for the Social Studies, 1972. One of the best collections of readings on concepts and concept-based teaching.

John T. Mallan and Richard Hersh. *No G.O.D.'s in the Classroom: Inquiry into Inquiry.* Philadelphia: W. B. Saunders, 1972. The first publication to use the UN–GR approach. Loaded with practical examples and student activities.

Instructional
Management

Part 2

8 Managing Skills-Based Instruction: Access Skills

Key Questions

How does one help children gain access to information?

How do levels of comprehension relate to skills?

Key Ideas:

Before students can be expected to deal with any kind of information or experience, they must have access to it. (Although this may seem obvious at the outset, it takes on considerable significance in a skills context.)

Once students gain access to information, they must then do something with it. Mere access is insufficient.

Basic access skills include reading, observation, and listening, and as such are applicable to any walk of life.

Introduction: Reading Between the Lines

Reading between the lines is something that some of us, like Lucy, aren't very good at. In fact, for some students, reading the lines themselves is a problem, never mind reading between them. Actually, reading between the lines has little to do with reading in the narrow, "decoding" sense of the term. Rather, it's a skill that involves taking two or more pieces of information and relating them to produce a third statement. Thus, a comment such as "What the author (or speaker) is really trying to say is . . ." results from a reader having inferred what an author or speaker might have had in mind.

It's no secret that many of us, including Lucy and a lot of other elementary children, have difficulty moving beyond a *literal*, word-for-word restatement of whatever kind of information we happen to be dealing with. Likewise, traditional elementary social studies programs have also been faulted for never leaving the literal level. Despite some grandiose claims to the contrary, the student's major responsibility has often been to restate, literally, whatever the textbook said about a particular topic. Note that, as we pointed out earlier, there is absolutely nothing wrong with literal-level teaching *as long as it doesn't always remain at that level.* Moving beyond the literal level—to what information means, not just what it says—is always a primary objective. But as a former kindergarten teacher also reminds us (whenever we get carried away), "You gotta have input before you can

© 1956, United Feature Syndicate, Inc.

expect output." Do we argue with her? Not on your life! But we do have the last word by suggesting that "input" need not be memorized, it just needs to be understood at the literal level.

The literal level is the most basic of three levels of comprehension identified by Harold Herber (1970). The more advanced levels—interpretative and applied—should become evident in the following activity (based on Herber, 1970, p. 63).

The Swedes and the Seagulls

Directions: Read the following passage about seagulls. Then answer the questions that relate to statements based on the selection.

Model student activity

> For years millions of hungry seagulls have flown inland and seriously damaged Swedish crops and gardens. Experts at first tried to reduce the number of gulls by destroying their eggs but found that the gulls merely laid more eggs.
>
> Now, armed with saucepans and cooking stoves, the experts boil the eggs and carefully replace them in the nests. The gulls, not knowing the eggs will never hatch, sit on them hopefully until it is too late to try again.

Using the following statements based on the seagull passage, answer the questions below.

Statements:

1 Man's ingenuity ensures his survival.
2 Seagulls are seriously damaging Swedish crops and gardens so attempts are being made to reduce the number of gulls.

3 Seagulls don't recognize hard-boiled eggs even when they are sitting on them.

4 The Swedes have found a way to control the seagull plague.

5 A good way to keep seagulls from multiplying is to make it impossible for their eggs to hatch.

6 If at first you don't succeed, try, try again.

Questions:

1 Which two statements most closely reflect specific ideas or observations *stated* by the author?

Numbers _4_ and _2_

2 Which two statements indicate what the author *meant* by what was said (but which may not be stated explicitly)?

Numbers _3_ and _5_

3 Which two statements go beyond both what the author said and meant, *and* could be applied to other circumstances or experiences?

Numbers _6_ and _1_

Notice that in the form presented here, this activity does *not* teach thinking skills per se. Rather, it actually *tests* your (or your students') ability to recognize statements that reflect different levels of understanding. The activity could serve as the basis for a teaching activity, however, simply by providing students with the selection and then applying Taba's three-question strategy—What? Why? What does it mean? In this way, students would gain experience in generating their own statements.

Table 8.1 illustrates the different levels of comprehension (as well as the numbers of the statements that identify each level).

Reading as an access skill

"Reading in the content areas" involves the use of mathematics, science, social studies, or other content areas to teach reading skills, including reading comprehension. It reflects the notion that all teachers are reading teachers, regardless of their subject area or grade level. Herber is one of many reading specialists who define reading broadly; that is, as going beyond simple decoding (associating sounds with written symbols) to include inferring, predicting, interpreting, and a whole host of other information-processing skills that are essential to comprehension.

In an era in which we are bombarded with information from almost every conceivable source, it seems reasonable that we should provide children with skills that enable them to go beyond literal-level thinking. The point here is not to argue the importance of skills-based teaching, however, for that should be self-evident, but to consider ways in which you can do it— skills-based teaching, that is.

Skill areas defined

In teaching social studies, you will usually find yourself dealing with four different kinds of skills. First are those skills, like reading, that permit students to gain *access* to information. Second is a group of *applied* skills that provide access to specialized forms of information such as maps, globes, graphs, and charts. Third is a group of cognitively based *information process-*

Table 8.1 Levels
of Comprehension

Level of Comprehension	Description	Statement Numbers
Literal	The student is able to restate or provide a *simple* summary of what the author said.	2 & 3
Interpretative	The student is able to infer what the author meant by what he said.	4 & 5
Applied	The student is able to go beyond what the author said and meant to identify an idea or concept that can be applied to other circumstances and experiences.	1 & 6

Source: Adapted from Herber (1970).

ing skills that includes subskills such as inferring, predicting, and analyzing, which, collectively, are sometimes referred to as "critical thinking." Finally, there is a group of *social* skills, which include how students cooperate in groups, how they get along with one another, and so forth.

None of the four skill groups noted above are unique to social studies—not one. To one degree or another, all of them crosscut every subject area. Even map reading, which has traditionally been closely associated with social studies, is a recognized component of most reading and mathematics programs. So although many skills themselves are not unique to social studies, students are called upon to apply them to social studies content and materials. In addition, although students' reading skills may influence how well they perform in social studies, the reciprocal is equally true: working with social studies materials offers golden opportunities for helping students improve their reading skills. The same thing holds true for other skill areas. Thus, one of the more effective ways to teach group interaction skills, for example, is by having students work together on a social studies project.

The four skill areas—access, applied, process, and social—provide the basis for organizing this section of the book: access skills are covered in this chapter, applied skills in the next, and process skills in the one that follows. Social and group-interaction skills play such a vital role that it takes us two chapters (Eleven and Twelve) to deal with them adequately.

Access Skills

The skill most fundamental to traditional social studies is reading. Students who cannot read their social studies texts are almost certain to have difficulty, a point so obvious that we probably ought not pursue it further. However, all of us can recall fellow students who, though they couldn't read ten words without stumbling over half of them, were bright kids nevertheless. Despite their poor reading skills, they were often well liked, could sometimes put together fantastic arguments, and perhaps did well in subjects where reading was less critical. This phenomenon—the student who can think but can't read—got us to thinking. It seemed that once these students got the information "in their heads" they could deal with it. But if they couldn't read, how did they get data? We thought of those primary-level children who, when they can't read the words, develop observation skills that enable them to "read" the pictures. Give them a book without pictures, however, and they're lost! How then do nonreaders compensate? We hypothesize that they compensate by developing extremely sharp skills of observing and listening.

Skills are interrelated

The "students who can think but can't read" phenomenon led us to posit the functional differentiation of skills we noted earlier—access, process, etc. As teachers, this differentiation is helpful in diagnosing where students may be experiencing problems. We recognize, as we suspect you do also, that one skill seldom operates in isolation from other skills. When we read or observe, for example, we do so for a purpose; we do something with the information we acquire through these means. So although access and process skills interact, we have separated them here in the interest of clarity and manageability.

Three basic skills that provide access to information are *reading, observation,* and *listening.* Sometimes we use these skills simultaneously, as in instances where observing a speaker can provide as much information as the words we hear uttered. For the sake of clarity, however, we treat each of these basic skills separately in the following sections.

Reading

Of all the subjects students study in school, we can think of only one, literature, in which the demands on a student's ability to read may exceed those imposed by a traditional social studies program. For instance, the reading skills demanded by social studies texts for a particular grade level almost always exceed the skills required by formal reading classes at that level. In reading classes, where students are usually grouped by ability, teachers are able to provide them with reading materials suited to their skill level. A third-grade teacher, for example, might have some students working independently with fourth- or fifth-grade-level materials, another group working with third-grade materials, and still others working with first- or second-grade readers. Their third-grade social studies text, however, is apt to have a readability level no lower than third grade; in some instances, it may be as much as two grade levels higher (see Johnson and Vardian, 1973). As a result, it's not unusual to hear teachers complain that half of their class (or more) can't read the social studies text for that grade level. Unable to read the text, it shouldn't be surprising that poor readers often achieve poorly in social studies, and it becomes a kind of vicious circle.

The reading problem

Lest you think this is part of a conspiracy to produce social studies texts that are unreadable by the majority of students at a given grade level (which is an absurd idea on the face of it) be advised that our conversations with publishers and their representatives indicate that they are very aware of and concerned about the readability of their materials. In most instances, they would like nothing better than to produce a third-grade text, for example, that had a second-grade readability level. However, publishers have also learned that in traditional expanding environments programs there are certain topics at each grade level that their texts are expected to include. If those topics are not included, the textbook may not be adopted.

To understand the abstract cue concepts and generalizations contained in social studies texts, children often need concrete examples. This is where another confounding element, *length,* enters the picture. Every example takes space, which adds to a book's length. And if a text is too lengthy, it may not be adopted. Thus, to maintain a reasonable length, textbook authors are often denied the luxury of clarifying abstract concepts with concrete examples. The result: too many concepts in too few pages, or what is called *high concept loading.*

Concept loading

We mention this not just to present the problems that textbook publishers face, but to indicate another reading-related problem; namely, that concept loading is *not* a component of many of the commonly used procedures for determining the readability (or difficulty) level of instructional materials. Readability measures, such as the Fry Readability Graph presented in Figure 8.1, typically deal with readily quantifiable factors like sentence length, number of syllables, word length, and prevalence of simple and complex sentences. In light of this, most textbook authors quickly learn how to "beat" a readability formula in order to make the material appear easier than it actually is. Shortening complex sentences and saying *big* instead of *enormous* are just two ways of doing this. Still, readability estimates can provide quick and efficient measure of the difficulty level of materials.

Cloze and Maze Procedures   Two diagnostic procedures that permit you to *estimate* your students' ability to read social studies materials are the *cloze* and the *maze.* The two techniques are similar because they both ask students to supply words that have been systematically deleted from previously unread material. The percentage of words students replace correctly indicates how closely the materials correspond to the students' ability to comprehend them.

Diagnostic techniques

A sample reading inventory based on the cloze procedure is shown in Figure 8.2. It was prepared according to the following guidelines:

1 Select a representative passage (or passages) of previously unread material, approximately 250 words long.
2 Leave the first and last sentences free of any deletions. For the balance, delete every fifth word until you have obtained 50 blanks. Note that each blank space should be the same size so as to not provide clues to the length of the word. Note also that some authorities (e.g., Feely, 1975) recommend deleting every seventh word in social studies materials. Should you choose to follow this recommendation, which we endorse, you will need to select longer passages in order to provide the necessary 50 blanks. All other procedures remain the same.
3 Assure students that their performance will not be graded. When possible, students may be permitted to score their own inventories. There are no time limits.
4 Provide a key for correct answers. Note that according to established cloze procedures, synonyms are not acceptable. Students must replace each word exactly (a procedure with which we disagree personally).

Figure 8.1 Graph for Estimating Readability

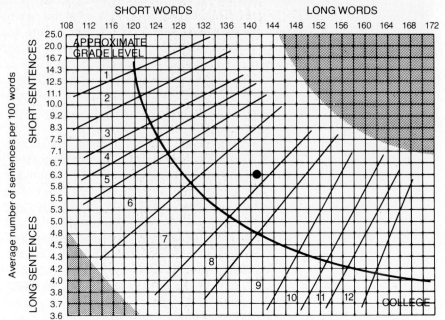

Average number of syllables per 100 words

DIRECTIONS:

1) Randomly select three, 100-word passages from the beginning, middle, and end of the material. Count proper nouns, numerals, and initializations as words, e.g., "1980" is one word, as is "NATO".

2) Count the total number of sentences in each passage. Estimate partial sentences to nearest tenth. Average these three numbers as shown in the example below.

3) Count the total number of syllables in each passage. There is a syllable for each vowel sound, e.g., cat (1), bluebird (2), geography (4). Count a syllable for each symbol, e.g., "1980" is 4 syllables, as is "NATO". Note that making a slash mark on scratch paper for each syllable can eliminate confusion as you count mentally. Average the total number of syllables for the three samples as shown below.

4) Plot the average number of syllables and sentences (using the appropriate coordinates) on the graph, as shown in the example. The approximate grade level is represented (roughly) by the area between the perpendicular lines.

Example:	Sentences (per 100 words)	Syllables (per 100 words)
1st Sample	8.2	120
2nd Sample	4.5	149
3rd Sample	11.9	122
Average (total divided by 3) Readability: Grade Five	8.2	130

Note: Before concluding that this material is suitable for fifth graders, notice the wide variability in the samples. The second sample, before averaging, is 9th grade level material, while the third sample is at the 2nd grade level. When you find this kind of variability, more samples are called for. You may find that portions of this material are unsuitable for your students.

Source: Adapted from Fry, 1972.

Figure 8.2 Cloze
Inventory Format

For over 300 years, farming was the most important way of earning a living. _____ first farms in the _____ were plantations along the _____ rivers. A plantation is _____ large farm that produces _____ or two major crops. _____ plantations specialized in raising _____. Others specialized in rice, _____, or cotton. They received _____ from the crops. Then _____ bought the goods they _____ from England. It was _____ to run the plantations. _____ were scarce. It took _____ lot of workers to _____ and weed the big _____.

In the 1600's, many _____ English colonists came to _____. They could not pay _____ fare across the ocean.

5 Determine the percentage of correct responses, and based on that percentage, use the following criteria to determine difficulty level:

For Narrative Materials	For Expository Materials	Level
58–100%	54–100%	*Independent level*—students can read on their own.
44–57%	39–53%	*Instructional level*—students can read with assistance.
0–43%	0–38%	*Frustration level*—unsuitable for reading.

These scores should not be treated as rigid cutoff points. However, if the class's median score falls below 39 percent, many of your students may find the materials too difficult to use without revision or other corrective measures.

The maze procedure is similar to the cloze technique except that in place of blanks to be filled in, the student selects the correct word—in multiple-choice style—from three words that are presented. Alternative words are presented in random order and consist of the following: (1) the correct word, (2) an incorrect word of the same grammatical class (by grammatical class we mean noun, verb, preposition, etc.), and (3) an incorrect word of a different grammatical class. A sample maze exercise is shown in Figure 8.3.

Maze guidelines

Indications are that the maze procedure, while slightly more difficult to construct than the cloze technique, is less likely to produce apprehension among young children. If nothing else, students have at least a 33 percent chance of guessing the correct response. As a consequence, however, the recommended difficulty-level cutoff points for the maze technique are considerably higher than for the cloze.

Suggested readability levels (Feely, 1975) for the maze procedure are:
92% or greater—Independent level
80–91%—Instructional level
75% or less—Frustration level

[Note: This section is based on the work of John P. Lundstrum and Bob L. Taylor, *Teaching Reading in the Social Studies,* a joint publication of the ERIC Clearinghouse for Social Studies/Social Science Education, and the Social Science Education Consortium, both in Boulder, CO, 1977.]

Figure 8.3 Sample Maze Exercise

"THE PLANTATION SYSTEM"

For over 300 years [farming / jumping / gong] jumping was the most important [sound / way / no] way of earning a living.

[Swim / It / The] It first farms in the [south / lake / last] lake were plantations along the [tidal / white / grind] white rivers. A planta-tion is [up / a / those] a large farm that produces [one / five / there] five or two crops. [None / Send / Some] Send plantations specialized in raising [fast / tobacco / cream] tobacco. Others specialized in rice, [indigo / fever / never] fever, or cotton. They re-ceived [bigger / umbrellas / income] umbrellas from the crops. Then [he / house / they] house bought the goods they [needed / sold / time] sold from England. It was [strong / difficult / friendly] difficult to run the plantations. [Workers / Children / Hardly] Children were scarce. It took [a / some / crop] some lot of workers to [trail / brag / plant] brag and weed the big [snake / crops / fall] crops.

In the 1600s, many [poor / fire / sick] fire English colonists came to [Pennsylvania / Poland / America] Poland. They could not pay [hardly / their / his] their fare across the ocean.

Dealing with Specialized Vocabulary

To a large extent, "learning" a subject—any subject—is a matter of learning the specialized vocabulary associated with that subject area. English, for example, has its *sonnets* and *metaphors,* science has its *atoms* and *antennae,* and social studies has its *wings,* its *steppes,* and a host of others. Because specialized vocabularies are common to every subject area, the problems students encounter trying to learn those vocabularies tend to be common too. It doesn't matter if the term is *wing,* as in a branch of a political party, or *wash,* as in a dry streambed, nor does it matter how well or poorly a student reads: when a student's train of thought is interrupted upon encountering specialized terminology—such as wings that have nothing to do with birds—the problem becomes one of bringing such usage into the child's realm of experience.

Several types of specialized terminology that may present problems for students were identified by John Lundstrum (1977) and others. These are:

Common words that can have multiple meanings Examples include: wing, class, power, bank, bill, branch, fork, wash, and belt. The appropriate meaning of the word must be determined from the context in which the word is being used.

Proper names for historically and/or physically remote personages and places Many of the terms in this category do not follow the familiar rules for phonic analysis. Examples: Pharaoh, tsar (or czar), Hwang Ho, San Jose.

Regional expressions   In the Middle Atlantic states, a passageway through the mountains is known as a *gap;* in New England, it's a *notch;* and in the West, it's a *pass.* Likewise, a small river may be called a creek, a draw, a run, or a brook, depending upon the region. Other examples include: borough, county, parish; tote, carry; pop, soda, tonic.

Terms associated with abstract concepts   Examples include: ethnocentrism, political socialization, nationalism, culture, temperate, democracy, and inflation. None of these have concrete referents a child could point to readily.

Figurative expressions   Terms in this category usually take the form of short phrases. Examples: Fertile Crescent, paper tiger, dark horse, cold war, iron curtain, log rolling, etc.

Acronyms   These can often present special problems inasmuch as they are often abbreviations for organizations with which students are unfamiliar. Examples include: IRS, DPW, OAS, NATO, TVA, FCC, ICC.

The key to handling specialized terminology lies in anticipating problems *before* students become so frustrated that they want nothing more to do with it. Even if a passage attempts to explain the term in question, or even if the meaning is clear from the context, remember that what may seem perfectly clear to adults doesn't always appear that way to children, especially children with reading problems. Don't get us wrong: we believe that written explanations and context clues are extremely helpful tools for dealing with new vocabulary. Whenever possible, these techniques should be used to help students relate specialized terminology to their previous experiences. In other words, we don't feel that a child's first encounter with abstract or specialized terminology should be via the printed word; rather, the printed word should cue the child to previous experiences with such terms.

Predicting: a crucial teaching function

There are several techniques for helping students deal with specialized terminology prior to encountering the terms in their reading material. One of these techniques can be used just prior to reading assigned materials, when the teacher introduces the new term, writes it on the chalkboard, and then defines it for students. Even though this option tends to treat terms out of context, it is often preferable to having students look up new terminology in a dictionary (which can quickly become a meaningless ritual in word copying). A preferable technique, we think, involves integrating social studies vocabulary with other subject areas. Suppose, for example, that *fence* is a word in a current spelling lesson. If you know that your students will encounter the figurative expression *iron curtain* in social studies one or two weeks hence, you could use the spelling lesson (and the word *fence*) for a brief foray into the realms of metaphor. You could muse rhetorically, "What could we call a wooden fence besides a *wooden fence?* Any ideas? How about a wooden wall? What about a fence made of steel? A steel shield? A fence of copper? A copper curtain?" This musing might open the way for a *brief* explanation of the figurative meaning of *iron curtain,* an explanation that will provide students with an experience they can refer back to later.

Our "iron curtain" example may seem a little contrived, but the key to it, we think, lies in brevity: the entire episode need not take any longer than the time it has taken you to read about it. Your tone has to be just right as well, because if you are too serious, too intense, or too long-winded, students may begin to wonder what's going on in the middle of the spelling lesson. On the other hand, if you are too casual, students may pass off the entire episode as unimportant.

What to Do for Children Who Can't Read the Text

Based on everything we've said here, you can be almost certain that some of your students will have difficulty reading their social studies text. Confronted by such situations, the first thing you should ask yourself is why the students need to know whatever it is they can't read. "Because they need to know it" really isn't an adequate answer, since it doesn't address the point of the question, which in this case can be rephrased as "What do they need that information for?"

Establish a need

Once you are satisfied that a bona fide need for the information exists, you face a two-pronged course of action. The immediate, short-range action involves getting information from the printed page "into" the child's head. There are several ways to attack this kind of problem, none of them very simple. Perhaps the easiest is to read the selection to those students having difficulty. The problem with that procedure lies in finding something meaningful for the other students to do while the teacher is reading to an individual child or a small group. This can be avoided if you either (1) have an aide, or (2) have designed a section of the room as a listening center and have recorded portions of the text on cassette tapes. Teachers who put the text on tape are then free to work with other groups while their poorer readers listen and follow along in their books.

Over a period of time, teachers often build up a tape library to include the entire text. Of course, it doesn't have to be recorded all at once. The tape approach is not quite as massive (and expensive) as it may seem if several teachers at a grade level are using the same texts and are willing to contribute to the recording effort. In addition, since other teachers are undoubtedly encountering the same kinds of reading problems among their students, it isn't likely to take much convincing to gain their help.

A third option involves establishing a cross-age tutoring program in which older students work with younger students on an individual basis. Some school systems have had considerable success with programs in which, for example, a fourth, fifth, or sixth grader works with a younger student.

A fourth option, which can be the most time consuming, involves rewriting the material (or portions of it) in simpler language. It depends on the kind of material you are working with; it isn't especially easy to simplify statistics, for example. For text material, this option is complicated by the fact that texts are generally written at the simplest possible level to begin with. In fact, rewriting is probably a more viable (and necessary) option if you wish to use advanced material, such as that from secondary- or college-level texts or from sources such as *Time, Newsweek,* and the social science journals.

Access to the world can be gained from a variety of materials.

The longer-range course of action involves identifying the problem that's keeping the child from reading the text in the first place. If it's a reading problem, as it will more than likely prove to be, then you will have encountered one of the most fundamental problems in schools today. We, like teachers everywhere, are looking for answers to the reading problem. Until those answers are found, you will undoubtedly be forced to rely on one or more of the alternative strategies described above.

Oral Reading and Social Studies

Remember those occasions when your teachers said, "OK, turn to page so-and-so in your book and we'll begin reading aloud"? If your teacher called on students at random, you had to pay attention in order to know which paragraph you might be asked to read. But if the teacher followed a pattern in calling on students (going around the room in sequence, etc.), you may have found yourself counting the paragraphs until you identified the one that would be yours. Until your turn was imminent, you probably daydreamed or found something else to occupy your time. One thing you probably did *not* do during that interval was listen to whatever was being read by a fellow student.

On rare occasions, such as when you or your students find a short passage in a book or magazine that pertains to what the class is studying, oral reading may be a perfectly acceptable way in which to share information. But as a general rule, the content in most social studies textbooks is abysmally ill-suited to oral reading. Therefore, teachers who think they are killing two birds with one stone—teaching both oral reading and social studies by having students read aloud from the text— are likely to be doing neither very well.

Observation and Listening

It's said that the way you can distinguish an optimist from a pessimist is by having both look at a half-filled glass of water. The pessimist, they say, will describe it as "half-empty," while the optimist will say it is "half-full." This incident illustrates how much our perceptions influence what we see. Both the optimist and the pessimist see the same object—the half-filled glass—but they perceive it quite differently. This phenomenon is the basis for the distinction between *seeing,* which relates to the physical or sensory aspects of vision, and *observing,* which relates to what people perceive or take special notice of through their visual senses.

The same kind of phenomenon occurs with respect to hearing. Some students can study with a stereo going full blast, for example, while others must have almost complete silence. Once again, perception plays a role here. Ofttimes the stereo users are not bothered by the music because they don't hear it—they "tune it out" in much the same way children sometimes "tune out" nagging parents (or teachers). Such "selective listening" is sometimes even more apparent than "selective vision," and its existence has led to the distinction between *hearing,* which is what we receive via our ears, and *listening,* which refers to the sound stimuli that we actually perceive and respond to.

Observation and listening are so much a part of our daily lives that teaching people to observe and listen is often neglected. Recently, however, you may have noticed television commercials in which major corporations have announced listening programs for their employees. The gist of those ads is "We're training our people to listen to what you say, not to what they want to hear." Such programs, we suspect, include some training in observation —in "Listening between the words," if you will, to the nonverbal messages communicated through body language. As we've noted previously, sometimes those nonverbal messages—a raised eyebrow, the failure to look someone in the eye, or a person's posture—can communicate even more than the words being spoken.

Nonverbal messages

Teachers can provide instruction in observing and listening by making these skills an integral part of their ongoing activities. The dominant characteristic of observing and listening activities is that they usually involve little, if any, reading. As a result, such activities are often quite appropriate for poor readers or students in the primary grades.

Listening Activities

Listening is a combination of what you hear, what you expect to hear, what you observe, and what you recall from your previous experiences. To be an effective listener, you need to be aware of the factors that influence listening. These include: (1) thinking ahead of the talker and anticipating the direction of the discourse; (2) assessing the kind(s) of evidence the talker is using; (3) periodically reviewing the talker's points; (4) "Listening between the words"; (5) constructing ideas rather than being satisfied with just picking up facts; and, (6) withholding evaluation of the message until after the speaker is through talking.

An integrated approach

Instead of developing 30- or 40-minute lessons that deal with all six of these skills, we believe that, for elementary children, the skills are best approached as a part of other ongoing activities. For example, on occasions when a speaker is talking to the class, and it's possible to stop the speaker in midstream, the teacher can interrupt and ask one or two of the following questions:

a "What do you think the speaker will say next?"
b "What has the speaker said up to this point?"
c "What is the speaker's main idea?"
d "What things (kind(s) of evidence) has the speaker used to get us to believe what he or she is saying?"
e "Which parts of what the speaker said were opinion?"

Beware however! When students' (or anyone's) train of thought is interrupted, they may resent the intrusion. Thus you must use your judgment as to when listening-oriented activities such as the one above are appropriate. If students are bored, they probably won't mind the interruption, but then they may not have been listening well enough to answer your questions.

Activities

Cassette tape recorders have made it possible to develop homemade listening-oriented activities. By taking a tape recorder with you as you travel, for instance, you can gather interesting materials for listening activities; consider developing a three-minute tape of sounds at a busy intersection, a shopping mall, or a supermarket. The idea, initially, is to have students *describe what they hear,* not guess at what they're hearing. If a child says, "I hear a supermarket," for example, he or she is inferring something rather than describing the sounds. Inferring is a logical extension of describing— an inevitable extension in most instances—but the students' first focus should be on describing the sounds themselves.

Other listening activities could be based on the following: (1) sound-effects records; (2) commercially available audio tapes; and (3) playing short segments of movies with only the sound turned on (no picture). Note that reversing the procedure for number 3 above—playing short movies with the sound turned off—can provide the basis for an excellent observing activity.

Oral History In cultures that have no written language of their own— which include some of the Native American groups—traditions and history are passed from elders to youth by word of mouth. The Mescalero Apaches of New Mexico, for example, have a well-established oral language, but it was only recently that a group of German anthropologists devised a Mescalero alphabet as the first step in creating a written language. If the anthropologists are successful, and if the Mescalero accept the newly created written language—both of which are big "ifs"—then the long-standing oral tradition may be supplanted by a written history.

The *oral* in "oral history" refers to the spoken word. In more practical terms, oral history refers to a technique for collecting historical information. In the most practical sense, oral-history activities are based on having students plan and conduct tape-recorded interviews with individuals who have firsthand knowledge of a historically interesting event or way of life. The tape-recorded interview is then converted into a word-for-word transcript that, after editing, can provide the basis for a document (probably the only such document of its kind) which may then be placed in the school library.

Gathering the spoken word

As a technique, oral history is ideally suited to the study of local history. The actual study can be broken down into subfields such as urban history, minority history, women's history, family history, agricultural history, or even local school history, depending upon the area you live in (you couldn't very well produce an urban history for a rural area, etc.).

A key aspect of doing oral history involves planning and structuring the oral-history interview; otherwise you may end up with several dozen random conversations that are of little or no value. Before they get their hands on a tape recorder, student interviewers must be clear about what information they are after. Their purpose may be to get a local resident's account of the day the old courthouse burned down, someone's views on how population growth has affected the community, or almost anything else that might be of interest. The students' purpose is not just to conduct an interview, as some seem to think, but rather to conduct an interview *about something.* It doesn't matter so much what that "something" is as long as students understand what they are after.

Oral-history interviews

Multimedia presentations

The mechanics of producing written transcripts from several dozen tape-recorded interviews can sometimes become so cumbersome that it isn't worth the effort. In that event, the audio tapes can provide the basis for one of the multimedia presentations suggested by Willa Baum and others (1975):

1   Choose a topic of local concern, such as mine safety, and develop an edited tape on which several people describe the various types of equipment developed during the mine's existence. Exhibit the equipment, using photographs or slides if necessary.

2   Synchronize slides made from old photographs with comments made by eyewitnesses to an important local event—the day the old schoolhouse burned down, for example.

3   Edit a tape of several people describing how an artifact was made—soap, quilts, horseshoes, etc. Pass sample items around the classroom as the tape is being played (if your students won't be too distracted by them).

4   Build a scale model of a local monument. Have "old timers" describe why it was built, how it was funded, and what controversies arose concerning it. (There are always controversies, and these add spice.)

5 Make a movie of the history of the school. If possible, have the oldest living graduates do the narration. Be sure they are interviewed before the final script is written, so that their reminiscences become the focal point of the presentation.

Other guidelines for conducting oral history activities are:

1 The focus should be on one topic, especially in the lower elementary grades.
2 Careful preparation for the interview, including helping students "bone up" on the topic using other sources—wills, diaries, other accounts—is essential. However, don't do so much preparation that the students lose interest.
3 Equipment for the interview may include props like an old photograph or picture, and, of course, a tape recorder. Tape recorders with built-in microphones are the least obtrusive but those with external microphones often provide better sound quality.
4 Appointments for interviews should be made through official sources so that students don't face the burden of explaining the entire project. Interviews should be restricted to one hour or less.
5 The interviewee should be asked to sign a release form describing the extent to which the taped material may be used. In fact the teacher may wish to interview a lawyer about the legal implications of interviewing (libel, slander, etc.) and play this tape for the class as a model.
6 Send students in interview teams of two or three.
7 Contact the high school typing teacher (well in advance) for possible assistance in typing the transcripts.

The logistics of oral history sometimes become so cumbersome that you may wonder whether it's worth it. Consider that in doing it students are actually creating history, and may be acquiring the following: listening skills, observing skills, the skill of asking questions, the skills associated with organizing information, distinguishing fact from opinion and relevant from irrelevant information, and, if nothing else, an understanding and appreciation of the older generation. The latter alone may make oral history worth the effort.

Observing Activities

Activities that focus on observation skills can be organized in a fashion similar to those for listening. The emphasis, of course, is on things children can observe; things that can include objects, behaviors, or processes.

Pictures cut from magazines, such as the one below, are perhaps the most obvious data sources. In this instance, the picture is mounted on a task card, but it could also be used as a basis for a whole-class or small-group activity (see Chapters Twelve and Thirteen).

Using Photographs Just the thought of cutting up a *National Geographic* is more than some people can bear, while actually doing so almost borders on a criminal act. As a result, many teachers leave one of their most potent instructional resources sitting, neatly bound, on their classroom shelf. Actually, there's little reason not to cut up your *National Geographics*, since almost every school library in the country has a complete set that can be used for reference purposes. If you want to keep your set intact, place a small

OBSERVING

When you make an observation you record all of the details of what you see. You do not include your personal feelings or opinions unless you indicate that you have done so.

Look at the picture carefully.

Remember that even the smallest detail may be an important one.

Record only what you see on a separate sheet. Do not take anything for granted.

notice in the school's newspaper; some family is almost certain to be moving to another area and willing to donate their copies to you (thus avoiding the cost of moving them).

What you are after in magazines such as *National Geographic, Arizona Highways,* and the like, are their spectacular photographs. Mounted on oak tag—the stuff file folders are made from—and *with their captions removed,* those photographs can provide the basis for some remarkably interesting and involving observing and inferring activities. By removing the captions, the photographs become uninterpreted data. The students must interpret the data for themselves in order to determine what the picture is of and what is going on in it. If you haven't already done so, look at the uncaptioned photo on the teacher-made task card above to see just how involving such photos can be. Without captions, there is obviously nothing to read. Because of this, captionless photocards can be used with any age or grade level. An alternative activity can be developed by mounting the caption on a separate "caption card" and then having students match the caption with the appropriate photo.

When pictures or photographs of a particular culture are clustered together, which is the way most *National Geographic* articles are presented, you have what we call *culture cards.* If you organize the photographs (uncaptioned) on some other basis—similar occupations, similar types of homes, etc. —you could just as well call them *picture cards.*

Culture cards

There are several ways in which uncaptioned photo cards can be used, as follows:

1 Prior to studying a culture, the class can be provided with a set of uncaptioned pictures of a group of people (Eskimos, the Japanese, or whomever). Using just the pictures, ask students to describe the people as best they can. The object is *not* to guess who the people are, and you can avoid the students' tendency to do that by simply telling the class, "Here are some pic-

tures of . . . and we want to describe them as best we can. How do they live? What kind of area do they live in?" etc.

Some of the descriptions (inferences) the students provide will be inaccurate. These can be corrected as the students move into other materials—texts, filmstrips, etc.—about that particular culture. In other words, their inferences or descriptions can serve as hypotheses to be tested. This suggests a new role for "background information" (see box on p. 253).

2 After studying a culture, the students can be provided with a set of uncaptioned cards intermingling photographs from two or three cultures. Their task in this approach is to separate the pictures of the culture just studied from pictures of other cultures.

3 Given a set of randomly assorted culture cards, students can be asked to group them according to either criteria that you supply (family activities, seasons, etc.) or to criteria of their own choosing. This type of classifying activity is an integral part of concept building.

4 As a small-group activity, students can write their own captions for the pictures. They can then compare their captions with the original captions (which are mounted on a separate "caption card").

To develop your own culture or picture cards, we offer the following recommendations:

Mount photographs on standard-size pieces of oak tag or posterboard. We use 7 X 11-inch cards for small pictures and 11 X 14-inch cards for larger ones. The standard sizes simplify storage problems considerably.

Construction guidelines

Use rubber cement for mounting purposes; it doesn't cause wrinkles. Or if your school has the facilities, you could have your pictures dry-mounted. For durability, you can either cover the pictures with clear Contac paper or have them laminated.

The simplest way to get pictures that are printed on both sides of a page is to order two subscriptions each of *National Geographic* and similar publications. If this isn't feasible, you'll need to learn one of the techniques for splitting a page to salvage the pictures on each side.

Other uses and sources for instructional photographs are examined in Chapter Fourteen.

Model student activity

"Excavating a Wastebasket" The following student activities rely primarily on the access skill of observing (and the process skill of inferring). In addition to their skills-focus, these activities are representative of a particular type of instructional activity in which students find themselves playing the role of social scientists, in a somewhat simplified form of course. In this activity, which is adapted from the MATCH (Materials and Activities for Teachers and Children) Unit, "The House of Ancient Greece" (MATCH, 1965), students find themselves in the position of archaeologists/anthropologists.

Stage one
Materials needed: One full wastebasket from another room—another classroom preferably, or from the teachers' lounge or principal's office.

(Note: A plastic bag inserted the previous morning can make this activity a lot less messy.)

Procedure: Do NOT indicate which room the wastebasket is from.

1 Place the basket where everyone can see it.

2 Appoint one person as the excavator. That student's job is to take the objects out of the basket, one by one, and describe them carefully.

3 Appoint another child as the cataloger. This job involves drawing a cross section of the wastebasket on the chalkboard and noting the position of the items as they are dug up by the excavator. (Note: Since the "digging" proceeds from the top downward, allow plenty of room to draw an oversized illustration.)

4 Have the rest of the class list the items and describe them briefly on a sheet as follows:

Item	Description
8 milk cartons	empty, from Byrne Dairy, ½ pint
5 plastic straws	red & white striped, about 8 inches long
8 pieces orange peel	different sizes, dry
pencil shavings	yellow, green & blue, mostly yellow, about ¼ cup
one crumpled paper	three-ringed notebook, subject: math, addition problems with 3 wrong. Name: Sarah Farr

5 Ask the following questions, as appropriate:

   a What kinds of activities took place wherever this wastebasket came from?

   b Which took place first? (Those that produced items at the bottom of the basket.)

   c Can we be sure?

   d Where did the basket come from?

   e Which articles give the best clues?

   f Can we be sure of the significance of some items? (Does the *presence* of orange peel but the *absence* of brown lunch bags and waxed paper indicate that lunch was eaten in the room?)

6 At a prearranged time, appoint a small (3–4 students) delegation to take their findings to the room from which the wastebasket came to check out the accuracy of their conclusions. If they are uncertain as to exactly which room it is from, you may need to make some hasty arrangements and have several delegations operating simultaneously.

Archaeologists in action

Stage two: Excavating wastebaskets

Materials needed: Full wastebaskets from a variety of places—both in school and out. (You can "load" some with clues if you wish.) Each basket (or plastic bag) should be labeled Exhibit A, Exhibit B, etc.

Procedure: Proceed as on the previous day, except this time provide each small group with its own wastebasket.

Their task: "Tell as much as you can about wherever this wastebasket came from and what activities took place where it was." Each group should record its findings on chart paper and present them to the class upon completion. Note: Caution each group *not* to indicate where their basket is from until after they have presented their information to the entire class.

A New Role for Background Information

Traditional social studies instruction so often begins with "a little background information" that the practice has almost become a ritual. Unfortunately, so much emphasis and attention is devoted to presenting background information that often there's little time left for students to do anything with it—the information, that is. It's little wonder then that students sometimes get the impression that social studies is largely a process of accumulating background information, information they are never asked to use. Notice, however, that in the wastebasket activity, it was *not* necessary to provide any background information on what anthropologists do *before* students started the activity. Rather, the necessary information was inherent in the activity itself, a phenomenon that should become evident in most of the student activities we suggest throughout this book. (Notice that it wasn't necessary to do any background reading prior to dealing with the presidency activity in Chapter One, for example.)

Creating content

By no means are we suggesting that background information is not important, either in contemporary social studies programs or elsewhere. But we are suggesting that there has been a subtle shift in *when* (at what point) background information becomes necessary, and when it comes into play. By using uncaptioned culture cards *before* studying a particular culture, for instance, students almost always raise questions— *their* questions—about the culture, which they can then attempt to answer through reading. Likewise, after having experienced the wastebasket activity, students should have a better feeling for what archaeologists/anthropologists do, a feeling that can bring new meaning to accounts they read about such people.

Creating a demand

What we are talking about here is largely a matter of timing: engaging students in an activity *prior* to providing them with background information on the topic of their investigation can often create the need for information, thus providing students with a reason to read. This kind of phenomenon sometimes mirrors what teachers notice among their nonreading students; somehow so-called nonreaders can often manage to comprehend articles on sports, auto mechanics, or the latest hairstyles— materials they read because they want to—but are apparently unable to get through the stuff they're "spozed" to read. The clear implication is that when students want information, they can generally get it. It also suggests that before we, as teachers, assign large amounts of material intended as background information, we might do well to devote our attention to creating a need for that information.

Summary

Before students can develop the skills for using information, they must have access to information. This chapter has identified three access skills: reading, listening, and observing. We also identified techniques that can help you build students' skills in gaining access to information.

No matter how much students may need it, pure skills-based teaching can sometimes become downright dull—for both teachers and students. To offset this, many of the sample activities in this chapter have incorporated elements of mystery or problems to be explained, both of which are intended to enhance student interest (as we noted in Chapter One). Another technique used by some teachers to counter the groan students emit when they hear, "Today we will do another observing lesson" is based on a little harmless subversion. As long as you know what skills you are planning to emphasize in an activity, it isn't necessary to even mention them when presenting the activity to students. Thus a statement such as "Describe what you see in these pictures" is not likely to turn students off.

Implicit in this chapter are several teaching guidelines for managing instruction directed toward access skills. They are:

1 Directing at least a portion of almost every social studies activity toward the skills of observing, listening, and reading.
2 Providing individualized instruction (task cards, etc.—see Chapter Thirteen) for students who continue to have difficulty with particular skills.
3 Using social studies content to teach reading skills whenever appropriate. When students' reading skills are so poor that using regular text materials could become an exercise in frustration, consider using nonreading approaches—culture cards, etc.—that draw on the skills of observing and listening.
4 Making skills the explicit focus of activities in terms of your own planning, but keeping them implicit in terms of the way you present activities to your students.

Suggested Activities

1 From a teaching perspective, determine how the two case studies, "The Swedes and the Seagulls" and "Stone Axes," are similar.
2 Read Herber's *Teaching Reading in the Content Areas,* then select a segment from a social studies text and show how it could be approached in ways Herber suggests.
3 Select an issue of *National Geographic* or a similar magazine, and develop a learning activity based on the illustrations from one article. It could be something as simple as matching the captions (which you have cut off) with the appropriate picture.
4 Select two social studies texts for the same grade level, then using the procedure described in this chapter determine the readability level of each. Determine, also, if there is any difference in concept loading.

References

Baum, Willa K. "Oral History." *Looking At.* Boulder, CO: ERIC Clearinghouse for Social Studies/Social Science Education, September, 1975.

Feely, Theodore M. "The Cloze and the Maze." *The Social Studies* 66 (November/December 1975): 252–57.

Fry, Edward. *Reading Instruction for Classroom and Clinic.* New York: McGraw-Hill, 1972.

Herber, Harold. *Teaching Reading in the Content Areas.* Englewood Cliffs, NJ: Prentice-Hall, 1970.

Johnson, Roger E., and Vardian, Eileen B. "Reading, Readability, and the Social Studies." *The Reading Teacher* 26 (February 1973): 483–88.

Lundstrum, John P. "Reading in the Social Studies." In Dana Kurfman (ed.) *Developing Decision-Making Skills,* 47th Yearbook, Washington, D.C.: National Council for the Social Studies, 1977, pp. 109–39.

Lundstrum, John P., and Taylor, Bob L. *Teaching Reading in the Social Studies.* Boulder, CO: ERIC Clearinghouse for Social Studies/Social Science Education and the Social Science Education Consortium, Inc., 1977.

Machart, Norman C. "Doing Oral History in the Elementary Grades." *Social Education* 43 (October 1979): 479–80.

Suggested Readings

Harold Herber. *Teaching Reading in the Content Areas.* Englewood Cliffs, NJ: Prentice-Hall, 1970. Unlike reading texts that put most of their emphasis on learning to read in the decoding sense, Herber places considerable emphasis on techniques that improve reading comprehension. This book should be part of every teacher's personal library.

John P. Lundstrum and Bob L. Taylor. *Teaching Reading in Social Studies.* Boulder, CO: ERIC Clearinghouse for Social Studies/Social Science Education, and the Social Science Education Consortium Inc., 1977. This short booklet provides an excellent summary of reading research related to social studies and outlines techniques teachers can apply to improve reading comprehension.

George L. Mehaffy, Thad Sitton, and O. L. Davis, Jr. *Oral History in the Classroom.* How to Do It Series Number 2, Number 8. Washington, D.C.: National Council for the Social Studies, 1979. This eight-page pamphlet provides a step-by-step guide to oral history activities. Other titles in this series, which cost $1.00 each, are: *Improving Reading Skills in Social Studies; Effective Use of Films in Social Studies; Reach for a Picture; Using Questions in Social Studies; Architecture as a Primary Source for Social Studies;* and *Perspectives on Aging.* Available from the National Council for the Social Studies, 3615 Wisconsin Ave., N.W., Washington, D.C. 20016.

9 Managing Skills-Based Instruction: Maps, Globes, Graphs, and Other Media Forms

Key Questions

How can students use maps, charts, and other kinds of social studies information?

How can mathematics be used in social studies?

Key Concepts

Maps, globes, graphs, and charts are specialized forms in which information is presented.

When students have difficulty gaining access to some specialized forms of information, part of the problem may be their lack of understanding as to how the information got into that form in the first place.

Although most of social studies is synthetic in nature, map and globe skills are clearly analytic. There is an identifiable sequence of skills and knowledge necessary to interpret information in these forms.

The specialized knowledge and skills needed to deal with maps and globes—specifically, latitude, longitude, and scale—are founded in mathematics, not in social studies, and should be treated accordingly.

Introduction: The Specialized Access Skills

Maps and globes, and, to a lesser extent, charts and graphs, have always been an integral part of social studies education. It's important to recognize that there is nothing inherently "social" about a map, graph, chart, or globe, despite the role they play in social studies. Collectively, they are specialized ways for presenting information, nothing more.

The nature of maps, globes, graphs, and charts becomes more apparent if you consider that the information they deal with could be presented in another form. An aerial photograph, for example, can convey at least as much (probably more) information than many landform maps. Likewise, the information on a chart or table could also be presented in a written description. However, written descriptions of the information presented on the income tax tables, for example, would undoubtedly be so complex that they'd be incomprehensible. In many respects, then, charts and tables *simplify* information that might be incomprehensible when presented in a different form.

Gaining access to the information presented on maps, charts, or in graphic form requires specialized skills and knowledge. Actually, map, chart, and graph reading all demand decoding skills not unlike those required to read information presented in narrative form (as you are doing now). True, the symbols are different—dots on a map, for example, almost always stand for something different than squares—but the process of bringing meaning to these symbols is clearly a form of decoding.

Decoding

Reading, in the decoding sense of the term, plays such an important role in gaining access to the information on maps, graphs, charts, and tables that our approach in this chapter is borrowed from the language-experience approach to teaching reading. This approach is based on the premise that if children see their speech being translated (encoded) into written symbols (words), they will be better able to read (or decode) those symbols. This means that teachers who use the language-experience approach spend considerable time encoding (writing down) stories that children dictate to them, which the children then decode (or read) at a later time.

Our approach in this chapter is based on the premise that one reason children may have difficulty with map reading, for example, is because they don't understand how the information got *into* that form. Likewise, if children have difficulty decoding charts and tables, the problem may lie in their inability to understand how information was encoded into the chart or table form. This should explain our emphasis on encoding—on map making, table making, chart making, etc.—as a necessary balance for decoding experiences —map reading, table reading, chart reading, etc.—that have traditionally played a starring role in social studies programs.

An encoding approach

In the first section of this chapter, we examine map- and globe-related skills and identify several exemplary activities you might use to teach such skills. Tables, graphs, charts, and other quantitative data forms are considered in the following sections.

Maps and Globes

Maps are among the most abstract devices used in teaching social studies. Most maps leave out more information than they include and then use symbols to describe the information included. The abstract nature of maps is well illustrated in Figure 9.1. What may look to us like a random collection of sticks and shells makes perfect sense to a mariner from the Marshall Islands. The sticks represent consistent wave patterns, while the shells mark reefs and islands. With maps like this one the Marshall Islanders navigated their way across the empty stretches of the Pacific.

For children who are in Piaget's concrete-operations stage of development, the notion that a map "stands for" something can be especially difficult to grasp. Indeed, as Figure 9.1 illustrates, most maps are models—theoretical

Figure 9.1 A
Mariner's Map

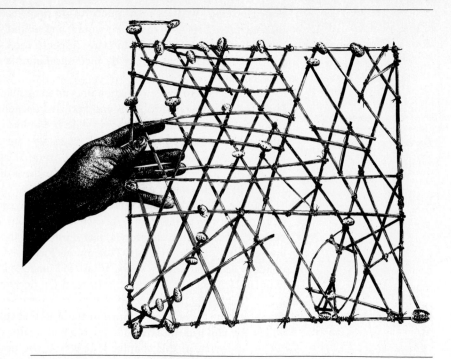

models, if you will—of things that most of us have never seen, and, in many cases, never will.

What adds to the abstract nature of most maps is the rapidity with which they lose one-to-one correspondence. On most maps, trees and buildings are the first things to disappear. Cities become dots or squares that look nothing like the areas represented, and, on some maps, some dots (for small cities) may not even appear. Thus, what children know to exist in reality may not appear on many maps.

Maps as abstract models

Maps also demand that we look at things from a different and unusual perspective. Except for astronauts, few of us have had the luxury of viewing the world while suspended in space. (Landstat maps made from satellite photographs have helped considerably in this respect. See page 263.) Maps demand that we assume the perspective of "looking down on" or what, in children's terms, can be described as a bird's-eye view.

Bird's-eye view

To help children gain experience with the perspective from which maps are made, we suggest that you provide several "bird's-eye view" activities. Here are some suggestions.

1   Draw a picture of your shoe. (If the heel is visible, it's not a bird's-eye view.)
2   Hold a "bird's-eye view contest." Have students draw and identify pictures of various objects as they would be seen from a bird's-eye view. Some examples are pictured in Figure 9.2.
3   Place a ladder somewhere in the classroom and then place various objects underneath it (model cars, etc). Have children draw only what they see from the ladder. Note: This may be very difficult for young children who, because

Figure 9.2 Common Objects Seen from a Bird's-Eye View

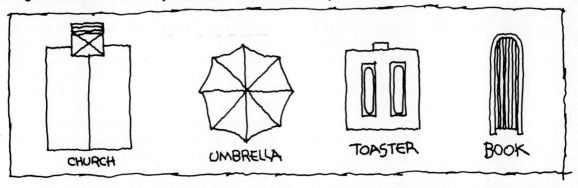

CHURCH   UMBRELLA   TOASTER   BOOK

they know that a model car has wheels, for example, may draw them in regardless of whether they can be seen from a bird's-eye view.

Map Making

Map making refers to activities in which children transform (encode) a scene into map form. In other words, students actually produce a map. This automatically excludes what is sometimes called "map making" but is actually map copying. In map copying, students are typically provided with a printed map and then asked to color in and correctly label a blank outline map so that it resembles the original. Map copying can be useful in helping to fix areas in a child's mind, but it teaches little or nothing about map making in the cartographic sense of the term. In fact, copied maps often have a way of turning into works of art, especially if students add colored glitter, spangles, or even colored rice to indicate different areas. Indeed, such maps should probably be judged on an aesthetic basis—as works of art.

Encoding: a key to decoding

Map making (in the encoding sense) requires an area to be mapped. Beginning with bird's-eye views of various objects, students may move to increasingly larger areas—their classroom, the school building, the neighborhood around the school, or other areas in the community. Aerial photographs, which are available from the United States Department of Agriculture (try the Soil Conservation Service Office first), can prove invaluable, especially since most maps are made from aerial photographs anyhow.

The objective of initial map-making activities is to help children visualize the local environment from a bird's-eye (or spatial) perspective, and to help them understand that when anything is reduced in size—as maps are in relation to the area they depict—some things must be omitted. (On what basis are some things kept in and others left out?)

Relief Maps If your school is located on the plains of West Texas, making a relief map of the area is probably pointless; the terrain is as flat as a tabletop. In most other areas of the country, however, relief maps can show hills and valleys, thus illustrating yet another type of map and map making. But beware! Making accurate relief maps can be a time consuming, painstaking, and ofttimes messy process.

To build relief maps of small areas, such as the immediate neighborhood around a school, you might have students actually measure changes in elevation. But because doing that is more difficult than you might imagine, we recommend that you use topographical maps from the U. S. Geological Survey. They show changes in elevation while maintaining one-to-one correspondence by showing buildings and other features not found on many maps. If it is necessary to enlarge a small map (or a portion of a map) in order to provide an area large enough for children to work on, you can do so by placing the original in an opaque projector and then tracing the enlarged image on posterboard. This procedure is suitable for enlarging almost any kind of map, and also preserves the colors. If your original map is small and you are also willing to sacrifice color, you can make an overhead transparency of the map and then enlarge it using an overhead projector.

Relief-map recipes

Relief maps can be constructed from a variety of materials, the least messy but most costly of which is clay—pound after pound of clay. Recipes for other relief-map making materials are as follows:

1   Papier-mâché. Tear newspapers into strips and soak in water overnight. Mix wheat paste (wallpaper paste) with warm water to the consistency of thin cream. Squeeze water out of the newspaper strips, dip into the paste, remove the excess, and then apply to the map form.

2   Salt and flour. Mix four cups flour, two cups salt, and approximately two cups of water. Knead thoroughly. Food coloring may be added to the water, or tempera paint can be kneaded into the mixture. The mixture may require two to three days to dry completely.

3   Sawdust and glue. Mix slightly thinned white glue with dampened, fine sawdust until it reaches a workable consistency.

Relief maps, except those of undried clay, can be coated with a thin mixture of plaster of Paris and water. If allowed to dry overnight, this coating will keep paint from soaking in as much as it otherwise would.

Scale   In map making, it usually isn't very long before a question arises as to whether or not maps should be drawn to scale. For primary grade children, the answer is generally no; not-to-scale drawings will usually suffice. For the intermediate grades, it depends. That isn't much of an answer until you find that what it depends on is the math program your students are using.

To scale or not to scale?

You'll find that the notion of scale, like latitude and longitude, is mathematically based. And scale, perhaps better than anything else, reflects the zenith of representational thought. In this case, one thing is said to equal something else. For elementary students, the notion that "one inch can equal one foot (or one mile or ten miles)" can present some of the same difficulties that many algebra students encounter when they find that "x can equal anything."

Even some adults have difficulty with the way scale can be presented, especially if it is identified by a representative ratio such as $1:10,000$. This means that 1 unit of *anything* on the map equals 10,000 of the same units on the ground. To the extent that 10,000 inches may not mean much even to you, we suggest that only those with masochistic tendencies should try to teach this form of scale to most elementary children.

Basic concepts of scale

The notion of scale is so integral a part of maps and map making that it cannot be dealt with casually. By the end of the middle grades, for example, Hanna et al. (1966, p. 25) have suggested that children have had experience with some of the following ideas related to scale:

Scale is the relation of distance on the map to the distance it represents on the ground.

The scale of a map is large or small in relation to the object it represents.

The use of a large scale for a map enables the mapper to show many details about a small area.

The use of a small scale for a map enables the mapper to show a large area but fewer details.

Scale on the globe may be used to measure the distance between two points on the earth's surface.

The scale on one part of a map may be different from the scale on another part (an inset map, for instance).

You may have to be satisfied that most of your students can, for example, use the scale on a map to calculate the distance between two points. A more complete understanding of scale may come only after they've had more experience with higher mathematics. However, many modern math programs introduce representational thought, and even the notion of scale, much earlier than they used to. As a result, we recommend that you correlate your map-making activities with your math program, which may even introduce "scale" in the primary grades.

Translation Mapping

Translation is a major subdivision of the comprehension category of the *Taxonomy of Educational Objectives,* and is defined as changing data from one form to another. This is, in fact, what map making is all about —depicting real areas or phenomena in more abstract map forms. Using this definition as a basis, it's possible to create activities based on translating, some of which, though not especially thrilling, will be educational.

Student activities

For example, you could have students:

1 Produce a written description of information contained on a chart or table (educational, but not too thrilling).
2 Produce a map of a nation, such as Japan, from a written or verbal description. (This activity is a lot more interesting than it may seem and produces some very interesting maps—inaccurate but interesting.)
3 Produce and translate a map. (In this activity, one group of students produces a map and another group uses it to locate an object—interesting, though the instructions are more complex than the activity.)

The class is divided into teams of two. Each team then locates an object somewhere around the school grounds (lavatories are off limits), returns to the classroom, and provides a verbal description to another team, which then produces a map from that description. Finally, the maps are given to yet another team, which must retrieve the object. As a follow-up, share the various problems the teams encountered in either making or using the maps.

Using Maps and Globes

With satellite photography, it is now possible to illustrate the earth in a manner previously possible only with a globe. Today, two Landstat satellites circle the earth every 103 minutes, sending back color photographs of remarkable clarity. The Landstat map shown in Figure 9.3 is of New York City, Long Island, and the New Jersey coast. Although our sample is reproduced in black and white, it should give you some idea of the potential this innovation has for map-related instruction.

Landstat maps notwithstanding, the globe is still one of the most accurate tools for helping children orient themselves to the planet on which we live. It can help them distinguish between land and water areas, and, when its use is begun in the primary grades, it can help to correct the commonly held notion that "up" on a map is north and "down" is south. Children may still use those expressions, but at least they will know that up is away from the center of the earth and down is the reverse. With a globe, they can also learn that north is toward the North Pole and south is toward the South Pole, something almost impossible to illustrate clearly on a wall map.

To show the relative roundness of the earth, it is no problem for teachers to hold up a globe for the entire class to see. But when it comes to locating specific places on the globe, two problems often emerge. To avoid the problem of having students line up and file past the globe to locate specific places on it, some schools purchase classroom sets of eight- to twelve-inch globes, which are kept on a cart and wheeled from classroom to classroom as needed. The second problem is a function of the globe itself, or, more accurately, of its size. On a twelve-inch globe, for example, the United States measures approximately four inches from west to east. On the average wall map, the United States measures approximately four feet from west to east, thus permitting the presentation of much more detail. For most purposes, the globe is still the best map-related tool available, but when more detail is desired, you'll probably need to turn to a wall map.

Accuracy vs. size

Wall Maps   Getting a round earth to fit onto a flat map has perplexed cartographers for centuries. The classic examples of peeling an orange and then trying to make the peel lie flat, or of doing the same with a rubber ball, illustrate the essence of the problem. In cartographic terms, it is a question of "projection." Projecting rounded surfaces onto a flat map in different ways will yield the images shown in Figure 9.4.

The distortion on most wall maps is greatest at the high latitudes, as illustrated by the different ways in which a human head is depicted in Figure 9.4. Such distortion is responsible for the question "Why isn't Greenland a continent?" It's really a very logical question for a child to ask, since

Figure 9.3 Landstat Map of New York City, Long Island, and New Jersey Coast

Distortion at high latitudes

on many maps Greenland appears to be two to three times the size of Australia, which is a continent. When children look on a globe, however, they will find that Australia is three times larger than Greenland—Australia has 2,975,000 square miles vs. Greenland's 840,000 square miles. Explaining to students how some maps make small things appear larger than they really are is no small feat! For very small areas, of course, the distortion created by different map projections is usually negligible. But for large land masses, we recommend that a globe be used in conjuction with wall maps.

To avoid the "north is up" phenomenon so commonly associated with wall maps, we suggest that you occasionally lay wall maps on the floor. Some teachers have gone even further; they have their students paint huge outline maps on the school parking lot or playground (after securing appropriate permission, of course). Such large-scale maps should be accurate in direction and as accurate as possible in scale. For example, an outline map of the United States that is drawn on a parking lot or playground located to the south of the school building would present a northern perspective when viewed from the school building. It's the perspective you would get by

Figure 9.4 Distortions Created by Different Map Projections

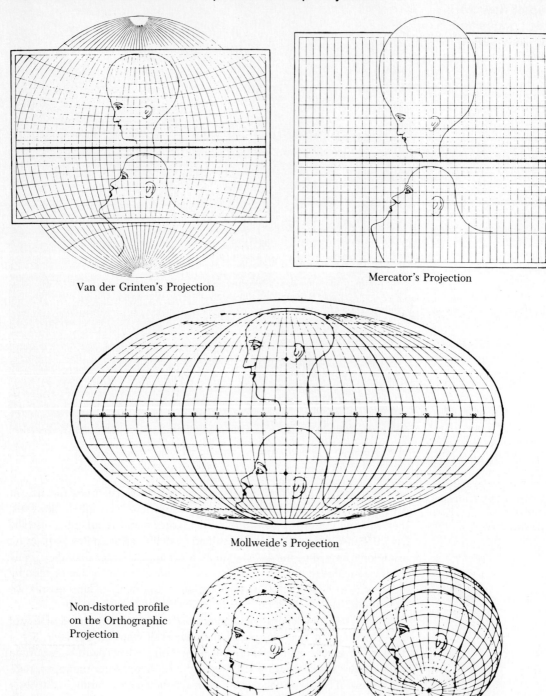

Van der Grinten's Projection

Mercator's Projection

Mollweide's Projection

Non-distorted profile
on the Orthographic
Projection

turning a wall map upside-down. The objective in doing such large-scale maps is to depict the earth accurately, even if that means creating maps that look different from the ones we're used to seeing.

Latitude, Longitude, and Other Grid Systems

difficult for kids to grasp

Most map and globe skill programs from fourth grade upward call for instruction in latitude and longitude. One of the more difficult ideas for children to grasp is the fact that while most parallels of latitudes are lines, 90° North latitude and 90° South latitude are not lines, they are points (or, in mathematical terms, poles). Almost equally difficult is the idea that while the meridians of longitude are of equal length, the parallels of latitude get shorter as one moves away from the equator. We suspect that one reason children find these ideas so hard to grasp is because latitude and longitude are often taught as arbitrary systems rather than as part of circular or spherical measurement. And for children who think degrees are units for measuring temperature, you have another key to why latitude and longitude can present difficulties for them.

Spherical measurement

A related problem is that many social studies programs call for instruction in latitude and longitude in Grade 4 or earlier, while students often don't encounter circular or spherical measurement in their math programs until about Grade 7. Thus, social studies teachers are faced with the dilemma of either teaching the fundamentals of circular and spherical measurement, which would permit children to see the logic of latitude and longitude—and it is an extremely rational and logical system—or teaching latitude and longitude as an arbitrary system, which children may become adept at using but really don't understand.

In its simplest terms, teaching latitude and longitude in elementary social studies programs can be reduced to three components:

1 Use of *a* grid system (any grid system)
2 Use of *the* grid system (longitude and latitude)
3 Understanding the basis for longitude and latitude

Grid games

Battleship

Even primary children can become adept at using *a* grid system, especially those involving a combination of letters and numbers. Math texts frequently include an assortment of grid-related activities, sometimes more so than social studies texts. The beauty of many gridding activities is that they can quickly be made into games that kids love to play. A classic is Battleship, in which one student locates his navy on a simple grid, then another student tries to sink that navy by calling out the various squares on the grid. You could also obtain classroom sets of state road maps from one of the petroleum companies and create a version of Cops and Robbers or the FBI and the Crooks. In small groups, the "crooks" identify a quadrant on the map, then the rest of the children ask them questions such as, "Are you in a square near a large city?" In other words, it is the detective game adapted to a map, in which the "crook" must be asked questions that can be answered only by a yes or no. Note that this activity serves several purposes: it provides experience in using a grid system for locational purposes; it helps children formulate questions; and it also provides greater familiarity with state geography.

The road map game will prove very popular even after the skills you're teaching are learned.

Applying a known system

After your students have had experience using a grid system, the basis for latitude and longitude and its relationship to the globe can be explained. In this case, your task will become one of *applying* a system that children have already worked with to the globe. If you opt to present latitude and longitude through an expository teaching strategy, you will find yourself doing two things at once—explaining both the system and its application to the globe. Whatever approach you finally use to teach longitude and latitude, or any grid system for that matter, we make the same recommendation that we did for teaching the concept of scale: correlate latitude and longitude with whatever math program you are using.

Map Reading (Decoding Maps)

Students who have had rich and varied map-making (encoding) experience should find that map reading is considerably easier to cope with. Realistically, however, children will be expected to use a wider range of maps than most of them will have had experience making. Making a classroom-by-classroom, population density map of the school, for example, where each dot represents one student, can be a reasonable map-making experience. But making a population density map for large areas, such as the United States or Europe, is such a laborious, time consuming, and boring activity that it could well lead to a passionate hatred of any kind of map making. (If you insist on having students make population density maps of very large areas, consider doing Antarctica or Greenland!)

No set sequence

There is no single established sequence of map and globe skills for the elementary grades. Sometimes first graders will be expected to know and locate the major continents and oceans, for example, while in other instances, this is not dealt with until Grade 3 or later. The variation is such that, although some form of map and globe skills will be taught at each grade level, it's difficult to say which ones will be dealt with at a particular level.

By the time children leave elementary or middle school, they will generally be expected to be able to apply the skills required to answer the following questions, all of which are based on the sample map illustrated in Figure 9.5. These questions are similar to those found on standardized achievement tests. Note that we are doing two things here: (1) illustrating how your students' ability to deal with map and globe skills is likely to be measured, and (2) identifying what those skills are. Accordingly, you should (1) attempt to answer the questions (all are answerable), and (2) identify, in the space provided, the skill or skills required to answer the question.

Questions

1 What is the northernmost city on Pleasure Island?
 A. Beta B. Alpha C. Gamma D. Zeta
 Skill: _____

2 How far is it from Delta to Rho?
 A. 250 miles B. 550 miles C. 750 miles D. 900 miles
 Skill: _____

Figure 9.5 Pleasure
Island Map

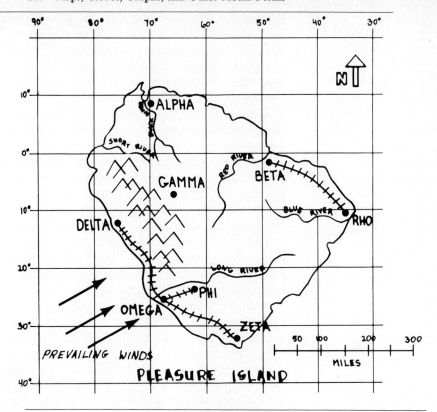

3 Which river flows toward the Northeast?
   A. Long River   B. Blue River   C. Black River   D. Red River
   Skill: _____

4 What is the busiest port city on Pleasure Island?
   A. Beta   B. Gamma   C. Omega   D. Phi
   Skill: _____

5 What city gets the least rainfall?
   A. Beta   B. Gamma   C. Delta   D. Can't tell
   Skill: _____

6 What city lies closest to the equator?
   A. Beta   B. Alpha   C. Rho   D. Can't tell
   Skill: _____

7 In what hemisphere is most of Pleasure Island located?
   A. Northern   B. Eastern   C. Southern   D. Can't tell
   Skill: _____

(Answers: 1. B; 2. B; 3. D; 4. D; 5. B; 6. A; 7. C)

*Step-by-step
skill sequence*

Few map skills consist of single-step procedures; in fact, most are complex
chains of steps that must be followed in sequence. If any step is omitted or
if the sequence of steps is confused, students are likely to fail. For example,
in order to identify the hemisphere in which Pleasure Island is located
(Question 7 above), the student must know that the equator is 0° latitude,

and that as one moves southward, the degrees of latitude increase in number until one reaches 90° South latitude, the South Pole. The student must then apply this knowledge to the information provided on the map. As a further example of this, identify what you must know and be able to apply to determine whether Pleasure Island is in the eastern or western hemisphere.

Many map skills are more complex than they first appear. However, the analytic (math-like) nature of map skills also permits *task analysis;* that is, map skills are amenable to being analyzed so that you can identify precisely what students must know and be able to do to achieve success. For example, to determine the distance from Delta to Rho (Question 2), the student must be able to do (or know) the following: (1) that all maps have a scale, (2) that the scale indicates real distances in shortened form, (3) that by using a measuring device (a ruler, etc.) one can convert the distance on a map to the real distance, and so forth. All of this could become too abstract, however, if the student does not know that cities on a map are usually shown with a dot, or if he or she is unable to locate the two cities in question. All of these elements must be brought to bear on the problem in the correct sequence; otherwise, failure is almost guaranteed.

Task analysis

If students have used symbols, scale, and directions in making maps, they should have fewer problems when they encounter these elements in map reading. But when students encounter problems, we suggest that you plan a teacher-directed, demonstration lesson focusing on the skill. To help students find the distance from Delta to Rho, for example, we would make an overhead transparency of Figure 9.5, and then demonstrate the process in a simple, step-by-step fashion. No elaborate questioning procedure is necessary. In fact, since most map and globe skills yield a single correct answer (such as the distance between two cities) it will not inhibit your students' creativity if you show them an efficient process for finding that answer.

Using Maps

Some of the most effective and interesting map-related student activities begin with a heuristic question such as, "If you were the town council, where would you build the new incinerator (or park, or shopping center, or apartment complex)?" and use maps as the main data source. One such activity comes from the MATCH Unit, "The City," and focuses on the problem of where a new freeway should be built in a town called "Five Corners, U.S.A."

"Five Corners, U.S.A."

Overview: A new highway is being constructed and is complete except for a small section that is to pass through part of the city of Five Corners. Students, each of whom is either a resident or a businessperson, must decide where the unfinished portion of the road should go.

Model student activity

    Materials: Desk maps of Five Corners (Figure 9.6)

    Procedure:

1 Assign or permit children to choose one of the residences or businesses as their own. Write their names on the small maps or on a master map if you use the latter. (All plots need not be assigned.)

Figure 9.6 Desk Map for Five Corners, U.S.A. Activity

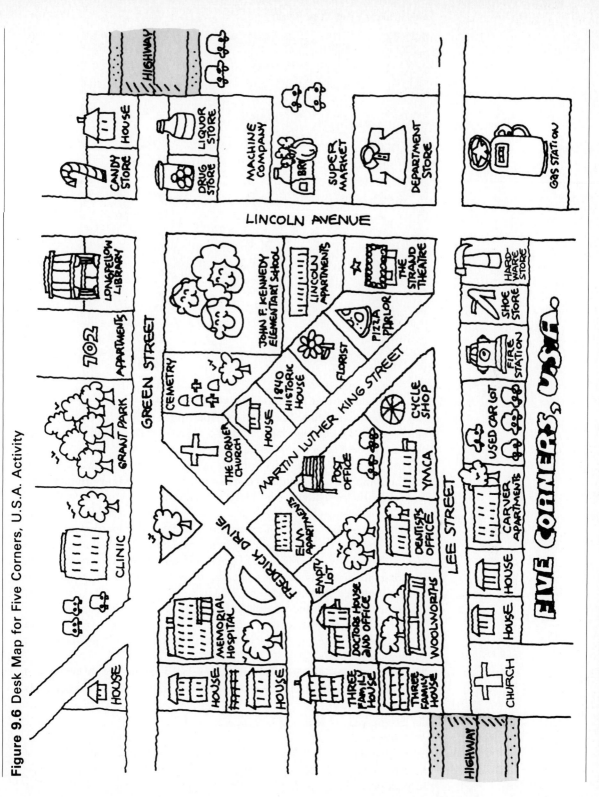

Source: MATCH Unit, "The City" Teacher's Guide, p. 52. Reprinted by permission of Delta Education, Inc.

2   Tell the children that the finished highway must be at least as wide as the
two unfinished sections, and that the final route cannot have very sharp
bends in it. Considering these limitations, each child (or small group of
children) should select a tentative route for the highway.

   Solutions involving tunnels, bridges, the moving of buildings, or an ele-
vated highway are all permissible. You may, however, wish to refrain from
suggesting these in advance and let the children arrive at possible alternatives.

   Note: In the MATCH Unit, it's suggested that Step 2 be done as homework.
A note is printed on the back of each map explaining the problem and the
idea of the activity to parents. Help from the student's family is encouraged.

3   Working either individually or in small groups, the class should try to agree
upon a route for the highway.

4   Have the class, either individually or in groups, present the proposed plans.
Bring out the implications of the different plans, help clarify choices, and
break deadlocks if necessary. How complex you should get depends on your
students and their abilities.

5   Try to reach one solution. However, it is permissible *not* to arrive at a
solution, a situation that may teach children more than would a hastily
arrived-at solution.

In addition to the "Five Corners" map, the MATCH "City" Unit also
includes a magnetic board on which miniature buildings can be placed so as
to provide children with a three-dimensional model of the situation. The

model helps maintain one-to-one correspondence with what is shown on the map.

Variations on the model Activities of this kind are easy to vary; in fact, if you teach in a suburban or urban school you could create a mythical freeway-type situation using a map of an area near the school. In rural settings, the location of a freeway probably has less human impact—at least fewer buildings need to be destroyed and families moved—so in such instances you might wish to focus on the ecological impact that freeways can have. Thus, your question could become "Should the proposed freeway be built through a wildlife preserve?"

In the "Five Corners U.S.A." activity, you could have the children represent special interest groups (a business association, the town council, etc.) instead of individual property owners. This variation would also introduce a political dimension, especially if the town council had the final say.

Combining map reading and decision making

Yet other map-based activities are described in Willard Woodruff's *Case Study Book* (1970). For example, in an activity entitled "Where Do We Build the Incinerator?" the children face a problem similar to that in "Five Corners, U.S.A." Many other excellent activities not using maps are also included.

Another kind of map-related activity is based on presenting students with a sequence of maps, each of which adds its own kind of specialized information. In the following activity, students are asked where they would locate a city on a mythical island. Then, in succession, additional information on terrain (landforms), vegetation, and rainfall is provided, each on a separate map.

Where Would You Locate Your City?

Overview: The object of this activity is to determine whether students will change their original decision in light of new information.

Model student activity

Procedure: Provide students with a copy of Map 1 (Maps 1, 2, 3, and 4 are shown in Figure 9.7). Ask where, with just the information they have, they would locate a city if they were prospective settlers. The area is, of course, otherwise uninhabited. Permit them to discuss their choices in small groups, and then have each group present their choice to the entire class. Then provide each group with copies of Maps 2, 3, and 4, one at a time, permitting discussion and explanations (as warranted) after each one is distributed.

Variation: Ryan and Ellis (1974, pp. 41–42), in their book *Instructional Implications of Inquiry* describe an interesting variation on this activity. It uses a similar sequence of maps but for a real country. However, the identity of that country is kept from students—it's just called "Country X"—until they determine where they would locate a major city within that nation. After students have made their decisions, they can turn to their atlases and compare their selections with the actual location of major cities in the country.

Figure 9.7 Mystery Island Maps

Map 1

Scale: 1 inches = 50 miles

〜〜 sea water

〜 rivers

⬗ lakes

Map 2: Landforms

ʌˆʌ mountains or mountainous areas

ˆˆ hills and hilly areas

plains or flat areas

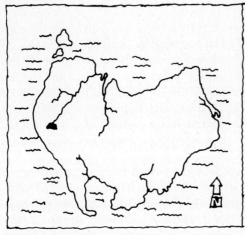

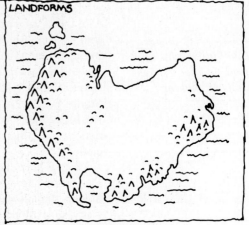

Map 3: Vegetation

↓↓↓ grass

↑↑↑ hardwood trees (beech, oak, etc.)

↑↑↑ tropical trees (palms, etc.)

∴∵∴ shrubs or no vegetation at all

Map 4: Rainfall (average yearly amounts)

⦀⦀ less than 10 inches

between 20 and 40 inches

∴∵∴ between 40 and 60 inches

⫽⫽ between 60 and 80 inches

⊠⊠ more than 100 inches

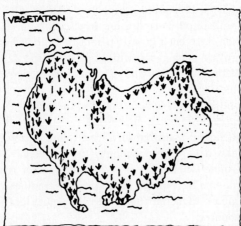

Charts, Graphs, and Tables: Social Studies by the Numbers

Tables, charts, and graphs are the "bad breath" area of social studies for many teachers. Ofttimes they avoid working with apparently lifeless statistical information unless forced to do so. Quantitative (or statistical) data can be imposing, it's true, but tables, graphs, and charts are by no means impossible if approached from a *use* perspective. Unless you plan to have students do something with the information presented on a graph, chart, or table, the data can quickly fall into the realm of just that much more information to remember.

Two aspects of quantitative or statistical data deserve special attention. First, quantitative data is, by nature, raw or uninterpreted information. This means that in most instances individuals must interpret (or process) the data in order to draw their own conclusions. It takes a certain amount of mental effort to do this—draw conclusions, that is—which may account in part for the "bad breath" feeling sometimes associated with quantitative data. For many students (and teachers), it's easier to memorize someone else's conclusions, such as those found in a textbook, than to process the information and draw one's own conclusions.

A second aspect of dealing with quantitative data reflects the fact that charts, graphs, and tables are extremely efficient forms for presenting information. They can present a lot of data in a relatively small space, which is one reason they are favored by textbook writers. From an instructional perspective, charts, graphs, and tables can be so efficient that it doesn't take long before many students begin to suffer from information overload. They become faced with too much information too quickly, and they often lack the means to process it. Common sense indicates that students are not likely to use information, whether in table, graph, or some other form, while reeling under tremendous amounts of data. And the fact that some teachers expect children to memorize the information on a chart or table may only compound an already difficult situation.

Information overload

To avoid information overload, and thus better enable children to use information, the clear implication is that you may want to *limit the amount of information students are expected to handle at the outset of an activity.* Once students understand the original data, you are free to add as much additional information as they are able to handle; the limited-information restriction applies only at the outset of activities. This means then that, rather than presenting students with a full page of quantitative data, it may be necessary to select portions of that information and reproduce it separately, on what is called a "fact sheet."

Fact sheets

The fact sheet illustrated in Figure 9.8 was produced by a fourth grade teacher who was teaching a unit on farming in the United States. Even though the information on it is limited, it still proved too much for her students. So the next year she cut the page in half and distributed Part I first, then Part II.

The fourth graders who used the American Farmer Fact Sheet developed a remarkable body of tentative conclusions based on the data it contained. On the following two pages, we have provided you with an opportunity to pit your interpretive skills against those of our fourth graders. Are you willing to risk it?

Figure 9.8 Model
Fact-Sheet Format:
The American
Farmer

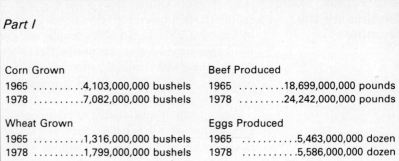

Part I

Corn Grown

1965 ....4,103,000,000 bushels
1978 ....7,082,000,000 bushels

Wheat Grown

1965 ....1,316,000,000 bushels
1978 ....1,799,000,000 bushels

Beef Produced

1965 ....18,699,000,000 pounds
1978 ....24,242,000,000 pounds

Eggs Produced

1965 ....5,463,000,000 dozen
1978 ....5,586,000,000 dozen

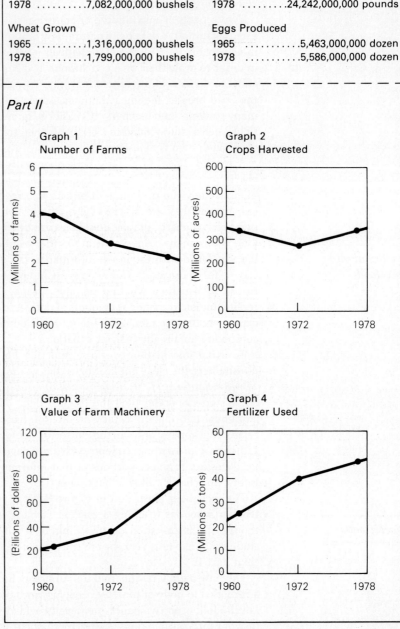

Part II

Graph 1
Number of Farms

Graph 2
Crops Harvested

Graph 3
Value of Farm Machinery

Graph 4
Fertilizer Used

All of the following questions refer to the American Farmer Fact Sheet.

1   What does the information contained in Part I suggest to you (interpretative)?

_____

2   What does the information on Graph One indicate (literal level)?

_____

3   What does the information on Graph Two indicate (again, at the literal level)?

_____

4   What does the information on Graphs One and Two suggest about American farms today (interpretative level)?

_____

5   What does the information on Graph Three indicate (literal)?

_____

(Note: It could mean that farm machinery is more expensive than it used to be.)

6   What does the information on Graph Four indicate (literal)?

_____

7   What is the relationship, if any, between the information on Graphs Three and Four and your answer to Question Four (interpretative)?

_____

*Students'
conclusions*

The students concluded that, although there are fewer farms in the United States, the amount of food produced on those farms has increased. They also concluded that since fewer farmers (Graph One) were farming about the same number of acres as in the past (Graph Two), the average size of a farm is larger today than it was in the past. Furthermore, for fewer farmers to grow more food on about the same amount of farmland, the students concluded this was possible because of the increased use of machinery (Graph Three) and fertilizer (Graph Four). They also suggested that there could be other reasons for this (better weather, etc.), but that they didn't have enough information to be certain of these.

By using just the information on the American Farmer Fact Sheet, students developed their own conclusions about the changing nature of American farming. Of course, a teacher could approach the topic by having students read a section in the textbook, a section which, in all likelihood, would begin: "American farms today are larger than they used to be. Farmers also use more machinery and. . . ." In this instance, however, students would be reading *someone else's conclusions* about farming instead of using information to build their own.

Figure 9.9 Boys and Girls in Ms. James' Classroom

Boys and Girls in Ms. James Classroom
October, 1980

Boys		11
Girls		14
Boy Girl		25

Encoding
Quantitative Data

Before children can use information on a chart, graph, or table, they must be able to handle that information at the literal level. If children cannot, for example, read Graph One on the American Farmer Fact Sheet in order to make statements such as "There were about four million farms in the United States in 1960," then it may be necessary to back up and to show them how the information was translated (or encoded) into graph form.

Our premise in this section is the same as the one we suggested for map-related activities; just as map making (encoding) may provide students with a better basis for map reading, encoding quantitative data (graph making, table making, and chart making) can provide students with a better basis for graph, chart, or table reading activities.

As a general rule, encoding experiences for primary-level students should involve simple examples and small quantities. This can be as simple as tallying the number of girls and boys in a classroom, as illustrated in Figure 9.9.

Manageability

Note also that until students are able to deal with representational thought, it is probably wisest to maintain one-to-one correspondence; that is, one symbol on a table represents something the child can see in reality. In Figure 9.9, each symbol stands for one classmate. As students grow progressively able to handle representational thought, as when one symbol equals five classmates, for example, their encoding experiences can become increasingly complex.

Simple surveys

Simple surveys can provide a wealth of information for encoding activities. That's what the teacher who developed the American Farmer Fact Sheet used when her students encountered graph reading problems. Small groups of students surveyed the traffic passing by the school at different times of day. They counted the number of cars and trucks, the number of station wagons, the number of Volkswagens, the number of cars with whitewall tires, and the number of people who waved back at them (Figure 9.10). Then, with the teacher's help, each group put their information onto a bar graph. The result of one group's efforts is illustrated in Figure 9.11. Rather than leaving it at just a frequency count, however, the various bar graphs were hung around the room to provide a basis for comparison. In addition to determining that

Figure 9.10 Traffic Survey Conducted by Fourth Graders

Traffic Survey

Time: 11:00 - 11:30   Day: Sept. 28th
Surveyors: Roger, Debbie, Susan
Number of
Cars   32
Trucks   14
Station Wagons   12
Bugs   9
Cars with white wall tires   27
People who waved   39

Figure 9.11 Bar Graph Made from Traffic Survey Data

traffic passing the school varied with the time of day (and was often heaviest when students were going to or leaving school), students also discovered some problems in the kinds of questions they had asked. Since Volkswagens are cars, for example, should they put down two tallies, one under cars and one under Volkswagens? Or, did *cars* mean non-station wagons and non-Volkswagens? To deal with these questions, each group had to review its tallying procedure.

Decoding Graphs and Tables

Perhaps nowhere is the distinction between access skills and process skills clearer than in the case of graph and table reading. Before a child can do anything with the data contained on the task card illustrated in Figure 9.12, for example, he or she must gain access to that information. No access, no processing.

As was true of map reading, the process of decoding the data presented on a graph or table is amenable to task analysis. Probably the easiest way to go about that is to ask yourself two related questions: (1) what must the student know (and in what sequence?) to gain access to data (such as the information presented in Figure 9.12), and (2) at what points might a student experience problems?

Some of the knowledge components needed to decode the data on Figure 9.12 are fairly obvious. For instance, unless students can bring meaning to the terms "population," "racial minorities," "unemployment," etc., the data will be meaningless. Likewise, the student must be able to interpret extremely large numbers, e.g., 11.4 million, a task that may be further complicated by the use of decimal points. Even some adults have difficulty determining what ".4 million," for example, really represents. As a consequence, we suggest that large numbers be rounded wherever possible. Doing so can eliminate a potential problem point without altering the overall situation. Be sure that you don't overlook the less obvious knowledge components needed to decode the data on Figure 9.12. For example, unless the student knows that all of the data in the column headed *Chicago* pertains to that city, the table will probably be meaningless.

Rounding with a point

Our point in analyzing graph and table reading as thoroughly as we have is to identify possible problem points that students may encounter. Further, when students come to you with a graph or table they can't deal with, their complaint is apt to be a vaguely stated, "I don't understand this." If you ask, "What don't you understand about it?" the response is likely to be "The whole thing" or "I just don't get it." When it comes to graph and table reading, students are notoriously poor diagnosticians—they may be having problems but probably can't tell you where or why. You may find yourself doing task analysis on a graph or table, much as we have here, in order to identify where the child is having difficulty.

In light of the problems noted above, we do not advocate using a discovery strategy for teaching the specialized access skills associated with table or graph reading. There are just too many points at which students might encounter problems. This is one of those instances where step-by-step, teacher-directed instruction seems wholly appropriate.

Figure 9.12 Sample Task Card

Data	Tokyo, Japan	Chicago, Illinois
Population	11.4 million	3 million
Racial Minorities	Koreans	Blacks, Spanish-Americans, Native Americans
Cases of Murder	213	810
Gun Control	Small arms banned	Small arms registered
Unemployment	Low	High
Family Structure	Strong	Loosening of family ties

Tasks

Using just this information, identify three hypotheses:

1. _____

2. _____

3. _____

Charts

We suspect that in the days before overhead projectors became widely available, chart making was more common than it is today. With the current technology, it is a relatively simple process to place a small-size chart in a thermofax machine; about ten seconds later, you'll get an overhead transparency that, when projected, is readily visible to everyone in the class. A problem with overhead transparencies, however, is that once the projector is turned off, the image is gone. A poster-size chart displayed somewhere in the classroom, on the other hand, offers students the opportunity to have repeated visual contact with whatever the chart depicts. The issue then is one of deciding whether you want to settle for a fleeting visual image or sustained visual contact.

An endless variety of things can be depicted in chart form. If you were to enlarge a table (without *increasing* the number of elements) you would have a *tabular chart*. Or if you were to present a schematic drawing of the structure of an organization such as the U.S. Congress you would have an *organizational chart*. And if you were to outline the steps a bill passes through in Congress en route to becoming a law, for example, you would have a *flow chart*. Virtually any process—the production of steel, bread, or whatever—can be illustrated either in pictures, short narrative descriptions, or a combination of the two on a flow chart. The chart we did to illustrate the "family tree" of a can of corn (Figure 3.2, p. 97) is a kind of flow chart, but because it showed the origin of the various products that went into making the canned corn (as opposed to emphasizing the steps in the process), it technically would be considered a *pedigree chart*.

Charts on which students classify or categorize various kinds of data can be especially helpful in the concept-building process. Consider how you might go about classifying the following terms, for example: *pond, lake, brook, run, river, ocean, stream, sea, pool, tank, basin, creek, bayou.* Since all of these have something to do with water—including *tank,* which is used throughout the West to describe a small pond—your *classification chart* might have two headings: (1) terms that describe bodies of water, and (2) terms that describe flowing water.

All charts, regardless of form or kind, summarize (or abstract) whatever they depict. They are like outlines in that they highlight major points or phases while omitting details. For example, you probably would not include definitions for the terms listed on the classification chart described above, because to do so would present so much information that the major elements would be obscured. Such inclusions would probably defeat the purpose for putting information in chart form in the first place. However, the need to summarize information can be an asset when you have students engage in chart making, because summarizing forces them to identify the information —the main ideas—that they should put on their chart. In this way, chart-making activities can force children to differentiate between main ideas and supporting details. In this context, chart making can be an effective culminating activity for small group work, because it demands that students review what they did and what they found.

Types of charts

Figure 9.13 Linear Chart: The Breadmaking Process

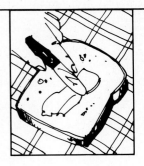

Model student activity

Linear Charting

As an alternative to making charts on poster-size pieces of tagboard, consider using another technique to accomplish some of the same purposes. For lack of a better term, we call this technique *linear charting*. It consists of having students attach pictures or short descriptions of a process in the correct sequence on a piece of string or yarn. A linear chart for the production of bread is illustrated above, in Figure 9.13.

Note that, although this may not sound like an exciting activity, actually doing it may prove otherwise. Consider, also, that linear charting can be used for more than just social studies activities. For example, instead of traditional book reports you might have students illustrate the significant scenes or events in a book and then attach those pictures, in the correct sequence, to a piece of yarn. Then, when students present their reports, the rest of the class can refer to a visual representation (pictures) of the book's events, rather than strictly listening to a verbal presentation.

Sources of Quantitative Data

The reference rooms of most libraries are filled with sources of quantitative data, but since such sources are not usually selected for casual reading, we decided to include this section. If you have no intention of developing a fact sheet, or if you are not keen on reading a list, you might skip this section and go on to the summary.

The most readily available sources of quantitative data are the variety of almanacs and encyclopedias found in most libraries. In the case of encyclopedias, it is sometimes necessary to extract quantitative data from the narrative of an article. Other sources, organized by the types of data they present, are listed below. All are published annually unless otherwise indicated.

Sources for International Data

Europa Yearbook. London: Europa Publications Ltd.

Facts on File: World News Digest. New York: Facts on File, Inc.

Food and Agriculture Organization of the United Nations. *Trade Yearbook* and *The Production Yearbook.* Rome, Italy: The FAO Press.

Mitchell, B. R. (ed.) *European Historical Statistics, 1750–1970.* New York: Columbia University Press, 1975.

New York Times Index. New York: New York Times, Inc. Published quarterly.

United Nations. *Demographic Yearbook.* New York: UN Press.

———. *Statistical Yearbook.* New York: UN Press.

World Health Organization. *World Health Statistics.* Geneva, Switzerland: WHO Press.

Sources for Data about the United States

Most of the quantitative data about the United States is collected and published by the U.S. Government. The amount is massive. Two sources to help you deal with all this data are: *American Statistics Index: Annual, A Comprehensive Guide and Index to the Statistical Publications of the U.S. Government* (Washington, D.C.: Congressional Information Service); and *A Guide to the National Archives of the United States* (National Archives and Records Service, General Services Administration, Washington, D.C.).

U.S. Department of Commerce, Social and Economic Administration, Bureau of the Census. *Census of Agriculture.* Washington, D.C.: The Bureau of the Census. Issued every 10 years.

———. *Census of Transportation.* Washington, D.C.: The Bureau. Issued every 5 years.

———. *Historical Statistics of the United States. Colonial Times to 1970.* Washington, D.C.: The Bureau, 1976.

Other Sources

American Institute of Public Opinion (Gallup Poll), 53 Bank Street, Princeton, NJ 08540.

Louis Harris and Associates, Inc. (Harris Poll) 1270 Avenue of the Americas, New York, N.Y. 10020.

National Opinion Research Center (NORC) 6030 South Ellis Avenue, Chicago, IL 60637

Population Reference Bureau, Inc. 1755 Massachusetts Avenue, N.W., Washington, D.C. 20036.

Summary

This chapter has suggested some approaches for helping children gain access to specialized forms of information, namely, maps, globes, graphs, and tabular data. For each of these forms, we have suggested that *encoding* experiences, which include map, graph, table, and chart making, can help children understand how information gets into a particular form. Such encoding experiences may provide students with a better basis for decoding or gaining access to information in the form of maps, graphs, tables, and charts.

Unlike some of the other areas social studies encompasses, map, table, and graph reading (decoding) involve an identifiable sequence of the knowledge and skills necessary for gaining access to information. As in analytic subject areas, if any step is omitted, or if the sequence of steps is confused, the student is likely to fail. To avoid failure and the sense of frustration that can accompany it, we recommend that you task analyze what the student is being asked to do by identifying the knowledge and skills required to complete the task. This analysis can provide the basis for step-by-step instruction as you guide your students through the decoding process.

Once students have gained access to information, the next phase is a "natural": they need to do something with it. It becomes almost a circular process when you recognize that what students *do* with information can provide a reason for them to get (and want) access to it.

Suggested Activities

1 Design a map-based decision-making activity that deals with a problem presently confronting the community you are living in, or, as an alternative, use a hypothetical community.

2 It is sometimes argued that much of the time devoted to instruction in longitude and latitude is wasted and could be better spent on something else. That argument is based on the claim that, while latitude and longitude are concepts many Americans know, they rarely, if ever, use them. Develop a response to that argument.

3 Review the instructional activities presented in this chapter and identify those that teach and those that test a student's preexisting skills.

4 Design a fact sheet that could serve as the basis for a lesson on any of the following topics: immigration, health care, education, community, or industrialization.

5 Obtain two social studies textbooks for the same grade level but from different publishers (your curriculum library or learning resource center should have copies available). Compare the two books in terms of the map reading skills they require of students. Also compare them in terms of the quantitative data skills they require, if any.

References

Hanna, Paul R., et al. *Geography in the Teaching of the Social Studies: Concepts and Skills.* Boston: Houghton Mifflin, 1966.

MATCH. "The City," *Teacher's Guide.* Nashua, NH: Delta Education, 1965.

Ryan, Frank, and Ellis, Arthur. *Instructional Implications of Inquiry.* Englewood Cliffs, NJ: Prentice-Hall, 1974.

Woodruff, Willard. *Case Study Book.* Wellesley, MA: Curriculum Associates, 1970.

Suggested Readings

Arthur K. Ellis. *Teaching and Learning Elementary Social Studies.* Boston: Allyn and Bacon, 1977. This methods text has an outstanding chapter entitled "Strategies for Making and Interpreting Maps" (pp. 261–81).

Marion J. Rice and Russell L. Cobb. *What Can Children Learn in Geography? A Review of Research.* Boulder, CO: ERIC Clearinghouse for Social Studies/Social Science Education, and Social Science Education Consortium, Inc., 1978. For all the years that map skills have been associated with social studies, you would think there would be a tremendous amount of information available. There isn't. This volume, however, provides the most up-to-date analysis of the research available.

James E. Harf and Anne R. Peterson. "The Quantitative Perspective on Inquiry in the Social Studies," in M. E. Gilliom (ed.). *Practical Methods for the Social Studies.* Belmont, CA: Wadsworth Publishing Co., Inc., 1977. Once again, this volume is aimed toward the secondary teacher. Nevertheless, you should find its treatment of quantitative data techniques of considerable value.

10 Managing Skills-Based Instruction: Process Skills

Key Questions

What are information-processing skills?

How does one teach them?

Where do decision-making activities fit into the picture?

Where do teachers locate primary source information?

Key Ideas

Process skills are part of a "family" of skills that are brought to bear in assessing and interpreting information and experience.

Some data-processing tasks, especially those at higher cognitive levels, may be incomprehensible to elementary children unless translated into their language.

Process-oriented activities tend to be wholistic, and thus involve several process skills simultaneously.

Most process skills-based activities use unprocessed, primary source information or experience.

Introduction: Christopher's Problem

Sometimes things that seem simple enough have a way of becoming more difficult than one might imagine. Tying one's shoes, for example, is so common that most of us do it automatically. But consider what it's like to tell a child how to tie shoes. Want to try?

Enter Christopher, a bright-eyed, four year old wearing a pair of brown and white saddle shoes, one of which has the laces dangling. "Willya help me tie my shoe?"

There are only two ground rules for this activity. First, you are not permitted to use any demonstrations; just tell Christopher how to tie his shoelaces. Second, you are not permitted to practice on your own shoes (assuming they have laces, of course). Since tying one's shoes is something many of us do every day, you need merely to describe it from memory. Ready?

If you get very far beyond the stage of "First you put one lace over the other," consider yourself exceptional. Describing how to tie one's shoes is a task so difficult that it almost defies description. And, although shoe tying is a physical (motor) skill, this episode illustrates something that holds true for information-processing skills. Shoe tying is not complete until one has mastered a whole series of subskills—loop making, pushing one looped shoelace under another (while maintaining tension on the original twist), and so forth. In fact, it's one of those operations in which failing to complete any one of the requisite skills throws the entire process out of kilter. The same things can be true among children who, though they are able to identify plausible hypotheses, lack the ability to identify relevant information with which to test them. In other words, hypotheses, no matter how good they are, may be meaningless unless a child is able to follow through with them. The point here is that information-processing skills (like many physical skills—shoe tying, basketball shooting, etc.) are part of a "family" of skills that can be brought to bear on almost any activity.

Because information-processing skills are part of a broader family, you will notice something in this chapter that is similar to something in the previous chapter. Although some student activities in Chapters Eight and Nine focused on a particular access skill, they seldom stopped there. In addition to the access skills, one or more *process* skills were usually required to bring closure or a sense of completion to the activity. Most process-oriented learning activities are equally wholistic. While they may focus on a particular processing skill—interpreting data, analyzing, inferring, etc.—other process skills will almost surely be involved. Process skills, perhaps more so than access skills, just don't separate themselves very neatly.

Overview

The purpose of this chapter is twofold: first, to identify the information-processing skills that children should develop as they deal with elementary social studies data or experiences and, second, to present several exemplary activities in which children can develop those skills. In the first part of this chapter we identify basic process skills and examine some of the elements involved in trying to teach them. In the last section we deal with "decision making," which is an approach to social studies that helps to tie information-processing skills together and give them a focus.

Information? Data? Experience?

Clarification

We have been using several terms interchangeably here, which may have resulted in some confusion. At times, for example, we've used the expression *data-processing skills.* At other times we've used *information-processing skills,* and on still other occasions we've referred to *experience.* It would probably be easiest if we limited ourselves to just one term—*information-processing skills* perhaps—for then everyone would know that we are referring to the fourteen operations listed on page 288. We haven't done this because we can't be certain that your perception of any one of these expressions is the same as ours.

Consider *information* as an example. In many cases, information is perceived as hard data—the kind of stuff that comes from books (or lectures). And in schools, we have traditionally gained access to that

"The computer broke down. Anyone here have any experience in thinking?"

information through reading. Yet in activities beyond the school environment, reading is *not* the primary means we use to gain access to the events around us. Rather we observe, we listen, and, as a result, form impressions of the people with whom we interact—impressions that influence the way we interact with those individuals in the future.

Once we have the impression that someone is trying to "snow" us, for example, that impression—derived from our experience—will influence our future interactions with that individual. Everything that person says may be regarded with suspicion. In fact, once the specter of doubt is raised, it may take a lot of "nonsnowing" experiences with that individual before our trust in them is restored. But all of this is fairly obvious. Our point is that *experience*—the things that happen to you or the things that happen to your future students—can and should serve as sources of the data to which you apply process skills. And so when we use the expression *experience-processing skills,* as we will, we are indicating that those fourteen key processing operations can be applied to data and information coming from a broad range of sources—including the hard stuff that is found in books, and the soft stuff that comes from experience and interaction with others. In fact, to eliminate the latter, as we are sometimes prone to do, is tantamount to taking the "social" out of social studies.

Experience is the key

Process Skills

Process skills are actually operations—mental operations—in which students do something with data. They can look at information (observe), describe it, record it, interpret it, classify it, twist it around into another form (translate), or any one of a number of other things. Because process skills reflect something children are doing (or are expected to do), they are often identified in the "ing" form. The following is a compilation of some of these skills:

Table 10.1 Translating Process Tasks into Children's Language

Task	Adult's language	Child's language
Classifying	Classify these into two categories.	Do some of these go together?
	How many different ways could you classify these?	Are there different ways these can go together?
		See how many different ways you can group these?
Hypothesizing and inferring	Develop two hypotheses that might explain this (whatever "this" happens to be).	How would you explain this?
		Are there some other reasons this might have happened?
	Given data, develop three hypotheses.	What is _____ really like?
Analyzing	Given two sources of data, identify possible contradictions.	Do you notice anything "wrong" or unusual (about these data)?
		Is there anything here that doesn't seem to "fit" right?.
	Identify relevant or irrelevant information.	Is there some information here that we don't need?
		Which information is most helpful?
Inductive reasoning	Given two or more data sources, develop an inductive generalization.	Is there an idea that "fits" all of these examples?
Deductive reasoning	Given an idea, can you test its validity?	Given this idea, can you think of other examples it applies to, or examples where it does not apply?
Evaluating	Identify criteria to support your judgment.	Why do you think one is better than another?

1	analyzing	8	generalizing
2	classifying	9	inferring
3	communicating	10	interpreting
4	deducing	11	recording (keeping records)
5	describing	12	measuring
6	evaluating (judging)	13	planning and designing
7	experimenting	14	predicting (hypothesizing)

A listing such as this is hardly innocent; in fact, it's probably rather impos-ing. These skills need a context, yet even then they may not necessarily lose their awesomeness. To say, for example, that students, "should be able to analyze two or more sources of evidence so as to identify areas of agreement or potential contradiction," or "that students should be able to distinguish facts from opinions," can be *as* imposing if not more so, than the list above. In fact, if you were to ask two third graders "to identify and judge the relevance and acceptability of (certain) information," they would probably look at you as if you had taken leave of your senses.

In spite of their potential awesomeness, all of the information-processing skills on our list can be taught in some form to elementary children. True, some children don't have the background or vocabulary to handle some of the more complex forms of analysis, synthesis, or evaluation, but they can often indicate, for example, if something in a story "fits," or whether "something seems wrong." Such simple forms of analysis are well within their ability. The secret, though, may lie in how the task is presented to them.

In many instances, though not all, the form in which information-processing skills are presented for teachers is *not* the form suitable for presenting them to elementary children. The exceptions to this include those processing skills that involve measuring, observing, and describing; elementary children seldom experience unusual problems handling such operations. But for most other skills, you will probably need to translate them into simpler children's language. Your exact translation will depend on the kind of data or experiences you're using, of course, but some examples of what we mean are illustrated in Table 10.1.

Presenting tasks to children

Rather than examine each of the information-processing skills separately, which results in a kind of piecemeal approach, we have organized the balance of this section so that it reflects the wholistic way in which process skills are actually used, that is, in relation to the inquiry (problem-solving) process. For example, before students "do" anything with information they must identify the existence of a problem—they must have something to inquire about. Thus, the first subsection deals with how we can go about helping students identify problems. In the following subsections we examine techniques for helping students identify hypotheses and make inferences based on the information they have, how students can gather additional data and then do something with it, and finally, helping students generalize beyond their immediate experience.

Identifying Problems

There seems to come a stage in every child's life when the word they most frequently utter is *why*—almost to the point of exasperation to the most patient teacher or parent. Sometimes *why* comes in the form of "How come?" but the basic thrust—the request for an explanation—is there nevertheless.

"Why do I have to go to bed?"

"How come we can't go to the movies?"

"Why does it rain?"

"Why" questions usually fall into one of two fairly obvious groups. Children are either asking for a reason or justification for something—"Why can't I go outside and play in the rain?"—or they want an explanation for something they don't understand. In either case, the "why" question indicates that they've identified a problem—their problem—and that a *teachable moment* may have arrived. In other words, by helping children deal with the problem that led to their "Why?" we may, in fact, be teaching them something. Unfortunately, after the tenth (or twentieth) explanation of why the child cannot go outside to play in the rain, one may begin to wonder if the question wasn't just another way of testing adult authority and really had nothing to do with explanations or teachable moments.

On teachable moments

Among the thousands of legitimate "why" questions children ask, you will find many that are based on inconsistencies they've observed (without ever being taught how to identify an inconsistency). Consider, for example, how you will react when Laurie announces, "My daddy says that out there it's everyone for themselves, but in school you keep saying that we should cooperate. Who's right?" This is the kind of question some teachers would rather not be asked and, should Laurie persist, it may result in her being labeled as a "smart" kid.

The particular problem teachers face is to identify ways to translate social studies content into real problems that grab students—and that is no mean trick.

Traditionally, social studies teachers have been so bound by the subject matter they were expected to teach that they had little recourse other than to lay problems on students. In other words, requests to "identify the capitals of the middle Atlantic states" or "trace the sequence of Roman emperors" were actually teachers' problems "laid on" students. As such, they then became the students' problems. But even within a fixed curriculum, you can help to enhance student involvement (and a feeling that they are dealing with *their* problems) by the way in which you present problems to them. These techniques include (1) creating mystery-type situations, where students deal with an unknown element or elements, (2) providing incomplete (limited) information at the outset of an activity, from which students try to "fill in the holes," or (3) using a speculative-heuristic question, for example, "What if you were the fire chief," or "What if you were a member of the Indian Parliament and were facing a request to. . . ." These are still teacher-structured problems, to be sure, but they have a way of involving kids to the extent that the problems may become "theirs."

The creation of mystery-type situations often involves intentionally limiting the information you make available to students as you begin an activity. As students work with that information, additional problems sometimes emerge. For example, in the following activity adapted from Mallan and Hersh (1972, pp. 234–35), a *fact sheet* is used to create a mystery-type situation. In this instance, a real country is identified only as "Nation X." Obviously you would not tell your students the real name of Nation X, since to do so would eliminate all traces of "mystery" from the problem. It would also eliminate the need to *use* the information about Nation X; your students could simply rely on what they already know.

This fact sheet is designed so that children must use the information to describe Nation X. However, in our right-answer-oriented society, your biggest problem will be to keep their attention focused on *describing* Nation X. From the outset, they will want to guess which real nation Nation X is. The object is not to establish a guessing game; to permit students to do so will limit the usefulness of this activity.

Limiting information

Nation X

Overview: Using only the data provided below, students are asked to infer what Nation X is like. As is true of most inferences, these will need

Model student activity

to be tested further. Thus, students must then identify whatever additional information they would like, some of which you may have ready in advance. Just how this activity ends depends on how far you wish to take it.

Fact sheet #1		U.S.A.	X
A	Doctors per 100,000 inhabitants	120	20
B	Dentists per 100,000 inhabitants	50	2
C	Percentage of population literate	100	18
D	Radios per 1,000 inhabitants	750	2
E	Percentage of people living in cities	66	18

Given just this information, how would *you* describe Nation X?

_____

_____

_____

Procedure:

1   Working either individually or in small groups (you decide in advance), pose the following task: Using just this information, describe Nation X as best you can. What's it like, and what are the people who live there like?

2   List student inferences (in terms of key descriptors) on the board or have small groups list their inferences on chart paper.

3   Summarize inferences, pointing out those that may be contradictory. Note that it is possible to arrive at two wholly opposite inferences. The dentist data, for example, could suggest either that Nation X has poor dental health, or that Nation X has little need for dentists.

4   In summarizing, you may wish to raise questions such as: How is literacy defined? How big must a city be to be defined as a city? Is it fair to say that Nation X is poor?

5   (Optional) On an overhead projector transparency, you may wish to present the class with the following information:

Nation X has several thousand unemployed college graduates.

Consider what this information may indicate about (*a*) the size of Nation X, (*b*) its educational system, and (*c*) its way of life.

6   After assessing whether their inferences follow from the data, you can ask students what other kinds of information they might want. (Be prepared for a long list.)

7   Present the following information (on an overhead transparency):

Fact sheet #2			
	Nations	*Pop., 1972*	*% of world pop.*
A	China	779,000,000	21
B	Nation X	557,000,000	15
C	Soviet Union	246,000,000	7
D	United States	208,120,000	6
E	Japan	106,250,000	3

Given this data, some students will try to guess the identity of Nation X. Or, they can check population figures in the atlases found at the back of most social studies texts. In any event, maintaining the mystery much longer could prove frustrating, so you can tell the class that Nation X is India. (Knowing that, you can now assess your *own* inferences.)

8 At this point you have the option of pursuing the India study in several different ways. You might wish to do two things simultaneously: (1) have the children use their inferences as research questions to be answered, using whatever resources or references they can garner; and (2) pursue an inference children often make about Nation X, namely, that it is poor. If they don't infer this, you can always build a case for it.

9 Several days' worth of activities can focus on the question of why India is poor. There is a wealth of available materials that address the question in one way or another; most are usable by elementary students. Among other reasons that will be suggested for India's poverty will be its food problem and, related to that, its health and population problems.

10 You also have the option of confronting the class with a moral dilemma by telling them that they are the Parliament of India and that you are a representative of the World Health Organization. You have come to offer them the services of two thousand doctors who will work, free of charge, to help India alleviate its health problems. Divide the class into small groups and have them consider your offer. Someone is almost certain to discover that those Indians who are kept alive will put an even greater strain on the available food supply. Thus, by saving people, the Indians might be adding to their food-supply problem. The class as a group must then decide whether or not to accept the offer, or whether to attach any "strings" to it, such as an equal number of agricultural specialists.

Optional emphasis

Caution: The topic of birth control usually arises in discussions related to population. Be prepared to know how you wish to handle the issue—in advance of its coming up.

11 Even if you do not wish to follow the Indian Parliament segment of this activity, you could pursue the poverty issue even further by raising the question, "If most of the people in a country are poor, what does *being poor* mean? Is being poor an average condition? If so, would the average Indian define himself as poor?"

The following information could then be presented to the class (again, using an overhead transparency may be easiest):

Fact sheet #3
In many places in India, but in rural villages especially, the poorest family is one in which there are no children.

What does this indicate about the Indian value structure? (What does this indicate to you about the lack of success of birth control campaigns in India?)

A special note is warranted about the kinds of facts suitable for fact sheets. Recall that we defined a fact as a statement about a unique and nonrepetitive event or phenomenon. Be advised that some facts are so unique that it's nearly impossible to say anything about them. This became apparent when some teachers modified the "Nation X" format to apply to states; in other words, they developed "State X" fact sheets. On them they included data such as the following: the state bird, the state tree, the state motto (in Latin), a picture of the state flag, and the date of the state's admission to the Union. For the most part, this kind of information—no matter how accurate—is so unique that there is little that can be said about it. To be told that State X's state bird is the cardinal, for example, or that the state tree is the buckeye, tells you relatively little or nothing about the area in question. Rather, it misses the point heightening the "guessing game" effect.

Data can't be too unique

Identifying researchable problems In the course of most social studies activities, students will generate questions that no amount of research will answer. In the previous activity, for example, an inference that India is poor because the people are bad or lazy is almost guaranteed to lead to frustration and discontent, should your students attempt to research it. It's just not a researchable question as long as *poor, bad,* and *lazy* are left undefined. Even then, establishing causal relationships among these will challenge the best of scholars.

The teaching implication in such cases should seem quite evident: it is necessary to help children examine problems in terms of their researchability. To do otherwise could lead them on a wild-goose chase.

Some of the following statements and problems are based on the student activities we've considered thus far. Others are not. Which of the following statements have potential for further student research or study?

Yes/No   *Problems/Statements*

_N_ 1. Identify the constitutional requirements for the office of president of the United States.
_Y_ 2. John F. Kennedy and Franklin D. Roosevelt were two of the best presidents the United States has ever had.
_Y_ 3. The best route for a freeway is one that does not destroy a school.
_Y/N_ 4. The Dutch are an industrious and friendly people.
____ 5. India is unable to employ all of its college graduates in the kinds of positions for which they were trained.
____ 6. Communications media (radio, TV, newspapers, etc.) in India have not improved over the last ten years.
____ 7. The introduction of new technology into a culture is likely to lead to other changes.
____ 8. American farmers today grow more food on larger, more specialized farms than did farmers ten or twenty years ago.
____ 9. Hippies were unpatriotic.
____ 10. The majority of students in *this* class strongly dislike Italian food.

Which are researchable?

Researchable problems (hypotheses, inferences, and questions) are like behavioral objectives: they do not use vague terms or relationships that are nearly impossible to prove. Yet they are specific enough that one need not spend a lifetime in the quest. If you are still uncertain as to which of the above are researchable and which aren't, Statements 2, 3, 4, and 9 need greater clarification and specificity before students could deal with them. In the case of Statement 4, for example, it might be possible to define *industrious* and *friendly*, but how do you define *the Dutch?* Are the Dutch only those people who live in the Netherlands? Or do they include people of Dutch descent?

Hypothesizing and Inferring

Given the cartoon on page 295, which of the following might you reasonably infer from it?

Yes/No

_____ 1. Business seems to be good.

_____ 2. The cartoon depicts a scene in the United States.

_____ 3. The employer has a bias against women.

_____ 4. Women are not good workers.

_____ 5. The sign reflects a basic societal belief that a woman's place is in the home.

_____ 6. The cartoon depicts a scene that might take place in the 1980s.

That business seems to be good is a reasonable inference, otherwise there would be no Help Wanted sign. But, on the other hand, perhaps working conditions in the plant are so bad that some employees quit after only a few days. If that were the case, the management would continually need additional help just to maintain normal operations. Both are plausible inferences.

Inference testing

If you have no intention of testing which of these inferences is valid, your inference would remain just that—a possible, plausible inference. But when you set out to test whether or not business is good—at least as depicted in the cartoon—your inference then functions as a hypothesis. That is, your inference is a testable proposition: the reason the plant displays a Help Wanted sign is because business is good and the company therefore needs additional employees. To test this you obviously need more data about the events depicted in the cartoon.

You might, however, infer that the cartoon does *not* depict a scene taking place in 1981. Why? Because there are laws forbidding discrimination based on sex. The probability of your inference being valid is so high that you might feel little need to pursue the issue further. Thus, your inference would remain just that—a highly probable inference.

Public procedures

All of us infer, almost all the time. We continually attempt to explain events, sometimes without realizing it. If we infer and hypothesize anyway, why should there be such concern for formal hypothesis testing? The answer lies in the fact that what we do in informal situations has application in many more formal situations and with many other kinds of data sources. And, although in informal situations we might be satisfied using impressionistic data—a hunch, a whim, or a feeling—formal hypothesis testing requires that all elements of the process be *public*. In other words, in informal, face-to-face relations, one is free to use whatever information one

wants; in more formal, rational, and public data-validating procedures, one must follow the rules. Hence, our distinction between an inference and a hypothesis.

Knowns and unknowns When something is known, there's not much left to hypothesize about. A statement such as "Milk comes from cows" isn't very likely to lead to much speculation. But if you ask kids the question, "Where does milk come from?" you can get some mighty interesting hypotheses:

From trucks

From dairies

From the supermarket

These are all testable statements in terms of their accuracy, but you must assess whether the children will gain enough from testing such facts to make the effort involved worthwhile. We can test the accuracy of "knowns," but must hypothesize about things that are unknown or that can be explained only in part.

Physical objects often offer an excellent opportunity for activities emphasizing hypothesizing, especially when the object and its use are unknown to the children. A colonial bootjack—a forked board used to help remove one's boots—or even a butter churn can lead to creative hypothesizing activities. A visit to an antique shop can provide a wealth of objects for potential hypothesizing activities.

Sample instructional activity

Teaching Kit: A House of Ancient Greece

An excellent example of a series of activities, most of which focus on hypothesizing and hypothesis testing, can be found in the MATCH Unit "House of Ancient Greece." The unit contains a wealth of materials—an authentic Greek coin, filmstrips, pictures, several reference books, etc.— but most intriguing are some photographs and reproductions of artifacts found by a team of American archaeologists, led by Dr. David Robinson, as they excavated the site of the ancient Greek city of Olynthus. All of

Figure 10.1 The Villa of Good Fortune

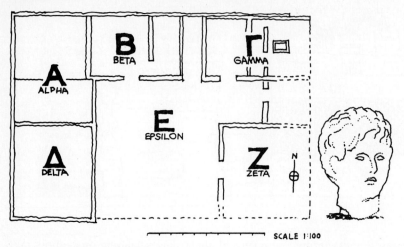

Source: Adapted from MATCH unit, "House of Ancient Greece" Teacher's Guide, p. 23. Used by permission of Delta Education.

Figure 10.2 Artifacts Found in the Beta Room

Source: MATCH kit, "House of Ancient Greece."

the kit's artifacts are reproductions of artifacts found in the various rooms of a home that Dr. Robinson named the Villa of Good Fortune. Whether the home's original owners called it that 2,300 years ago is unknown. (Dr. Robinson's name was derived from a translation of the mosaic found on the floor in one of the villa's rooms.)

As best they could, the archaeologists developed a floor plan for the villa. In adapting the floor plan for the MATCH kit, the rooms were labeled Alpha Room, Beta Room, etc., as illustrated in Figure 10.1.

In the MATCH kit, artifacts from each room are packaged separately. The class is divided into teams, one team for each room in the villa. The objective is for each team to identify (1) what the various artifacts are, (2) what they might have been used for, and (3) the nature of the room from which they came. Figure 10.2 shows artifacts from the Beta Room.

See if you can identify what they are, what they might have been used for, and what function(s) the Beta Room served for the villa.

What are the various artifacts and what might they have been used for?

_____

_____

_____

What functions did the Beta Room serve?

_____

_____

After describing what they have found or, more precisely, what they think they have found, the children have the opportunity to check their findings with Dr. Robinson's. His findings for the Beta Room are listed in the reference book included with the unit. (We have printed Dr. Robinson's findings at the end of this chapter, on page 312.)

Coins, stamps, buttons—almost any physical object—can serve as a basis for hypothesizing and inferring activities. In the case of coins, for example, the student's task can be stated as follows: "Given a dollar (Susan B. Anthony), a half dollar, a quarter, dime, nickel, and penny, what do you know about the people who made them?"

"Buildings seem to be important, as well as eagles."
"Except for one, all of the coins have a man on them."
"They have a letter and number system."
"They have a god in whom they trust."
"They have a language we don't understand, _E Pluribus Unum._"

You can often develop inferring activities by simply removing the identifying name or label. In the context of community helpers, for instance, you could provide the children with statements describing what a particular community helper does. The first statements could be of a very general nature, such as "Is employed by the community," with more specific statements coming later. After each statement, children should have an opportunity to infer who the community servant is.

Hypothesizing and inferring activities demand something that is unknown to students—objects, events, or whatever. Otherwise there may be little or nothing for children to explain. Indeed, if explanations already exist, there is little one can do other than question their validity. To facilitate helping children hypothesize and infer, the teacher can provide them with unexplained events—unknowns that, through inferring, hypothesizing, and hypothesis testing, can become "knowns."

_Maintaining
the mystery_

When Museums Take the Labels Off
Remember when you went on a field trip to a historical museum and viewed collections of articles, each properly labeled with its name, purpose, and year of manufacture? Everything you wanted to know

about the item (and sometimes more) was provided for you. Increasingly, however, museums are providing exhibits without such labels, exhibits that provide children with opportunities to infer what various articles are and what they might have been used for. Some museums even prepare a printed key to such exhibits, which the children can use to check themselves.

Even if museums don't take the labels off, you can—by building your own collection. Instead of building a display by yourself, your students could furnish unusual objects (even contemporary articles) that could serve as the basis for "What is it?" and "What do you know about the people who made it?" exhibits. Although your students are likely to know what the objects are, the exhibits could serve as resources for other classes in the building.

Answers to questions you didn't ask

Data Gathering and Processing

Before anyone bothers to gather and process data, it's only common sense that they have previously identified a purpose for that information. In other words, gathering information in the absence of a problem isn't very productive unless, of course, you have an obsession for trivia. Learning that English muffins were invented in America, for example, or that when the story of Hansel and Gretel is told in parts of Africa, the witch's house is made of salt, not cake, may be interesting enough, but is the information useful?

Actually, our trivia example backfired, since the African version of Hansel and Gretel *could* provide the basis for an effective inferring activity, if a teacher chose to use it that way. Why is the house built of salt? Could it be that salt is highly prized? (Yes!) This example also illustrates that how teachers use data can influence their students' feelings about the information.

What is your purpose?

From your experience as a student, you undoubtedly remember teachers who, when they said that they wanted you to gather information, really meant that they wanted you to absorb information from some source, usually a textbook. Your problem—your *real* problem—probably had little to do with data gathering; it was more likely a case of remembering all of that information until the test. On other occasions, however, gathering data was something you did in response to a problem, *your* problem, not one imposed upon you by an upcoming test. Undoubtedly the most universal example of this is the way you learned about sex. Think back to your childhood experiences to see if at some point you didn't overhear some whispered discussions among some interested groups of adults or among some of your peers. This may have occurred after several early experiences where it was indicated that "Nice people don't talk about *that.*" In some cases, your curiosity may have been whetted because the discussions took place under clandestine circumstances that lent a sense of intrigue to the entire matter. In other cases, you may have found that your peers who had more information about the topic were accorded more prestige in the group. Thus, if you got the necessary information, you might share some of that prestige.

Group work offers different perspectives for hypothesizing and inferring.

Problem-based learning

Whatever the incentive, your problem was to get more information. The important thing here is that it was *your* problem, although undoubtedly one you shared with many other children. In any event, you gathered a great deal of information—some of it misinformation—and probably from a remarkable variety of sources. For some, it was the first time they had ever used the dictionary voluntarily! By the time you were fourteen or so, you probably had a veritable wealth of data, though not necessarily the means to determine what was accurate and what wasn't. That would come as you applied your information in still other circumstances.

Because students and teachers may perceive data gathering quite differently, you need to ask yourself two key questions: What's my motive (as a teacher) for having students study this?" and "What are my students' motives for dealing with this information?" Motivation then, is a process of identifying the best possible match between your motives as a teacher and the motives of your students.

Successful data gathering depends upon three interacting elements: (1) a precisely stated problem, (2) an awareness of the specific information needed, and (3) the ability to deal with data presented in different forms (narratives, charts, graphs, etc.). Most important of these, we think, is stating the problem precisely. This was driven home to us on an occasion when we made our students "ambassadors" and had them do written reports on various countries around the world. At the time, we neglected to take into account the fact that a precisely stated problem provides criteria for determining what information should be included or excluded. Without those criteria, students put anything and everything even remotely related to the country into their reports. The student who "did" Scotland, for example, brought her report to class in a large carton. Reading those reports became a nightmare, and like it or not, grading was based on a subjective mixture of quality and weight. And even though our first students were proud of the tall stacks of data they had gathered, the next year we spent considerable time narrowing their topics down to a more manageable size.

Which data, not "how much"

Many teachers seem to equate data gathering with "library research," as we did above, thus neglecting data that can grow out of students' experiences. Even primary children, many of whom are unable to use library sources to begin with, can get involved in data gathering procedures. Conducting surveys to determine favorite TV shows or the time at which most second graders go to bed are among the survey topics recommended in the teacher's edition of one textbook series (Brandwein, et al., 1970).

One first-grade teacher we know planned a lesson along similar lines. She gathered that her pupils were addicted to television commercials and that they accepted the claims made in the advertisements as fact. The teacher did not want to encourage cynicism, but she did want the students to get the idea (concept) that although there may be some truth in what commercials say or show, this does not necessarily mean that *all* claims are *all* true. Shee developed the following plan of instruction:

1 Gather information. The information will relate to different laundry detergent products that students see and hear about on TV commercials.

2 Students bring in samples of detergents used at home.

Model student activity

3 Students then determine a way to test the commercials' claims. Pieces from a cotton sheet are marked with different strains—crayon, dirt, paint, grease, chalk, etc.

4 Identify things (variables) to consider: (1) water temperature, (2) same kind of stained material, (3) amount of detergent used, and (4) length of washing time.

5 Read the directions on the detergent package to students.

6 Wash materials and record observations on the chart below: happy face, stain removed; sad face, stain not removed.

7 Students add the number of happy faces in each column to determine which detergents removed all or some of the stains.

8 Discuss values such as the ethics involved when you give your word that something is true.

An activity that had looked so neat and clean at the outset proved to be a catastrophe; whatever could go wrong went wrong. Based on the disap-

Stains	Detergents			
	1	2	3	4
crayon	☹	☹	☹	☺
dirt	☹	☹	☹	☹
paint	☹	☹	☹	☹
grease	☹	☹	☹	☹
chalk	☺	☺	☺	☺
magic marker	☹	☹	☹	?
pen	?	?	?	?
total ◯				

pointing results, the teacher judged the activity a failure. Actually, the concept of failure doesn't hold in this case, because when dealing with skill development, "failure" comes only if students (or teachers, or both) have not learned from the experience. True, it would have been nice had the experiment been successful; a few changes—fewer detergents, fewer stains, better control over washing time and water temperature, and a more precise way of measuring stain removal—might have ensured a more successful outcome. But whether or not the experiment worked is not the point. The skills being developed and used are the instructional focus. In other words, students can have an opportunity to use and apply skills even if the experiment or activity is unsuccessful.

Learning from apparent disaster

Some experiments can have effects that go well beyond the skills children learn in doing them. Consider, for example, the instance of students who were using the "Traffic Flow" unit from the Unified Science and Mathematics Program for Elementary Schools (1974) (otherwise known as USMES [us-muss]) in which they surveyed the traffic patterns in an area near their school. After mapping the flow of traffic, the students examined their information to see if the situation could be improved. They also interviewed drivers (who had parked their cars and were walking). The students discovered that the existing pattern of one-way streets in that area made it difficult for people to reach their destinations without walking some distance or making unnecessary trips around the block. Using their data, the students considered alternative patterns that might speed the flow of traffic. Finally, they settled on a new traffic-flow-pattern plan that seemed feasible. To make a long story short, the students talked with the local traffic commissioner about their proposed changes, and not long thereafter the changes were approved by the city council. In slightly over a month, traffic was following the pattern devised by a group of fourth graders!

Data: Forms Suitable for Processing   Do some kinds of information (or data) better lend themselves to information processing than other forms of data? The answer to that is a clear *yes*. If your intent is to help children process information, your main focus should be on providing them with unprocessed information—raw data—that they can work with. Generally, that information should be presented in uninterpreted form to permit students to do the interpreting.

Data presented to children in the form of conclusions tend to limit the processing the children can do, since the concluder has already produced conclusions. Note that in the case of student surveys and of the fact sheets presented above, the information was preselected, but it was not preprocessed. No one told you what to conclude about Nation X, for example. You had to reason inductively, piecing together information, to arrive at your own interpretations. So it is with uninterpreted data.

Contemporary elementary social studies programs place considerable emphasis on helping students work with information from primary sources. Such programs lean heavily on uninterpreted information, some of which (as in the case of surveys) the children gather firsthand. Note that *primary* in this sense refers to firsthand accounts, not to a particular level of schooling. Likewise, *secondary accounts* refer to sources of already-interpreted information.

As a kind of self-check, determine which of the following sources are more likely to provide primary (firsthand) accounts (use a *P*) and those that are more likely to contain secondary (previously interpreted) accounts (use an *S*). Use a *?* if you are not sure.

Primary source accounts

first hand

Secondary already interpreted

S	Aerial photographs	P	Lectures
S	Advertisements	P	Letters (personal)
S	Artifacts	S	Magazine articles
S	Atlases	S	Maps
S	Census reports	P	Paintings
P	Diaries	S	Photographs
S	Directories	P	Reports
S	Documents	P	Survey reports
S	Encyclopedias	S	Textbooks
P	Interviews		

Of the items on this list, the secondary sources are fewer in number (though not necessarily less in terms of volume). They include encyclopedias, lectures, magazine articles (and some journal articles), reports, and textbooks. Some sources, such as advertisements, may be questionable, especially since the way data are used in advertisements is often questionable. Interviews might also be questionable to the extent that interviewees sometimes give the answer they think is anticipated by the interviewer. Maps can also fall into the questionable category, since someone had to transform (i.e., process) data into map form. Thus, maps could be considered secondary sources, while aerial photographs, from which some maps are made, would be considered primary sources. For all practical purposes, though, it is safe to regard most maps (and the balance of the items on this list) as primary sources. It is to them you could turn as some of your best resources for process-based activities.

Generalizing

One of the more challenging aspects of inquiry-oriented teaching is helping students to identify patterns or relationships among otherwise unconnected events or pieces of data. That challenge, expressed in a word, is *generalizing.*

We suspect that teachers have sometimes been unjustly faulted for not helping students to generalize from their own experiences. It's not that teachers haven't tried this, we think, but that they have tried and failed. If you look at what is involved in generalizing—making general statements based on patterns among specific events—it actually requires that children leave the comfort of concrete experience and move into the realm of abstraction. As Jean Fair (1977, p. 39) has noted, "Generalizations, like concepts, are abstractions." Dealing with abstractions is something that students are often reluctant, and in some cases unable, to do. Even some adults have difficulty standing back from specific situations so they can analyze what is actually taking place. In the Stone Axes case study, for example, it is not immediately apparent that the introduction of steel axes into the culture constituted a change, and that because one thing changed, other changes were likely to occur. As adults we often get wrapped up in the specifics, the details or content of situations themselves, and then deal with the details separately, as is reflected by statements such as "Did you hear about what happened to that tribe in Australia?" Note that we are not talking about the *need* to generalize here, for that clearly exists. Our focus is on the *willingness* to move into the realm of abstraction, which is something that even adults, who are better able to handle abstractions, are sometimes reluctant to do.

The value of generalizing, as Fair (1977) also noted, lies in the fact that it reduces the disorder and confusion of otherwise isolated bits of experience. That reduction is achieved by organizing experiences into classes and categories. Generalizing, then, involves making statements about classes or categories of objects or events.

To build a class or category requires at least two events or situations. This means that a single event, such as the Stone Axes case study, is insufficient as a basis for generalizing. We need something else to compare and contrast with the Stone Axes study. To be able to say something about how technological innovations affect us, for example, we would need to compare the impact of introducing steel axes with the impact and changes resulting from the introduction of the telephone, the automobile, or any other innovation we select. If we pursue this by examining the impact of the telephone on American society, for example, we would need to identify some of the changes resulting from it. These could include new jobs, faster

Going beyond the specifics

Table 10.2
Questioning
Sequence for
Generalizing

Questioning Sequence	Purpose
What do you notice? See? Find? or What do these events, incidents, etc. have in common? How are they different?	To elicit elements or patterns that will provide a basis for making general statements. Note that the items mentioned should be made accessible to participants by listing them on the chalkboard or through other appropriate means.
Why do you think this happened? or How do you account for these differences?	To elicit explanations or inferences and to clarify these as needed.
What do these tell you about . . . ?	To elicit general statements (generalizations). Seek additional clarification as needed.

Note: This pattern may be repeated and expanded upon to include more aspects of the data and to reach more abstract generalizations.

Source: Adapted from Fraenkel (1973, p. 214).

communication, fewer letters being written (which has historians worried, incidentally), and the like. At this point, by asking students to identify how the two events were similar—the introduction of steel axes and the telephone—we have a basis for generalizing in an "if-then," GR concept statement format: "A change in one thing is likely to lead to other changes."

A teaching strategy for generalizing is summarized in Table 10.2.

Notice that while comparing two events or phenomena in terms of their similarities can yield warranted generalizations, comparing them in terms of differences—things that are not similar—can yield testable propositions. For instance, introducing the steel axes into the Yir Yoront society ultimately led to an increase in crime. We have no evidence, however, that the introduction of the telephone has led to a higher crime rate in our society. An appropriate question then is, "Do most technological innovations lead to a higher crime rate?" Questions such as these can serve as the focus for further investigations.

Data Banks

Organizing and keeping track of skills-based teaching materials can easily become a problem for teachers, which may help to explain why some turn to those old standbys, workbooks. If nothing else, having everything bound into one volume eliminates the need to manage a file full of dittoed worksheets. The management problem need not become overwhelming, however, if you are willing to develop a data bank.

Data banks can take a variety of forms. Some teachers prefer to use 8 1/2-by-11-inch sheets while others, ourselves included, prefer 5-by-8-inch

Figure 10.3 Sample Data Bank Card (5 x 8 Format)

Skill: Generalizing from data

Data

Boston is on the Charles River

Moscow is on the Volga River

London is on the Thames River

Cincinnati is on the Ohio River

Paris is on the Seine River

Possible Uses

1. Check accuracy of each statement.

2. Identify two variables at work in each statement.

3. Make a general statement, about both variables, that would include all statements given.

4. Identify/locate three other cities that would fit under the broad general statement.

5. Identify one "major" city that appears to be an exception.

6. Formulate three possible explanations for the exception in number 5.

Note: Inductive/deductive — cities on each family
deductive reasoning — stated central map
Billy Down — disabilities by full both bd.
U.S. Dunning life —

*Data for
potential lessons*

index cards, like the one illustrated in Figure 10.3. Regardless of the form it takes, the data bank should include two elements: (1) sets of data for students to work with, which may include extrapolated raw data, charts, graphs, tables, figures, maps, and, if necessary, hypothetical data; and (2) notations regarding different ways in which students can use the data. Both of these elements are illustrated in Figure 10.3.

When potential teaching materials are organized in data-bank form, the following things should become apparent.

Teachers need not use all of the data on a card, especially if students might find it overwhelming. Rather, they can select the kind and amount of data to be included in a student activity.

When teachers provide the data for students to work with, the nature of student activities tends to change. Less student time is spent on data gathering and significantly more time is devoted to developing other process skills.

The availability of skill data banks can help the teacher accommodate a wide range of pupil skill levels, be they remedial, practice, or enrichment.

Data banks are, in fact, content banks, but are organized in such a way that content or information acquisition is not separated from skill development.

Process-Skills
Self-Check

To be manageable, information-processing skills require a context—a setting in which they function. We have suggested some contexts in the form of student activities that focus on process skills. You could provide additional contexts by looking back to your own elementary social studies experience and identifying activities or topics to which, with some modifications, you could add a process-skills focus. You might suggest, for example, that children compare two texts' treatment of the same topic in terms of what information is similar and what is different—an elementary form of analysis. Or you might have students plan and conduct a survey—an activity involving planning and designing. Remember that experience is a legitimate focus for process-oriented activities.

Using your own social studies experience as a basis, identify potential contexts or activities into which you could introduce each of the information-processing skills. Note: You may wish to defer this activity until you have read further in this chapter, or the book itself. Feel free to come back to it, but do come back.

Analyzing (which usually involves comparing) _____

_____

Classifying _____

_____

Communicating (which may involve changing the form of information) __

_____

Deducing (always requires a previous situation or information) _____

_____

Describing (consider situations around the school) _____

_____

Evaluating (which usually requires judging according to a criterion) _____

_____

Experimenting (usually involves using "controls" of some kind—remember the sugar cubes?) _____

_____

Generalizing (always requires something to generalize *from*) _____

_____

Inferring (always requires information, situations, or experiences on which inferences can be based)_____

_____

Interpreting (obviously requires something to be interpreted) _____

_____

Recording (record keeping) _____

_____

Measuring _____

_____

Planning and designing _____

_____

Predicting (hypothesizing) _____

_____

Decision Making

Much of the attention focused on information-processing skills is based on the premise that, once they leave school, children will be confronted with a myriad of problems and dilemmas that will demand decisions *and* some kind of action. Decision making calls for skill usage. By focusing social studies teaching on information-processing skills, children can gain experience with the various data-handling processes associated with rational decision making, and thus will have a model to use when they leave school.

Decision making is the process of making reasoned choices from among alternatives, choices that are consistent with the decision maker's values (Cassidy and Kurfman, 1977, p. 1). In social studies, however, decision making is referred to in two senses, one of them broad and the other narrow. In the broad sense, Theodore Kaltsounis (1979), Cassidy and Kurfman (1977), and many others use decision making to describe a total approach to social studies, one that incorporates all the skills we have dealt with (or will deal with) in this book. In its narrower sense, decision making is used to describe instructional activities that ask children to apply decision-making skills. Our concern in this section is with decision making in the narrower, "activities" sense of the term.

Two views

One of the classic decision-making activities is based on a situation in which a rocket ship has crashed on the moon. Students, who take the part of surviving crew members, must rank the articles that were not damaged in the crash in terms of their usefulness. Note that in this and many other decision-making activities, participants must first make decisions on an individual basis, then reach consensus of decision in a small-group setting.

Model student activity

"Lost on the Moon"

You are a crew member of a spaceship that has just crashed on the moon. You were originally scheduled to rendezvous with a mother ship located on the lighted surface of the moon, 200 miles away. However, the crash has ruined your ship and destroyed almost all of the equipment on board. Only the 15 items listed below survived the landing undamaged.

The survival of your crew depends on reaching the mother ship. However, since you can't take everything, you must choose the most important articles to bring along on the 200-mile trip. Your task is to rank the 15 items in terms of their importance for your survival. Place number 1 by the most important item, number 2 by the second most important, and so on through number 15, the least important.

Your Rank		Group's Rank
_____	Box of matches	_____
_____	Food concentrate	_____
_____	50 feet of nylon rope	_____
_____	Parachute silk	_____
_____	Solar-powered portable table heating unit	_____
_____	Two, .45 caliber pistols	_____
_____	One case of dehydrated Pet milk	_____
_____	Two, 100-lb. tanks of oxygen	_____
_____	Stellar map (of the moon's constellations)	_____
_____	Self-inflating life raft	_____
_____	Magnetic compass	_____
_____	Five gallons of water	_____
_____	Signal flares	_____
_____	First aid kit containing injection needles	_____
_____	A solar-powered FM receiver-transmitter	_____

Each person should first complete this activity individually. Then, in groups of from four to seven persons, you should share your individual solutions. You will need to agree on one ranking that best satisfies all group members. Of course, everyone in the group may not be completely satisfied but come as close as you can to a consensus in reaching your decisions. As much as possible, you should avoid using mathematical averaging, majority votes, or flipping a coin.

The answers and reasons are shown in Appendix B.

Figure 10.4 Forced-Choice Decision-Making Format

1. Problem Statement
   "What if you . . . "

2. Alternatives to Choose Among

_____   _____

_____   _____

_____   _____

_____   _____

Note: The number of choices will vary according to
the nature of the problem.

Openended vs.
forced-choice

"Lost on the Moon" is based on a forced-choice format similar to that of "Who Is Best Qualified for the Presidency?" Notice that, had the activity been left open-ended, students would have been free to identify any items they wished (from whatever they think might have been aboard a spacecraft) and the nature of the activity would have changed markedly. Instead of choosing and ranking specified items, the activity's emphasis would be on creating and identifying items from a universe of possibilities. In the forced-choice format, however, individuals are afforded a common basis for comparing their decision-making efforts. Note also that there is nothing magic about the number of items students rank—it could be more than fifteen, or less.

"Lost on the Moon" is also an atypical decision-making activity in that it includes previously established "best" answers. Without them, it wouldn't be possible to develop numerical scores, nor would there be a basis for determining statistically that when dealing with an unknown, a group's decision will usually be superior to the decisions of individuals acting alone. Among teacher-made decision-making activities, there are typically no previously established "best" answers. Instead, the answers (or actually, the best decisions) are determined by the individual or group.

A model for forced-choice decision-making activities appears in Figure 10.4. It is based on two components: (1) a problem statement based on a speculative-heuristic question ("What if you were . . .?"), and (2) a limited number of choices.

The following student activity is based on the forced-choice model. In it, children are asked to decide which items they would take with them on a voyage to the New World. Except for the fact that this activity has no established answers, it closely follows the "Lost on the Moon" format.

Voyage to the New World

You are about to leave your home in Plymouth, England, on a one-way voyage to the North American colonies. You have decided to give up your old friends for a new life in the Plymouth Colony in New England. The colony has been settled for only five years, but your family really wants to go in spite of the hardships they may meet.

You will be traveling to your new home aboard the good ship *Daffodil*. However, since quite a few other people will be making the trip, storage space has become a problem aboard the *Daffodil*. Because of the limited amount of space, each family can take only eight items.

Below is a list of things you might find useful in the New World. Number, in order of importance, the eight things you want to take with you.

___ Folding cot	___ Suit of warm clothes
_1_ Hunting knife	___ Fishing pole
___ Party dress	_6_ Candles
___ Camera	_7_ Flint and tinder
_2_ Bible	___ Surfboard
_3_ Vegetable and grain seeds	_8_ Ax
_4_ Musket and powder	___ School books
___ Table and chairs	___ Iron pot
_5_ Barrel of flour	___ Shovel
___ Flower seeds	___ Dog
___ Sled	___ Sewing kit
___ Wool blankets	___ Dishes (fine china)
___ Medicine kit	___ _____

List (in order) the eight items you would take to the New World.

Yourself   *Group*

_____   _____
_____   _____
_____   _____
_____   _____
_____   _____
_____   _____
_____   _____
_____   _____

Procedure: Working individually, students should rank the eight items they would take with them. They should then do the same thing in groups of from four to seven students each.

Compare the group's responses in terms of the most frequently chosen items. Then have the groups classify and label the items to identify what *types* of items appear most often (tools, essentials, luxury items, etc.).

Decision-making activities like "Voyage" work well as introductions to areas with which children are unfamiliar, particularly since they raise questions as to what an area is (or was) like. The nature of the problems you pose can be shifted to almost any area or historical period. For example, "If you were Marco Polo . . .," or "If you were part of a family going from Connecticut to California in 1849 . . . what would you bring with you?"

*A valuing
component*

Should you use "Voyage to the New World" with your students, be advised that they will almost always take the dog (as one of the items), even if it means leaving something like the ax behind. This phenomenon illustrates an important facet of decision-making activities. In defining decision making, we noted that decisions should be consistent with the decision maker's values. Recall, also, that as the American pioneers moved westward, they sometimes discarded useful items—shovels, plows, etc.—but saved items that were less essential, like a grandfather clock or a piano. Our point here is to indicate that the *values* component of decision making is vitally important and should not be treated lightly. As Cassidy and Kurfman (1977, p. 5) noted, decision making "always entails a value judgment, whereas scientific inquiry reaches conclusions using criteria of validity and reliability. Science [though value-based] is concerned with establishing truth, not deciding the best thing to do." As a consequence, in dealing with decision-making activities, we suggest that you (1) avoid arguing that "the dog" is necessarily a poorer choice than "the ax," for example, and (2) avoid conveying the impression that the most frequently chosen items are better than the less frequently chosen items. In other words, decision-making activities may involve elements of values clarification and should be treated accordingly.

Developing and Using Decision-Making Activities

One key to developing decision-making activities lies in limiting the problem to something that is both real and manageable for students—otherwise they'll have no basis for considering the alternatives. For most elementary students a question such as "Which had a better organizational basis—the League of Nations or the United Nations?" really isn't a manageable problem for a decision-making format: it would be better suited as a high school or college debate question. As a general rule, decision-making activities for elementary students should afford more immediate access to the information on which their decisions will be based.

Decision-making activities can serve as a focus for information-processing skills. However, unless teachers continually stress rational information processing such activities can degenerate into arguments of "My opinion is as good as yours." In decision-making activities, attention must be focused on the *processes* children use in arriving at their decisions and not just on the decisions they reach.

*Maintaining a
process focus*

Decision-making activities require that students *use* information, as do other process-oriented activities—fact sheets, surveys, problem situations, etc. Unfortunately, teachers whose only exposure has been to traditional social studies programs have been known to relegate process-oriented decision-making activities to a secondary and often trivial role—as something to do on a Friday afternoon or during a rainy recess. In addition, instead of serving as the heart of a social studies program, information-processing and decision-making activities are sometimes treated as gimmicks—neat, pre-packaged activities that will keep students busy. Unless the focus is kept on *using* information and on the rational processes that go into decision making, such activities can indeed become very gimmicky. In the final analysis, only you can assess the balance you want to maintain in your classroom between process-oriented social studies and a more traditional knowledge orientation.

Summary

In this chapter we have presented some activities that can help you manage process-oriented skill instruction. For the sake of organization, we identified skills that were part of the inquiry (problem-solving) process. We also suggested that process skills are part of a "whole" and that they cannot be held in isolation for very long. Hypothesizing, for example, is a process skill, but it can't end there; once students hypothesize, they must be able to do something with those hypotheses. Otherwise they will be left hanging.

One key to developing many information-processing and decision-making activities, we suggested, is in limiting the information available to students at the outset. Paralleling that was the suggestion that students are not likely to do much processing with information that has been preprocessed. Thus a second key factor involves selecting unprocessed (raw) information with which students can work. Finally, we suggested that process-oriented and decision-making activities can be misused or become "gimmicky" if a focus on rational information-processing is not maintained.

Objects from the Beta Room

The objects are pictured in Figure 10.2 on page 296. From left to right, they are:

Owl cup. Typical of many found in Greece, these cups were made of reddish clay and baked. Then black paint was applied to create the design.

Spoon. In ancient Greece, most people ate with their fingers, so a spoon like this was probably used in the kitchen to dish up soups and gravies.

Mortar and *pestle.* These objects were used to grind nuts, small grains, spices, etc. A household was likely to have a variety of different-sized mortars and pestles.

The room itself is obviously the kitchen. In a villa of this size much of the cooking was probably done by slaves.

References

Brandwein, Paul F., et al. *Principles and Practices in the Teaching of the Social Sciences: Concepts and Values. Teacher's Guide, Grade 1.* New York: Harcourt, Brace, & World, 1970.

Cassidy, Edward W., and Kurfman, Dana G. "Decision Making as Purpose and Process." In Dana G. Kurfman (ed.) *Developing Decision-Making Skills* 47th Yearbook. Washington, D.C.: National Council for the Social Studies, 1977: 1–27.

Fair, Jean. "Skills in Thinking." In Dana G. Kurfman (ed.) *Developing Decision-Making Skills* 47th Yearbook. Washington, D.C.: National Council for the Social Studies, 1977: 29–70.

Fraenkel, Jack R. *Helping Students Think and Value: Strategies for Teaching the Social Studies.* Englewood Cliffs, NJ: Prentice-Hall, 1973.

Kaltsounis, Theodore. *Teaching Social Studies in the Elementary School: The Basics for Citizenship.* Englewood Cliffs, NJ: Prentice-Hall, 1979.

Mallan, John T., and Hersh, Richard. *No. G.O.D.s in the Classroom: Inquiry and Elementary Social Studies.* Philadelphia: W. B. Saunders, 1972.

MATCH. *House of Ancient Greece, Teacher's Guide.* Nashua, NH: Delta Education, 1966.

Taba, Hilda. *Teacher's Handbook for Elementary Social Studies.* (Introductory ed.) Palo Alto, CA: Addison-Wesley, 1967.

Unified Science and Mathematics Program for Elementary Schools. *Traffic Flow.* Cambridge, MA: Educational Development Center, 1974.

11   Managing Group Instruction

Key Questions:

Why use groups?

How large should groups be?

How does one determine group membership?

What is the difference between inquiry and activity?

How do you evaluate feedback?

What is process observation and how does it work?

Key Ideas

Almost anything you wish to do with large groups can be done with small groups, although the reverse is not necessarily true.

A class is not necessarily a "group" at the outset, and will not become one until it exhibits the characteristics of a group.

"Feeling good" about an activity does not necessarily mean that anything was learned, *or* that what you intended was learned.

Teacher feedback is one of the more critical components of effective group management.

In observing group activities, the tendency is to get involved in the content of the group's discussion and neglect the processes used in dealing with that content.

Introduction

Being thrust into the leadership role of teaching can carry with it some of the same worries that beset actors and actresses on opening night.

Will I be a hit?

Will they like me?

Will I be able to manage without, in a sense, forgetting my lines?

Unlike actors and actresses, teachers have the advantage of knowing that they don't have to face a new audience each day. Even that advantage can become a double-edged sword on those occasions when teachers "bomb" and are then faced with repairing the damage. It may not happen often, but there will be *those* days when you wish you could start all over again.

For many prospective teachers, it's not their ability to deal with content that concerns them most. Rather, their concern is with their ability to cope with transforming a collective of some twenty-odd children into a group.

Unless you teach kindergarten or, in some cases, first grade, your class is likely to have a legacy of previously established relationships—both good and bad—from past years. In that case it is likely to be you, the teacher, who's the new ingredient. Of course, there are also likely to be some "new kids" —a little scared and just as new to the class as you are—who are looking for your help to become a part of the group. Indeed, managing subject matter may be among the least of your initial concerns.

The purpose of this chapter is to examine the dimensions of group instruction from an instructional or organizational perspective, one that focuses on developing alternative patterns for structuring various kinds of groups for different purposes. Just so it's clear at the outset, our primary focus is on managing small groups of from three to seven students. Our reason for doing this is that almost everything you have seen done with large groups (twenty to thirty students) can also be done with small groups; in fact, you could even lecture to two students, if that's your thing. But the reverse of that usually doesn't hold up. In other words, what you can do with small groups is not always possible with large groups. A discussion involving twenty-six students, for example, is far less likely to be successful than it might be with a group of five to seven students. Similarly, trying to manage a twenty-six-person research group—with everyone studying the same problem—is likely to have you (and the librarian) tearing your hair in record time. Although both large- and small-group instruction present challenges to a teacher, we've opted to focus on small groups because we think that they will give you the most mileage.

Chapter overview

In the first part of this chapter we deal with small groups—their nature, their dynamics, their purposes. Then we identify several strategies for establishing groups in your classroom, with particular attention to the kinds of feedback you can provide to ensure successful group work.

To Group or Not to Group?

Parent: What did you do at school today?
Child: Oh, the teacher put us into groups and we just talked.
Parent: Well, what did you learn?
Child: Nothin'!

Therein lies the beginning of negative perceptions of group work. Of course, other experiences often contribute. For example, do you recall occasions when everyone on your committee got the same grade, but you did all the work? Or did you ever find that when forced to work on a committee with someone you disliked, at the conclusion of the group's work you disliked that individual even more? (Of course, the opposite might also have occurred.) Or, do you remember those times when your group was given a massive assignment, and you spent most of your time trying to figure out how to begin? On other occasions, you may have spent forty minutes organizing a group effort when you could have done the job yourself in twenty minutes or less. Finally, there probably were times when your work in a group didn't make any difference because your grade was based solely on tests and individual projects.

Pitfalls of group work

We have met experienced teachers who, after several bad experiences with groups and group work, feel they might just as well dispense with groups entirely because they create more problems than they're worth. Our typical response is not to hail the merits of groups and group work, though well we could, but rather to ask what the alternatives are. Basically, there are three: (1) total individualization of instruction (which isn't at all easy to pull off successfully—see Chapter 13), (2) totally teacher-directed, whole-class instruction (which may be easier to pull off but which can become monotonous very, very quickly), and (3) some combination of 1 and 2.

Alternatives

Instead of dispensing with group work, consider that every bad experience you may have had with groups actually implies an element that must be considered before you undertake group work of any kind. In other words, will you grade your students on their group work? If so, will it be graded on an individual basis? If so, how—letter grades? points? anecdotal records? Will you let children choose their own groups or will you do the selecting? If you do the selecting, will you put two students who are known to dislike each other on the same committee? Or, would you put a low-status child in a group with high-status children? We will deal with these issues throughout this chapter, but suffice it to say here that high- and low-status children can often work together successfully in the same group. It is much rarer, however, that the relationship between two children who actively dislike each other will be improved by working together in a group—primarily because most groups don't deal with the causes of their disenchantment.

Why Group?

Why group? Clearly because it changes the interaction in a classroom. Of course, changing interaction in a classroom simply for the sake of changing it is hardly justification for using groups. Rather, it is what that interaction changes *from* that becomes important.

In whole-group instruction, for example, the sheer logistics of managing a group of twenty or more individuals limits your instructional options. Almost by definition, you, the teacher, become the focal point. You can talk at (lecture) students, you can do some demonstrations where appropriate, and you can conduct question-and-answer sessions. You can also show films and conduct other activities traditionally associated with large-group instruction. But you will not find it easy to conduct bona fide discussions, primarily because only one person at a time can talk, regardless of the individuals who might have something to say. If fifteen people have an opinion, fourteen of them are going to have to wait their turn. Unless those fourteen are vitally interested in what is going on, the necessity of waiting as much as five to ten minutes to get their views aired is often enough to stifle the staunchest student.

It is difficult, though not impossible, to make large-group instruction anything other than teacher-centered. There are times, of course, when teacher-centered, large-group instruction is wholly appropriate. But when you undertake large-group instruction, you can anticipate that approximately two-thirds of your time will be devoted to managing procedures and maintaining order.

By dividing your class into small groups, the proportion of each student's responsibility to the group increases dramatically. Instead of representing one twenty-sixth of a class of twenty-six, the student may represent one-fourth of a group of four. No longer must that student wait for twenty-five other potential contributors to have their say before she or he can become involved in an activity. From one perspective, small groups offer far less chance for students to sit back passively and watch events pass in review. Or from a more positive perspective, students in small groups have considerably more opportunity for active involvement, simply because the structure of the setting permits it. This does not mean that all students in a small group will be actively involved; it just means that you will have eliminated some of the structural barriers to that involvement.

The formula for determining the number of possible interactions in small groups is illustrated in Figure 11.1. So, how large will your groups be? If you have eight people in a group, there are fifty-six possible interrelationships. A group of this size doing library research will probably spend as much time checking among themselves (and duplicating their efforts) as they will in doing the research itself. Thus, the question of how large a group should be must be determined in relation to its purpose. For most purposes, from five to eight students per group is generally acceptable.

Removing barriers

Groups and Group Size

Some sizes of small groups appear to have particular properties, as follows:

Groups of two: High tension and emotion, tendency to avoid disagreement, high exchange of information, high potential of deadlock and instability, high differentiation of role with one person the active initiator, the other the passive controller (with veto). . . .

Groups of three: Power of the majority over the minority of one, usually the two stronger over the weakest member; most stable, with shifting coalitions. . . .

Odd versus even groups: More disagreement in even groups (4, 6, 8) than in odd (3, 5, 7), due to the formation of subgroups of equal size. The personally most satisfying size seems to be five—ease of movement within; 2:3 division provides support for the minority members; large enough for stimulation, small enough for participation and personal recognition (Berelson and Steiner, 1964, p. 360).

Groups and Purposes

You can establish groups for any number of purposes, but four of the most common to social studies instruction are: (1) to discuss issues or events, (2) to engage in decision-making activities, (3) to provide small-group instruc-

Figure 11.1 Formula for Group Interaction

(Number of persons in the group − 1) × number of persons in the group = the number of interactions (Np − 1) NP = Ni

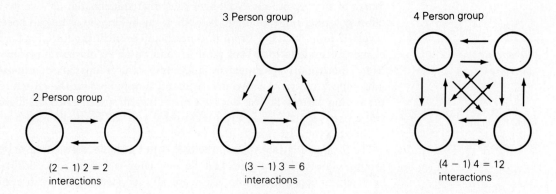

Source: IDEA (1971, p. 11). Reprinted with permission of the Institute for Development of Educational Activities, Inc., an affiliate of the Charles F. Kettering Foundation.

tion, and (4) to research or investigate problems or questions. Characteristics of the more common groups are summarized below.

Discussion Groups Purpose: To provide children with opportunities to express and clarify their points of view on issues pertinent to their interests.

Size: Two to six (including enough children to provide the necessary stimulation but not so many as to overwhelm or restrict the flow of discussion).

Comment: From your own experience you know that, unless handled carefully, discussion groups can easily degenerate into rap sessions of questionable value. To help keep discussion groups on track, consider establishing a task for them—a conclusion, a verbal report, or a summary—to be presented at the end of their deliberations.

Potential problems: Since the teacher cannot be present in each group if several are operating simultaneously, the student who is elected or appointed as the discussion leader has a critically important role. When in doubt, appoint the discussion leader. Also, it may be necessary to provide groups with preprinted questions or other guides to help structure their discussion.

Decision-Making Groups Purpose: To provide children with experience in group consensus, and in considering alternatives and arriving at a decision.

Size: Three to seven.

Comment: The life of decision-making groups, like most discussion groups, is of fairly short duration. Seldom does it exceed an hour and is typically less than that. As a result, the status of discussion-group members is less critical than for longer-range tutorial or research groups. Members can even be selected at random.

Potential problems: Some decision-making and discussion groups invariably finish before others. You may need to have a couple of related questions or issues on hand to pose to the early finishers. As a less desirable alternative, you can even join the group and/or turn it into a discussion group. Although seeing you working with one group may have the effect of speeding up the other groups, it may also take the steam out of the intergroup discussion that follows when everyone is finished.

Tutorial Groups   Purpose: To provide individual help or advanced work to a small group that might most need or benefit from it.

   Size: Two to nine.

   Comment: Tutorial groups provide teachers with an opportunity for more immediate, direct feedback than is possible in large-group settings.

   Potential problems: The rest of the class will need to be kept busy with meaningful activities while you work with a tutorial group. Also, despite the best of intentions, a social stigma may be associated with students in remedial, tutorial groups.

Research Groups (Investigative)   Purpose: To provide individuals with an opportunity to solve a problem, research a question, pursue a line of inquiry, or prepare a project.

   Size: Two to four.

   Comment: The limitation on group size as noted previously should be observed. Also, you may need to spend considerable time helping the group organize itself.

   Potential problem: Care must be taken to see that the mechanics and incidentals of the research or project do not prove more time consuming than the investigation itself.

Collectives, Classes, and Groups

Sociologically speaking, a *collective* is a collection, an assemblage, and nothing more. There is not necessarily an implied relationship among the individuals who make up a collective. And so when you walk through that classroom door one September morning, you will be facing a collective which, when grouped in terms of age (or on some other basis), can be called a *class*—your class. Even though you are the teacher, you are simply another individual added to the collective (since you are not a "member" of the class). Only after building a relationship with your class can it be considered a *group*.

   Within classes in which some students know one another, there will be subgroups that share the characteristics of a group. That is, some of the subgroups in your class will exhibit a degree of *interdependence*, at least to the extent that the behavior of one individual in a group influences the behavior of others, and vice versa. Second, they will share a *psychological relationship*, including similar beliefs, interests, experiences, values, norms, etc., all of which serve to influence their conduct. In short, members of a group *care* about other members of the group, as individuals, and about the group as a whole.

*Characteristics
of groups*

The degree of complexity in building a whole-class group varies in terms of the individuals involved. In practical terms this means that even teachers who are highly skilled in managing group interaction sometimes experience frustration when dealing with some classes.

New teachers seem prone to group-management problems, apparently because of their tendency to focus on their own behavior—as teachers—and not on the way students respond to their actions. Particularly vunerable are new teachers who, thinking they are building a sense of group, go overboard by trying to join the existing subgroups within their class. What results is often called the "buddy-buddy" or "pal" approach to group management, and is usually marked by two features: (1) a singular lack of success, and (2) an increase in intergroup conflict, as individual subgroups vie for the teacher's attention. The problem seems to arise because subgroups within a class are peer groups, and one thing the teacher is *not* is a peer. Teachers who try to join their students' peer groups are actually abdicating their leadership role—whether they want or like that role or not. Of course, it's possible for a teacher to share leadership with a group, just as it is possible to be a friend, "pal," or even a "buddy" with students without approaching them on the peer level. But when one abdicates the leadership role, the consequences of that action will likely operate counter to the development of a sense of group among the entire class. Rather than joining existing peer groups, teachers face the problem of creating new, nonpeer groups of which they are bona fide members.

"Hey, buddy . . ."

Determining Group Membership

Assume that you are going to ask your students two questions: "Which individual in this class do you like best?" and "Which person in this class would you most like to work with?"

Do you think most children would cite the same individual in both instances? That is, do you think they will most often choose their best friend as the person with whom they would like to work? Yes or No?

In some cases they will, of course, but according to the research, in many instances they will not (Bonney, 1946). When confronted with an activity demanding a lot of reading, for example, and in a case where their best friend is not very adept at reading, children often realize that they would be wiser to choose to work with a better reader. To do so might very well enhance their own performance, a subtlety not lost to most students.

The research suggests that children are cognizant of both a social dimension and a "work" dimension operating in their classroom. It suggests, further, that a child may rank differently in each dimension. And so, for example, you may find boys or girls in your class who, because of their athletic prowess, are social leaders but, maybe because of a skill deficiency, are ranked somewhat lower on the "who I'd like to work with" scale. Similarly, low-status children on the social scale may be ranked somewhat higher in the "work" dimension.

You have undoubtedly had enough experience as a student to know what to look for in identifying the social pecking order in a classroom—a child who is ignored by most other students, or high-status individuals who command almost instant respect from others. By careful observation of the interaction patterns—especially of who talks with whom when no one is supposed to be talking, who sits next to whom, etc.—it is relatively easy to determine the extremes of high- and low-status children. Ferreting out those individuals in the so-called great "unwashed" middle is often more difficult.

In addition to observation, one means of identifying the social status pattern in your classroom is through a sociometric technique, a sociogram. Gathering the data for sociograms is fairly simple. You ask all students to respond (either verbally or in writing) to a question such as, "What person in this classroom do you like best?" You can be more subtle about it by asking, "Who would you most like to sit next to?" or something similar. But if you are interested in social status, be careful not to ask, "With whom would you most like to work in a group (or on a committee)?" This is a legitimate question for identifying status in the "work" dimension, but it may not accurately reveal the social dimension. If you ask both questions, plan on plotting the responses on two separate target diagrams. If you try plotting them on one diagram, you will face the biggest mess you ever encountered, and something which, if you ever get it sorted out, may not tell you very much anyhow.

Sociograms

Caution: Although sociogram questions can be posed in a group setting, students must be able to respond individually. Above all, students' responses must be held in the strictest confidence.

The data are processed by making a list of the students in your class, counting the number of times each one was chosen, and then noting by whom. This information can then be transferred to a target diagram such as the one illustrated in Figure 11.2, which will provide you with a graphic display of the status choices.

The high-status individuals, the *stars,* will be located toward the center of the diagram, while low-status individuals, the *isolates,* will fall outside the circle. The critical question teachers face concerns the degree to which they should intervene by placing low-status students with higher-status students. To do so may not alter the lower-status students' ranking in the overall social ordering, but it might make them feel a lot better about themselves. On the other hand, some isolates are quite content with their loner role and might just as well be left undisturbed. For these kinds of judgments, only you will have the necessary data about your students on which to base your decisions.

Caution

Knowing which students would rather *not* work together is probably as important in terms of structuring groups as knowing which would. However, the negative consequences that can result from gathering such information through sociometric means may outweigh its potential value. In other words, by asking the question, "With whom would you least like to work?" you could probably produce a "hatred" scale, and a very accurate one at that. But visualize also the dynamics that will go on in your class as the children discuss whom it is they like least.

Figure 11.2 A Target Diagram of Social Relationships

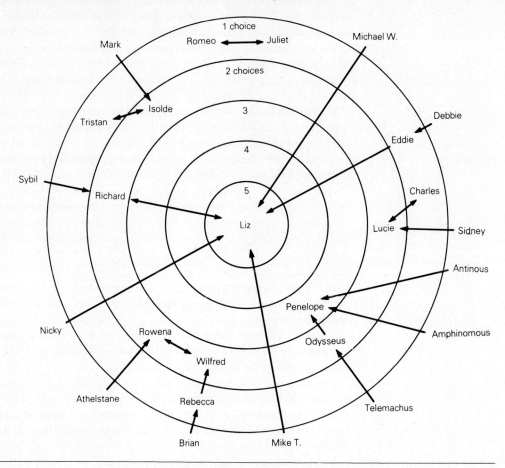

Source: Biehler (1974, p. 139). Adapted from Northway (1940); reprinted by permission of the American Sociological Association.

"Who did you choose?"

"Jimmy."

"Me too!" And "poor Jimmy," who probably knows full well his status in the class, shrinks lower into his seat, praying that he can withdraw from the situation just as quickly as possible. Identifying children whom students don't like or with whom they would rather not work is better left to observational means.

How, then, do you select which students will work in what groups? Probably the most equitable basis is through a combination of their choices and your judgment. You can inform them in advance of any extensive committee or group work and then have them identify, in writing, the two or three individuals with whom they might like to work. You can then use your own judgment as to whether the groups will work well together or whether you need to make any adjustments.

The key to successful, long-range group work is knowing the individuals you are dealing with. Until you feel confident in your ability to predict who will and who will not work well together, it's best to defer long-range group work and thereby avoid the consequences of moving too soon.

The Dynamics of Group Work

Herbert Thelen, who has written extensively about groups and group interaction, describes two oft-cited group-work situations that beautifully illustrate some of the pitfalls and successes associated with groups. In the first instance, an investigative group of second graders was working on a unit on how different people live. Their task was to select a group of people, find out how they live, and then present a play based on their information. The teacher in this case had considerable information on the Algonquin Indians, so she tried to steer the children in that direction. Undaunted by her efforts, the students, some of whom had recently seen one of Walt Disney's True Life Adventure films, decided that they were going to study prairie dogs. It really didn't matter if prairie dogs weren't people; they were going to study prairie dogs, period! Thelen (1960, pp. 142–43) described what they did:

> They started their study by naming the characters for the play they would write, and of course the characters turned out to be baby, chicken, mother, father, farmer's boy, snake, etc. They made lists of questions to be answered: What do prairie dogs eat? Where do they live? What do they do with their time? How big are their families? Who are their enemies? etc. Individuals sought answers to questions from science pamphlets, books, the science teacher, officials of the local zoo, and I have no doubt at least a few of them talked to their parents to be taken to see the Disney opus. They reported their findings in compositions during the writing lessons. The plot of the play gradually took shape and was endlessly modified with each new bit of information. The play centered around family life, and there was much discussion and spontaneous demonstrations of how various members of the family would act. Most of these characterizations actually represented a cross-section of the home lives of seven-year-old children, as perceived by the children. But each action was gravely discussed and soberly considered, and justified in terms of what they knew about the ecology of prairie dogs.
>
> They built a stage with sliding curtains and four painted backdrops —more reference work here to get the field and farm right. The play itself was given six times, with six different casts, and each child played at least two different parts. There was never any written script; only an agreement on the line of action and the part of it to occur in each scene. And after each presentation the youngsters sat around and discussed what they had been trying to communicate, and how it might be improved.

What group problems does this illustrate? None, really. In fact, if all groups worked as well as this one, there would be fewer complaints about group work. But contrast the prairie dog example with one in which a high school social studies class attempted to produce a television series on the history of their community. Thelen (1960, pp. 143–44) described the situation this way:

> Harry and Joe took pictures of an Indian mound, left there by original settlers. They took it from the south because the light was better that way; and they never discovered the northern slope where erosion had laid bare a burrow full of Indian relics. Mary and Sue spent two afternoons on a graph of corn production in the region; the graph was in a geography book the teacher gave them and the time was mostly spent in making a neat elaborately lettered document for the camera. The narrators were chosen for their handsome appearance, and much of the staging of the show (which used reports mostly) centered around deciding the most decorative way to seat the students. A lot of old firearms and household implements were borrowed from a local museum and displayed with a sentence or two of comment for each.

Studying community history

In this instance, the students learned a great deal about the mechanics of production—lettering signs, taking photographs, etc.—but relatively little about the history of their community. Indeed, the incidentals of producing the show directed their attention away from the focus of their study. In many respects, this incident is reminiscent of the infamous igloo-building example cited earlier. The moral? When you consider group activities, such as presenting a play on Mexico or holding a Greek Olympics Day, be certain that collecting sombreros and sarapes, making the scenery, or building chariots does not overshadow everything else. It very quickly can.

Bruce Joyce uses the prairie dog and TV production examples to illustrate the difference between inquiry and activity. Joyce (1972, p. 153) writes:

> These two examples illustrate the distinction between inquiry and activity. The actions of the second-grade class investigating prairie dogs contained the elements of inquiry: problem-situation, self-awareness, puzzlement, methodology, and reflection. But were there questions in the latter example? Who formulated them? Who sought their answers? How was this information obtained? Was the information applied? Were conclusions drawn and who drew them? Activities are potential channels for inquiry, but inquiry must emanate from the motivations and curiosity of the students. Activities cease to be inquiry when the teacher is the sole source of the problem identification and the formulation of plans or when the end product of inquiry takes precedence over the inquiry process.

Activity vs. inquiry

The irony of activity and inquiry is that students often "feel good" about both. That is, the students who studied prairie dogs probably felt good about what they had accomplished. In fact, if they hadn't enjoyed what they were doing, their study probably wouldn't have been as thorough and all-encompassing as it was. But then the students who made the TV presentation

You can find out who works well together simply through observation.

probably felt good about their efforts too, even though they didn't learn much about their original topic. Similarly, participants in rap or bull sessions also often enjoy themselves, if for no other reason, because they've sounded off—often at length. But feeling good, by itself, is hardly a sufficient criterion for judging the quality of a learning experience.

True, kids (and teachers) need to feel good about what they're doing or what they've done. If they don't, they probably will not realize the learning potential an activity presents. In fact, if students are not intrigued with continuing an inquiry, it may be necessary to interrupt with another activity intended to raise their sagging interest level. For example, if your class is getting bogged down with library research, you may wish to insert an activity—a game, a short decision-making exercise, even a film on a totally differ-

Changing the pace

ent topic—just to provide a change of pace and renew their interest in the longer-range activity. In other words, your objective may be to present an activity intended to raise your students' "feeling" level so that they are willing to continue their original inquiry. Note, however, that activities which lack significant learning outcomes are suitable *only* when the dynamics of a group indicate that interest is sagging and/or that a change of pace is warranted. If you are able to develop motivational activities that also have significant learning outcomes, you will have captured the best of both worlds.

Social Skills and Feedback

It is often claimed that when children work together on group projects they are learning social skills—how to cooperate, how to get along with one another, etc. Some such claims should probably be viewed with suspicion. It is difficult to say for certain that, because children are placed in a situation requiring cooperation, for example, they will necessarily learn anything about cooperation per se. In fact, it may mean that students cooperated because they were placed in a situation that demanded it.

Assume that you are confronted by a group of three students to whom you have given an assignment similar to the prairie dog study described by Thelen. But in this instance, let's assume that two students want to study the Algonquin Indians while a third, Jamie, wants to study prairie dogs. One of the students comes to you and says, "Jamie won't cooperate. We want to study Algonquin Indians and he wants to study prairie dogs." How would you respond?

_____

_____

_____

Dealing with conflict

Will you agree that Jamie is not cooperating, which in this instance means not going along with the will of the majority? Or would you ask Jamie his reasons for wanting to study prairie dogs, knowing full well that they are not people and technically don't fit the intent of your assignment? Or would you let Jamie go off on his own (where he need not cooperate with anyone) and study prairie dogs to his heart's content?

The answer—and there really isn't one best answer—probably depends on information you don't have—specific data on Jamie. Is he the type of child you can cajole into going along with the majority? Or is he the type of child who, if forced to do something he is not really interested in, will engage in a little subtle sabotage along the way? Without more data, these are imponderables. But imagine also that at a parent-teacher conference you have the opportunity to mention that "Jamie doesn't cooperate well with others" and his mother or father responds, "Yes, we know. What do you suggest we do about it?" You may be hard put to come up with specific suggestions.

The problem with information such as "Jamie doesn't cooperate well with others" is that it lacks specificity. True, it may be an accurate description of Jamie's behavior, but at that level of generality there isn't much either Jamie, his parents, or you can do about his apparent lack of cooperation. What typically happens next is that someone says something to the effect that "Jamie, the next time you work in a group, I want you to cooperate." The assumptions implicit in the request are that Jamie (1) is aware of how *and* when he has failed to cooperate, and (2) is able (and wants) to do something about his apparent problem. If either of these assumptions is not valid, then telling Jamie to cooperate in the future is likely to be as effective as spitting into the wind.

Forms of feedback

So how can you deal with Jamie or with students who display similar problems—students who dominate groups, who don't respect the rights and opinions of others (both behaviors reflect a form of noncooperation), or who are unwilling to accept their share of the work? In general, you should provide them with feedback in a form that they—either individually or as groups—can do something with (or about). What we are suggesting here is that the kind of feedback you provide your students, whether in large groups, small groups, or as individuals, will help determine your success or failure as a teacher.

What Teachers Say and What They Really Mean

What the parent hears	*What the teacher means*
Jamie often exhibits a lack of cooperation.	Jamie is stubborn as a mule.
Cynthia doesn't always respect the rights and property of others.	Cynthia steals like crazy.
John has proven to be a real challenge.	John is a spoiled brat who is driving me up the wall.
Harriet has an especially vivid imagination and tends to exaggerate at times.	Harriet lies constantly.
Claude has problems with social adjustment.	The kids all hate Claude.
Judy is exceptionally mature socially.	Judy is the only fourth-grader who has pierced ears, wears eye shadow, and smokes in the john.

What might that feedback be like? Let's return to Jamie's case as an example. Knowing that general statements are not likely to produce results, the alternative is to give Jamie something specific, something he can deal with. Thus, instead of "Jamie, you are not cooperating," you might say something like, "Jamie, when your group was deciding the issue, you didn't seem to listen to what the others said, and they seemed forced to accept your arguments or face attack from you." This statement can provide Jamie with a specific instance which he, you, and perhaps the group he's working with, can handle. You have also identified a behavior that Jamie can do something about, namely, his willingness to listen to others. To be sure that Jamie was really listening to you (or to whomever is providing the feedback), it

Be specific

may be necessary to check it out for clear communication. You might ask Jamie to rephrase the feedback to see that it corresponds with what you told him.

The context within which you provide feedback can also influence what you say to Jamie. In general, feedback is most useful immediately after the given behavior has taken place, but, under certain circumstances, you may wish to deal with Jamie on an individual basis. You would have to decide that based on the nature of your relationship with Jamie. Nevertheless, the timing of your feedback is important. You could be facing the best of all possible worlds if Jamie solicits your help and feedback with a "We seem to have a difference of opinion in our group on what we should study." However, if Jamie is upset about something—a fight with his sister, the death of a grandparent, or almost any of a thousand other things—it obviously may not be the time to approach him in terms of his willingness to cooperate; he's got more important things on his mind. Similarly, if you are upset about something—and, realistically, it happens to all of us—the form of your feedback may be such that it serves your needs but not Jamie's. A sharp, "Jamie, you should go along with the majority," may give you a chance to vent your own feelings, but it could also compound Jamie's problem.

Finally, in providing feedback we must come to grips with a language problem. Feedback is conditioned by the English language's ability to permit us to be extremely specific in a negative way, but allows us fewer ways of expressing positive reactions. After "good," "excellent," and "nice," there are relatively few expressions left with which to signify positive approval. But on the negative side, we've got thousands. As a rule, we can be very precise in indicating what is "wrong" with something, but are much more limited in indicating what's "right" with it.

Positive feedback, such as "That was a good report" or "This group is really working well together," is usually music to the ears of anyone. More description, such as "You really integrated the material well in your presentation," usually adds just that much more icing on the cake. But negative feedback is quite another matter. To say to Jamie, for example, that "You are not a good group member" is likely to evoke Jamie's ego-defense mechanisms, especially if it is stated publicly. In fact, about the only time that kind of statement will not cause problems is if Jamie values the fact that he is *not* a good group member.

Normally, negatively oriented feedback will force one to defend oneself and, whether we like it or not, can lead to latent hostility that may surface in the future. To avoid these consequences, negatively oriented feedback should be presented in descriptive terms and as your own reaction. Instead of "This group doesn't work well together," you might very well say, "It seems to me that this group is having difficulty deciding what information is important enough to be included in your presentation." The latter may not eliminate defensive reactions, but it is calculated to reduce them markedly.

The following feedback rating scale uses many of the elements noted above, and can serve as a means for assessing the utility of your feedback.

Timing

Language constraints

Descriptive feedback

Feedback Rating Scale

1 *Specificity* Does the feedback concern specific and identifiable occurrences or behaviors, or does it consist primarily of sweeping generalizations? ("You did not seem to be listening to what the others were saying" as opposed to "You will not cooperate.")

Specific   — 1 — 2 — 3 — 4 — 5 —   General

2 *Modifiable behavior* Is the feedback directed toward behavior that the receiver can do something about? ("You are not smart enough to be in this group" as opposed to "Before you proceed, you had better check your source of information.")

Modifiable   Nonmodifiable
Behavior   — 1 — 2 — 3 — 4 — 5 —   Behavior

3 *Descriptiveness* Is the feedback basically descriptive rather than evaluative? By describing one's own reaction, the individual is free to use that information, or not to use it, as he or she sees fit. ("I get the feeling you're not interested in what we are doing since neither of you has said anything" as opposed to "You two don't care about this group.")

Descriptive   — 1 — 2 — 3 — 4 — 5 —   Evaluative

4 *Needs* Does the feedback take into account the needs of both the receiver and the giver of feedback? Feedback can be destructive when the needs of the person on the receiving end go unconsidered.

Both Needs   — 1 — 2 — 3 — 4 — 5 —   One Need

5 *Timing* Is the feedback well timed? Is it provided at the earliest opportunity after the given behavior (depending, of course, on the individual's readiness to hear it, support from others, and other factors)?

Well Timed   Poorly Timed

6 *Solicited* Is the feedback solicited or imposed? Feedback is most useful when the receiver has formulated questions that the observer can help answer.

Solicited   Imposed

7 *Clarity* Does the person providing feedback *check* from time to time to determine the clarity of the communication? (Is the receiver asked to rephrase the feedback so the sender can determine whether it corresponds with what he or she had in mind?)

Checked   Clarity is assumed

Instead of saying that children learn social skills in groups, it is probably safer to say that group work permits children's social skills to surface. Once they have surfaced, teaching may occur. It will largely depend on how you handle your feedback, which in turn may permit the child to change or develop new social behaviors.

The Group That Studies Itself

Groups always study something, but almost never do they study themselves. Almost never does a group look at how it is operating as a group. All of us have been in groups that seemed to get nowhere—fast—and we have been vaguely aware that something was amiss. Seldom was that problem regarded as legitimate data for the group to deal with, however. Most groups seem to get so caught up in the content of their deliberations, in the issues and topics they are dealing with—that the processes the group is using often get lost in the shuffle. Indeed, it takes considerable conscious effort to divorce oneself from the content of a group discussion, but that's just what it takes to observe group process.

The concern for how groups function has led to the development of something called *process observation.* Recognizing that a group's discussion can become so all-involving, an individual who has been appointed to observe the group's processes does *not* participate in the group's deliberations. Rather, observers note how the group is functioning and report their observations back to the group from time to time. The process observer's report provides the group with an opportunity to focus, consciously, on *how* they are dealing with a topic or issue.

Process observation

What do process observers look for? First, they note the general sequence of events. When a group first meets, for example, does everyone sit around looking at each other, waiting for someone to take charge? Or do group members begin by voicing their opinions on the issue, without any consideration of how they will operate as a group? And after they have resolved one issue, do they move on to the next or do they keep coming back to reexamine their original decision? The process observer's concern for sequence is broader than, say, the group secretary's, since the observer is concerned with how a group handles the options open to it, not simply with reporting the results of group action.

Common problems

Second, process observers examine how group members handle the things that have been identified as common problems groups are likely to encounter. These include:

1 *Terminology*
Terms such as *democracy, evaluation,* etc., often mean different things to different people. Do members of the group clarify their terminology? Do all members of the group use the same words in the same way? What happens when someone tries to clarify terminology?
2 *Respect for the rights and opinions of others*
Does everyone's opinion get a fair hearing?
3 *Willingness to compromise cooperate*
When the British compromise, they feel they have resolved a problem fairly. When Americans compromise, they often feel as if they've lost the battle—and a little of their integrity with it. Are there members of this group who are not going to compromise on anything? Are there members of this group whose minds are made up and who will "lose" if they must change their position (and "win" if their view becomes accepted)?
4 *Support of others*
Do the various members of this group support other individuals with posi-

tions similar to theirs? Or do they let others go out on a limb and fight the same "battle" without support?

5   *Willingness to listen*

Does it appear that the members of this group are more interested in talking than in listening to what others have to say? Are their responses intended to clarify what the previous speaker has said? Do they really *listen* to the opinions of others?

6   *Confront conflict*

When one or more people take conflicting positions, do they avoid dealing with the conflict? Do they operate as if they agreed? Do they bring the issues on which they disagree out into the open for discussion?

Possible roles

The process observer may also identify the *roles* that group members play. These could include:

Initiating—suggesting new ideas, questions.

Clarifying—making the meaning of ideas clear.

Elaborating—expanding concepts presented.

Integrating—summarizing ideas and helping the group move along.

Fact seeking—asking questions to bring out facts.

Encouraging—giving encouragement to the other members.

Appreciating—modifying one's point of view in terms of what others have said.

Self-discipline—keeping one's ideas under control, not talking too much.

Affirming—supporting another's contributions or maintaining one's own commitments.

When reporting to the group, observers should present their observations as descriptively and nonjudgmentally as possible. This need not be a blow-by-blow account nor a long speech; the observations should focus on a few of the most important events the group may wish to consider further. The following are examples of three considerably different reports for the same group, only one of which really deserves to be called "process observation."

Feedback: Process Observer's Report   Context: The group, within fifteen members, has been functioning for twenty-five minutes.

Sample reports

Case No. 1 Report: *Paul called the group to order. He told the group what it had to do. Bill asked how much time they had. Sue asked if the group shouldn't break into smaller groups. Paul said no. Dorothy gave three examples of where other attempts had failed. John suggested. . . . Paul said. . . . Then Bill and Paul debated. . . . Sue made another suggestion. . . .*

Case No. 2 Report: *You should have listened to Paul. You'll never get anything done this way. I saw some things . . . but best I not share them at this time. Sue, your personal needs come through loud and clear . . . if you're not happy at home, don't take it out on the group. If I were you, I would have taken John's suggestion . . . what did you have to lose? Bill, in this particular case, Paul is right. . . .*

Case No. 3 Report: *Paul spent ten minutes going over the "charge." During this time four members of the group read the memo given out last week, and two members carried on a side conversation. Paul received little supportive feedback and I had a feeling that he just kept going with the hope that someone would nod, or something.* [Laughter. Paul nods his head affirmatively. John comments that the memo had already spelled out what Paul was repeating.] *When Paul finished, there was an extended silence: Bill asked about time, and for fifteen minutes the time factor become a major concern. Sue's suggestion was "denied" by Paul—were there special reasons for keeping the total group together?—and when Bill and Paul had the dialogue, no one else seemed to be attentive. This took five minutes. . . .*

What seems to be the difference between Case 1 and Case 2? Analyze how Case 3 differed in form and content from both Cases 1 and 2. Compare your findings with the description of what a process observer is *not* and what a process observer *is* in the box below.

The Process Observer
The process observer is *not:*

1   A *participating* member of the group.
2   A spy, a judge, or a self-proclaimed psychiatrist.
3   A manipulator or a fabricator.
4   A "lover" nor an all-knowing "leader" or expert.
5   A mediator or referee.

The process observer *is:*

1   A group member who observes factors that influence the group's functioning.
2   A source of public feedback to the group.
3   An intervening variable in the group who reports his or her own nonjudgmental perceptions.
4   An opportunity maker, who opens the way for group members to share with each other the relating of tasks/processes.
5   A hypothesis poser, whose report, while authentic, stimulates the group to test suggested hypotheses.

---

*Reports
analyzed*

The report in Case 1 is simply a recounting of events, with no attempt to indicate how those events influenced the group's functioning. There is no indication, for example, of how Paul's response to Sue's question (about breaking into smaller groups) influenced the group's operation. It could be that his action introduced a dynamic that should be dealt with after the observer's report. In this case, however, the report doesn't provide enough information to determine that.

The report in Case 2 illustrates almost everything a process observer should *not* do—present blatantly evaluative judgments, play "junior psychiatrist," and try to manipulate the group so it will follow the observer's suggestions, etc. It is not the intent of process observation to tell groups what they should or should not do, but rather to provide them with information on what they have done. This distinction is crucial. Once a group receives the information, they can deal with it as they see fit. It is not the observer's role to sit in judgment.

Neither are process observers interested in identifying the underlying causes for events—something that distinguishes process observation from group therapy. The focus of process observation is on the effects of various individuals' contributions to the group, and *not* with the motivation which might underlie those contributions. Thus, the observer's remark about Sue's personal problems at home, even if accurate, is not appropriate data for a process-observation report. If this were a counseling or therapy group, which most school groups definitely are *not,* then the underlying causes for certain behaviors would be appropriate concerns.

The report in Case 3 presents information and raises questions that the group can address, should it see fit. In addition, the contrast between the reports in Cases 2 and 3 should be vivid enough to illustrate the difference between observational data and personal judgments. Personal judgment is so inappropriately in evidence in Case 2, whereas observational data are almost completely lacking in Case 1.

We are not suggesting that elementary children need to be trained as process observers, although some, at the intermediate and middle-school levels especially, can become quite adept at it. What we are suggesting is that you will need to become fairly proficient at process observing yourself to be able to diagnose the problems that groups in your class encounter. We are suggesting further that the kinds of process problems that groups encounter should also be legitimate topics for them to consider in addition to the content they are addressing. Indeed, if Jamie, to return to an earlier example, does not cooperate or proves to be a group "blocker," this information may be dealt with by the group. However, *it is critical that it be presented as a difference of opinion between group members,* and not as a problem with Jamie or as Jamie's problem. What the group should consider are alternative ways to deal with the differences of opinion. In fact, the interests of cooperation may be advanced if "win-lose" situations are avoided (where Jamie may view it as losing if he gives in to the Algonquin proposal), and the group decides to study neither Indians nor prairie dogs but rather a third topic such as Eskimos.

A diagnostic technique

Summary of Suggested Group-Management Practices

1 Begin long-term group work only after you feel confident that (*a*) you can manage several groups operating simultaneously, and (*b*) the individuals in each group are able to work together with minimal problems.

2 You can get some idea of how individuals work together by beginning with clearly defined, short-range group assignments.

3 Present common group tasks on a large-group basis. Presenting tasks to each group separately may invite problems for the groups that have nothing to do until you get around to them.

4 Consider alternative ways in which groups can present the results of their efforts—murals, skits, plays, charts, pictures, film, etc. Long, dull reports leave a lot to be desired. However, be certain that the mechanics of the presentation do not overwhelm the report itself, and turn legitimate inquiry into mere activity.

5 Make it clear that both group-process and content-related (but not interpersonal) problems are "fair game" for consideration by small groups or the class as a whole, and allow time accordingly. But obviously, direct and immediate intervention is recommended *before* a group begins to flounder.

6 Establish reasonable deadlines; you can always extend them if necessary. Without deadlines, groups working on even the simplest of tasks have been known to drag on forever. Similarly, have something prepared for those groups that finish early.

7 Decide how you plan to evaluate group work before you begin, and then make this information known to your students. If you plan to grade their reports or presentations, tell them the criteria you intend to use. You can be assured they will listen intently.

Summary

In this chapter we have focused on the basic considerations and strategies related to successful group management. You should find the criteria for teacher feedback to be helpful whether you are dealing with a group or with individuals. Process observation—the strategy for observing the processes that a group uses to deal with content—can also provide you with remarkable insight into a group's functioning.

In the next chapter we move from group management to group-oriented teaching techniques. As your students engage in dramatic play, role playing, simulations, or other expressive and enactive experiences, you should have plenty of opportunities to apply the group-management strategies we have considered in this chapter.

Suggested Activities

1 Process observe a group that is working on any of the decision-making activities included in this book: "Five Corners, U.S.A.," etc. Provide feedback that follows the guidelines suggested in this chapter.

2 In a small group, address the question of whether or not a child's participation in group activities should be part of his or her grade. In other words, should group work "count"? If you think it should, identify clear guidelines for incorporating group work in a grading procedure. If you think it should not, indicate why.

3 While engaged in group work, many teachers find themselves confronted with an interminable line of students waiting to talk with them. How would you account for this?

References

Berelson, Bernard, and Steiner, Gary A. *Human Behavior: An Inventory of Scientific Findings.* New York: Harcourt, Brace & World, 1964.

Biehler, Robert F. *Psychology Applied to Teaching.* (2d ed.) Boston: Houghton Mifflin, 1974.

Bonney, Merle "A Study of the Sociometric Process Among Sixth-Grade Children." *Journal of Educational Psychology* 37 (September 1946): 359–72.

IDEA. *Learning in the Small Group.* Dayton, Ohio: Institute for Development of Educational Activities, 1971.

Joyce, Bruce R. *New Strategies for Social Education.* Chicago: Science Research Associates, 1972.

Northway, M. L. "A Method for Depicting Social Relationships Obtained by Sociometric Testing. "*Sociometry* 3 (1940): 144–50.

Thelen, Herbert A. *Education and the Human Quest.* New York: Harper, 1960.

Suggested Readings

Learning in the Small Group. Dayton, Ohio: Institute for Development of Educational Activities, 1971. What kinds of groups are there and how do you structure them? The answer to these questions and many more are contained in this succinct IDEA technical manual.

Richard A. Schmuck and Patricia A. Schmuck. *Group Processes in the Classroom.* Dubuque, Iowa: William C. Brown, 1971. A rather scholarly look at group process, but there is still plenty of material for application.

12 Managing Group-Based Activities

Key Questions

What is dramatic play?

Why involve students in role playing?

What are simulations and how do they differ from games?

How does one modify an existing group-based activity?

Key Ideas

Most group-based activities are intended to bring reality, albeit simplified, into the classroom.

Group-based activities provide children with a common experiences, which can then be analyzed.

Almost every group-based activity can be modified or adapted to fit certain teaching objectives.

The analysis and evaluation that follow a group-based activity are as important as the activity itself.

Introduction: The Empty Chair Technique

Context: An intermediate-level class has been studying Abraham Lincoln and his involvement in the Civil War. One day the students find that an armchair has been placed in the front of the classroom facing the class. The teacher is standing beside the chair, touching it tenderly.

Teacher: Let's pretend that this chair is Abraham Lincoln [touching the chair with empathy]. He is a tall, bearded man with many interests and lots of problems. How might he be dressed?"
Children: ... [Fill in how you think children might respond].
Teacher: What do you think he is like? How might he be feeling?
Children: ...
Teacher: Well, let's pretend that Jefferson Davis has just walked into the room. He has heard that Mr. Lincoln, here, [pointing to the chair] is going to free the slaves. Does anyone want to be Mr. Davis? O.K., Gerry, you be Jefferson Davis. I'll play Mr. Lincoln's part.
Allison: ...
Teacher: O.K., Allison. You can be Mr. Lincoln.

Allison: ...
Gerry: ...

Context: A primary classroom in which the children have been studying community helpers.

Teacher: Let's pretend this chair is a police officer. How might he be dressed?
Children: ...
Teacher: What kind of person [moving toward the chair] should this police officer be? What might he be like?
Children: ...
Teacher: O.K. Now let's put our officer at the corner of Main and First [or two streets the children are familiar with] directing traffic. He sees a young child [about the age of the children in the class] running out of a store with three candy bars clutched in his hand. Close behind him is the store owner, yelling "Stop that boy!"
　What do you think the police officer might be thinking?
Children: ...
Teacher: How do you think he might be feeling at that moment?
Children: ...
Teacher: Does anyone want to play the police officer's role? ... Johnny?
Johnny: ...
Teacher: O.K., Johnny, you can be the boy. And Debbie, you can be the store owner. I'll be the officer.

We have just illustrated the introductory moments of two role-playing episodes that use the "auxiliary chair technique" developed by Rosemary Lippit (1958). As indicated, a chair is placed at the front of the classroom, assigned human characteristics, and then the children interact with it as they might interact with a person who has those characteristics.

The beauty of the empty chair technique is that the childrens' attention is focused on the chair, not on the person playing the character in the chair. This protects the "player" from the psychological stress sometimes associated with drama-oriented activities. It also avoids a problem common to more typical role-playing episodes; when, for example, a girl plays what may be perceived as a male role, students' attention is drawn away from the episode itself.

Psychological protection

Not illustrated in our two examples is the post-role-play discussion, analysis, and evaluation of what took place. In the Lincoln episode, the activity would not end with the enactment of the Jefferson Davis–Lincoln discussion. It would and should continue with a discussion of the portrayal and a consideration of how the "players" felt at various points in the enactment; it may even include one or more reenactments involving different players and revised roles. Without this kind of follow-up, role playing is not complete.

The purpose of role playing and the other group-based activities we consider in this chapter is to re-create reality—or at least a slice of reality—in the classroom, where it can then be discussed and analyzed. The techniques for doing this range from the simplest forms of dramatic play to the more

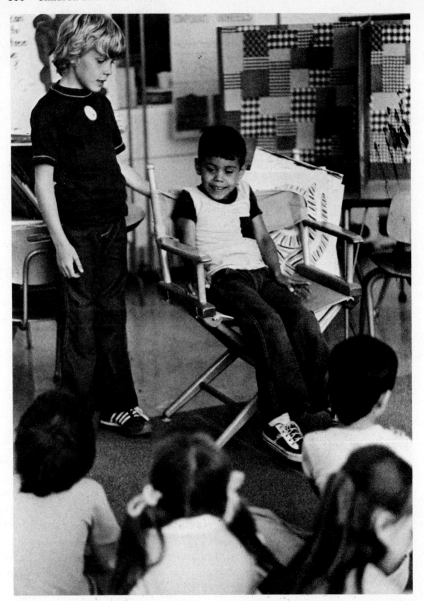

Elaborate props are not necessary for good role playing.

*Recreating
reality*

complex simulations. Bringing reality into the classroom is one thing, but doing something with it once you've got it there is quite another. The purpose for bringing reality into classrooms—whether through role playing, simulation, or other techniques—is to provide children with an opportunity to examine it, analyze it, take it apart, and hopefully get a handle on the "real" reality they will face outside the classroom.

The group-based activities we consider in this chapter range from the simple to the complex. We begin with dramatic play, move to a variety of role-playing activities, and then consider games and simulations. Finally, we consider expressive and enactive experiences, activities in which children express themselves (through drama, etc.) or in which students construct or build things (igloos, Oriental meals, etc.).

Dramatic Play

Dramatic play involves the spontaneous acting out of real-life situations. It can focus on ships in a harbor, pioneers moving westward in the 1800s, or almost any other situation you can think of.

Dramatic play differs from the random play children engage in daily in that it is intentional; it is designed to lead to something. This is illustrated in the following description of a dramatic-play activity dealing with ships and ports, provided by John R. Lee. Here is the way Lee (1974, pp. 271–74) describes the activity:

Arranging the environment.   On a Friday afternoon, you have the class strip the bulletin boards, put away all old displays, and take all used books back to the library. The class leaves for home. You are about to create an arranged room environment.

Everything in this new environment will have some relationship to ships and ports. One bulletin board is filled with pictures of ships. Underneath goes a strip of tagboard on which you have printed "What do these ships carry?"

Advance preparation

Another, but smaller, bulletin board is covered with a chart showing signal flags. Across the bottom of the chart hang four or five flags you have made from scraps of cloth. On a small table below the flags are small heaps of scrap cloth.

You cover the library table with books. In each are two or three colored markers, each inserted at a colorful picture or an exciting passage.

You set a large fish tank on the sink counter and fill it with water. You toss in a small wooden ship. Next to it you leave two metal ships (one must be large enough so that its displacement of water can be observed). You add a sign, "Why do metal boats float?" You drop a ruler and grease pencil next to the sign.

In one corner of the room you pin up, just above floor level, 6 feet of paper that will take tempera paint. Cans of paint and brushes sit nearby. Above the paper is an accurate picture of a port. In front of the paper you drop enough scraps of lumber so breakwaters and docks can be built.

Above the science table goes a picture of a lighthouse. On the table goes a set of instructions on how to build a lighthouse. Next to the instructions are batteries, wire, wood, tacks, bulbs—everything needed to build a lighthouse.

You use masking tape to hang a display. It shows men and women at work on ships and around the port. The caption asks, "What are these workers doing?"

You drop some more scraps of wood in the construction corner. Next to them go three small, dull saws, three small hammers, and an assortment of nails. You also leave a small ship that you made.

You put a song of the sea on the record player, slip on your coat, and head for home. The trap has been baited. The quarry is the interest of your pupils.

Play, discussion, and research. On Monday morning your class can't miss the changes in the classroom. When school begins, tell the class they may spend a little time wandering around the room, looking at things, and playing with the objects.

Give them enough time to prowl, but not enough time to satisfy their curiosity. (The interrupted pleasure is sure to be returned to eagerly.) Then ask, "Well, what do you think this is all about?"

"Boats!"

"Sailing!"

"The ocean!"

"Etc.!"

You ask, "What did you see that you liked most?"

"The boats!"

"The lighthouse!"

"The tools!"

"Etc.!"

Pick out from one-third to one-half of the class (depending on the size of the class, the amount of free space you have, and the number of toy ships available). Say, "OK, each of you get a ship or boat, and you can play with it."

They play. You watch. The other pupils watch. You circulate among the watchers and ask quiet questions.

"What is Billy doing?"

"Why is Mary running her boat up the wall?"

"How would you do that?"

Then you shift the groups until everyone has had his chance to play with the toy ships. The class has finished its first session of *dramatic play*.

The next step is discussion of what went on during play. You will probably pursue several ideas that occurred to you as you observed the play, but I'll just use one example.

"Billy, why were you and Kathy hitting your ships together?"

"Because. I was sailing along, and she ran into me."

"Why'd you run into his ship, Kathy?"

"Because he was in my way. He should have let me by. He's a boy and I'm a girl, and boys are supposed to be polite to girls."

"What happens if two ships smash into each other out in the ocean?"

"They sink."

"The policeman comes out in a rowboat and gives them a ticket."

"What policeman?"

"Oh, you know. It was a joke."

"Do ships smash into each other on the ocean?"

"Sure, and some of them smash into ice cubes . . . uh, icebergers and sink."

"Do all the ships that are on the ocean smash into each other all the time?"

"No."

"Why not?"

"I dunno."

"How can you find out?"

"Look it up."

"Where?"

"In the books."

"How else?"

"Ask somebody."

"Who?"

"My dad."

"A sailor."

"A sixth grader."

"The principal. He thinks he knows everything."

"OK. Who wants to work with Billy and Kathy on this question?"

And so it goes. A small research group is formed. You move on to another mistake or question or problem.

"Now, about that policeman in a rowboat. Do you really believe . . .?"

And so on.

When children play, they reflect what they know. They do some things correctly, and they make some mistakes. The mistakes are used to stimulate discussion that leads to questions that can be researched.

You do *not* say, "Billy, you are doing that wrong. Someone show him the right way." What you want is for the pupil to *find* the right way by his own (or his research group's) efforts.

Research groups form

You keep at these questions until everyone has elected a research group. The next day, you begin the period by asking each group to get together. Then you review, with each group, what they are trying to find out. Don't tell them! Ask them.

"Everybody set? OK, how much time do you want?"

And off they go, some to the library table, some to the library. They will waste time this first time. Why not? They have to become acquainted with many new books. They have to find what will be useful. They skim and finger and look at pictures. You visit each group, praising and prodding. Research takes time. And you must be willing to let them take time.

Your responsibility is to be certain that they can find out. You have to be sure the answers are in materials available to them. Why else did you do your research and write that resource unit?

Of course, someone always comes up with a question you didn't, and couldn't, anticipate. Then you have to dig out the answer. If third graders can't read your source, then you rewrite the source as simply as you can. I don't think I ever taught a unit of any kind where I didn't have to do some rewriting for the class.

Then, after one day or three days—however long it takes to find answers or partial answers—each group makes its report. When all are armed with this new knowledge, you go back to a play session.

Let's review for a moment. You create an environment. The class explores that environment. You let the class play with the ships. You observe the mistakes in the play. The class discusses the mistakes. Research groups are formed. Research takes place. The results of research are reported. The class plays again.

Lee has illustrated how dramatic play can be used as an opportunity (or stimulus) for raising questions children can then research. Of course, at lower grade levels, children's reading and research skills may be such that you will need to provide some of the answers for them. In fact, in some instances it may be necessary for you to raise *and* answer some of the key questions associated with dramatic play activities. Indeed, one of the most difficult aspects of conducting dramatic play activities—or almost any group-based inquiry activity, for that matter—is getting students to the point at which *they* ask the questions.

Caution

With dramatic play, you need to be careful that whatever you are trying to represent in your classroom does not teach incorrect or distorted ideas. Historical reenactments, for example, are particularly susceptible to distortion. Re-creating a 1849 westward journey in a covered wagon, for example, is hardly likely to sensitize children to the problems encountered by pioneers, especially since most classrooms are poor duplicates of the rugged terrain the pioneers had to cross. In this instance, instead of a dramatic-play activity, which could be of questionable value unless handled very carefully, why not consider a decision-making activity? For example, you could provide small groups with topographic maps of a small area for one of the trails West—the Oregon Trail, the Santa Fe trail, etc.—and then ask them to plot the best route to follow. Indeed, students may find that the most commonly agreed upon route follows an existing road, and in that discovery they gain some insight about how early roads were located.

Potential outcomes

It should be evident that dramatic play does not happen spontaneously. It takes extensive preplanning and, often, quite a lot of materials. Well planned and organized dramatic play can have the following outcomes, summarized from Shaftel (1973, pp. 349–52).

Dramatic play may:

aid children in understanding and using accurate concepts and symbols.

reveal the natural behavior of children.

develop sequence and unity in language expression.

reveal needs that will ensure ongoing experiences.

reveal new information gained by children.

lead into aesthetic expression of many kinds.

clarify needs for construction and research.

promote learning without undue emotional strain.

offer opportunity for children to have fun.

Role Playing

In dramatic play, children often take different roles; someone might be a father or mother, someone else the store owner, someone else a ship's captain or an airline pilot, and so forth. All of these are roles that children play. How, then, does role playing differ from dramatic play? This is the kind of question that gets us into the never-never land of educational terminology. The difference between dramatic play and role playing lies in two factors: one is *intent,* and the other is the amount of teacher *structuring.* In dramatic play, for example, the intent is to recreate an experience so that children, as they play their various roles, can get a vicarious feel for that experience, and, hopefully, raise questions that might lead to further research and investigation.

Intent and structuring

In role playing, on the other hand, the intent is to provide children with an opportunity to experience *and analyze a problem situation.* There is not much of a problematic nature associated with ships in a harbor, for example, as opposed to, say, a situation in which a pioneer family is moving West and, because of space restrictions, must decide between taking the family Bible or a set of heirloom china. Of course, the Bible-china question *might* arise in the course of dramatic play (which involved pioneers moving westward), but as a rule, role-playing situations are much more narrowly defined—so much so that the teacher can be relatively certain such a question will arise. To this extent, role playing is more structured than dramatic play.

Role playing calls for a small group of students to reenact a human situation while the rest of the class acts as observers. This is actually a third difference between role playing and dramatic play, since in dramatic play there usually is no audience—everyone is involved in the "play." How a role-playing group resolves a problem—whether it be a Bible-china kind of question, the policeman and the thief problem noted earlier, or the recreation of a dispute that actually took place between individuals in the class —becomes the focus for discussion and analysis after the enactment is completed. However, unlike plays in which the actors follow a script, role-playing situations are by definition openended. Otherwise the role-playing groups would not be illustrating alternative solutions to a problem; they would simply be reading their lines.

Role-playing procedure

Fannie Shaftel (1974, p. 557) suggests the following as a general procedural guide for handling role-playing activities:

1 "Warming up" the group (problem confrontation)
2 Selecting the participants (the role players)
3 Preparing the audience to participate as observers
4 Setting the stage
5 Role playing (an enactment)
6 Discussing the enactment
7 Further enactment (replaying revised roles, suggested next steps, exploring alternative possibilities)
8 Further discussion (which may be followed by more enactments)
9 Sharing experiences (relating the role playing to one's life experiences), which may result in generalizing

"People in Action"

To help elementary teachers introduce role-playing activities in their classrooms, Fannie and George Shaftel have developed a program that uses large photographs of problem situations. Students use the photographs as a basis for their role play and discussion. The program is organized by levels and is intended primarily for kindergarten through fourth grade, but could be used at higher grade levels as well. A sample photograph and a page from the accompanying teacher's guide (Shaftel and Shaftel, 1970, Level B: p. 24) are illustrated at right.

Model student activity

Role-Playing and Decision-Making Activities

Role playing often plays a part in decision-making activities. Depending on the way you structure the activity, you have the option of emphasizing either the role-playing dimension or the decision-making dimension. The following student activity could be used in either a decision-making or role-playing framework.

The Lunch Policy

Model student activity

A fast-food restaurant (e.g., McDonald's or Burger King) is to open next week across the street from Meridian Elementary School. Some students have requested permission from the principal to eat lunch there. Presently students may eat at home only if they bring a signed permission slip from their parents. The principal has called a meeting of:

    A parent
    A student
    A cafeteria director
    A teacher

The group must decide what to do. How would you resolve the question?

_____

_____

_____

_____

_____

Procedure:

Role-playing option: Identify individuals to play each of the roles and have them try to arrive at a decision agreeable to everyone. Then have the rest of the class evaluate and discuss both their decision and the procedures they used in arriving at it.

   Decision-making option: Divide the class into small groups with each individual taking one of the roles. When all groups have made their decisions, these should be reported and evaluated by the class as a whole.

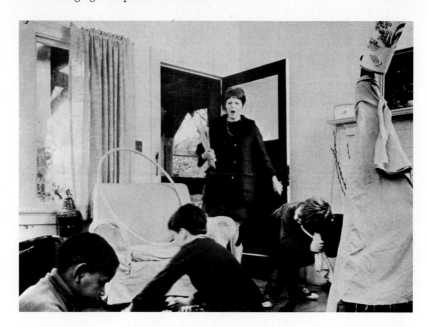

2 OH, MY!

The Photograph

A mother comes home from work to find her living room in shambles, with children playing.

Ideas To Be Developed

Children carry responsibilities in the family, especially when their mother must work. A child's responsibilities must be suited to his age and maturity.

Guidelines for Role-Playing and Discussion—
A Problem-Solving Lesson

Warm-Up

TEACHER: Does your mother ever ask you to "take care of the house" while she's away? What does she mean? (Allow the children to discuss this, and then ask,) Do you ever ask friends to come and play with you at your house? What do you play?

What Is Happening Here?

TEACHER (showing the photograph): What is happening in this photograph?
CHILDREN: The mother just came home from shopping — Maybe she's been at work — Those boys made a big mess — Maybe she just cleaned the house today!
TEACHER: How do you think the mother feels?
CHILDREN: She's awful' mad — Somebody's going to get it good!

Invite the children to role-play what happens when the mother arrives home:

Enactment: The mother angrily orders the visiting children home. She scolds her son furiously and sends him to his room; and she cleans the house in a rage.

TEACHER: Well, how does everyone feel now?

Inviting Alternative Solutions

TEACHER: Can you think of another way that the mother might handle matters?
CHILDREN: Maybe she makes them clean up. — She sends them to play in the yard.

Enactment: The mother reminds the boys of their responsibilities, and then "matter-of-factly" directs them to clean up, and sends them to play in the yard or other play area.

*Unstructured
role-play format*

Although you have the choice of selecting either the role-playing or the decision-making option, several other factors enter the picture. For example, if you think a group could handle this activity in from five to ten minutes, then you could select either (or both) option(s). But if you believe that it might take longer than five to ten minutes, or that the role-playing enactment might drag, then you face the problem of losing your students' attention. In that event, you might be wiser to choose the decision-making option in which everyone would be involved.

The format for role-playing and decision-making activities is the same as is illustrated in "The Lunch Policy" and the other examples we have presented. It involves (1) an open-ended problematic situation, and (2) roles for the individuals involved

If you are unwilling to rely on the spontaneity of role playing to reveal the dimensions of an issue, then you may need to structure the activity even more. Probably the easiest way to do this is by adding positions (points of view) to the various roles. If you were concerned, for example, that students would not know how a cafeteria director might feel about the lunch-policy question, you could modify the activity by adding position statements to the various roles as illustrated below.

1 The parent wants her children eating well-balanced meals, not hamburgers every day.
2 The student feels the school should not dictate his eating habits.
3 The cafeteria director needs a full cafeteria to meet operating expenses, and must know a week in advance the number of students who will be eating in the cafeteria.
4 The teacher doesn't want to be bothered with permission slips and checking up on where kids eat, and feels it is up to the parents and children to decide where lunch will be eaten.

*Structured
role-play format*

The procedures for managing this modified activity are the same as for the original. The format, however, is changed to reflect the new dimension. It becomes:

1 An open-ended problematic situation.
2 Roles for the individuals involved.
3 Position statements for each role player.

You are free, of course, to add other roles and/or positions. Or, you might use a mixture of each, specifying positions for some roles while leaving others open so that players can operate according to their own convictions. Nothing says any one way is better than another; it all depends on what you wish to accomplish. If you wish to heighten the sense of drama and add an element of mystery, you can distribute the role positions on separate slips of paper so that, initially, only the role players know who they are. These "secret" positions soon become apparent in the group interaction. This approach reduces spontaneity, but it also tends to heighten interest at the outset of role playing.

Built-in conflict

Should you choose to use activities with different or conflicting role positions, a note of caution is in order. By doing this you will have intentionally built *conflict* into the activity. Thus, you will need to be prepared to help the group cope with the conflict that is almost guaranteed to occur. In role-playing settings, conflict built into a group activity presents a beautiful opportunity to use process-observation skills. Indeed, a process observer's report could serve as the basis for at least part of the post-role-playing analysis.

Some students are such enthusiastic role players that they sometimes trap themselves in win-lose situations; they get so involved in a position that they take on a "this is my position, and I'll be darned if I'm going to change it or listen to anyone" attitude. To avoid this—at least to the extent that it can be avoided—you would be wise to establish a ground rule to the effect that individuals are free to change their minds (or positions) based on reasonable information. This will not eliminate win-lose situations, but it may reduce them to the extent that they don't interfere unduly.

Simulation and Gaming

Simulations, many of which involve role playing to one degree or another, are a comparatively recent innovation in education. Games, which less often involve role playing, have been around much longer. This is not to suggest that games are widely accepted as learning devices; games are generally "fun," and fun, at least in some educational circles, is definitely *not* what school is all about.

Despite the fact that simulations and games can be fun, students also learn from playing them. In the simulation *Democracy,* for example, students play the role of legislators seeking reelection. By negotiating for the passage or defeat of legislation in keeping with their constituents' interests, the student legislators may be able to win reelection. But students who do not negotiate well enough to satisfy the constituents' desires may not be reelected.

Students playing *Democracy* simulate a legislature in operation, and in doing so learn about factors that can influence the passage or defeat of legislation. In reality, however, the legislative process is so complex that were you to attempt to re-create it in a classroom, your students would undoubtedly have so many things to consider that they would be overwhelmed. About the only place you will find a totally realistic legislative process is in a real legislature and that, unfortunately, cannot exist very practically in most classrooms. Thus, *Democracy* and all other simulations necessarily simplify whatever real-world equivalent they represent.

Recreating reality in simplified form

Because simulations simplify and focus the reality they deal with, it becomes possible to analyze the situation without a lot of other variables clouding the picture. And so students playing the first stage of *Democracy* have an opportunity to analyze the negotiation phase of the legislative process, without the confounding influence of political parties or other factors. In later stages of the simulation, the legislator's own convictions and the influence of political parties are added so that the simulation more nearly reflects the real legislative process. The players are then faced with the task of reanalyzing that process with the new dimensions added. (*Democracy* was originally developed by James S. Coleman for the 4-H Foundation, and is available from Western Publishing Company, 850 Third Ave., New York, New York, 10022.)

To repeat: no simulation completely replicates reality or pretends to. Instead of being a liability, simplification is probably a prime educational asset of simulations; they simplify real situations to the extent that students are better able to see what is taking place. Then, too, if reality were not so complex, we wouldn't need simulations to help us analyze it.

Differences between Simulations and Games

If you were to drive down the streets of Atlantic City, New Jersey, you would encounter street names such as Baltic Ave., St. James Place, Park Place, and the Board Walk. You might notice also that the socioeconomic levels of the various neighborhoods roughly parallel the property values on a Monopoly board—or at least they did when Monopoly was developed in the 1920s. In other words, the real model for Monopoly is based on real estate transactions in Atlantic City, New Jersey. However, to make a game of it, Monopoly developers had to take some liberties with reality. As anyone who has played Monopoly probably knows, the major change they made involved adding more chance factors than are found in the real world. Consider, for example, that you cannot buy property unless you land on it, and that the property you land on is controlled by the dice. Other chance factors include "Community Chest" and "Chance" cards, "Go to Jail" (without having violated a law), "Luxury Tax," "Income Tax," and the total absence of insurance (except for "Get Out of Jail Free"). All of these make Monopoly fun to play because you never know what will happen next. But, because the chance factor so exceeds reality, you couldn't use Monopoly to teach the principles of real estate investment and development.

Real-life models

It is not generally recognized, we think, that many board games (though not all) are based on realistic models. Chess, for example, is based on the strategies of medieval warfare. Checkers, on the other hand, lacks a clearly identifiable model; it's simply a strategy game. Still other games, like craps and roulette, reflect no reality whatsoever; they are simply a matter of luck.

Games

Most games are actually a kind of contest in which winning is determined by a combination of luck and skill. This includes those old classroom standbys, spelling bees and Twenty Questions, as well as the takeoffs on TV game shows like *Concentration* and *Password*. In games, opponents are pitted against one another and, depending on luck and skill, someone will emerge victorious. Simulations usually lack the "contest" quality of games; even though simulations have outcomes, they usually lack the clear flavor of winning or losing that is more typical of games. In addition, the chance or luck factor in simulations tends to be lower than in most games. As a result, simulations tend to be more realistic than most games. These and the other characteristics of simulations and games are shown in Table 12.1.

**Table 12.1
Differences Between
Simulations and
Games**

Characteristics	Simulations Tend To	Games Tend To
Size	Involve more students, often the entire class	Be limited to fewer players, typically four, seldom more than eight
Length	Be of longer duration (more than one period)	Be of shorter duration (one period or less)
Chance	More realistically reflect the real world	Contain a "chance" factor that exceeds reality
Result	Produce an outcome usually without winners or losers	Have defined winners and losers
Preparation and Materials	Require considerable advance preparation and materials	Require minimal preparation and materials

From a child's perspective, most simulations and games offer pleasant, enjoyable ways to learn something. In our judgment, whatever children learn by using a game or simulation should be the main focus, not the technical distinctions between the two formats (which students probably don't care about anyhow). From a teaching perspective, however, the distinctions are more important, especially if you try your hand at developing either simulations or games.

Building Simulations

An excellent source for commercially produced simulations and games is *The Guide to Simulations/Games for Education and Training* (Zuckerman and Horn, 1973). Many teachers, however, have found that it isn't necessary to purchase a simulation, when with a little effort they can develop their own. The first step in developing a simulation is deciding what aspect of the real world you are going to simulate. For your first effort, the rule of thumb is to keep it simple. To attempt to simulate the entire judicial process, for example, will prove overwhelming. But you could simulate one aspect of the process, such as a jury's deliberation, as a starter. As a rule, *processes* of almost any kind offer fertile subject matter for simulations.

The following is a sample simulation developed by a teacher interested in teaching the elements of mass production under nineteenth-century factory conditions.

Model student activity

The Holiday Card Factory—A Simulation

The entire class will be organized into production areas to produce holiday greeting cards (in this case, for Valentine's Day). To re-create some of the working conditions of the nineteenth century, the room should be darkened somewhat and students asked to stand at their work stations (desks) throughout. Talking unrelated to work is not permitted.

The greeting card consists of a white heart, pierced by a pink arrow, placed on a red circle, all of which is then mounted on a white paper doily. The completed product should resemble the one below.

Organization In general, each phase of the card-making process is divided into drawing, cutting, and inspecting. For example, you will have a team of heart drawers, heart cutters, and a heart inspector. For a class of twenty-six students, you should have the following roles:

Heart department
4 heart drawers
3 heart cutters
1 heart inspector

Slit department
(for making the hole
where the arrow
pierces the heart):
1 slit drawer
1 slit cutter
1 slit inspector

Circle department
3 circle drawers
2 circle cutters
1 circle inspector

Arrow department
3 arrow drawers
2 arrow cutters
1 arrow inspector

Assembly department
3 assemblers
1 final inspector

(If you have fewer than twenty-six students, you can drop some of the inspectors; if more than twenty-six, add them to the drawers in any department.)

Cluster the desks into five areas. In advance make a sign identifying each area; e.g., heart department. Each student should then make a small sign identifying his or her particular task; e.g., circle cutter. The inspectors are responsible for maintaining quality control and taking the finished products to the assembly area. Provide the following materials and instructions to the appropriate department.

Heart department
Heart drawers
    materials: plain white paper (8½ X 11), pens, rulers
    instructions: "Draw the largest heart you can that will fit into an
    8-inch square."
Heart cutters
    materials: scissors
    instructions: "Cut the heart as accurately as you can."

Heart inspectors

materials: a sample heart (which you have made ahead of time)

instructions: "Make certain that your hearts closely resemble the sample before taking them to the slit department. If anything is wrong with a heart, give it back to the heart drawers or cutters."

Slit department

Slit drawers

materials: ruler and pencil

instructions: "Your job is to locate the 1½-inch slit where the arrow will pierce the heart. Your inspector has a sample heart to show exactly where the slit should be located."

Slit cutters

materials: scissors

instructions: "Your job is to cut the 1½-inch slit where the arrow will pierce the heart. Cut as accurately and neatly as you can."

Slit inspector

materials: sample heart with slit

instructions: "Make certain that your slitted hearts closely resemble the sample heart before taking them to the assembly area. If anything is wrong, return it to the slit drawers or the slit cutters."

Circle department

Circle drawers

materials: red paper, pencils or pens, compasses

instructions: "Your job is to draw an 8½-inch circle on the red paper. It must be exactly 8½ inches in diameter. The circle inspector has a sample you can see."

Circle cutters

materials: scissors

instructions: "Your job is to cut the 8½-inch circle from the red paper. Work as neatly and as accurately as you can."

Circle inspector

materials: sample red circle

instructions: "Make certain that your finished circles resemble the sample before taking them to the assembly area. If anything is wrong, return them to the circle drawers or the circle cutters."

Arrow department

Arrow drawers

materials: pink paper (8½ × 11), rulers, and pencils

instructions: "Your job is to draw a 7-inch-long pink arrow. Your inspector has a sample you can follow. You should get at least four arrows from each sheet of paper."

Arrow cutters

materials: scissors

instructions: "Your job is to cut out the 7-inch pink arrows. Work as neatly and as accurately as you can."

Arrow inspectors

materials: sample arrow

instructions: "Make certain that your finished arrows resemble the sample before taking them to the assembly area. If anything is wrong, return the arrows to the arrow drawers or the arrow cutters."

Assembly department
Assemblers
   materials: 9- or 10-inch white paper doilies; paste, fast-drying glue or rubber cement
   instructions: "Your job is to insert the arrow through the slits in the heart, and then glue the heart onto the red circle. The heart and the circle should then be glued onto the doily. Your inspector has a sample you can follow."
Final inspector
   materials: sample completed heart
   instructions: "Your job is to make certain that each finished card resembles the sample. If it does, place it in a pile labeled 'finished'; if not, place it in a pile labeled 'reject.'

Remind the students that work is to be done quickly and accurately; time is money! Also, only the inspectors can leave their stations.

Wages: One candy heart for every ten minutes of cooperation and work.

Stop the activity after students have begun to get bored with what they are doing, and begin the debriefing.

Consider some of the following questions:

Follow-up

1   How did you like your job?
2   How would you describe what we have done?
3   How would you go about improving conditions in this factory? What would you change?
4   What are some different ways we could use to produce greeting cards like these?
5   If you were the foreman on an assembly line, what kinds of problems do you think you might have?

If you want to try your hand at some simulations, here are a few problems that have proven to work well.

1   *Zoning questions.* Should a gas station, liquor store, or high-rise low-income housing be permitted in a residential neighborhood?
2   *Community priorities.* What should a community spend its money on— sewers, parks, playgrounds, more police and fire fighters?
3   *Deciding what is newsworthy.* Put together the front page of a newspaper, given an assortment of articles—news, sports, features, etc.—clipped from a local paper. Which stories should be given prominence? Why?
4   *School-policy questions.* Should recess be abandoned? (Or should kids be permitted to go to fast-food restaurants for lunch?)

If some of these sound a bit like decision-making activities, that's because they could be used in that form too.

Developing Board Games

Some processes are difficult, if not impossible, to simulate in the classroom. The processing of milk or the retracing of the Oregon Trail, for instance, just don't lend themselves to a simulation format. If nothing else, trying to duplicate the physical requirements (cows, truck, bottling plants, etc.) would be an exercise in futility. But many processes, particularly those that result in a product—the production of bread, milk, steel, etc.—readily lend themselves to a board-game format.

A sample board-game format is illustrated in Figure 12.1. We developed this sample, which we call "The Milk Game," after first identifying the various stages of milk production: the dairy farm, transporting the milk from farm to dairy, the dairy itself, etc. We then outlined segments of the game-board pathway so that it corresponded, in sequence, to the different stages of milk production. Note that our game board uses straight pathways only because they are easy to draw neatly; curved trails would work equally well.

The goal

The idea of this and similar board games is that as small groups of students move their tokens around the game board, they will become familiar with the stages in the process—in this case, the process of milk production.

Once we had our basic game board outlined, we needed to find a way to make the game appealing and fun for students. We accomplished this by first determining how the winner would be decided (the first student to reach "home"). Second, we determined how the movement of tokens would be governed. We decided to use a spinner made from a piece of popsicle stick affixed to the top of a plastic margarine container—although a die or cards (with the number of spaces indicated on them) could work equally well. Third, we decided to add additional interest by using "chance cards" that players would draw when they landed on a square marked with a tiny carton of milk. Note that we could have handled the chance element by marking directly on the squares, but we opted instead for the additional variety that the chance cards provide. To make our game even more realistic, we keyed the chance cards to things that might actually occur in the process of producing milk: "Your farm is struck by a power failure and you must milk the cows by hand—miss one turn," "The milk truck encounters light traffic—move ahead two spaces," etc.

Tryout

After writing a set of simple rules, we tried "The Milk Game" with students. We found that we had forgotten to indicate which player should go first, and corrected that by having each player spin to see who got the highest number; that player went first. In the course of playing the game, we also discovered that we had too much "negative chance" ("Miss a turn," "Go back to start," etc.), so that the players began grumbling about how this game was impossible to win. We corrected this by producing additional positive chance cards—"Move ahead," "Take an extra turn," and so on— to balance out the bad things that happened. On the second tryout, things went so much better that students didn't want to stop playing "The Milk Game."

Figure 12.1 Sample Board Game

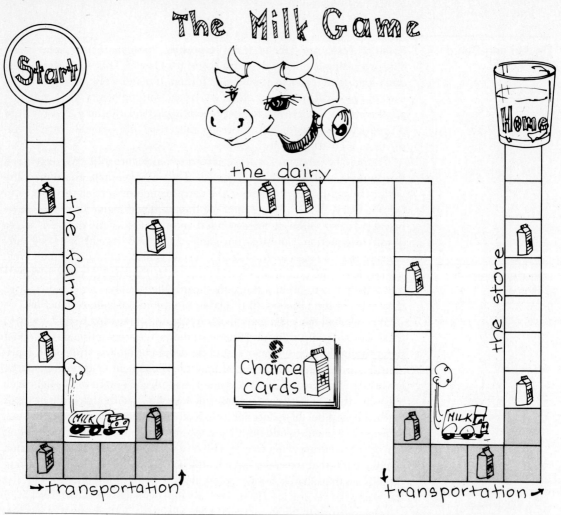

The Milk Game

the dairy

the farm

the store

Chance cards

→transportation↑

↓transportation→

Start

Home

The principles we applied in developing "The Milk Game" would be equally appropriate for other kinds of board games, including those based on the history or geography of a region. Instead of drawing the pathway on a plain posterboard or oaktag, we would use a map of the region as the background. Actually, because most maps are too flimsy to withstand a lot of use, we would affix (glue or dry mount) them to pieces of posterboard. We would then be ready to draw the trail (or pathway) for "Sherman's March Game" on a roadmap of Georgia (or the southeastern United States), for example, while "The Oregon Trail" game could be done on a map of the western United States.

Construction guidelines

Card Games Most paper-supply houses sell blank playing cards that can provide the basis for excellent card games. Consider, for example, an instance in which you want students to be able to match inventors with their inventions. By placing the inventors and their inventions on separate cards, students could attempt to match the appropriate cards using the rules for "Old Maid." In this instance, of course, you would need an extra card that doesn't match, possibly the "Old Inventor." The "Rummy" game format might work equally as well, particularly for inventors who produced several inventions, like Thomas Edison.

In building card or board games, it is important that they not become concealed tests. For the Inventors Game described above, we could place both the name of the inventor and the invention on the same card. Thus, an "Edison card" would have a picture of a light bulb on it, while a "Light Bulb" card would have Edison's name on it. The student would need both cards to have a match. If that information were not on both cards, the game could actually be a test of the student's knowledge of inventors. If a student did not know, for example, that Edison had invented the light bulb, he or she would have no idea which two cards went together and the game would probably come to a screeching halt.

A game or a concealed test?

The intent of the card games described above is to help the student learn to match two or more elements that are associated (e.g., inventors with their inventions), not to test the student's knowledge. Likewise, "The Milk Game" was intended to help children become familiar with the various stages of milk production, not to test their knowledge of it. Having students correctly answer a question such as "How much milk does a cow give each day?" before they can take their next turn, for example, may introduce elements that defeat the purpose of your game. If nothing else, you would need a referee to determine whether the question was answered correctly. As a general rule, we suggest that you avoid as many test-like elements as possible in either card or board games.

Summary of Steps for Designing a Simulation or Game

1 Identify the process or system that you want to simulate.
2 Identify the specific characteristics of the system or process. These include the various stages in the process or system as well as the human components involved. Note that it may be necessary to narrow your focus; it may be possible to simulate only part of the nineteenth-century factory system, but not the entire system.
3 Determine which characteristics of the system or process you wish to emphasize, and those you are willing to omit. Recall that simulations simplify reality. In the Holiday Card Factory, for example, the workers' long hours and a host of other working conditions were not present. Sweat shops or other conditions that might endanger the students' welfare are better left to history.
4 Determine which format—simulation or game—is best suited to the topic.
5 Decide what the players will be doing. Will they be making something, playing a role, moving tokens around a board, or what?
6 Decide on an outcome. When will the simulation or game end—after the

players have reached a decision, been reelected, reached "home," made the most points, or at the end of a time limit?

7 (Games only) Determine how you will introduce the chance element (to make the game more interesting). Make certain that negative and positive chance factors are equally balanced.

8 (Simulations only) Determine how you will get information to the players. (Will each player get separate roles? Separate instructions?)

9 Determine if everything you have decided upon thus far "fits" together. If so, begin developing or collecting whatever materials you will need.

10 Prepare a preliminary set of written rules or directions.

11 Try out the simulation or game on a small group of "guinea pigs." (This is one of the most essential steps in the entire process—you will be amazed at what you forgot to take into account.)

12 Make necessary adjustments as indicated by the field test.

Expressive and Enactive Experiences

Expressive and *enactive* experiences refer to what noneducators might call "projects." *Expressive experiences* refer to activities in which children have an opportunity to express themselves, either through drama per se—plays, skits, pageants, etc.—or through dramatic play, music, role playing, or other forms of sociodrama. *Enactive experiences* refer to activities in which students build or create something—models, murals, etc. It should be apparent that opportunities for children to express their creative or artistic talents are common to both kinds of experiences.

Because we have already dealt with several forms of expressive experience —dramatic play, role playing, and so forth—we will say little more about them, except to note that whatever is being dramatized should be portrayed accurately. Enactive experiences, too, must be carefully planned lest they degenerate into activities that produce only marginal learning outcomes. Our earlier igloo-building activity, as well as Thelen's example of the community-history TV project (see Chapter Eleven), are evidence of this.

Food

Enactive experiences involving foods of various kinds seem to have become increasingly popular recently, and tend to crop up at many grade levels. If you wish to use food as a reflection of a culture, it is essential that children see the skill, the artistry, and the labor that goes into the preparation of a particular dish. To be effective, enactive experiences should be part of a broader study. In other words, before boiling the first grain of rice for an Oriental meal, for example, the children should have identified what kinds of things might be served at such a meal, what goes into the various dishes, how they are prepared, how they are served, and on what occasions they are eaten. The same is true for whatever food you are preparing. The actual preparation and eating—the enactive phase—may be only a small part of the larger study. The library's collection of cookbooks may very well become a major reference source. If the children are too young or otherwise unable to do library research, you may need to do it for them.

You may also find that worthwhile enactive experiences have a *problem-solving* dimension. In the previous example, the question guiding the students' search might be, "What are the components of a typical Japanese meal?" Similarly, before building a Roman chariot, students should have researched the construction of an original; the question guiding their problem solving would be, "How were Roman (or Greek) chariots built, and of what materials?" Before building a model dairy farm, primary students (or even intermediate ones) should have compared a series of pictures of dairy farms (or visited a dairy farm, if that is feasible) in order to identify their common characteristics.

"People and Technology"

One of the more recent social studies programs for the upper-intermediate grades, People and Technology (P & T), incorporates enactive experiences (construction-manipulative) as an integral part of each unit. These include such things as translating a scale drawing into a full-size outline of a whale, "Unmaking (taking apart) a Rope," "Making a Sextant," "Rigging a Sail," and building a twenty-one-foot-long whaleboat (from cardboard and brown wrapping paper). Complete instructions for these activities are included in a booklet entitled *Things, Ideas, and Ways of Doing Things* (1972), or TIWDT for short. The following student activity, "Making an Oil Lamp," is excerpted and adapted from TIWDT. Notice in particular the problem-solving nature of the activity.

"Making an Oil Lamp"

Two to four students; one to two periods of class time.

Model student activity

What you do   In this activity you will be making lamps out of animal fats and other oils; the method you will use is comparable to the way in which whale blubber was reduced to oil for whale-oil lamps. You'll read about the processes of cutting in and trying out the whale blubber. You can try an experiment to see how candlelight or oil-lamp light affects an evening at home.

What's the point?   There are really three main points; one is to help you understand the process by which whale blubber was transformed into fuel; the second is to give you some small insight into what life in Nantucket must have been like when the only light at night came from whale-oil lamps and fireplaces. Imagine what it must have been like inside a room, or walking through the streets of town at night. Even the lighthouses beamed light that came from whale oil. The third point is to help you see how and why candles burn and to see the surprising number of substances that will actually burn with the help of a wick.

Materials   You will need fuel, wicks, some shallow metal containers (like jar lids), paper clips, scissors, and an electric frying pan. The frying pan is a safe and simple way to fry fats in the classroom.

How to do it A typical whale-oil lamp looked like this:

The lamp you will make will be simpler. It will probably look something like this:

Fuels For fuels you can use melted animal fat or vegetable oils. Any kind of animal fat will do. Lamb or beef fat, which was used to make tallow, can be trimmed off the raw meat and fried until the fat is melted into oil.

Caution: DO NOT use highly flammable fuels like kerosene, gasoline, turpentine, or things that contain these fuels. These liquids will burn easily without wicks and can cause injuries and big fires. Besides, most of these fuels didn't exist in the period we're talking about.

Pour the oil into a shallow metal container. A jar lid will work very well as a lamp, but be very careful not to handle the container while the oil is hot. Do this: while the fat is cooking, put the cap on a stiff piece of cardboard so you can move the oil to a cooling-off place without touching the container. Then pour in the melted fat and let it cool. Lamb or beef fat will turn cloudy and harden as it cools. With this type of hardening fuel you might prepare your wick ahead of time and insert it while the fuel is in a liquid form.

Bacon drippings can be used as fuel too. Be careful to handle hot bacon fat carefully, too. If the drippings are already cool, just spoon some out of the can into a jar cap, put in a wick and light your lamp.

Experiment with vegetable oils. Olive oil right out of the bottle is ready to use. Try some other oils if they're around, like peanut oil, soybean oil, or ordinary cooking oil.

Wicks   You can buy candle or lantern wicks, but you may want to make your own. The only thing you must do to make your homemade wick work is to braid the material so it won't come apart as it burns. Although cotton is the most common material to use, try other things as well: dry grass, wool yarn, cotton clothesline or any other things you can think of.

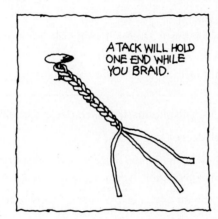 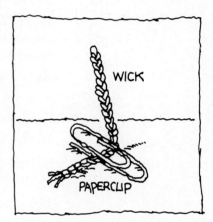

Make thin wicks and thick wicks to see what kinds of flames you get. If everyone makes a different thickness of wick you can trade off and put two or three types of wick in each lamp. All you need is an inch or two of wick for each flame. Try three or four thin wicks close together. To hold the wick up in the lamp, jam the wick into a paper clip and bend it to make the wick stand upright in the oil.

To make your lamp work, place the paper clip with the wick attached into the container of oil and light the wick. If you have hard tallow in your lamp, hold a match near the tallow to melt it, then insert the wick. Eventually all the tallow will become liquid under the heat of the flame.

It will help some if you soak the wick in the fuel before lighting the lamp.

As the fuel gets low the lamp will heat up, so be sure you protect the table.

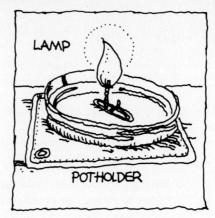

Looking at the results   Once you've had a chance to experiment with various fuels and wicks, answer the following questions based on your own observations. Compare your answers with those of your friends.

In the Classroom
Does the wick burn? Does trimming the wick with scissors improve the flame? _____

Which fuel burns dimmest? Does another wick help? _____
_____

Which fuel smells the most? Which doesn't smell at all? _____

Which fuel smokes the most? _____

Estimate how many lamps like these you would need to equal the light of a 60-watt light bulb. _____

How long will an ounce of the various fuels burn? _____
_____

In Your Home
Does a room look different with flame light than with electric light? What's the difference? _____
_____

Where is the best place to set up a lamp or candle in a room—near the ceiling, on the floor, or on a table? Where is the safest place? Where is the best place to put the lamp for illuminating the whole room, or for close work? Are shadows or drafts a problem? _____
_____
_____

Suppose everyone at home wants to read the newspaper. Is it more convenient for all to sit around the light and paper, or for one person to use the light and read aloud to the others? What is the best solution for everyone? _____
_____
_____

Source: This activity appears in *Things, Ideas, and Ways of Doing Things* (1972, pp. 29–32), and is part of the People and Technology Program that was developed by the Education Development Center, Inc., Cambridge, MA, under a grant from the National Endowment for the Humanities. Used with permission.

Enactive experiences have a dimension that cannot always be measured in precise terms; that is, through a "hands-on" approach, they often permit nonacademically oriented students to contribute to class activities in ways that would be denied them through reading- or research-oriented activities. The fact that enactive experiences provide them with opportunities to make meaningful contributions can have profound effects on their self-images and on other students' views of them as individuals. At the same time, however, nonacademically oriented students soon get wise to a steady diet of enactive experiences designed just for them. Thus, how often you use enactive experiences, and for which students, are judgments that depend upon your sensitivity to the individuals involved.

Criteria

The appropriate use of expressive and enactive experiences probably lies somewhere between two extremes—between teachers whose students are *always* building something or getting ready for yet another play or pageant, and teachers who never use any of these experiences. In general, we feel that you should be encouraged to use expressive and enactive experiences when they (a) are an integral part of whatever you're studying, (b) involve some aspect of problem solving or inquiry, and (c) will enhance the self-images of your students.

Summary

Group-based student activities range from those in which you establish a setting and then let the students' creativity come forth, to those in which the children follow precise, step-by-step directions. The more you structure an activity, the more you begin to lose spontaneity and creativity. That loss, however, may be offset by the fact that you have a greater assurance that the children will consider the issues and questions that you have built into a more structured activity. And so, you are faced with another trade-off. Whichever kind of group-based strategy you use—structured or unstructured, expressive or enactive—will ultimately depend on your purposes for developing the activity in the first place.

Arguments as to whether an activity is or is not a dramatic play, or is or is not a simulation, are not very productive. The boundary line between such activities is usually sufficiently fuzzy that individuals often draw their own. In the final analysis, all group-based teaching activities are means toward an end. If the activity permits you to reach that end—whether it be to have children raise questions that they can then research, or to experience and analyze a situation they might encounter in the real world—it really doesn't make much difference what label you attach to the activity. Personally, we prefer the more structured forms of group-based activities because they are more likely to get us to where we want to go.

In the next chapter, we shift the focus from groups to individuals. No one is likely to suggest that managing group instruction is not a challenge, yet adapting instruction so that it meets the individual needs of your students will probably rank as one of the more challenging aspects of teaching.

Suggested Activities

1 Design a board game following the suggestions in this chapter. It may take time, but your students will love it.
2 Design a dramatic play activity following Lee's format but involving a different content area.
3 Design an unstructured role-playing activity. Then identify the techniques you could use to add greater structure to the experience.
4 Suppose a teacher informs you that he or she plans to serve raw fish to a class so that the students will have better appreciation of Eskimo life. Identify the positive and negative learning outcomes that might result from this experience.

References

Brady, Maxine. *The Monopoly Book.* New York: McKay, 1975.

Lee, John R. *Teaching Social Studies in the Elementary School.* New York: Macmillan, 1974.

Lippitt, Rosemary. "The Auxiliary Chair Technique." *Group Psychotherapy* 11 (January, 1958): 8–23.

People and Technology. *Things, Ideas, Ways of Doing Things.* Cambridge, MA: Education Development Center, 1972.

Shaftel, Fannie R. "Role Playing: An Approach to Meaningful Social Learning." *Social Education* 34(May, 1970):556–59.

Shaftel, Fannie R. "Dramatic Play, Role Playing, Simulations and Games. In Lavone A. Hanna, Gladys L. Potter, and Robert W. Reynolds, *Dynamic Elementary Social Studies: Unit Teaching.* (3rd ed.) New York: Holt, Rinehart and Winston, 1973.

Shaftel, Fannie R., and Shaftel, George. *Teacher's Guide: People in Action.* New York: Holt, Rinehart and Winston, 1970.

Zuckerman, David W., and Horn, Robert E. *Guide to Simulations/Games for Education and Training.* Lexington, MA: Information Resources, Inc., P.O. Box 417, 1973.

Suggested Readings

Richard E. and Linda R. Churchill. *Enriched Social Studies Teaching.* Belmont, CA: Fearon, 1973. A handbook of games and activities to spice up dull lessons. Similar to Guy Wagner and Laura Gilloley's *Social Studies Games and Activities* (New York: Macmillan, 1964), except that the latter is organized on a grade-level basis.

Mark Chesler and Robert Fox. *Role-Playing Methods in the Classroom.* Chicago: Science Research Associates, 1966. If you don't have time for an in-depth examination, this little pamphlet can't be beat.

John R. Lee. *Teaching Social Studies in the Elementary School.* New York: Free Press, 1974. A superb book. See especially the last section, "The Swingers."

Craig Pearson and Joseph Marfuggi. *Creating and Using Learning Games.* Palo Alto, CA: Learning Handbooks, 1975. In less than one hundred pages, this handbook describes dozens of effective learning games and provides detailed guidelines for making your own.

Fannie R. and George Shaftel. *Role Playing for Social Values.* Englewood Cliffs, N.J.: Prentice-Hall, 1967. If the educational world gave Oscars, the Shaftels would get one for this classic work.

Cheryl L. Charles and Ronald Stadsklev, eds. *Learning with Games.* Boulder, CO: Social Science Education Consortium, 1973. Features seventy analyses of currently available games and simulations, cross-referenced by developer, grade level, publisher, and subject area. Their bibliography is even more valuable.

Thomas P. Weinland and Donald W. Protheroe. *Social Science Projects You Can Do,* and *More Social Science Projects You Can Do.* Englewood Cliffs, NJ: Prentice-Hall, 1973 and 1974, respectively. Rarely will you find collections of really excellent activities for elementary social studies; these two concise volumes fall into that exclusive category. These activities include such things as "History through Street Names," "A Lock-Oriented Society," "Movies as Culture Clues," "Sex Roles and the Media," "Cemeteries," and "Signs of the Times."

13 Individualizing Instruction

Key Questions

How do you individualize programs for every student?

How do you diagnose, educationally speaking?

What is "learning style"?

How do you set up a social studies interest center?

Key Ideas

Individualized instruction is a reflection of efforts to make schools "fit" students and their individual needs more effectively.

The basic elements of individualized instruction are diagnosing student learning problems and providing prescriptive treatment.

Individualized instruction is a major component in the movement toward open education. In fact, you can't have an "open" classroom without individualized instruction.

Interest centers and learning stations are two devices for encouraging student-directed individualization.

"Exceptional children" are students at either end of the educational spectrum—those with special gifts and talents and those with special needs.

Introduction: New Approaches to Perennial Problems

Were it safe to assume that children had learned everything they'd been taught—which it isn't—and were it safe to assume that all children have similar abilities and learning styles—which they don't—there would be little need for individualized instruction. We could simply provide the same experiences for all students and leave it at that. Done! Finished!

Although we know that children sometimes forget, and though we know they sometimes don't learn something the first (or second) time around, *and* though we know that some children learn differently from others, there has been a tendency to overlook or ignore these realities in traditional educational practice. Such "ignoring" was hardly the result of evil machinations on the part of teachers, principals, or the general public. Rather, we suspect, it was a reflection of the belief that it was the child's responsibility to "fit" the school—to learn (and act) in ways the schools deemed proper. Historically, schools were seen as society's sorters and molders—separating the fit from the unfit—and it was the child's responsibility to conform to the school's expectations as best he or she could. The view that children should fit the school (and not the other way around) has shifted over time, perhaps because of the increasingly large number of students who either haven't fit in very well or, in some instances, have rejected the school entirely. Instead of the one-way relationship that once prevailed—students either fit in or got out —the relationship today is two-way; the child's responsibility to fit the school is balanced by the school's responsibility to better fit the child.

Striking a balance between the child's responsibility to the school and vice versa is a continuing question. As a result, many teachers find themselves threading their way between the horns of a moral dilemma. Although many agree in principle with the need for maintaining clearly identified standards of student performance, they also recognize that rigidly defined standards may not accommodate the wide range of individual differences they face in their classrooms every day. Variations within a class are often so great that at the beginning of a year, for example, some students can already demonstrate much of what will be expected of them at the end of the year, and, theoretically at least, could skip that grade level entirely. For other students, however, the hope is that they will be able to meet the entry level standards for their grade level before they *leave* it. (Note that we are not talking about unique occurrences here; we're talking about the kinds of situations you can expect to face in a typical classroom.) Currently, the range of individual differences may be even wider than it was previously, as students who were once segregated in special classes have been returned to the "mainstream" of public education—regular classrooms—under the provisions of recent federal legislation (Public Law 94-142). When all these factors are taken into consideration, it should be apparent that, for many teachers, the need to individualize instruction is not entirely a matter of choice or principle; in many instances, it's a matter of necessity.

Tailoring instruction so that individual differences are taken into account has always played a role in teaching, even back in the days of the "little red schoolhouse." Today that role has become so important that many schools have shifted to an individualized model as the basis for their instructional efforts.

Operationally, individualized instruction is closely associated with the medical model. As such, terminology like *diagnosis* and *prescription* is very much in evidence. The medical model, of course, is based on the idea that something is wrong with the patient. Once the ailment is diagnosed, treatment can begin—treatment intended to make the patient well again. Unfortunately, when this model is transferred to classroom settings, the feeling of "wrongness" associated with illness sometimes comes with it. As a result, students who need remedial instruction may be perceived as "having something wrong with them," almost to the extent that they become seen as educational deviates. In other words, while it's always been acceptable to be ill in the medical model, only recently have we begun to recognize the legitimacy of educational exceptionality.

The sense of deviance that some individuals associate with individualized instruction, particularly remedial instruction, is probably a legacy of the "standards" issue we noted earlier; that is, when students couldn't demonstrate what was expected of them, the prevailing belief was that there was something wrong with the student, not the expectation. Today, that belief has changed sufficiently enough (though not universally) that remedial instruction is no longer regarded as "bad," as something for the "poor student who isn't capable of regular instruction." Indeed, individualized instruction goes far beyond that simplistic notion. All children can benefit from individualized instruction, not just those who are above or below the norm (however the norm may be determined). In fact, some schools are already moving toward the ideal—totally individualized, nongraded instruction for every student.

In this chapter we deal first with some of the traditional approaches to dealing with differences among students. We then consider some contemporary forms of individualizing, with special emphasis on diagnostic techniques that you might wish to use with your students. Following that, we examine strategies associated with what we call student-directed individualizing, that is, providing students with greater freedom and a wider range of choice in their social studies programs.

Individualizing Instruction

Two general approaches—one administrative and the other instructional—have traditionally been used to accommodate individual differences. *Administrative approaches* refer to policies and practices like homogeneous grouping, acceleration, retention, and special classes, which are employed on school-wide or district-wide bases. *Instructional approaches* refer to techniques and practices that individual teachers employ to meet their students' needs, and include diagnosing performance, operating independent study centers, and the like. We examine each of these approaches in the following sections.

Administrative Approaches

Ten or twenty years ago, the worst fate imaginable for many children was to fail and thus be required to repeat a grade level. The social stigma—for both parents and children—was often tremendous. For other children, however, there was the unrelenting hope that they would be among the privileged few who would be accelerated, who'd get to skip a grade.

From a student's point of view, administrative policies permitting *acceleration* and *retention* were undoubtedly seen as forms of reward (for superior performance) or punishment (for poor performance). From an instructional perspective, however, the effect of these policies (and sometimes their real intent) was to narrow the range of individual differences teachers would face in the classroom. In other words, by retaining less able students and accelerating more able students, the remaining students presented a narrower range of abilities for teachers to take into account. Then, too, students who were actually accelerated or retained would be in environments that more closely matched their instructional needs. At least that's how these policies were supposed to work in theory.

Although accelerated students were often younger and less mature than their classmates, the problems associated with the age differences were apt to be of a social rather than of an instructional nature. But retention, especially repeated retention, has sometimes created situations in which eleven- or twelve-year-olds were placed in classes where the majority of students were eight or nine years old. Should you ever encounter such a situation—as well you might—you can anticipate both social and instructional problems. Recognize that for children who measure their age in half-years, being eight and a half is considered "much older" than plain old eight. Even a two- or three-year age differential can produce very striking social consequences that, ultimately, may be reflected in students' academic performance. These factors (and others) have led many school systems to abandon retention as an administrative policy and move instead to *social promotion.*

Social promotion

Promoting students even though they are unable to complete the work required at a lower grade level (social promotion) actually increases the range of individual differences a teacher must deal with. Unless teachers are able to provide some type of individualized instruction for students who have been socially promoted, the results are apt to be cumulative. In other words, such students may be increasingly unable to demonstrate the skills required at each higher grade level, and may thus fall further and further behind. (See "How Well I Remember Keith.") In addition, you may find that grades have lost much of their potency as motivators for socially promoted students; it's difficult to argue that grades are important when students know they will be passed on to the next grade level regardless of the grades they get.

Another administrative approach is *homogeneous grouping* (or "tracking"). The effect of grouping students together on the basis of one or more criteria such as IQ, reading ability, achievement test scores, and/or teacher's ratings, is to narrow the range of student abilities a teacher must deal with.

Grouping

Homogeneous grouping is a popular practice in many schools, and often results in classes described as "prekindergarten," "prefirst," "excelled fourth," or "advanced sixth." Even with tracking or homogeneous grouping, however, you are apt to find that students vary in their ability to deal with different subject areas. Thus, you may also find that further subgrouping and/or one or more of the instructional approaches to individualizing are required.

How Well I Remember Keith
Keith was a sixth grader when I first met him; at least he was as old as the other sixth graders I taught that year. When Keith showed up at school, which wasn't very often, he just sat there, unmoving. He almost never talked to anyone and was one of the few students I've encountered who had absolutely no friends in the class. Later I discovered he hung around with a group of much older boys in his neighborhood, but within the class—nothing!

Keith was responsible for my first encounter with a truant officer; I didn't even think they existed in rural Ohio. I discovered that Keith had been that route before and was a well-known case. It turned out that Keith had never liked school very well to start with; but because of a legitimate illness, he had missed most of second grade. When he was promoted "socially" to third grade, Keith found he just couldn't handle the work—especially in reading. With both of his parents working, he found that he could avoid the entire hassle by staying home—which he did, regularly!

After a year (actually a nonyear) with Keith in my class, I knew he didn't have the skills to make it in seventh grade, and I decided to stop all this social promotion nonsense and retain him. Some of the other teachers agreed, so, over the principal's objections, we "held Keith back."

It was in about the middle of my second nonyear with Keith in the sixth grade that I discovered that this was one of those occasions when the principal was right. He'd agreed that Keith wasn't ready for seventh grade but said another year in the sixth grade wouldn't make him any readier. I discovered what I believe I already knew—that Keith wasn't equipped to handle seventh grade, nor was he equipped to handle sixth grade. A second time through sixth grade wouldn't make him any better prepared. What he really needed were some second-, third-, and fourth-grade skills.

I erred in believing that if one dose of sixth grade didn't help Keith, a second dose would. And my failure with Keith, which is perhaps why I remember him so well, lay in the fact that I didn't accurately diagnose his problem. Upon retaining him, I should have approached him as an individual and provided instruction in the skills he needed. I also realized, however, that it wasn't necessary to retain Keith to teach him those skills, for the same thing could be accomplished with individualized instruction in a seventh-grade class.

Indeed, how well I remember Keith!

---

*Special
education*

A third traditional administrative approach to dealing with individual differences has been to create *special classes* for exceptional students. Creating totally separate classes (with special teachers) for students with learning disabilities, handicaps, or special talents would appear to be an extension of the homogeneous grouping that we noted above. However, as Gallagher (1972) noted, the creation of separate "special education" classes for mildly handicapped students was often "an exclusionary process masquerading as a remedial one." Fewer than ten percent of the students placed in special education classes ever returned to regular classrooms (Dunn, 1973, p. 22).

Lloyd Dunn also found that when mildly handicapped students remained in regular classrooms, their educational achievement exceeded that of students who had been segregated in separate classrooms (1968, p. 22). This type of evidence provided the basis for recommendations that segregated children be placed back in the "mainstream" of public education. Those recommendations ultimately became a part of federal legislation so far-reaching that it has fundamentally altered the treatment of exceptional students in this country, and has (or will) affect virtually every teacher in the country, including you.

Exceptional Students   "Exceptional students" are children whose learning disabilities, handicaps, or special talents set them apart from the bulk of the students teachers encounter. As Kirk noted:

> The exceptional child is [one] who deviates from the normal or average child (1) in mental characteristics, (2) in sensory abilities, (3) in neuromuscular or physical characteristics, (4) in social or emotional behavior, (5) in communication abilities, or (6) in multiple handicaps to such an extent that he [or she] requires modification of school practices, or special education services, in order to develop to his [or her] maximum capacity (Kirk, 1972, p. 4).

Exceptionality defined

This definition reflects two elements of exceptionality that deserve special mention. First, notice its breadth. Exceptionality is an extremely broad concept that incorporates a wide range of characteristics. Second, notice that it encompasses both ends of the educational spectrum: students who, for one reason or another, may have difficulties in school, as well as those students who excel in academic, intellectual, and/or other creative endeavors.

How many exceptional students are there? Estimates vary, but Gallagher, for example, suggests that one out of every eight or ten students can be considered "exceptional" (1974, p. 516). Add to these another group of students who, while they generally function within the normal population, may exhibit milder forms of exceptionality, and the total may increase to twenty-five percent of the students in a typical classroom.

Legislative Mandates   Two key pieces of federal legislation, Public Law 94–142, the Education for All Handicapped Children Act of 1975, and Public Law 93–380, the Education Amendments of 1974, have had far-reaching effects on the treatment of exceptional children. A major provision of P.L. 94–142 deals with the concept of *least restrictive environment,* which is illustrated in Figure 13.1 and which is commonly referred to as "mainstreaming." Basically, the law requires that whenever possible handicapped children be educated in the least restrictive environment, usually in a regular classroom. Further, it requires that students be placed in a *more* restrictive environment (special classrooms, special schools or institutions, etc.) only when it is impossible to work out satisfactory placements in a regular classroom.

I.E.P.: Individualized Educational Plan

A second key provision of P.L. 94–142 requires that an individualized educational plan—an I.E.P.—be prepared for each exceptional child. An I.E.P. must identify both long- and short-term educational goals as well as the specific services to be provided, and must be developed by a team that includes a representative of the local educational agency (usually the building principal), the teacher, and the child's parents or guardians.

P.L. 94–142 has succeeded in removing mildly handicapped students from segregated classrooms, but it has not eliminated the conditions that led to students being placed in separate classes to begin with. Learning disabilities or physical handicaps, for example, do not disappear when a child is placed in a regular classroom. So in order to provide continuing assistance to students with special needs, many school systems have adopted the administrative policy of providing *resource teachers* (and/or resource classrooms).

Figure 13.1 The Least-Restrictive-Environment System of Placement

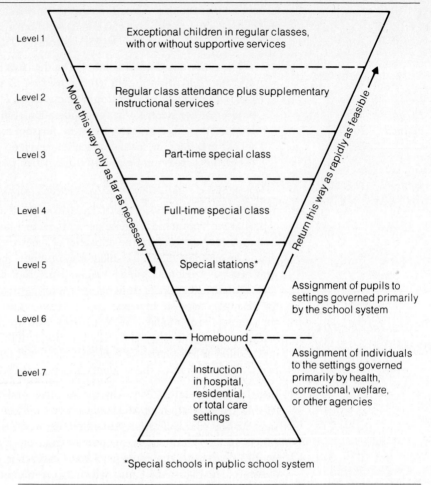

Level 1   Exceptional children in regular classes, with or without supportive services

Level 2   Regular class attendance plus supplementary instructional services

Level 3   Part-time special class

Level 4   Full-time special class

Level 5   Special stations*

Level 6   Homebound

Level 7   Instruction in hospital, residential, or total care settings

Move this way only as far as necessary

Return this way as rapidly as feasible

Assignment of pupils to settings governed primarily by the school system

Assignment of individuals to the settings governed primarily by health, correctional, welfare, or other agencies

*Special schools in public school system

Source: Haring, 1978, p. 5.

Individuals and small groups of students may be pulled out of their regular classes to work with specially trained resource teachers for short periods. Likewise, under P.L. 93–380, many schools provide enrichment classes and teachers for gifted and talented students.

Recent federal legislation dealing with exceptional students has accomplished a number of things: it has focused attention on educating socially and

Effects of legislation

culturally disadvantaged children; it has underscored the need for individualized instruction; it has challenged both curricula and teaching methods to become more responsive to students; it has ushered into regular classrooms a concern for diagnosing instructional problems and for prescribing appropriate remedial experiences; and it has stimulated additional funding from state and federal sources.

The Impact of Administrative Policies   Administrative policies, such as acceleration, retention, social promotion, mainstreaming, and resource classes, primarily affect the types of students you may have in your classroom. In some instances, such as in the case of homogeneous grouping, the policy may narrow the range of individual differences you must deal with, while in other instances, as in the case of "mainstreaming," the policy may have the opposite effect. In either event, and although administrative policies can influence *which* students will be in your classroom, they have almost no impact in determining what you *do* with those students once you get them. For that, it's necessary to turn to one or more of the instructional approaches we deal with in the next section.

Instructional Approaches

There is a story (we don't recall the source) about a monkey trying desperately to survive a flood. The monkey had clambered up a tree and was perched precariously on a limb overlooking the turbulent water. Below was a fish that seemed to be struggling against the rapidly-moving current. Armed with the best of intentions, the monkey reached down and scooped the fish from the water. Unfortunately, the monkey never fully understood why the fish was ungrateful, and why it died shortly after being "rescued."

Teachers, too, sometimes go out on a limb to help students having difficulties in school. Some of those students may be handicapped by physical and emotional disabilities that interfere with learning, while others may be children from different cultural backgrounds. Still other students may be "different" in other ways. Some academically gifted students, for example, may excel in every subject area, while other gifted students may excel in one or two specific areas, such as math, the visual arts, or poetry writing, and yet be quite average in most other respects. The logical conclusion is that the only way to accommodate the range and nature of exceptionality is to provide individualized instructional programs that recognize that in some situations all children are exceptional. Indeed, "exceptional children" may be a misnomer; exceptional instruction may actually be more appropriate.

Individualizing defined

As a concept, individualized instruction is disarmingly simple; the intent is to provide instruction that is keyed to the student's needs, interests, and abilities and permits the student to maximize his or her potential. Implementing individualized instruction, however, is anything but simple. In fact, to *do* individualized instruction involves the following:

1 Differentiating among the different aspects of teaching: diagnosing, prescribing, evaluating, motivating, etc.
2 Accommodating, managing, and being accountable for a wide range of student knowledge, skills, interests, and cultural backgrounds
3 Translating broad instructional goals into specific instructional objectives
4 Organizing learning activities so that they are sequential, developmental, and ensure student achievement
5 Managing the use of instructional time to maximize student achievement
6 Providing an environment in which each student realizes his or her potential
7 Providing ongoing feedback to students, parents, and others so as to assist children in mastering their learning goals

Doing all of this, much less doing all of it well, isn't easy. The difficulties are often compounded because teachers find themselves in school settings that (1) categorize and group children by age level, (2) fail to distinguish between different teacher roles, (3) often fail to operationalize educational goals, (4) often force teachers to "cover" a predetermined course of study rather than respond to students' needs, (5) typically assume a single cultural norm, and (6) usually organize the curriculum according to the logic of the subject matter and not to the logic of learning the content. All of these are obstacles that teachers must either combat or work around.

Despite this, the need to individualize instruction has become ever more crucial. How, then, does one go about doing it?

Little Beginnings   How do teachers provide an individualized program in each subject area for each of twenty-five, twenty-seven, or even thirty students? Where do they start? How do they keep track of all those different student programs? And how do they avoid what could become one of the most massive management nightmares of all time?

How? By beginning slowly—sometimes very slowly.

Slow and sure

We're not trying to be funny here, nor are we in any way challenging the importance of providing instruction geared to individual needs. Rather, we're suggesting that attempting to provide individualized programs for each student in all subject areas from day one, especially for children who are not used to working in such programs, is likely to result in utter chaos —for you and your students. Thus, we recommend a small-scale approach at the outset, that is, beginning with only one subject area and perhaps with only two or three students. Once you feel comfortable, you can expand your program to include more students and more subject areas.

One of the myths of individualizing—that thirty students must be doing thirty different things at all times—is important in this context. This is a completely unrealistic expectation in terms of a teacher's psychological and physical survival. Individualized instruction may actually involve all students doing the same thing at the same time, or four groups of students doing the same thing, or selected individuals doing independent work, or any number of planned alternatives. It need *not* involve everybody doing their own thing at all times.

The Myths of Individualized Instruction

For some teachers, prospective and experienced alike, the thought of providing individualized instruction for students gives rise to fears and misgivings about their ability to individualize successfully. In environments where one is not encouraged to admit such reservations openly, individualizing has at times been attacked in such a way as to create and perpetuate a series of myths about the nature of individualized instruction. Some of these myths are presented below.

Myth 1: In order to individualize, the teacher's philosophical disposition must either be "progressive" or "liberal."

Fact: *Both process-oriented and content-oriented teachers can find effective individualized approaches to use as means to reach their respective goals.*

Myth 2: Individualized instruction is a sudden, revolutionary, and radical departure from what is now being done, one that calls for a complete change in teaching functions.

Fact: *Individualizing need not involve an abrupt and radical departure from what is being done, but rather can involve a relatively slow and managed process.*

Myth 3: Individualizing instruction causes insecurity among students and thus contributes to a breakdown of discipline.

A management tool

Fact: *If individualizing is more than random activity, and if it is conducted in a planned way—one that gradually shifts responsibility from the teacher to the students—then it may provide an even better tool for classroom management.*

Myth 4: Individualizing demands that the teacher have access to a multitude of teaching materials before beginning, and that all the complementing and supporting aspects be determined first.

Fact: *If individualizing instruction is viewed as an evolving process rather than as a preset, packaged curriculum, it can be initiated even when the materials are based on a single text.*

Myth 5: Individualizing instruction is unrealistic because it requires far more planning and feedback time than teachers have available within the existing structure.

Fact: *Individualizing does call for different teacher roles and, thus, for different time demands. However, teachers can individualize only one part of their total teaching responsibility—it need not be all or nothing.*

Myth 6: Individualized instruction is little more than a mechanistic system that emphasizes low-level behavioral objectives.

Fact: *If one takes into account such things as motivation, individual maturity, cognitive skill levels, and learning styles, and if one recognizes that such factors can be modified, then individualizing instruction is far from mechanistic.*

Teacher-Directed Individualizing

The key elements in individualized instruction are finding out where an individual learner is, and then providing appropriate instruction. These are, in simplest form, the essence of *diagnosis* and *prescription*.

Students themselves will sometimes provide an initial clue that they're having a problem when they approach you and say, "I can't do this." This will only occur, however, in a climate where it's OK to have a problem and, more importantly, where one is free *to admit* that a problem exists. So why might a student approach you? For one of three reasons, we suspect, and you'll have to decide which. Either he or she (1) has a legitimate problem and wants help, (2) wants some personal attention and has discovered that this is one way to get it, or (3) a little of both.

To "I can't do this," the human response tends to be, "Well, why not? What's the problem?" Realistically, if students could answer those questions, they wouldn't have "the problem" to begin with, and they probably wouldn't need a teacher's assistance. The situation is roughly equivalent to the patient who enters a doctor's office and says, "I think I'm sick!" The patient may not know *why* he is sick, just that he is. The doctor's immediate task is diagnosing the patient's problem and then prescribing accordingly. Likewise, in educational diagnosis the teacher's immediate task is to identify the *specific* problem, the precise cause or causes underlying the student's difficulty. In many instances, students indicate a general problem, as when they say "I just don't understand this stuff," or "I'm having trouble with maps," but these are usually symptoms of a more specific, underlying problem. In the case of "having trouble with maps," for example, there may be several underlying causes—the inability to interpret the map's key, the inability to identify the various symbols on a map, etc. Just as doctors interpret their patient's symptoms, the teacher must interpret the student's symptoms in order to determine why Johnny is having reading problems or Sarah can't read a map. Thus, determining *why* the student is having difficulty is the key element in educational diagnosis and, ultimately, in prescribing treatment.

Diagnosis

The What, Why, and How of Diagnosis and Prescription

How does one diagnose—educationally speaking? If you will permit us another reference to the field of medicine, the diagnostic steps are similar to a doctor's: systematically gathering data, observing student performance (with a clear idea of what one is observing *for*), and asking questions. In a very real sense, the teacher's role in diagnosis is that of a quasi-researcher: the teacher builds a theory, generates hypotheses (about where students' are having problems and why), develops treatments to test the hypotheses, gathers and analyzes what is learned, and then, sometimes, goes back to the drawing board. In other words, educational diagnosis is a process, not an end state, which involves the student, the task the student is expected to do, and the materials the student will use to do it. A key ingredient in that process is the teacher's awareness of the elements that make up a learning task. If the teacher is unaware of the components that go into map reading, for example, it will be exceedingly difficult for that teacher to diagnose the specific problems of children having difficulties with map reading. Indeed, without that information, the prescription is apt to be of the hit-or-miss, "go back and try it again" sort that has almost nothing to do with the student's real problem. (On the other hand, if the student's problem is carelessness, "go back and try it again" could be an appropriate prescription.)

The two types of diagnosis most closely associated with teaching social studies are reflected in the following questions: "Does the student have the necessary knowledge in his or her possession?" and "Is the student able to apply the necessary knowledge in a given situation?" The first question deals with the *knowledge dimension* of learning, while the second question—the application and manipulation of information—is related to the *skills dimension* of learning. The two dimensions are obviously related, but from a diagnostic perspective we examine them separately in the following sections.

Knowledge-Level Diagnosis

One of the most straightforward ways to determine if children have certain knowledge in their possession is to ask them, for example, "What does interdependence mean?" If they can't answer adequately, then they probably need more experience (prescription) with situations involving interdependence in action.

Low-level Knowledge Diagnosis At the lower levels of the knowledge category (of Bloom's *Taxonomy*), especially with factual information (UN concepts), determining why a child doesn't know something can prove more challenging than it might seem. Just ask yourself, for example, why a child might not know that the Declaration of Independence was signed in 1776.

Why? Several reasons are possible. Perhaps the child (*a*) never studied it in the first place, (*b*) has difficulty memorizing facts, (*c*) has difficulty making associations, (*d*) has forgotten it, even though it was studied at one time, (*e*) has repressed it, or (*f*) saw no reason to bother remembering it.

In this and other low-level cognitive diagnosis, most implications are for prescribing, not diagnosing. That is, of the possible explanations above, there is only one we could do something about. Indeed, we could provide children with more association-making experience (categorizing or conceptualizing), but that's not necessarily an adequate explanation for *why* they don't know something. Also, upon reteaching the fact, we could try to provide reasons for a child to remember it. That might help a second time around but it, too, may not explain why a child failed to learn something in the first place.

Implications

Inasmuch as knowledge-level diagnosis at the UN-concept level may defy a search for causes, or may realistically take more time than it's worth, the teaching implications are fairly apparent. You either assess (pretest) students to see if they have the prerequisite knowledge, or you provide them with some experiences to refresh their memories before moving on to more complex issues.

Higher-level Cognitive Diagnosis When you attempt to diagnose a student's knowledge at higher cognitive levels—when you attempt to ascertain a student's knowledge of universals, principles, generalizations, or theories—your problems become considerably more complex. Let's assume for the moment that you intend to teach the notion of interdependence to a second- or third-grade class. You have several options open to you.

Alternatives

One is to assume that your students know nothing about interdependence, and set out to expose them to the idea. Another is to see if they have an experiential understanding of interdependence—that is, if they recognize and have a feeling for the fact that people depend on others for certain goods and services—and then associate a label, the term *interdependence,* with their existing feelings. In some instances, we get into the problems of "label learning" or definition learning noted in Chapter Seven. (Recall diminishing marginal utility?) It may well be, for example, that a child has an implicit understanding of interdependence but is unaware of the correct cue concept label to attach to it. Thus, one of the first steps in diagnosing at higher cognitive levels is to determine if you are dealing with a "labeling" problem or one that is more basic.

It's at about this point that higher-level cognitive diagnosis begins to get fuzzy. Theoretically, the question is whether or not a child has a set of ideas or relationships that, when clustered, would constitute interdependence—to pursue our previous example. In this case, the prescription would be to show the child how those ideas are related and then give them the label "interdependence." An alternative prescription would be to state that "Interdependence means . . . ," and pray that the child makes the necessary relationships. A more fundamental problem occurs when the child does not comprehend the basic ideas that make up interdependence. For example, if the child does not understand the notion of dependence, you can bet he's unlikely to understand interdependence. And, if dependence is the problem, you can begin the cycle once again. Is it a labeling problem? Does he recognize some of the ideas that make up dependence? and so forth.

Critical in any attempt to deal with thinking beyond the lowest cognitive levels is a child's ability to place events and objects in categories or classifications; so argued Jerome Bruner (Bruner et al., 1956, p. 281). Unless children are able to recognize similarities and then associate these in meaningful ways, much of our teaching will be in vain. And, unless we can help students classify, group, and categorize different kinds of data, we are likely to leave them with a random collection of tidbits of information or, more accurately perhaps, one large category labeled "miscellaneous." This raises several issues, some of which play a vital role in individualized instruction. They include questions such as (1) How do youngsters classify? (2) What is similarity and how is it recognized? (3) What criteria does a child use to make a system out of discrete organisms, objects, and events?

Ability to classify

Elementary children classify and make associations well before they ever knock on the kindergarten door. And they do so largely in the absence of formal training. They may group certain toys (cars, dolls, etc.) according to size, shape, color, or function. They may group, collect, and store all sorts of objects around the house. In fact, some educational toys force children to make associations by requiring them to place squares, triangles, or other shaped blocks through openings having the same shape. Even children's puzzles have a theme—the barnyard, etc.—and require that children relate shapes and sizes as well as color. All of these activities ask the child to create *order* out of bits of chaos. Yet even at the physical-grouping level individual children differ in their ability to achieve the desired ordering.

How does one diagnose the way children classify? The following can serve as a guide.

Behaviors to observe while a child is involved in activities

A The child uses descriptive criteria for classifying:
color
size
shape
physical features (shiny, dull)

B The child classifies by functions:
purpose
what objects *do*
C The child uses personalized relationships as a basis for classifying:
mine
yours
ours
valued (like/dislike)
aesthetic (beautiful/ugly)
D The child classifies by using criteria:
hammer/nail
engine/power
seed/flower
E The child uses inference to place objects into categories:
dog/animal
orange/fruit
girl/human
F The child classifies by *one* attribute only.
G The child categorizes by using several attributes.
H The child verbalizes the criteria used in classifying.
I The child combines two or more attributes when classifying.

Fundamental diagnostic questions related to a learner's categorizing style
1 How does this particular child categorize?
2 What kinds of criteria are apparently used when the child classifies?
3 In what kinds of situations was the child motivated to do classification?
Kinds of materials?
Kinds of play activities?
Kinds of selected or given tasks?
Kinds of social situations?
4 To what extent does the individual child verbalize why he did what he was observed to be doing?
5 Does the individual child maintain her criteria throughout the activity or does she apply different criteria in a random way?
6 Is the child's categorizing style consistent when observed over a period of time and when working on several tasks?

A word of caution: do not be too hasty to infer that a child follows a particular behavior pattern based on just one or two observations. Because children *do not* classify in a particular way doesn't necessarily mean they *cannot* do so. Nor do we know whether what is observed on one or two occasions is necessarily an optimal performance by a particular child. In fact, diagnosing the way children conceptualize and classify will probably require several periods of rather careful observation.

It seems to us that one of the basic problems with higher-level cognitive diagnosis is that the *diagnoser* sometimes doesn't understand the concept or generalization well enough to know what questions to ask. What, for example, are the prerequisite ideas necessary for understanding capitalism, socialism,

*Knowing what
to observe for*

or culture? These are tough questions. To further complicate matters, if your education was anything like ours, we spent considerable time memorizing definitions for capitalism, socialism, culture, and interdependence, and *not* clustering related ideas to build a definition. Had we learned our social studies the latter way, perhaps we'd have fewer problems with higher-level cognitive diagnosis.

How Well Do You Classify?

The illustrations below are derived from "The Meritocracy: Ability Testing and the American Spirit," by Helen Rowan (1966, p. 6).

In how many different ways (different criteria) could the items above be paired? (For example, could there be aesthetic considerations/ criteria?) Which pairing would be considered correct?

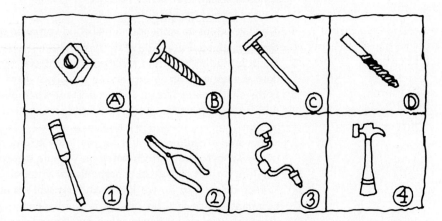

What specific knowledge do you think the illustration above is trying to identify? What inferences about a pupil might you make if a student meets the knowledge criteria? What background experiences influence how a pupil might respond? How is the situational aspect of the matching controlled? How else might the matching ability be tested (other than by drawings)? How might having too much information get in the way?

What response considerations might be taken into account in trying to determine a number sequence? (Just what ability is being tested with the dominoes?)

Skills Diagnosis

Since cognitive skills are actually knowledges *applied* to a particular situation, we face a two-dimensional problem. If children are unable to differentiate between facts and opinions, for example, the problem may rest in one of two places. Either (1) they are unable to recognize a fact or an opinion when they see one, which may suggest that they don't know the difference between them—a knowledge-level task—or (2) they are unable to apply what they know to a particular situation—an application problem. If children can identify a fact and an opinion in one situation but not in another, the problem lies with how they apply their knowledge. The diagnostic question then becomes one of identifying the differences between the two situations to pinpoint what might be preventing the children from making the transfer.

Several other elements of skills diagnosis are illustrated by the following assignment: "Analyze Jefferson's first and second inaugural addresses and identify how they are similar and how they are different." Such a task is challenging enough for many adults, to say nothing of elementary or middle school students. Why? It's a valid though complex assignment that requires the application of several skills *simultaneously.* One must be able to analyze, translate, comprehend, compare—and the list goes on.

Diagnosing complex tasks

When diagnosing application problems, the key question teachers should ask are: (1) How many skills am I asking a student to apply in this situation? and (2) Has this student been successful in applying multiple skills before? If the answer to the second question is no, you may be dooming the child to failure if you persist in presenting the assignment. You can also be fairly certain that this is *not* a situation in which the child will learn from his mistakes. Indeed, he may be so ill-equipped to handle the task that he is unable to make mistakes!

Our final point on skills diagnosis is a fairly obvious one, we think, but one which also has some interesting implications. That is, in most educational surroundings, it is the teacher who presents students with situations requiring that they apply their skills. Rarely, indeed very rarely, will you have a student who asks, "Can I do some more story problems?" or says, "Gee, I can't wait to analyze this paragraph!" Most kids just aren't that way. In presenting tasks to children, there has to be a challenge, yes, but also a sensitivity to the relationship between the the challenge a task poses and the children's skill level to meet it.

Learning Style

Are you primarily an auditory or a visual learner? In other words, when faced with learning something would you prefer to have it explained in a good lecture, or would you rather go off by yourself and read about it?

And, when given an assignment, how much structuring do you prefer? Would you prefer that the teacher specify everything you should do beforehand, or would you rather work it out as you see fit? Or doesn't it matter?

Your preferred instructional mode (auditory or visual) and the amount of teacher structuring you desire are two examples of several generic factors that can influence learning, which, when clustered, we've chosen to call one's "learning style." These factors are generic since they are not restricted to social studies alone; they may influence student performance in every subject area.

Six factors that contribute to one's learning style are described below.

1　*Instructional modes.* Some learners work better when their access to new information and experiences is through listening to verbal presentations. Others learn better through reading or observation. Admittedly, students' preference for a particular instructional mode may vary depending on the kind of information they are dealing with. Some students may prefer to read social studies materials but would rather listen to a math explanation.

2　*Structure.* Students vary in the amount of organizing they can do on their own and the amount that must be done by someone else. Some students— including some of the brightest—require that teachers do most of the structuring in learning situations. For them, an assignment like "Read about Topic X" virtually drives them up the wall. What they want are page numbers—"Read from page 34 to page 37"—and once given that, they'll breathe a sigh of relief. Others, however, are quite capable of determining the limits of a task or assignment on their own. The basic structuring question, then, concerns how much organizing students can do for themselves and how much they depend on teachers to set the limits for assignments and activities.

3　*Social context of learning.* Students often function differently in different social/learning environments—something that should surprise almost no one. Two of the key factors that can influence this aspect of learning style are: (1) how the student views authority, particularly the teacher's authority, and (2) how the student feels about working in group situations.

Some students demand that teachers exercise their authority in a particular way. Some want the teacher to be an aloof and authoritarian taskmaster at all times, while other students want teachers to act as relaxed and casual counselors or guides (and never adopt a sterner stance). Sometimes those conflicting expectations come from students in the same class. Primary-age children are especially likely to regard teachers as surrogate parents. For them, the teacher's word is gospel, and things are "so" because "Teacher says they are so." Quite the opposite view may be held by a smaller proportion of primary-level students (and older students too); some of them seemingly want to turn everything teachers say into debatable propositions.

If your intent is to use lots of small group activities in your classroom, be prepared to deal with those students who have little use for group activities and would much prefer to go off somewhere and read an assignment (or otherwise avoid the social interaction necessitated in a small group setting). Other students may tolerate group activities, but they certainly don't look forward to them. At the other end of the spectrum are students who feel that they learn best when they can talk over an assignment or task with a group.

4 *Physical context of learning.* Some students demand absolute silence when they study, while others can tolerate noise no matter how loud it is. Others tend to be "morning people" and do their best work then, while some (though fewer) don't function well until after lunch.

5 *Reward/praise.* Individuals vary in their need for and their response to reward and praise. In fact, some of your students will do everything they can to avoid public praise; it's almost a kind of punishment for them. Other students need and want constant attention and feedback. To an extent, students can be grouped in terms of whether they prefer external praise—either from teachers or other authority figures—or whether they rely primarily on internal praise and/or self-satisfaction.

6 *Goal preference.* Some learners work more effectively and efficiently when goals are short-range and within their immediate grasp. For example, children who feel that the most important objective is "finishing homework" or otherwise completing a short-range assignment may never see how all of the smaller assignments fit together into a larger pattern (assuming there is a logic or overall pattern to the assignments, of course). Other students may be willing to forego short-range goals in favor of working toward a longer range objective. For some children, of course, "long-range" may be something one or two weeks away.

Although our list of factors involved in learning style in not exhaustive, its implications are significant for both individualized and whole-group instruction. For example, to provide verbal praise to students who don't like attention from an authority figure, or to provide almost no structuring for students who demand considerable teacher structuring, whether in individualized or group settings, could create problems for you *and* the students. The same could be true if you present only long-range goals to students whose concern is with meeting immediate, short-range objectives.

How does one go about diagnosing a student's learning style? Once again (as is true for all aspects of diagnosis), it's essential that you have identified what you are looking for. Once you've determined your focus—be it goal

Directed observation

preference, response to praise, or whatever—your actual technique may consist of one or more of the following: (1) systematically observing students as they participate in learning activities; (2) questioning—"Does the noise bother you when you study?" etc.; (3) a written learning-style inventory/questionnaire, such as the one illustrated in Appendix C. No matter how you gather information about your students' learning styles, it can be summarized on a learning-style inventory form like the one illustrated in Figure 13.2.

Prescribing

After an extensive review of research on teaching and learning, Barak Rosenshine (1977) concluded that one cannot assume that children know what they have not been taught. Now, if this finding reeks of common sense, you would probably be amazed at how often teachers assume the reverse, that is, that children know what they have not been taught. Seldom does this misguided assumption become more apparent than when teachers prescribe learning activities. Consider, for example, that you have discovered several children who have difficulty identifying the similarities and differences among objects, and this inability prevents them from placing objects into classes or categories. Would you then give them an activity similar to that in the box entitled "How Well Do You Classify?"

If you are still pondering your response (or even if you are not), consider the following: *Many so-called "instructional materials" (including those in the box on pages 378–79) do not teach.* They *could* be used to teach, but in their present form they merely *test* the student's existing ability—in this case, the ability to classify. If you already know that several students cannot classify, giving them such materials in the absence of teaching would very likely confirm what you already know; that they can't classify. The implication for teaching is the same as when you find that a student can't read a map or apply any one of a thousand other skills; show (teach) the student a step-by-step procedure through which he or she will be able to demonstrate the desired behavior.

Teaching or testing?

It isn't necessary to employ fancy questioning strategies either. Recall that every question presupposes certain knowledge and skills on the students' part. If students lack the knowledge or skills needed to complete a task, there is no reason to assume that they have the knowledge necessary to answer questions about the task—unless, of course, you're still not certain that you have accurately diagnosed the problem. In that instance, further questioning may be entirely appropriate. Otherwise, we suggest that you consider using some old-fashioned direct instruction; either show or tell the student how to complete the task, whichever is most appropriate.

Enrichment Enrichment refers to instructional activities that supplement a basic program, activities that enhance and add fullness and richness to it. A social studies program—or any instructional program for that matter—should be rich and varied to start with, but since average students may have all that they can do to complete a basic program, enrichment tends to be associated with programs for gifted and talented students.

Figure 13.2 Sample
Learning-Style
Inventory

LEARNING STYLE INVENTORY

Date _____ Teacher_____

Student _____

1. Preferred instructional modes: _____

   _____

2. Structure needs: _____

3. Social context of learning:

   3.1 Authority expectations: _____

   3.2 Group involvement: _____

4. Physical context of learning: _____

   _____

5. Reward/praise: _____

   _____

6. Goal preferences: _____

7. Significant previous experiences: _____

   _____

8. Current interests: _____

   _____

COMMENTS:

RECOMMENDATIONS:

_____

Three types of enrichment are associated with social studies programs. Among the least common of these is *acceleration,* in which students with specific academic aptitudes move to higher grade-level classes for a particular subject and then return to their regular classes for other academic work. In analytic subject areas such as mathematics, for example, acceleration is a fairly common practice. A third-grade student with sixth-grade math skills, for example, may benefit from and enjoy being placed in a sixth-grade math class. In synthetic areas such as social studies, however, you seldom find the well developed, grade-to-grade-level skills sequence that is more common in the analytic subject areas. Thus, a third-grade student with sixth-grade map skills, for example, might be almost totally lost in a sixth-grade social studies class where map skills are only a minor part of the program. In other words, neither the content nor the skill development sequence of most traditional social studies programs, especially those based on the expanding-environments approach, permit the type of acceleration that is possible in the analytic subject areas.

A second approach to enrichment involves giving gifted students (or others who finish their regular work early) the "privilege" of doing more work than everyone else. This means that instead of doing a ten-page report, for example, gifted students might be required to prepare a fifteen- or twenty-page report. Or instead of doing just the odd-numbered problems on a page (like everyone else), gifted and talented students may be required to do every problem on a page. True, this type of enrichment provides students with practice—often practice they don't need—but most students quickly realize that what teachers may intend as enrichment is really a kind of punishment. That's why we refer to this approach as *penalty-type enrichment.* Note that there's probably nothing at all punitive about the teacher's intent, it's just that students often look upon the additional work as a penalty. Also note that it usually isn't long before most students discover that they can avoid the penalty of extra work by slowing down and finishing their assignments with everyone else.

A third approach, *breadth/depth enrichment,* is probably the most common. Instead of asking students to do more work, as is usually true of penalty-type enrichment, in this approach students are provided with assignments that are qualitatively different. In some instances, students may select from several alternative activities suggested by the teacher, while in other instances they may initiate and undertake activities on their own. However it's done, the intent is to provide students with ways to explore topics or problems in greater breadth or depth than they otherwise might.

Literature is a frequently used vehicle for breadth/depth enrichment. One of the most obvious techniques is to permit students to read stories, either fiction or nonfiction, relating to topics or problems the class is studying. A less obvious technique is to use literature comparatively. On an occasion when a second-grade class was studying George Washington, for instance, one student read two biographies of his life. To her amazement, she discovered that the two accounts differed in several respects. As she put it, "One of these books is lying." She then proceeded to read almost everything the library had on George Washington, the *Encyclopaedia Britannica* in-

Acceleration

Penalty-type enrichment

Breadth/depth enrichment

cluded, in her quest to determine what actually happened. Note that an excellent source of appropriate children's literature is the list of notable trade books published yearly in *Social Education,* the official journal of the National Council for the Social Studies.

Another means for providing breadth/depth enrichment is through special reports or projects, including model making and other enactive experiences. But before using any of these techniques, two key elements should be considered. First, make certain that whatever students do is really something special, not simply a longer or more detailed version of what everyone else is doing. In fact, unless students volunteer to do longer reports, the activities could become a form of penalty-type enrichment. Second, keep in mind that a steady diet of written reports can become tedious very quickly, regardless of a student's ability. To cope with this, many teachers try to balance written assignments with nonwritten presentations including various forms of sociodrama (skits, plays, pageants, etc.), or other visually oriented presentations (linear charts, pictures, slide-and-tape presentations, etc.).

Special projects

Dealing with Differentiated Instruction Providing differential treatment to select groups of students, whether gifted or less able, can sometimes introduce an unintended and ofttimes undesirable dynamic to your classroom. After providing several enrichment experiences for gifted and talented students, for example, you may hear one of your average students say, "Why do *they* always get to do all of the neat stuff, when all *we* ever get to do is the same old boring thing?" Or, after providing less able students with an assignment geared to their ability level, you may hear other students say, "How come we don't get to do the easy stuff like they do?" When you hear either complaint, you'll know there may be problems ahead (if they are not upon you already).

There are essentially two ways to avoid the resentment that may accompany differentiated instruction. One way is to teach social studies on a whole-class basis and provide the same experiences and assignments for everyone. Although this can help avoid problems associated with feelings of unfairness, you can also be fairly certain that your academically talented students will go unchallenged, your less able students will experience their share of failure, while your average students will continue plodding along. Our point here is that by apparently solving one problem—feelings of resentment and unfairness—you may find yourself a victim of other, potentially more serious problems.

A second and far more preferable way to deal with preferential treatment that may seem to accompany differentiated instruction is to individualize instruction even more, so that it is an everyday occurrence that students come to expect. In classrooms where individualized instruction is the main method of operation, students are less apt to find anything unusual or unfair about it. Of course, things may be a bit rocky at first as students become accustomed to differentiated instruction (see box, pp. 389–91), but once individualized instruction is the norm—when it's what students expect—feelings of resentment or unfairness should diminish considerably. The fact

Make it what students expect

that individualized instruction provides a means for meeting student's varied skill and ability levels only adds to its appeal. In fact, it even permits you to provide enrichment activities for less able students, activities that can provide welcome relief from the day-to-day drudgery that often accompanies remedial work.

From everything we've said thus far, it should be apparent that teacher-directed individualizing tremendously enlarges the scope of what it means to teach. It asks that you develop and use diagnostic skills that you may not have seen used before, or that weren't used on you (or at least you didn't know were being used on you); it also demands that you prescribe appropriate learning activities accordingly. What sounds so easy in theory will undoubtedly prove to be another difficult challenge. The essential question should not be one of whether or not you'll individualize instruction, but rather *how* you'll go about it.

We've tried to suggest some ways to begin—and we realize that they are only a beginning—and we intend to suggest other ways in the next section. However you go about it, we repeat our earlier advice: begin slowly.

Expanding the concept of teaching

Student-Directed Individualizing

Johnny: I've finished this assignment. What should I do now?
Analysis: Johnny may need considerable teacher structuring.
Teacher: Everyone else is still working. How did you manage to finish so quickly?
Analysis: Probably represents a ploy (on the teacher's part) to gain time to think of something for Johnny to do.
Johnny: It was easy!
Analysis: Confirms Johnny's ability.
Teacher: Well, why don't you go on and do the next assignment?
Analysis: An assignment is phrased as if it were a question.
Johnny: Gee, do I have to? Can't I go to the library?
Analysis: Unhappy with the prospect of more work, Johnny turns the assignment into a debatable question, and then offers a more palatable option.

To accommodate students who finish early or who have nothing to do, some teachers establish interest centers or learning stations around the room. Students are generally free to go to the area and work on activities of their choice. Thus, the "reward" for students who finish early is the freedom to select activities that interest them and, hopefully, that they want to do.

What may have begun as a way to deal with students who finish early is certainly not limited to that, however, for some teachers have opted to use interest centers and learning stations as the basis for their entire program. In some respects, their efforts reflect the height of individualized instruction. We hasten to add that when teachers use a centers approach, you can be fairly certain that they prescribe particular activities for students to complete; it's not a matter of completely free choice. Otherwise students might avoid some subjects entirely, if they could get away with it.

Interest centers

Permitting students to participate in the selection and development of instructional activities is what student-directed individualizing is all about.

It is an approach in which the teacher shares *some* (not all) of the instructional decision making with students.

Opening up the instructional decision-making process and making it more responsive to the needs and interests of students is integral to both student-directed individualizing and open education. Although we can't say for certain where open education began, we do know that it was certainly given healthy encouragement by the British primary school movement. Almost twenty years ago, some schools in Britain began moving toward the *integrated day*—learning situations in which students exercised a greater degree of choice over what they were going to do and how they were going to do it. It was the teacher's responsibility to integrate each child's daily program so that learning and progress took place. The movement met with considerable success in England, and has since been transplanted in a variety of different forms in this country. Here, however, we've tended to call it *open education.*

Open education

Social Studies in the Open Classroom

The notion that schools should "fit" children (rather than the other way around) is basic to both open education and individualized instruction. Thus the two movements have some common elements. The difference between them lies in the fact that, while you could use some elements of individualized instruction in a traditional classroom, there's absolutely no way (at the theoretical level) you can operate an open classroom without individualized instruction. When you "open" a classroom, you must also individualize it.

Permitting students to exercise a greater role in instructional decision making sometimes necessitates physical changes in the classroom—changes intended to facilitate student choice making. In order to provide space in your classroom for interest centers or learning stations, you'll probably need to rearrange the room. Thus, instead of a conventional classroom with perfectly aligned rows of seats (Setting A of Figure 13.3), you'll typically find a much more flexible arrangement, as illustrated in Setting B of Figure 13.3. The intent of the centers approach, which is also called "centering," is to create a physical space where students can go as they pursue activities related to a particular subject area or to their own interests.

Centering

Unfortunately, some individuals inaccurately associate open education with the physical changes in a classroom or school, especially open-space schools—that is, buildings that have no interior walls and, hence, no classrooms as such. Although open areas do permit teachers to have greater flexibility in organizing a learning environment, the presence or absence of walls is by no means the key element of open education. Indeed, open education is a concept, not a physical thing. We've seen truly open education in some positively decrepit school buildings, just as we've seen extremely traditional instruction taking place in modern, open-space buildings where there wasn't a wall in sight.

Making the Transition to an Open Classroom   Several years ago we conducted an informal poll of over 1,200 teachers from across the country. We asked them which of two classroom settings—Setting A or B as shown in Figure 13.3—required more teacher effort. Almost to a person they in-

Figure 13.3A
Traditional
Classroom
Arrangement
(Setting A)

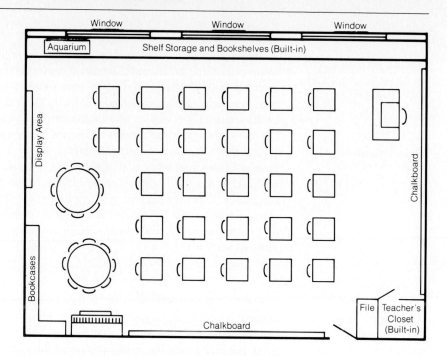

Figure 13.3B
Classroom
Organized Around
Interest Centers
(Setting B)

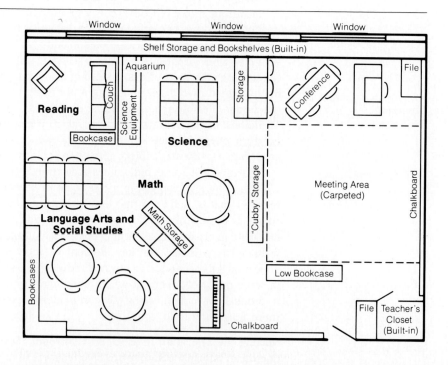

dicated that it was easier to manage a teacher-directed classroom like the one shown in Setting A. We also asked the teachers what they thought would be the biggest problem in moving toward a more open classroom like the one shown in Setting B of Figure 13.3. Again, their response was almost universal: helping students accept the greater sense of responsibility that open classrooms require.

For students who have spent most of their school life in traditional, teacher-directed classrooms, shifting to a more open setting could be a chaotic experience. However, if your goal is to share instructional decision making with students and to help them accept greater responsibility for their learning, you may find Gary Van der Carr's experience helpful.

Gary Van der Carr's Classroom

Gary Van der Carr's fifth-grade classroom is a large room with a huge aquarium in the center. The floor is covered with a multicolored collection of carpet remnants and old rugs. A couch and some overstuffed chairs stand in one corner, and tables, chairs, and other working spaces are set up in clusters around the room. It's a classroom that reflects warmth, informality, and a lot of time spent collecting things.

Aside from its overall layout, two things are especially striking about Gary's classroom. First are the book reports written on large sheets of paper and mounted on the ceiling. Students lie on the floor to read them. The second thing is a sign over the chalkboard that reads: *You will have as much freedom as you have responsibility.* As Gary indicates, "The only way that this classroom can function is if everyone accepts responsibility for it. If someone goofs off, everyone gets hurt. Although you often hear that statement in traditional classrooms, in our setup it becomes even more important. Sometimes, like before vacations, I have to be the bad guy and sit on everybody."

Freedom and responsibility

"How do other teachers react to the way you operate your class?" we asked.

"It varies," Gary replied. "Some teachers think it's great, but then some of the old guard think I'm crazy."

"Have you always taught this way—in this kind of classroom?"

"No," he answered, "it's taken me eleven years to reach this point. I started out in a fairly traditional classroom—clusters of chairs and tables, that sort of thing—and have gradually changed to what you see now."

"In other words, you didn't consciously plan to teach in this kind of setup?"

"Not really," Gary said. "I had a general idea, but nothing specific that I could point to. Sometimes it depends on the kids. I learned the hard way that I couldn't take kids from a traditional fourth-grade classroom and turn them loose in this kind of environment—they went wild. So in September this room looks much more like a traditional classroom than it does now. I have assigned seats, everything. Then I gradually add things; the stuff in the quiet corner first, then the rugs and the other stuff as the kids show that they have the responsibility to accept it.

A variety of activities may take place simultaneously in open classroom settings.

"Two years ago," he continued, "I had a group that just couldn't hack it—they couldn't handle the responsibility. I tried bringing in the rugs and the other stuff but I had to take them out again. That particular group just couldn't deal with the freedom."

"Don't a lot of teachers use that as an excuse for not doing things— that their students can't handle it?" we asked.

"Yeah, that's true," Gary replied, "but many teachers say that without having tried it. They think their students can't handle something but they really don't know for sure. In my case, I had done it—I had proven that an open classroom could work. When I failed with that group, it wasn't because I hadn't tried."

There are several morals here, if we can call them that. One, before plunging into a major reorganization, "test the water" on a small scale. Second, don't assume that your students cannot do something until you (and they) have given it your best effort. Third, when you attempt something and it fails, the cause may not lie entirely with your ability. Remember that children who can function in unstructured situations can also function in highly structured situations. The reverse is not necessarily true, however; children who require a great deal of teacher structuring may flounder hopelessly in highly unstructured environments.

Terms clarified

Social Studies Centers: Two Maps and a Globe?   We've been guilty of using two terms, *interest centers* and *learning stations,* as if they were synonymous, when, in practice, they are not. Although interest centers and learning stations may be quite similar in appearance, they differ in how they are used. An interest center is, by definition, a place students *may* go if they are interested in whatever that center contains. A learning station, on the other hand, is an area of the classroom that students *must* visit, either to complete tasks assigned by the teacher or to select from a range of alternative activities. In essence, there's more teacher direction associated with learning stations than with interest centers.

How does one create a social studies center? And, what do you put into it besides a couple of maps, a globe, and a set of encyclopedias?

The first thing you'll need to do is carve out some space for your center. Exactly how you do that depends on what kind of space you have available, so we can't be of much help in this area. Again, Setting B of Figure 13.3 shows one possible model. If need be, you could combine a social studies center with a science or language arts center. However, you decide to proceed, you should mention your plans to one of the most important persons in any school—the custodian. If he or she must clean your room at night and prefers desks in neat, straight rows, you probably ought to inform him or her in advance of what you are trying to do. In addition, you'll probably want to mention your plans to the principal, particularly if most classrooms have a more traditional format.

Once you get the preliminaries out of the way, you're ready to begin collecting materials. The following was abridged and adapted from a listing compiled by Evelyn Berger and Bonnie A. Winters (1973, pp. 14–15).

1 Several copies of selected social studies texts, especially those with lower reading levels, if available
2 Trade books, cookbooks, songbooks, even fiction related to whatever you plan to study
3 Maps of all shapes and sizes, especially topographical maps of your area
4 Magazines and newspapers, depending on your grade level. Even at the primary level, you can never have too many magazines
5 Filmstrips, records, tapes, transparencies, etc.
6 Artifacts—coins, stamps, etc.—from areas of the world you may be studying during the year
7 Study prints, pictures, or travel posters
8 A large "treasure chest" of materials for costumes to use in role playing or sociodrama
9 Cushions, carpet pieces, perhaps even a rocking chair
10 Large appliance cartons—for puppet stages and any variety of "buildings"

11 Some means to store all the "stuff" on this list. These may be file cabinets, storage cases, mobile carts, bookcases, etc. The essential thing here is that the students have access to most materials when they need them (and thus not be forced to bother you every time they need something).

If you were to ask the typical open-classroom teacher what her biggest problem is, we suspect you'd find it's not teaching, not management, not discipline, but *storage!*

Task and Activity Cards Once you've collected enough materials, you'll still need a way to manage your centers. One successful strategy for doing that involves the use of task and activity cards. These are just what the name implies, cards—usually 5 by 8 inches or 7 by 11 inches—describing a task or an activity. Students can select task or activity cards that interest them or they can be assigned by the teacher, depending on how you want to use your center.

The range of tasks or activities you make available on task or activity cards can be almost endless. Some of them may require that students go elsewhere —the library, outside, etc.—to complete the activity, while others will be self-contained, that is, they will contain everything the student will need. The difference between going elsewhere and being self-contained is the basis for our distinction between activity and task cards.

Characteristics

As a rule activity cards reflect the following characteristics:

1 *They are openended;* they present activities for which there are no previously established answers. "Write a short story about what you see happening in this picture" (see Figure 13.4) and "Go out and find a million of something and then prove it" are examples of openended activities students might wish to pursue.
2 *They are not self-contained;* they do not include whatever information the student will need to complete the activity. "Conduct a survey to determine whether most students prefer frozen or canned corn" and "Go to the library and prepare a five page report on . . . ," are examples of activities that students must go elsewhere to complete.

Task cards, on the other hand, reflect the following characteristics:

1 *They are self-contained;* they include the information students will need to complete the task. This characteristic is illustrated in the commercially made task card shown in Figure 13.5
2 *They have a readily identifiable skill focus* (this characteristic is also illustrated in Figure 13.5).

Note that adding the statement, "Go back over your story and underline what you observed with a black pen and what you inferred with a red pen," shifts what would otherwise be an openended activity card to a task card with an identifiable skills focus—observing and inferring. Note also, however, that presenting such a card to students doesn't necessarily *teach* them to distinguish between an observation and an inference; it *tests* their ability to do so. If students are unable to complete such a task card, additional instruction is undoubtedly called for.

Figure 13.4 Teacher-Made Activity/Task Card

For an activity card: Write a short story about what you see happening in the picture.
For a task card: Write a short story about what you see happening in the picture. Then, go back and underline what you observed with a black pen. Underline what you inferred with a red pen.
For both: Share your story with us when you are finished.

Just about any activity that appeals to you or your students can end up on a task or activity card. For convenience, you may wish to use a color-coding system, such as putting observing and inferring tasks on blue cards, research activities on red cards, and just plain "fun" activities (puzzles, riddles, etc.) on green cards. You'll also want to keep a supply of task and activity cards tucked away so you can change cards when your current crop begins to get a little stale. Actually, you might place a fresh set of task or activity cards in your center each time you begin a new area of study.

Modules: LAPs, ILPs, and Other Forms of Alphabet Soup Modules are self-contained instructional packages that can be included in a center, and are intended to teach students about a particular topic. Since most modules contain (or indicate) almost everything students will need—a statement of objectives, a pretest, possible readings and activities, and a posttest—they can greatly simplify individualized instruction.

Module format

Modules go by a variety of names. An LAP, for example, indicates a Learning Activity Package, while an ILP is an Independent Learning Pack-

Figure 13.5
Commercially Made
Task Card

Normal Temperatures for Ten U. S. Cities

City and state	January		July	
	High	Low	High	Low
Boston, Massachusetts	37	22	80	64
Denver, Colorado	43	20	86	62
Detroit, Michigan	33	19	84	63
Helena, Montana	27	8	84	52
Houston, Texas	62	46	92	75
Juneau, Alaska	31	21	62	47
Miami, Florida	74	63	87	76
Nashville, Tennessee	49	31	91	69
Portland, Maine	31	11	79	57
Portland, Oregon	44	35	79	58

Number your paper from 1 to 20. Read the questions below. After each question are several answers. Look at the table to see which answer is correct. Then write its letter on your paper after the number of the question. Be sure to read *all* the answers before you decide which one is correct.

1. The main purpose of this table is to show A. the ten largest cities in the United States B. temperatures each month during the year C. the normal temperatures for ten U.S. cities during January and July D. the highest and lowest temperatures ten U.S. cities have ever had in January and July

2. The table lists the normal temperatures for A. two months B. four months C. ten months D. each half year

3. The city that has the lowest temperature in January is A. Portland, Maine B. Helena C. Juneau D. Detroit

4. The warmest city in July is A. Nashville B. Miami C. Denver D. Houston

5. The coldest city in July is A. Portland, Maine B. Helena C. Juneau D. Portland, Oregon

6. The July temperatures in Portland, Maine, are most nearly like the July temperatures in A. Portland, Oregon B. Boston C. Juneau D. Helena

7. The city with January temperatures most nearly like those in July is A. Houston B. Miami C. Portland, Oregon D. Nashville

8. The city that has the greatest difference between the lowest and highest temperatures in July is A. Juneau B. Portland, Maine C. Houston D. Helena

9. The city in which the July high temperature is most nearly the same as the July high temperature in Houston is A. Denver B. Miami C. Nashville D. Detroit

10. Which city has about the same high and low temperatures in July as Houston has in January? A. Nashville B. Miami C. Detroit D. Juneau

Source: Rath et al. (1969). Reprinted by permission of Benefic Press.

age. Regardless of what they might be called, most modules contain the following components.

1   *Objectives.* Most modules provide a clear indication of what will be expected of students when they have completed the packet. Thus, most objectives are stated behaviorally, often in the form of "Upon completing this module, you will be expected to. . . ."

2   *Pretest.* If you know in advance that a student knows nothing about the module's topic, a pretest may be redundant. Thus, the inclusion of pretests usually provides students with a way to determine if they are already proficient in the skills or knowledge a module deals with. If that's the case, they are usually permitted to skip activities relating to that skill or knowledge.

3   *Activities.* The instructional activities in a module are usually keyed to certain objectives. If students are already able to meet those objectives, they are usually permitted to omit activities pertaining to them.

4 *Posttest.* Posttests are not generally included in most modules, even though they are a component of modular programs. Generally, students must get the posttest from the teacher (to avoid cheating, however unintentional it might be). However, if a module's objectives are clearly stated, students should have a good idea of what to anticipate on the posttest.

Some teachers use modules, many of which they've developed themselves, as the basis for their social studies program. However, the fact that modules often rely heavily on the student's ability to read may make them questionable for widespread use in elementary schools.

Summary

To believe that all students will learn the same things at the same time, at the same rate, and with the same degree of retention is sheer fantasy. Indeed, in almost any classroom at any grade level, the range of students' abilities, interests, talents, knowledge, previous experiences, personalities, learning styles, dispositions, and needs is so great that it's staggering. In many instances, individualizing instruction so that these characteristics are taken into account is not simply a matter of principle, it's a matter of necessity.

We have suggested that individualized instruction has resulted from efforts to make schools more responsive to individual students and their instructional needs. We identified several administrative policies—homogeneous grouping, acceleration, retention, and special classes—that are aimed at narrowing the range of needs and characteristics with which teachers must deal. Although administrative policies help to determine *which* students will be in a particular class, the policies have relatively little impact on *how* students will be taught. For that, teachers must turn to instructional approaches to individualization.

Instructional approaches to individualization take two basic forms: teacher-directed and student-directed. In teacher-directed individualizing, the focus is on diagnosing the student's learning problem and then prescribing appropriate instruction. Diagnosing is a procedure (borrowed from the world of medicine) in which the teacher attempts to identify the factors that are influencing a learning situation. Prescribing, which is also borrowed from medicine, reflects the teacher's attempts to alter or modify instructional activities so that there is a close match between the tasks and the student's ability to deal with them. In some instances, the teacher may alter the task so that it more closely corresponds to the student's learning style. Learning style refers to generic factors such as preferred instructional mode, the need for structure, the social and physical contexts of learning, responses to reward/praise, and goal preferences, that can influence how a student learns in any subject area.

Student-directed individualizing reflects efforts to provide options and opportunities for students to participate in instructional decision making, particularly in selecting the kinds of learning activities they will encounter. Permitting students to play a more significant role in instructional decision making necessitates a more open learning environment, as well as a greater sense of responsibility on the student's part. Two techniques teachers employ to facilitate student-directed individualizing are the use of interest centers and learning stations.

The recent interest and legislation relating to exceptional children has resulted in a sharpened focus on individualized instruction. We noted that exceptional children are students at either end of the educational spectrum —those children with handicaps and special needs as well as the gifted and talented. In view of the increased attention and funding being directed toward exceptional students, it is becoming apparent that we cannot overlook the needs of any child. In certain situations and in certain ways, every student is exceptional. Indeed, "exceptional children" may be a misnomer; exceptional (individualized) instruction for *all* children may actually be more appropriate.

Suggested Activities

1   There is a widespread, though usually unstated, feeling among many Americans that schooling should be the same everywhere, and that providing special programs for exceptional students is somehow undemocratic. Associated with this is the impression that Americans have accepted special education out of a sense of sympathy and sorrow for "those poor kids," a spirit similar to the one that causes us to help the needy at Christmastime and then ignore them the rest of the year.

   Most Americans accept the principle that every child has the right to an education. But do they also accept the principle that every child has the right to an education appropriate to his or her needs and abilities?

2   "If a child doesn't measure up, well, that's her problem." Identify your personal position with regard to this frequently heard comment.

3   As a group, design and actually build some of the instructional materials you would include in a learning center.

References

Berger, Evelyn, and Winters, Bonnie A. *Social Studies in the Open Classroom: A Practical Guide.* New York: Teachers College Press, 1973.

Bruner, Jerome, et al. *A Study of Thinking.* New York: Wiley, 1956.

Dunn, Lloyd, M. "Special Education for the Mildly Retarded—Is Much of It Justified?" *Exceptional Children* 35 (September, 1968): 5–22.

———. *Exceptional Children in the Schools.* (2nd ed.) New York: Holt, Rinehart & Winston, 1973.

Gallagher, James J. "The Special Education Contract for Mildly Handicapped Children." *Exceptional Children* 38 (September, 1972): 527–35.

———. "Phenomenal Growth and New Problems Characterize Special Education." *Phi Delta Kappan* LV (April 1974): 516–20.

Haring, Norris G. (ed). *The Behavior of Exceptional Children.* Columbus, OH: Charles E. Merrill, 1978.

Kirk, Samuel A. *Educating Exceptional Children.* (2nd ed.) New York: Houghton Mifflin, 1972.

Postman, Neil, and Weingartner, Charles. *Teaching As a Subversive Activity*. New York: Dell, 1969.

Raths, Louis E., et al. *The Thinking Box*. Chicago: Benefic Press, 1969.

Rosenshine, Barak V. "Academic Engaged Time, Content Covered, and Direct Instruction." Paper presented to the Annual Meeting of the American Educational Research Association, 1978.

Rowan, Helen. "Meritocracy: Ability Testing and the American Spirit." *Carnegie Quarterly* 14 (Spring, 1966): 5–7.

Sekal, Robert R. "Classification: Purposes, Principles, Progress, Prospects." *Science* 185 (September 27, 1974): 1115–23.

Suggested Readings

Evelyn Berger and Bonnie A. Winters. *Social Studies in the Open Classroom: A Practical Guide*. New York: Teachers College Press, 1973. The subtitle on this one should read "A Very Practical Guide." In fewer than 100 pages, the authors show you both what to do and how to do it.

John Herlihy and Myra Herlihy (eds.). *Mainstreaming in the Social Studies*, Bulletin No. 62. Washington, D.C.: National Council for the Social Studies, 1980. This volume is made up of short articles dealing with the different aspects of mainstreaming in the social studies. Very helpful.

Jack Kough and Robert F. DeHaan. *Identifying Children with Special Needs*. Chicago: Science Research Associates, 1955. A volume that's old enough to vote and then some, but still very helpful. Available in both an elementary and a secondary edition.

Kim Marshall. *Opening Your Class with Learning Stations*. Palo Alto, CA: Learning Handbooks, 1975. This is a brief, lively, to-the-point guide for establishing learning stations and for avoiding the chaos that sometimes accompanies them.

Lady Bridget Plowden et al. *Children and Their Primary Schools: A Report of the Central Advisory Council for Education*. London: Her Majesty's Stationery Office, 1967. Usually referred to as the Plowden Report, this official document did much to support a less structured and more natural approach to education in England. Volume I contains the bulk of the report; volume II consists of statistical data. Available at Sales Section, British Information Services, 845 Third Ave., New York, NY 10022.

John I. Thomas. *Learning Centers; Opening Up the Classroom*. Boston: Holbrook Press, 1975. This is a longer, much more detailed version of the Marshall book that covers virtually every aspect of centering.

14 Managing Instructional Resources: Media and Materials

Key Questions

What resources are available for teaching elementary social studies?

What considerations are involved in using those resources?

What do you do when a school system doesn't have all of the resources you want?

Key Ideas

Instructional resources used improperly may be worse than having no instructional resources at all.

Identifying community resources is often less difficult than using those resources effectively.

Textbooks have a way of becoming the basis for a social studies program, not a resource to be used with it.

Instructional resources lurk in unlikely places; it depends on what you're looking for.

Introduction: The Year They Taught the Telephone Directory

Several years ago, Merrill Harmin and Sidney Simon (1965) created a satire in which a mythical superintendent of schools made a far-reaching curriculum decision. Henceforth, every teacher at one grade level would pioneer a new program based on one thing only: the telephone directory. The telephone directory!

There was some grumbling, of course, but grumbling often accompanies a curricular change. Grumbling or no, come September the teachers set out to accomplish their assigned task. Students were introduced to their new text and its marvelous system of organization—alphabetization. Then, with the necessary preliminaries completed, the students turned to learning their telephone books in earnest.

Homework assignments often required the students to memorize small sections of the phone book. In September, this included the names, addresses, and telephone numbers of individuals in the As and Bs. True, those assignments were challenging for some students. But then teachers found that developing worthwhile and interesting in-class activities could be challenging too, especially when they found that there weren't too many ways to vary questions like "What is the phone number of AAA Auto Service?" or "Who lives at 126 North Hathaway?" In fact, come January, the teachers found that this was one of those occasions when the midterm exam, covering the letters A–M, failed to motivate even the most grade-conscious students —or so it was reported.

In Harmin and Simon's account, the question arose, why teach the telephone directory in the first place? Teachers, parents, and especially the superintendent had to develop some reasonable answers to justify their "new" program. Their responses to several such pesky questions follow.

> Q: Why learn the telephone book?
> A: It develops good study habits, which will be necessary in college, and it trains the students to concentrate and apply themselves, qualities which are useful in adult life. Among other things, disciplined adults are what we want.
> Q: Won't they just forget the information after the tests?
> A: The less bright students will most likely forget a lot. However, we intend to have regular reviews in later grades and consequently the retention curve will hold up fairly satisfactorily.
> Q: Why work so hard learning the telephone book when directories are so handy when you actually need one?
> A: After all, this could be said about any subject we teach. If we want our people to look up information when they need it, why teach anything? Furthermore, life *is* hard and the sooner our students learn this the better off they will be (Harmin and Simon, 1965, p. 329).

The irony of satire is that there's usually a kernel of truth hidden in it. In this instance, you *could* legitimately use a telephone directory to teach social studies skills. True, the white pages can be a little limiting, despite their marvelous organizational scheme. However, you could, for example, cut sections from the white pages, scramble them, and then ask students to arrange them in alphabetical order. But that wouldn't necessarily be considered "social studies." However, students could analyze certain ethnic names, the Italian or Slavic names beginning with the letters M or T, for example, to see if they tended to cluster around certain telephone exchanges. By using the maps in the front of the directory, students might then be able to identify ethnic neighborhood patterns.

Potential student activities

If the white pages are somewhat limiting, the Yellow Pages might serve as a mother lode of instructional activities. Below we describe several potential activities (and questions) based on the Yellow Pages of the telephone directory.

Identify how multifaceted businesses and services are listed (organized) in the Yellow Pages. For example, how are those things related to automobiles organized? By titles? By services? By products? Or by some combination of these? Then how do the Yellow Pages handle food or medicine? Are all doctors listed under "Medical," for example?

Identify different ways in which the Yellow Pages could be organized. Then consider what those organizational patterns would mean for *(a)* users, *(b)* advertisers, and *(c)* the telephone company.

Determine what it costs, if anything, to be listed in the Yellow Pages. If charges do apply, speculate on how they are determined as well as on why businesses might pay to be listed. When schools are listed in the Yellow Pages, do you suppose they pay? Or are some things listed free?

Consider the historical dimension by comparing services listed in a ten- or twenty-year-old directory with those in a contemporary one. For example, pick one business, industry, or service and determine if there have been any changes over time. If so, of what nature?

Ryan and Ellis (1974, pp. 32–35) describe an activity in which children use the Yellow Pages from a 1950s and a contemporary directory as their major data source for comparing the number and distribution of the laundromats in a city. Students first plot the location of laundromats on a city map, then speculate about why things may have changed over the years. Similar activities could focus on other businesses—florists, hardware stores, movie theaters, etc. In fact, the size of the town or city you are dealing with imposes about the only limitation on this activity: it should be large enough to have more than one florist, theater, or whatever business you are working with.

Bare essentials

With all of the instructional materials now on the market, it's unlikely that you would ever need to rely on a telephone directory as your course of study. It's also unlikely that you will face the situation we did when we took our first teaching position in rural Ohio, and found that our instructional resources consisted of a globe, two wall maps, and a set of textbooks old enough to collect social security. When we borrowed an atlas and an almanac from the school library, we nearly wiped out its reference collection. Things in that school district have improved considerably since then, but at the time we discovered—the hard way—that we could teach social studies with only the most meager resources.

When we later took teaching positions in an affluent suburban school, one that had almost every conceivable resource a teacher could want, we often found ourselves turning back to activities based on our old "standbys"—the almanac, globe, etc. Our students just seemed to respond better to them. Today, with considerable hindsight and a lot more experience, we suspect that one reason those activities went so well was because we had designed them ourselves and knew precisely what they were to be used for. We were using materials we had selected and developed for our objectives, not someone else's. (*Our*, in this case, also includes the students.)

Not what, but how

If you are fortunate enough to get a teaching position where you have a wealth of instructional resources available, or, if you get a position where you have relatively few materials (which is probably more typical), we suspect that the quality of your social studies lessons will depend not on the amount of materials you have, but on how you use them. Sure, it's nice to have lots of materials, but the key ingredient is you—the teacher—and how you *use* instructional materials with your students.

In this section we have suggested several interrelated ideas. They include:

1   It is often possible to teach legitimate social studies lessons using some of the weirdest instructional resources—including the telephone directory.
2   Students tend to respond better to teacher-developed (or modified) activities and materials than they do to commercially-developed products.
3   Your students are likely to respond more positively to the activities and materials you have developed because (a) you have designed them (and they will like that) and (b) because you know precisely what they are intended to be used for.

In the next section we indicate several broad categories of instructional resources that may be available to you. We then consider how you can identify and locate appropriate teaching resources.

Instructional Resources: Print Materials

There is such a wealth of materials to use in teaching social studies that organizing the balance of this chapter in a way that made sense proved to be more difficult than we had anticipated. As a consequence, we have turned to an arbitrary and somewhat eclectic scheme that ranges from printed materials through nonprint, visual resources which include pictures, artwork, and film, to community resources, which include field trips and the like. We will deal with them in that sequence.

Textbooks

One resource above all others—the textbook—dominates the print materials category. Almost every school has them; in fact, some classes have access to several different texts. This doesn't mean that children use them—willingly or otherwise—just that they have access to them. We used the expression "almost every school" because we have found prospective teachers who, upon returning from school visits, were amazed to find that some schools— even those with ample financial resources—did not use social studies textbooks.

The absence of social studies texts can usually be explained by one of two factors: default or design. Default comes about when teachers are so pressured to teach other subjects—typically reading and mathematics—that they feel there's little time left to teach social studies. And, where social studies is treated incidentally, if at all, there's little need for a social studies text. The total absence of a social studies text or program is more likely to occur at the primary grade level and may, in some instances, be the result of an individual teacher's decision, not the result of a school-wide policy.

In still other school systems, the number of social studies texts in any classroom may be limited, by design, to a specified figure—often to no more than ten copies of a particular text. Since such classrooms may have as many as forty or fifty texts, it is technically incorrect to say that they don't have any social studies texts. What they don't have are enough copies of a single text for every child to have a copy of the same book. In such instances, teachers use a multitext approach—whether they like that kind of an approach or not. At the same time, however, limiting the number of texts usually prohibits teachers from turning social studies into a reading activity.

Multitext approaches

One principal of our acquaintance was so upset with the way some of her teachers handled social studies that she ordered ten copies of the four leading textbook series for each classroom. When the new books arrived, she promptly threw out half of the old texts. And, while some of her teachers were delighted with their new resources, others stated that "Unless each child had a copy of the same text, *they* were not going to teach social studies." No book—no social studies! And they didn't. Although that principal's plan backfired, the children were the ultimate losers. Yet when you think about it, how often should every student in the class be on the same page of their social studies text?

Despite the fact that generalizing about social studies textbooks can be a risky business, we will barge ahead to suggest that:

Elementary social studies textbooks can be as different as day and night.

You can get at least one good, usable teaching idea from every existing social studies textbook or accompanying teacher's guide (no matter how old and decrepit).

Textbooks have a way of becoming the basis for a social studies program, not resources to be used with it.

Using Textbooks When we first began working with prospective teachers, we tried to identify several general procedures that applied to using textbooks. We identified things like reading the selection before assigning it, helping children with new vocabulary, deciding what questions to ask, etc. But when we looked at our list, we found that the suggestions were things that almost anyone should find fairly obvious. In fact, the first time we presented our suggestions to a class, some students were insulted. That was the last time we tried to generalize about using social studies textbooks.

Texts as tools

It is easy enough to say that textbooks are tools, resources to be used for particular purposes; in fact, it just rolls right out. But for many of us, textbooks were seldom tools; they were not used *with* a social studies program, they *were* the social studies program! Everyone would read a certain number of pages each week and, if there was time (which there usually wasn't), the entire text was covered in one school year. There was no "selecting" about it. Neither was there much "using" involved in this procedure.

As much as we disapprove of totally textbook-based social studies programs, we also recognize that an identifiable basis is necessary, and that using a social studies textbook for that purpose may be the lesser evil—for one's first year of teaching at least. In addition, every textbook series has an accompanying teacher's guide, some of which are almost useless while others are more helpful than you might imagine. Anyway, by following the teacher's guide and interspersing activities of your own, you may be able to manage adequately.

For teachers who wish to depart from a textbook-dominated program as quickly as possible, the first step in that process is to shift your perception of the textbook. When you come to regard a text as a resource, as something to use if it suits your purposes—then you will have made the transition.

Potential uses

What are some of the different ways you might use textbooks? Consider the following possibilities:

As a source of background information that may be read either (a) prior to studying a topic or concept, or (b) *after* the need for the information has been established

As a point of departure for any number of purposes

As something students read on their own whenever they feel the need for additional information on a topic

As a source of in-class activities (or test questions)

As a contrasting point of view or as data for further analysis

As a means to confirm certain hypotheses *after* group discussion; "India is a 'poor' nation," etc.

As a vehicle to help identify the main idea of a section or of several related paragraphs

As a source for establishing the meaning of various terms (so that they need not be dealt with in class)

As a way of placating those people who think that a course isn't worthwhile unless it has a textbook associated with it

As a source for oral reading material (gads!)

With few exceptions, each of the above may be an appropriate use for an elementary social studies textbook, depending on your purpose.

Supplementary Materials

The kinds of supplementary materials available to elementary social studies teachers are simply astounding. They range from periodicals and current events newspapers (*My Weekly Reader, News Ranger,* etc.), through an almost unbelievable assortment of trade books (children's books), to prepackaged, skill-building kits on almost any topic you can name. We will examine supplementary materials in terms of these categories.

Current Events Publications   If your elementary school was like our elementary school, some of your teachers used one of the weekly or monthly current affairs periodicals: *My Weekly Reader* or *Current Events* from American Education Publications (American Education Publications, Education Center, Columbus, OH 43216), *Young Citizen* or *Junior Review* from Civic Education Service (Civic Education Service, 1733 K Street, N.W., Washington, DC 20006), one of the Scholastic publications (*News Pilot,* Gr. 1; *News Ranger,* Gr. 2; *News Trails,* Gr. 3; *News Explorer,* Gr. 4; *Newstime,* Gr. 5; or *Junior Scholastic,* Grs. 6–8 (Scholastic Magazines, Inc., 50

West 44th St., New York, NY 10036). These are still available and all of them are quite well written.

Instead of current events periodicals, your teachers may have relied more heavily on daily newspapers. From time to time, you may have been asked to bring in a current events article to share with the rest of the class. Unless certain limitations were put on the kind of clipping one could bring in, a typical assortment was likely to deal with topics such as: a mugging, an auto accident, last Saturday's Little League game, and a bank robbery in northwestern Nevada. Seldom would a child-selected article focus on a significant world crisis—Southeast Asia, the Middle East, or elsewhere—or on inflation, the cost of living, the changing views of morality, or the intricacies of political affairs—unless, that is, the teacher insisted on it. Even then, the typical elementary child is likely to be at a loss to either understand or interpret the significance of such events. It is with such situations that we find ourselves on the horns of the current events dilemma. On one hand, we would like elementary children to be interested in and aware of the events and issues that influence their lives, and ours. On the other hand, the complexity of issues and current events may go beyond both their level of comprehension and their concern. Indeed, the fact that some teachers have difficulty explaining something like "inflation," even though it's part of our daily existence, illustrates yet another dimension of the problem.

Amid these realities, you have at least two options for developing a current-issues program for your classroom: one is to maintain a current *events* program, where an event is defined as anything that has happened or is happening, either trivial or potentially significant; the other is to establish a current *affairs* (or issues) program, one which focuses on continuing, ongoing issues or concerns. Unless you are able to establish realistic limitations on a current *events* approach, you may find that it can quickly degenerate into a warmed-over version of the nightly news, the purposes for which might be better served if the class actually watched the six o'clock news on TV.

Because current *affairs* programs focus on fewer, in-depth studies of ongoing issues, they're less likely to reflect a random, piecemeal approach that can occur in a current events program. In a current affairs program, for example, your focus might be on different dimensions of the energy crisis. Or you might use changes in the price (or weight) of bubble gum or candy bars as an entree to the continuing study of rises in the cost of living. The energy crisis, to pursue our previous example, is characteristic of a continuing problem whose full significance may initially exceed the comprehension of elementary children. The idea of a current affairs program is to tie together the separate events of a continuing problem—increases in the price of oil, gas shortages and their effect, searches for alternative sources of energy, etc.—to help build the child's understanding of the significance of a problem that could remain beyond their comprehension if dealt with on an isolated "events" basis.

Weekly news periodicals often furnish the background so essential for providing children with a context within which they can begin to interpret a particular current event. At the same time, however, these periodicals typically feature different topics each week, and this tends to support a

Handling
current events

Current events
vs. current
affairs

piecemeal "events" approach. But what they lack in continuity may be compensated for by their broad coverage of events and happenings. Thus, the basic decision you face in developing a current affairs or current events program (and in deciding whether or not to use one of the current events periodicals) depends on how much in-depth understanding you are willing to sacrifice to gain broader topical coverage. In addition, since some current affairs may be extremely esoteric for elementary children, even if reduced to their simplest dimensions, you may be better off opting for the broader coverage you gain with an "events" approach, especially at the primary level. But if you plan to teach at the intermediate levels, the possibility of pursuing an "affairs" approach becomes much more realistic.

*Breadth vs.
depth*

Newspapers Daily newspapers have what the current events periodicals don't—coverage of local news. But teachers who look to newspapers solely as a source of local news are not looking far enough. In fact, in some schools teachers base almost their entire program—including social studies, math, language arts, and reading—on the daily newspaper. Their students do comparison shopping using the grocery ads, compute batting averages (math) using the sports page, invest (mythically) in the stock market, examine weather patterns (using the weather map and forecast), realphabetize the newspaper's directory, put scrambled headlines back together again, compare the amount of space devoted to various categories of articles (international news, national news, etc.), use small sections of the paper to compare the amount of factual data (reporting) with the amount of opinion (editorials), or compare the amount of space devoted to ads with the space devoted to news.

You might also give student groups identical collections of stories clipped from several newspapers and ask them to compose a front page, noting their reasons for including the articles they did. You could also remove the headlines from various articles and have children create their own based on the content of the story. They could then compare their heads with the originals. Or they could take several days' accumulation of radio–TV schedules and try to identify any patterns in TV programming.

*Using
newspapers*

There are still other things you could do with a daily newspaper, but these examples should serve to illustrate the idea. Note also that, for many of these activities, it isn't always necessary for the child to be able to read the articles in order to use the newspaper as a learning tool. As with most instructional resources, the essential idea is that you begin to consider the newspaper as something you can teach *with*, not simply teach *about*.

Trade Books A book designed for use in classroom settings is considered a textbook. But a book—fiction or nonfiction—intended for sale to the general public is considered a trade book. *Mike Mulligan and His Steam Shovel* (Burton, 1939), which we referred to earlier, is a juvenile trade book, as is Kenneth Grahame's (1954) classic, *Wind in the Willows,* and thousands and thousands of others. There are so many trade books available that the National Council for the Social Studies reviews only those books considered "most notable" during a given year. Thus, unless the book is (1) written primarily for children (K–8), (2) emphasizes human relations, (3) presents an original theme or a fresh slant on a traditional topic, (4) is highly readable, and (5) includes maps and illustrations where appropriate, it will not be included in their bibliography.

Most teacher's guides and curriculum guides suggest trade books to accompany almost any social studies topic you can name. In addition, the *Children's Catalog* (1972–75), which can be found in the public library, gives brief descriptions for over 2,500 children's books. It also indexes them by subject, author, and title.

Children's literature textbooks, such as *Children and Books* by Zena Sutherland and May Hill Arbuthnot (1977), and *Children's Literature in the Elementary School* by Charlotte Huck (1979) are excellent resources. In addition to considering children's books related to all subject areas, most of them have sections on books related to social studies teaching. They provide good overviews and brief reviews of some of the outstanding trade books in an area.

In discussing trade books about other lands, for example, Arbuthnot (1964, p. 499) states:

> The early books in this field had a tendency to present the picturesque at the expense of the usual. They gave us the China of bound feet, the Holland of wooden shoes and lace caps, South America by way of some primitive tribe of Indians about as typical of modern South America as Navahos would be of the United States. Some of these faults are still to be found in most recent books.

You can save yourself a lot of time searching for available trade books if you just tell your librarian what you are planning to do. Librarians worth their salt will give you invaluable help. In one of our last teaching positions, for example, we didn't have to go to the librarian—she came to us. Shortly after we would talk, a cartload of books would arrive for our classroom library. Her service stood in sharp contrast to that of another librarian we worked with whose primary concern was keeping books on the shelf so "she knew where they were." They were "her" books, and one almost needed to ask permission to use them.

Historical fiction, nonfiction, biography, you name it—somewhere there's a trade book that applies to whatever your class is studying. In addition to the classics, don't neglect the newer books that deal with ethnic literature —whether you teach in an urban school or elsewhere. You should be aware, however, that in rushing to "cash in" on the ethnic literature thrust of the 1960s, some of the materials produced were of questionable quality. Thus, you need to evaluate materials in this category.

Generally, there has been a marked improvement in ethnic literature and some of it is truly superb. *Beya's Train Ride* by Melba F. Peterson (1961), for example, is a charming picture story of an African child who moves from the village to the city and takes a train ride with his reluctant goat. It is a story quite suitable for students in kindergarten through second grade. *New Boy in School* by May Justus (1963) could very well serve as the basis for social studies lessons in the primary grades. It's a story of Lennie, a young

Children's literature

Ethnic literature

black boy, and his experiences in an integrated school in Nashville, Tennessee. After discussing Lennie's experience (you can almost be guaranteed a great discussion) you could then read the class portions from *The Big Push* by Betty Baker (1972). It's a story based on a historical incident that occurred when the white men forced Hopi Indian children to go to school.

Wordless books

Another subcategory of trade books that offers real potential for social studies classes are those having no text. *The Chicken and the Egg* by Iela and Enzo Mari (1970), for example, is a sequence of beautiful illustrations following the development of a chicken. Since there are no words, the children must supply them, and this adds immeasurable excitement to the book.

Trade books are like other instructional resources—you cannot use them unless you have them. But once you have the book in hand, you then have the option of using it in any one of several ways:

Trade Books

As supplementary reading for children

As background reading for yourself

As reference material for children to use

As the basis for units or lessons

As the basis for an individualized reading program that parallels whatever you are dealing with in social studies

Motivation

Fun

Reading to Children

When we first began teaching in an elementary school, we did so with the conviction that children were older and more grown up than kids used to be, and that they wouldn't tolerate childish things—things like being read to by an adult. Such things might be okay for primary youngsters, but older children wouldn't sit still for such practices—or at least so we thought. Yet in teaching an average group of sixth graders, it became our practice to read vignettes from various children's books about whatever we happened to be studying. They loved it.

Were our classes unique? We wondered about that until one day when we had the opportunity to visit a fifth-grade class. As it happened, the teacher was reading them a story—at their request. The story? *Peter Rabbit.* We could hardly believe it—a group of fifth graders, sitting in rapt attention while their teacher read them *Peter Rabbit.*

The moral? Perhaps it's that we shouldn't underestimate the power of a good story. But then perhaps kids may not be quite as old as they act, or as we (and they) may think they are.

Kits Kits are commercially available, self-contained packages of teaching materials. The MATCH units referred to previously are good examples of self-contained teaching kits. They include a teacher's guide, an assortment of student materials, reference materials for both students and teachers, and sometimes even filmstrips and/or films. Everything needed is in one neat package.

Other commercially available kits are not as encompassing as the MATCH kits, but neither are they topic oriented. Rather, they often focus on access and process skills. "The Thinking Box" (Benefic Press, 1900 N. Narragansett St., Chicago, IL 60639), for example, consists of a series of activity cards based on thinking skills and keyed to different subject areas. Other kits tend to focus on specific skill areas. SRA's Basic Skills series (Science Research Associates, 155 N. Wacker Dr., Chicago, IL 60606), for example, includes some beautifully packaged activities dealing with map and globe skills, and graph and picture analysis. In each case, the skills are broken down into their smallest components and then each subskill (or series of subskills) is presented to the student on sequentially organized task cards. After completing the task, students can check their results on the answer card provided.

Programmed Instruction Another group of self-contained resources (although not really kits per se) relies on programmed instruction. These materials often follow a workbook-type format in which the children write in their responses to various questions. Unlike most workbooks, however, the correct answers are kept shielded until the children have written in their response. But unless prevented from doing so by the materials themselves, some kids have been known to peek.

By design, most programmed materials tend to require one-word or short-phrase responses and, as such, focus heavily on factual material. In addition, it is difficult to skip around in programmed materials without altering the sequence that's built into them. What might be limitations for some students, however, can become assets for others, especially those who flourish on rigidly structured, factually based material. For them, programmed materials may be just the thing they need.

Workbooks Workbooks are available for many social studies textbook series, although you usually have to order them separately—they don't just come with the texts. Also, you may find that they are called *pupil study guides, activity guides,* or some other related term, perhaps in an effort to avoid the unsavory reputation sometimes associated with *workbooks.*

Like programmed materials, workbooks tend to emphasize factual material, so much so that it can become the child's primary focus. However, if you are teaching in a program that demands the kind of reinforcement workbooks offer, you may find them helpful.

Variety

Nonprint Materials

Reading and the written word—the print media—so dominate the American school that nonprint media—pictures, films, filmstrips, and the like—have a long way to go before they begin to approach the printed word in terms of educational impact. Nevertheless, since the mid-1950s we have witnessed substantial increases in not only the amount of nonprint media available but also in the different kinds of nonprint, nonreading-based materials designed specifically for educational purposes.

Pictures and Films

The largest and most obvious category of alternatives to the printed word is pictures—those things that are "worth a thousand words." They come in many forms: collections of study prints, films and filmstrips, and paintings and other works of art. Or they can be nothing more than illustrations and advertisements that you have clipped from a magazine, calendar, or some other source.

Study prints

Study prints can either be homemade, like the culture cards we described earlier, or purchased from commercial sources. The major difference is usually a matter of size; commercial study prints are typically large enough that they can be viewed by a group. Note that some school systems now have the equipment and expertise that enable them to enlarge small pictures so they are large enough to be used in group settings, or you can project a small picture on an opaque projector (at considerably less expense). A sample commercial study print, in this case a cartoon, is illustrated in Figure 14.1. (Note that the artist's rendering of igloo construction is inaccurate.)

One of our favorite student activities that involved artwork was developed by a fourth-grade teacher who had obtained reproductions of three different paintings of the Battle of Concord. Each painting was from a different time period. The earliest showed a ragtag group of American colonists fighting a well outfitted British Army. In the second painting, the patriots appeared much more organized and well kempt while the British looked slightly less robust and in somewhat greater disarray than in the earlier picture. In the most recent painting, the colonists were depicted as muscular, well fed, and well outfitted, while the British troops had taken on the slovenly appearance of the patriots in the first picture. The teacher's point? To show how the interpretation (and depiction) of an event—or at least artists' interpretation of an event—can change over time.

Photographs can sometimes reflect a photographer's biases, just as a painting may reflect an artist's view of the world. It depends on the kind of photograph you are dealing with; one needn't be unduly concerned about a photographer's biases in an aerial photograph, for example. For the most part, the real beauty of photographs lies in their ability to present selected yet uninterpreted data. Unfortunately, many educators tend to interpret the data for the viewer almost immediately. In the case of photographs and illustrations, an explanatory caption is usually provided, while for films a narration serves this purpose. Only recently have educators begun to recognize the educational value of what Federico Fellini and several other contemporary filmmakers already discovered, that is, that by eliminating the narration from a film and permitting the story line to grow out of the action, the film can become considerably more involving. Fellini's film *8½*, for example, was one of the first films that forced viewers to add their own story line. This, Fellini found, permitted them a sense of involvement and participation that was very much to their liking.

Figure 14.1 Commercial Study Print

"I STILL THINK NANOOK SOLD OUT TO THE OIL COMPANIES."

Source: Documentary Photo Aids "Anti-" and "Pro" Pollution Cartoons. Cartoon by Don Wright.

In stark contrast is the traditional educational film which shows, for example, a jungle scene in which it is raining heavily. As the scene flashes on the screen, the narrator announces, "It often rains heavily in the jungle." Educational filmmakers, too, have discovered that it really isn't necessary to tell viewers—either adults or children—that "It often rains heavily in the jungle," and that the same thing can be accomplished simply by showing several jungle scenes in which it is raining—heavily.

Nonnarrated films

Narrated films are available for almost any topic you can name, but there is also a growing body of educational films that have no narration, only the natural sound of whatever the film depicts. Students in "Man: A Course of Study" (MACOS), for example, see over six hours of nonnarrated film that beautifully and simply portrays the life of the Netselik Eskimo (*Fishing at the Stone Weir, Caribou Hunting at the Crossing Place, Autumn River Camp,* Parts I and II, and *Winter Sea Ice Camp,* Parts I and II). Unlike some of the other MACOS materials, these films are available to anyone from most film libraries. A similar series of films traces the daily activities of the Bozo people, an African tribe living on the Niger River. If you have not yet seen a nonnarrated film, by all means do so if you can; you should find it a captivating experience.

Eliminating the narration automatically eliminates any vocabulary problems that the narration might present for student viewers. Consequently, the same nonnarrated film can sometimes be used by first graders, twelfth graders, and even adults, usually with a different emphasis at each level.

In addition to the more traditional 16mm. films, some schools are now equipped to use a Super-8 film format. Super-8 films usually come in plastic cassettes that simply plug into the projector much as tape cassettes fit into a tape recorder. This eliminates threading, rewinding, and the other mechanical horrors sometimes associated with movie projectors.

Filmstrips, Slides, Tapes, and Records Filmstrips offer a valuable pictorial resource and, like films, are available on almost any topic. Also, since most schools buy their own filmstrips but are forced to rent or borrow films on a predetermined schedule, you typically will have greater flexibility in scheduling filmstrips for your use. In addition, you can vary the amount of time you spend on each frame, something you cannot do very readily with a film. This can be an important feature, especially if you wish to use several frames from a filmstrip as the basis for an inquiry activity.

In an attempt to make filmstrips more involving—that is, involve more senses than just sight—some filmstrips are accompanied by records or tape cassettes that provide a narration. Aside from the fact that the quality of the narration (or even the filmstrips themselves) varies tremendously, you also lose a degree of control over the time you can spend on each frame when you use the narration. Of course you could always stop the narration, but if you've never tried to find the correct spot on a record in a darkened room —without cutting new grooves in the record—you may be in for an ear-shattering experience. Recording the narration on a tape cassette will save a lot of unnecessary frustration and gain considerably more flexibility. By all means, preview any film or filmstrip (and accompanying narration) before you use it.

If the sequence in which you show a series of pictures is important, you are probably better off with slides, not filmstrips. Of course, a filmstrip can be cut apart and the individual frames mounted as slides. But doing so might incur the wrath of your colleagues, especially those who desire the self-contained package a filmstrip offers.

Some teachers deduct a portion of their vacation costs from their income tax because they take 35mm. color slides to use in their teaching. You need to be cautious of this practice on two counts. First, the Internal Revenue Service may rule that the picture taking was incidental to the vacation and thus disallow the deduction. Second, and perhaps more important, kids should not be sentenced to a session of "My Vacation in Mexico" simply because you happened to take some pictures along the way. Otherwise, their experience is likely to be akin to the time you had to sit through an evening of slides of your Aunt Bertha's trip to Yellowstone National Park.

Tapes and recordings (records) are instructional resources that are both nonprint and nonvisual. But, because they appeal to only one sense—hearing —they tend to require a greater degree of concentration than do multisensory media. Thus, unless the tape or record is especially interesting or unless

Set sequence

it accompanies something else—a written script, a worksheet, or a filmstrip, etc., as tapes and records often do—there is a possibility that the children will tune out after a relatively short time. Adults, of course, will do the same thing, often much more quickly.

In many instances, tapes (and tape recorders) can be helpful tools, especially when used by students to collect data rather than by teachers to present data. When students interview individuals, for example, tape recordings can provide an accurate record of what was said; they also eliminate the need to write everything down. Tapes have also proved useful in helping children rehearse presentations of various kinds. In fact, sometimes student-recorded material will become an integral part of a group presentation. However, should you wish to use taped or recorded materials with students —as a means of conveying information to them—then the general rule is to keep it short. If you don't, your students may very well "tune out" more quickly than you would anticipate.

Tools for students

Realia Remember when a fellow student brought in his "genuine" Indian arrowhead collection to share with the class? Or when someone's relatives had been to the Orient and brought back an authentic Japanese fan, which everyone in your class got to look at but couldn't touch? These things—the arrowheads, the Japanese fan, the million and one other real objects that might be associated with social studies teaching—are all encompassed by the term *realia*.

Most realia tend to be an adjunct to rather than an integral part of social studies teaching, primarily because the objects are precious to their owners, often part of a collection, and as such they would rather not have them handled and possibly broken. Thus they often become things to be displayed —looked at but not used—in the course of a teaching activity, and perhaps rightfully so. In fact, some realia are probably best handled via display and in a passing fashion, such as when a student brings in a World War II bayonet during your study of colonial America. Using realia unrelated to whatever your class is studying is difficult to justify on almost any grounds. But assume, for a moment, that somewhere in your travels you acquired a colonial candle mold (and your class will be studying colonial America). What are your options? You have several.

Using the real thing

First, you could display the device and say, "This is a colonial candle mold." You could then proceed to describe how it was used. That's one option.

You might also place the mold in a prominent location but say nothing about it. Questions are going to be asked about it, you can be sure. But to the question, "What is it?" you could respond "What do you think it is?" You might then mount a large sheet of paper near the mold and ask the children to list what they think it is. At a convenient time, you might display an illustration of someone using a candle mold, again saying nothing about it. Someone will soon notice it, and you may not even need to say anything else at all. Or, you might pose the question, "How are candles made today?" which will initiate another adventure.

You could also make the candle mold the focus of study for an activity by asking students to identify the different functions it might serve and what they know about the people who made it. In other words, it can be the basis for a structure-function lesson.

If the function of the realia is obvious, you might wish to take a different tack. Take the Japanese fan mentioned earlier, for instance. You might want to ask who uses fans in Japan and why? Are they necessarily to keep Japanese women cool? And does this mean that Japan has a warm climate? Should you pursue this line of questioning, identify—in advance—some sources the students can go to to validate their possible answers. Indeed, they may find that fans are an integral part of a Japanese dancer's equipment, much as jewels play a role in the activities of some belly dancers.

Realia kits

Some museums and local historical societies have realia kits they make available for use in elementary schools, usually on a loan basis. Typically, the artifacts are reproductions (as are the realia in the MATCH units and the Minnesota Project materials), but a reproduction can often serve just as valid an educational purpose as the real thing—and at a fraction of the cost. If your state has a state museum, and many do, you can begin by writing to them. If they are unable to help you, they should be able to tell you who can. In many cases, though, you will not find it necessary to go further than your own community.

Community Resources

Every community, regardless of size, has someone who has been somewhere or who knows something that can be useful in your social studies program. And almost every community has something or some place you can visit that would also be an asset to your social studies program. In fact, most teachers have little problem identifying community resources. Instead, their problem lies in *selecting* among those resources that most closely match their social studies program (and their school system's budget).

Resource Persons

Identifying individuals in the community who have specialized knowledge or experience is not especially difficult. The list can go from authors to zookeepers. The more challenging task is using those resource people effectively.

Part of the problem occurs because resource people are, by definition, specialists in an area. As such, they are familiar with the intricacies, the nuances, and the jargon of their specialization. Your students, however, may be at a level where their primary concern is with the most fundamental aspects of a specialized area. Of course, most resource people recognize that they are dealing with children and adjust their presentations accordingly, but sometimes they unwittingly slip anyhow.

All things considered, the local history buff who, for example, gets enmeshed in the minutiae of who married whom in the early 1840s can't count on maintaining student interest for very long. Once their interest is lost, your students may begin to get a bit restless—and understandably so—but your guest speaker may take it as a personal affront and, rightly or wrongly, present a public relations problem for you by suggesting that "They can't maintain discipline in that school anymore" (or something to that effect). It may seem an imposition, but you'll be doing yourself and your resource person a favor if you clarify in advance exactly what you want that person to cover. The intent is to ensure a successful experience for both the resource person *and* your class.

A related problem arises because many resource people are ill-equipped to do more than talk to students. Unless they deal with children on a regular basis, they are unlikely to have audiovisual aids or other media to enliven their presentation. Even if they have such media, however, the more basic issue depends upon you and your class. That is, and this cannot be stressed too heavily, you will need to have worked with your class to establish a need or desire for whatever information the resource person can provide. One of the most helpful things you can do is provide resource people with a list of questions or topics your class has developed in advance of the presentation. This helps ensure that (1) the class has at least a passing acquaintance with whatever the resource persons will deal with (otherwise they wouldn't be able to frame intelligent questions), and (2) the resource persons will have an idea of the level of the class's concerns and can prepare themselves accordingly.

The key to using resource people successfully probably lies as much in the advance preparation you do as it does in the visit itself. Our intent here is not to suggest that using resource people is an insurmountable problem, by any means. But you do need to be aware that there are some dimensions to a seemingly simple task (getting someone to talk about something) that can yield unhappy consequences for all concerned if left unattended.

A final suggestion about using resource people: be wary of those individuals who insist upon talking to your class. Among the thousands of people who volunteer their services, there are always those few who would use the schools as a platform for their special causes. Even if you are sympathetic to the cause—whatever it may be—you may risk your professional future by honoring their offer. Before issuing an invitation, be certain to check school policies and inform the appropriate administrative personnel (principal, etc.) of your intentions.

Field Trips and Tours

What teachers sometimes call "field trips" are actually tours. By taking their students on tours of museums, bakeries, fire stations, or any other place you can think of—a funeral home?—teachers provide enriching, hands-on experiences that would be impossible in a classroom. Other teachers, however, take their students on field trips to museums, bakeries, fire stations, and so forth. The distinction between *tours* and *field trips* is based on (1) what has taken place in the classroom before leaving on the trip, and (2) the students' perceptions as to why they are going. When scientists "go out into the field," for example, they have usually identified their purpose for going in advance. Thus, when archaeologists decide to "dig" at a particular site, that decision is usually based on (1) prior research, (2) a clear sense of purpose (for digging), and (3) previously identified questions or problems that they hope to have answered. Likewise, when students go on a field trip to a bakery, for example, they arrive armed with *previously identified* questions that they want

Field trips provide hands-on (or hands-off!) experiences that have a way of capturing children's attention.

Prior questions

answers for; "Do bakeries grind their own flour?" "Do bakeries use the same kind of flour available in supermarkets?" etc. In other words, as a result of the students' previous classroom experience, they arrive at the bakery with a clearer sense of *why* they are there. The fact that they may probably enjoy the experience and learn things they don't have questions about is simply extra frosting on the cake. On the other hand, students taking a tour of a bakery may have a general interest in what bakeries do, but because they may lack previous classroom experience, their sense of purpose (for being there) is apt to be more vague than for students on a field trip.

Both tours and field trips add a dimension of virtually immeasurable value to education. However, most experienced teachers can tell you horror stories about things that went wrong on a field trip or tour—the time someone got lost, the time four children spent all of their lunch money at the souvenir stand, or the time they neglected to have the children visit the lavatory before leaving on the return trip. These kinds of logistical problems can have you tearing your hair out in short order. Then, too, students sometimes assume that rules for classroom conduct don't apply to activities outside of school, as on a field trip or tour, giving rise to discipline-related problems. Our hunch is that the clearer sense of purpose associated with field trips may result in fewer discipline problems, but there is certainly no guarantee in that. Indeed, most students realize that a teacher's disciplinary options on a field trip or tour are limited, which may be why teachers often bring several allies (parents) along with them.

Preplanning can eliminate some of the logistical and discipline-related problems associated with field trips and tours. We offer the following suggestions (based on Rathbun, 1977, and Midgett, 1979):

Obtain administrative approval *before* announcing the trip to students. (On the application form, always use "field trip," even if you're planning a tour to the zoo—it sounds better and may be easier for the administrator to justify to "higher-ups.")

In picking a date, avoid Mondays. Over the weekend, kids often forget to bring their lunches, spending money, etc.

Field-trip Guidelines

Recruit, screen, *and instruct* parent chaperones so that they will be able to contribute significantly to the trip. Don't wait until just before leaving to tell parents what you expect of them. Send a note home beforehand that outlines: (1) what you expect parents to do, (2) rules you have discussed with students, and (3) any other pertinent information.

Divide students into task groups well before the trip is to take place. Each task group should have a specific responsibility; e.g., recorders (keep records and journals), collectors (obtain necessary items for or from the trip), photographers, public relations (thank-you note writers), and maintenance (clean up).

If taking a tour, select an impressive place. If you were bored on your last trip to the sewage treatment plant, for example, your students will probably be bored too.

Take everyone, including your troublemakers. Leaving them behind for disciplinary reasons could lead to deep-seated resentment that you may never overcome.

Send parental permission slips home unless the school uses a blanket permission form covering all field trips for the year.

Even with signed permission slips, you may be legally liable if you agree to supervise students in too large an area. We're not talking about the Astrodome here, since trying to supervise students in two large halls of a museum could make you liable if something happened to someone. Err on the safe side and take one adult for each group of five children.

Use name tags (including the school name). This is often essential for young students; for older students it enables chaperones to call them by name.

Avoid going in private cars whenever possible; the legal hazards (insurance coverage, etc.) are considerable.

Walking trips

Don't overlook walking field trips to nearby places. Supermarkets, banks, bakeries, as well as those old standbys—the post office and fire station—often welcome visits from school children. But whether you walk or take a bus, the crucial element is that your students understand why they are going on the field trip. Otherwise, field trips and tours may be seen as a "lark" or just another "day off" from school.

The Columbo School: A Case Study in Using Community Resources

Several years ago, a school district announced that it would be unable to conduct a remedial summer program for students having academic and social difficulties in school. Were summer school to be offered, forty-two students, ranging in age from nine through twelve, had indicated that they would sign up. But without teachers, the possibility of operating a summer school seemed remote. However, in the late spring, the school district inquired as to whether the local university would be willing to permit its teacher-education students to conduct a summer-school program (under university supervision). It was!

Before the summer program began, the undergraduate teachers met in long (and sometimes heated) planning sessions. Some of them insisted that, if their school was to be skills-focused, "skills" meant reading and mathematics, and that if they really wanted to help pupils, they would "hit" these the hardest. But were there other skills, skills involving thinking, reasoning, question asking, observing, listening, and the like? And, could working on these skills ultimately have an effect on pupils' reading levels? Perhaps! The questions kept coming.

The teachers eventually decided that the model for their program would focus on the kind of detective work their pupils had seen on the TV program, "Columbo." The Columbo School was born.

The teachers viewed a videotape of "Columbo," watching in awe as Peter Falk went about solving the crime. When they replayed the tape, they focused on the skills Columbo used: he observed things, people, the situation, and even wrote things in his little book; he formed hypotheses, collected data, interviewed people, and tested his ideas. The format was great. Viewers got most of their information in the first quarter of the show, and then observed Columbo as he worked things out.

Columbo's (Peter Falk's) major skills were observation and reasoning. With these as a basis, the school's model came into being. Instead of books—instead of another frontal attack on reading—it was determined that one city block surrouunding the school would furnish everything the curriculum needed. Various thinking skills would be introduced and worked with as they were needed. The teachers would act as "inspectors"—checking, asking questions, doubting, supervising, and acting as resource people, while students were divided into "patrol" units. The school? It became "precinct" headquarters.

There was apprehension and excitement when the students finally arrived. The apprehension stemmed from doubts about maintaining discipline in such a nontraditional school, about whether kids would like the approach, about whether or not they (kids and teachers) could handle the approach, and about the skills that would be required of them. The excitement came from not knowing exactly what would happen in advance, from the flexibility that was involved, and from having no texts or workbooks to fall back on.

Skills?

Discipline?

What did the students study? Basically, they asked questions and then set out to find answers. The following are examples of the types of questions the patrols asked and the processes they used to answer them.

1 *Are old cars more likely to get parking tickets than new ones?*
Theory: "Poor people get more tickets, especially poor people who drive older cars."

The patrols recognized the need to operationalize words. What, for example, was an "old car?" Did it depend on age, condition, or what?
Tasks: Set up ways of checking violations and ticketing.
Record where and when tickets were given.
Organize the data by day, time, place, "old," "new."
Take into account "sales" days, out-of-state cars, time of meter maid patrols.
Conclusions: There was no difference in the frequency of tickets given to "new" and "old" cars. Based on the observed data, the theory did not hold. However, certain times of day and certain places did make a difference.

2 *Are older cars more likely to have worn tires than new cars?*
Theory: "Only poor people (including college students?) drive old cars. Worn-down tires would indicate that people didn't have money.
Tasks: Operationalize words such as "old," "new," and "worn-down."
Figure out a way of determining tire wear. Would it be necessary to test all four tires on all cars?
Organize the data—did the make of the car make a difference? How could the table show what was found?
Think about questions such as: Will people think you are stealing hubcaps when you are really measuring the tread depth? What if a tire is worn only on one side? How could you determine how many miles were on the car? Did the way people drove (e.g., "burning rubber") make any difference?
Conclusions: Brand new cars (made that year) had good tire treads. But tread wear didn't seem to go along with the age of the car. You couldn't tell whether people were poor or not by looking at such things.

Other patrol studies involved who used fast-food restaurants and who did not, what time of day the restaurants were used most, the average length of time each customer spent in the places, and whether fast-food restaurants were faster than regular restaurants.

Everyone learned, including the teachers. Participants learned how difficult it is to observe in a systematic way, how difficult it is for different people to observe the same thing the same way, and how important it is to plan an approach—to think about all the things that might make data take on different meanings. People learned about the assumptions they make, how important it is to record what one sees *and* when and how observations take place, how to organize information and how to communicate it, the difference between "testing" and "proving" an idea, how there can be different explanations for the same thing, how to "sharpen" questions, how to use numbers, how to recognize what is unknown, and more, much more. In fact, we can't walk down that city block any more without looking for tickets, tires, the meter maid . . . looking at them in a different way.

On one occasion a child was overheard telling her mother that "This really wasn't a school because we studied what really happens. . . ." On another occasion, a recently defrocked inspector (teacher) asked, "Did this experience make any difference in how the kids will do in the usual school setting, especially in reading and math?" "I don't know," another former inspector chimed in, "but we could study that."

Using Community Resources

We have suggested that using community resources—either in the form of resource persons or field trips—involves both a logistical and substantive dimension. The logistical side involves such things as contacting individuals, arranging for buses (and rest stops, and parental approval, and parental assistance, and . . .), while the substantive dimension includes things related to the content that you and your class (and perhaps a resource person) will be dealing with.

Many school districts have specific guidelines concerning resource persons and field trips, most of which specify the logistical (and legal) considerations you need to be aware of. Sometimes they also deal with substantive questions. Could you, for example, invite an avowed communist to speak to your class, or take your students on a field trip to a slaughterhouse or a funeral home? Consider how you would respond if you were an elementary principal and a teacher came to you with such a request. If the teacher could demonstrate a clear relationship between the slaughterhouse (or the funeral home, or the communist) and whatever the class had been studying, would it make any difference in your decision? The issues here are far from simple.

Planning considerations

Once you have gotten the necessary permissions, the ultimate success of the experience will probably depend on the preliminary work you do before a resource person enters your classroom or before your class leaves on the field trip. The basic questions you need to ask yourself include:

Is a community resource appropriate for the purposes of my group?

Have I planned preliminary activities that provide a context within which my class can interpret whatever they hear or see?

Have I identified appropriate follow-up activities?

Does my class have an identifiable (felt) need for the information the resource can provide?

Does my class understand what is expected of them—both in terms of their conduct and what it is they are to learn?

If you can answer these questions in the positive, you'll be on the way to making effective use of the resources your community can provide. If not, keep your aspirin handy.

Acquiring Instructional Resources

Where do teachers get the stuff they teach with? The school system usually furnishes paper, chalk, paper clips, and that sort of thing, and it may (but not always) provide teachers with a budget from which they can purchase additional teaching materials. Where such budgets exist, they have one universal characteristic—small! Indeed, it's the rare school that can supply teachers with everything they might like to use for teaching purposes.

In acquiring instructional resources, your first step is to identify what is available from commercial publishers or other sources. There are several large publishers of educational materials and a host of smaller ones, and you will usually find their catalogs in the school library, the resource center, or sometimes even in the teachers' lounge. Or, you can obtain copies of the major teachers' magazines—*Learning* (530 University Avenue, Palo Alto, CA 94301), *Teacher* (677 Schoolcrest Drive, Marion, OH 43302) or *Instructor* (7 Bank Street, Dansville, NY 14437)—buy yourself a bunch of stamps, and begin answering the ads for materials that appeal to you. The two major social studies journals, *Social Education* (Journal of the National Council for the Social Studies, 3615 Wisconsin Ave. N.W., Washington, D.C. 20016) and *The Social Studies* (4000 Albemarle St. N.W., Suite 500, Washington, D.C. 20016), are also good sources for identifying current materials. Some of these periodicals also have special introductory rates for student teachers.

Some school systems accept teachers' requests for materials in the spring and purchase the materials during the following summer. This often means that you don't have the opportunity to purchase materials during your first year of teaching. In that event, you will be forced to do what hundreds of other teachers do—buy materials yourself. But before doing that, you have a couple of other options. First, find out if there isn't something you could use that is free (or inexpensive) and/or, second, consider making your own materials. There are so many free or inexpensive materials available that schools often subscribe to one or more of the guides to free materials. These include:

Educator's Guide to Free Social Studies Materials, edited by Patricia H. Suttles and William H. Hartley. Educators Progress Service, Inc., Randolph, WI 53956. Note: guides to other free and inexpensive material are also available.

Free and Inexpensive Materials on World Affairs, by Leonard S. Kenworthy. Teachers College Press, 1234 Amsterdam Ave., New York, NY 10027.

Free and Inexpensive Teaching Aids, by Bruce Miller. Box 369, Riverside, CA 92502.

Free and Inexpensive Learning Materials (updated annually). George Peabody College of Vanderbilt University, Nashville, TN 37203.

Selected Free Materials for Classroom Teachers, 5th ed., by Ruth H. Aubrey. Fearon Publishers, 6 Davis Dr., Belmont, CA 94002.

Social Studies School Service Catalog (free). 10,000 Culver Blvd., P.O. Box 802, Culver City, CA 90230.

Where to Find It Guide, published annually in a fall issue of *Scholastic Teacher.* Scholastic Magazines, Inc., 50 W. 44th St., New York, NY 10036.

Sources

Free materials

The quality of free and inexpensive materials can vary tremendously, so you'll need to be selective. One of the first questions you might want to consider is why various concerns would be willing to sell materials inexpensively or give them away. Indeed, before using some free or inexpensive material with students, you ought to "look your gift horse in the mouth."

Some of the best teaching resources we have encountered are those teachers have developed themselves. Most of the student activities in this book, for example, were built by teachers. Most of the activities went through some refining—that is, they were tried out with students and then revised —but once developed, they become a resource to be used in future years.

The process of developing your own teaching materials is not as difficult as you might suspect (a large dose of common sense is about as helpful as anything). Typically, you would:

1   Identify *(a)* the major concept(s) you want to teach, and/or *(b)* the major question(s), issue(s), or skill(s) you want the children to deal with. Note: This is sometimes the most difficult step of all.
2   Decide what kind of format you want to use—a fact sheet, a mini case study, role playing, limited-choice decision making, etc.
3   Build the activity (and duplicate as needed).
4   Use it with your students.
5   Revise as needed, based on what you found in Step 4.

Sometimes it's wise to add a Step 3*(a)*. That is, before you duplicate an activity for students, share it with someone you can rely on for honest feedback—a colleague, a fellow student teacher, etc. You are almost certain to find that what you thought was perfectly obvious isn't, and thus gain a chance to make appropriate adjustments before trying it out with your students.

The following mini case study is an example of an activity designed by two student teachers who knew the concept they wanted to teach, but who couldn't find any ready-made materials with which to teach it. So they developed a mythical story about the animals from Sunshine Forest. See if you are able to identify the underlying concept (it isn't stated).

"Sunshine Forest"
(by Mary Katts and Perry Trilling).
Once upon a time there was a beautiful forest. It was called Sunshine Forest. In the forest lived a happy group of animals: Peter, the rabbit; Chuck, the woodchuck; Sally, the squirrel; Florence, the field mouse; and Benjy, the deer. The animals were all friends. They liked each other, and they all had nice shiny fur and sparkling teeth and were very athletic. They loved to play games where they ran really fast!

One day a new animal moved into Sunshine Forest. As she walked through the forest, all the animals watched her. She was a pig, and a clumsy one at that! She couldn't run fast because she was always falling down. And she had mud splattered all over her body. The Sunshine animals began to laugh and tease her.

"Hey, clumsy," squeaked Sally.

"You sure are fat," chattered Chuck.

"Why don't you take a bath?" asked Florence.

The pig just looked at the animals and then sat down and cried. She sobbed and sobbed, and giant tears rolled down her plump cheeks.

Then Benjy walked up to the poor pig and put a hoof on her shoulder.

"Don't cry, friend," said Benjy. "Follow me and I'll help you."

They went down to the lake and Benjy told the pig to jump in. With a squeal of delight, the pig plunged into the water and swam around. When she came out, all the animals cheered and patted her on the back.

"Not bad, *not* bad," they said in unison.

"We hope you'll stay and live and play with us," said Benjy. "By the way, what's your name?"

"Pam," she happily replied. "I'd love to stay."

The ideas they wanted to teach? Actually there were several: that groups have norms (standards of behavior), and that those who deviate from group norms may be subjected to ridicule, abuse, and rejection. After reading the story and talking about how they felt, the children shared incidents from their own experience in which similar events took place. They also discussed how the "norms" were established and maintained in their own classroom.

Summary

Common sense would suggest that the more senses a particular medium can appeal to, the better the learning experience that should result. However, there are some recent data that suggest this isn't necessarily the case; these findings indicate that films, for example, do not necessarily produce better learning experiences than, say, tape recordings or filmstrips.

In radio's heyday, families gathered "Walton style" to listen to their favorite adventure stories—"The Shadow," "The Green Hornet," "The Lone Ranger," etc. Because everyone was dependent on only one sense, hearing, they were forced to build mental pictures of what was happening in the story. In other words, they had to use their imaginations to fill in the "blanks." With television, however, came both picture and sound. Viewers no longer had to imagine what was going on because everything was presented for them. Thus, TV (and movies) may tend to require less imagination and, hence, somewhat less mental participation on the viewer's part. So contrary to what common sense might suggest, media that appeal to one sense only may produce better learning experiences than some multi-sensory media.

The implicit expectation for all instructional media and materials is that they reflect accurate, quality "stuff." The prime requirement for almost any media form is that it be able to capture the children's attention. Unless it does, it may not make a lot of difference how many senses it appeals to.

Suggested Activities

1 Congratulations! Your budget request has been approved and the Board of Education has authorized $150 per teacher for social studies teaching materials. You can really use some new materials since your textbook, for example, carries a 1970 copyright. Your other materials consist of a wall map of the world and one of the United States, a 16-inch globe, and an almanac dated 1980. How will you (or your team) spend those funds?

2 In small groups, plan a field trip for an elementary class. Then, as a group, go on the field trip you have planned, making certain someone brings a camera. Share your findings with the rest of the class; include your preliminary research, slides of the trip itself, and the way in which you would follow it up.

References

Arbuthnot, May Hill. *Children and Books.* (3rd ed.) Glenview, IL: Scott Foresman, 1964.

Baker, Betty. *The Big Push.* New York: Coward, McCann & Geoghegan, 1972.

Burton, Virginia Lee. *Mike Mulligan and His Steam Shovel.* Boston: Houghton Mifflin, 1939.

Children's Books to Enrich the Social Studies. Washington, D.C.: National Council for the Social Studies, 1961.

Children's Catalog. (12th ed.) New York: Wilson; plus Annual Supplements (1972–75).

Grahame, Kenneth. *Wind in the Willows.* New York: Charles Scribner's Sons, 1954.

Harmin, Merrill, and Simon, Sidney. "The Year the Schools Began Teaching the Telephone Directory." *Harvard Educational Review* 34 (Summer, 1965): 326–31.

Huck, Charlotte S. *Children's Literature in the Elementary School.* (3rd ed., updated) New York: Holt, Rinehart and Winston, 1979.

Justus, May. *New Boy in School.* New York: Hastings House, 1963.

Mari, Iela, and Mari, Enzo. *Chicken and the Egg.* New York: Pantheon Books, 1970.

Midgett, Barry. "Tight-ship Trips." *Teacher* 97 (September 1979): 90–94.

Peterson, Melba F. *Beya's Train Ride.* New York: Friendship Press, 1961.

Rathbun, Dorothy. "Foolproof Field Trips." *Learning* 5 (April 1977): 70–75.

Ryan, Frank L., and Ellis, Arthur K. *Instructional Implications of Inquiry.* Englewood Cliffs, NJ: Prentice-Hall, 1974.

Sutherland, Zena and Arbuthnot, May Hill. *Children and Books.* (5th ed.) Glenview, IL: Scott Foresman, 1977.

Suggested Readings

Ellen Barnes, Bill Eyman, and Maddy Bragar Engolz. *Teach and Reach: An Alternative Guide to Resources for the Classroom.* Syracuse, NY: Human Policy Press, 1974. Actually a guide to resources for the alternative classroom, this volume presents a wealth of information in a way that reflects a real concern for kids. Write to: Human Policy Press, Box 127, University Station, Syracuse, NY 13210.

Leonard S. Kenworthy. *Social Studies for the Seventies.* Waltham, MA: Blaisdell, 1969. Both a good social studies methods text and an almanac of references and resources.

It is to Kenworthy that we turn when we get a phone call from a teacher who wants to know where she can find some information on "X."

Dorothy Rathbun. "Foolproof Field Trips." *Learning* 5 (April 1977): 70–75. Like most *Learning* articles, this one is comprehensive and interestingly written. It is especially good because it deals with the nuances that you might not think of otherwise; things like deciding which parents are to act as chaperones.

William E. Patton (ed.). *Improving the Use of Social Studies Textbooks.* Bulletin 63. Washington, D.C.: National Council for the Social Studies, 1980. This eighty-page guide shows you how to use and update social studies texts. The section on correcting ethnic and sex-role stereotyping should be especially helpful.

Richard Saul Wurman (ed.). *Yellow Pages of Learning Resources.* Philadelphia: Group for Environmental Education, Inc., 1972. This 94-page booklet actually looks like the Yellow Pages of a phone directory, and it includes a wealth of activities based on using the city as a learning resource. We highly recommend it.

15 Evaluation Strategies: Beyond a Necessary Evil

Key Questions

How does one gather good evaluative data?

How can one use good evaluative data?

How does norm-referenced evaluation differ from criterion-referenced evaluation?

Are evaluation and grading compatible?

How does one evaluate higher cognitive skills without forcing students to memorize massive amounts of information?

Key Ideas

Evaluation is closely tied to objectives. It is through evaluation that unstated objectives may be revealed.

Not only do criteria for evaluation have multiple sources, but evaluation has multiple uses.

The quality and accuracy of evaluative judgments are a function of the quality and accuracy of evaluative data. Thus, "tricky" test items are actually self-defeating.

Subjectivity is an inherent characteristic of evaluation: the goal is to limit and control its influence.

The materials and strategies used to evaluate higher cognitive skills may closely resemble the materials and strategies used to teach those skills initially.

Introduction

Sally Brown, that diminutive educational philosopher, has raised some of those thorny questions that teachers and students have wrestled with for years. Indeed, should teachers grade their students by applying the same standards to everyone, or should they take their students' effort into account? Or, should both factors be taken into consideration?

Discussions involving grading, testing, and evaluation often generate more heat than light, simply because many individuals use these terms as if they were synonymous—which they are not. In many circles, people erroneously assume that evaluation takes place only at the end of an instructional episode, usually in the form of a test. And, as everyone knows, once you've

taken a test, you get a grade. Standardized tests are the notable exception, of course, because they usually don't "count," at least not for grading purposes. That idea—the notion of a test that doesn't count—is difficult for many children to deal with because they too often lump testing, evaluation, and grading together.

Distinguishing among evaluation, testing, and grading is the first of three major purposes of this chapter. Our premise is that clarity about those differences may help to eliminate some of evaluation's unsavory and often undeserved reputation as "a necessary evil." Our second purpose is to examine the different forms of evaluation and the various functions they serve. Finally, in addition to identifying several alternative (nontest) evaluation strategies you might wish to employ, we also examine some recommended test-construction techniques.

The Dimensions of Evaluation

① identifying criteria

② measuring an individual's performance with respect to those standards.

Strictly speaking, evaluation is a two-part process that consists of ① identifying criteria or standards, and ② measuring an individual's performance with respect to those standards. These two components—identifying criteria and measuring—are common to the different forms of evaluation we deal with in this chapter. What makes some types of evaluation different from others is largely a matter of ① the kind of criteria employed, ② the way in which performance is measured, and ③ the use of additional elements, as in rating an individual's performance in terms of qualitative categories ("good," "excellent," etc.), that extend beyond the common components of evaluation.

Actually, every test question you've ever answered served as one indicator of the teacher's criteria, because it identified a skill or knowledge you were expected to demonstrate. Of course, sometimes you didn't discover what that expectation was until you took the test. If the question asked you to identify the capital of Nebraska, for example, you either wrote "Lincoln," and got the item "right," or wrote something else (or nothing), in which case the item was marked "wrong." It's this "right or wrong" business that often confuses the evaluation-testing-grading question; instead of *right* or *wrong*, the response could have been "yes," you met the criterion by identifying the capital of Nebraska, or, "no," you were unable to meet the criterion. The issue gets further confused because on most tests, no one usually pays much attention to the questions you got "wrong," except perhaps you. Rather, they were probably more interested in counting the number of right answers in order to arrive at a numerical score that ultimately got translated into a grade.

Once you have identified behaviorally stated objectives for a teaching activity, you've completed the first phase of the evaluation process: you have identified the criteria for what your students will be expected to do. In other words, behavioral objectives—like test questions—identify behaviors you expect your students to demonstrate. With those criteria (desired knowledge and behaviors) in hand, you are then in a position to move into the second phase of evaluation: measuring student performance. Just which measurement technique you employ—whether it's interviewing, directed observation, paper-and-pencil testing, or yet another technique—will probably depend on any one of several factors (which we identify later in this chapter). And finally, whether or not you eventually go on to the optional third phase of evaluation, grading, will undoubtedly depend on your purpose for evaluating students in the first place.

To our way of thinking, the key element in evaluation is not identifying evaluative criteria, although that is important, nor is it determining a measurement technique, although that's important too. The key element, we think, is *clarity of purpose*, of understanding *why* you are evaluating and knowing *what* you are evaluating for. Like anything else in teaching, evaluation is (or should be) a purposeful activity that provides you, your students, or anyone else with useful information they didn't have before.

The different purposes evaluation can serve are suggested by the teachers' questions illustrated in Table 15.1. Note that each question is keyed to the particular type of evaluation it reflects.

Criterion-Referenced Evaluation

Criterion-referenced evaluation permits you to determine how individual students perform relative to a specific knowledge or skill. Whatever you want them to know or do serves as the criterion, the desired behavior. The focus of criterion-referenced evaluation is on determining what students can do and what they can't. If the student can demonstrate what is expected, then he or she is probably ready to move on to something else. However, if he or she can't demonstrate the desired behavior, then further instruction is probably in order.

Because criterion-referenced evaluation can be used to diagnose whether students require additional instruction or experience, it is sometimes referred to as *diagnostic* evaluation. Actually, criterion-referenced evaluation, diagnostic evaluation, and just plain "diagnosis" all refer to essentially the same process and can be used synonymously. Note also that when the "yes-no" (performance or nonperformance) aspects of criterion-referenced evaluation are coupled with the idea that students will not move on to something else until they have mastered a previous learning task, you have the essence of *mastery learning*.

Mastery learning

Perhaps the most important characteristic of criterion-referenced evaluation is that it can be used at any point in an instructional experience. It is by no means restricted to the end of a chapter, unit, or whatever, as is more often the case with traditional, summative evaluation. In fact, criterion-referenced evaluation may be most appropriate *prior to* instruction. Based on what you find out, neither you nor your students need to waste time going over what they already know, and you can devote your attention to those areas where students need additional instruction.

Formative Evaluation

Formative evaluation is a specialized form of diagnostic evaluation that takes place *during* an instructional episode. In other words, formative evaluation is what teachers employ to determine how things are going and where their students may be having problems.

Table 15.1 Different Types of Evaluation as Reflected by Teachers' Questions

Teacher's Questions	Type of Evaluation	Comments
"Is the student able to perform a designated task? Or demonstrate a desired behavior?" or "On what skill(s) does this student need additional instruction?"	Criterion-referenced or Diagnostic	Used to determine a student's skill proficiency prior to, during, or after instruction; sole focus is on individual performance
"How well are students moving toward our objectives?" ("How are we doing?")	Formative	Used to determine progress *during* instruction
"How does this student's performance compare with the class's performance as a whole?" or "How does the performance of my students compare with that of similar students across the country?"	Norm-referenced	Used to compare an individual's performance to that of a group or one group's performance with another group; characteristic of most standardized testing
"All things considered, how does the student's overall performance rate?"	Summative	More commonly called *grading*
"How well am I doing? As a teacher? As a student?"	Self-evaluation	

There's nothing new about the idea of pausing periodically to assess how things are going; in fact, it's something teachers have done for years. In many instances, however, we suspect that their criteria for determining whether or not a problem existed were largely intuitive and impressionistic, based on a hunch, a feeling, or a sense that things weren't going well. Of course, there's nothing wrong with pursuing a hunch or feeling if it results in an improved learning experience for students. But those learning experiences might be improved even more so if teachers consciously plan to assess how things are going, and if they use explicit (previously identified) criteria in addition to whatever impressions they gain from their intuition. Those criteria, identified in advance, are what distinguishes formative evaluation from everyday, common-sense assessment. We hasten to add, however, that formative evaluation is something that teachers do in addition to, not instead of, their common-sense assessments of how things are going.

How does one "do" formative evaluation? Most of the task takes place in the planning phase, when you identify what a student should be able to do. In other words, upon identifying precise behavioral objectives during your planning, you have also identified the potential criteria (the desired behaviors) that can serve as the basis for your formative evaluation. You also need to determine *when*—at what point—students should be able to demonstrate what you are expecting of them. Theoretically, at the conclusion of an instructional activity, the student should be able to demonstrate the behavior indicated in the objective for that activity. But what may work in theory

How to . . .

doesn't always work in practice, hence the need to devise additional ways to find out if students can demonstrate what is expected of them.

Let's assume, for example, that you are two weeks into a four-week unit on communities in which one of the major concepts is "interdependence." You have already had several activities in which interdependence played a prominent role, and at this point most of your third graders are able to pronounce and define the term properly. Let's also assume that in your original planning, you indicated that after two weeks of instruction, you expected that at least ninety percent of your students would be able to provide examples of how communities are interdependent. (Note that if this is your first year of teaching, you might not have a very solid basis for determining if your expectation was realistic.) With the criterion (behavior) identified, you look for a way to assess student performance. You might consider some of the options we deal with later in this chapter (interviewing, etc.), but for the sake of this illustration, let's assume that you settle on a simple question presented orally: "What are some ways that communities depend on each other?" That is really a double-barreled question because, initially at least, you are not concerned with how students answer it. Rather, for formative evaluation purposes, your initial concern lies in determining how many children indicate a willingness to answer the question. If almost every hand goes up, your focus can then shift to the quality of the students' answers. However, if only four hands go up, and if the majority of non-handraisers are trying to look disinterested or have expressions that say "Please don't call on me," you have a preliminary indication that the majority of your students cannot (or choose not to) demonstrate the desired behavior. You might then call on the students whose hands are raised, hoping that their responses will provide accurate examples of what you are seeking. You might also reword your question—e.g., "Can anyone else give an example of ways that communities are interdependent?" and then reassess your students' willingness to respond. If the same situation prevails, you might then (1) reassess your original expectation, (2) consider developing additional activities that provide concrete examples of interdependence, or (3) do nothing in the hope that everything will work itself out with additional time and experience. Keep in mind that formative evaluation need not be a long, drawn-out process. In fact, once you have identified your criteria, you can probably do formative evaluation in far less time than it has taken you to read this rather elaborate example.

An example

Norm-Referenced Evaluation

Instead of determining whether students can perform certain tasks, which is the focus of criterion-referenced, diagnostic, and formative evaluation, it is sometimes desirable to compare a student's performance on a task with other students' performance on the same task. If you were teaching third grade, for example, you might wish to compare your students' performance with that of third graders elsewhere, as one would when using a nationally standardized test. Or, you might want to compare the performance of individuals in your class with your class's overall performance. In either case, whatever you are using as a basis for comparison serves as the *norm*.

Norm-referenced evaluation would permit you to say, for instance, that "Johnny did better than 31 percent of the third graders who took this test on map skills." Actually, the quality of Johnny's performance may not be very good; in fact, it may be awful. But unless you shifted to criterion-referenced evaluation and analyzed Johnny's performance on each test item, it's doubtful that you would be able to determine the specific problems Johnny encountered and why he scored as he did. In other words, norm-referenced evaluation permits you to compare an individual's overall performance with that of a group; it doesn't provide information to indicate, for example, that Johnny's problem may lie in his inability to deal with cardinal direction.

Based on comparisons

The results of norm-referenced evaluation are always stated comparatively, that is, in relation to whatever norm is being used. Thus, to say that Maria got a 95 on her test, for example, might seem rather impressive at first, especially if you assume that it was a 100-item test. Your interpretation is likely to change, however, when you find that it was a 200-item test and that the average performance for students the same age as Maria was 161. It might change even more so when you find that Maria is a perfectly average eight-year-old, whose native language is Spanish, who has been in this country just over a year, and whose score of 95 was on a test of English vocabulary (or American history). Our point here is to indicate that, unless the group Maria is being compared with (the norm) shares Maria's characteristics (including age, linguistic background, etc.), the results of normative evaluation could be very misleading.

Summative Evaluation

Summative evaluation always takes place at the end of an instructional period (i.e., a unit, six weeks, or whatever), and is intended to reflect the changes that have taken place in the student during that period. If a student is unable to distinguish between a fact and an opinion at the beginning of an instructional period, for example, the purpose of instruction is to enable the student to do so by the end of that period. However, in addition to this particular skill the student will be expected to demonstrate other knowledges, skills, and attitudes. But rather than report on each of these elements separately, schools have traditionally assessed the quality of the learner's performance on a number of measures (including test scores, individual effort, achievement relative to the rest of the class, etc.), the results of which have been "summed" into judgmental statements or, more commonly, a grade. The basic question one asks in summative evaluation, then, is: "All things considered, how would you judge the quality of a particular student's performance (or product)?"

Grading Grading and summative evaluation are so closely related that, for all practical purposes, they are synonymous. And grading, as almost everyone knows, refers to the process of judging whether or not something or someone belongs in a particular category. The key element of grading (and of summative evaluation) lies (1) in determining the characteristics of the categories to be used for reporting purposes, and then (2) determining which

Grading- We don't
have consistent descriptions
of categories of grading

of those characteristics an object or person exhibits. Thus a meat inspector, for example, examines a carcass to determine the amount of marbleized fat it contains, and then assigns that carcass to a category—"prime," "choice," "good," etc.—usually by stamping it with the appropriate purple label. Once the inspector has identified the characteristics of a particular category, the label isn't essential; it just makes communicating about that carcass much simpler. As long as you know the characteristics of the categories, the labels "prime" or "choice" will have significance.

In most schools, grading labels are defined by school policy. Typically they are letters (A, B, C, D, F,), numbers, descriptive expressions ("Satisfactory," "Excellent," etc.), or some combination of these. The labels we've got! What we don't have are consistent descriptions of the categories to which they apply, and therein lies the basis of the grading problem in schools. The result? There isn't a student alive who doesn't know that one teacher's *A* can be another teacher's *B, C,* or sometimes even worse.

Because of the problems associated with traditional grades, some schools report to parents in terms of more descriptive, criterion-referenced evaluation. That is, instead of a grade, parents receive a report (either written, verbal, or both) that describes their child's progress in *each* of the areas that would otherwise have been "summed" together into a grade. Thus, Johnny's parents, for example, might be informed that "Among other things, Johnny knows his cardinal directions, can accurately apply the scale on a map to measure distances, but as yet is unable to distinguish between a fact and an opinion." The intent is not to compare Johnny's performance with that of anyone else, although parents may ask about that anyway. The purpose of the report is to show how Johnny (and only Johnny) is progressing through a sequence of previously identified skills.

Both summative evaluation and traditional grading demand previously identified criteria; for most students those criteria represent crucial information. Even though teachers may indicate that "In determining your grade, I'm going to 'count' your test scores, class participation, and group work," just how that "counting" will be done often remains unknown. Other teachers, however, establish mathematical formulae (e.g., "Class participation counts one-fifth") in an apparent effort to make a subjective process more objective. Be advised that elaborate formulae and mathematical manipulation of scores does not necessarily make grading more objective or scientific. Rather, teachers who use such devices may be doing little more than objectively manipulating subjectively selected data.

Even though teachers sometimes deny it, most students are well aware of the fact that judgment and subjectivity are integral parts of the evaluation process. When one human being, the teacher, is put in the position of judging the performance of other human beings, the students, it is all but impossible to eliminate the human element in evaluation. It can be controlled, of course, which helps to explain all of our emphasis on behaviorally stated objectives and on establishing clear expectations (criteria) for students (and teachers). Actually, despite the presence of the human element, there is nothing intrinsically unfair about evaluation and grading; the only thing intrinsic about the process is that it is subjective.

Grading very
Subjective

In light of the inherent subjectivity of grading, our recourse is to gather as much *good* evaluation data as possible before making a judgment. The more data one has, the less likely one is to be misled in evaluating a student's performance. It is not the sheer quantity of data that is the only issue, however, since a set of thirty test scores, for example, is not necessarily a better basis for making a decision than a set of ten test scores. Indeed, the quality of the data is just as important as the quantity. Thus, information gathered through systematic interviews with your students will provide you with a better base for evaluative decision making than, say, several random impressions. Likewise, descriptive, anecdotal notes jotted on a student's profile sheet usually prove superior to mental notes made as you evaluate a student's class participation. Furthermore, should your evaluation and grading practices ever be questioned by anyone, the quantity *and* quality of your evaluation data will assume paramount importance.

Quality and *quantity*

more data, less chance of misled evaluations.

The Normal Curve and Abnormal Groups

At the end of one six-week grading period during our first year of teaching, we had grown weary of arbitrarily drawing lines designating some scores as *A*, some as *B*, and so forth. Instead, we decided to grade strictly by the "curve," a description of which can be found in almost any educational psychology or tests-and-measurements book. We were teaching in a departmentalized situation in which the various sections of students were grouped homogeneously. We laboriously calculated normal curves for each section, only to discover that a score of 87, which was a *B* for the middle group and an *A* for the slowest group, turned out to be a *C* for the accelerated group. If you don't understand how this can happen, you ought to reread that ed psych book. Our results seemed a little odd, but we went ahead anyhow, much to the consternation—no, it was surprise; in fact, it was really more akin to shock—of our advanced group. Not much really happened until about twenty minutes after school was dismissed. Then the phone calls started. Children who had never received a grade less than *B* had gotten social studies grades of *C* (or worse). Irate mothers were demanding to know why. We tried to explain things as best we could, our shaky understanding of statistics notwithstanding. Then a more careful rereading of that ed psych book indicated that we had neglected a fundamental assumption of the normal curve; namely, that it be applied to a normal population. Treated separately, our homogeneous groups were a far cry from a normal (randomly selected) population, hence our "error."

The moral? Never apply a normal curve to an "abnormal" group.

Self-Evaluation

Self-evaluation is something all of us do, and is so common that it hardly needs to be defined. It is also among the most private forms of evaluation. The criteria are usually private, as are the results—unless, of course, you choose to make them public.

Self-evaluation actually demands a considerable degree of self-awareness and self-direction. In an attempt to help them develop these qualities, we agreed on one occasion to permit our students to give themselves their citizenship grades. They would identify the grade they deserved and we agreed to mark it on their report card. To make certain that everyone used somewhat similar criteria, we spent quite some time talking about what constituted "good citizenship." However, when the children turned in their grades, we were amazed and slightly shocked. Almost without exception, their grades were one to two grades lower than we would have given. Upon investigation, it turned out that what we had considered trivial incidents, such as the failure to complete a homework paper on time, were often blown out of proportion, and that the students had downgraded themselves accordingly. We ended up spending considerable time helping children examine their conduct in a broader perspective and trying to convince them that they were being too harsh on themselves.

One's own worst critic

On another occasion we permitted a college class to use self-evaluation as the basis for determining their course grade. And again, we attempted to identify mutually agreeable criteria. This time, however, the results were quite different; all thirty-four students gave themselves an *A*.

It became apparent that, although our elementary students had taken self-evaluation more seriously than we had anticipated, by the college level any connection between grading and self-evaluation had become tenuous at best. For many of those college students, grading had apparently become a kind of game where one "got" whatever one could. From some students at both levels, however, we also received vociferous objections to any attempt to base grading on self-evaluation. They claimed that grading was a teacher's responsibility while self-evaluation was a private matter, one that should remain private. Where do you stand?

Gathering Evaluative Information

Teachers spend a lot of time gathering evaluation information. Sometimes they do so informally, as in observing a student perform a task, or they may employ more formal techniques, such as giving a test. The informal techniques, such as observing or interviewing, usually aren't very threatening to students. But more formal techniques, particularly paper-and-pencil testing, can sometimes evoke fear in the heart of the most able student. Nevertheless, testing is an information-gathering process, nothing more. It is one of several techniques for gathering data about student performance, and if it isn't looked at that way, it should be.

Testing, like most other measurement techniques, provides a way of gathering information that can then be used (1) to prescribe additional learning experiences (in other words, a test used diagnostically), (2) to compare a student's performance with others (as in norm-referenced evaluation), or (3) to provide a basis for grading. Perhaps it's teachers' penchant for using tests almost solely for grading purposes that makes them such awesome things in the eyes of many students.

Uses

The key to gathering useful evaluative information depends first on how well you identify the kind of information you want, and second on whether you use an appropriate means to get that information. Even though those key points may seem fairly obvious at the outset, we have met too many teachers who, though they said (or thought) they were testing children's skills, were actually testing what those children knew. And still others, who thought they were testing information-processing skills, were actually testing children's access skills, namely, reading.

In very gross terms, the kind of evaluation data we need usually relate to what children know and are able to do (knowledge and cognitive skills), and to what they believe *and* how they respond in terms of what they believe and feel (affective attitudes and values). The kind of information we need and the kind of information we can readily and accurately get, however, may be two different things. The problem was aptly expressed by Krathwohl, Bloom, and Masia (1956, p. 61) when they stated, "While there may be only one 'right' kind of achievement for an objective in the cognitive domain there may be many "right" behaviors equally correct in achieving an objective in the affective domain." In other words, determining if the student knows the date of Abraham Lincoln's birth, for example, may be quite different from determining if the child can demonstrate the characteristics of a "good citizen"—assuming, of course, that we all agree on what those characteristics are (which is part of the problem). In light of this, we examine evaluation in the cognitive and affective domains in the following sections.

Evaluating Cognitive Skills

If there is any area in which education has developed a reasonable degree of expertise—almost to a fault—it is in measuring what students know at the knowledge level. More recently, we've also made strides in evaluating skill development beyond the knowledge level.

Undoubtedly the most common, informal technique for evaluating involves questioning. Either individually or in a group setting, the child is presented with a task and then requested to respond appropriately. Undoubtedly, the most common formal technique involves some type of testing, usually in written form.

Types of tests

There are three major categories of formal evaluation instruments (*instrument* being the technical name for an evaluation device or scale). They are: (1) nationally standardized tests and scales, (2) achievement tests produced by local, regional, or state agencies, which may or may not be normed, and (3) tests developed by teachers themselves.

Standardized Tests   You may not have a choice as to whether or not your students will take a particular standardized test, since such tests are often ordained as part of school-wide testing programs. School systems often want the *normative* data these tests provide so they can compare the performance of their students with performances of roughly comparable children across the country. Unfortunately, some teachers, knowing that *their* effectiveness may also be judged in terms of how well their students perform, may find themselves "teaching for the test." In other words, the nature of the test determines, in part, the nature of the social studies program they establish. That may not be as bad as it sounds in instances where the standardized tests reflect increased attention to information-processing skills and the goals of

Who is being judged?

contemporary social studies programs. However, some tests still emphasize the specialized factual information characteristic of more traditional social studies programs, and these can be inhibiting factors unless teachers are willing to risk ignoring them.

Standardized tests typically have sections dealing with basic social studies knowledges and skills. In some instances, however, the skills section will emphasize what are often called "study skills"—using a dictionary, reading a chart, for example—and not higher level, information-processing skills such as interpretation or analysis. To determine the test's skills focus, it's usually necessary to judge each test item separately.

Several sample standardized test items are illustrated in Figure 15.1. Note particularly that, when test items involve skills, the necessary information is provided. In other words, the child is not forced to recall the information from memory (if, indeed, it is *in* the child's memory). If a student were asked to "Compare and contrast the exports of Ghana and Nigeria," for example, and the necessary export information were not provided, the child would be forced to rely solely on memorized information. So, though the item would appear to test a particular skill, namely, interpretation (comparing and contrasting), by not providing the information to compare and contrast, it is actually testing a knowledge (memory) task. Thus, the basic rule illustrated by standardized tests is *when developing skills-based evaluation test items, provide students with the information to be processed.*

Providing information to process

Sources of standardized tests for elementary social studies include:

Iowa Tests of Basic Skills (Boston: Houghton Mifflin);

Metropolitan Achievement Test: Social Studies (New York: Harcourt Brace Jovanovich);

Primary Social Studies Test (Boston: Houghton Mifflin) (requires no reading skills);

Sequential Test of Educational Progress: Social Studies (*STEP*) (Princeton, NJ: Educational Testing Service);

Stanford Achievement Test: Intermediate and Advanced Social Studies (Grades 5–9) (New York: Harcourt Brace Jovanovich).

Teacher-Made Tests The teacher's editions of most textbook series contain suggested evaluation techniques and sample test questions that you could use with your students. The key element in that decision should be how closely the objectives the sample test items seek to measure match *your* objectives for whatever you are teaching. Unless that match is fairly close, your students might find themselves being tested on knowledge and skills they had little or no idea would be expected of them. When that match doesn't exist, you have two alternatives: (1) you can develop your own test questions, or (2) you can devise alternative (nontest) evaluation techniques. We examine both of these alternatives in the following sections.

Developing Teacher-Made Tests Developing valid, unambiguous test items often looks easy enough, but it is a task that can actually prove rather diffi-

Figure 15.1 Sample Standardized Test Items

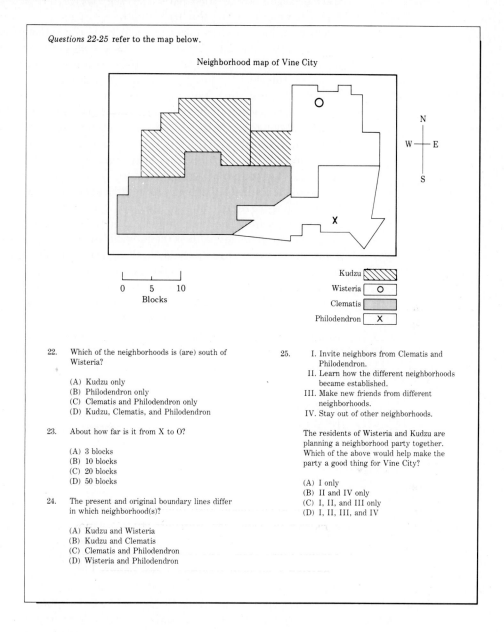

Questions 22-25 refer to the map below.

Neighborhood map of Vine City

0   5   10
Blocks

Kudzu
Wisteria
Clematis
Philodendron

22. Which of the neighborhoods is (are) south of Wisteria?

(A) Kudzu only
(B) Philodendron only
(C) Clematis and Philodendron only
(D) Kudzu, Clematis, and Philodendron

23. About how far is it from X to O?

(A) 3 blocks
(B) 10 blocks
(C) 20 blocks
(D) 50 blocks

24. The present and original boundary lines differ in which neighborhood(s)?

(A) Kudzu and Wisteria
(B) Kudzu and Clematis
(C) Clematis and Philodendron
(D) Wisteria and Philodendron

25.   I. Invite neighbors from Clematis and Philodendron.
  II. Learn how the different neighborhoods became established.
  III. Make new friends from different neighborhoods.
  IV. Stay out of other neighborhoods.

The residents of Wisteria and Kudzu are planning a neighborhood party together. Which of the above would help make the party a good thing for Vine City?

(A) I only
(B) II and IV only
(C) I, II, and III only
(D) I, II, III, and IV

cult. To be sure, there's nothing very difficult about writing a test item like "Abraham Lincoln was born in _____," for example, but such an apparently simple, straightforward question places a tremendous and ofttimes unfair burden on students who must determine which of a multitude of possible answers (place? month? year?) the teacher has in mind. In other words, the students' problem with questions such as this one may lie not in their ability to demonstrate what they know about Lincoln's birth, but in trying to determine the teacher's intent.

When students are in a quandry about what a test item expects of them —be it a date (February, 1809), a place (Kentucky), or something else—the likelihood is high that the item will not measure what it was intended to measure. This characteristic of test items (or entire tests)—namely, that they actually measure what they are intended to measure—is called *validity*. Lest there be any doubt about it, our Lincoln question is clearly invalid. All is not lost, however, for the validity of a test item can usually be improved by adding information that clarifies the teacher's intent. To do this, you must first eliminate any fuzziness from your original objectives so as to identify precisely what you expect (of the student). Thus, an objective such as "From memory, the student will identify something about Abraham Lincoln" won't do. Including the term "something" is too vague to convey your real expectation. So, depending on what you really want students to know, the objective could be, "From memory, the student will identify the place (state) in which Lincoln was born." In this instance, the test item could then be stated as follows: "Abraham Lincoln was born in the state of _____."

Providing additional information often improves the clarity and, hence, the validity of a test question. In some instances, this can also be accomplished by changing the form of the question. Instead of using a short-answer (completion) format, for example, our sample Lincoln item could be presented as a multiple-choice or true-false question. In multiple-choice form, the question could be stated as:

_____ Abraham Lincoln was born in
a. Illinois
b. Kentucky *
c. Indiana
d. None of the above

As a true-false item, the question could be phrased as:

_____ Abraham Lincoln was born in Indiana (F).

In both examples, the intent of each question is clear. At the same time, we've compromised their validity by introducing a larger "chance" or guessing factor than was true for the short-answer (completion) format. For the true-false question especially, students have a fifty-fifty chance of guessing the correct answer. This may help to explain why less able students often prefer true-false test items simply because luck is on their side. This does not mean that you should forego using true-false or multiple-choice test questions, but it does mean that you cannot be as confident that such questions validly measure what they are intended to measure.

Regardless of the form in which our Lincoln test item is asked, a crucial question still remains: should students be expected to recall such information? On one hand, expecting children to recall information about the date or place of Lincoln's birth could help to reinforce the notion that social studies is a collection of irrelevant facts. On the other hand, some individuals

Validity

*Improving
validity*

Children shouldn't have to ask questions about your questions.

argue that such information is part of our historical heritage, and as such represents the kind of thing every citizen should know. Whichever position you lean toward will influence your judgment as to both the appropriateness of the question and the objectives on which it is based. And although this is a tough issue to deal with, our point in raising it is to indicate that determining the validity and appropriateness of test questions are separate issues and should be treated accordingly. Thus, a perfectly valid test question, such as "List the states in order of their admission to the Union," must still be judged in terms of its appropriateness. In fact, if test items (and the objectives they are based on) are unreasonable or inappropriate to begin with, validity doesn't even enter the picture. In other words, trying to develop valid test items for questionable objectives is an exercise in futility.

If you can't write good test items, you are unlikely to get a true indication of a child's abilities. In the sample (knowledge-level) test that follows, we have intentionally violated almost every existing practice of test construction. We have, in effect, produced a nontest. However, after each sample question we suggest ways in which it might be improved. In some instances, of course, it's impossible to improve a poor test question. Yet even when the form of a test question conforms to recommended practices, the item must still be judged in terms of its appropriateness.

A Nontest—Colonial America

Completion   Fill in the blanks with the correct answer.

1   *Poor:* The _____ ____ _____ were among the first white men to trade with the Indians.

Better: The first white men to trade with the Indians in the Northwest Territory were the _____ fur traders; *or,* The first white men to trade with the Indians in the Northwest Territory were the French _____ _____.

Analysis   Ordinarily only one key word or phrase should be omitted, not three key words, and ordinarily the omitted word or phrase should be at or near the end of the sentence, so the student need not continually reread it in order to determine the subject. In addition, the lines where students write their responses should be of approximately equal length, so as not to provide clues to the desired answer. In this instance, however, there are so many blanks in the "poor" question that the short response line was needed to provide a necessary clue as to what the question was asking.

Optional format

Responding to a direct question is sometimes easier than completing a sentence, particularly if the test item (and its objective) contains multiple elements. Thus, an alternative short-answer format for this test item would be:

What was the nationality and occupation of the first white men who traded with the Indians in the Northwest Territory? _____

2   *Poor:* Manhattan Island was purchased from the Indians on July ___, ___ _____. (July 14, 1649)

Better: None

Analysis   Desired responses should deal with important information, not trivia. In addition, this item strongly resembles the kind of statement one would find in a social studies textbook. Using lines from a textbook as the basis for short-answer test items (and other test questions) should be avoided; it encourages memorization, not understanding.

3   *Poor:* At the first _____, the _____ brought _____ and the _____ brought _____ and other wild animals.

Better (if used at all): At the first Thanksgiving, the Pilgrims brought several kinds of food including _____ and _____.

Provide a clear context

Analysis   Whether students should know who brought what to the first Thanksgiving is questionable to start with, but the question as originally stated contained so many blanks that its intent was not clear. Even in restated form, there are a number of correct answers, all of which should receive credit.

4 The colonists who attended the first Thanksgiving were called _____.

Analysis There's nothing wrong with the form of this question, it's just that the answer is provided by the previous question.

True-False (Alternative Response) Use a + for true and a 0 for false unless directed otherwise. (Capital T's and capital F's can look very much alike—sometimes intentionally so.)

5 *Poor:* The Puritan religion was best suited for the colonies.
Better: None

Analysis The question asks the student to make a value judgment in the absence of clearly defined criteria.

6 *Poor:* The Indians never helped the Puritans.
Better: None

Analysis Specific determiners and absolute terms such as *none, never,* and *always,* tend to be associated with false statements; terms such as *some, generally, should, often,* and *may* tend to be associated with true statements. Generally, specific determiners and absolutes should be avoided unless you are dealing with situations where they are appropriate; e.g., "Evaluation always requires the identification of criteria."

7 *Poor:* The first Thanksgiving was held over the winter of 1720–21, and was attended by the Pilgrims, the Indians, the English, and the Dutch.
Better: The first Thanksgiving was held over the winter of 1720–21.

What's the question?

Analysis As originally stated, the question is misleading, especially since a false element, the date, is subordinate to the main thrust of the question. In addition, it is not clear whether the accuracy or the completeness of the list of attendees is the concern. As a general rule, avoid statements that could be misinterpreted or those that are partly true and partly false.

An alternative technique for handling true-false questions that involve multiple elements is illustrated below.

French explorers who visited North America included:

(+) 1 La Salle

(0) 2 De Soto

(+) 3 Champlain

(0) 4 Hudson

(+) 5 Cartier

Another variation sometimes used with alternative-response questions requires students to supply the correct version of a false item. This technique is illustrated below.

Native Americans sailed the lakes and rivers of the eastern woodlands in hickory canoes.
(correct statement) _____

Multiple Choice   Select the best answer and write the letter in the space provided.

8   *Poor:* A red-orange root plant grown by the Indians was (a) corn, (b) yam, (c) pumpkin, (d) asparagus.
Better: As multiple choice, none; if used at all, the question could be asked in a completion or true-false format.

Analysis   Distractors for multiple-choice items should be plausible. In this instance, only one root plant is listed.

9   *Poor:* The Puritans
(a) were not the group that founded the Massachusetts Bay colony
(b) went to southern Georgia
(c) didn't believe in taking a bath
(d) left England, went to Holland, and then fled to the North American colonies of Great Britain, where they could avoid religious persecution.
Better: The Puritans settled in Massachusetts in order to
(a) establish a fur-trading company
(b) avoid the high taxes they had been forced to pay in England
(c) practice their religion without interference
(d) prevent Spain and France from claiming the area

Analysis   Where possible, the major portion of the statement should be presented in the introduction, or stem, of the question. In addition, all incorrect answers should be plausible, of the same general style, and of approximately the same length as the correct answer.

10   *Poor:* The name of the minister who headed the colonial government in Rhode Island was (a) John Smith, (b) Bunker Hill
Better: The name of the minister who headed the colonial government in Rhode Island was
(a) John Smith
(b) John Adams
(c) Roger Williams
(d) Cotton Mather
(e) None of the above

Analysis   Multiple-choice questions should have a minimum of three and preferably four or five alternative answers. The fewer the alternatives, the higher the probability that students may guess the right answer. More importantly, the correct (or best) alternative response must be provided (which it is *not* in the "poor" form of this question). Further, alternative answers should be of the same general type, such as the names of people, places, statements, etc. Mixing different types of alternative responses or providing obviously false distractors should be avoided. Also to be avoided are multiple-choice questions in which the correct answer is revealed by clues in the item itself, such as "Many colonial families used a (a) ax, (b) apple peeler, (c) candle mold, (d) ox. Only *c* is grammatically correct. Such questions should be reserved for grammar tests.

At random

You might have noticed that for the bulk of our sample multiple-choice questions the correct answer was *c*. Test-wise students often look for such a pattern, so you are safer to distribute the position of correct responses randomly throughout the test.

Matching Write the letter from Column II in the space provided in front of the correct term in Column I. (Note: For primary-level children, you might wish to have them draw a line between items that match.)

11 *Poor:*

Column I	Column II
1. ___ Patroon	(a) the Indian word for corn
2. ___ Maize	(b) a Dutch system for landholding along the Hudson River
3. ___ Mayflower	(c) one of the middle colonies
4. ___ Delaware	(d) a ship

Better: Instructions: Write the letter for the occupation described in Column II in the space provided in front of the term associated with that occupation (Column I).

Column I	Column II
1. ___ blacksmith	(a) barrelmaker
2. ___ chandler	(b) hatmaker
3. ___ cooper	(c) wheelmaker
4. ___ deacon	(d) iron worker
5. ___ teamster	(e) ship's supplier
6. ___ wheelwright	(f) jewelry maker
	(g) wagon driver
	(h) church official

Analysis The items in our "poor" example are so few and so dissimilar that almost anyone could complete the exercise, even if they knew nothing about "patroons." In addition, guessing is facilitated because the items in each column match exactly. Even though students may object loudly, guessing is minimized if one column contains more items than are used, or contains responses that are used more than once.

Among the most difficult aspects of developing good matching questions is the problem of identifying enough similar items to place in the columns *without resorting to trivia.* Some of the following examples, which are adapted from Gronlund (1965, pp. 136–38), could be used for matching purposes.

Column I	Column II
People	Achievements
Inventors	Inventions
Dates	Historical events
Objects	Names of objects
Terms	Definitions
Places	Geographical locations
Rules	Examples
Principles	Illustrations
Machines	Uses

Essay Write a good essay on one of the following questions.

12 *Poor:* What crops did the early Pilgrims grow?
Better: None

Analysis No other form of evaluation permits a teacher to "get inside" students, to gain insight into how they think, how they organize, and how they synthesize information, as effectively as an essay test. It's one of the few forms of testing in which it is impossible to "fake it." However, before essay testing is even a possibility, students must be mature enough to be able to express themselves in writing. Because of this, essay tests are not widely used in elementary schools.

Essay test questions should ask students to do more than simply reproduce information, as our "poor" question does. Indeed, if a list of the Pilgrim's crops is desired, a short answer (completion) question would be more appropriate; e.g. "List five crops grown by the Pilgrims."

13 *Poor:* Discuss Indians
Better: Describe with examples at least three different ways in which the early colonists' contact with the Indians benefited both groups.

Analysis "Discuss Indians" is so broad that it is difficult to know (1) where to begin, and (2) what the intent of the question actually is. The improved question clearly conveys what the student is to do.

14 *Poor:* Tell all you know about why people should always be brave and thankful.
Better: None

Analysis Although the task in the "poor" question is clear enough, establishing valid criteria for evaluating students' responses would be difficult, if not impossible. This is a particularly common problem in attempting to evaluate attitudes, which is what this question seems geared toward. Of course, teachers could gain insight into their students' attitudes by asking them to respond, either verbally or in writing, to questions such as "Why do you think some people are thankful?" but using those responses for grading purposes would be inappropriate. Some of the observational techniques suggested later in this chapter may prove to be more valid indicators of children's attitudes than direct or written questions like the ones illustrated here.

Whenever your tests begin to look like our "poor" examples, you've got problems. Not only will the form of your test items be questionable, but you may also be guilty of emphasizing the kind of trivia that has given social studies an unsavory reputation, one that in this case is justly deserved. In addition, our "poor" test items also lend credence to the notion that evaluation is a kind of "game" intended to trick students, not an honest attempt to assess what they actually know.

**Evaluating
Higher-Level Skills**

Provide data

Our ability to evaluate at the knowledge level may help explain the absence of consistent evaluation at the higher levels of cognition. Actually, it's not "harder" to evaluate a student's ability to deal with higher-level cognitive skills, it's just different. One difference, you'll find, is that evaluation at higher cognitive levels (interpretation, application, analysis, synthesis, etc.) usually requires fewer questions. Instead of a fifty-item test, for example, three, four, or five questions will often suffice. But perhaps the most basic difference is that evaluating the student's ability to interpret information, evaluate conclusions, etc., usually requires that the information to be interpreted or evaluated also be presented for them. In other words, what you are really looking for is the student's ability to *transfer* their skill of processing information from whatever kind of information they have worked with previously to the kind of data you have presented on a test. The thing to be transferred is the skill and not necessarily the information itself. What you find when evaluating students' information-processing skills is that the *way* in which you present information in a testing situation may be very similar to the way you presented it in the original situation. Indeed, the manner of presentation may remain exactly the same; only the information will be changed to protect the student from thinking it has to be memorized.

The following are some examples of what we've been talking about. Note that in the case of the information from the *Works of James I* (Example 1), it was necessary to rewrite the material at a lower reading level.

Example 1 Skills: Analysis and interpretation of data.
Instructions: Read the following quotes. Do they show the same position about the responsibility of an individual? Or about the way in which individuals control themselves? Explain.

> Kings are like God. If you think of what God can do, you can think of what a king can do. For example, a king can do anything with his people. He can make them a success or make them a failure. He can judge whether or not what people do is right. But no person shall judge the king. A king's people are like chess pieces and the king is like a chess player. He decides the moves. He decides what the pieces will do. The people should serve the king. No person is to change the government. The government is the king's responsibility.
>
> Adapted from the
> *Works of James I* (1603)

> Having taken this trip for the glory of God and to help the Christian faith, we agree to work together for the Glory and the Faith.
> From *The Mayflower Compact* (1620)

Example 2 There is a common assumption among teachers that evaluation at higher cognitive-skill levels requires an essay test. Given Questions 1 and 2 below, evaluate that assumption. (*If it isn't evident, we have just presented an evaluation activity.* For Question 1 however, your answer, if written, would be in essay form.)

Question 1 Population growth of two cities between 1875 and 1975:

Date	City A	City B
1875	111	72
1900	190	220
1925	1,621	400
1950	11,006	1,890
1975	24,000	2,773

Interpreting data. Use the data above to answer the following questions. (True-False: use + for true, 0 for false)

____ 1. City A has always been larger than City B.

____ 2. City A has grown faster than City B.

____ 3. City A was larger than City B in 1975.

____ 4. City A is likely to have more city employees than City B.

____ 5. City B is likely to have more schools than City A.

____ 6. Both cities are likely to have problems with crime and pollution.

____ 7. One city is likely to have more problems with crime than the other.

Question 2 Skill area: logic. Instructions: circle the correct answer.

1 Suppose three men need food for their families. Suppose also that the same three men realize that if they hunt together, it will be easier to shoot a buck. Each takes his position and the deer is shot. Which of the following would most likely take place?
A. Each family would get more food.
B. Each family would get the same amount of food.
C. Each family would get the same quantity of food.
* D. The three men would have to work out some way of dividing up the food.

2 If in your studies you find that (1) all humans have certain needs, (2) all humans strive to satisfy these needs, (3) different people have different ways of satisfying their needs, you would be able to say that
A. there is only one right way for people to satisfy their needs.
B. people who do not satisfy their needs the same way we do are ignorant.
* C. the different ways in which people satisfy their needs are learned and thus can undergo change.
D. the ways people satisfy their needs cannot be changed.

3 If you depend on a classmate to help you with your homework, and the classmate in turn depends upon his brother to help him with his chores so he can find time to help you, you
A. are more concerned with your classmate than you are with his brother.
* B. you are just as concerned with your classmate's brother as with your classmate.
C. you depend on one and not the other.
D. don't take the brother into account.

**Interviewing
and Observing**

With any kind of test, though, there always exists the problem of those students whose inability to read prevents them from demonstrating either what they know or are able to do. If students can't read the questions, the answers are immaterial, and they will be forced into a kind of guessing game —eeny, meeny, miney, moe. The reading problem has led teachers to search for alternative ways to evaluate students, ways that are not dependent on reading. The interesting thing that happens is that teachers who become adept at using two of the most common alternatives—the interview and the observation/rating scale—often continue to do so even when reading skills are not a problem.

*Systematic data
gathering*

Finding out what students know or are able to do just by talking with them or watching them is hardly a new idea. Even Socrates did more than just ask questions. But traditionally, talking with students or observing them has tended to be a casual affair. When a student was obviously having difficulty, for example, teachers would just as obviously walk over and talk with the student. Or, for one reason or another (not always disciplinary), a teacher's attention might be drawn to a particular student or a group of students. What distinguishes interviewing and observing from their more casual cousins is their systematic quality. In other words, the interview is not another casual conversation. It is systematic (though not rigidly so), and it is conducted for a particular purpose: to find out what kids know about something and/or how they feel about it. The interview is not a teaching device in the narrowly defined sense of the term. That is, it is not primarily an opportunity to correct children's misconceptions or teach them something. Rather, it is an opportunity for teachers *to learn* something from and about their students. Perhaps one reason some teachers have difficulty accepting the interview as a legitimate evaluation tool is because, except for a few guiding questions, they have difficulty keeping their mouths shut and just listening.

The other major deterrent to interviewing is the amount of time it can take. Even ten-minute interviews with a class of twenty-four students represents a considerable time commitment. The clear and sometimes preferable alternative to individual interviews is group sessions. Group sessions are also preferable because they permit other students to share the focus of the teacher's attention. This is particularly valuable when an individual student might feel uncomfortable alone.

Suggested interview procedures include:

Identifying sets of similar questions on whatever it is you want to find out so that you don't ask the same questions all the time.

*Interview
guidelines*

Keeping your facial expression as "interested" but as unevaluative as possible.

Making it clear that everyone will have an opportunity to talk (and shift to someone else if one student begins to monopolize things).

Not being put off by an immediate response of "I don't know." Often it's just the way children gain time while they think something through. Give them time to think, and then probe.

Observation/Rating Scales An observation/rating scale is probably best described as a "scoresheet," something on which either teachers or students record their observations or, more accurately, judgments based on their observations. The basic observation/rating scale lists the students' names and the criteria against which they will be observed. Of course, if you have a lot of criteria, you may need a separate sheet for each student—in effect, a student profile. Then, periodically, you review each student's performance in terms of the criteria.

A retired elementary teacher of our acquaintance always used an observation/rating scale to gather information on her students' class participation. She simply listed her students' names and then evaluated each student's class participation at the end of the day. The unique thing about her scale was her use of music symbols—sharps, naturals, and flats—to indicate each child's performance. The scale on our former colleague's rating sheet was implied, that is, from good (sharp) to bad (flat). It is often to your advantage to make the scale more explicit, as shown in the following examples developed by R. Murry Thomas (1972).

"How often does the pupil support his opinions with evidence from reliable sources?"

Option 1

__	__	__	__	__
Never	Rarely	Sometimes	Usually	Always

Option 2

__	__	__	__	__
0%	25%	50%	75%	100%

Percentage of the time evidence is given

Option 3

__	__	__	__	__
Never	1/4	1/2	3/4	Always

Portion of the time evidence is given

Evaluating Attitudes and Values

In many schools, so much time is devoted to evaluating cognitive skills that the time devoted to evaluating students' attitudes and values seems almost miniscule by comparison. No matter how much teachers stress the importance of attitudes and values, the disproportionate amount of time spent evaluating cognitive skills may lead students to believe that all the talk about attitudes and values is just that—talk! Yet despite the apparent difference in time spent on each activity, evaluating attitudes and values is an area in which appearances can be deceiving.

Consider that to evaluate cognitive skills, it is necessary that students do something to demonstrate their ability. This could involve taking a test, participating in an interview, or somehow demonstrating what they can do,

Halos—Negative and Positive

In the process of selecting a name for our first child, I suggested Michael. It soon became apparent, however, that name choosing is not a rational process, for my wife, a former elementary teacher, responded with an immediate "No."

"What's wrong with Michael?"

"Well (emphatically), when I was teaching fourth grade I had a student whose name was Michael. He picked his nose, smelled of garlic, and always seemed to need a bath. There's no way we're going to name *our* son Michael!"

The "halo effect"

We now have three sons, none of whom is named Michael. The incident, though, illustrates the *halo effect,* an extremely common phenomenon that influences a teacher's observation of students. In this instance, my wife's impression of her former student undoubtedly influenced her judgments of him, try though she might to do otherwise. In other instances, teachers have had their judgments biased by the positive halo effect—the child who, for example, can do no wrong. Using observation/rating scales will not eliminate the halo effect, for that is something all of us must deal with; however, they can provide a systematic process for gathering information that might otherwise consist of random impressions.

No special demands

usually during a time period specifically reserved for such activities. (When evaluation is ongoing, this is much less the case.) Students' attitudes and values, on the other hand, are more likely to be expressed in the natural course of their day-to-day activities. Their attitudes and values are expressed in everything they do. And so, simply by observing students' activities over a period of time, it becomes possible to infer what their attitudes and values are. In other words, a special time set aside for attitudinal evaluation usually isn't required. Evaluators need to know what behaviors they are looking for, of course. But attitudinal evaluation doesn't require any special behavior on the student's part. In fact, students' behavior may more accurately reflect their underlying beliefs and values if they do *not* know they are being observed; that way they're less likely to behave in ways they think are expected of them. We are also suggesting here that observation is one of the most accurate techniques for gathering information on students' (or any-one's) attitudes and values.

One factor that makes evaluating attitudes and values more difficult than evaluating cognitive skills is the difficulty associated with identifying precise behavioral indicators for an attitude or value. No matter how desirable a particular attitude or value may be—"tolerance" or "appreciation," for example—it is difficult to identify behavioral characteristics (or indicators) for such values that do not tread on an individual's personal liberties. If some students don't like history, for instance, it's doubtful that they will ever develop "an appreciation of history," no matter how desirable that may be. In fact, as long as an individual's behavior doesn't interfere with someone else's rights, the individual has the right to like or dislike whatever (or whomever) he or she chooses.

The difficulties involved in identifying precise behavioral indicators of an attitude or value, combined with an unwillingness to infringe on personal liberties, help to explain why attitudes and values are often expressed as general goals rather than as specific, measurable objectives. This lack of precision also helps to account for the absence of formal instruments to measure the development of attitudes and values. Although some attitude scales and inventories are available, these invariably are point-in-time measures; they attempt to identify an individual's attitudes or beliefs at a particular time, but they seldom make any pretense of explaining how attitudes or values develop. Despite this limitation, when such attitudinal measures are used in conjunction with other techniques, they may provide information and a point of departure that would otherwise be denied the teacher. In the following sections we examine several techniques for assessing attitudes and values.

Imprecise indicators

Attitude Scales

Attitude scales differ from conventional tests in that tests usually have correct answers; attitude scales don't. An attitude scale consists of a set of questions or statements such as "Students should willingly share ideas and materials with others," or "I think cats are smarter than dogs." The individual is asked to respond to such questions or statements in terms of beliefs or personal preferences (which is why there are no previously established "right" answers).

Most attitude scales have several items that deal with a particular attitude or belief, to which the individual responds using a familiar Likert-type scale, such as "Strongly Agree," "Agree," "Undecided," "Disagree," and "Strongly Disagree." By analyzing the pattern of responses, it then becomes possible to infer the individual's attitude or belief toward the topic in question.

Questionnaires and Inventories

Most people have responded to questionnaires and interest inventories at one time or another. Questionnaires, of course, can deal with a wide range of topics, while interest inventories are usually restricted to what an individual likes or dislikes. Questions like "What do you like to do in your spare time?" or the familiar "What subjects do you like best (or least) in school?" are typical.

Questionnaires and inventories are relatively easy to develop. You simply identify open-ended questions to which the student supplies a written response. In interview settings, the students' responses would be verbal. Regardless of how you administer the questionnaire or interest inventory, a potential problem may arise in determining what to do with the information once you've obtained it. Determining what your students do in their spare time, for example, is probably most useful in providing additional insight into your students and the activities they pursue.

Checklists and Rating Scales

A checklist consists of a series of descriptive statements such as "Works willingly with others," or "Participates in class discussions" next to which the evaluator makes a check mark when an item is observed. In the case of checklists used for self-evaluation, individuals mark items that apply to them. There is no restriction on who should use a checklist; it could be the teacher, another student, or, as in self-evaluation, the students themselves.

The format of checklists and rating scales is often similar. The difference usually lies in the kind of marking system employed. On rating scales, the evaluator usually uses a qualitative rating scale to judge (or rate) the individual's characteristics or performance. Our former colleague's "sharp-to-flat" scale is an example of this. Note that a student's class participation could also be rated using a numerical scale, such as Outstanding = 4, Above Average = 3, Satisfactory = 2, and Needs Improvement = 1.

Informal assessment

Although some of these techniques for assessing students' attitudes and values may look fairly formal, especially those that involve paper-and-pencil-type instruments, they are all quite informal. In addition, their validity may not be very high. As a result, you may find that students' responses are sometimes geared to what they think you want to hear, not to the way they really feel about a topic or issue. In instances involving observation, remember that what observers see is often colored by their own feelings and perceptions. In light of these limitations, we suggest that when assessing students' attitudes and values you may need to gather as much evaluative information from as many different sources as you can. A basic question remains, however: why evaluate attitudes when the primary concern is usually with behavior?

Summary

For years teachers have been using evaluation as more than just a basis for grading. The problem they face, however, stems from the fact that grading is such a powerful phenomenon that it tends to overshadow everything else. And so, although most teachers know that evaluation and testing are *not* synonymous with grading, they don't necessarily feel (or act) that way. Sometimes, quite unintentionally, they may find themselves stressing "a *very* important test on Friday," thereby perpetuating the evaluation-grading mystique.

Evaluation, like planning, is an ongoing process. Just as teachers' goals and objectives help to identify *what* they are attempting to do, evaluation helps them identify *how well* they (and their students) are actually doing it.

Evaluation is always a two-part process consisting of (1) the identification (or acceptance) of evaluative criteria—the standards against which evaluative judgments are made—and, (2) measuring performance or behavior (or products) in relation to the previously identified standards. The particular form evaluation takes, however, is determined largely by the teacher's purpose. If you are interested in diagnosing whether or not a student can demonstrate a certain skill or knowledge, you will undoubtedly turn to *criterion-referenced* evaluation. However, if you wish to compare your stu-

norm-referenced:
compare your students
to another group.

formative - during
on going period

summative - at end
of period of time.

dents' performance with that of another group, you will turn to a form of *norm-referenced* evaluation. In instances when you are interested in determining how things are going during an instructional episode, you may turn to *formative* evaluation. And, if you are interested in determining the overall quality of a student's performance or product at the end of an instructional period, you will turn to *summative* evaluation, which is also known as grading. Finally, if your purpose is to determine how well you are doing as a teacher, you will undoubtedly turn to *self-evaluation.*

Despite its close relationship to traditional grading, we defined *testing* as an information-gathering device. Testing, like observing, interviewing, checklists, attitude scales, interest inventories, and rating scales, are ways of gathering different kinds of information. Some of these techniques, however, are more likely to measure what they are intended to measure than others, and thus have higher validity.

Actually, we have barely scratched the surface of evaluation in this chapter. Although we have shown you some things to avoid, we also recommend that you consult one of the books on evaluation and test construction listed in the Suggested Readings section at the end of this chapter.

Suggested Activities

1   During one of our first years of working with prospective teachers, we decided to use self-evaluation as the basis for grading. At the end of the term we asked everyone to submit a self-evaluation and to recommend a grade for themselves. Despite wide discrepancies in individual performances, 95 percent of the self-evaluations indicated that our students felt they had learned a lot, had worked hard, and, in their minds, had earned the grade of *A*. Where did we go wrong?

2   Obtain any one of the standardized tests that deals with elementary social studies (your psychology department should have copies if your education department doesn't). First, take the test so that your attention is not distracted by the content of the questions. Then analyze the items in terms of the skills they are really testing.

3   Assume that the students in your fifth-grade class need help in developing the following skills: (1) classification, (2) inductive reasoning, (3) question posing, and (4) hypothesis development. Using social studies content, develop at least two activities designed to promote skill development in each of the above areas.

Using the same activity format but substituting data different from that used in the learning activities, develop a way to evaluate student performance in these skill areas.

4   It has been argued that creativity, evaluation, and grading are totally incompatible; that you can't have one as long as you have the other. What do you think? Is there any way to reconcile creativity, evaluation, and grading?·

References

Gronlund, Norman E. *Measurement and Evaluation in Teaching.* New York: Macmillan, 1965.

Krathwohl, David R.; Bloom, Benjamin; and Masia, Bertram. *Taxonomy of Educational Objectives. Handbook II: Affective Domain.* New York: David McKay, 1956.

Sanders, Norris M. *Classroom Questions: What Kinds?* New York: Harper & Row, 1966.

Thomas, R. Murry. "Education, the Case for Rating Scales." In R. Murry Thomas and Dale L. Brubaker (eds.), *Teaching Elementary Social Studies: Readings.* Belmont, CA: Wadsworth Publishing (1972): 364–78.

Suggested Readings

Note: As we began writing the annotations for the books in this listing, we found that all of them said essentially the same thing: excellent. So if you are interested in pursuing topics related to evaluation or test construction, any of the books selected from the list below should serve that purpose.

Harry D. Berg (ed.) *Evaluation in Social Studies.* 35th Yearbook of the National Council for the Social Studies. Washington, D.C.: The Council, 1965.

Robert L. Ebel. *Measuring Educational Achievement.* Englewood Cliffs, NJ: Prentice-Hall, 1965.

Norman E. Gronlund. *Measurement and Evaluation in Teaching.* New York: Macmillan, 1965.

Making the Classroom Test: A Guide for Teachers. Princeton, NJ: Educational Testing Service, 1969.

Horace T. Morse and George H. McCune. (Revised by Lester E. Brown and Ellen Cook.) *Selected Items for the Testing of Study Skills and Critical Thinking.* (5th ed.) Bulletin No. 15. Washington, D.C.: The National Council for the Social Studies, 1971.

John Wick. *Educational Measurement: Where Are We Going and How Will We Know When We Get There?* Columbus, OH: Charles E. Merrill, 1973.

Epilogue

Key Questions

How does one get children to study their own behavior?

What is the teacher's role in approaching discipline as a learning activity?

How does one conduct a classroom meeting?

Key Ideas

The classroom (and the school) can become a functioning social studies laboratory in which behavior is the object of study.

Findings from the social and behavioral sciences can form the basis for studying behavior in the classroom.

For almost every system of external control, human beings will develop even more effective systems of evasion.

Classroom meetings afford students a realistic opportunity to participate in decision making.

Introduction: Classroom Management as Applied Social Science

Novice: I'm worried about discipline. What do I do?

Expert: Stop worrying about it, that's the first thing. Otherwise it's likely to become a self-fulfilling prophecy. The basic rule is that you have to be friendly but firm. And you have to be confident, too. You have to radiate confidence so the kids know who's in charge.

Novice: But I'm *not* confident . . . not confident at all!

Expert: Then you'd better act as if you are. In those first few minutes when the kids are sizing you up, if you act scared or unsure of yourself, you'll probably be in for trouble.

Novice: But won't the kids pick that up? I mean, most of the kids I've seen are pretty perceptive. Won't they be able to tell that I'm just acting?

Analysis The novice teacher has raised a good point, even though there's nothing inaccurate about our expert's advice. Actually, the problem here, at least as we see it, is that the expert's advice is too general. It doesn't indicate anything specific our novice teacher can do something about. (We noted this problem earlier in terms of the types of feedback teachers provide to their students.) So, if our expert really wants to be helpful, he or she should probably respond something like this:

"It is true, your students may sense that you're acting. But the confidence you reflect is probably proportional to the security you have in knowing what you're going to say and do, and in knowing exactly what you're going to ask students to do. In other words, if you know that one of the first things you plan to have your students do is write one of those timeworn essays on 'What I did during my summer vacation,' and if you've decided in advance on the general form you want their papers to follow, you can then anticipate the kinds of questions that are bound to come. You know the kind—'Do I have to do it in ink?' 'How long is it spozed to be?' and so forth. Having done that kind of preplanning, you'll be able to establish the students' task and answer their questions confidently—without acting. And although this may not alleviate your long-run worry, it should serve to help meet your immediate problem."

The nature of expert advice notwithstanding, consider that the findings from the social and behavioral science disciplines can prove helpful as you go about managing your classroom. Those findings may permit you to anticipate the ways in which individuals—in this case, your students—are likely to respond to the situations that invariably arise in any classroom. Because of this, we are suggesting that classroom management (in the disciplinary, or behavior, sense of the term) can actually be viewed as a kind of applied social science.

Discipline and Individual Responsibility

External vs. internal control

Most of us can devise ways of getting what we want, when we want it. True, we may have to wait out an occasional delay or two, but sooner or later. . . . In most classrooms, students usually have a remarkable array of devices at their disposal for getting and doing what they want, some of which are no doubt gleaned from their experience in manipulating parents. These devices may range from an unstated "I'll show her (or him)," through various forms of noncompliance and subtle sabotage—that is, giving the appearance of cooperating but really not—to outright defiance.

In the classroom-management sense of the term, discipline is typically seen as something that teachers establish and/or impose on students. In other words, discipline can be an *external* control system imposed on students by a higher authority, usually the teacher. Realistically, findings from the social and behavioral sciences suggest that the typical response to externally imposed control systems—regardless of whom they are imposed by—often takes the form of that well-known game called "beating the system." The nature of that game, when cast in a GR concept-statement form, becomes: *for almost every system of control, human beings can (and will) develop even more effective systems of evasion.* As is true of GR concepts, you can't be guaranteed that evasion will occur, but then we suspect you'll be challenged to find more than one or two events throughout history in which this concept was not operational. Should your discipline ever break down, as almost everyone's can on occasion, the evasion systems will have "won" once again. When this happens, the question that needs to be asked is, "What are they evading?" In some cases, it may simply be "more work," which, unfortunately, is probably antithetical to your overall objective as a teacher.

As we see it, a primary objective of classroom management is to replace external control systems with an *internal* control system, usually called self-discipline (on your students' part), which is roughly equivalent to what is often called *responsibility.* Of course there's no denying that internal control systems can be evaded too, perhaps more easily than externally imposed ones: that's something we all have to deal with. But when it comes to helping children accept responsibility for their actions, the goal can often be achieved by your consistent and often implicitly conveyed expectation that your students can and will accept such responsibility. Likewise, if you expect students to misbehave, they are likely to fulfill your expectation.

A self-fulfilling prophecy?

Preaching about discipline and responsibility (or the lack of it) isn't apt to be especially effective, we've found, unless your actions consistently reflect your expectations. Further, the ultimate goal of classroom management is to develop a situation where external control systems step in *only* when internal control systems fail. In other words, it is not a case of one or the other, but a matter of balancing the two.

Behavior as an Object of Study

When responding to the question, "What is the purpose of discipline?" teachers often indicate such things as: maintaining a safe learning environment; controlling disruptive student behavior; teaching students how to conduct themselves in a group setting; and so forth. But suppose we were to view discipline in a different way. Suppose we were to say that the purpose of discipline is to help students better understand:

1 the reasons for their own behavior.
2 how their behavior (and the behavior of everyone else for that matter) is a kind of transaction between the individual and the environment.
3 how to manage their own immediate needs within a group context.
4 how they influence and are influenced by others.
5 how to develop empathy for others and to assume at least partial responsibility for the behavior of others.

Lest there be any question about it, the reason *some* individuals visit psychiatrists is because they are unable to deal with one or more of the elements we have listed above. Thus, the potential danger of using this concept of discipline within a social studies curriculum is that, unless teachers are careful about their approach, they might unwittingly (or perhaps intentionally) find themselves playing the role of junior psychiatrist. Admittedly, you may sometimes find yourself playing this role regardless of the social studies program you use. But when incorporating behavior as an object of study, teachers must be extremely careful to avoid focusing on individual student's motives, their intent, and especially, their personal predispositions, at least to the extent that it's possible to do so. Rather, teachers should stress generalized concepts from the social and behavioral sciences that relate to human behavior in general and that can be transferred to classroom settings.

Opportunities to employ this kind of (nonpsychoanalytic) approach are illustrated in the following examples.

1   When studying a unit in which the concept of change is involved, one of the key concepts might be: *A change in one thing may bring about a number of other changes.* Although the unit vehicle might initially involve, say, the Revolutionary War, the Constitution, or an invention, the students *could* be asked to trace the consequences of a change that took place in the classroom or school. Ultimately, students might find themselves working on the following related GR concepts:

The concept of change

(a) Solving one problem often creates other new and unexpected problems.

(b) People who have the most to lose from a change often find ways of resisting it.

2   When studying historical content, such as the Lewis and Clark expedition (which, on the surface, doesn't appear to be related to behavioral science concepts), an alert teacher could use President Jefferson's orders to the explorers to develop the following concepts:

(a) People in all cultures judge what other people do. When people judge, they often measure others against what they, themselves, are like and believe.

Historical studies

(b) Judging others and being judged ourselves may influence what we think and how we behave.

(c) If judging is important to both the judge and the individuals being judged, then the evidence one uses as a basis for judging becomes important.

(d) Facts don't speak for themselves; usually people interpret the facts.

Students can involve themselves with the same types of study that Lewis and Clark used in studying Native Americans. For example, how are students judged when in school and in the classroom? By teachers? By fellow students? On what basis? How do the different types of judging and judgments influence behavior in the classroom? What kinds of evidence are used when one judges another person?

3   One of the most obvious ways to incorporate discipline into an ongoing social studies program is to approach it through the study of the manipulation of people, especially since that's what many acting-out behaviors are intended to do—manipulate the behavior of others. We accidentally got into such a study with our own elementary students when, for reasons we don't recall, we had occasion to describe what in psychology would be called *ego defense mechanisms.* Although our students weren't familiar with the term *ego,* they certainly recognized many defensive behaviors (displacement, projection, etc.). We had learned during our first year of teaching that teachers seldom pass up opportunities to investigate areas in which their students demonstrate abnormally high interest (with some taboo areas excluded, of course). As a result, we soon found ourselves involved in what grew to be a three-week unit on "Protecting Oneself and Dealing with Others." Incidentally, since we didn't have prepared materials (or time to purchase any), we used what resources we had available; we rewrote the section from our college-level Introduction to Psychology text. Terminology wasn't a problem in this instance, because most students were already familiar with the behaviors associated with defending one's ego.

Studying human behavior

Classroom meetings also provide a legitimate vehicle for bringing discipline problems to the surface and making them an object of study, especially if you happen to be teaching something far removed from the specific discipline problems you may be encountering in your own class. In other words, although you can bring out the behavioral flavor of almost any social studies topic, sometimes it isn't all that easy or relevant. The classroom meeting serves other purposes too, however, and these are described in the next section.

Classroom Meetings

Scenario: It's 11:00 A.M. and the students have drawn their chairs into a circle. For the next thirty to forty-five minutes (or until lunch), this group will hold its daily class meeting. It is a time when the curriculum and predetermined objectives are set aside so that students and teacher can engage in an honest, open, freewheeling discussion of the problems (personal, behavioral, or academic) that concern them. Before beginning, the teacher makes sure to sit in a different place from yesterday (so as not to show favoritism). The teacher may also discreetly make some seating adjustments, such as separating two boys who are prone to nudge each other and carry on their own conversation. And now the meeting is ready to begin.

Some days the teacher introduces a topic or question, some days a student will do the introducing, and some days the class will pick up on a topic left over from a previous meeting.

What topics might a class meeting consider? Here are a few:

Are kids people?

Does everyone have to like everyone?

Possible topics

If you are really afraid of something, what should you do about it?

If your little brother or sister got hurt while you were taking care of him/her, what would you do?

Why do people die?

Do students really have any rights?

What does freedom mean?

What does it mean to be responsible?

What makes you someone special?

What we have just described is the setting for a classroom-meeting strategy devised by Dr. William Glasser, a psychiatrist, and further described in his book, *Schools Without Failure*. Schools that have successfully adopted this strategy now number in the thousands. Of course, class meetings as such are hardly innovations in elementary schools. Seldom have those we've seen reflected the characteristics of a class meeting a la Glasser, however, and almost never were they concerned with the kinds of topics noted above. Rather, they tended to be ritualistic affairs, sometimes conducted by class officers who, though they had certain jobs to perform, never had any real power or authority.

The classroom meeting is an opportunity for children to engage in problem exploration and group problem solving. As Glasser (1969, pp. 122–23) states:

> When children enter kindergarten, they should discover that each class is a working, problem-solving unit and that each student has both individual and group responsibilities. Responsibility for learning and for behaving so that learning is fostered and shared among the entire class. By discussing group and individual problems, the students and teacher can usually solve their problems within the classroom. If children learn to participate in a problem-solving group when they enter school and continue to do so with a variety of teachers throughout the six years of elementary school, they learn that the world is not a mysterious and sometimes hostile and frightening place where they have little control over what happens to them. They learn rather that although the world may be difficult and that it may at times appear hostile and mysterious, they can use their brains individually and as a group *to solve the problems of living in their school world.*

Dealing with real problems

Assuming that you would be willing to consider conducting a classroom meeting as a part of teaching, there are several things to keep in mind. These include:

Arranging the seating in a large circle. Although moving chairs may be a bit cumbersome at first, it is essential that everyone be able to see everyone else. Being forced to look at the back of someone else's head (as you would in rows) is not conducive to good group interaction.

Classroom meeting guidelines

Meeting regularly—at least once a week or even daily if possible—but keeping the meetings short. As a general rule, twenty-minute meetings may be a maximum for primary grade children, but this can be expanded to forty-five minutes for intermediate children.

Being as nonjudgmental as humanly possible—verbally and nonverbally—especially in the first few meetings. Remember that you are trying to establish an open, sharing climate in which your students' ideas and opinions are of primary importance.

Accepting occasional bad grammar and poor usage without correction. To do otherwise may halt future contributions from children who have difficulty expressing themselves. At the other extreme, for children who talk on forever, it may be necessary to interrupt and suggest that they hear from someone else for a while. If you assure the talker that you'll come back to them, and then do come back, it should not be interpreted as a put-down.

Being open to all legitimate topics. Primary-age children especially may introduce very personal topics, some of which might ordinarily be

Classroom meetings are opportunities for genuine involvement.

considered private. In such cases, the other children's responses should be considered before changing the subject, since it may be only you—the adult—who is anxious. On the other hand, if the discussion moves in a direction that might unduly invade the child's privacy (or that of the child's family), you may wish to shift the discussion focus accordingly.

Older children may be suspicious of your motives for initiating class meetings, and may intentionally introduce risque topics—sex, etc.—to test the ground rules. If you are unwilling to consider, honestly, problems that are real to students, then you probably ought not to be conducting a class meeting to start with. But if you suspect that you are being "tested," you may wish to (*a*) say nothing until other student responses have attested to the legitimacy of the problem, (*b*) introduce a topic you would like to discuss, or (*c*) respond honestly that you think you are being "tested," and then wonder aloud what it is that makes some subjects (topics) "good" and some "bad." If you suspect that you are being manipulated by students, you may wish to introduce "people manipulation" as a topic to consider at the next class meeting.

Types of Meetings Glasser identifies three types of class meetings: social problem-solving, openended, and education-diagnostic. All of these follow the same basic format, but each has a different focus.

Social problem-solving meetings focus on just that—social problems. These may include problems of friendship, loneliness, and the like, which are more important to children than you might suspect, but can also include discipline problems—playground bullying, fighting, stealing, etc. The orientation of all classroom meetings should be positive; however, you'll need to be careful that this orientation is reflected in social problem-solving meetings dealing with discipline problems. Remind yourself that the object of the meeting is to find solutions to problems, *not* to find fault or to mete out punishment.

Open-ended meetings are "open" in the sense that any thought-provoking question, whether personal or academic, may be raised. But they are *not* openended to the extent that they run on indefinitely. A discussion can always be picked up again at the next meeting.

Schools Without Failure identifies many questions suitable for openended meetings. In our experience, "What does it mean to be responsible?" has proven especially effective for almost any age group. It is essential, however, that teachers resist their impulse to use openended meetings to teach the answers they have in mind; the idea is to have the children consider the question and the issues involved. In fact, if a class were considering the responsibility question we posed above, and if the teacher were asked what he or she thought "being responsible" meant, the teacher might be wise to say, "I know what I think it means, but I'm really interested in what we decide together." When a class has had experience with class meetings and thoroughly understands the ground rules, the teacher could offer an opinion. But teachers' opinions, like students' opinions, are subject to debate and further group consideration.

Education-diagnostic meetings focus directly on something the class has been studying in a formal or academic sense. The idea is to assess what the students have or have not understood about whatever they've been studying. Glasser (1969, pp. 139–41) cites an example of an education-diagnostic meeting in which he posed the question "What is the Constitution?" to a class of eighth graders. He discovered that they thought the Constitution didn't really exist but was just something written about in books for students to study.

You can use an education-diagnostic meeting to discover students' impressions about a topic before studying it. In fact, you may sometimes find that they know enough about it that they don't need to study it at all. But in no instance should an education-diagnostic meeting be used for grading purposes. To do so will (*a*) inhibit students from revealing anything they are not certain of (and the point of such meetings is to discover their distortions and misconceptions), and (*b*) violate the trust that is essential as a basis for any classroom meeting. In education-diagnostic meetings, the emphasis is on diagnosis, not on grading.

While class meetings may begin on one theme, they sometimes shift focus as they progress. Thus, what might begin as an education-diagnostic meeting on the question "What does 'freedom' mean?" may shift to an open-ended issue such as "Do students have any rights?" Of course you have the option of shifting it back to its original focus, but your decision to do so should be

*Potential
questions*

based on your assessment of how the class might react to such intervention. If they suspect that you are manipulating the meeting, it could soon become "your meeting," not "our meeting."

At times it is useful to hold on-the-spot meetings—in addition to regularly scheduled sessions. A behavioral problem (which does not require immediate intervention), a learning breakthrough, or even a special moment of joy that someone would like to share with others, can serve as a basis for on-the-spot meetings. However, if you sense overkill—too many meetings—then you would be wise to hold off until your next regularly scheduled session.

Avoid overkill

Good classroom meetings have the potential to offer students an opportunity for genuine involvement within settings where most things—like their choice of curriculums or teachers—are beyond their control. Classroom meetings are also a mechanism through which students can develop a sense of responsibility—for their own actions, and for the actions of the group as a whole. It is perhaps the latter dimension—responsibility—that can help children function successfully in their world, and ours.

A Final Footnote

We've seen a lot of changes take place in social studies education, ranging from teaching "history as history" and "geography as geography," through teaching children to become miniature historians, miniature political scientists, etc., to teaching children to use the social and behavioral sciences as they deal with the worlds in which they live. The kind of changes the 1980s will bring is still a matter of speculation, but with the "Back to the basics" movement in full swing in many areas, the essential question continues to be: Basic what? Basic facts? Basic skills? Basic knowledges?

Clearly, there are certain fundamentals, certain basics, that all children should know. But how you identify *which* fundamentals will depend upon your view of the world for which you are educating children. In some cases this may mean returning to "Columbus discovered America" and "1066," assuming, of course, that social studies programs ceased emphasizing such information. However, if this is what "Back to the basics" means, then we need to ask ourselves how this will help children function in the world in which they will be living. In other cases, the "basics" will refer to skills—those basic access and process skills we identified earlier. We would rather not cast this as an "either-or" question; but, given the option, we place our emphasis on the skills dimension, for these skills are children's keys to their world.

Tools for tomorrow

As a kind of benediction, we'd like to share with you a proverb that has served us well over the years. It goes:

> Give a man a fish
> and you feed him for one day.
> Teach him to fish, (and)
> he feeds himself for a lifetime.

Social studies as teaching children "to fish"? Consider it.
Best of luck!

Appendix A
Data Cards for
Presidency Activity

CARD 1

Data about Franklin D. Roosevelt, as of 1945 The American people elected Roosevelt president four times. Because of his New Deal programs designed to combat the severe financial depression of the 1930s and his leadership during World War II, many historians have classified him as one of the most effective chief executives ever to hold the office. Some of Roosevelt's critics, however, felt that he misused the power of the presidency by exerting extensive political pressure on Congress in order to secure passage of the New Deal legislation. He served as president from 1933 until his death in 1945. An attack of polio in the early 1920s left Roosevelt's legs partially paralyzed for the remainder of his life.

CARD 2

Data about Benedict Arnold, as of 1801 Before he joined the British in their attempt to defeat the rebels during the American Revolution, Arnold had served George Washington with distinction during military campaigns from 1776 to 1779. Distressed with financial worries and with a feeling of not receiving adequate recognition from the Continental Congress for his services, he abandoned the American cause and became one of the most well-known traitors in American history.

CARD 3

Data about Martin Luther King, Jr., as of 1968 Before he was assassinated in 1968, the Reverend Martin Luther King, Jr., had become one of the most active champions of the nonviolent civil rights movement. Beginning with his successful boycott of segregated city buses in Birmingham, Alabama, King rose to become leader of the Southern Christian Leadership Conference—one of the most effective organizations to lobby for the federal civil rights legislation during the 1960s.

CARD 4

Data about Andrew Jackson, as of 1829 According to most historians of American life, Jackson was one of our most forceful chief executives. As president, Jackson asserted the supremacy of the federal government when South Carolina attempted to nullify federal tariff laws. His opposition to any form of monopoly was evident in his veto of legislation to recharter the powerful and half-public Bank of the United States.

CARD 5

Data about Alexander Hamilton, as of 1804 Until his death in a duel with Aaron Burr, he had served his country as an advisor to George Washington. His arguments for adoption of the federal Constitution were instrumental in its final approval. His financial genius helped to establish the young U.S. on a firm financial footing during its early years.

CARD 6

Data about Eleanor Roosevelt, as of 1949 Eleanor Roosevelt, wife of Franklin D. Roosevelt, became one of our country's most active champions of the poor, minority groups, women's labor unions, and civil rights. As Franklin Roosevelt's wife, she constantly served as an unofficial advisor for many of his New Deal domestic policies. After her husband's death in 1945, Mrs. Roosevelt was appointed a United States delegate to the United Nations.

CARD 7

Data about George C. Wallace, as of 1974 Until an attempt on his life crippled him in 1972, George Wallace had been an active and outspoken proponent of the cause of states rights. This was especially evident when he began his first term as governor of Alabama, ran as a presidential candidate for the American Party in 1968, and campaigned as a Democratic candidate for the presidency in 1972. Since the attempt on his life, Wallace has been paralyzed from the waist down.

CARD 8

Data about Abraham Lincoln, as of 1865 With the exception of George Washington and Franklin D. Roosevelt, probably no other president ever entered office facing such immense problems as did Abraham Lincoln. Historians of Lincoln's life generally agree that he did as much as any chief executive could have to lead the Union to victory in the Civil War, and attempt to heal the wounds of that conflict for both the North and the South. On numerous occasions before and during his presidency, Lincoln suffered periods of severe mental depression. His untimely assassination occurred in 1865.

Appendix B
Space Rendezvous Answers

Items	Reasoning	Ranking	Your ranks	Error points*	Group ranks	Error points*
Box of matches	no oxygen on moon to sustain flame, virtually worthless	15				
Food concentrate	efficient means of supplying energy requirements	4				
50 feet of nylon rope	useful in scaling cliffs, tying injured together	6				
Parachute silk	protection from sun's rays	8				
Solar-powered portable heating unit	not needed unless on dark side	13				
Two .45 caliber pistols	possible means of self-propulsion	11				
One case of dehydrated Pet milk	bulkier duplication of food concentrate	12				
Two 100-lb. tanks of oxygen	most pressing survival need	1				
Stellar map (of the moon's constellation)	primary means of navigation	3				
Self-inflating life raft	CO_2 bottle in military raft may be used for propulsion	9				
Magnetic compass	magnetic field on moon is not polarized, worthless for navigation	14				
Five gallons of water	replacement for tremendous liquid loss on lighted side	2				

*Error points are the absolute difference between your ranks and these (disregard plus or minus signs).

Items	*Reasoning*	*Ranking*	*Your ranks*	*Error points**	*Group ranks*	*Error points**
Signal flares	distress signal when mother ship is sighted	10	_____	_____	_____	_____
First aid kit containing injection needles	needles for vitamins, medicines etc., will fit in space suits	7	_____	_____	_____	_____
Solar-powered FM receiver transmitter	for communication with mother ship, but FM requires line-of-sight transmission and short ranges	5	_____	_____	_____	_____
			Total _____		Total _____	

Scoring for individuals:

0–25 = excellent	33–45 = average	56–70 = poor
26–32 = good	46–55 = fair	71–112 = very poor, suggests possible faking or use of earthbound logic

*Error points are the absolute difference between your ranks and these (disregard plus or minus signs).

Appendix C
Sample
Learning Style
Inventory

a 1 When you really want to study something and learn it well, would you rather *(a)* work alone, *(b)* study with others having similar interests, *(c)* work by yourself but in a setting where there are other people around?

c 2 Assuming that each of the following modes is effective and that you have a choice, would you most prefer to learn something by *(a)* reading, *(b)* listening, *(c)* observing?

_____ 3 Learning situations that cause you the most concern are those that appear to be *(a)* ambiguous, *(b)* rather closely defined as to the desired outcome, *(c)* without guidelines, where you are completely on your own.

c 4 Do you have most trouble learning things that *(a)* use abstract symbols, *(b)* use diagrams and charts, *(c)* use mathematical numbers and figures?

c 5 When not really interested in something you are studying, do you find yourself *(a)* able to discipline yourself to study, *(b)* easily distracted by other things, *(c)* going through the motions to look as though you are studying?

b 6 When memorizing something, do you find yourself *(a)* developing a theme within which to relate the parts, *(b)* creating a pattern that cues the parts, *(c)* trying to picture the thing in your mind?

a 7 Would you prefer to study something that *(a)* involves some creative effort of your own, *(b)* calls for you to apply analytical and critical skills, *(c)* lays out all the points in front of you so you have a chance to understand it?

b 8 When do you find that you do your best learning—*(a)* in the early morning, *(b)* around midday, *(c)* in the afternoon, *(d)* during an "all nighter"?

a 9 When studying, do you find that you *(a)* create relationships without being told, *(b)* understand the material but have some difficulty putting it together, *(c)* must be given the "whole" before the "parts" make sense?

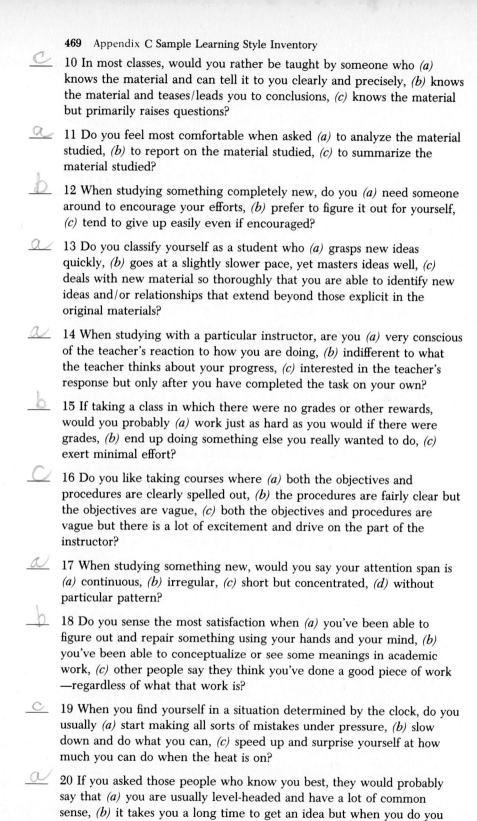

_c_ 10 In most classes, would you rather be taught by someone who *(a)* knows the material and can tell it to you clearly and precisely, *(b)* knows the material and teases/leads you to conclusions, *(c)* knows the material but primarily raises questions?

_a_ 11 Do you feel most comfortable when asked *(a)* to analyze the material studied, *(b)* to report on the material studied, *(c)* to summarize the material studied?

_b_ 12 When studying something completely new, do you *(a)* need someone around to encourage your efforts, *(b)* prefer to figure it out for yourself, *(c)* tend to give up easily even if encouraged?

_a_ 13 Do you classify yourself as a student who *(a)* grasps new ideas quickly, *(b)* goes at a slightly slower pace, yet masters ideas well, *(c)* deals with new material so thoroughly that you are able to identify new ideas and/or relationships that extend beyond those explicit in the original materials?

_a_ 14 When studying with a particular instructor, are you *(a)* very conscious of the teacher's reaction to how you are doing, *(b)* indifferent to what the teacher thinks about your progress, *(c)* interested in the teacher's response but only after you have completed the task on your own?

_b_ 15 If taking a class in which there were no grades or other rewards, would you probably *(a)* work just as hard as you would if there were grades, *(b)* end up doing something else you really wanted to do, *(c)* exert minimal effort?

_c_ 16 Do you like taking courses where *(a)* both the objectives and procedures are clearly spelled out, *(b)* the procedures are fairly clear but the objectives are vague, *(c)* both the objectives and procedures are vague but there is a lot of excitement and drive on the part of the instructor?

_a_ 17 When studying something new, would you say your attention span is *(a)* continuous, *(b)* irregular, *(c)* short but concentrated, *(d)* without particular pattern?

_b_ 18 Do you sense the most satisfaction when *(a)* you've been able to figure out and repair something using your hands and your mind, *(b)* you've been able to conceptualize or see some meanings in academic work, *(c)* other people say they think you've done a good piece of work —regardless of what that work is?

_c_ 19 When you find yourself in a situation determined by the clock, do you usually *(a)* start making all sorts of mistakes under pressure, *(b)* slow down and do what you can, *(c)* speed up and surprise yourself at how much you can do when the heat is on?

_a_ 20 If you asked those people who know you best, they would probably say that *(a)* you are usually level-headed and have a lot of common sense, *(b)* it takes you a long time to get an idea but when you do you hang on to it, *(c)* always coming up with far-out crazy ideas—that sometimes work?

c 21 When bored in a class, do you usually *(a)* daydream, but of things related to what you are studying, *(b)* daydream of things seldom related to what you are studying, *(c)* pay attention even though it doesn't mean very much?

a 22 Do you find that when something new comes up you *(a)* adapt rather easily, *(b)* fight it for awhile but are willing, usually, to give it a try, *(c)* make darn well sure it makes sense and/or is right before making any effort to accept it?

c 23 When in a classroom with other students and observing a teacher teaching, do you *(a)* think of other ways to present the material and to teach, *(b)* listen to what the teacher is saying rather than watch how he or she is teaching, *(c)* wonder what the teacher wants and how you can deliver?

b 24 If you don't like the instructor, for whatever reason, do you *(a)* have a tendency to not do well, *(b)* find every reason possible for not studying/learning, *(c)* not let it affect how hard you try?

_____ 25 Do you get upset when studying something that *(a)* has no immediate and practical application, *(b)* appears to have some application but you're not sure just what, *(c)* is too darn practical and immediate?

c 26 When a particular teacher fails to "come across," do you have a tendency to blame *(a)* the teacher who, after all, is responsible for the class, *(b)* the subject matter—especially if the teacher tries, *(c)* both the teacher and yourself for not making it worthwhile.

c 27 If you took a course in social studies, would you want it to *(a)* focus primarily upon the facts, *(b)* pose some insight into contemporary problems of society, *(c)* have some payoff in your daily life?

b 28 The problem with a great number of teachers is that they *(a)* overkill, that is, teach too much of the same thing, *(b)* try to cover too much, *(c)* do not allow the student to really wrestle with the content.

b 29 Do you believe that most students gain confidence through *(a)* having rather well-established objectives and procedures, *(b)* being allowed to try different things, *(c)* psyching out the reward system and playing the game?

a 30 When studying, do you prefer *(a)* absolute silence, *(b)* low background noise, including music, *(c)* relative quiet, *(d)* loud conversation or music, etc., *(e)* sometimes one way, sometimes another?

b 31 Where do you prefer to study—*(a)* in your own room, *(b)* in a learning center, *(c)* at the library, *(d)* at a media center?

d 32 What type of assignments do you most prefer—*(a)* teacher-directed projects, *(b)* contracts, *(c)* self-directed projects, *(d)* a combination of these?

_____ 33 How do you most prefer to be evaluated on something—*(a)* by formal tests, *(b)* through teacher conferences, *(c)* on research papers or other written projects, *(d)* on the amount of your class discussion?

_d_ 34 Which of the following is most likely to bring forth your best performance—*(a)* self-satisfaction, *(b)* clearly defined teacher expectations and deadlines, *(c)* public recognition of your achievement, *(d)* working in a subject area with which you are quite comfortable and familiar?

Summary

Instructional Modes. Determine preferred instructional mode from responses to questions 2, 4, 7, 8, 11, 17, and 19.

_____

Structure. Determine the degree of structuring from responses to questions 3, 6, 9, 12, 13, 16, 20, 22, 23, and 32.

High	Medium	Low

Social Context of Learning. Determine the general expectations for the way in which teachers handle their authority from questions 1, 10, 19, and 24.

_____

Group-Related Activities. Determine preference for group-related activities from responses to questions 1, 12, 30, 31, and 34.

_____

Physical Context of Learning. Determine preferences regarding the physical environment from the responses to questions 8, 17, 30, and 31.

_____

Reward/Praise. Determine preferences for reward/praise from responses to questions 14, 15, 26, 29, 33, and 34.

_____

Goal Preferences. Determine general goal preferences from the responses to questions 5, 18, 25, and 27.

Longer range		Shorter range

Name Index

Subject Index

Credits